Professional Services:
Text and Cases

Professional Services: Text and Cases

Thomas DeLong
Harvard Business School

Ashish Nanda
Harvard Business School

Boston   Burr Ridge, IL   Dubuque, IA   Madison, WI   New York   San Francisco   St. Louis
Bangkok   Bogotá   Caracas   Kuala Lumpur   Lisbon   London   Madrid   Mexico City
Milan   Montreal   New Delhi   Santiago   Seoul   Singapore   Sydney   Taipei   Toronto

The McGraw·Hill Companies

 Irwin

PROFESSIONAL SERVICES: TEXT AND CASES
Published by McGraw-Hill/Irwin, a business unit of The McGraw-Hill Companies, Inc., 1221
Avenue of the Americas, New York, NY, 10020. Copyright © 2003 by The McGraw-Hill
Companies, Inc. All rights reserved. No part of this publication may be reproduced or distributed
in any form or by any means, or stored in a database or retrieval system, without the prior written
consent of The McGraw-Hill Companies, Inc., including, but not limited to, in any network or
other electronic storage or transmission, or broadcast for distance learning.
Some ancillaries, including electronic and print components, may not be available to customers
outside the United States.

This book is printed on acid-free paper.

1 2 3 4 5 6 7 8 9 0 FGR/FGR 0 9 8 7 6 5 4 3 2

ISBN 0-07-255920-9

Sponsoring editor: *Ryan Blankenship*
Editorial coordinator: *Tammy Higham*
Marketing manager: *Lisa Nicks*
Media producer: *Todd Labak*
Project manager: *Jim Labeots*
Production supervisor: *Gina Hangos*
Designer: *Adam Rooke*
Supplement producer: *Matthew Perry*
Senior digital content specialist: *Brian Nacik*
Cover design: *Ryan Brown*
Typeface: *10/12 Times New Roman*
Compositor: *ElectraGraphics, Inc.*
Printer: *Quebecor World Fairfield Inc.*

Library of Congress Cataloging-in-Publication Data
DeLong, Thomas.
    Managing professional services / Thomas DeLong, Ashish Nanda.
        p. cm.
    Includes index.
    ISBN 0-07-255920-9 (alk. paper)
    1. Professions—Marketing. 2. Consultants—Marketing. 3. Service
industries—Management. I. Nanda, Ashish. II. Title.
    HD8038.A1 D456 2003
    658—dc21   2002070132

www.mhhe.com

About the Authors

Thomas DeLong is the MBA Class of 1957 Professor of Management Practice in the Organizational Behavior group at the Harvard Business School. Before joining the Harvard faculty, Professor DeLong was chief development officer and managing director of Morgan Stanley Group, Inc., where he was responsible for the human capital of the firm. He focused on issues of organizational strategy regarding people, organizational change, and globalization at Morgan Stanley.

Professor DeLong has created a course for MBA's entitled *Managing Human Capital: Keeping Hope Alive in Organization.* He has also taught the course focused on leadership in professional service firms. He teaches in the following executive education programs: Leadership in Professional Service Firms, Senior Human Resource Management, and a number of custom executive education programs. Professor DeLong has taught in various executive education programs in the United States, Europe, and Asia. He obtained his undergraduate and master's degree from Brigham Young University and his PhD from Purdue University in industrial supervision. He was also a Visiting Scholar at the Sloan School of Management at the Massachusetts Institute of Technology. He has worked with financial services, management consulting, law firms, and a myriad of organizations in leadership and organizational behavior issues.

Ashish Nanda is an associate professor of the Harvard Business School. A member of the Negotiations, Organizations, and Markets unit at the Harvard Business School, Professor Nanda teaches MBA courses entitled *Professional Services* and *Leadership Values and Decision Making.* He teaches in the Harvard executive education program *Leadership in Professional Service Firms.* His research focuses on management of professional service organizations. Nanda is also affiliated with the General Management unit and has taught *General Management* in the MBA curriculum and led doctoral seminars on *Joint Ventures* and *Administrative Theory and Practice.*

Nanda has taught in executive education programs on management of professional service organizations, general management, business ethics, and international management in North America, U.K., India, France, Switzerland, Brazil, Venezuela, and Colombia. He has advised law, financial services, management consulting, technology consulting, human resource, and advertising firms. Prior to coming to Harvard University, he worked for several years as an executive with the Tata group of companies in India.

Nanda received a bachelor of technology degree (first rank) in electrical engineering from the Indian Institute of Technology at Delhi and a postgraduate diploma in management (first rank) from the Indian Institute of Management at Ahmedabad. He was awarded an AM in economics from Harvard University in 1990 and a PhD in business economics from Harvard Business School in 1993.

Nanda has received several academic awards, including Henry B. Arthur Fellowship, Harvard University Center in Ethics and the Professions Faculty Fellowship, McGillicuddy Fellowship, IIM Director's Gold Medal, Air India Industrial Scholarship, President of India Gold Medal (twice), Raman Subramanian Memorial Prize, Science Talent Award (twice), and All India Merit Certificate.

Table of Contents

Preface

As professional service firms become ever more prominent in economies the world over and highly motivated professionals gravitate to them in growing numbers, insights into the world in which the former compete and the latter build careers become increasingly important. *Professional Services: Text and Cases* acquaints readers intimately with the landscape in which some organizations succeed and others flounder, some careers flourish and others fail. Case studies and technical notes elucidate the processes by which professional service firms conceive, refine, and deliver services, their managers organize and lead professionals who are often disinclined to be led, and the highly autonomous and self-directed professionals thrive or are thwarted.

Organizing into professional service firms enable professionals to complement one another to offer a broad range of services, achieve scale and scope economies, and jointly develop a shared reputation that leverages their collective efforts. But they also pose unique challenges related to coordinating, often globally, the activities of many, highly autonomous professionals; ensuring that intra-organizational tensions are value enhancing rather than value destroying; and guarding against becoming excessively internally focused at the expense of maintaining client focus.

The nature of the professionals who deliver service poses particular challenges for those who hold leadership positions in professional service firms. The professionals who self-select into these organizations are highly skilled, have multiple affiliations, tend to be achievement oriented, seek little direction, are highly task driven, seek constant positive feedback, and have little tolerance for processes that inhibit their drive to achieve.

A number of assumptions run through the pages of this book. A key assumption is that successful professional service firms deliver service that exceeds client expectations and satisfies the personal and career ambitions of the professionals who provide it. We further assume that its unique nature renders the delivery of professional service difficult to scale.

This book is organized in seven modules that address the foregoing considerations in a way that unfolds for the reader in a logical progression. Each module corresponds to a unique set of challenges, organizing principles and concepts, and critical processes that correlate with the central organizing framework for the graduate course developed by the authors. The first module offers an overarching view of the challenges that face professional service firms, articulates the vision and desired outcome of the book, and establishes a rationale for why it is essential to understanding and succeeding in these firms.

Every professional service firm must make strategic decisions that will have short-term and long-term ramifications for its success. The second module presents various approaches to developing and sustaining externally focused strategies, a crucial starting point in light of our observation that many professional service organizations hesitate to plan strategically partly because of the rapidity of change in their external domain. The cases in this section explore the external dynamics that affect professional service firms.

The third module addresses internal strategy, specifically, the governance, systems, and structures that support a professional service firm's philosophy and values. Case studies illustrate how to leverage the financial and human capital that comprise these systems and emphasize the important role organizational strategy plays in the effective functioning of professional service firms.

The fourth module addresses the tendency of many professionals to be impatient with organizational processes. We emphasize as critical to the success of professional service firms the three key processes related to recruiting, developing, and retaining professionals; decision making; and managing knowledge. Case studies in this section emphasize the importance of leadership in driving processes in these firms.

As important as its internal processes are the external processes that connect a professional service firm with its clients. These firms leverage the knowledge and experience of their professionals to produce service that is largely intangible. Case studies in Module Five illustrate how client satisfaction can be assured or lost through investment in or misuse of relationships.

Module Six takes a broader perspective than the previous four modules by asking how professional service firm leaders balance all four of these considerations—external strategy, internal strategy, internal processes, and external processes—to lead their organizations through change and toward success. The module segues studies of how leaders manage internally and interact externally simultaneously and how they set direction and establish a long-term view while simultaneously managing professionals and clients for short-term results.

The book's concluding module encourages individuals interested in professional success to focus on some issues that we believe are critical for long-run success as professionals—learning strategies, being ethical, and balancing private and professional life.

It has only been in recent years that doors have been opened to those of us deeply interested in the phenomenon of professional service firms. Our research and field observations over that period suggest that professional service firms are complex systems that warrant in-depth study.

We believe that professional service firms have the potential to serve as model organizations for the future. The protagonists in the cases exemplify how leaders of tomorrow's organizations are likely to confront challenges that will lead to the success or failure of their organizations.

Acknowledgments

This book is a product of the efforts of many visionaries who perceived the need to teach future leaders about the world of professional service firms. Harvard Business School (HBS) faculty have been particularly supportive of our endeavor. Leonard Schlesinger, former colleague and head of the Service Management area and currently COO of The Limited, was adamant that a contribution be made by HBS in this arena. Understanding HBS students and wanting them to be better prepared for the professional services world, Dean Kim Clark supported us with enthusiastic encouragement. George Baker and Nitin Nohria contributed time and energy to this undertaking.

Colleagues who played an integral role in the development of this book include Jack Gabarro and Jay Lorsch, who engaged us in discussions about the phenomenon of professional service firms, encouraged us to write cases that would serve both executives and graduate students, and involved us in the executive courses of the Leadership in Professional Services Firms program. We are also grateful to our colleagues Diane Burton (The Firmwide 360-Degree Performance Evaluation Process at Morgan Stanley; Rob Parson at Morgan Stanley), John Gabarro (Brainard, Bennis & Farrell; Cambridge Consulting Group: Bob Anderson), James Heskett (Shouldice Hospital), Herminia Ibarra (Charlotte Beers at Ogilvy & Mather Worldwide), and Jay Lorsch (Cambridge Consulting Group: Bob Anderson) for sharing with us cases written and co-authored by them.

Research associates and graduate students played a key supportive role in developing cases and pushing us to think more clearly about where we wanted to go with the enterprise. Scot Landry, Boris Groysberg, Monica Mullick, and Ying Liu all helped develop materials for this book. Our administrative assistants, Nancy Lund and Laura Macaluso, were indispensable in processing the work flow between sources of information and people.

The endeavor would never have been as rewarding as it turned out if it were not for the constant support of our families. Camille and Shubha were unwavering sources of encouragement. Sara, Catharine, and Joanna (Tom's children) and Pranav (Ashish's) helped make this an enjoyable journey for both of us.

In essence, we get the credit for the accumulated efforts of many.

Thomas DeLong

Ashish Nanda

An Overview of the Professional Services Book

This book is designed to help MBA students understand *professional service firms* (PSFs). It is meant to be useful whether you lead or start one, work for one as an employee or contractor, or hire and work with them as a client. The course studies how to create, manage, and thrive in these firms through understanding their internal and external dynamics and developing skills that are essential to succeeding in these organizations.

WHAT IS A PROFESSIONAL SERVICE FIRM?

A professional service firm provides professional service to its clients (Figure 1).

The two dimensions we use to characterize professional service are *output* and *provider expertise*. On the output dimension, service, as opposed to products, is an intangible "experience." Professional, as opposed to nonprofessional, providers have particular expertise (usually certified through membership in, and accreditation with, professional associations). Following are some examples of

Professors Thomas DeLong and Ashish Nanda prepared this note with the assistance of Research Associate Monica Mullick and Ying Liu (MBA 2001) to serve as an aid to readers beginning the casebook on professional services. It presents a structure and an outline intended to serve as a reference and provide orientation to readers.

FIGURE 1

		Product	Service
Provider	Professional	**I** (software, pharmaceutical)	**IV** (financial services, consulting)
	Nonprofessional	**II** (consumer goods, steel manufacture)	**III** (hotel, fast food)

Output

professional service providers: accountants, actuaries, architects, consultants, doctors, lawyers, teachers, engineering consultants, investment counselors, hedge fund managers, money managers, and investment bankers.

Some providers lie on the interface of product delivery and service provision and so have some but not all characteristics of PSFs. Private equity and venture capital providers, for example, offer not only advisory services but also a tangible product—money. Other providers lie on the interface of professional and nonprofessional service. The guilds and associations of their providers may be striving for, but are not recognized as, professionals. Travel agencies, advertising agencies, executive recruiters, and public relations counselors fall into this group.

Whereas professional service providers can, and often do, offer their services as solo-practitioners, often they group together into firms. Grouping together in PSFs enable practitioners to (1) complement one another so as to offer a broad range of services; (2) achieve scale economies (typically through back-office efficiencies) allowing them to spend time more productively at their vocation; and (3) jointly develop a shared reputation. Working together in a firm, however, poses unique challenges as well that solo practitioners may not face, specifically the challenges of (1) coordinating the activities of different professionals; (2) ensuring that intraorganizational tensions are value enhancing rather than value destroying; and (3) guarding against becoming too internally oriented (versus client focused).

UNIQUE CHARACTERISTICS OF PROFESSIONAL SERVICE FIRMS

PSFs have the following distinguishing characteristics:

• Their primary assets—knowledge, experience, and reputation of the people who work in them—are *intangible*.

• The service delivered is *intangible* and difficult to evaluate.

- The service providers are typically highly *skilled people* with multiple affiliations—to the firms as employees and often as owners and to their professions.

These characteristics imply PSF leaders have to be particularly sensitive to the following dimensions:

1. *Client relationship management.* PSFs essentially make, and then deliver on, promises to their clients. Clients' perceptions of service are influenced by the nature of service offered, nature of relationship developed, and delivery versus promise. Effectively managing client relationships and expectations is often key to building a sustained professional service business.

2. *Management of human capital.* Because they depend on their employees for asset development and service delivery, PSFs compete with one another not only in the service market for clients but also in the labor market for capable professionals. Competitive advantage in service business is usually rooted in the ability to attract, nourish, and motivate the best talent in the labor market. Human capital, unlike physical capital, is not easily quantified, necessitates assessment based on assumptions and predictions, can be leveraged through organizational alignment, is often not fungible, can have multiple applications without reducing value, and can depreciate if underused or disused.[1] Successful PSFs employ professionals who combine the analytic talent to do the technical work with the human qualities to support relationship development and the entrepreneurial instincts for organization building.[2]

3. *Value creation.* PSFs, like other business organizations, have the key objective of economic value creation. To ensure that value is generated, PSF leaders must ensure that the economies of working together (scale, scope, complementarities, shared aspirations) outweigh the diseconomies (complexity, dissension, politicking, strife).

PSFs that effectively address the above three considerations enter into a *virtuous cycle* in which the three primary constituencies operate in harmony to create shared value (Figure 2).[3] We will examine in this book how PSFs develop and maintain virtuous cycles and also how some PSFs slip into vicious cycles in which dissatisfaction of one of the three constituencies leads to overall breakdown.

QUADRANTS OF PROFESSIONAL SERVICE FIRMS

Leaders of PSFs have to be concerned with managing at both the 50,000-foot level of strategy and vision and the ground level of tactics and execution. PSF

---

[1] D. H. Maister, "Balancing the Professional Service Firm," *Sloan Management Review,* vol. 24, no. 1, Fall 1982.
[2] T. A. Stewart, *Intellectual Capital/The New Wealth of Organizations* (Doubleday 1997).
[3] J. L. Heskett, T. O. Jones, G. W. Loveman, W. E. Sasser, Jr., and L. A. Schlesinger, "Putting the Service Profit Chain to Work," *Harvard Business Review,* March–April 1994.

FIGURE 2

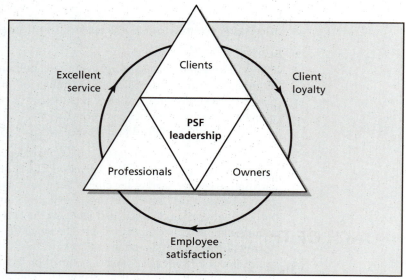

leaders have to manage both the external environment of clients and competition, and the internal environment of people and processes.

The book develops a framework around these two dimensions. Juxtaposing these two dimensions—*level* and *focus*—orthogonally yields four quadrants (Figure 3). We assert that *to be successful, a PSF needs to achieve balance across these four quadrants.*

FIGURE 3

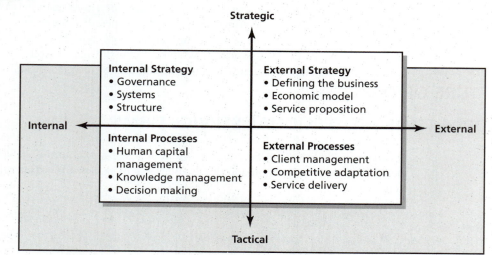

Following are the descriptions of the four quadrants:

- **External strategy** involves developing and sustaining a unique vision that is compelling to target clients and creates economic value for the providers.

- **Internal strategy** relates to the deployment and administration of mutually consistent governance mechanisms, formal and informal structures, and performance evaluation and compensation systems.

- **Internal processes** connect strategy with implementation; these include human capital management (recruitment, training, retention, and motivation), decision making, and knowledge management.

- **External processes** are concerned with ensuring delivery of promised service through client and project management and nimble adaptation to competitive dynamics.

APPROACH OF THE BOOK

The book employs primarily the inductive learning approach. The frameworks are used as "lenses" rather than "theorems." The primary learning tool is the case study method. The case studies typically take a longitudinal perspective that follows professionals and their enterprises over extended periods of time. This affords readers the opportunity not only to determine the sources of high performance at any given time, but also to identify the strategic capabilities and processes that sustain success over time, and to learn how PSFs react to change. To benefit from inductive learning, students are expected to take a personal approach to case examination through understanding the case from the perspectives of the protagonists.

Virtually all the professional service businesses (e.g., consulting, investment banking, law, money management, etc.) will be represented through cases. The book will study entrepreneurial PSFs operating with new models and in new spaces as well as established industry leaders in more traditional businesses.

STRUCTURE OF THE BOOK

The book takes a two-step approach. We first introduce the four-quadrant framework to identify the drivers of PSF success and study each of the four quadrants through an introduction to a module followed by cases that illustrate the overall model. The second part of the book identifies and elaborates the skills professionals must develop and refine to succeed in PSFs. The learning trajectory the book follows is from the outside in. It begins with a broad understanding of the external environment in which PSFs operate, deepens the perspective by looking inside PSFs first at their systems, people, and processes, and eventually personalizes the learning by studying skills needed for individual success.

The book is organized in seven modules. The purpose of each of these modules, and the primary purpose and/or setting of each case are discussed below. (Exhibit 1 provides the book outline.)

Module One: Introduction to the Challenges Facing PSFs

First, in *Hambrecht & Quist* we will discuss the changing balance, as the market evolves, between the benefits of scale and advantages of remaining independent. In the second class, by tracking entrepreneurs Chan Suh and Kyle Shannon's start-up of their interactive consulting firm, *AGENCY.COM,* we will discuss the challenges of launching and growing a PSF.

We will conclude the module by (1) defining PSFs, (2) examining their key differences from other organizations, and (3) introducing the four-quadrant framework. Each of the next four modules examines a particular quadrant. We also describe the history of investment banking as well as the rise and decline of the e-consulting space.

Module Two: External Strategy for Sustained Competitive Advantage

This three-case module examines approaches to developing and sustaining PSFs' external strategy. We emphasize the importance of simultaneously ensuring (1) clarity on one's positioning within the spectrum of service providers; (2) relative attractiveness of the service proposition to target clients; and (3) pricing that ensures clients receive value for the service offered even as the service providers earn economic returns. These cases will also emphasize the trade-offs, and necessity of balancing, between (1) being adaptive and focused, and (2) leveraging scale economies and ensuring speed of delivery.

In the first case, we will discuss various success factors that would determine the fate of newly launched *Thomas Weisel Partners,* an entrepreneurial, niche-focused investment bank during a time when the banking industry was rapidly consolidating. In *Woodland Partners,* we will discuss the relative advantages of various growth strategies that faced the founders of the investment management firm in 1995.

The *Shouldice Hospital* case will emphasize that to make capacity expansion decisions, leaders have to give serious considerations to the firm's value proposition to clients, the culture of the organization, and the importance of preserving the culture in its service delivery system.

Module Three: Internal Strategy of Organizational Design

This six-case module, focuses on the second quadrant of internal strategy, opens with the observation that, whereas in product firms owners, managers, and employees tend to be different groups of people, in PSFs these groups tend to overlap (Figure 4). This overlap demands careful attention to organizational governance, structure, and systems since they simultaneously impact on all three key

EXHIBIT 1   Professional Services Book Outline

Module One: Introduction to the Challenges Facing PSFs

Hambrecht & Quist
AGENCY.COM (A): Launching an Interactive Services Agency
The Rise and Decline of E-Consulting
History of Investment Banking

Module Two: External Strategy for Sustained Competitive Advantage

Thomas Weisel Partners
Woodland Partners: Field of Dreams
Shouldice Hospital Limited

Module Three: Internal Strategy of Organizational Design

Morgan Stanley Dean Witter Private Client Services
Diamond in the Rough (A)
The Goldman Sachs IPO (A)
Family Feud (A): Andersen versus Andersen
The Saga of Prince Jefri and KPMG (A): Mystery of the Missing Billions
International Profit Associates

Module Four: Managing the Organization through Processes

Rob Parson at Morgan Stanley
Strategic Services at Andersen Consulting
Bain & Co., Inc.: Making Partner
Venture Law Group

Module Five: Serving Clients Effectively

&Samhoud
The Union Carbide Deal (Abridged)
Jill Greenthal at Donaldson, Lufkin and Jenrette (A): The TCI/AT&T Deal

Module Six: Leadership and Change Management in PSFs

Cambridge Consulting Group: Bob Anderson
Charlotte Beers at Ogilvy & Mather Worldwide
Lehman Brothers (A): Rise of the Equity Research Department
Alexander Bandelli (A)
Tom Tierney At Bain & Co. (A)
Infosys

Module Seven: Becoming a Professional

Tim Hertach at GL Consulting (A)
Professionals' Quandaries
Tradeoffs: Juggling Careers in PSFs with Private Life
The First Six Months: Launching a PSF Career

FIGURE 4

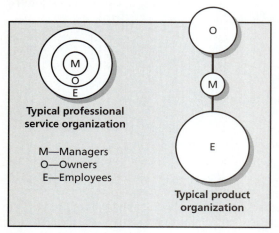

Typical professional
service organization

M—Managers
O—Owners
E—Employees

Typical product
organization

resource providers. Only through alignment of its systems, structure, and governance can a PSF sustain its competitive advantage.

In the *Morgan Stanley Dean Witter Private Client Services* case we will highlight the interlinkages between internal cohesion and market success by discussing the challenge of postmerger integration. In *Diamond in the Rough,* we will explore the benefits and risks of pursuing Diamond Technologies founder Mel Bergstein's chosen approach of focusing first on organization building and only later on market opportunities. Following the IPO decision process of *Goldman Sachs* will allow readers to study the comparative benefits of a private versus public ownership structure and how different incentive affects two governance mechanisms. The *Family Feud: Andersen versus Andersen* case will help readers explore the internal tensions that can be occasioned in a multipractice PSF. The *Prince Jefri* case, by distinguishing between circumstances in which organizational synergies benefit from those in which they adversely affect client interests, will help readers understand the reasons for, and benefits and limitations of, "Chinese walls" in PSFs. In the *International Profit Associates* (IPA) case, we will introduce the 7-S model for organizational alignment in a PSF and highlight the importance of dynamic interactions among internal systems.[4]

This module will emphasize the interlinkages between PSFs' external and internal strategies and also shed light on the dynamics of competition between professions. Some of the cases in this module will help readers elucidate competitive as well as organizational implications of running multidisciplinary practices.

Module Four: Managing the Organization through Processes

The four cases in this module will underscore that successful PSFs derive sustained competitive advantage from developing and maintaining effective processes. Implementing key processes can ensure that a PSF simultaneously delivers high-quality service for its clients, creates value for its owners, and builds capability for its employees. We will focus on the three key processes in PSFs: human capital management, decision making, and knowledge management.

We include the *Rob Parson at Morgan Stanley* case as a follow-up case to highlight the complex managerial challenges associated with performance management.

[4] The description of the 7-S model was presented in R. H. Warterman, T. J. Peters, and J. R. Phillips, "Structure Is Not Organization," *Business Horizons,* 1980.

A well worn, but ultimately true cliché, is that the strategic assets of PSFs walk out of the elevator every day. Leaders of the most effective PSFs pay particular attention to the processes of recruitment, selection, socialization, and development of professionals. The *Bain & Company: Making Partner* case, by focusing on the decision choices facing the firm's partner promotion committee, will help readers explore the processes of professional development and career progression in a management consulting firm. Craig Johnson's approach to hiring and retaining top-notch lawyers in the Silicon Valley law firm, *Venture Law Group,* will introduce readers to some relatively unique methods of recruitment and retention emerging in progressive PSFs.

The *Strategic Services at Andersen Consulting* case addresses issues of internal capabilities and external opportunities and the tension between them to illustrate that organization theory, socialization, organization economics, hiring, retention, and decision making all affect the nature of a high-performance PSF.

We intend to emphasize through this module that as information availability, scale, scope, and geographic dispersion increase rapidly, PSFs face the challenge of ensuring that their professionals work together effectively without being unduly burdened by the process that connects them.

Module Five: Serving Clients Effectively

This three-case module focuses on the client service process. The module emphasizes the importance of building and leveraging relationships to achieve results that are valuable for both clients and providers. The module focuses on the externally oriented process of investing in clients and building mutual trust. The cases in this module help readers understand marketing in both relationship and transactional businesses and the relationships between service promise and delivery and client satisfaction and loyalty.

In *&Samhoud,* we will introduce the linkages between employee productivity, satisfaction and loyalty; customer satisfaction and loyalty; and firm profitability and growth, while exploring the dilemma of whether or not to continue a relationship with a major client. In *The Union Carbide Deal* and *Jill Greenthal at DLJ* cases, we will examine the relationship between client relationship management and deal transaction. In *The Union Carbide Deal* we will follow an investment banker's efforts to woo a client away from a competitor. In *Jill Greenthal at DLJ* we will discuss how investments in client relationships can be leveraged into business opportunities.

Module Six: Leadership and Change Management in PSFs

Module Six moves from analysis of the individual quadrants to putting it all together in leading a PSF through change and organizational development.

The first case in the module deals with the dilemma of being a producer-manager. The *Cambridge Consulting Group: Bob Anderson* case introduces the dilemmas facing *Bob Anderson* and the challenge of achieving the "best of both worlds," excellence in both client service and managing internally. The case will pose the question of how this balance can be achieved for both organizational and personal success.

Three cases in this module, *Charlotte Beers at Ogilvy & Mather Worldwide, Alexander Bandelli,* and *Tom Tierney at Bain & Co.,* will focus on the challenge of managing change in PSFs. Change is particularly difficult to manage in PSFs because professionals are often invested in their positions and hence become rigid and protective of territory. In the *Charlotte Beers at Ogilvy & Mather Worldwide* case, we will emphasize not only the importance of having a vision of the firm, but also the process of operationalizing the vision over an extended time period to achieve the desired outcome. In *Alexander Bandelli* we will follow the efforts of a real estate firm office head to change the culture of his office. In *Tom Tierney at Bain & Co.* we will follow a chief executive's efforts to rotate office heads in his consulting organization to keep his professionals learning and developing.

The *Lehman Brothers Equity Research Department* and *Infosys* cases will focus on leading PSFs to successful transformations and highlight the elements of leadership. In *Lehman Brothers Equity Research Department* we will follow the spectacular rise of Lehman's equity research department under the leadership of Jack Rivkin. In *Infosys* we will follow the growth to prominence of India's premier software firm under the stewardship of Narayan Murthy.

Module Seven: Becoming a Professional

Module Seven moves the unit of analysis from the organization to the individual. This four-session module emphasizes the skills and values that we believe successful professionals must possess for optimal effectiveness: an ethical perspective, constructively giving and accepting feedback, balancing private and professional lives, and coping with demands early in one's career.

In *Tim Hertach at GL Consulting* we will confront the dilemma faced by Tim Hertach, HBS MBA '88. Should he confront senior management over a billing practice that he considers wrong or should he protect his career in order to fight more meaningful battles later? In *Professionals' Quandaries* we will study five caselets where professionals confront ethical dilemmas. We intend to promote understanding of ethical situations confronted by professionals and encourage proper actions when professionals face ethical situations.

The concluding two sessions in this module are concerned with launching careers in PSFs and maintaining balance between professional and personal lives. In *The First Six Months: Launching Your Career in PSFs* case, we will study two caselets. The first case illustration will allow readers to consider an effective strategy in achieving success in the first six months of their careers. In the second caselet we will discuss some of the challenges people face when giving and receiving feedback with superiors, subordinates, and other colleagues.

In the *Trade-offs: Juggling Careers in PSFs with Private Life* case, we explore the myth that professionals, by working harder and longer and traveling farther and more frequently, dedicate more of their lives to work than do others. We will discuss the dilemmas of launching one's career versus not working unrealistic hours and giving one's best to the job versus commiting to one's family. We will offer some strategies to help confront professional/private life trade-offs and cope with the myriad demands that successful professionals face.

Module Summary Notes: Professional Services Casebook

CASE NAMES AND ABSTRACTS

Module One

1. Hambrecht & Quist

Hambrecht & Quist (H&Q), an investment bank headquartered in San Francisco, has a unique culture relative to its Wall Street counterparts. Firm members and even competitors describe the culture as entrepreneurial, team-driven, nonbureaucratic, and change-oriented. H&Q's unique culture has given it a number of competitive advantages, including the ability to attract high-quality staff, the ability to win business among its target group of emerging growth companies, and the ability to maintain below-average SG&A costs. However, competition in the investment banking industry is intensifying in 1997–98 due to an unprecedented wave of megamergers between investment banks and commercial banks. The new combined banking entities are able to offer customers a broader array of products and services than H&Q is able to offer, creating a significant amount of pressure for H&Q to sell to, or merge with, another financial institution itself. Industry analysts believe it is not a question of whether but rather when H&Q will lose its independence. However, H&Q management believes that "selling out" would destroy the very culture that made the firm successful. What action should Dan Case, the CEO and chairman of H&Q, take to balance the seemingly competing demands of maintaining the firm's culture and positioning the firm for future growth?

Teaching purpose: To highlight the challenges of competing in the financial service space where scope and scale become more important to some clients. The challenge of serving customers and remaining focused on firms' vision is highlighted.

2. AGENCY.COM (A): Launching an Interactive Service Agency
Having recently launched one of Silicon Valley's first start-ups, co-founders Chan Suh and Kyle Shannon ponder whether their interactive consulting firm is prepared to bid for work from a very large client.

Teaching purpose: To study the strategic, organizational, and managerial challenges facing an entrepreneurial professional service firm offering Internet-related services.

3. History of Investment Banking
This note gives the reader a basic understanding of how the investment banking industry has evolved in the previous century. Students interested in careers in professional service firms will see patterns in the industry that cross over to other service arenas. This awareness adds depth and breadth to professionals already in the business who are seeking insights into career choices and alternatives.

4. The Rise and Decline of e-Consulting
The cyclical nature of market forces come into play as readers become aware of the delicate nature of this market niche. The various forces that come into play to create consulting firms as well as those that created the demise of these institutions is studied.

Module Two

1. Thomas Weisel Partners (A)
Thomas Weisel, longtime leader of Montgomery Securities, realizes that the sale of Montgomery to NationsBank was the biggest mistake of his life. After his exit from NationsBanc Montgomery Securities, Weisel develops a business plan for a new merchant bank, Thomas Weisel Partners.

Teaching purpose: To discuss competitive strategy in the financial services industry, specifically focusing on comparing circumstances when scale is critical versus when a niche strategy is viable.

2. Woodland Partners: Field of Dreams?
Elizabeth Lilly, Richard Rinkoff, and Richard Jensen are pondering whether to launch a new investment management firm and if so, what growth strategy to chart for the potential firm.

Teaching purpose: To understand the interrelation between growth strategy, organizational processes, management challenges, and personal goals in an entrepreneurial professional service firm.

3. Shouldice Hospital Limited

Various proposals are set forth for expanding the capacity of the hospital. In assessing them, serious consideration has to be given to the culture of the organization and the importance of preserving it in a service delivery system. In addition to issues of capacity and organizational analysis, this case describes a well-focused, well-managed medical service facility that may well point the way to future economies in the field.

Teaching purpose: The importance of complete alignment inside the organization to create opportunities for superb customer service.

Module Three

1. Morgan Stanley Dean Witter Private Client Services

The 1997 merger of retail giant Dean Witter and investment bank Morgan Stanley was a year old when Bob Sculthorpe was appointed director of Private Client Services (PCS) at Morgan Stanley Dean Witter (MSDW). The firm was still operating under two separate broker-dealer registrations, and there had been no satisfactory resolution to the dilemma facing the leaders of the retail securities division of MSDW. Where did Morgan Stanley PCS and its high net worth focus fit into the retail/investment banking giant? Should Morgan Stanley PCS be merged with the 10,000 account executives of Dean Witter? Sculthorpe faced several dilemmas: Would the highly compensated MS PCS brokers stay in an integrated brokerage unit? Client retention could also be a problem if the two salesforces were merged in a manner inconsistent with the branding of either. With several key PCS investment professionals in various stages of considering whether to leave for competitors, he knew that he must act quickly and decisively.

Teaching purpose: The impact of mergers on culture is emphasized through the teaching of this case. An excellent example of clashing cultures and what leaders can do about it.

2. Diamond in the Rough (A)

Diamond Technology Partners, a consulting firm based in Chicago, was founded in 1994 by Mel Bergstein and Chris Moffitt, with investment from founding partners and Safeguard Scientifics. In April 1996, just after fiscal year-end, the two largest clients withdrew from projects representing 50 percent of the previous revenues. A few weeks earlier, management had put together a $50 million revenue forecast for the year, had hired 28 new employees to start the following September, and had promised employees year-end bonuses. Management also anticipated that the company would go public within the next 12 months. Bergstein wonders whether there is a future for Diamond.

Teaching purpose: To explore how to start and bring a professional service firm public and how to manage crises in the first two to three years.

3. The Goldman Sachs IPO (A)

This case addresses the proposed IPO and raises questions regarding how agency costs may rise or fall as Goldman converts from a private partnership to a public limited corporation.

Teaching purpose: To elaborate on agency theory and corporate governance in a professional service organization.

4. Family Feud (A): Andersen versus Andersen

This case traces the history and development of consulting within Andersen and the history of the schism between Arthur Andersen and Andersen Consulting. It ends with the two units seeking external arbitration of their dispute.

Teaching purpose: To study the internal tensions of management of a multidisciplinary professional services firm.

5. The Saga of Prince Jefri and KPMG (A): Mystery of the Missing Billions

Accounting and law firms around the globe are following with great interest the progress through British courts of a lawsuit. Those familiar with the suit, filed by Prince Jefri of Brunei against the professional service firm KPMG Peat Marwick, remark that its judgment will be "a landmark ruling with profound implications." At stake is nothing less than how professional service firms conduct their business.

Teaching purpose: To explore how professional service firms should think about conflict of interest in deciding whether to accept engagements. The case highlights (1) the emerging tension between how accounting firms and law firms view their responsibility to clients; and (2) the use and limitations of Chinese walls in managing potential conflicts within firms.

6. International Profit Associates

IPA, one of the fastest-growing private organizations, targets small business owners and offers consulting services. The firm measures employees' performances closely and links compensation with those numbers. What kind of work environment will this measurement focus create? How do leaders motivate professionals? Is IPA's strategy sustainable?

Teaching purpose: The importance of finding a niche market and staying consistent. Case raises ethical and incentive issues in a midmarket area where customers may not be that sophisticated.

Module Four

1. Rob Parson at Morgan Stanley (A)

Rob Parson was a star producer in Morgan Stanley's Capital Markets division. He had been recruited from a competitor the prior year and had generated substantial revenues since joining the firm. Unfortunately, Parson's reviews from the 360-degree performance evaluation process revealed that he was having difficulty adapting to the firm's culture. His manager, Paul Nasr, faces the difficult decision of whether to promote Parson to managing director. Nasr must also complete

Parson's performance evaluation summary and conduct Parson's performance review.

Teaching purpose: To explore managerial problems associated with performance appraisal and performance management.

2. Strategic Services at Andersen Consulting

Bill Copacino, Andersen Consulting's managing partner of Strategic Services Americas, needed to submit his recommendation to Peter Fuchs, Strategic Services worldwide director, for the operating plan for Strategic Services Americas for fiscal year 1999. Strategic Services had grown by over 40 percent per year in headcount since 1989, but it remained a relatively small part of Andersen Consulting. Copacino and Fuchs were challenged to grow Strategic Services at the level required to increase its relative position in the firm to 10 percent of its people and 15 percent of its revenues. As they discussed options, there were no easy answers. Should Strategic Services continue to try to grow at 30 percent plus per year? Would Strategic Services be able to find enough new and experienced hires to continue to grow? Could the unique culture be maintained? Should they consider acquisitions? Was there an effective way to meet their growth targets?

Teaching purpose: The challenge of keeping a professional service firm in balance in order to mentor and teach junior professionals. How do you deal with the challenge of lateral hires?

3. Bain & Company, Inc.: Making Partner

In June 1998, Bain's Compensation and Policy Committee meets to review candidates for elevation to partnership. The case presents the profiles of four candidates and ends with the promotion committee debating the merits of the candidates.

Teaching purpose: To explore the issues that have to be considered in deciding whether to promote a PSF employee to partner.

4. Venture Law Group

Craig Johnson's approach to hiring and retaining top-notch counselors in the Silicon Valley law firm introduces some relatively unique methods of recruitment and retention emerging in professional service firms.

Teaching purpose: Understand how progressive professional service firms can be in order to encourage long-term commitment and loyalty through incentives.

Module Five

1. &Samhoud Service Management

A Dutch consulting firm uses the service profit chain theory to advise clients and build its own organization. Employee's satisfaction and work environment are the firm's top priorities.

Teaching purpose: Highlight the importance of being internally focused on employees in order to serve clients.

2. The Union Carbide Deal (Abridged)

On November 3, 1986, after a three-hour board of directors meeting, Union Carbide decided to accept First Boston's proposal to embark on a $2.5 billion recapitalization program. Jamerson and his associates' efforts had paid off. Jamerson had reason to be excited. He had changed a weak relationship between First Boston and Union Carbide into one that would generate tens of millions of dollars in revenues for his firm. In the highly competitive world of investment banking, it was a particularly sweet victory, since First Boston had won the business from Union Carbide's traditional banker, Morgan Stanley.

Teaching purpose: To emphasize the key variables in creating and maintaining long-term relationships in professional service firms.

3. Jill Greenthal at Donaldson, Lufkin & Jenrette (A): The TCI/AT&T Deal

Jill Greenthal, managing director at Donaldson, Lufkin & Jenrette, is leading her team of investment bankers to negotiate on behalf of Tele-Communications, Inc. (TCI) on a potential landmark deal with AT&T. Representing TCI in the negotiations is the culmination of relationships that Greenthal has nurtured over the course of a decade. Despite the best efforts of her team, negotiations appear poised on the edge of an impasse. Greenthal wonders what, if anything, her team can do to help find a better alternative.

Teaching purpose: To help students explore (1) how a "relationship manager" in a professional service firm builds and leverages relationships (externally with the key client and internally with team members and complementary departments) to execute critical transactions that are beneficial to the clients as well as the professional service firm, and (2) how effective investment banking teams work together intensively to close potential deals.

Module Six

1. Cambridge Consulting Group: Bob Anderson

This case describes the situation facing the head of a rapidly growing industry-focused group within a consulting company. It highlights the dilemmas of being a "producing manager" (i.e., a professional who has both individual production as well as management responsibilities). Issues raised include delegation, developing subordinates, developing an agenda, and building an organization.

Teaching purpose: To demonstrate dilemmas of the producing manager's role.

2. Charlotte Beers at Ogilvy & Mather Worldwide (A)

This case examines Beer's actions on assuming leadership of Ogilvy & Mather Worldwide, the world's sixth-largest advertising agency, during a period of rapid industry change and organizational crisis. It focuses on how Beers, the first outsider CEO, engages and leads a senior team through a vision formulation process. The case chronicles closely the debates among senior executives struggling to reconcile creative, strategic, and global versus local priorities. Sixteen months later, with a vision statement agreed upon, Beers faces a series of implementation problems. Turnaround has begun, but organizational structures and systems are not yet aligned with the firm's new direction. The case concludes as Beers must decide how to work best with her senior team to achieve alignment in 1994.

Teaching purpose: The case gives the instructor the opportunity to discuss leadership and change in the context of a professional service firm.

3. Lehman Brothers (A): Rise of the Equity Research Department

This case describes the rise of Shearson Lehman's research department under Jack Rivkin's leadership from relative obscurity to the highest ranking research department on Wall Street within three years. In the spring of 1990 Rivkin is promoted to co-head the firm's equity division and his associate, Fred Fraenkel, is named the new head of equity research. Stepping into the shoes of a charismatic leader, Fraenkel is pondering over what changes, if any, he ought to introduce to the research department's practices.

Teaching purpose: To highlight the steps taken over a five-year period to build a high-performing professional service organization; to emphasize the importance of (1) leadership, (2) alignment, (3) strategy implementation, (4) processes of recruiting, developing, and retaining star professionals, and (5) establishing a strong culture to encourage enterprise and teamwork; also to explore the challenge of maintaining a high-performing professional service organization once it has been established.

4. Alexander Bandelli (A)

Alexander Bandelli has the opportunity to redefine the way real estate business is done in the Northeast region. He has just joined Ronsini and Fitch and has been asked by senior management to move to a client focus rather than the older, traditional transaction focus. Alexander has many challenges before him. How should he prioritize his work? Does he focus outside the organization or internally? Is the organization prepared for this change project? What should he do first?

Teaching purpose: Highlights the challenge of leadership, project management and time management in a professional service firm. The reader must wrestle with prioritization, change and decision-making processes that have long-term implications.

5. Tom Tierney at Bain & Company (A)

Bain managing director Tom Tierney is contemplating how best to rotate the office head position between two partners at one of the firm's offices. The case provides background information on Bain's governance structure and Tierney's management style.

Teaching purpose: To explore (1) governance systems, (2) career planning, and (3) succession dynamics in a professional service firm.

6. Infosys Technologies, Limited

Infosys, an Indian software start-up, has been under the leadership of CEO N. R. Narayana Murthy for decades. Murthy and his team dealt with important challenges regarding future growth and financing.

Teaching purpose: To introduce the elements of leadership that lead to successful professional service firms.

Module Seven

1. Tim Hertach at GL Consulting (A)

Ten years into his career after graduating from HBS, Tim Hertach discovers billing irregularities at his consulting firm. He must decide whether (and how) to challenge senior management or to stay quiet and protect his career.

Teaching purpose: (1) To explore how to negotiate an ethical dilemma; (2) to study the flexibility and initiative of professional service firms' billing practices.

2. Professionals' Quandaries

Five caselets allow considerations of five important questions: (1) Why are ethics particularly critical for professionals? (2) In what circumstances do ethical quandaries seem to arise more often? (3) Must all professionals "grow up" and lose their "innocent" ethics in favor of adopting a professional ethics-in-use or relative ethics? (4) How should professionals ensure that they don't slide down an ethical slippery slope? (5) What do professionals gain by being ethical?

Teaching purpose: Each professional must wrestle with the dilemma of making decisions that challenge ethical practices. The case pushes the reader in unconventional ways.

3. Trade-Offs: Juggling Careers in PSFs with Private Life

Balancing professional and private lives continues to challenge single and committed partners alike. Professionals are expected to work long hours. It is simply part of the ethos of professional service firms. This case focuses on the lives of three couples connected to professional service firms and their ensuing challenges in balancing professional and private life.

Teaching purpose: Highlight the complexity of managing the myriad roles that a professional faces every day. What are the trade-offs in making decisions that impact so many in so many ways?

4. The First Six Months: Launching a PSF Career

This case presents two situations: (1) two graduating MBAs from Harvard Business School compare and contrast their strategies for getting off to a good start in consulting; and (2) a junior consultant has to deal with the reception of difficult feedback in his very first performance review.

Teaching purpose: To help students reflect on (1) developing a strategy to ensure a good start in professional services, and (2) ensuring a quick turnaround if they do not start well.

Introduction to the Challenges Facing Professional Service Firms

A NEW PERSPECTIVE

During our first two cases in the first module, we have attempted to explain the vision of this casebook, detail its uniqueness, explain why readers should spend time and energy focused on the book's content, and hopefully, demonstrate that the cases will not only present specific information but will also cumulate to a knowledge base that will help you understand professional service firms better.

The goal in presenting the first two cases of the book is to expose you to many of the subjects that will be discussed in depth later in the book. PSFs of all sizes face many challenges of growth and evolution. These challenges often lead firms to difficult choices regarding how best to compete and structure themselves for the future. Whether these choice points are driven by external or internal factors, a PSF's decision will impact how the PSF performs externally or internally, both on strategic and tactical levels. The point of view we want to convey clearly with

This note was prepared by Professor Thomas DeLong, Professor Ashish Nanda, Dean's Research Fellow Scot Landry, and Ying Liu (MBA 2001).

this book is that high-performing PSFs (and the professionals that run these firms) must become skilled at understanding and addressing these challenging decisions.

We also believe that by understanding the world of PSFs, readers will have much greater understanding of the business world in which they may live. PSFs are becoming more central and important to the global economy. PSFs remain an enticing career path for many of the world's brightest business minds who are attracted by working with highly motivated and talented colleagues, developing deep expertise, earning outstanding compensation, and helping other organizations grow and thrive. However, since a PSF career can be incredibly demanding, we believe that the thorough examination of PSFs conducted in the book's 30 cases will allow readers to make more informed and more satisfying career choices.

This initial module is meant to clarify how the book would be useful to readers who would be starting PSFs, working for them as an employee or contractor, managing them, or hiring them from the client side. Through AGENCY.COM and Hambrecht & Quist we will touch upon how to create, manage, and thrive in these firms through understanding their internal and external dynamics, and the skills that need to be developed that bring success in these organizations. In Hambrecht & Quist, we will also discuss the changing balance, as the market evolves, between the benefits of scale and advantages of remaining independent. These cases will emphasize the trade-offs, and necessity of balancing, between (1) being adaptive and focused, and (2) leveraging scale economies and ensuring speed of delivery.

SETTING THE CONTEXT—THE UNIQUENESS OF PSFs

Selling and Delivering on Promises

We begin the book by explaining that PSFs are organized to serve clients and to sell credible promises, deliver on those promises and help their clients learn from past experiences to deliver future value. In most cases, PSFs meet these promises and expectations by harnessing internal expertise (intellectual capital) and capabilities to help client organizations understand and capitalize on business opportunities (improving a client's probability of success) or address challenges (limiting a client's risk). The turbulence and velocity in most business markets increased significantly in the 1990s, leading clients in those markets to seek more and more PSF expertise.

Intellectual Capital/Intangibility

PSFs create value through intellectual capital (the ability to think, conceptualize, and put those thoughts into action) and thus differ from other business organizations that create value by machines and tangible resources.[1] The intangible nature of PSF work makes it nearly impossible to reverse engineer the production of professional services and makes it difficult to evaluate the quality of those services. Additionally, most work in PSFs is performed real time with clients, leveraging the interaction between the client and the professional. The interaction is so dynamic that the value of the interaction often cannot be predicted or measured. Because of this intangibility, high-performing PSFs must excel at managing client expectations.

Human Capital Management

Another element of PSFs that is different from many other business organizations is that PSF assets are nearly entirely human (knowledge, expertise, and reputation of its employees). A cliché often used in PSFs is that their assets ride up and down the elevator each day. This fact necessitates a strong recruiting and retention program for high-performing PSFs. It also necessitates a strong knowledge-management program, in which PSFs ask their professionals to codify project learnings to share with the broader organization. In this way, firms can take individual-specific learning and expertise, and make it firm-specific and able to be shared with all the firm's professionals. Successful knowledge-management programs allow firms to conduct engagements more profitably and quickly. They also protect a firm's expertise when professionals leave the firm.

Relationships

Since a PSF's most important assets are human, the relationships professionals have within their firm, within their professions, and with their clients are critical to achieving competitive advantage. Many PSFs are organized as collegial partnerships that place great demands on the relationships among the partners within the firm. We will see this interaction effect with Chan Suh and Kyle Shannon in the AGENCY.COM case. Firm professionals form close bonds with a firm's clients. It is often unclear until a given professional leaves a PSF, whether a client's loyalty is to the individual professional or to the firm. High-performing PSFs often succeed in either attracting professionals who have these client relationships, or in making a client's relationships firm-specific versus professional-specific.

THE FOUR QUADRANTS OF A PSF

We introduce in this module a four-quadrant lens organized around two dimensions—level and focus (see Figure 1). The lens highlights the four main areas PSFs must get right to have a sustainable, successful, and well-functioning firm. We assert that high-performing PSFs need to achieve not only success in each of

---

[1] In brain-driven organizations human assets are most critical.

FIGURE 1.1

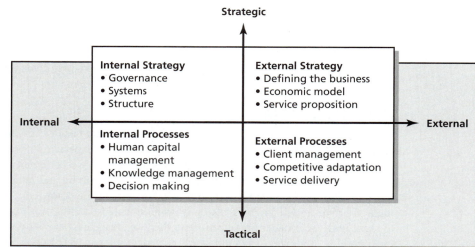

the individual quadrants but also balance among these four quadrants. In other words, PSF leaders must be concerned with managing both at the 50,000-foot level of strategy and vision and the ground level of tactics and execution. PSF leaders have to manage both the external environment of clients and competition and the internal environment of people and processes. We believe this model will be a useful tool for students as you analyze not only where a PSF's challenges are emanating from, but also how you think different decisions will impact other parts of the organization.

This opening module emphasizes that highly performing PSFs balance the internal–external paradigm. Too often PSFs only focus on the external markets and do not strategically connect how the professionals within them create value. These two cases provide examples of firms that have a clear sense of the internal value proposition and how to execute on the strategy.

We highlight this model in this module because it serves as a foundation for the first five modules of the book. Our intention is to have the readers take the model to memory and use it as a lens in which to create, design, and lead PSFs.

We emphasize that PSF leaders must manage both the external environment of clients and competition and the internal environment of people and processes.

The next four modules focus on each of the quadrants individually and deal with how PSFs must build capabilities in each of the four quadrants to be successful. The protagonists introduced in the first two cases must guide their firms around the barriers and through the jungle, and keep balance and perspective regarding the four quadrants. In Modules Six and Seven, we will again look at the model holistically from the perspective of firm leaders (Module Six: *Leadership and Change Management in PSFs*) and of beginning professionals in those firms (Module Seven: *Becoming a Professional*).

HAMBRECHT & QUIST

The first case of the module centers on the dramatic actions of Hambrecht & Quist (H&Q) as it confronted the marketplace and how it fit in that competitive space. H&Q in the middle and late-1990s was a successful firm. Their positioning as a top boutique firm with a collegial employee culture was well understood in the marketplace. But changes in the market for financial services made it challenging for H&Q to look toward the future. This case highlights not only the characteristics of a successful PSF but also the importance of offering a differentiated service and of evolving a business model and positioning if the marketplace heads in a different direction.

In understanding its current and future potential positioning, H&Q must consider many questions. What are the advantages and disadvantages of scale in the market? Is the market mature enough to support heavy vertical integration? How can you determine whether externally driven changes will make sense internally? How do you know when the time is right for the change?

What lessons can H&Q learn from previous mergers? Why were the other HARMs selling?[2] Why had H&Q not sold? Was H&Q missing opportunities or just waiting for the optimal time to exploit the opportunity? Having differentiated itself by focusing solely on growth companies, can H&Q offer the full range of services customers want (if they do)?

Focusing on internal questions, H&Q must consider how important its culture was to its business success and to its ability to attract and retain talented recruits? How would this change if H&Q merged or was acquired by a big bank? If it chooses to merge or be acquired, would the benefits of increased scale and scope offset changes in the H&Q culture? Would H&Q's customers prefer a more one-stop shop portfolio of products from H&Q, or would they continue to prefer a focused boutique? Who is H&Q's primary target customer going forward (money managers, venture capitalists, individual investors, or big institutions)? Who would a merger benefit most (officers, investors, mid-level managers, new recruits, large clients, or small clients)? Who would it hurt most?

Dan Case must decide how to create a strategy that is consistent both externally and internally. He must create and gain consensus to a strategic vision about how the market will evolve in the future. If he determines that scale is important, he should seek a partner. If he decides to seek a partner, he must be clear to customers, employees, investors, and other stakeholders how the move benefits them. The case also begins to address the challenges of a merger and the consequences of being clear about strategic capabilities through the merger process.

These decisions drive the business model that Dan Case has created. After agreeing to be acquired by Chase Manhattan Bank, he now must work to preserve these values and beliefs. This challenge creates a useful segue into the next mod-

---

[2] The four HARMs are Hambrecht & Quist, Alex. Brown, Robertson Stephens, and Montgomery Securities.

ule, which focuses on the importance of creating internal systems and structures that are consistent and in alignment with the external strategy discussed in this note.

AGENCY.COM

By tracking entrepreneurs Chan Suh and Kyle Shannon's start-up of their interactive consulting firm, AGENCY.COM, we discuss many of the challenges of launching and growing a PSF. AGENCY.COM is illustrative of the new world of PSFs. The interactive consulting world hardly existed 10 years ago. In 1999, 130 of the 500 fastest-growing companies in the United States were consulting companies focused on technology or strategy consulting. Chan Suh and Kyle Shannon began one of the nation's first interactive consulting firms and soon realized how difficult it is to balance capabilities with opportunities. This realization smacked them in the face as GE asked them for a request-for-proposal (RFP) that if accepted would have changed the horizon for these two naïve enthusiastic entrepreneurs.

Suh and Shannon must learn quickly about scale and scope, about technical expertise, and about defining the business. In short, they must build into AGENCY.COM the fundamentals that will allow for future business success. How will they differentiate their service? How do they create an integrated delivery process that delights the customer when the customer is not sure what the desired outcome is? How will they manage relationships over time, adapt to the competition if appropriate, and provide the service they have promised? How will they manage costs and hire the best people who will be committed to the vision of the firm? How will they decide on the best way to govern the firm? How will they create systems and structures within the firm that take into consideration the needs and personalities of all the professionals? How can they build their firm for the long term?

HISTORICAL NOTES

We introduce two specific notes that give the reader a historical perspective of investment banking and the world of e-consulting. These notes give context and understanding to a number of the cases we introduce in the book, including Hambrecht & Quist and AGENCY.COM. They also stand alone as information that will help professionals in the field understand how the organizations for which they work have evolved.

The second note serves as a primer for those professionals who have experienced or will experience the world of consulting in context to the Internet space. Although this arena grew overnight and has seen dramatic shifts in the last two years, it is important to have context and perspective of this domain.

HISTORY OF INVESTMENT BANKING

Few professionals choosing investment banking as a vocation know the history of the world in which they enter. This background material focuses on the evolution over the past 100 years of investment banking in the United States and describes the scope of products and services offered by these institutions. The note highlights the functions performed by these institutions, like the transference of economic resources, risk management, and mitigating the impact of asymmetric information on interactions among parties. The document also defines clearly what is in the purview of financial institutions and what is not. For example, some professionals may not be clear about how venture capital, private equity firms, and asset management functions differ from the role of investment banks.

The note provides a detailed summary of the history of banking, beginning with an international perspective and evolving up through the European family banks, to the emergence of Wall Street. In the note we highlight the impact of the Glass-Steagall Act and how this legislation affected how institutions defined their role in making markets. We conclude the document with a description of how institutions define themselves by how they compete, what functions they provide, how they make profits, and how they react to environmental conditions.

E-CONSULTING

The rapid growth of e-consulting and its rather marked decline is important to understand in the context of current market realities. While the e-consulting world has recalibrated in the past two years, there is an underlying body of knowledge we have attempted to capture. Organizations continue to spend capital on e-consulting, trying to leverage their Internet capabilities.

We have defined e-consulting as those services that help conceive and launch an e-commerce business model and integrate it, if necessary, with an existing business. We explore the e-commerce opportunities between businesses and between businesses and consumers. The number of firms that are reconsidering their positioning and investments in the e-consulting world are considerable. Many firms worry about how this arena will grow, or whether it will consolidate even more and in what directions. Firms, incumbents, and new entrants are all rethinking the extent to which they want to commit financial and human capital in the arena.

We focus on the competition among new entrants into the space and how they may address competition from larger entrants. It is evident that incumbents are considering to what extent they want to invest in the space. The challenge we address is whether or not incumbents should change organizational practices that will be consistent with core principles, practices, and values of the firm.

We also address the challenge of building partnerships and alliances to leverage the strengths of each provider. Strategic arrangements provide them with access to the contacts, expertise, infrastructures, scale, and resources that firms already have. The incumbent firms gain by enhancing their e-consulting knowledge, skill, and credibility through their association with the Internet firms.

The centerpiece of the e-consulting note focuses on longer-term issues such as the changing market because of the Internet or whether the Internet consulting space can endure long term. We try and address how both the firm–client relationship and the firm–employee relationship may change because of the Internet. We finally address to what extent the Internet consulting space will enhance centralization and globalization opportunities. The challenge will be to determine to what extent firms will enter this space based on current market conditions.

SUMMARY

We see through these two introductory cases the complex world of PSFs. We see that the internal and external considerations of these firms must be intertwined to create organizations that are able to manage people and processes effectively. The protagonists must define their businesses, understand the strategic demands, and develop an economic model that serves their business proposition. They must proactively manage the organizational demands through the systems and structures they create. They must manage the human capital, decision-making, and knowledge management processes that drive the tactical/operational dimension of the firm. In addition, they must connect the internal processes with the external ones that serve and surpass client expectations.

The first module of the book provides readers with an introduction into the world of PSFs. We have employed the inductive learning approach to introduce the challenges inherent in these organizations. We have used two cases that are examples of the kinds of cases that will follow in order to teach the concepts and perspectives and acquaint readers with skills that are necessary to acquire to be successful. We have tried to create a rationale for not only why we need to study PSFs but also why readers need to know this information to make more informed career decisions. We know that we join these firms because they are a magnet for intellectual capital (community), because of the warranty function (branding), the financial function (security), and the learning function (capabilities). It is in part due to this confluence of motivations that makes the understanding and mastery of the skill competencies imperative in order for readers entering into PSFs to become effective in leading, creating, and thriving in these dynamic systems.

QUESTIONS ARISING FROM THE CASES IN THIS MODULE

While we do not pretend to have covered all the questions listed below, we at least have attempted to push readers to raise at least a number of them in the first two cases:

- How do PSFs work?
- How are these firms different and unique from other firms?
- How are PSFs changing with the changes in the global economy?
- How do PSFs relate with the world of e-commerce and the world of technology?
- How do PSFs add value, and how will I create value in them?
- If I wanted to create my own PSF, how would I go about doing it?
- How do I balance the internal and external markets of a firm simultaneously? How do I get the supply and demand right?
- What are the processes that are crucial to get right in a PSF firm?
- Do I really want to work in the professional service arena? If so, for how long?
- Why have so many of my colleagues joined them in the past?
- How do I choose the right firm if I choose to work in a PSF?
- How do I develop the professional skills I will need to be successful?
- How do I manage my career within the firm and leverage my own capabilities?
- How do I progress through the PSF to assume leadership responsibility?
- How do I share knowledge throughout the firm that helps both my colleagues and me?
- How do I continue to learn and grow and develop?
- If I want to leave the firm, how do I do it the right way?
- How do I balance all the pressures in my professional and private life?

These questions are the heart of the concerns readers have about the world of PSFs. The opening module attempts to touch upon these myriad concerns through introducing the readers to three protagonists who must confront many of these issues as they make critical decisions that determine firm success or failure.

Hambrecht & Quist

Dan Case, the CEO of Hambrecht & Quist (H&Q), welcomed 30 MBAs who had come to a recruiting event at the home of one of H&Q's managing directors in December 1997. While other investment banks hosted similar parties at local restaurants, Case felt strongly that the H&Q event should be at a senior firm member's home since it reflected the close knit "family" atmosphere of H&Q. Case considered H&Q's culture one of its biggest competitive advantages in the recruiting process.

Interest from MBAs had escalated in recent years. Headquartered in San Francisco, H&Q had become a leader in financing high-growth, entrepreneurial companies and had recently received attention for its involvement with a series of high profile initial public offerings (IPOs) such as Netscape, Siebel Systems, and Amazon.com (see Exhibit 1 for a partial list of H&Q clients). Also, H&Q had grown significantly, with revenues tripling and the number of employees doubling since 1992 (see Exhibit 2 for selected financial information).

Now, at the end of 1997, H&Q was at a crossroads. Case knew that it was important for the firm to continue to grow in order to provide career and financial opportunities for its employees, and attractive returns for its shareholders. But he wondered if he could maintain H&Q's culture if the bank grew much larger.

Also, H&Q was a ripe acquisition candidate. Similar sized banks such as Robertson Stephens & Co., Alex. Brown, and Montgomery Securities had been acquired earlier in 1997. Opinions varied on whether H&Q's shareholders and employees would be better served over the long run if H&Q remained independent or were acquired by a larger financial institution.

Case gazed at the MBA students and wondered whether H&Q would be the same firm next year when they joined.

DAN CASE

For Dan Case, entrepreneurship began at a young age. Steve Case, Dan's younger brother by 13 months and CEO of America Online, recalled:

> Dan and I were both interested in business at an early age, coming up with new ideas all of the time. None of them amounted to much, but we learned a lot—including what each of us was best at. It quickly became apparent that I was better at coming up with the ideas and Dan was better at coming up with the money and the discipline needed to nurture the ideas into reality. And that pattern, established when we were around 10 years old continues to exist today. I'm more the entrepreneur and marketer, and Dan is more of the financier and strategist. The great thing about this is how well we complement each other, so sibling rivalry has been replaced with trust and mutual respect.

The two grew up in Honolulu along with an older sister and a younger brother. Case, whose fa-

Nicole Tempest, associate director of the HBS California Research Center, prepared this case under the direction of Professor Thomas DeLong as the basis for class discussion rather than to illustrate either effective or ineffective handling of an administrative situation.

EXHIBIT 1   Partial List of H&Q Clients

H&Q: Investment Banking for the New Economy

EXHIBIT 2   Hambrecht & Quist: Financial Highlights, for Fiscal Year Ending September 30
(in thousands, except per share and other data)

	1993	1994	1995	1996	1997
Operating Results					
Total Revenues	$110,547	$119,330	$220,839	$392,702	$346,232
Expenses:					
Compensation and benefits	54,917	60,175	105,370	198,613	178,873
Other	29,386	33,118	43,570	67,022	90,262
Income before income tax					
provision	26,244	26,037	71,899	127,067	77,097
Net Income	15,304	15,918	49,438	88,601	43,174
Pro forma net income[1]	—	—	—	71,158	
Per Share Data					
Earnings per common share	—	—	—	—	$1.68
Pro forma earnings per					
common share[2]	—	—	—	$3.27	—
Book value per					
common share[3]	$3.94	$4.43	$6.31	$9.99	$12.51
Financial Condition					
Total Assets	$131,878	$155,160	$319,630	$537,917	$678,937
Debt Obligations	16,913	12,684	13,771	8,365	2,700
Stockholders' equity and					
partners' capital	50,290	63,591	105,462	226,711	297,378
Other Data					
Number of common shares					
outstanding[3,4]	12,760,336	14,353,884	16,720,804	22,693,930	23,768,722
Return on average					
stockholders' equity					
and partners' capital	37%	28%	58%	60%	16%
Pro forma return on average					
stockholders' equity and					
partners' capital	—	—	—	47%	—
Number of employees[5]	350	426	498	685	823

[1]1996 pro forma net income includes taxes on LP earnings as if LP's earnings were subject to an effective tax rate of 44 percent.

[2]Pro forma earnings per common share is determined by dividing pro forma net income by the weighted average number of common shares, including common share equivalents, outstanding during the year. Pro forma earnings per common share are not shown prior to 1996 because the amounts would not be meaningful.

[3]Includes equivalent shares related to LP units outstanding at September 30, 1994 and 1995. Shown at end of period.

[4]Shown net of treasury shares.

[5]Shown at end of period.

Source: 1997 Annual Report.

ther was a corporate lawyer and mother a teacher, teamed up with brother, Steve, at age 11 to form several small businesses, including Case Enterprises—a mail-order company that sold a wide variety of products from seeds to greeting cards through the mail and door-to-door—and the Aloha Sales Agency, which sold ad circulars. While none of their ventures was a major financial success, they gave Case a taste for the excitement and challenge involved in starting a company. Case went on to Princeton University where he graduated Phi Beta Kappa with a degree in economics and public policy from the Woodrow Wilson School in 1979. Following college, he joined H&Q for the summer before completing a Rhodes scholarship at Oxford University focusing on management studies. Case reflected on his decision to join H&Q in 1981:

> I wanted to work in finance at the intersection of strategy and entrepreneurial activity. When I got here this place was a crazy, small, wonderful, loosely organized firm, with close ties to Silicon Valley, that worked with early stage companies that the rest of Wall Street was ignoring. We had an "around the edges" business strategy, focused on a few high-growth industries, and we had a culture that was not afraid of change.

Unlike many of his peers in the banking industry, Case did not hold an MBA and had spent his entire career at just one firm. Case rose quickly at H&Q; he was tapped to lead H&Q's merger and acquisition (M&A) business in 1986, then the investment banking division in 1988, followed by promotions to co-CEO in 1992, CEO in 1994, and chairman of the board in 1997.

H&Q: THE FIRST 10 YEARS: 1968–1978

The firm's founders, George Quist and William Hambrecht, met in the mid-1960s. The son of a San Francisco milkwagon driver, George Quist got his first taste of growing a business as president of Mandrel Industries, a manufacturer of precision instruments. He grew the company from $600 thousand to $20 million in sales and ultimately sold it to Ampex, the maker of videotape recorders and data processing equipment. He later joined Bank of America in San Francisco as president of the venture capital division. Bill Hambrecht became interested in high technology through his job with Security Associates, a Florida investment bank, where he worked with small technology companies. In 1965, Francis I. du Pont & Co. acquired the firm and Hambrecht was tapped to open up their corporate finance office in San Francisco.

During the mid-1960s, Hambrecht and Quist collaborated on several West Coast venture capital deals. In 1968, the two met at the Kona Kai Club in San Diego and discussed the idea of starting their own investment bank. On the plane back to San Francisco they drafted the business plan and on the same day raised their first $1 million. They primarily focused on investing in new technology ventures on the West Coast, but to cover their overhead, they underwrote equity offerings for companies that the larger investment banks considered too small or too risky. When the equity market faced a major downturn in 1974, Hambrecht & Quist underwrote just two offerings all year. Under mounting pressure from their limited partners, Hambrecht & Quist liquidated most of their venture-capital portfolio and took out a $2 million personal loan to pay back the limited partners. As Quist commented in 1981: "In 1974 we used to sleep every other night."[1]

H&Q survived this period by taking aggressive steps to reduce overhead. The corporate offices were starkly furnished and institutional salespeople were expected to pay for half their expenses, including assistants' salaries, phone bills, and airplane tickets.

---

[1] "The Folks Who Brought You Apple," *Fortune,* January 12, 1981.

H&Q: THE SECOND 10 YEARS: 1978–1988

H&Q experienced rapid growth during the late 1970s and early 1980s. However, when the technology market turned down in 1984–1985, H&Q's business slid with it, resulting in significant turnover at the firm. Of the other banks that competed in H&Q's market niche at the time, LF Rothschild Holdings Inc. was hurt the most by the market downturn—they had underwritten too many deals without paying close enough attention to quality. LF Rothschild never fully recovered from the technology downturn when the broader stock market collapsed in 1987. Ultimately the firm filed for reorganization under Chapter 11 of the federal bankruptcy code in 1989. Robertson Stephens & Co. took advantage of the fact that it had fewer client problems to address, since it was smaller than the other firms, to focus on new business development. As a result, Robertson Stephens gained market share during this period. Alex. Brown & Sons came out of the 1984–1985 downturn the biggest winner since its broader product base and industry focus better insulated the firm from the problems in the technology sector. Case reflected on this period:

> It was a very difficult time for H&Q. Basically the firm divided into two groups—one group consisted of people who were new or less committed to H&Q who quickly washed out. The other group consisted of loyalists to H&Q and Bill Hambrecht. I was part of the latter group. At the age of 30, I was put in charge of investment banking. I was the seventh head of Corporate Finance in seven years, I had 21 people reporting to me and turnover was running at about 40 percent. It sounds pretty bad, but in many ways it was still fun. I like new things and

fixing things that are broken, and we had plenty of both.

H&Q: THE LAST 10 YEARS: 1988–1997

Because many of the small companies with whom H&Q worked moved on to larger banks as their needs outstripped H&Q's capabilities, H&Q had been accustomed to relatively high client turnover. However, when the firm recovered from the 1987 market crash, management realized that they needed to develop greater continuity with clients and greater diversity within its revenue base to give the firm additional stability. To achieve this, between 1988 and 1990 H&Q invested heavily in research, developed its M&A practice, expanded its health care practice, and built its institutional sales and trading business.

By 1991, all of these investments were paying off. However, that same year a crisis at MiniScribe, an H&Q venture-backed disk-drive company shook the firm. Q.T. Wiles, the nonexecutive chairman of H&Q from 1983 to 1987, had taken on the added responsibility of serving as chairman and chief executive of MiniScribe in 1985 in a "corporate doctor" role to revitalize sales. While under Wiles's leadership, MiniScribe was found guilty of engaging in fraudulent activities to boost reported sales, including shipping bricks to customers and counting shipments to MiniScribe warehouses as sales. Wiles, who had served as CEO remotely, spending only a few days a month at the company, resigned from MiniScribe in 1989 amid the turmoil. MiniScribe filed for Chapter 11 bankruptcy protection in January 1990, and later, filed for Chapter 7 liquidation.[2] MiniScribe stockholders and bondholders filed over 20 lawsuits against directors and officers of the company, including Bill Hambrecht, Coopers and Lybrand—MiniScribe's accounting firm—and H&Q.[3] While

---

[2] "Corporate Doctor' Loses a Patient—Wiles Fails to Revive MiniScribe," *San Jose Mercury News,* September 18, 1989.
[3] "Miniscribe Auditors Settle," *San Jose Mercury News,* October 30, 1992.

many believed H&Q would have eventually won its case, and, in fact, H&Q was never found guilty of wrongdoing, there was an initial finding by a Texas jury that prompted the firm to settle the litigation in 1991–1992 at an aggregate cost, including expenses, of $59.8 million. The largest component of the settlement was a $30 million term note issued by the litigation creditors, which, if paid all at once, would have bankrupted the firm, since H&Q's book value was only $30 million or so at that time.

Following the MiniScribe incident, H&Q effectively did a leveraged buyback of itself by offering significant equity stakes to professionals as part of its compensation policy. In addition to providing H&Q with the cash needed to pay the creditors, the equity component served to make H&Q look more like its Silicon Valley clients. While modified over time, H&Q's compensation structure in 1997 still included a significant equity portion. Case reflected:

> The way we describe it is that we pay 80 percent Wall Street and 20 percent Silicon Valley. At times for senior professionals we are slightly behind from a W-2 standpoint, but if the firm wins and is successful in the marketplace, you advance faster and have a much higher net worth opportunity—from H&Q stock and venture capital investments—than at a typical Wall Street firm.

MiniScribe also gave H&Q a healthy dose of fiscal conservatism. From decisions made regarding the amount of capital retained in the firm each year, to H&Q's austere offices, the firm adopted a more conservative approach to doing business.

In 1992, Case, just 34 years old at the time, was named president and co-CEO, alongside Hambrecht. After two years as co-CEOs, Hambrecht and Case made the decision to reevaluate and formalize the firm's strategy. After an in-depth strategic planning process, the group concluded that H&Q should differentiate itself from other investment banks by focusing solely on growth companies and investors seeking to capitalize on growth opportunities. Ironically, the firm decided that to do this effectively, H&Q would need to become a growth company itself to have the products, distribution capabilities, and capital required to meet the needs of clients as they grew. Pleased with the firm's new strategic focus, Hambrecht stepped aside as co-CEO in 1994, giving Case full CEO responsibility.

Between 1993 and 1997, H&Q's revenues grew at an annual rate of 33 percent, from $111 million to $346 million, and the number of employees grew from 350 to 823. The growth of H&Q's over the counter trading (OTC), M&A, and executive financial services business, combined with a continued focus on underwriting, contributed to the firm's rapid growth during this period. Between 1995 and 1997, H&Q ranked sixth among all banks in the United States in the total number of IPOs underwritten and first in the number of IPOs underwritten in the technology sector—its primary focus (see Exhibit 3 for 1995–1997 IPO league tables).[4] In August 1996, H&Q made the decision to seek a public offering to provide capital for additional growth and to provide improved liquidity for its founders and employees. H&Q sold 4,025,000 shares of common stock to the public at $16 per share, representing a market value of $405 million on a fully diluted basis. By the end of 1997, H&Q's shares, which were valued at under $2 per split-adjusted share in 1992, were trading between $30 and $40 per share.

H&Q's BUSINESS PHILOSOPHY

H&Q typically established contact with companies at a very early stage in their development—sometimes through a venture capital investment—and continued to service their needs as they grew by providing research coverage, equity and convertible debt offerings, brokerage services, merger

---

[4] CommScan Equidesk.

EXHIBIT 3 All IPOs: 1995–1997

Bank	Number of Deals	Rank by Number of Deals	Dollar Volume	Rank by Dollar Volume	After Market Performance %	Rank by After Market Performance
Salomon Smith Barney	230	1	$31,506	4	27%	14
NationsBank Montgomery Securities	186	2	9,557	10	36	9
BT Alex. Brown	183	3	11,338	9	64	2
Morgan Stanley Dean Witter	183	3	49,100	2	38	8
DLJ	156	5	20,224	7	53	6
Hambrecht & Quist	**153**	**6**	**6,667**	**12**	**51**	**7**
BankAmerica Robertson Stephens	152	7	7,760	11	57	3
Goldman Sachs	147	8	47,914	3	54	4
Merrill Lynch	133	9	52,458	1	35	10
Cowen & Co.	117	10	5,546	13	27	14
Lehman Brothers	100	11	21,073	6	29	12
CS First Boston	90	12	26,726	5	54	4
Bear Stearns	72	13	12,612	8	73	1
CIBC Oppenheimer	71	14	2,796	15	32	11
UBS Securities	65	15	2,991	14	29	12
Volpe, Brown	65	15	2,167	16	18	16

Source: Securities Data Company.

and acquisition, and general corporate advisory services. H&Q prided itself on balancing the continual hunt for high-profile transactions with a deep-rooted orientation to investment quality.

H&Q believed that industry specialization was critical to meeting the needs of its clients. Accordingly, H&Q made research a priority, hiring analysts with industry and technical expertise. Research analysts were divided into tightly defined industry groups which were frequently reevaluated to ensure adequate coverage of emerging subsegments.

H&Q's strategy also involved actively developing its international banking business by assisting non-U.S. companies in raising capital both in the United States and in their own countries. However,

international underwriting activities represented less than 10 percent of H&Q's underwriting revenue in 1997, leading management to view international markets as a significant growth opportunity for the firm.

Through its industry-focused research and banking teams, its close relationships with the venture capital community, and its proximity to Silicon Valley, H&Q believed it was uniquely positioned to identify the next generation of winners. A managing director reflected on this aspect of H&Q's strategy:

We would rather be a co-manager on the Netscape IPO than lead-manage the IPO for one of Netscape's competitors who was not

EXHIBIT 3   All Technology IPOs: 1995–1997 (continued)

Bank	Number of Deals	Rank by Number of Deals	Dollar Volume	Rank by Dollar Volume	After Market Performance %	Rank by After Market Performance
Hambrecht & Quist	**103**	**1**	**$4,596**	**6**	**54%**	**6**
BankAmerica Robertson Stephens	99	2	5,071	5	52	7
BT Alex. Brown	80	3	3,934	7	74	4
NationsBank Montgomery Securities	76	4	3,140	9	29	11
Cowen & Co.	74	5	3,069	10	28	12
Morgan Stanley Dean Witter	42	6	6,744	2	69	5
Goldman Sachs	36	7	7,669	1	116	1
Volpe, Brown	33	8	1,142	13	16	14
CIBC Oppenheimer	27	9	814	16	28	12
Lehman Brothers	24	10	1,052	14	16	14
DLJ	22	11	1,427	12	52	7
UBS Securities	22	11	932	15	34	9
Salomon Smith Barney	21	13	1,875	11	-16	16
Merrill Lynch	18	14	5,327	4	30	10
CS First Boston	12	15	6,088	3	87	2
Bear Stearns	10	16	3,682	8	76	3

Note: Based on H&Q's internal classification of technology companies.
Source: Securities Data Company.

nearly as well positioned for success. H&Q's philosophy is a reflection of senior management and our heritage in the venture capital business. Everyone at H&Q loves growth companies—we're not transaction junkies. Most companies will chase transactions; we want to find the next Apple, the next Genentech.

H&Q'S CULTURE AND PEOPLE

H&Q was known in the banking industry for having a distinctive culture. As one senior director at Morgan Stanley observed:

H&Q is a more genuine place to work than many other investment banks. Case and Hambrecht demand that professionals balance the tension between internal pride and external arrogance. H&Q has little time for "stars" who are absorbed with neon lights. They do excellent work and take themselves a little less seriously than at the traditional Wall Street firm.[5]

Many employees felt that H&Q's small size relative to its Wall Street competitors gave the firm a competitive spirit reminiscent of the David

[5] Case writer interview.

and Goliath battle. A managing director explained:

> Our balance sheet isn't as big as other banks', which often puts us in an underdog role. But, people here relish that. At H&Q, the people have to be good because although there are rationalizations why we should win the business, there are also rationalizations why we shouldn't. It comes down to this: is it your team or the firm name that wins the big deals? At H&Q it's the team.

Perhaps most important, H&Q's unique culture played a significant role in the economics of the firm. Case observed:

> Our culture impacts the bottom line in four distinct ways. First, the culture at H&Q makes it a fun and stimulating place to work, which results in below-average turnover, and in a professional services firm, turnover can be extremely costly from a recruiting, training, and client continuity standpoint. Second, we have a culture where senior managers roll up their sleeves and work with bankers and analysts to win and service business. As a result, we have less true senior manager overhead than some other banks. Third, going back to the roots of the firm, there has always been close coordination between research, venture capital, and corporate finance, resulting in less functionalism and greater efficiency—you don't have to duplicate overhead between departments. [For example, the corporate finance group doesn't necessarily need a technologist on staff because research won't talk to them, which happens elsewhere in the industry. We actually leverage our venture and research resources to help qualify a lot of banking business for us.] Fourth, our culture and our brand allow us to attract quality people who deliver a consistent, quality product. As long as we keep building that brand, customers find us, and when they do that we have a lower cost per qualified lead. So in terms of traditional service chain management we have lower SG&A costs—and lower SG&A means more money left for research, market making, venture investments, compensation, and profits.

H&Q's management tried to hire people who fit the culture. Prior to 1994, H&Q did not actively recruit MBAs. Instead, professionals with relevant experience were brought in from a variety of sources, including high-tech companies, law firms and other banks. H&Q's management believed the diversity of backgrounds was an asset and put greater emphasis on intellect, creativity, and integrity than on prior banking experience.

However, the firm believed that its focus on diverse backgrounds had resulted in too few people with finance experience at a time when the firm was growing fast and needed bankers who required minimal training, who could be staffed on deals quickly. As a result, starting in 1994, the firm consciously focused on hiring more professionals with previous securities industry experience to balance the expertise on staff. In fact, of the eight MBAs who started at H&Q in 1997, five had previously worked in the investment banking industry.

A common theme among the people H&Q hired was their passion for financing entrepreneurs and their interest in thinking like an investor. Case reflected:

> We value good investment discipline. We like people who have good investment judgment, because if you're a good investor, then you're going to be good at figuring out which companies we should recommend. Our mind-set here at H&Q is "think like an investor." If you think like an investor you can filter out transactions that you shouldn't do.

For the most part, H&Q steered clear of hiring "rainmakers," preferring instead to hire mid-level professionals and give them the opportunity to grow into senior roles. While the strategy of building from within had worked well for H&Q to date, some employees believed that as the market became more and more competitive, H&Q would need to hire some well-established and well-known industry players if the firm wanted to efficiently establish a presence in new product or industry areas.

THE INVESTMENT BANKING INDUSTRY: GROWTH AND CONSOLIDATION

A merger and acquisition wave came over the investment banking industry in late 1996, in part due to an easing of the restrictions set forth in the 1933 Glass-Steagall Act, which aimed to segregate commercial and investment banking activities. In 1996, the Federal Reserve Board raised the limit on the amount of underwriting business a bank affiliate was permitted from 10 percent to 25 percent of revenues.[6] Commercial banks were eager to take advantage of this regulatory change since they were facing slow growth and decreasing margins in their core commercial lending business. On the other hand, investment banks sought the lending capabilities of commercial banks in order to keep pace with client growth in an increasingly capital-intensive economy.[7]

Several major acquisitions took place in 1997. In April 1997, Bankers Trust New York Corp. purchased Alex. Brown & Sons Inc. of Baltimore, the nation's oldest brokerage firm, for $1.7 billion, or approximately 2.7 times book value.[8] That left only three independent players among the group of firms known on Wall Street as the "HARMs" (H&Q, Alex. Brown, Robertson Stephens & Co., and Montgomery Securities). Then in June, BankAmerica Corp. announced a $540 million purchase of Robertson Stephens. Not even a month later, NationsBank of Charlotte, N.C., acquired Montgomery Securities for $1.2 billion, or 8.7 times its book value—a price so rich that many analysts questioned the growth assumptions underpinning the deal.[9] In other deals, SBC Warburg announced the purchase of the investment bank, Dillon Read & Co, for $600 million, or approximately 3 times book value in May 1997.[10] In August 1997, ING Group of the Netherlands, announced plans to purchase Furman Selz, a research-focused New York investment bank, for $600 million, and Travelers Group announced in September 1997 that it would acquire Salomon Brothers for more than $9 billion in stock, almost 2 times Salomon's book value, in a bid to create a financial powerhouse that would rival Merrill Lynch & Co. and Citicorp.[11] By the end of 1997 H&Q was one of the few boutique investment banks that remained independent.

While on paper the rationale for these mergers made sense, in practice it had often proven difficult to blend the distinctive cultures of commercial banks and investment banks. Due in part to cultural differences, past commercial bank and investment bank combinations had often failed to meet expectations.

H&Q: AN ACQUISITION TARGET

Opinions varied both inside and outside H&Q about whether it would be in H&Q's best interests to stay independent or be acquired by another bank. Case believed that recent industry consolidation gave H&Q an even greater strategic advantage; its

---

[6] "Behind the Deal—Bank Has Opportunity, Challenge with Storied Investment House," *San Jose Mercury News,* June 10, 1997.
[7] "Bank Buyouts Could Pinch Small Start-Ups," *San Jose Mercury News,* July 6, 1997.
[8] "Swiss Bank Unit to Buy Dillon Read," *The Wall Street Journal,* May 15, 1997.
[9] "Montgomery OKs Sale—NationsBank Gets Securities Firm For $1.2 Billion," *Mercury News Wire Services,* July 1, 1997.
[10] "Swiss Bank Unit to Buy Dillon Read," *The Wall Street Journal,* May 15, 1997.
[11] "Travelers to Join Financial Powerhouses—It Will Combine with Salomon Brothers in $9 Billion Merger Deal," *New York Times,* September 25, 1997.

competitors—who had previously focused on emerging growth companies—would be pressured to put more capital to work in larger deals for larger companies. In doing so, he reasoned they would face increasing conflicts of interest and risk losing their identity and point of differentiation. Case explained the strategy for staying independent:

> We have an extremely viable independent strategy, but it isn't "don't change." It involves reinventing ourselves again, focusing on the balance between venture capital, underwriting, brokerage and M&A, focusing on contribution margin instead of revenue, and focusing on life-cycle return on equity (ROE). As an independent investment bank we may not offer certain products which only a small fraction of our clients need, and that's fine, but we better have high share of mind for the products we do offer.
>
> As an independent investment bank we have some advantages and disadvantages relative to our regional competitors who have been acquired by large commercial banks. The advantages are that we maintain our culture and we have the ability to stay focused, which in turn, protects the identity of the brand. It makes differentiation a lot easier—we'll become even better known for the products and industries which we do cover, whereas the acquired firms risk losing their identity and focus. They'll be forced to move up-market and compete against the special bracket Wall Street firms in new product areas, which is not an enviable position. And when the compensation guarantees expire in a few years, turnover will go way up. The disadvantages of staying independent are that we have less capital and a narrower product line. However, emerging growth companies in search of transitional financing before, or shortly after, an IPO usually need a few million, or occasionally a few tens of million, but rarely a few hundred million dollars.
>
> We should stay independent as long as the advantages outweigh the disadvantages. Obviously, if somebody can figure out how to give us all the advantages and none of the disadvantages, we'd have to listen, but nobody has so far. Even if it were a close call, history and emotion would suggest you shouldn't sell. You can only do it once and it's an irrevocable decision. It took us three decades to get to $100 million in revenue, but only three years to triple that. So we need to think about the long term. We shouldn't make the stay-independent-or-not decision based on a two-year outlook.

Bill Hambrecht was an even stronger proponent of H&Q's independence:

> H&Q was built around an investment orientation. We start with the premise that we are going to do the best deals, not the biggest deals. There are many ways to get paid if you focus on doing high-quality deals, regardless of size. However, deal size is extremely important to the larger Wall Street banks. If H&Q were to a be acquired by one of these banks, we would no longer be able to work with the small entrepreneurs which has been our point of differentiation. In fact, you see what has happened to our regional competitors who have been acquired by larger banks—they have moved upstream and are finding it harder to be responsive to smaller clients. H&Q's culture is unique because people are proud of what they do—they are proud of the firm's performance record. If the focus switches to deal size and transaction volume, H&Q's culture will surely suffer.[12]

Evidence suggested that H&Q's focus on deal quality, rather than deal size, had paid off in terms of stock price appreciation following the IPOs

---

[12] Case writer interview.

they underwrote ("after market performance"). Whereas the firm ranked fifth in the number of IPOs it underwrote in 1996 and eleventh in dollar volume, H&Q ranked first in after market performance for the year. Similarly, in 1997, while H&Q ranked eighth in the number of IPOs it underwrote and thirteenth in dollar volume, it ranked second in after market performance (see Exhibit 4 for 1996 and 1997 IPO league tables).

Other Perspectives on a Potential Acquistion or Merger

Many **senior firm members** shared Case and Hambrecht's stand on independence, arguing that an acquisition would cause H&Q to lose its unique culture, which was the glue that kept many of them at the firm. As one managing director commented:

"There are 500 reasons not to sell from a lifestyle and 'fun in coming to work every day' standpoint. I don't think you can buy the soul of the firm."

At the same time, however, some senior firm members were concerned that their newly acquired regional competitors, BankAmerica Robertson Stephens and NationsBank Montgomery Securities, would be able to market an expanded set of products and services to the same emerging growth companies which H&Q was targeting. Evidence of the impact of this could be seen in the change in technology sector IPO rankings between 1996 and 1997; while BankAmerica Robertson Stephens and NationsBank Montgomery tied for the third place ranking in 1996 behind H&Q and Alex. Brown, the two firms tied for the first place position in 1997, participating in more technology IPOs in 1997 than in 1996, even though the over-

EXHIBIT 4   All IPOs: 1996

Bank	Number of Deals	Rank by Number of Deals	Dollar Volume	Rank by Dollar Volume	After Market Performance %	Rank by After Market Performance
Salomon Smith Barney	96	1	$11,476	4	8%	14
NationsBank Montgomery Securities	91	2	4,830	9	23	4
BT Alex. Brown	88	3	5,169	8	26	2
Morgan Stanley Dean Witter	83	4	29,675	1	24	3
Hambrecht & Quist	**67**	**5**	**3,160**	**11**	**27**	**1**
DLJ	63	6	7,951	6	21	6
BankAmerica Robertson Stephens	60	7	2,598	12	16	9
Goldman Sachs	59	8	24,529	3	16	9
Merrill Lynch	57	9	25,926	2	11	13
Cowen & Co.	50	10	2,446	13	13	12
Lehman Brothers	46	11	4,030	10	4	15
CIBC Oppenheimer	40	12	1,569	15	21	6
CS First Boston	32	13	9,774	5	19	8
Bear Stearns	29	14	6,286	7	16	9
PaineWebber	21	15	2,129	14	22	5

Source: Securities Data Company.

(continues)

EXHIBIT 4   All IPOs: 1997 (continued)

Bank	Number of Deals	Rank by Number of Deals	Dollar Volume	Rank by Dollar Volume	After Market Performance %	Rank by After Market Performance
NationsBank						
Montgomery Securities	62	1	$2,825	10	26%	9
Salomon Smith Barney	61	2	6,164	6	12	14
Morgan Stanley						
Dean Witter	51	3	10,273	3	30	6
DLJ	49	4	5,307	7	27	7
Goldman Sachs	43	5	10,047	4	39	4
BankAmerica						
Robertson Stephens	42	6	2,974	9	33	5
Merrill Lynch	41	7	14,805	1	27	7
BT Alex. Brown	38	8	2,199	11	72	1
Hambrecht & Quist	**38**	**8**	**1,519**	**13**	**49**	**2**
Lehman Brothers	32	10	10,466	2	11	15
CS First Boston	30	11	7,250	5	21	10
Cowen & Co.	28	12	1,557	12	20	11
Bear Stearns	24	13	3,134	8	44	3
UBS Securities	21	14	975	15	14	12
CIBC Oppenheimer	18	15	619	16	14	12
Prudential Securities	18	15	1,177	14	7	16

Source: Securities Data Company.

all technology IPO market was weaker in 1997 (see Exhibit 5 for 1996 and 1997 technology IPO league tables). Senior firm members also feared the encroachment of major Wall Street banks into H&Q's territory of emerging growth companies, and questioned whether H&Q could be as successful in the future as some of the clusters of companies on which they focused no longer represented a niche.

Many **vice presidents** and **principals**—neither the most senior, nor the most junior level—viewed an acquisition as an opportunity to cash out a portion of their options at an attractive price and have the opportunity to achieve more favorable pay packages with the larger acquirer. This was important to them since many in this group believed H&Q's "W-2 compensation" was not competitive with larger Wall Street investment banks.

Most **recent hires** lined up on the side for independence, noting that a primary reason they had joined H&Q was to have more responsibility and greater opportunity to directly impact the bottom line earlier in their careers than they would have had at larger banks. If H&Q became part of a larger financial institution, they believed these advantages to working for the firm would be lost.

From a **shareholder** perspective, there were many reasons to be in favor of a sale. H&Q's stock price had appreciated significantly from its public offering—rising from $16 per share in August 1996 to between $30 and $35 per share in November 1997, before takeover rumors drove the price up as high as $45 in December 1997. At $30–35 per share H&Q was trading around 2.5 times the firm's book value—equal to many of the recent acquisition multiples in the industry (see Exhibit 6 for H&Q's share

EXHIBIT 5   All Technology IPOs: 1996

Bank	Number of Deals	Rank by Number of Deals	Dollar Volume	Rank by Dollar Volume	After Market Performance %	Rank by After Market Performance
Hambrecht & Quist	**43**	**1**	**$1,939**	**4**	**29%**	**3**
BT Alex. Brown	37	2	1,840	5	20	6
NationsBank Montgomery Securities	30	3	1,305	6	34	2
Cowen & Co.	30	3	1,303	7	16	8
BankAmerica Robertson Stephens	30	3	1,204	8	15	9
Morgan Stanley Dean Witter	16	6	4,028	2	76	1
Goldman Sachs	16	6	4,360	1	22	5
CIBC Oppenheimer	15	8	451	10	17	7
Lehman Brothers	12	9	461	9	-12	12
Merrill Lynch	10	10	4,018	3	9	10
DLJ	8	11	432	11	26	4
Salomon Smith Barney	6	12	419	12	9	10

Note: Includes only banks that completed at least five technology IPOs during 1996; technology sector based on H&Q's internal classification of technology companies.

Source: Securities Data Company.

All Technology IPOs: 1997

Bank	Number of Deals	Rank by Number of Deals	Dollar Volume	Rank by Dollar Volume	After Market Performance %	Rank by After Market Performance
BankAmerica Robertson Stephens	31	1	$2,202	2	36%	5
NationsBank Montgomery Securities	31	1	1,170	4	27	7
Hambrecht & Quist	**23**	**3**	**974**	**5**	**51**	**4**
Cowen & Co.	14	4	521	7	30	6
BT Alex. Brown	11	5	555	6	140	1
Goldman Sachs	8	6	2,290	1	93	2
UBS Securities	8	6	280	10	13	8
Morgan Stanley Dean Witter	7	8	1,180	3	67	3
Salomon Smith Barney	6	9	307	8	-36	11
CIBC Oppenheimer	5	10	159	11	13	8
Lehman Brothers	5	10	286	9	-6	10

Note: Includes only banks that completed at least five technology IPOs during 1997; technology sector based on H&Q's internal classification of technology companies.

Source: Securities Data Company.

EXHIBIT 6   H&Q's Share Price History, from August 9, 1996 to December 31, 1997

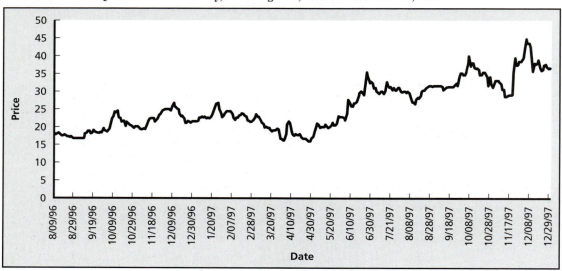

Source: Bloomberg.

price history). At $30 per share, H&Q's market value was close to $800 million—almost twice its value at the time of its IPO just over a year earlier. Some industry observers believed that if H&Q did not take advantage of its high market value in the near term, the stock market might turn down, causing deal flow to slow, which could turn H&Q's niche player strategy into a less valuable franchise until the next growth cycle.

Several **industry analysts** believed that it was not a question of whether, but rather of when, H&Q would succumb to the pressure to merge with, or be acquired by, another investment bank. As one industry reviewer explained:

> It's only a matter of time before Hambrecht & Quist goes the rest of HARM's way . . . size matters in investment banking because huge firms can offer a full range of trading, research, and financial-instrument services to clients. H&Q can continue to thrive serving the smaller

end of the spectrum, but bigger deals can be elusive. For example, despite H&Q shepherding U.S. Robotics Corp. through two highly lucrative public offerings, the Skokie, Illinois, firm chose Morgan Stanley & Co. to advise it on its merger with 3Com Corp.[13]

Many **competitors** also believed that H&Q would have to expand its product offerings and geographic reach to compete effectively in the future. However, they cautioned that if H&Q followed this strategy the firm would risk losing its point of differentiation. A senior member of a competing Wall Street investment bank discussed H&Q's predicament:

> H&Q has been chosen to manage the first round public offerings for a number of successful growth companies. However, the question is whether they will be selected to play in the second round where the margins

---

[13] "Hambrecht & Quist: Is It 'Dead Meat' in Takeover Frenzy?" *San Jose Mercury News,* September 29, 1997.

EXHIBIT 7   Letter from Bill Hambrecht, Chairman of the Board of H&Q

Almost 30 years after co-founding Hambrecht & Quist with the late George Quist, I am retiring as Chairman. Every entrepreneur I have ever known has had a dream, and George and I were no exception. Thirty years ago we set out to do something different. Of course, we wanted H&Q to be a financial success, but we also wanted H&Q to be a firm we were proud of, and that added real value. Perhaps most important, we hoped to create challenges and opportunities that would attract other talented people and make H&Q an exciting place to build their careers.

We were extremely fortunate because we succeeded beyond my wildest dreams. Together with the extraordinary people who have joined us, we were part of something very special that I will always treasure. We have helped our clients succeed by financing their dreams to change the world with their innovative technologies and ideas. And we have shared that success with our employees and stockholders. I take great pride in this success and know that it will continue under superior leadership.

Five years ago, when Dan Case became Co-Chief Executive Officer, we started a transition process that I now feel is complete. H&Q has made enormous progress, and has an exciting future that is in the hands of a great leader and an exceptional management team.

I leave with deep love and affection for everyone at H&Q.

Bill
William R. Hambrecht
Chairman of the Board of Directors
Hambrecht & Quist Group

Source: 1997 Annual Report.

are more attractive. H&Q has played at the beginning of the food chain, but the margins are at the other end. H&Q will have to add products and services and expand globally to be successful. The future is pushing them to become a full service bank, but as they do so, they become more like a Goldman Sachs or Morgan Stanley and they lose their specialness.[14]

LOOKING AHEAD

At the end of 1997, Bill Hambrecht retired as chairman of H&Q, making Case both CEO and chairman of the firm (see Exhibit 7 for Bill Hambrecht's letter to shareholders). Case knew that 1998 would be an important year for H&Q. Not only did it mark the beginning of H&Q's fourth decade, but it also would be the year in which Case would need to decide among three growth paths: (1) be acquired or merged with a larger bank; (2) add additional industry groups to compete with larger banks; or (3) embrace the status quo, remain independent and grow organically.

As Case looked at H&Q's potential new recruits, he wondered which option would be in their best interests, as well as the best interests of H&Q's shareholders, customers, and current employees.

[14] Case writer interview.

AGENCY.COM (A):
Launching an Interactive Service Agency

Chan Suh checked his watch and saw that it was two A.M. Suh and Kyle Shannon, co-founders of AGENCY.COM, were working together into the early hours of that June morning in 1995 to prepare a response to a request-for-proposal (RFP) for General Electric. Suh was surprised not so much by the hour of the morning—late hours were very much a part of AGENCY.COM's "spirit of getting things done"—as by the speed at which the past several hours had flown by. Other than his watch, he had no measure of the passage of time, as AGENCY.COM's headquarters was a windowless inner office above the loading dock at Time's midtown Manhattan headquarters.

Although tired, Suh and Shannon were exultant about AGENCY.COM's early success; they had won four of their five pitches in May, their third month of operations. "Because of our success in May," remarked Suh:

> we were confident in our chances and excited about the opportunity of winning the GE account. GE would be the biggest account ever in the industry—most previous jobs had budgets around $100 thousand. The GE contract was worth about $4 million. Winning an account that size definitely would solidify our positioning as a leading player in the industry.

As they prepared to finalize the GE RFP before the 8 A.M. submission deadline, Suh, focusing on the one question they still needed to address, called across the room: "Kyle, GE has a question on what we think the future of the Internet is. Can you whip up a little something?" Shannon surprised Suh with his response:

> I'm not sure if I want to do that Chan. I'm tapped out and it's two A.M. in the morning. If we win this account we'll likely have years more of these two A.M. nights. I'm starting to be more concerned that we'll win this account versus lose it. Are we ready to win this account now? Chan, are you *sure* that we want to submit this RFP?

THE FOUNDERS

Kyle Shannon: From Yo-yos to *Urban Desires*

Upon graduating from Penn State in 1987, Kyle Shannon went directly to New York to become a professional actor and screenwriter. (Exhibit 1 provides biographical information on the key protagonists.) "I found it necessary to work at odd jobs," he recalled,

> such as selling yo-yos at FAO Schwartz and bartending to make ends meet. In 1990, sick of bartending, I switched to desktop publishing. I liked the work much more because

Dean's Research fellow Scot Landry prepared this case under the supervision of Professors Ashish Nanda and Thomas DeLong as the basis for class discussion rather than to illustrate either effective or ineffective handling of an administrative situation.

EXHIBIT 1
Background of Key
AGENCY.COM
Personnel

Chan Suh
- Co-founder of AGENCY.COM, February 1995.
- Marketing director of *Vibe* in 1994. Helped launch Time's Pathfinder site and was eventually charged with bringing *Vibe* online.
- Led marketing efforts for various magazines including *Details, Life,* and *Vibe.*
- Nine years in marketing positions at Conde Nast and NewsCorp.
- Studied creative writing at Sarah Lawrence College in New York.

Kyle Shannon
- Co-founder of AGENCY.COM, February 1995.
- Created *Urban Desires* (first Web culture e-magazine) in 1994 *(www.desires.com).*
- Founder and president of World Wide Web Artists Consortium, 1994–1998 *(www.wwwac.org).*
- Director, image processing, YAR Communications, 1993–1995.
- Co-founder, artistic director, New Voice Theater Company, 1991–1998.
- Professional actor and screenwriter, 1987–1994.
- BFA in acting, Penn State, 1987.

Ken Trush
- Founded and operated independent accounting practice specializing in growing entrepreneurial companies, 1984–1997. Contributor to first AGENCY.COM business plan.
- Ernst & Young, 1981–1984.
- Goldstein, Golub, and Kessler, 1980.
- Eugene V. Rose & Co., 1978–1979.
- Certified public accountant, 1981.
- BBA in accounting from Baruch College, 1978.

it engaged both sides of my brain, allowing me to use both logical and creative skills. After freelancing for two years, I realized that I probably worked much harder and many more hours as a freelancer, because I also had to drum up work, than I would in a full-time position. So, in 1992 I took a full-time job doing desktop publishing at an advertising agency.

About a year later, I started to get interested in interactive stuff and I recommended to my boss that the company explore interactivity. When he responded "show me the bottom line" I got fed up and left. Actors are always looking for an excuse to quit our day jobs! I took another job as a manager at YAR Communications in early 1994. At this point, new media was starting to catch on. Later that year, while I was giving an impassioned speech to all the account executives, saying that "we must get on the Internet," my boss interrupted and asked me to "show him the bottom line." Frustrated, I quit two weeks later.

While at YAR Communications, Shannon received a flyer promoting a friend's band concert. He started investigating the possibility of saving the printing and distribution charges by posting the flyer on the Internet. Shannon considered starting an agency to represent and promote unsigned bands on the Internet. Working with a friend, he calculated that he would need about 150 bands to break even. Considering this a difficult proposition, he asked his friend to run an analysis to determine whether he could transform the idea into a webzine (an online magazine). Because of the potential for advertising revenue, the idea seemed as if it could be profitable. In November 1994 Shannon launched *Urban Desires,* a webzine devoted to promoting events and discussing artists' issues. A month later, he learned that the Parisian newspaper *Libération,* after accessing the site, had raved about *Urban Desires* in a full-page article. Recalled Shannon:

> At that moment I experienced an epiphany and realized how powerful the Internet was. The effort and time involved in creating websites was similar to staging artistic productions, but the impact was far larger. I couldn't believe that I could program HTML in my living room in Brooklyn, put it on a server in Los Angeles, and then have people access the site in Paris!

Chan Suh: Recognizing the Internet as a Great Equalizer

Chan Suh was born in Korea and spent much of his childhood in Paris. He arrived in New York City in 1980 to study creative writing at Sarah Lawrence College with the goal of becoming a fiction writer. "After graduating from Sarah Lawrence in 1984," Suh recalled,

> I spent a few years finding myself. I worked for a year as a bouncer and night manager at the Reggae Lounge in New York. Then I spent a year fishing for shrimp and crabs in Georgia. After that, I came back to New York and worked as an accounting assistant for a year. At the end of that job, in 1988, I still had a strong desire to enter publishing. To get my foot in the door at a publishing house, I decided to temp at *New York Magazine.* My task was to enter addresses into a database. When I realized that the magazine had at least five months worth of names, I suggested to them that it would be cheaper to hire me full-time for a year than to pay the temp agency for five months. They agreed and I was hired into the marketing department.

> I was dirt poor at the time. On my second day as an employee I had only $5 in my pocket, which I spent on a pint of ice cream. Desperate to get out of this financial hole, I worked incredibly hard. I found a great boss to work for and became a general gofer for him. Most of the other folks in the department disliked him because he was moody at times, but I loved working for him because he was fair, completely transparent, and always let people know where they stood with him.

> After about three years in the marketing department I was promoted to manager. My time there was short, though, as after my boss was fired in 1991 the new director cleaned house and let me go. I took a job as a manager of the startup magazine *Details.* Because it was not well funded I remained there only a short time and then moved on to Time Inc. to work on *Life* magazine. At this point I started to settle into thinking that my career would be in publishing though I hoped to do some writing eventually.

After a year at *Life,* Suh was promoted to marketing director of *Vibe,* a music magazine with a hip-hop and R&B urban youth focus. Suh thought one way to steal readers from competitors *Rolling Stone* and *Spin* would be to launch an online version of *Vibe.* Suh recalled:

> I looked at who was on the Web and it was all colleges and college students. They took it up really quickly, as soon as Mosaic, the first graphical browser, came out; first the tech people, but then everyone else. I thought: "This is the perfect market for *Vibe*—young, urban—the kinds of people we want to take away from *Rolling Stone."*

> However, nobody could tell me how to get on the Web so I had to learn the technology myself. I found that among the best sources of information were online bulletin boards that had dedicated areas to discuss the Web. As soon as I understood how to communicate online, I immediately fell in love with the

medium. It was a forum to exchange ideas without their being colored by perceptions of race, gender, or appearance. The Internet had the potential to transcend the way people treated each other and overcome biases. It could serve as a great societal equalizer.

One of the first graphical publishing sites, the *Vibe* site generated substantial traffic. Recalled Suh: "Thousands of people visited the site, which back then meant it was hugely successful, and we got a ton of subscriptions out of it. Fortunately, it was also profitable from day one because I got advertisers to sponsor sections." Suh was soon working 16 hours per day—8 hours at his marketing director's job and another 8 hours on his Web projects. But he was thrilled: "I felt like a master of the universe, because I could change what was on the Web."

A Meeting of Minds

Shannon and Suh met through *Echo,* an online discussion group both had joined to learn more about the Web. Suh became a key source of answers to Shannon's questions regarding the launch of *Urban Desires.* Meeting to discuss a particularly difficult query from Shannon, the two found that they shared many similar passions. One of these was the video game *Myst,* which they found "compelling," according to Shannon, because

> it worked well within its constraints. At that time most other games were incredibly slow because their flashy graphics didn't work within the constraints of the technology. Upon reflection, Chan and I agreed that most Web designers similarly functioned without taking into account the Web's constraints. The consequence was many websites that functioned poorly or were too slow.

In October 1994 Shannon—"for selfish reasons, so that I could surround myself with people who knew more than I did about the Web"—founded a focused discussion group for Internet issues, the World Wide Web Artists Consortium

(WWWAC). Network members, including Suh, began to work together on freelance projects. Shannon loved the work so much that he quit his job at YAR and began working full-time on the Internet. "Kyle is an anarchist at heart," Suh remarked. "He said, 'To hell with my day job, we can go start something.'"

In December 1994 Shannon prodded Suh to join him in "starting a company doing Internet stuff." Suh and Shannon joined a few friends at a planning meeting over beer at TGI Fridays to discuss starting a company to produce Web content. "If we don't suck," argued Shannon, "then we'll be leaps and bounds ahead of everyone else." But Suh wanted to ensure that their ideas went beyond "just doing Internet stuff" and real clients were attracted to their business concept before he would consider leaving Time. Recalled Suh:

> Everyone wanted to do content because they all came from artistic backgrounds. At one point I said, "Nobody's going to pay us for content. I know because I'm working on *Pathfinder,* Time's Internet project. So, either we're going to build content as a hobby, or we're going to do something else." The one thing we all knew was that the Internet was going to be big, I mean *huge;* this was going to take over everything . . . and the consultants and the advertising agencies and the IBMs of the world didn't know anything about it. So we decided that we would be a group of people who could help companies do stuff on the Internet. Then we could use some of the proceeds to fund our creative interests, like Kyle's *Urban Desires.*

THE BIRTH OF AGENCY.COM

The *Sports Illustrated* Swimsuit Site

Suh's wait for breakthrough clients was short. In January 1995 two Time divisions familiar with his success with *VibeOnline* and his involvement in Time's development of its *Pathfinder* website, sought Suh's help with Internet related projects. The consumer marketing division wanted to study how it might increase subscriptions via the Internet, while *Sports Illustrated* (SI) sought to develop a website to promote its pay-per-view broadcast of the *Sports Illustrated Swimsuit Video* in mid-February. Suh negotiated a $20,000 fee from Time, half to be paid up-front and hired Shannon to help with these projects. "The number was very much of a guess," recalled Suh. "I had no real idea how much this work would cost and I just suggested $20,000 when they asked me for a price. With no delay or negotiation, they accepted it! Kyle and I thought that the profit from these gigs might be more than our combined savings from all of our years working!"

Shannon quickly set up three ethernet-connected computers in his Brooklyn living room, an arrangement affectionately referred to as their LRAN(living room area network). "My wife helped us out with the meals," he recalled, "and our dog helped keep us down to earth by continually tripping over our ethernet cables." Shannon began working full-time on the project; Suh joined him after his full days of work on *Vibe*. "We worked until about 4 A.M. each morning," Shannon described the experience, "particularly after the *Sports Illustrated* folks gave us a video on the first of February and told us to do whatever we thought would look good. With only two weeks before site launch, it was a big challenge to turn the video into pictures and then build the site."

As a result of viral marketing—intense word-of-mouth marketing that spread quickly, like a virus, with those exposed to the site "infecting" friends with information about it—the *Sports Illustrated* site became so popular that it crashed two servers within its first 12 hours of operation. Swimsuit models drew traffic, but the site's pinwheel design and extensive use of QuickTime video clips impressed prospective clients. The buzz created by the site and the news of the crashed servers generated tremendous publicity

for the pay-per-view broadcast and for Suh and Shannon.

Incorporation

While working on the *Sports Illustrated* site, Suh and Shannon engaged certified public accountant Ken Trush, with whom Shannon had worked at YAR Communications, to begin the process of incorporation. "To get paid for our work at Time, we needed to set up processes for invoices, obtain permits, and name our company," recalled Suh.

> Ken told us to set up two checking accounts, one for payroll and one for general expenses. So we went to the bank in the bottom of the Time building. They said that there was no minimum balance for the accounts so I looked into my wallet, found $80, and put $40 into each account. Our company was founded with $80!
>
> We also needed a name for the company. Our first choice was "The Agency." I liked it because in publishing we worked with many different agencies that had a variety of talented people to help out businesses. Kyle liked the name because it would imply that we were a "Central Intelligence Agency type of operation that would send in agents to fix corporate problems." Unfortunately, though, a Boston company had already registered the domain name theagency.com. But, in the process of discovering that, we found that the domain name agency.com was available. When I heard it, I liked it immediately because it was exactly what we did; we were an agency that helped companies get on the Internet. Our domain name became our company name. Kyle suggested that we make the name all capital letters to stand out in press releases and news articles.
>
> We were one of the first dot.com companies ever, because when we tried to register the company name with the state of New York, they didn't know what to do with the

period in the middle! After the paperwork cleared, I quit my position at Time.

THE FIRST THREE MONTHS

Capitalizing on Initial Success

Thrilled with the results of the *Sports Illustrated* site, Time executives approached Suh about researching issues and developing websites for other Time properties. Shannon recalled Suh's response.

> Chan insisted that to make this work for us Time would need to swap office space in exchange for our work and he demanded that Time provide space in their building and lease us computers by the following Monday [it was a Thursday]. When Time's director of consumer marketing, Marjorie Rich, replied that it would take longer than a few days to make that happen, Chan pounded his fist on the wall, angrily asked her, "Then where do you want us to work, on benches in Central Park?" and bolted out of the room. But Marjorie chased him down and promised us that she "would make it happen somehow."
>
> By the middle of the next week, Time came through with 10 computers and a space above the loading dock that formerly was Time's travel office. Although the space was dark and cavernous, we were psyched to be on the Avenue of the Americas, an address that we knew would help business.

After witnessing these negotiations, Shannon came to appreciate "Chan's awesome business instinct, particularly his guts to lay the company on the line in order to exert pressure. Chan was able to look people in the eyes and not break down. In the big leagues, people sense weakness. Chan's display of confidence led companies to have confidence in us." "AGENCY.COM was able to avoid bank or private financing," noted Trush, "because they did not have to buy expensive computers or pay high monthly rent and a hefty rent deposit."

Building Momentum

AGENCY.COM was hired as a subcontractor in March 1995 to build parts of the Zima and MasterCard websites. Impressed with its work, the firm to which it had subcontracted recommended AGENCY.COM when MetLife sought help with a small budget project. "The MetLife account," recalled Suh,

> allowed us to establish a foothold in the *Fortune* 500 by giving us credibility with other *Fortune* 500 companies. These were the types of companies we wanted to work with. I knew that $50,000 for website development was not a big deal for these large companies and I felt really comfortable working with them, since I myself had worked in a few.
>
> Also, winning business on our own allowed us to say no to more subcontracting work. The firm we initially subcontracted for had asked us to partner with them long term to do subcontracting. But we didn't want to become factory workers for another firm and build up their reputation instead of our own. We knew our work was good, and we vowed that we would never subcontract again if we could build a site as good or better.

AGENCY.COM began aggressively pitching business. Although Shannon felt "like David versus Goliath going in to pitch large companies," Suh did not consider the selling process particularly difficult. "Most sales were aspirational in nature," he recalled. "We just went in, presented slides of our previous work, and listened as clients asked us to 'do that for them too.'" In April 1995 AGENCY.COM won four of five pitches, adding Hitachi, American Express, GTE, and Columbia House to its client list. "The domino effect really helped us," Shannon recalled. "Once we got in the *Fortune* 500 club it was easy for big companies to trust that we could deliver strong results for them too."

Shannon and Suh did not concern themselves with competition. "We had enough work to keep us busy seven days per week, 14 hours per day," recalled Suh. "There was plenty of business to go around. Most web-design firms just decided which business they wanted and they were successful at getting it."

By requiring clients to pay half the total fee up front, AGENCY.COM achieved positive cash flow early (see Exhibit 2). Moreover, recalled Trush: "Chan, unlike some of his competitors, refused to take on business at a loss to land major accounts. After listening to him, most of AGENCY.COM's potential clients were persuaded by his logic that they wanted us to make money so that we'd still be around to serve them in six months."

Although prepaid fees and reinvested profits assured AGENCY.COM a steady cash inflow that facilitated staffing and avoided incurring heavy debt to finance growth, problems continued to crop up. "We were sleeping in the office, on the couch, and that's all we were doing besides working," explained Suh.

> My investment in a co-op was foreclosed because I couldn't afford to pay the mortgage, as all my money went into the company. The day they foreclosed, the marshals were coming to move me out. I packed all my stuff in a van and came to work. I had no

place to go. One of our clients, who had a brownstone in Manhattan, lent me her basement so I could live there until I found a place to live. Apparently it didn't undermine her confidence in our company!

Trush, who worked with Suh together on business administration while the rest of the team focused on delivering client work, became a trusted advisor to the founders. Shannon called him "the secret ingredient behind our success in the early days."

A Team of Pioneers

"We learned virtually everything on the fly," recalled Shannon, "not only how to build certain tricks into websites, but even business fundamentals such as scoping out projects, billing, and recruiting. A mantra that was echoed frequently when we tried new things was 'this just might work.' Fortunately for us, it often *did* work." "We were in a survival mode all the time," recalled Suh.

> Yet it was exhilarating because we were doing things nobody else in the world was doing. We probably felt the same way that Steve Jobs and Steve Wozniak did while

EXHIBIT 2

AGENCY.COM 1995

Forecast Income Statement

	$000	%
Revenue	2,162	100.0
Less: Direct expenses		
Labor	789	36.5
Gross margin	1,373	63.5
Less: Indirect expenses		
Labor	86	4.0
Depreciation and amortization	6	0.3
Other operating expenses	413	19.1
Total indirect expenses	505	23.4
Operating profit	868	40.1
Less: Other expenses	0	
Profit before taxes	868	40.1

they launched Apple computer. And, like Apple, the process was fun because people didn't "wear hats" here. We pitched in where we were needed and tried to learn from one another.

Suh and Shannon hired friends, former colleagues, members of WWWAC, and friends of current employees. "There was only a small community of people who knew how to do this stuff, so we brought on everyone we could," explained Suh.

But people we hired quickly self-selected into our organization or opted out of it. We tended to attract "doers," those with a "can-do" attitude who really sought to make things happen. "Manager-types" tended not to last long because of their frustration with the ambiguity of tasks and roles. A few times, we chose to let them go. We had to fire a guy in our first month. There were only five of us then, including Kyle and me, and the first thing this guy wanted to do was draw up an org chart. There were only five of us!

AGENCY.COM added 10 employees during its first three months. By the end of May its office above Time's loading dock was becoming crowded and cluttered. The spider web of cables that comprised the company's intranet, taped helter-skelter to the walls and ceilings of the office, was termed its "tape-net." This makeshift headquarters contributed to AGENCY.COM's "wartime mentality" whereby everyone pitched in and did whatever it took to deliver projects on time.

"The pay was terrible," recalled one of AGENCY.COM's earliest hires, "much less than publishing. Nor was there an IPO hysteria or huge desire for stock ownership. But I didn't come here for the money. I just wanted to do something exciting." Most of the employees were quite young, many having recently graduated from college. One recent graduate recalled that "the Internet was becoming the rage in computer science programs and many of us thought it would turn everything upside down. It's potential was exponential. We

knew that we were literally creating an industry." "I felt like a pioneer at AGENCY.COM," remarked another early employee.

I remember the first time I saw an innovation that I developed appear on *somebody else's* website—what a compliment to see your creativity copied elsewhere! I knew that type of experience was enriching my soul, even if it wasn't building my checking account. It made the long hours and the intense time pressure worth it.

Suh pointed out that being located in New York was a major positive for the firm. "New York is the center of talent," he explained,

not only for business and communications, but also for creative folks. If you're a true thespian, you'll be here. If you're a playwright or graphic artist, you want to be here. If you're a financial wizard, you want to be in New York. There are a lot of people like that pursuing those kind of dreams in New York.

Similar personalities and interests supported AGENCY.COM teamwork. "Almost everyone who liked working here," reflected Shannon,

tended to be beer drinkers, not martini lovers. We also were night owls and we all tended to dislike "big talkers": consultants, MBAs, or anyone who wanted to get their hand on the AGENCY.COM joystick, thinking that they could run our firm better than we could. We enjoyed knowing that we controlled our own destiny. That in itself was great fun and an awesome motivator.

One of the internal programs that reflected the spirit that Shannon and Suh infused in AGENCY.COM was "dress-up Fridays." CNN covered this novel concept and the *New York Times* wrote a feature article about it. "AGENCY.COM team worked much longer hours than our Time counterparts," said Suh, describing the origins of the "dress-up Fridays," and we all joked that because of our long hours we were often the ones who tended to stink in the elevator. When Time decided to make a big deal about introducing casual Fridays, we thought it would be funny for us to introduce dress-up Fridays. Then perhaps we could somewhat approach our Time neighbors in dress and looks.

THE GENERAL ELECTRIC DEAL

General Electric, one of the first companies to want to establish an interactive agency of record, asked AGENCY.COM and other companies to reply to its RFP in the first week of June 1995.[1] GE wanted to build 88 interconnected websites in only eight months.[2] The opportunity was very attractive; winning the GE account would go a long way toward establishing AGENCY.COM as an industry leader.

To win the account, Shannon and Suh would first have to complete and submit the RFP within the next six hours, including an answer to the "future of the Internet" question. Although he wondered whether "slicker" companies might be more capable and comfortable answering such a question and servicing the GE account, Shannon was "enthusiastic and confident about our chances of winning." He asked Suh: "If we pitch this business, we'll likely win it. Chan, are we ready to win this account now?" "GE is the biggest contract ever in the industry," reflected Suh, pondering Shannon's question.

We can increase our revenues tenfold overnight and likely gain the reputation as the biggest player in this space. On the other hand, I wonder whether we really can staff up quickly enough to service both GE and our current clients with the quality of service that they expect. We have only 12 full-time employees now. We still haven't figured out how much work is needed to service the four accounts that we just won. Also, since GE would be at least 90 percent of our revenues, won't that take away our independence?

The clock was ticking. As Suh wondered whether the concerns expressed by the normally enthusiastic Shannon were simply the result of many nights' sleep deprivation or warranted careful consideration, Shannon asked again: "Chan, are you *sure* we want to submit the RFP?"

---

[1] An "agency of record" relationship is much like the relationships that most advertising agencies establish with *Fortune* 500 companies, whereby the agency is expected to partner with a client for the long term and develop a deep understanding of the client's business. Agencies of record are normally placed on retainer and expected to not work with competing firms.

[2] Katherine Cavanaugh, "The Wizards of Web Site Design," *Newark Star-Ledger,* January 13, 1997, p. 1.

History of Investment Banking

> The investment banker was a breed apart, a member of a master race of deal makers. He possessed vast, almost unimaginable talent and ambition. If he had a dog, it snarled. He had two little red sports cars yet wanted four.
>
> *From* Liar's Poker, *Michael Lewis, 1984*

INTRODUCTION

This note focuses on the evolution over the past 100 years of investment banking in the U.S. and describes the scope of products and services offered by investment banks.[a]

ACTIVITIES OF INVESTMENT BANKS

Functions Performed by Financial Institutions

Investment banks perform a subset of the activities that fall under the umbrella of banking. Lord Rothschild (1910–1990) of the famed European banking dynasty, explained that banking "consists essentially of facilitating the movement of money from Point A, where it is, to Point B, where it is needed".[1] More formally, Bodie and Merton (2000) identify the six functions performed by financial institutions as:[2]

1. *Transfer of economic resources* through time, across borders, and among industries;

2. *Risk management;*

3. *Clearing and settling payments* to facilitate trade;

4. *Resource pooling* and the *subdividing of ownership* in enterprises;

5. Providing reliable *price information* on securities to help decentralized decision making in securities markets; and

6. *Mitigating the impact of asymmetric information* on interactions among parties, that is, overcoming the problems of hidden information (adverse selection) and hidden action (moral hazard).

Role of Investment Banks

Investment banks perform these six functions in their role as intermediary between issuers of securities and investors in securities. Their role as intermediaries implies that investment banks serve two clients in every deal—issuers and investors. An issuer can be a public or private company, or any other entity that sells financial assets in the form of stocks or bonds (i.e., securities). An investor can be a company, an institution, or a person who buys these assets. Alternatively, an issuer can be viewed as a buyer of capital (i.e., it issues

[a] The terms "investment banking firms," "investment banks," and "banks" are used interchangeably in this note. Lynn Villadolid Roy, HBS MBA 2001, and Professors Ashish Nanda and Thomas DeLong prepared this note as the basis for class discussion.

securities because it needs externally generated funds) and an investor can be viewed as a provider of capital.

Although it is possible for issuers to bypass the services of an investment bank by accessing the capital markets directly, the large number and wide dispersion of potential issuers and investors makes the market for securities trade fragmented. Fragmented markets can function well if the characteristics of items being exchanged are easily observable to market participants. But securities are complex, partial financial claims on running enterprises. The securities market suffers information asymmetry—issuers know the intrinsic value of the securities they are offering, investors have relatively less information. This can lead to "adverse selection"—potential buyers of securities shying away from purchasing them because they are not sure of the value of the securities. Investment banking firms reduce the information asymmetry by gathering and disseminating information to both issuers and investors and matching issuers with investors by executing transactions.

In addition, investment banks help securities issuers manage risk by underwriting, providing insurance to the issuers by committing to buy the securities from the issuer at a predetermined price prior to reselling them to investors.

Scope of Investment Banking Activities

"Full service" investment banks offer a range of services—financing, underwriting, investment research, private placement, mergers, acquisitions and restructuring, venture capital, market making, proprietary trading, financial engineering, asset securitization, clearing and settlement, and money management—that span all six of the functions outlined above. Within a bank, the groups that handle each of the services tend to be organized in separate divisions, performing their own specialized set of activities.

Investment banks are compensated for their activities primarily through fees and commissions.

Merger and acquisition advice generates advisory fees; stocks, bonds, and private placements bring securities placement fees; principal transactions (proprietary trading and principal investment) are rewarded by appreciation of the banks' own capital; sales and trading generate commissions; and asset (money) management yields fees and commissions. Because most compensation systems generate rewards only upon execution of transactions, investment banks are motivated to execute as many transactions as quickly as possible.

Noninvestment Banking Financial Institutions

Investment banks comprise only a part of the universe of financial intermediaries. The following provides brief descriptions of financial intermediaries that are not investment banks.

- *Commercial banks* act as conduits between sources and applications of funds. Their primary business is accepting deposits and making loans. Other depository savings institutions such as savings banks, savings and loan associations, and credit unions compete with commercial banks.

- *Pension and retirement funds* combine private savings and social security retirement benefits of individuals, thereby mitigating individuals' risk through pooling, invest these funds on behalf of the individuals, and distribute the returns to the individuals upon their retirement.

- *Mutual funds,* through pooling investors' cash, spread the impact of fixed costs on small investors and offer them the benefits of sharing the services of professional management of their funds.

- *Insurance companies* help individuals and institutions manage risk by accepting annuity streams of payments from them in exchange for promised lump-sum compensation upon the occurrence of particular events.

- *Venture capital and private equity firms* raise finance for equity investments in early-stage firms and start-ups, provide expertise to help grow the companies, and then "harvest" or exit the investments after some time, typically through liquidity events such as initial public offerings of stock or acquisition of the firms.

- *Asset management and investment management firms* advise and administer mutual funds, pension funds, and other pools for investors.

- *Securities broker-dealers* facilitate secondary markets trading.[b] Broker-dealers include "specialists," firms that take on the responsibility of "market making" particular securities—ensuring liquid markets in those securities by offering to buy or sell securities at their listed price.

- *Finance and credit card companies* extend individuals and institutions credit and, in the case of credit cards, function as a form of payment (a substitute of cash).

- *Financial information services firms,* such as rating agencies (e.g., Moody's, Standard & Poor, Fitch IBCA, and Duff & Phelps for the securities business; Best's for insurance; and Morningstar, Lipper and SEI for mutual funds), financial data analysis firms (e.g., Value Line), and real-time information networks (e.g., Bloomberg and Reuters), offer comprehensive specialized financial information that is of use to other financial institutions.

HISTORY

There are six great powers in Europe: England, France, Prussia, Austria, Russia, and Baring Brothers.

Attributed to Duc de Richelieu, prime minister under Louis XVIII

International Banking History

The Sumerians in Mesopotamia are documented to have used credit around 3000 B.C., when barley and silver were the medium of monetary exchange. The first documented banking regulations were contained in Hammurabi's code, around 1800 B.C. in Babylon.

The first European banking institutions emerged in the Italian city states of Genoa, Florence, and Venice in early twelfth century. The first securities—financial instruments that signified ownership position in corporate entities (stocks, options, warrants) or presented creditor claims on assets of corporate entities (bonds and other forms of debt)—emerged in these Italian city states in the thirteenth and fourteenth centuries. The Republic of Venice, for example, issued long-term loans called the "prestiti," which were widely held by the public and whose prices were listed as a matter of public record.[3] The Medici bank of Florence became the first bank to overcome local barriers, establishing a network of banks and alliances in Venice, Rome, Milan, Bruges, Avignon, London, and Geneva. It later fell into insolvency in 1494, as a result of overextending its credit.

The first major bankers were "merchant bankers," traders of commodities and goods besides capital. Merchant bankers' earliest activities included advancing farmers money against future crop deliveries and extending loans to businessmen in exchange for security in the form of shop merchandise. Although banking had early roots, it was not until the late Middle Ages and the Renaissance that the Catholic Church's criticism of money lending waned and banking began to prosper.[4]

The European financial centers moved from Northern Italy, first to Spain and Portugal, and then to France and Amsterdam. In the 1600s, Amsterdam became a major securities exchange, where futures contracts and derivatives were

---

[b] Primary markets are the capital markets for new securities, such as IPOs. Secondary markets involve transfer of ownership (trading) in securities previously issued in the primary markets.

traded. A futures contract is an agreement that obligates the sale of a commodity or a financial instrument at a particular price on a stipulated future date.[5] Derivatives are contracts of various types (including options, futures, forwards, and swaps) whose value is based on the performance of underlying financial assets, indices, or investments.[6]

EUROPEAN FAMILY BANKS

"Investment" banking or "wholesale" banking (as distinct from "commercial" and "merchant" banking) emerged in the late eighteenth and early nineteenth centuries. Initially, investment banks were private partnerships that pooled large amounts of capital, typically by floating bills in capital-surplus nations, to fund projects, usually for governments. Often these banks were used by monarchs and sovereigns to discretely fund immense projects, including military campaigns, that would have otherwise required public funding through increased taxation. These capital pools were raised usually and invested. The complexity of raising, transferring, and applying capital across international borders posed a formidable barrier to entry because it required the establishment of a vast, cross-border network of information and relationships. Only a few banks were able to emerge and dominate what the French called "high finance."

Among the most successful investment banks to emerge in the first half of the nineteenth century were the family banks of the Rothschilds and the Baring Brothers. Both families understood the interactions between international politics and finance and were very reliable in meeting the terms of their contracts.

The Rothschilds, in particular, formed a particularly effective network. The five sons of the patriarch, Meyer Amschel Rothschild, established offices in Frankfurt, London, Paris, Vienna, and Naples. These five establishments were depicted as five interlocking arrows in the family insignia. To maintain cohesiveness of their investment banking business, the Rothschilds married amongst themselves and partnerships were kept strictly within the family. Recognizing the power of up-to-date information, the family employed pigeon post to receive and send reports of intraday stock movements. At the height of the Rothschild's power, from 1815 to 1860, the combined capital of the five partnerships made it the world's largest bank. The colossal fortune that the Rothschilds amassed primarily from lending to governments and speculating in existing government bonds led to the founding of a new breed of aristocracy whose wealth came from capital as opposed to landownership. In 1830, a journalist marveled: "Not a cabinet moves without their advice. They stretch their hand, with equal ease from Petersburg to Vienna, from Vienna to Paris, from Paris to London, from London to Washington."[7]

Other great banking families that emerged during the era of unprecedented prosperity in Europe between the eighteenth and the mid-nineteenth century were the Warburgs, the Lazards, and the Schroders. The family banks that dominated the major financial centers of Europe became "universal banks," offering a broad range of financial services, and played a major role in the capitalization of the industrial revolution.

Pax Britannica

Napoleon's defeat in 1815 propelled the city of London to become the dominant financial center of the Western world. It would remain so for the next 100 years. Britain's policy of extending property rights to foreigners enabled the Rothschilds, in particular, to conduct their business safely in London as opposed to central Europe, where anti-Jewish violence was commonplace.[8] The Rothschilds and the Baring brothers developed a strong partnership that dominated investment banking activities.

By the late nineteenth century, colonial Britain had accumulated so much savings that the city of London was able to export prodigious amounts of capital.[9] British investors financed foreign bonds from Spain, Chile, Peru, Mexico, Brazil, and Colombia, and railway bonds from France, China, and the United States.

America's vast need for capital lured European investment houses, notably the Barings, the Rothschilds, and the Speyers, to establish American offices. In 1820 the Baring Brothers solidified their American ties by sending Thomas Ward as a permanent representative. In 1837 the Rothschilds sent as their New York representative August Belmont, who became one of the wealthiest Americans in the nineteenth century.

While the European houses were establishing their American offices, an American from Danvers, Massachusetts, named George Peabody made the opposite move—he relocated to London in 1838 to sell American bonds in Europe. In 1854, he partnered with another American, Junius Spencer Morgan, founding the House of Morgan, an American banking dynasty that would become instrumental in shifting the balance of financial power from London to New York.

By the late 1870s, the House of Morgan had established itself in the U.K. and had begun to outshine the power of the Rothschilds and the Barings. Contributing to its demise in power, the seemingly infallible Rothschilds had committed one fatal lapse of judgment: discounting the potential of default-ridden United States, they had reduced their commitment to the country.[10]

The Emergence of Wall Street

Philadelphia was the financial capital of the United States until 1825. The opening of the Erie Canal contributed to New York's emergence as a powerhouse and catapulted Wall Street into prominence. By the mid-1830s, New York was the largest securities market in the United States. The depression of 1837 caused Philadelphia to default on its state debts, bringing down many Philadelphia-based banks and causing Philadelphia to fall farther behind New York in financial activity. By 1850, the development of the telegraph allowed New York securities prices to be communicated instantly to all the other centers, making New York the undisputed financial capital of the United States. The term "Wall Street" came to symbolize the American financial system as a whole.

Joseph Seligman and Jay Cooke, prominent among the early nineteenth century founders of American banks, amassed vast fortunes, thanks to their innovative and aggressive financial deals in an unregulated environment. Besides Seligman and Cooke, many of the early American banking families initially flourished because of their strong ties to European investors.

In 1861, the House of Morgan founded a New York office led by Junius's 24-year-old son John Pierpont (J.P.) Morgan. During the great financial panic of 1873, Wall Street experienced its first major upheaval as the mighty House of Jay Cooke failed, and the House of Morgan gained undisputed supremacy in American banking. Apart from the Morgans, other prominent families also began to establish banking operations as an outgrowth of their successful mercantile activities. Besides the Seligmans, these houses included the Lehman Brothers, Solomon Loeb, Abraham Kahn, and Marcus Goldman.[11] Other Yankee houses, notably the Lees and the Higginsons, also emerged from mercantile roots.

After the Civil War, the atmosphere in the United States was one of unbridled optimism. America's financial power was growing. Investment banks came to be sought more by private sector corporations, such as rail and canal companies, than by their traditional clients, sovereign states. The importance of government bonds declined as private companies' stocks and bonds entered the financial market.

By 1900, the United States had surpassed Great Britain as the foremost industrial power in the world. Investor interest was in the U.S. economy, and reliable information was hard to find. Only the best banking partnerships, such as Morgan's, had access to important and timely information from issuers and investors. Similar to the Barings and the Rothschilds, Morgan's bank and other prominent investment banks in the United States often held the upper hand against issuers, including sovereign governments.

J.P. Morgan

Biographers of J.P. Morgan (1837–1913) have conjectured that there will never be another financier exercising as much power as Morgan did at the turn of the twentieth century. He controlled one-third of America's railroads at a time when railroads comprised 60 percent of all New York Stock Exchange stocks and 19 of the 20 most actively traded bonds were railroad instruments. Using his deal-making prowess, Morgan convinced competing railroads to collude by carving out specific territories of operation. Subsequently, he consolidated the railroads into trusts that he controlled.

Morgan applied the same approach to consolidate the steel industry, creating U.S. Steel in 1901 (when U.S. Steel, the world's first billion-dollar corporation, was created in 1901, Morgan controlled about 70 percent of the steel industry); the shipping industry, creating International Mercantile Marine (IMM) in 1902; and the farm equipment industry, creating International Harvester in 1902. He also figured prominently in the affair of three leading insurance companies, including Aetna. In the banking industry, besides Morgan Bank, he controlled Banker's Trust and Guaranty Trust (later folded into the Morgan Bank) and held major stakes in the banks that later became Chase and Citicorp.[12] The process by which he reorganized and consolidated several industries into trust structures came to be dubbed "Morganization."

Historians credit Morgan's success to his dominant personality (Morgan flaunted Wall Street's power to everyone, including U.S. presidents), stellar connections (being the son of a top banker from the city of London), and sheer audacity (in his first job at Wall Street with Duncan, Sherman,

Morgan, during a visit to New Orleans in 1859, decided to stake without authority the firm's entire capital on a boatload of Brazilian coffee that had arrived without a buyer; although his gambit reaped a financial windfall for the firm, it cost Morgan a promotion to partnership).

Morgan masterminded the unofficial cartel among Wall Street banks that gave birth to the "gentleman banker's code." Under the rules of the code, issuers agreed to exclusive relationships with banks and banks restricted competition by not openly soliciting for other banks' business or employees. Many prominent Wall Street firms chose not to have nameplates on their headquarters, the prevailing attitude being that it was beneath the dignity of banks to solicit business and, instead, issuers ought to feel honored to be represented by prestigious banks.

The bankers' code ensured the continued domination of the banks over the issuers and raised formidable entry barriers into investment banking. Despite its success in commercial paper, Goldman Sachs, for example, was rebuffed in its bid to enter into the lucrative railroad underwriting business, dominated by the established underwriters at the time—the Morgan Bank, Kuhn Loeb & Co., headed by the legendary Jacob Schiff, and Speyer & Co. Speyer is reported to have informed Henry Goldman that the three established banks would handle all the railroad business and that newcomers were not wanted.[13]

Similar to the Rothschilds a century ago, Morgan's empire comprised of four partnerships in New York, Philadelphia, London, and Paris.[c] His mammoth deals included lending to the French government during the 1870 Franco-Prussian war and the financing of AT&T. He also orchestrated the rescue of the General Electric Company upon its failure in 1893, the 1895 rescue of the Gold Standard, and the historic rescues, in the wake of the 1907 financial panic, of New York City, the

---

[c] The New York and Philadelphia branches remained to become part of JP Morgan, the London branch was sold in 1975 to Deutsche Morgan Grenfell, and the Paris arm was bought by Morgan Stanley in 1975.

New York Stock Exchange, and several major banks and trusts.

Although these rescues gained him the respect of the federal government and the financial community, as he "brought on an atmosphere of integrity and solidity that had been conspicuously missing earlier on the Street," Morgan was reviled among popular Americans.[14] Ironically, it was Morgan's success as a financier and power broker that led to increasingly strident calls for greater regulatory oversight of the finance industry. The press dubbed him the "trust king," and by 1912, the public outcry against his various trusts reached a "thunderous crescendo" as a result of the Titanic disaster, one of two superships owned by Morgan's shipping trust.[15] Many believed that Morgan had amassed power because federal regulatory oversight was weak.

Evolution of U.S. Securities Regulation

Prior to 1913, the United States had experienced frequent banking panics, notably in 1819, 1837, 1840, 1857, 1861, 1873, 1884, 1890, 1893, 1896, and 1907.[16] Depressions followed many of these panics as frightened creditors called in bank loans, and businesses were hard-pressed to repay their loans due to declining asset values. Despite the frequency of those panics, moves to institute federal regulatory oversight and establishment of a central bank came to naught primarily because of the populace's aversion to centralized control. The Bank of the United States' charter was voted down twice, in 1836 and 1911. States were reluctant to cede regulation of state banks to a centralized authority and opposed branch banking, which they felt concentrated financial power in large cities at the expense of developing local communities. The aversion to centralized control hindered not only securities regulation but also general business regulation. It was not until 1887 that the Interstate

Commerce Commission (ICC) was established to regulate the railroads. In 1890, the Sherman Antitrust Act was passed.[d]

The absence of a central bank and a fiscal agent, and the curbed power of state commercial banks led the U.S. government to rely on private financiers such as J.P. Morgan to stabilize the national economy against boom-and-bust cycles. In 1895, after President Grover Cleveland asked Morgan's assistance in rescuing the gold standard, the public became concerned at his growing power relative to the federal government.[17]

In 1904, the Justice Department sued one of Morgan's trusts, the Northern Securities Corporation, under the Sherman Antitrust Act. Caught by surprise that a fellow gentleman and patrician would take the public's side against him, Morgan asked President Theodore Roosevelt to "send your man to my man and they can fix it up."[18] Roosevelt refused, choosing to focus his administration instead on breaking up Morgan's trusts and increasing federal government's regulation of the economy.

Despite the animosity between the two, Roosevelt was forced, during the 1907 banking panic, to rely on Morgan to employ his power and prestige to command the cooperation of all of Wall Street.[19] Morgan's success in stemming the effects of the panic, led even the most ardent detractors of a centralized banking system to recognize the need for a central agency, preferably under federal control, to function as the lender of last resort.[20]

Through a series of legislations, the government fortified regulation of the securities markets, Congress passed the Aldrich Vreeland Currency Act in 1908, creating the National Monetary Commission to study changes in the banking system. Early securities regulation, however, were enacted on a statewide level, notably the "blue sky" laws, initiated in 1911 and still in force in some states. Blue sky laws regulated the sale of in-state securities by out-of-state issuers. Though intending to protect investors, these regulations were inconsis-

---

[d] In 1914, the Clayton Act enlarged the scope of the Sherman Act's antitrust regulations.

tent and haphazardly implemented across states, resulting in only the most sophisticated investors and bankers being able to properly handle nationwide securities offerings.

In 1910, Senator Nelson Aldrich presented a bill proposing the creation of a central bank. By 1912, Woodrow Wilson singled out financial reform as a major part of his presidential campaign and that same year, the House Banking and Currency Committee, led by Arsene Pujo, summoned JP Morgan to testify regarding his interests and portrayed Morgan as the "bankers' bank" to demonstrate his disproportionate power over the government, other banks, and issuers.

Nineteen thirteen was a watershed year in American financial history. On March 31, J.P. Morgan, the most powerful individual on Wall Street, died. Aldrich's 1910 bill was resurrected and, on December 23, passed into law as the Federal Reserve Act. The central bank would have two main responsibilities: to provide stability to the nation's banks as the lender of last resort, thereby supplanting the power of private financiers; and to provide stability to the economy by controlling the money supply and key short-term interest rates so as to be responsive to changes in demand for credit.

To limit excessive centralization of power, the act established not one but 12 district Federal Reserve banks in major cities around the country, with a seven-person board of governors that would meet regularly in Washington and take joint action by majority vote. National banks were required to join the Fed, but the state banks could join if they met standards. As a result of this policy, numerous state banks, especially the weakest ones, were inadvertently excluded from the discipline and the protection of the new system.

Fed officials came to pride themselves on their independence—no members of the executive, legislative, or judicial branches of government were allowed to serve on the Fed to shield it from political pressure. The Fed was made controllable by the executive branch indirectly by the stipulation, as with the Supreme Court, that the president ap-

point all seven Fed board members, subject to Senate approval. The Congress also required the Fed chairman to deliver, semi-annually, a report to Congress called the Humphrey-Hawkins testimony.[21]

The Roaring Twenties, the Great Crash of 1929, and the Great Depression

By the end of the First World War, Wall Street's transition into the dominant financial capital of the world was complete, with the United States becoming a net exporter of capital. At this time, two important financial intermediaries competed in the marketplace: the private banks, most prominent of which were the House of Morgan and Kuhn Loeb and Co., and the commercial banks, foremost of which were the National City Bank (forerunner of Citibank), the Chase National Bank, and the First National Bank of Boston (First Boston).

The 1920s was a period of tremendous economic expansion. Wall Street soared with the economy, and from 1922 to 1929 (with the exception of 1923), the Dow Jones Industrial Average rose in every single quarter (compared to the same time in the previous year).[22] To take advantage of the heady growth of activities of the bull market, banks began the refinement and widespread use of syndication—a group of banks sharing in the underwriting of securities for initial public offerings—allowing them to underwrite ever larger securities offerings. Speculation became rampant and by September 3, 1929, stocks had reached stratospheric heights.

After the Labor Day holiday in September 1929, stock prices began to fall as investors began profit taking—cashing in on gains from stocks owned because their market price has risen—thereby pushing prices down. As prices declined, short sellers jumped in. On October 24, Black Thursday, prices began collapsing under pressure of sell orders. Record trading volume prevented the ticker tape from keeping up with price changes.[23] The price decline finally stopped on

November 13, having wiped out all the stock market gains of the previous two and a half years.

The 1929 stock market crash was followed by the banking panics of 1930, 1931, and 1933. These panics, along with an international currency crisis that forced the United States to keep interest rates high, contributed to the banking collapse of 1933.[24]

Depression Era Regulation[25]

Although disputed by some academics, the prevalent perception among the public was that Wall Street's securities abuses of 1929 had been the major contributing factor to the failure of many banks that directly led to the Great Depression.[26]

From 1933 to 1940, Franklin D. Roosevelt's administration passed a series of laws designed to increase financial disclosure requirements and regulatory oversight of Wall Street: the Glass-Steagall Act of 1933, the Securities Act of 1933, the Securities Exchange Act of 1934 (which led to the creation of the Securities and Exchange Commission), the Public Utility Holding Company Act of 1935, the Trust Indenture Act of 1939, the Investment Company Act of 1940, and the Investment Advisers Act of 1940.

The Glass-Steagall Act (1933) and Its Impact

The separation of commercial from investment banking, which had been championed by Senator Carter Glass, had not received much support prior to 1933. However, in the prior year, flagrant abuses of power by Wall Street banks were unearthed in Senate committee hearing on stock exchange practices. In particular, the conduct of National City Bank (precursor to modern-day Citibank) in failing to disclose negative information when it repackaged bad Latin American loans that it sold to investors elicited widespread condemnation. In light of the Senate committee hearings' findings, the provisions that eventually became part of the Glass-Steagall Act were directed to curb the following abuses.[27]

1. Banks were investing their own assets in securities with consequent risk to commercial and savings deposits.

2. Unsound loans were made to shore up prices of securities or the financial position of companies in which banks had invested their own assets.

3. Commercial banks' financial interest in the ownership, price, or distribution of securities tempted banks to sell to their depositors securities that they had underwritten.

Although the Banking Act of 1933, commonly referred to as the Glass-Steagall Act, comprised several measures, including the establishment of the Federal Deposit Insurance Corporation (FDIC) to stem bank runs, it is primarily remembered as the act that forced banks to choose between two very different identities. They could engage in either deposit taking and loan-making ("commercial banking") or securities dealing and underwriting ("investment banking"). The assumption was that preventing commercial banks from trading in securities would prevent fraud and promote their soundness.[28]

The Glass-Steagall Act was devastating for universal banks such as the House of Morgan. Their lobbying effort in 1934 to defeat the act having failed, senior partners of the House of Morgan decided in August 1935 that their future lay in commercial banking (the commercial bank would retain the name J.P. Morgan and Company) and voted to spin off an investment bank, Morgan Stanley & Company. To some, the 1935 decision by the Morgan Bank to spin off Morgan Stanley was "a shocking failure of vision" for a firm that had sponsored US$6 billion in securities for blue-chip companies and foreign governments between the end of the First World War up until the time of Franklin D. Roosevelt's inauguration in 1932.[29] To others, the decision was a conservative move to retain the stable part of the business, which employed approximately 90 percent of its staff, and give up the relatively more unstable and unpredictable business.[30]

As commercial banks divested or terminated their U.S. underwriting business, stand-alone investment banks were born, including First Boston Corporation, Lehman Brothers, and Dillon Read.[31] Since only the United States and Japan (which was forced to adopt laws similar to the U.S. banking statutes after World War II) among the world's major economies required this separation, commercial banks such as Citicorp and Chase, forbidden from underwriting and dealing in securities in the United States, maintained leadership in the underwriting of Eurobonds (bonds denominated in U.S. dollars or other currencies issued to investors outside the currencies' home countries).[32]

Whether the Glass-Steagall Act achieved its objective of increasing the safety and soundness of banks is debatable. But the act did succeed in breaking the power of the top banks on government and the economy. Observed an historian: "Such was the power of Glass-Steagall that. . . . Wall Street executives in the 1950s would be a colorless breed, unknown to the general public, like so many gray-haired bureaucrats."[33] Subsequent attempts to repeal or draft exceptions to those sections of the law that mandate separation of commercial and investment banking were not successful over the next several decades. Because the focus of Glass-Steagall was on regulating potential financial industry abuses, it did not address other potential causes of U.S. bank failures: unit banking structure and the prohibition of nationwide banking.[34]

Post–World War II Investment Banking Environment[35]

Investment bankers, not commercial bankers, emerged as principal counselors to U.S. corporations. With the Glass-Steagall act insulating the investment banks from commercial banks, the only other group of financial intermediaries that could mount an effective competitive challenge, the industry became concentrated and began to assume collusive characteristics.

Similar to the structure of banks prior to Glass-Steagall, underwriting syndicates continued to have a hierarchical structure, with power disproportionately held by a few top firms (the so-called bulge bracket firms). Bulge bracket firms shared the largest participation of stocks to be distributed by an underwriting syndicate and commanded the lion's share of fees. By 1940, four firms commanded bulge bracket status: Morgan Stanley, First Boston, Dillon Read, and Kuhn Loeb.

Immediately after the Second World War, the U.S. Justice Department unsuccessfully filed an antitrust suit on 17 leading securities firms. By 1971, Salomon Brothers and Merrill Lynch had replaced Dillon Read and Kuhn Loeb as bulge bracket banks, and upstart Donaldson, Lufkin and Jenrette, founded in 1959, began to be considered just one rung below.

Some observers argue that well into the 1970s, the financial services industry protected incumbents from competition by adhering to anticompetitive rules of marketplace operation. The exchanges, for example, operated with fixed commissions (fees to brokers). Only in 1975, when the Securities and Exchange Commission (SEC) mandated a "national market system" and abolished fixed commissions, was competition in commissions introduced in the exchanges.[36]

Also in the early 1970s the Securities Investor Protection Act was enacted. The securities industry's equivalent of FDIC insurance for commercial banks, it stipulates that the SEC can enforce the amount of capital that securities firms must possess to protect the liquid assets of their customers.[37] The strict requirements of the SEC in maintaining the safety and soundness of securities' firms, coupled with firms' self-regulatory mechanism, have allowed the SEC to quickly flag down firms that are in trouble. The early warning mechanism has allowed some weaker firms to merge with stronger firms to avoid failing.[38]

By 1980, corporations' allegiance to single banks began to be challenged in favor of multiple banking relationships. A landmark event was the 1980 securities offering by IBM Corporation in which the issuer demanded the inclusion of Salomon Brothers as a co-manager in the offering alongside traditional banker, Morgan Stanley. Morgan Stanley refused to cede its longstanding tradition of sole managing its offerings and withdrew, but IBM's defiance had broken banks' stranglehold in demanding the loyalty of corporations to single underwriters.

The Bull Market of the 1980s and the 1990s

The 1980s and 1990s were decades of a heady bull market, punctuated by few hiccups. These two decades saw several innovations in financial markets, including the creation of a multimillion dollar mortgage and asset-backed securities market, spearheaded by Salomon Brothers in the early 1980s; the junk bond (high yield) market, spearheaded by Drexel Burnham Lambert, and the use of financial engineering (corporate derivatives) in the 1990s. Firms that brought products or services first to market benefited for a short window of time from high profits but lost their advantage quickly to competition.[39] New products and services that entered the market, because they dealt with information processes and methodologies, were generally not patentable and hence were easily copied by competitors. However, being first to market gave firms the market recognition for being on the cutting-edge of innovative thinking and attracts clients seeking new ideas and instruments. Regional firms tended to follow the lead of the big firms in adopting innovative products and services once they have proven successful.

Black Monday, 1987

On August 25, 1987, the stock market peaked at 2,722.42. Then began a precipitous decline in prices. On October 19, 1987, global markets experienced a massive sell-off. By market's close, the Dow Jones was down 22.6 percent on six times the normal trading volume. Sixty investment banking firms, including the respected E.F. Hutton and L.F. Rothschild, had failed.[40]

Despite the gravity of the situation, quick intervention by the Fed and concerted announcements of major blue chip corporations of stock buybacks orchestrated by major investment banks saved the markets from total meltdown.[41] The markets bounced back quickly and continued sustained growth through the 1990s.

The strength of measures enacted to counteract crashes such as Black Monday were again tested during the long economic expansion of the United States during the nineties. The 1990s also saw bargaining power shift from corporations and banks to retail investors, represented by mutual funds. The Asian financial crisis of 1997 and the 1998 Russian crisis threatened to disrupt the stability of the markets. But the markets bounced back quickly.

The Glass-Steagall Repeal

The Depression-era regulation and subsequent amendments during the 1960s and 1970s had made the financial services industry one of the most highly regulated in the United States. But the 1980s and 1990s were decades of more liberal oversight. By the mid-1980s, recognizing that the increasingly global and competitive financial environment had rendered provisions of Glass-Steagall unworkable, the Federal Reserve and other government agencies began to relax regulations that separated the businesses of many of these institutions. In 1999 legislators "struck a midnight deal to repeal Glass-Steagall, setting the stage for the enactment of the most important piece of financial legislation since the Great Depression."[42] Ironically, the main reasons espoused for the demise of the act are similar to the rationale for why the act was instituted in the first place—promoting the soundness and health of U.S. banks by leveling the playing field, and protecting consumers' rights.

The Glass-Steagall Act repeal removed the last legal impediments for commercial and investment banks to jump into each other's turf. Commercial banks were eager to enter the higher-margin, less commoditized investment banking business through greenfield entry or through merger with existing investment banks. Investment banks, meanwhile, needed access to much greater capital than before to compete effectively. The large, global clients with whom investment banks wanted to work most were seeking large, global financial advisors that could take significant financial positions for extended periods of time. Besides, technical advances had lowered data processing and communication costs, opened new markets, fostered new financial instruments, and provided instantaneous links among global financial markets. However, the benefits of technical advances were available only to firms that invested aggressively in technology. Seeking access to more capital, several investment banks turned to commercial banks to form large, global financial monoliths. Other investment banks, seeking to retain their independence while also needing a large capital base, converted their ownership structures from partnerships to public firms.

Seeking to reduce risk, some investment banks became diversified financial services companies, operating in businesses such as asset management to stabilize firm earnings, as well as traditional investment banking businesses, such as underwriting and trading, that underwent business cycles. This increase in scope of services was complemented with the use of technology to predict and manage firms' exposure to risk. By the mid-1990s, some investment banks were also offering lines of credit, including credit cards, commercial banks were selling stocks and mutual funds, and credit card issuers were selling insurance.[43] Universal banks, offering "full-service," were reemerging in the form of financial behemoths such as Deutsche Bank, Credit Suisse, and the Travelers Group.

Evolving Roles of the SEC and the Fed

The bull market tested the strength of regulation as financial innovation; globalization of markets, increased technology, and heightened speculation produced lofty stock prices similar to that seen in the '20s. Spectacular insider trading scandals erupted, and the SEC indicted prominent Wall Street superstars, including Michael Milken, the creator of the junk bond market, and Ivan Boesky, a prominent arbitrageur. The Milken/Boesky scandal would eventually taint many leading Wall Street firms and lead to the 1990 demise of Milken's firm Drexel Burnham Lambert. In 1993 Salomon Brothers, stung by a scandal in its treasury bond trading, came close to failure. In 1994 Kidder Peabody, a leader in mergers and acquisitions, was sold to GE. Appendix I delineates the key initiatives underway at the SEC at the turn of the century.

During the 1990s, the lawmakers, realizing the need to contain the budget deficit, became reluctant to steer the economy using long-term levers such as tax changes and spending and relied instead on the Fed to use its short-term levers (the money supply and short term interest rates) to manage the economy. The Fed, under the leadership of chairman Alan Greenspan (since 1987), carried out its mandate to maintain economic growth, a high level of employment, stable prices, and moderate long-term interest rates very effectively by actively managing the country's money supply and key short-term interest rates. Congress largely let the Fed's actions go unquestioned, as it was widely credited for sustaining the long run of the bull market and engineering one of the friendliest economic environments that Americans have enjoyed in decades, a period of modest inflation and relatively low interest rates.[44] With lawmakers moving slowly on overhauling the financial system, the Fed often stepped in to correct short term imbalances.[45] An example of the Fed's interventionist approach was the 1998 bail out of Long-Term Capital Management (LTCM), a US$100 billion hedge fund that teetered on the verge of bankruptcy as a result of market dislocations in the summer of 1998. Fearing a global market meltdown if LTCM declared bankruptcy, the New York Fed, led by William McDonough, organized a US$4.0 billion bailout from major Wall Street firms.[46] The net result was increasing power of the Fed during the 1990s. Chairman Greenspan's every speech came to be analyzed and closely followed by Wall Street to foresee future Fed moves and how these moves might impact the state of the economy.[e]

The U.S. Securities Industry in 2000[47]

As of 2000, the U.S. securities industry could be characterized as a loose oligopoly with each firm having multiple product lines.[48] The industry had an "hour-glass structure"—many small firms on a regional basis, few and often changing middle-bracket firms, and a stable set of bulge bracket firms. The structure of the securities industry was somewhat puzzling—some elements point to the industry being collusive; in many aspects, however, marketplace competition was very intense. The industry seemingly had low barriers to entry for small, upstart players but very high barriers to catapulting firms into bulge bracket status. And yet, it was an enticing industry—one that attracted entrants from other industries and other geographies because Wall Street was considered the most important financial center in the world, a model for other financial markets, and a gateway to America's huge domestic financial market.[49]

The participants in this industry had one of the following profiles.

1. **The full service firms** compete against one another in virtually all securities lines of businesses. They are the biggest and most diversified companies and believe that they can compete by offering a comprehensive set of services (one-stop shopping) as well as having a strong capital base to undertake the largest securities transactions. This approach is most personified by Merrill Lynch & Co. (Merrill Lynch), which has become a full-line firm through organic growth.

   Several firms have tried to compete with Merrill Lynch in offering full services by merging with other firms. Some of the 1980s merger behemoths, notably Shearson Lehman Hutton, did not succeed and subsequently dissolved. In 1997 the investment bank Morgan Stanley merged with the retail brokerage Dean Witter, and the trading powerhouse Salomon Brothers merged with the retail brokerage Smith Barney to try and offer full service. 1999 and 2000 brought another round of mergers, notably of Salomon Smith Barney with the Travelers Group (which included Citibank) to form the nation's largest securities firm, UBS (a foreign "universal" bank) with Paine Webber (a retail brokerage), JP Morgan with Chase (both of whose roots are in commercial banking), Credit Suisse First Boston (whose roots were in investment banking but which belonged to a foreign universal banking group, Credit Suisse) and DLJ (a trading and investment banking house), and Wasserstein Perella (an investment bank) with Dresdner Kleinwort Benson (a foreign universal bank).

2. **The investment banks** focus on investment banking business. They are best personified by Goldman Sachs, which has concentrated on investment banking services and resisted expanding into full-fledged retail services on its own or through merger with other financial services firm, in the belief that it can provide superior services by remaining independent and focusing only on areas of its core expertise. Goldman has pursued a policy of selective acquisitions only in businesses that it feels it can dominate.

3. **The retail brokerage houses** primarily offer securities products and services to retail investors. The best example of a retail brokerage house is Prudential Securities.

4. **The trading firms** derive most of their profits by putting their own capital at risk through the

---

[e] A famous incident involving the ability of chairman Greenspan's words to move markets worldwide involved a December 1996 dinner party where he remarked that he thought the markets were in a phase of "irrational exuberance." The comment sparked a major sell-off in the capital markets worldwide.

buying and selling of securities. The most prominent examples of trading firms are Bear Stearns and Lehman Brothers.

5. **The commercial banks,** ever since the demise of Glass-Steagall prohibitions, have been leveraging their corporate relationships to participate actively in securities underwriting. Examples of commercial banks that have catapulted to major underwriting status are JP Morgan, Chase, and Citibank (now part of Salomon Smith Barney).

6. **The online banks** emerged as a result of the rise of the Internet in brokerage services in the 1990s. The most prominent of these firms are Charles Schwab and Wit Capital.

Despite dropping technology markets, Wall Street's investment banking divisions finished a remarkable year in 2000, breaking many records. On the mergers and acquisition front, over US$3.5 trillion of deals were announced in 2000, including some of the biggest mergers and takeovers in corporate history.[50] In the bond market, records were also broken. International bond issuance reached an all-time high of US$1.4 trillion and a series of huge financing included Deutsche Telekom's landmark US$14.6 billion bond offering. In the equity markets, the United States alone produced a new high of US$96.8 billion of new issues.[51]

However, the outlook for 2001 looked murky, as Wall Street's biggest banks were unanimously downbeat in their earnings reports. Overall levels of trading remained depressed as the stock market declined. The number of new issues declined as the year 2000 wore on. Volatility in the equity markets ground equity underwriting to a halt. Since many M&A deals were financed by high-yield (junk) bonds, slowdown in M&A transactions contributed to a marked slowdown in the junk bond market. The sliding stock market also lowered asset management businesses' earnings forecasts, although firms with significant private client asset management businesses forecast ongoing profits for that sector.[52] The stock market decline

of the twenty-first century had led some to question Fed's continuing control over and understanding of the economy and express the concern that perhaps too much economic power had come to be vested with the Fed.

As activities in the financial markets continued to slow, the industry contracted. Middle-sized firms, realizing that they could no longer stomach the costs of playing in a consolidating, increasingly global game, began tying up with other investment banks. A wave of consolidations occurred, including the mergers of UBS and Paine Webber, Credit Suisse and Donaldson, Lufkin and Jenrette (DLJ), and Chase and JP Morgan.

APPENDIX I

SEC Focus, Circa 2001

Following the Securities Act of 1934, enforcement of the nation's securities laws had been assigned to the SEC. The SEC was governed by Congress and was subject to Congress's budgetary discretion and oversight, which on occasions had been problematic for the SEC. Apart from its duties to enforce laws, the SEC oversaw the capital markets' self-regulatory organizations such as the NASD as well as the conduct of market participants and investors. During the long bull run of the 1990s, the SEC, led by chairman Arthur Levitt, Jr., pursued several initiatives to level the playing field for all market participants, especially individual investors.[53]

Curbing Insider Trading

The SEC is the primary watchdog against insider trading. Historically, insider trading has been difficult to detect and prove, although there have been signs that insider trading is rising. During the 1990s, the SEC filed an increasing number of insider-trading cases, culminating in 57 fresh cases in 2000.[54] But the agency was still criticized for a perceived lack of enforcement in suspicious instances where call or put options soared prior to a major announcement that affected the stock.

Insider trading particularly hurts options traders who are obliged to execute trades for their customers and take the opposite position for 40–100 percent of the trades, a significantly greater risk than taken by stock traders who typically put their capital at risk for approximately 10 percent of the transactions. In 1997 options traders called for changes in exchange rules that would allow options-trading halts even in the absence of trading halts in the underlying stocks and for speedier recouping of their losses in the event that insider trading had been proven.

The SEC had moved to clarify and strengthen its rules on insider trading. It expanded the definition of insider trading to include "misappropriation," the use of material, nonpublic information to trade stock in a company by anyone, even if that person does not have a legal relationship to work for the company whose stock is misappropriated. In October 2000 the SEC clarified insider trading rules further by issuing directives 10(b5-1) to allow prosecution of insiders based simply on awareness of material, nonpublic, market-moving information and 10(b5-2), to elucidate the specific family relationships not exempt from insider trading rules.[55]

IPO Process

In the red-hot market for technology stocks during the late 1990s, allegations arose that the IPO share distribution process had become unfair and nontransparent to individual investors. The SEC is probing the "spinning" of IPO shares, a process whereby corporate executives and venture capitalists received free or unusually large, solicited or unsolicited, shares of upcoming IPOs with the understanding that they would profit from the allocation by cashing out of the shares soon after the IPO. These executives were then expected to "return the favor" by giving the particular firm future business.[56]

A focus of investigation was the IPO of VA Linux Systems, in which two funds, namely GLG Partners and Chelsey Capital, received relatively large chunks of the IPO offering from the under-

writer of the offering, Credit Suisse Group. SEC investigators and the U.S. attorney's office in Manhattan launched a joint investigation into whether unusually large commissions were paid. In December 2000, the SEC widened its investigation to include IPO allocations by Goldman Sachs, Bear Stearns, and Morgan Stanley.[57] In 2001, expanding its investigation to include one step after the IPO to study how money managers distribute stocks to individual clients, the SEC was uncovering evidence of money managers favoring IPO allocations to clients who paid performance-based fees.[58]

Disclosure

The SEC has aimed to improve the quality of information flowing to all market participants. One major issue that the SEC has attempted to address has been "selective disclosure," a practice whereby corporate insiders release information only to a select few information mediators, such as broker-dealers and analysts, thereby giving an arbitrage advantage of access to market-moving information to those mediators and their clients ahead of individual investors.[59] The SEC's Regulation FD (fair disclosure) went into effect in October 2000, mandating that any news with the potential to move a stock must be released to every concerned party at the same time.[60] Some information mediators complained that regulation FD could potentially chill the relationship between corporate insiders and analysts, hurting the overall quality of information released to the public and potentially making all analysts' calls less accurate.[61]

In November 2000 the SEC, responding to complaints that execution has been one of the murkiest aspect of stock trading and the cost of sloppy execution has often been hidden from investors, instituted new rules requiring Wall Street firms to disclose the quality of trade execution they provide to investors for both stocks and options.[62] The SEC also took initiatives to improve disclosure in US$3.2 trillion corporate bond market, including a new system and new disclosure requirements.[63] The SEC was also planning implementation, beginning winter 2001, of rules for options exchanges to disclose trading and order-execution data in a standardized fashion.[64] Beginning February 2001, the SEC also instituted strict new public-disclosure requirements of firms that engage their auditors to also provide consulting services.[65]

Monitoring Conduct in Financial Markets

Apart from instituting new rules, the SEC attempts to ensure that participants in the financial markets behave in a manner commensurate with the existing rules. This has meant careful policing of areas in financial markets that have seen intense activity and innovation. In recent years, this has meant careful monitoring and governance of financial markets impacted by the Internet revolution.

Employee stock options, which give workers the right, but not the obligation to buy a set number of shares of company stock at a given price for a certain period, are widely used as a form of incentive pay.[66] At the height of the Internet stock run, options induced many employees and executives to give up financial security for the chance to benefit from the options upside. With the fall in price of most technology stocks, most options are now "under water" and many firms have resorted to "reprice" employee stock options to adjust employee compensation. The SEC has imposed strict filing requirements for companies that reprice options, to make the cost of repricing transparent to owners of the firms' stocks and to curb indiscriminate revisions.[67] The SEC has also been investigating instances where some insiders were allowed to cancel or back out of unprofitable stock purchases.

The SEC has been supervising online IPOs, alternative exchanges, and online brokerage and trading systems and has been on the alert for "cyber rogues," who promote investment schemes over the Internet although they are not registered with the SEC as "broker-dealers."[68]

The SEC also intends to intensify surveillance of the mutual fund industry to ensure it becomes more friendly to the average investor. One area that the SEC has been probing is "portfolio pumping," executing end-of-quarter trades to artificially lift funds' quarterly performance results.[69] The SEC is also asking that mutual fund managers be no longer allowed to trade for their own account and has approved rules to strengthen the role of independent directors on the boards of the mutual-funds.[70] The SEC has also launched an investigation into "soft dollar" arrangements, often secret arrangements for money managers to receive funds or benefits such as research at discounted prices from brokerage firms for brokerage services presumably in return for directing trades their way.

The SEC actively disciplines rogue brokers. Prosecuting rogue brokers is challenging given the difficulty in linking payments to investment schemes, the statute of limitations for filing suits, and the relative insularity of the industry to outside interference. Besides directly disciplining rogue brokers, the SEC, in a controversial move, has even fined sales managers that hire rogue brokers.

The SEC has also been cracking down on the "pay-to-play" practice, particularly prevalent in municipal bond business, where municipalities award business related to municipal bonds to banks in exchange for political contributions from these banks.[71]

References

1. Niall Ferguson, *The House of Rothschild: Money's Prophets (1798–1848),* Viking Penguin, Inc., 1998.

2. Zvi Bodie and Robert C. Merton, "The Functional Perspective," part I, section 2.3, *Finance,* Prentice Hall, Inc., 2000.

3. Robert C. Merton and Zvi Bodie, "A Conceptual Framework for Analyzing the Financial Environment."

4. Samuel L. Hayes III and Philip M. Hubbard, *Investment Banking,* Harvard Business School Press, 1990.

5. John Downes and Jordan Goodman, *Dictionary of Finance and Investment Terms,* 5th ed., 1998 Barron's Educational Series, Inc.

6. Ibid.

7. Ferguson, *The House of Rothschild.*

8. Chapter 3, Thomas K. McCraw ed., *Creating Modern Capitalism,* Harvard University Press, 1997, p. 64.

9. Ibid., p. 70.

10. Ron Chernow, *The Death of the Banker,* Vintage, 1997.

11. Hayes and Hubbard, *Investment Banking.*

12. Chernow, *The Death of the Banker.*

13. Lisa Endlich, *Goldman Sachs: The Culture of Success,* Alfred A. Knopf, 1999.

14. John Steele Gordon, *The Great Game,* Scribner, 1999.

15. Ron Chernow, *The House of Morgan,* Simon & Schuster, 1990.

16. "The U.S. Banking Panic of 1933 and FDIC," HBS Case No. 9-799-077.

17. Gordon.

18. Chernow, *The House of Morgan.*

19. Gordon.

20. Ibid.

21. Ibid.

22. Ibid.

23. "The U.S. Banking Panic of 1933 and FDIC."

24. For a more complete discussion of the events surrounding the 1933 banking panics, see "The US Banking Panic of 1933 and FDIC."

25. This section draws upon Hayes and Hubbard.

26. Hayes and Hubbard, p. 99; Gordon, pp. 234–35.

27. See *www.cftech.com/BrainBank/SPECIAL REPORTS/ GlassSteagall.html.*

28. Hayes and Hubbard.

29. Chernow, *The Death of the Banker.*

30. Chernow, *The House of Morgan.*

31. Hayes and Hubbard.

32. For a more detailed discussion of the provisions within the Glass-Steagall Act that deals with the separation of commercial and investment banking, see *www.cftech.com/BrainBank/SPECIALREPORTS/GlassSteagall.html.*

33. Chernow, *The Death of the Banker.*

34. Ibid.

35. Hayes and Hubbard.

36. Hayes and Hubbard, p. 49.

37. Charles R. Geisst, *Wall Street: A History,* Oxford University Press, 1997.

38. Ibid.

39. Ibid.

40. Gordon.

41. "Terrible Tuesday, How the Stock Markets Almost Disintegrated a Day after the Crash," *The Wall Street Journal,* November 20, 1987.

42. Brian Nottage, "Glass-Steagall Dies, and None Too Soon," *www.Economy.com,* October 25, 1999.

43. "Wells-Fargo Online Financial Services (A)", HBS Case No. 9-198-146, 1999.

44. "The Federal Reserve," *Who's Who and What's What on Wall Street,* The Editors of the Wall Street Journal, 1998, Ballantine Books, New York.

45. Ibid.

46. *When Genius Failed: The Rise and Fall of Long-Term Capital Management,* Roger Lowenstein, 2000, Random House New York.

47. John O. Matthews, *Struggle and Survival on Wall Street,* Oxford, 1994.

48. Ibid.

49. "Wall Street: Tomorrow the World," *The Economist,* April 15, 1995.

50. FT Survey: Global Investment Banking, *The Financial Times,* January 26, 2001.

51. Ibid.

52. "Private Clients Are a Bright Spot in Banking Gloom," *The Financial Times,* March 23, 2001.

53. "Situation Vacant," *The Economist,* February 24, 2001.

54. Ibid.

55. "New SEC Rules in End Will Aid Firms' Insiders," *The Wall Street Journal,* October 18, 2000.

56. "SEC Targets IPO Process with Probes," *The Wall Street Journal,* December 16, 2000; "NASD Would Bar Some Big Investors from All IPOs, Not Just the Hot Ones," *The Wall Street Journal,* August 18, 2000.

57. "SEC Probes Two Funds' Role in IPO Stakes," *The Wall Street Journal,* January 8, 2001; "Linux Deal Is Focus of IPO-Commission Probe," *The Wall Street Journal,* January 12, 2001.

58. "SEC Uncovers New Evidence of Wrongdoing in Share Distribution Probe," *The Financial Times,* March 7, 2001.

59. "SEC is Divided on Proposed Rule Covering Disclosure to Analysts," *The Wall Street Journal,* August 7, 2000.

60. "The SEC Wants to Open the Info Vault," *Fortune,* October 2000.

61. " 'The Big Chill': Street Feels Effect of 'Fair Disclosure' Rule," *The Wall Street Journal,* October 23, 2000.

62. "New SEC Rules on Execution Disclosure Will Tell Investors of Hidden Trade Costs," *The Wall Street Journal,* November 16, 2000.

63. "SEC Clears System to Collect, Distribute Bond-Trading Data," *The Wall Street Journal,* January 23, 2001.

64. "SEC Plans to Launch Rules That Require Exchanges to Disclose Trading, Order Data," *The Wall Street Journal,* February 16, 2001.

65. "SEC's Auditor Rules Could Pose a Dilemma for Big Client Firms," *The Wall Street Journal,* November 16, 2000.

66. "Unlike Most Investors, Some Insiders Can Cancel Unprofitable Stock Purchases," *The Wall Street Journal,* February 15, 2001.

67. "SEC Curbs Rules for Employee Stock Options," *The Wall Street Journal,* March 22, 2001; "Tech Firms Object as SEC Gets Tougher on Their Practice of Repricing Options," *The Wall Street Journal,* February 7, 2001; "Unlike Most Investors, Some Insiders Can Cancel Unprofitable Stock Purchases."

68. "SEC Ponders Definition of Broker as Web Sites Offer Similar Services," *The Wall Street*

Journal, January 10, 2001; "SEC Probes US Mutual Funds," *The Financial Times,* January 16, 2001.

69. "SEC Probes 'Portfolio Pumping' at Funds," *The Wall Street Journal,* January 15, 2001.

70. "SEC Clears Rules on Independent Directors," *The Wall Street Journal,* January 4, 2001.

71. "SEC Chief's Valediction: Beware of Investment World's Pitfalls," *The Wall Street Journal,* January 17, 2001.

The Rise and Decline of E-Consulting

> What happened is that everything—how you sold chemicals or bought bolts or administered 401K plans or almost anything else—started to become an e-thing. We had just come through the Christmas of '98, the first Internet Christmas, and 10 days later Jack Welch mobilized 340,000 employees to make General Electric an e-company immediately. Suddenly thousands of organizations realized they were late to the party and needed to get there fast.
>
> *Geoffrey Colvin, "Old Consultants Never Die: They Just Go 'e,'"* Fortune,
> *June 12, 2000*

> E-commerce is an important channel, and in some cases an important business model, but it doesn't replace strategy . . . A lot of these e-consulting firms or e-strategy firms are helping in that piece, but it does not supplant what we do.
>
> *John Donahoe, managing director, Bain,* Consulting News,
> *June 2000, p. 8*

INTRODUCTION

In August 1998 International Data Corporation (IDC) estimated that within four years the worldwide market for e-consulting would grow 753 percent versus an increase of 83 percent in the traditional systems integration market. In 1999 Kennedy Information Group expected the global market for e-consulting at $37.5 billion by 2003. Forrester Research estimated that the U.S. market alone would reach $47.7 billion in 2002, whereas IDC predicted a more conservative U.S. market of $30.6 billion that year (see Exhibit 1). Though the specific forecasts varied, two of their attributes were consistent; e-consulting was perceived to be destined to grow quickly and become a huge busi-

ness for those consulting firms willing and able to capitalize on the opportunity.

In January 2000 more than 100 companies were named as e-consultants; 57 percent were publicly traded. By December 2001, more than 50 percent had disappeared. This note tracks the rapid rise and sharp decline of e-consulting.

THE CONTEXT

The Management Consulting Industry

Management consulting is a service provided to organizations by qualified persons who assist management, in an objective and independent manner,

Doctoral student M. Julia Prats and Professor Ashish Nanda prepared this note as the basis for class discussion. It draws upon "e-Consulting," HBS No. 800-312, prepared by Thomas Agan, HBS MBA 1989, and Dean's Research Fellow Scot Landry under the supervision of Professors Ashish Nanda and Thomas DeLong.

EXHIBIT 1 E-Consulting Market Forecasts

Forecaster—Year of Forecast	Worldwide Forecast ($ billion)							U.S. Forecast ($ billion)					
	1998	1999	2000	2001	2002	2003	2004	1999	2000	2001	2002	2003	2004
Industry Standard—98	4.0												
Dataquest—98		23.6			15.0								
Hambrecht & Quist—99							157.9						10.8
KIRG—99		6.1	11.7	18.9	27.0	37.5	50.0					4.4	
IDC—99	7.9	11.8						0.7					
IDC—00	16.1	27.0	42.2		43.6	78.5	99.1		3.0				
Dataquest—00			20.5										
InfoTechTrends—00			60.0				124.0						
Forrester—00		10.6	19.6			64.8							

Source: Casewriters.

1999 Breakdown of U.S. E-Consulting Market Forecast

	Category	1998 ($ billions)	2002 ($ billions)	Percent of Total (%)	CAGR (%)
Strategy	Internet strategy	0.2	2.1	4.4	77
	Brand strategy	0.1	2.9	6.1	130
Implementation	Business process reinvention	0.04	2.9	6.1	200
	Change management strategy	0.02	2.1	4.4	226
	Campaign analysis and tracking	0	0.8	1.7	—
	Creative development	0.07	2.6	5.4	149
	Content management	0.002	0.9	1.9	336
	User interface design	1.2	8.1	16.9	63
	Application integration	0.2	11.3	23.6	165
	E-commerce package implementation	0.2	3.8	7.9	118
	Custom software development	2.1	10.3	21.5	49
	Total market	4.132	47.8	100.0	85

Note: CAGR stands for compound annual growth rate.
Source: Forrester Research.

(continues)

EXHIBIT 1 (continued)

U.S. Internet Services Spending by Service Type, 1997–2004 ($ million)

	1997	1998	1999	2000	2001	2002	2003	2004	1999–2004 CAGR (%)
Consulting	—		$1,266	$2,010	$3,024	$3,024	$6,212	$7,155	41%
% of total	—		14%	15%	16%	16%	16%	16%	
Implementation	—		$6,339	$9,311	$13,583	$19,747	$26,406	$29,860	36%
% of total	—		72%	71%	70%	69%	68%	68%	
Operations	—		$1,153	$1,869	$2,865	$4,326	$6,191	$7,012	44%
% of total	—		13%	14%	15%	15%	16%	16%	
Total	$2,912	$4,642	$8,758	$13,190	$19,472	$28,525	$38,808	$44,026	38%

Source: Morgan Stanley Dean Witter, Industry Report, Internet Consulting and Application Services, April 2000. IDC & MSDW Research.

to identify and analyze problems, recommend solutions, and help, when requested, to implement these solutions. Management consulting projects are characterized by clearly recognizable "start" and "finish" milestones, established prior to the outset of the engagement. The project may involve services such as strategic planning, analysis, design, implementation, and testing. However, management-consulting services do not include the long-term management of a particular system, function, process, or business unit of an organization. These services, commonly referred to as "outsourcing," require different skills than consulting and are subject to unique cost and profitability drivers.[1]

Appendix I tracks the evolution of management consulting. During the 1980s, and continuing into the 1990s, the management consulting industry was one of the fastest-growing sectors of several advanced economies. In 1980 worldwide industry revenues were estimated to be $3 million. By 1999 this figure had grown to about $60 billion.[2] (See Exhibit 2 for the evolution of worldwide consulting industry revenues.)

During the 1980s information and communication technologies radically restructured entire industries, from financial services to manufacturing, not only making firms more efficient in carrying out their traditional activities but changing the form of competition in many industries. Wal-Mart, P&G, and other firms became the models for creating strategic advantage through the implementation of sophisticated enterprise resource planning (ERP) systems. This restructuring fueled the need for technology-rich consulting. "Technology is driving strategy in a way it hasn't since the dawn of the industrial revolution," observed PriceWaterhouseCoopers' consulting practice head Scott Hart. "The line between management consulting and IT has disappeared," observed CSC CEO Van Honeycutt. "The strategic integration of technologies and processes enable today's business leaders to not only compete more effectively and reduce cost, but to propel them to new solutions not yet envisioned."[3]

The demand for consulting exploded during the 1990s. Information technology had become increasingly central and strategic for management and, therefore, for management consulting. Besides, consulting services benefited significantly from the longest economic expansion in U.S. history (107 months), helped along by mega-mergers, deregulation (particularly the Telecommunications Act of 1995), globalization, restructuring, technological advances, and the increasing adoption of the Internet by corporations.

A New Technology Standard

The development of the Internet brought a unified protocol for communication and subsequently to an explosion of business applications. With the introduction of the Transmission Control Protocol/Internet Protocol (TCP/IP) in 1983, the Internet was in operation. The system for sharing documents over a network through the Internet was publicly demonstrated in 1991. Berners-Lee named the system the World Wide Web (WWW). In 1983 the National Center for Supercomputing Application (NCSA) at the University of Illinois released Mosaic, a "browser" to read WWW documents. Netscape sold its first commercial browser in 1995, soon followed by Microsoft. The introduction of the Web had a dramatic impact on Internet growth as defined by the number of linked computer hosts—from less than 2 million in 1993 to more than 44 million in January 1999. Directly related to this growth was the diffusion of relatively inexpensive home computers.

The Internet came to be recognized as an "enabling general purpose technology" with a potential for pervasive use in a variety of applications. It appeared obvious that the Internet had the potential to profoundly change the world through greater computing power, ease of communication, and the host of technologies that could be built upon it. Opportunities to build new services and technologies appeared boundless and global in scale. The benefits of these new technologies were expected to translate into greater economic pro-

EXHIBIT 2 Evolution of Worldwide Consulting Industry Revenues, 1997–2004

Worldwide Consulting Services Revenue by Region, 1997–2004 ($M)

	1997	1998	1999	2000	2001e	2002e	2003e	2004e	1999–2001 CAGR (%)
Worldwide	46,368	52,530	60,098	69,321	80,379	93,097	107,650	124,467	15.7
United States	23,962	27,453	31,450	36,210	41,920	48,410	55,790	64,278	15.4
Western Europe	14,037	16,064	18,479	21,314	24,542	28,127	32,131	36,633	14.7
Japan	3,303	3,303	3,485	3,768	4,129	4,558	5,059	5,651	10.2
Latin America	755	956	1,091	1,320	1,639	2,056	2,582	3,239	24.3
Asia/Pacific	767	786	939	1,161	1,485	1,910	2,427	3,072	26.8
Canada	2,462	2,695	3,108	3,608	4,217	4,919	5,721	6,645	16.4
ROW	1,082	1,273	1,546	1,940	2,447	3,117	3,940	4,949	26.2

Worldwide Business Consulting Services Revenue by Region, 1997–2004 ($M)

	1997	1998	1999	2000	2001e	2002e	2003e	2004e	1999–2001 CAGR (%)
Worldwide	19,956	22,444	25,464	29,140	33,399	38,259	43,729	50,017	14.5
United States	10,445	11,835	13,480	15,435	17,683	20,210	23,008	26,170	14.2
Western Europe	6,538	7,367	8,334	9,494	10,785	12,230	13,820	15,620	13.4
Japan	1,294	1,335	1,394	1,495	1,641	1,812	2,015	2,257	10.1
Latin America	244	314	370	446	547	674	840	1,052	23.2
Asia/Pacific	294	325	396	490	614	780	994	1,261	26.1
Canada	763	835	975	1,145	1,341	1,563	1,812	2,093	16.5
ROW	378	433	515	635	788	990	1,240	1,564	24.9

Worldwide IT Consulting Services Revenue by Region, 1997–2004 ($M)

	1997	1998	1999	2000	2001e	2002e	2003e	2004e	1999–2001 CAGR (%)
Worldwide	26,412	30,086	34,634	40,181	46,980	54,838	63,915	74,450	16.5
United States	13,517	15,618	17,970	20,775	24,237	28,200	32,782	38,108	16.2
Western Europe	7,499	8,697	10,145	11,820	13,757	15,897	18,311	21,013	15.7
Japan	2,009	1,968	2,091	2,273	2,488	2,746	3,044	3,394	10.2
Latin America	511	642	721	874	1,092	1,382	1,742	2,187	24.8
Asia/Pacific	473	461	543	671	871	1,130	1,433	1,811	27.2
Canada	1,699	1,860	2,133	2,463	2,876	3,356	3,903	4,552	16.4
ROW	704	840	1,031	1,305	1,659	2,127	2,700	3,385	26.8

e: estimated.

Note: The Business Consulting category includes consulting related to any business issue. Business Consulting encompasses services such as strategy, process improvement, capacity planning, best practices, business process reengineering, knowledge management, needs assessment, and change management. The IT consulting category includes IS strategy, IT and network planning, architectural assessments, IS operational analysis, technical system and Network design, supplier assessment, and maintenance planning. IT consulting covers the complete spectrum of technologies from mainframe, midrange, and small-scale multiuser systems to servers, workstations, personal computers, portables, networking equipment, operating systems, databases, packaged software applications, custom software, development tools, printers, and the Internet.

Source: IDC, Consulting Services: U.S. and Worldwide Forecast and Analysis, 1997–2004, April 2000.

ductivity through the lowering of communication and transaction costs. Furthermore, it would be the base to gain competitive advantage through the improvement in economic and quality terms with suppliers, to increase customer satisfaction through comprehensive websites to track order status, configure and place orders, and answer frequently asked questions. Executives began rethinking their business and technology strategies, reformulating their marketing, sales, and pricing activities, revamping their operations and organizational structures, and changing their relationships with customers, suppliers, alliance partners, employees, and even competitors. Organizations felt themselves under considerable pressure from "new economy" firms, new competitors exclusively based on the new technology, to reinvent themselves quickly so as not to lose their competitive edge.

Rising Expectations

Just as Apple, Microsoft, Intel, and Dell had been at the forefront of a new wave of technology in the 1980s, the 1990s ushered in a new wave of companies that were based on information networks. Capital markets recognized the potential value that was being created by these companies and channeled funds into these high-tech start-ups. To help speed up the integration of the new technology in existing businesses by carrying out complementary innovations, training and employing a new generation of employees, and helping organizations learn the new technology and engage in risky experimentation, capital was made available to e-commerce businesses in record amounts.

Venture investments in Internet companies reached $4.1 billion in the first quarter of 1999, representing 58 percent of the quarter's total venture investments and an increase from $1.6 billion in Internet investing in the fourth quarter of 1998. That was only the beginning of the venture investing wave. In the third quarter of 1999 equity invested in venture-backed Internet firms increased to $17 billion, rising to $21 billion in the first quarter of 2000. Most of the increase in dollars was attributable to a trend of ballooning deal size rather than the number of deals closed. In the first quarter of year 2000, for example, venture capitalists inked 464 deals, representing an increase of just 2.2 percent over the fourth quarter 1999. According to a PriceWaterhouseCoopers Money tree survey, an average individual VC placed an investment of about $4.8 million in 1997 in a U.S. Internet start-up; in 1998 the investment per start-up was $5.9 million; in 1999 it was $10.5 million. (See Exhibit 3 for details.)

In the late 1990s the stock market was bullish on technology stocks. From July 1999 to February 2000, as the NASDAQ Composite Index, which is heavily weighted with technology and Internet stocks, rose by 74.4 percent, the Dow Jones Industrial Average, composed mainly of old-economy stocks, fell by 7.7 percent.[4] In the four years following the Netscape IPO of August 1995 more than 400 Internet firms went public, in many cases achieving astronomic valuations. In 1999, 248 Internet-related firms went public, raising $48 billion. In the first quarter of 2000 alone, 119 companies went public with a total offering volume of $35 billion. Many of the firms that went public didn't have a track record of profitability.

Internet business potential and availability of capital created huge expectations among investors and the public in general. The pace at which the Internet affected business was dizzying, partly driven by real change (within four years the Internet had achieved 30 percent penetration of businesses) and partly by rising expectations and hubris.[5] (Exhibit 4 presents forecasts on the Internet's growing importance in the economy.) Appelations such as the "new economy" (as opposed to the "old economy") and "clicks and mortar" (as opposed to "bricks and mortar") began to be used increasingly frequently in business news and firm announcements. More than five new business publications were born between 1998 and 2000 to emphasize news related to the new economy. Observed *Fortune* in June 2000:

> Its [*Business 2.0*'s] first bimonthly issue is the June 13 edition, weighing in at 408

EXHIBIT 3 Capital Availability for Internet Companies

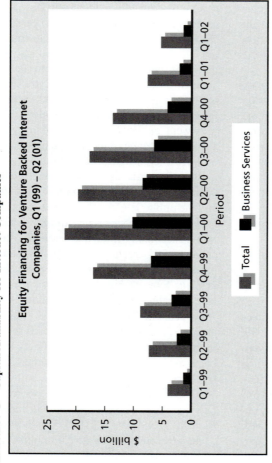

Equity Financing for Venture Backed Internet Companies, Q1 (99) – Q2 (01)

Legend: Total, Business Services

Source: VentureOne; PricewaterhouseCoopers.

* Equity financing include cash investments by professional venture capital firms, corporations, venture lessors, other private equity firms, and individuals into companies that have received at least one round of venture funding.

Worldwide Internet Related Financing, 1995–2000

	1995	1996	1997	1998	1999	2000	Q1 2000	Q2 2000	Q3 2000	Q4 2000
Total offering volume ($M)	1,495	2,531	1,987	4,066	47,918	46,295	35,398	4,238	5,368	1,291
Number of deals	15	19	20	43	330	187	119	24	38	6
Average deal size ($M)	100	133	99	95	562	247	297	177	141	216
Number of IPOs	9	14	12	24	248	118	64	16	33	5
Average IPO market cap ($M)	318	513	318	370	548	821	706	1,137	700	2,090

Source: Equidesk, Morgan Stanley Internet Research. Data as January 26, 1991.

EXHIBIT 4   The Growing Importance of Internet Commerce, circa 1999

Estimate Size of Internet Commerce as a Percentage of GDP (1999 est.)							
	1996	1997	1998	1999	2000e	2001e	2002e
U.S. GDP ($billions)	$7,636	$8,053	$8,415	$8,802	$9,223	$9,672	$10,160
Y/Y change	6.2%	5.5%	4.5%	4.6%	4.8%	4.9%	5.0%
Internet commerce	$2	$13	$40	$95	$187	$299	$446
% of GDP	0.0%	0.2%	0.5%	1.1%	2.0%	3.1%	4.4%

Source: The Keenan Report and MSDW Research.

pages—up from its 128-page inaugural issue of July 1998. What's true for *Business 2.0* is true for virtually every magazine covering this space, including *Fast Company, The Industry Standard, Red Herring,* and *Upside.* The June issue of Silicon Valley tech veteran *Upside* was 360 pages long. In June *Fast Company,* a self-improvement manual for new-economy middle managers, was 418 pages big. *Red Herring* had 628 pages in June, and by the way, it too is going biweekly. Meanwhile, *The Industry Standard,* "the news magazine for the Internet economy," has been topping them all, publishing as many as 360 pages every seven days.[6]

THE E-CONSULTING OPPORTUNITY

The Market Opportunity

The e-consulting segment was born in the mid-1990s as a management consulting service to help managers take advantage of new business opportunities enabled by the Internet. E-consulting comprises the services consulting firms provide to help conceive and launch an e-commerce business model and integrate it, if necessary, with an existing business.

The revolution that the Internet wrought in the corporate world had an enormous impact on the growth of e-consulting. Both the "old economy" and the "new economy" worlds were hungry for advice and expertise to succeed in their Internet endeavors. Managers of both traditional businesses and start-up firms were confronting several challenges because of the rapid integration of Internet in day-to-day business. First, as with any technological innovation, most executives felt uncertain about the potential of the new technology. Second, managers felt that their firms were not staffed with the right personnel to develop IT capabilities even as the labor market for IT professionals was very tight. A survey of 50 firms, for instance, found that in 44 percent of cases, IT projects had been delayed due to a lack of the right personnel.[7] Managers felt that despite the uncertainty and the tight labor market, they were being forced by competition and capital market infusions to make fast decisions committing their firms to Internet strategies. "These days clients have more money than time. That's a fundamental change," observed Steve Ariana of Scient. "You don't have to be right when you get it done. Early is better than accurate." The urgency, the uncertainty, and the lack of resources together created a tremendous demand for management advice.

Capital availability to technology companies also impacted e-consulting firms. On the one hand, Internet-based start-ups had sufficient cash to spend on external advisors. On the other hand, VC money was also made available to start new technology-focused consulting firms and finance their path towards an IPO. Zefer, a Boston-based Internet services start-up, raised $100 million from Chicago-based investment firm GTCR Golden

Rauner in 1999 and $48 million in new funding from NES and GTCR Golden Rauner in March 2001. Viant raised $10 million in two rounds from Mohr Davidow Ventures, Kleiner Perkins Caufield & Byers, and Trident Capital/Cognizant Enterprises. Scient garnered $5 million from Benchmark Capital, Sequoia Capital, and Stanford University. Both Scient and Viant were among the several e-consulting companies that went public in 1999. (Exhibit 5 lists VC Investments in selected e-consulting firms.)

Client Needs for E-Consulting Services

"There's been a cataclysmic shift in what clients are buying," noted Accenture CEO Joe Forehand.[8] Clients were looking for solutions to their problems rather than purchasing particular services. Traditional IT consulting had focused on using IT to improve a company's speed and efficiency. The opportunities opened up by the Internet were broader. For example, implementing e-commerce—the most obvious service facilitated by the Internet—introduced new competitive and strategic considerations. Remarked an e-consultant:

> When a company needs help with e-commerce, it is not just about implementing hardware, software, or even integrating systems. You have to start thinking how e-commerce could reshape your company, and within five minutes you're questioning your most basic strategic assumptions. What business are we in? How do we add value? Who are our customers? Who are our competitors?[9]

Hence, e-consulting came to comprise not one but a range of services, including strategy, implementation, and outsourcing. (See Exhibit 6 for a description of e-consulting services.) Forrester

EXHIBIT 5 Venture Capital Investments in Selected E-Consulting Firms, 1995–2000

Company	Venture Capital Investors
Answerthink	Golder, Thoma, Cressey, Rauner Inc., Miller Capital Management Inc.
Diamond	Safeguard, Technology Leaders Offshore C.V., CIP Capital L.P.
iXL	Greylock Management, Chase Capital Partners, Flatiron Partners, GE Capital, Kelso & Co., TTC Ventures, CB Capital, Portage Venture Partners, Transamerica Technology Finance
Mainspring	Highland Capital Partners, Crosslink Capital, Greylock, Flatiron Partners, MIT, Softbanck Venture Capital, Chase Capital Partners, GE Equity, Sandler Capital Management, J&W Seligman & Co., Essex Investment Management, Chemical Venture Partners
Razorfish	Seneca
Scient	Sequoia Capital, Benchmark Capital, Stanford University, Capital Research, Morgan Stanley Venture Partners, Amerindo Investment Advisors, Palantir Capital
U.S. Interactive	Safeguard Scientific, Technology Leaders
USWeb	Crosspoint Venture Partners, SOFTVEN No2 Investment Enterprise Partnership, 21st Century Communication Partners, The Cutler Group
Viant	Kleiner Perkins Caufield & Byers, Mohr Davidow Ventures, Information Associates, Trident Capital, BancBoston Capital, General Motors, Technology Crossover Ventures
Zefer	GTCR Golden Rauner, NES

Source: VentureSource, SEC filings.

EXHIBIT 6   E-Commerce Client Needs and Consulting Services

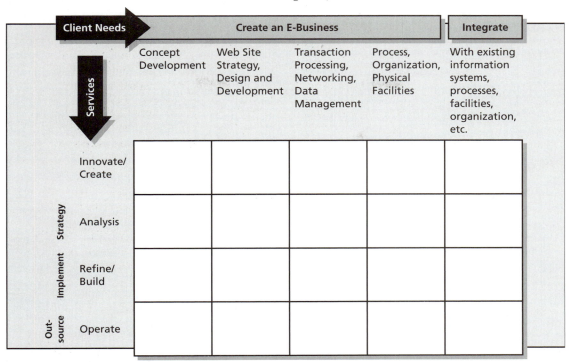

Source: Agan, Landry, Nanda, and DeLong, "e-Consulting," HBS 800-312, p. 17.

Industry Standard E-consulting project phases

Strategy phase	Strategists research and analyze a client's business, brand, and industry. Working with their findings, they define the scope and makeup of the project. This phase usually lasts three or four weeks, although a larger client may need more time. By the end of this phase, a detailed budget and work plan has emerged.
Architect phase	This involves the creative and technology departments working together to translate the strategy, developed in phase one, into a workable site. Tasks include specifying functional requirements, finishing the technical architecture, and determining content strategy and overall creative requirements. By the end of this phase, you may have a fully designed and working beta site that can be run though usability testing and review.
Implementation phase	Technologists build the final product and, if necessary, integrate it with the client's legacy systems. Once the product is built, you test it to see if it meets specifications. You also train the client's staff so they understand how to operate and manage the system.
Post-launch phase	This is the period after the launch of a site when a company monitors the site's performance and fulfills the criteria outlined in the strategy and architect phases. You might also work with the client to decide what upgrades and maintenance the site will need in the future.

Source: WetFett.com, Inc.

(continues)

EXHIBIT 6 (continued)

Service Methodologies of Some E-Consulting Companies

	Discovery	Define	Design	Production	Deployment
Agency.com	Explore, analyze, and categorize options	Develop concept plan and demo	Develop seed plan, launch plan, and execute prototype	Market test and calibrate	Scale, operate, and tune
Diamond	Consulting	Strategy, planning	Building and distribution	Continuous program management	
iXL	Discover; collect data	Define strategy	Design	Develop	Deliver final solution
Proxicom	Define strategy	Design solution	Develop solution	Deploy solution	
Razorfish	Clarify	Architect	Design	Implement	Enhance
Scient	Conceive	Architect	Engineer	Extend	
USWeb	Strategy	Analysis	Design	Technology development	Implementation and integration
US Interactive	Business case	Audit	Prototyping	Development	Implementation and tracking
Viant	Envision	Experience	Launch	Grow	
Xpedior	Imagine	Define	Architect	Build	Deliver

Source: Company and analysts reports.

Research estimated that only 11 percent of e-consulting would be strategy consulting. The remainder, 89 percent, would be implementation services, that is, services related to the refining and building an e-commerce business model and integrating it with existing processes and systems. (See Exhibit 1 for a detailed breakdown of the U.S. e-consulting market.) Organizations were also expected to spend heavily on the third category of e-commerce services, outsourcing. Outsourcing services include web hosting, Application Service Providers (ASPs), network management, logistics, fulfillment, call centers, and financial transaction processing.

Not only were the clients asking the e-consultancies to provide advice on a wide range of subject areas, but they were also asking the consultants to integrate their advice with implementation and often maintenance and support services. Observed Mercer Consulting vice chairman James Down:

Clients no longer say, "Thanks for the recommendations. We'll take it from here." Now the question is, "How can you help us make this a reality?" This has resulted in a broadening of services and in larger, longer-term relationships, new skill sets, and fee arrangements.[10]

COMPETITION IN E-CONSULTING

The market opportunity attracted very different players to the e-consulting arena. Between 1998 and 2000, strategy consultants, the Big Five accounting firms, software developers, hardware companies, systems integrators, advertising agencies, and professional service firms each claimed to be engaged in e-consulting. Systems integrators and the Big Five consulting firms focused on technology implementation, management consultants on business strategy, and interactive strategists on web design (see Exhibit 7).

The Challenge of Delivering E-Consulting Services

To deliver the broad range of services they were expected to provide, e-consulting firms brought together creative, technology, and strategy consult-

EXHIBIT 7   **Competition in Providing E-Consulting Services**

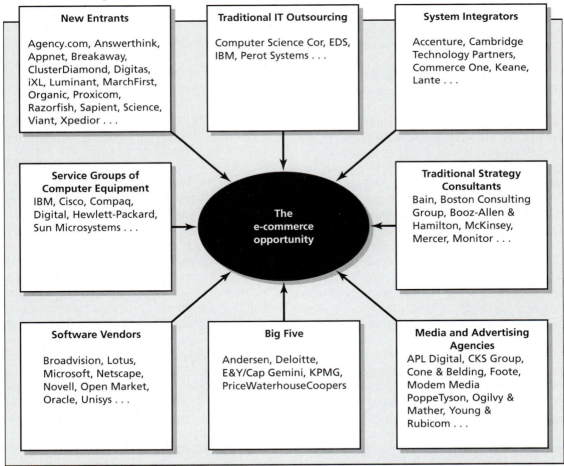

New Entrants

Agency.com, Answerthink, Appnet, Breakaway, ClusterDiamond, Digitas, iXL, Luminant, MarchFirst, Organic, Proxicom, Razorfish, Sapient, Science, Viant, Xpedior . . .

Traditional IT Outsourcing

Computer Science Cor, EDS, IBM, Perot Systems . . .

System Integrators

Accenture, Cambridge Technology Partners, Commerce One, Keane, Lante . . .

Service Groups of Computer Equipment
IBM, Cisco, Compaq, Digital, Hewlett-Packard, Sun Microsystems . . .

The e-commerce opportunity

Traditional Strategy Consultants
Bain, Boston Consulting Group, Booz-Allen & Hamilton, McKinsey, Mercer, Monitor . . .

Software Vendors

Broadvision, Lotus, Microsoft, Netscape, Novell, Open Market, Oracle, Unisys . . .

Big Five

Andersen, Deloitte, E&Y/Cap Gemini, KPMG, PriceWaterhouseCoopers

Media and Advertising Agencies
APL Digital, CKS Group, Cone & Belding, Foote, Modem Media PoppeTyson, Ogilvy & Mather, Young & Rubicom . . .

Source: Casewriters.

ants. The creative professionals in e-consulting firms included the graphic designers, marketers, copywriters, and informational designers who would work with clients to design the look of websites and develop web brands for firms. On the technology side were professionals that developed web software applications, integrated them with other operations of the companies, and ensured that they ran on the available hardware. Technology professionals included specialists in the back-end—software behind the site, such as customer databases, fulfillment systems, and visitor-tracking software—and in the front-end—design of the navigation and interactive elements of the websites experienced by visitors. Strategy consultants helped clients understand their e-business needs and helped develop e-business strategies to meet those needs.

Existing consulting organizations typically did not possess all the skills required to provide the entire range of e-consulting services. Most advertising and marketing communications agencies lacked the technical skills, such as application development and database integration, required to produce the increasingly complex and yet functional solutions demanded by clients. Most large technology product and service vendors lacked the creative and marketing skills required to deliver unique and compelling content and were further constrained by their need to recommend proprietary brands. Internet access service providers, whose core strength lay in providing Internet access and site hosting rather than solution development, typically lacked both the necessary creative and application development skills.

Further, strategists, creative branding and marketing, and technology groups often lacked the experience of working together and mutual understanding. Working cooperatively to create seamless business solutions proved a difficult challenge. Apart from skill differences, e-consulting also had to grapple with the cultural differences between advice-focused and technology implementation-focused consulting.

The New Entrants

Several new consulting firms were born to meet the demand for e-consulting services under the belief that traditional consulting would not be able to provide the desired services (see Exhibit 8). The Internet was "too different," requiring a mix of skills, business models, and advice that were all very different from those available with traditional consulting firms. The new breed of consultants promised to develop deep and broad capabilities in technology, strategy, and creativity to offer clients "one-stop shops" for strategy, implementation, and outsourcing consulting. Even more audaciously, several of the new e-consulting boutiques challenged the partnership model of traditional consulting firms by going public soon after incorporation.

The new e-consulting firms were built on three premises—flexible teams, global scope, and public ownership. First, e-consulting companies wanted to build flexible teams that combined multiple skills to successfully execute e-business projects from beginning to end. Each firm employed a combination of strategy, marketing, and technological professionals to fully serve their clients (see Exhibit 9). The entrepreneurs leading these new firms hoped that their smaller size compared to the incumbents and lack of institutional history would enable these firms to integrate professionals across disciplines more easily, be more creative, develop deeper expertise in Internet technology, and deliver faster on projects than the incumbents. For instance, several of the new firms claimed that they would complete strategy projects in six weeks in contrast to the six months typically required by the older, established firms.

For example, Sapient, one of the biggest and most established of the e-consultancies at nine years of age, had begun with client-server solutions, then moved into enterprise resource planning services, and eventually began offering Internet integration. The firm began pursuing a full-service strategy in earnest in 1998, picking up

EXHIBIT 8   **E-Consulting Companies**

Public			Private		
Company Name	**Founded**	**Employees in 2000/2001**	**Company Name**	**Founded**	**Employees in 2000/2001**
1 Agency.com	1995	1,500	1 Berbee Information Networks		300
2 answerthink, inc.	1997	1,650	2 Context Integration	1992	333
3 Applied Theory	1996	721	3 CyberSight	1994	75
4 Appnet Inc.	1997	650	4 e-built		
5 Breakaway Solutions		338	5 Emerald Internet Services	1996	5
6 BrighStar Info Technology		140	6 Extraprise	1997	300
7 Cambridge Technology Ptnr.	1991	4,200	7 Fort Point Partners, Inc.	1996	177
8 C-bridge Internet Solutions	1996	501	8 Fry Multimedia		
9 Ciber		5,000	9 Giant STEP	1991	140
10 Circle.com	1998	560	10 Greenwich Technology		
11 Cognizant Technology Solutions		3,164	11 Iconixx		
12 Computer Sciences Corp.	1959	58,000	12 Inventa		
13 Cyberplex	1998	320	13 Logica		
14 Cysive	1994	291	14 Logical Design Solutions		
15 DiamondCluster Int'l, Inc.	1994	576	15 Macquarium intelligent Commu		
16 Digex	1996	1,315	16 Magnet Interactive Group		
17 Digital Island	1994	900	17 NerveWire, Inc.	1999	210
18 Digital Lighthouse Corporation			18 Nexgenix		
19 Digital River			19 NOVO Corp.	1994	180
20 Digitas			20 Osprey Systems		
21 Exodus Communications			21 R/Greenberg Associates Interactive		
22 FutureLink			22 Redsky		
23 GenesisIntermedia.com			23 Renaissance Solutions		
24 Globix			24 Risdall Linnihan Advertising Int		
25 Idea Integration			25 Siegel & Gale Interactive		
26 Inforte			26 Snickelways Interactive		
27 Integrated Information System			27 SolutionBank		

(continues)

EXHIBIT 8 E-Consulting Companies (continued)

	Public				Private		
	Company Name	Founded	Employees in 2000/2001		Company Name	Founded	Employees in 2000/2001
28	Interliant			28	Tvisions		
29	iXL Enterprises, Inc.	1996	2,399	29	Unisys		
30	Lante Corp.	1984	345	30	Xcelerate		
31	Luminant Worldwide Corp.	1998	879	31	XOR Inc.	1991	391
32	Mainspring			32	ZEFER Corp.	1996	575
33	MarchFirst	2000	8,900				
34	Modem Media	1984					
35	Navidec						
36	Nextera						
37	Organic, Inc.	1993	954				
38	Primix Solutions						
39	Proxicom, Inc.	1991	1,194				
40	PSINet						
41	Qwest Communications Interna.						
42	Rare Medium Group						
43	Razorfish, Inc.	1995	1,800				
44	Sapient Corporation	1991	2,100				
45	Scient Corp.	1997	885				
46	Seranova						
47	Tanning Technology						
48	U.S. Interactive, Inc.	1994	700				
49	US WEB/CKS	1995	300				
50	Usinternetworking						
51	Verio						
52	Viant Corporation	1996	405				
53	Xceed						
54	Xpedior						
55	Zentropy Partners		300				

Source: 19 source/year combination
Years 1998, 1999, 2000, 2001
From 12 independent sources: Jupiter, KIRG, Fortune, Info TechTrends, Varbusiness, Upside, Red Hearring, Stephens Analysts, Forrester, Morgan Stanley, Lehman Brothers, The Industry Standard.

complementary skill sets such as design and experience modeling through acquisitions. Later, Sapient began to organize professionals around vertical industries such as financial services and communications. At the other end of the spectrum, four-year-old Viant and two-year-old Scient were born as full-service stables.

However, delivering end-to-end e-business consulting presented real challenges to the new firms. A Forrester Research study of 40 e-commerce-consulting shops concluded that "no service provider demonstrates excellence across all categories. Nearly all demonstrate biases and knowledge gaps that stem from their radically different origins."[11] Furthermore, their positioning as full-service providers led to a lack of differentiation in the industry.

The second principle on which new firms were built was that, because of the pervasive effect of the Internet technology, new consulting firms

EXHIBIT 9   Performance of New E-Consultants

E-Consulting Industry—Sequential Revenue and Head Count Growth

Quarter Ending	Mar. 00 Revenue	June 00 Revenue	Sept. 00 Revenue	Dec. 99 Head Count	Mar. 00 Head Count	June 00 Head Count
Agency.com	22.5%	50.0%	14.0%			
Answerthink	7	7	3	2%	4%	3%
Breakaway Solutions	66	96	-2	na	34	27
C-bridge Internet Soln	42	54	38	29	56	37
Cysive	50	24	-12	12	15	21
Diamond Technology	16	20	15	4	6	25
IXL	36	17	na	31	19	na
Luminant WorldWide	6	20	-5	6	8	-7
MarchFirst	9	8	-3	4	5	3
Mainspring				126	49	32
Organic	11	27	1	19	18	5
Proxicom	29	33	18	17	26	14
Raremedium	38	28	na	22	18	na
Razorfish	18	13	1	5	5	11
Sapient	18	25	10	7	10	4
Scient	70	39	12	21	20	27
US Interactive	60	59	na	175	10	na
Viant	29	26	-14	16	18	28
Xpedior	26	23	na	9	13	na
Average	*31%*	*31%*	*5%*	*30%*	*19%*	*16%*

Proportion of Dot-Coms in Client Mix

Quarter Ending	Mar. 00	June 00	Sept. 00
Answerthink	15%	10%	8%
Breakaway Solutions	28	20	20
C-bridge Internet Soln	2	2	4
Diamond Technology	5	8	5
IXL	20	10	na
Luminant WorldWide	7	7	5
MarchFirst	9	9	7
Organic	25	25	8
Proxicom	5	2	2
Razorfish	10	10	6
Sapient	19	16	9
Scient	16	10	6
US Interactive	11	11	na
Viant	18	15	32
Xpedior	20	20	na
Average	*14%*	*12%*	*9%*

(continues)

EXHIBIT 9   Performance of New E-Consultants (Continued)

E-Consulting Industry—Number of Billable Employees

Quarter Ending	Dec. 99	Mar. 00	June 00	Sept. 00
Answerthink	1,396	1,426	1,483	1,529
Breakaway Solutions	na	376	505	641
C-bridge Internet Soln	147	208	324	445
Diamond Technology	433	452	506	632
IXL	1,358	1,778	2,182	na
Luminant WorldWide	677	722	791	736
MarchFirst	6,700	7,245	7,645	7,895
Mainspring	68	101	133	165
Organic	na	666	816	855
Proxicom	568	678	853	989
Raremedium	443	540	661	na
Razorfish	na	na	1,448	1,605
Sapient	1,666	1,786	1,980	2,250
Scient	609	828	1,040	1,324
US Interactive	245	509	561	na
Viant	311	362	439	561
Xpedior	1,045	1,139	1,304	na
Average	*1,119*	*1,176*	*1,334*	*1,510*

E-Consulting Industry—Staff Mix September 00

	Technology	Creative	Strategy	Others*
Agency.com	35%	35%	20%	10%
Diamond Technology	33	0	67	0
Digitas	23	46	15	17
IXL	35	27	18	20
Luminant	43	27	15	16
MarchFirst	50	25	25	0
Organic	30	55	15	0
Proxicom	65	15	20	0
Razorfish	38	27	35	0
Sapient	48	20	10	22
Scient	50	25	25	0
US Interactive	36	16	13	34
Viant	50	25	25	0
Xpedior	90	5	5	0
Average	*45%*	*24%*	*22%*	*8%*

* Others includes project management, sales and marketing, and executive support

EXHIBIT 9   Performance of New E-Consultants (continued)

E-Consulting Industry—Gross Margins (%)

	Dec. 98	Mar. 99	June 99	Sept. 99	Dec. 99	Mar. 00	June 00	Sept. 00
Agency.com	38%	43%	47%	45%	46%	49%	51%	52%
Answerthink	53	44	41	41	41	45	43	44
Breakaway Solutions	32	55	62	54	60	60	55	49
C-bridge Internet Soln	22	42	46	47	0	47	51	51
Diamond Technology	48	49	46	47	48	49	46	47
Digitas	29	49	33	42	36	50	46	44
IXL	36	52	50	43	44	53	53	29
Luminant WorldWide	46	51	37	35	53	49	47	36
Mainspring	na	16	33	51	29	32	41	44
MarchFirst	na	39	49	43	46	51	49	48
Organic	19	51	47	25	18	44	51	45
Proxicom	41	41	45	49	50	52	53	53
Razorfish	57	57	58	50	52	58	53	46
Sapient	52	51	52	51	51	52	52	51
Scient	52	54	52	54	54	57	58	55
US Interactive	43	49	46	44	49	56	52	na
Viant	41	48	49	57	60	59	61	50
Xpedior	41	42	43	42	47	48	48	na
Average	*41%*	*47%*	*46%*	*46%*	*43%*	*51%*	*51%*	*46%*

E-Consulting Industry—Utilization

Quarter Ending	Sept. 99	Dec. 99	Mar. 00	June 00	Sept. 00
Agency.com	61%	65%	na	na	na
Answerthink	na	62	64	65	63
Breakaway Solutions	na	75	80	79	53
C-bridge Internet Soln	71	66	72	68	60
Diamond Technology	na	na	65	67	55
Digitas	na	62	64	65	60
IXL	na	69	69	66	na
Luminant WorldWide	na	68	66	66	59
Mainspring	66	54	61	60	54
MarchFirst	na	67	67	67	66
Organic	na	62	62	62	47
Proxicom	78	70	73	72	67
Raremedium	na	66	67	66	na
Razorfish	na	64	64	67	50
Sapient	na	75	77	77	69
Scient	71	68	76	77	69
US Interactive	na	67	69	67	na
Viant	na	59	67	67	5
Xpedior	na	72	70	64	na
Average	*72%*	*66%*	*69%*	*68%*	*56%*

(continues)

EXHIBIT 9 Performance of New E-Consultants (continued)

E-Consulting Industry—Staff Turnover

Quarter Ending	Sept. 99	Dec. 99	Mar. 00	June 00	Sept. 00
Agency.com	na	17%	na	na	na
Answerthink	na	27	32%	32%	24%
Breakaway Solutions	na	20	11	20	9
C-bridge Internet Soln	8%	15	16	17	12
Diamond Technology	12	14	15	15	11
IXL	18	24	19	18	na
Luminant WorldWide	19	19	19	20	na
Mainspring	13	3	10	10	15
MarchFirst	na	26	28	22	22
Organic	na	30	30	31	30
Proxicom	15	15	15	14	14
Razorfish	na	18	18	16	11
Sapient	15	15	14	15	15
Scient	9	10	11	12	14
US Interactive	na	20	22	25	na
Viant	na	4	11	17	12
Xpedior	na	22	28	26	na
Average	*14%*	*18%*	*19%*	*19%*	*16%*

Note: Sapient's turnover figures only include voluntary turnover.
Source: Company reports.

could be, and indeed needed to be, global from the beginning. (See Exhibit 10 for international revenue mix of the new e-consultants.) IXL, Razorfish, Scient, and other new entrants spent vast sums expanding internationally, through acquisitions and office expansions.

Offering one-stop shopping, in addition to expanding geographically pushed these new firms to

EXHIBIT 10
International Revenue of New E-Consulting Firms

Source: Company reports.

Quarter Ending	Mar. 00	June 00	Sept. 00
Answerthink	2%	2%	1%
C-bridge Internet Soln	0	8	8
Diamond Technology	10	4	7
IXL	0	8	na
Luminant WorldWide	17	2	na
MarchFirst	22	18	15
Organic	10	10	12
Proxicom	39	13	16
Razorfish	6	38	28
Sapient	7	8	10
Scient	20	10	16
US Interactive	18	25	na
Viant	0	4	17
Xpedior	3	7	na
Average	*10%*	*14%*	*12%*

grow very fast either organically or through acquisitions and partnerships to fill skill and geographic gaps. Revenues of the 24 major web shops, firms that concentrate solely on Internet consulting, doubled in 1999 to about $3 billion. Firms such as Scient and or Breakaway experienced 60 percent growth in revenues within one quarter in 1999. Margins fluctuated from 40 percent to 52 percent from 1998 to March 2000. Utilization rates averaged 73 percent in September 1999 for these new firms. As of May 2000, MarchFirst had 8,000 employees; Sapient and iXL had 2,100 each. Answerthink was born in April 97 and in less than three years had 18 offices in three countries. MarchFirst, the firm created in January 2000 as a result of the Wittman-Hart and USWeb merger, had 70 offices in 14 different countries.

The new breed e-consulting firms diverged in their growth strategies, with some, such as Organic, Scient, Viant, and Proxicom attempting to grow organically, others, such as Agency.com and Razorfish doing selective acquisitions, and yet others, such as iXL and Marchfirst, growing primarily through roll-up strategies. For instance, USWeb, one of the companies that merged into Marchfirst, acquired 28 Internet consultancies across all segments of the business within 18 months. Consequently, mergers and acquisitions in the management consulting industry more than doubled from 105 in 1997 to 221 in 1998.[12] The 63 merger deals made in the first quarter of 1999 alone surpassed the annual totals for each year before 1997.

Each growth strategy decision presented different challenges. In firms following growth through acquisition strategy, if management did not focus on post-merger integration, the various parts of the firm could have very different service offerings, methodologies, practices, infrastructure, culture, and professional expectations. However, focusing on integration could detract from client-service focus. Organic growth strategy required striking a careful balance between maintaining high standards to preserve their reputations for quality and achieving sufficient scale to meet demand and be competitive with other e-consultants in delivering complex and sophisticated applications.

Another approach chosen by firms to cover their skill gaps was to sign partnership agreements with software vendors, hardware providers, or other consultancies. Conditions for those contracts varied widely. Some partnerships share commissions, others cross-sold products and services, yet others received licensing discount or served as a beta testing of partner's software products.

A significant proportion of the new firms went public. Of the 90 e-consultant firms, almost all of which were born in the mid 1990s, about 60 percent went public in the late 1990s. As of July 1999, e-consultants, including USWeb/CKS, Proxicom, Sapient, Diamond Technology Partners, Razorfish, and Scient, had returned 25–30 percent on investments made in them at the time of their going public.[13] The leaders of the new firms believed that they needed large amounts of capital to grow quickly in scale and scope. Public firms also had access to a liquid and, for many, rapidly appreciating, noncash currency—common stock—that enabled them to make acquisitions relatively easily. Being publicly quoted also allowed these firms to offer stocks and options as compensation to attract and retain motivated and skilled professionals. Additionally, venture capitalists that had backed some of the e-consulting companies pushed them to go public to take advantage of the bull market. Reflected Answerthink chairman and CEO Ted Fernandez:

> The marketplace was changing very quickly, the competition for talent was only going to increase, and the demand for technology-related consulting services was going to increase. I felt an equity model was more appropriate given all of those changes, and just did not believe that the partnership cash model was going to be the best way to attract, retain, acquire, and do all the things you needed to do to compete."[14]

New e-consulting firms also introduced other novel business practices in the consulting industry.

For example, consultancies that were born to serve the e-business space engaged intensively in offering consulting in return for equity and performance-based pricing (taking a share of the revenue streams that they had helped clients create). "In the future we are going to get a lot more serious about not only taking equity but taking an active part in the funding [of clients]," observed Viant CEO Bob Gett, as the firm announced in December 1999 an alliance with Technology Crossover Ventures and Hewlett-Packard to help create and spin off Internet businesses.[15]

These web consultants caught the investors' eyes when some of these still small firms began to capture some of the most lucrative web engagements. In 1997, for instance, Viant's clients already included J.P Morgan, American Express, General Motors, Deutsche Bank, and Standard & Poor's among others. Creating a respected brand and building a roster of respected clients came, however, at a significant cost. Whereas major consulting firms typically spent 6–10 percent of revenues on marketing, e-consultancies spent double that percentage.[16] "From proactive selling all the way to print and television, we're focused on driving awareness around our name," remarked MarchFirst CEO Bob Bernard.[17]

The new e-consultants were very successful. Growth from 1998 to 1999 averaged approximately 200 percent and their average market capitalization was approximately 20 times revenue in early 2000. Revenues of the incumbents consulting firms, in contrast, grew in the 10–15 percent range during 1998–1999 and the market capitalization-revenue multiple was approximately 2_x. The new firms developed a powerful presence in the e-consulting marketplace. In February 2000 Forrester Research reported that 76 percent of interviewed firms were using an e-consulting firm whereas 54 percent were using the Big Five or other management consultants (multiple answers accepted).[18] Ninety percent of website developers felt that the Big Five consulting firms "do not grasp issues as well as the pure-play web developers."[19] Yet the advantages of better execution—

lower costs, better integration across disciplines, greater creativity, deeper knowledge of Internet Technologies, and faster delivery of services—was perhaps only half the reason why the entrants were so successful. The other half had to do with the failure of the incumbents to respond actively to the e-consulting market opportunity when it had first emerged.

And yet, the new e-consultants were facing enormous challenges. Although they had professionals who understood the power and opportunity of the Web, they lacked professionals who had sufficient vertical industry experience to offer industry-specific strategy advice.[20] In addition, these new firms were grappling with the challenge of managing hypergrowth. It was still unclear whether the newcomers could deliver on increasingly complex projects that melded their creative and technology skills with the in-depth industry-specific knowledge, understanding of legacy systems, and global reach, the possession of which the more established consulting companies could boast.

Incumbents' Reaction

E-business has changed the rules about strategic plans, operations, supplies, production, sales, distribution, and customer service. E-business has stolen time from every player in the market place, and it is forcing companies to transform their businesses and to act faster with more agility, flexibility, and anticipation. While the consulting industry has to help companies through this transformation, they must also become e-business.[21]

PricewaterhouseCoopers Management Consulting Services managing partner Scott Hart

During the mid-1990s, with clients procuring complex ERP software that took years to implement and could easily cost over $100 million in consulting services to install, the incumbent technology-oriented consulting firms were experiencing unprecedented growth in demand and attendant high profitability. Strategy firms, although in a slower-growth market segment, were also engaged in large-scale projects, such as Booz Allen's re-engineering project with Universal Studios and McKinsey's cost reduction project with Time-Warner.

With such mammoth and highly profitable opportunities abounding, many of the incumbent firms simply did not want to bother with the much smaller projects that e-consulting initially offered. For example, a typical e-commerce initiative at Cisco took six months, a staff of three to six, and cost $350,000 to $500,000 to complete. When a manager at a leading consulting firm brought forward a $500,000 e-consulting opportunity in 1997, his partner responded, "Bring it back after it has another zero after it." This attitude, common among the major consulting firms, allowed new entrants to offer e-consulting without significant competition from incumbents in the early stages of the development of the e-consulting market.

Moreover, business strategy firms such as Bain, Boston Consulting Group, Booz Allen Hamilton, and McKinsey were fighting competitive battles with the technology-focused consulting firms such as Andersen Consulting and Pricewaterhouse-Coopers. In the early 1990s strategy services from technology-focused companies, specially the consulting arms of accounting firms, were viewed as inferior to strategy services offered by focused strategy consulting firms. However, competition began intensifying as the technology-consulting firms, increasingly populated with alumni from the strategy-focused firms, promising close integration of strategy and technology consulting, and offering strategy services at discounted prices, were increasingly successful at winning high-quality strategy work in head-to-head competition with the strategy-focused firms.

Even as they were competing with one another for share of consulting services to large clients, the incumbents were experiencing increasing defections of both clients and professionals to nimbler

start-ups. A particularly dramatic example was the mid-1999 departure of Andersen Consulting managing partner George Shaheen to join the Internet e-commerce start-up Webvan. Andersen Consulting also lost the head of its e-commerce practice Rudy Puryear, who joined Lante as CEO.[22] In 1997 four of the key professionals in KPMG's IT practice left to found Answerthink. McKinsey also was hit by defections to dot-coms, losing the heads of its technology and insurance practices, as well as leaders in its retail, consumer goods, and media businesses.[23]

As clients increasingly turned to e-consulting firms in the second half of 1999, traditional consulting firms that had not been "quick-footed" enough to meet the demand for e-consulting services began losing market share and even suffering declining revenue.

Trying to cope with the new reality, many of the incumbents initiated plans to make massive investments in their consulting practices. In 1999 alone:

- PricewaterhouseCoopers announced plans to invest $3 billion over the next three years (2000–2003) in new products and services, particularly to boost its e-consulting business, and train 10,000 of its consultants on Nestcape products;[24]

- McKinsey launched a new practice, @McKinsey, focused on start-ups, with the expectation that it would have 500 professionals in several locations by early 2000;[25]

- Booz-Allen, Bain, and Boston Consulting Group were reported to be investing "a lot of money" into their Internet practices;[26]

- Ernst & Young launched a $100 million marketing effort touting its expertise in helping companies enter e-commerce;[27]

- Deloitte Consulting spent $100 million to advertise its e-business unit;[28]

- EDS announced a major restructuring creating a new "e-business solutions" unit with 20,000 employees;[29]

- Mercer Management Consulting announced an e-consulting alliance with IBM;[30] and

- Andersen Consulting created a joint venture with Microsoft, named Avanade, to offer e-consulting services.[31]

In response to the increasingly tight labor market for professionals, Andersen Consulting increased the number of its partners, reversing a 25-year trend of increasing ratio of professional staff to partners at the firm. In addition, the firm modified its up-or-out career progression policy to allow talented individuals to stay with the firm even if they were not promoted to partner. McKinsey responded to the competition by agreeing to accept equity from start-ups in exchange for consulting services, by engaging in implementation before the strategic analysis was totally complete, and by building up its business technology offices (BTO), launched in 1997, to 12 locations and 270 consultants worldwide within two years.[32]

Even as incumbent strategy firms were waking up to the opportunities of e-consulting and the challenges posed by the new entrants, several hardware, software, and network firms were also seeking to enter the field of consulting by offering e-consulting services.

- IBM initiated a $75 million campaign to advertise its Internet consulting business as it integrated its relatively tiny strategy-focused consulting division into its gigantic systems integration practice to create a single organization called Business Innovation Services.

- Hewlett-Packard formed a new consulting division to focus entirely on enterprise application and process integration.

- 3Com invested $40 million into USWeb/CKS and an additional $60 million to develop web-based technology to be co-marketed by the two companies; 3Com also acquired Interactive Web Concepts, an e-consulting firm, and incorporated its professionals into 3Com Consulting Services.

- Microsoft planned to hire 200 IT professionals for its consulting division by June 2000.

- Michael Dell told reporters at the Comdex conference in November 1999 that Dell Computer would make deeper forays into consulting, noting that his company's services group was growing faster than all the rest of Dell.

- MultiSoft formed a new consulting division to take advantage of the growing market of legacy to web integration.

The Incumbents' Advantage

The absence of fierce competition from incumbents during the early stages of the development of the e-consulting market allowed the new entrants to grow quickly and be perceived as better understanding the Internet and its issues than the incumbent firms. Although growing at a rapid clip, they remained small compared to the incumbents, which placed them at a disadvantage when trying to bid on large e-consulting projects for a global corporation. In addition, their smaller size and younger workforce was perceived as lacking the insight and experience required to develop detailed strategies for companies particularly when they required industry expertise. Admitted a senior executive in a new entrant: "In terms of services, when it comes to technology, among this group of players, we would be number one, or near it. But our strategy capabilities need some growth and improvement going forward."[33] Besides, the new e-consultants faced the challenge of building their intellectual capital to allow them to go beyond individual projects and create repeatable high-quality solutions for multiple clients.

Beyond their greater size, deeper industry knowledge and more project management expertise, the incumbent firms had the benefit of their networks of contacts and relationships. Over the years they had built relationships at multiple levels with major clients. Their alumni were in decision making positions with several client firms. This network provided the incumbents with invaluable inside information and political support, sources of significant competitive advantage when it came to selling consulting services. And their long track record of successfully delivering results gave the incumbents greater credibility with clients than the new entrants whose track record was less extensive.

Adding to their credibility disadvantage, some of the new entrants were not able to keep their promises. Several customers of Internet consulting firms expressed dissatisfaction with the execution of consulting projects and depth of business consulting and system integration skills. The following remarks of a dissatisfied client were not atypical:

> In May 1999, I hired iXL to write a business plan for the company, create a CD-ROM to show investors, and build the site. The total project was to be $893,000. A year and a half later, the website was still a shell, the CD-ROM has been canceled, and the business plan, completed in September 1999, was dead on delivery. It was pure college material. I had to pay Ernst & Young another $175,000 to start over. It was a complete disaster. . . .[34]

Rather than continue to compete head-on, several Internet-focused firms began to build alliances with incumbent firms to leverage their strengths. These arrangements provided the new entrants with access to the contacts, expertise, infrastructure, scale, and resources of the incumbents. The incumbents, in turn, gained by enhancing their e-consulting knowledge, skills, and credibility through their association with the Internet firms. In 1999 alone Bain struck an alliance with e-consulting firms Cysive and Mainspring, McKinsey and Proxicom agreed to jointly serve as consultants to new financial services company efinanceworks, KPMG entered a joint venture with Cisco to jointly develop e-consulting capability, IBM Global Services and Mercer Management Consulting formed a global alliance to offer e-consulting services, and Deloitte Consulting en-

tered an alliance with US Interactive. However, such partnerships were proving difficult to manage and make successful for both parties. The CEO of one Internet technology firm with partnerships across several consulting firms commented, "partnerships make acquisitions look easy."

THE FALL

On April 14, 2000, Nasdaq suffered its biggest point loss in history. From mid-March to late May 2000, the high-technology sector experienced a substantial decline in market value, with the Nasdaq dropping 34.7 percent and the Internet Stock Index (ISDEX) falling 55.3 percent. Viant shares fell by 41 percent on one day. Suddenly, industry analysts were questioning the long-term viability of firms in the Internet sector based on their cash flows and downgrading e-consulting stocks.[35] Several of the e-consulting firms that were preparing to go public were not able to debut in the capital markets (see Exhibit 11 for a list of firms).

Along with other Net companies, most of the newly public e-consulting firms were grievously hurt by the April correction in tech stocks. But the correction further hurt them because it slowed the inflow of their business. Demand for e-consulting services suddenly shrank as companies scaled back their Internet ambitions and decided that they could after all afford to take their time in implementing their Internet strategies. This shrinkage in business came about even as most e-consulting firms were struggling to digest their extraordinary growth over the past months. "When you are a small company and growing at the rate they were growing and receiving so much unsolicited business," admitted an e-consulting executive, "you just don't have the business operations set and processes in place to deal with any type of change in the market."[36]

Before the market turned on dot-coms, e-consultants were capitalizing on the fear of the Internet among incumbent "brick and mortar" firms,

EXHIBIT 11   E-Consulting Firms That Were Unable to Go Public

S. No.	Company	Founded	Headquarters	Description
1	Context Integration	1992	Burglington, MA	Provider of systems consulting full-cycle application development and training services. The company delivers web-enabled applications, including Internet, intranet, and extranet. Products and services are sold to multiple industries.
2	c-quential	1999	Cambridge, MA	An ADL spin-off (French consulting group for advertising firms).
3	Emerald Solutions	1996	Greenwood, SC	Provider of Internet services, including T-1, dial-up, e-mail, hosting, consulting, and web page design; products and services are sold to multiple industries; the company was capitalized by private investment.
4	Fort Point Partners	1996	S. Francisco, CA	Provider of Internet marketing services. The company provides strategy, technology, and program management services to help companies combine their existing capabilities with web-based technologies. Products and services are sold to multiple industries.
5	Greenwhich Tech Partners	1997	New York	Provider of design implementation, security, and management of website infrastructures. Products are sold to multiple industries. This company was capitalized by venture capital.
6	Iconixx	1995	Vienna, VA	Provider of e-commerce solutions, technology planning, and business process planning, specializing in web page design and development, Internet systems consulting, network consulting, and software custom applications development and consulting services. Products and services are sold to multiple industries. This company was capitalized by private investment.

EXHIBIT 11   (continued)

S. No.	Company	Founded	Headquarters	Description
7	Idea Integration	1996	Jacksonville, FL	The company specializes in the design and development of applications for online business, but it also offers its clients a variety of other services including strategy consulting, creative design, and web branding. A subsidiary of Modis Incorporated, the IT services arm of Modis Professional Services, Idea Integration has performed work on behalf of clients such as Hewlett-Packard, Merrill Lynch, Qwest Communications, and Time Warner Telecom. The company has offices in the UK and the United States.
8	Inventa	1993	Redwood, CA	Provider of b-to-b e-commerce integration services and solutions. Manages web services, including Internet applications performance monitoring, reporting, analysis, preventive maintenance, tuning, improvement, and upgrade. The company also provides monitoring, reporting, and statistical analysis software to provide integrated solutions. Products and services are sold to multiple industries. This company was capitalized by private investment and venture capital.
9	Logical Design Solutions	1990	Morristown, NJ	Developer of custom self-service web application software for Fortune 1,000 companies. Developer of TeleTrac^{tm}, a software which gives a detailed analysis of telephone tracking. Provider of custom telecommunication management software programming services. The software runs on Windows 95 and Windows NT. This company was capitalized by private investment.
10	Nexgenix	1990	Irwin, CA	Designer of websites and applications for companies. Provider of Internet website-related services. Services are provided to Fortune 1,000 companies and emerging e-businesses.

(continues)

EXHIBIT 11 (continued)

S. No.	Company	Founded	Headquarters	Description
11	Novo	1994	San Francisco, CA	Provider of e-business strategy and planning solutions. Services include Internet frame relay and ISDN access, Internet hosting, Internet consulting, web page design, web security consulting, and web marketing services. Services are provided to Fortune 1,000 companies. This company was capitalized by private investment.
12	Participate.com	1997	Chicago, IL	Provider of Internet community services. The company enables e-business strategies by offering an integrated management solution for online communities. The company develops, manages and hosts online communities utilizing its proprietary services delivery.
13	RDA	1988	Timonium, MA	Provider of database development and custom windows applications software development and engineering services.
14	Thrupoint	1996	New York	Computer network consulting service.
15	Zefer	1996	Boston, MA	Provider of Internet analysis, planning, and technical support services for e-commerce. Parent/holding company with a high-tech unit that provides Internet services. Products and services are sold to multiple industries. This company was capitalized by venture capital.

Source: Consultants News, 2001, Kennedy Information, Inc.

the chaos created by the frenzy to get on the Internet bandwagon, and the seemingly unlimited capital available to nurture the frenzy. Their sales teams didn't need to be particularly strong or skilled because the demand for their services was so great. Once the market turned soft, most e-consultants were unequipped to generate new business.

The difficult market conditions pushed several web consultancies (including, as of August 2001, Marchfirst and Xpedior) into bankruptcy. Others (including Organic, Rare Medium Group, Razorfish, and Scient) watched their stocks trade below a dollar for weeks, putting them at risk of delisting from Nasdaq. Yet others were acquired. Mainspring was acquired by IBM, Proxicom by South Africa–based Dimension Data Holdings, Seneca Investments took a major stake in floundering New York–based e-services company Agency.com, Cable & Wireless bought all outstanding shares of struggling web-services firm Digital Island, and mobile telecommunications services firm Motient bought Rare Medium.

In the free fall that followed, layoffs at e-consulting shops were legion. "Has there ever been another sector that's gotten wiped out in nine months like this?"[37] observed an e-consulting firm executive. iXL announced 350 layoffs in September 2000 and another 850 in November. In November MarchFirst announced the layoff of 1,000 consultants. Several senior executives left their firms. Bill Nussey abruptly resigned as president of iXL in a week in which e-consultants took beating on Wall Street (see Exhibit 12).

Potential survivors would have a combination of strong cash position, seasoned management, well-established and loyal customers, and a history of doing business before the Internet boom. Future e-consulting projects were likely to be fewer and more complex. "The easy stuff has by and large been done already," observed analyst Karl Keirstead. "The next phase of projects is larger, more complex, and requires better integration."[38] Observed Razorfish COO Jean-Philippe Maheu:

> When you're very successful, you grow very fast and you're well respected by your clients; you do tend to try a lot of things. But things are much tougher than they were a few months ago. We're definitely focusing on a more narrow service offering right now.[39]

Admitted Viant CEO Bob Gett: "This fits the Big Five model a lot more than the early innovation stages. Now the technology is mature enough to make room for the big guys."[40] (Appendix II provides a timeline of the evolution of the e-consulting business.)

EXHIBIT 12   **The Market Downturn**

Stock Prices						
Company	IPO Price	Oct. 99	Jan. 00	Apr. 1, 2000	Apr. 14, 2000	May 00
Appnet	$12	$26				
iXL	12	33.50	$55.50	$28.00	$19.50	$23.75
Proxicom	13	51				
Razorfish	16	47	95.13	27.50	15.63	19.06
Sapient			140.93	83.88	59.18	78.63
Scient	20	67	86.44	90.69	39.50	50.00
US Interactive	10	20.75				
Viant	16	48	99	33.50	20.81	25.50

Source: SEC filings.

(continues)

EXHIBIT 12   **The Market Downturn (continued)**

Number of Dot-Com Shutdowns

Month	Number	% of Total	Month	Number	% of Total
Jan. 00	1	0.2%	Dec. 00	49	7.6
Feb. 00	2	0.3	Jan. 01	55	8.6
Mar. 00	2	0.3	Feb. 01	60	9.4
Apr. 00	1	0.2	Mar. 01	44	6.9
May 00	13	2.0	Apr. 01	59	9.2
June 00	17	2.7	May 01	61	9.5
July 00	20	3.1	June 01	60	9.4
Aug. 00	10	1.6	July 01	39	6.1
Sept. 00	22	3.4	Aug. 01	38	5.9
Oct. 00	36	5.6	Unknown	2	0.3
Nov. 00	50	7.8	Total	641	100.0%

Source: WebMergers.com.

Layoffs at Selected Consulting Firms, Sept. 2000–Sept. 2001

Firm	Approximate Number of Positions Eliminated	Date Layoffs Announced	Comments
IXL Enterprises, Inc.	350	Sept. 00	14% of staff due to restructuring
U.S. Interactive, Inc.	124	Sept. 00	15% of staff due to restructuring
Razorfish	37	Sept. 00	2% of staff due to reduced dot-com spending
Luminant Worldwide	70	Oct. 00	7% of staff. Continued layoffs due to third quarter revenues
Razorfish	120	Oct. 00	7.5% of staff; streamlining and realigning business in response to market needs
Breakaway Solutions	90	Oct. 00	9% of workforce
Luminant Worldwide	174	Nov. 00	18% of workforce; lower than expected third quarter revenues
U.S. Interactive, Inc.	225	Nov. 00	28% of staff
marchFirst, Inc.	1,000	Nov. 00	Conserving funds because of lower-than-expected demand
Proxicom, Inc.	60	Nov. 00	5% of workforce due to soft market conditions
IXL Enterprises, Inc.	850	Nov. 00	35% of workforce to focus on serving larger clients in financial services, travel and retail and consumer packaged goods.
Scient Corporation	460	Dec. 00	25% reduction in worldwide staff; closed offices Silicon Valley and Austin, TX
Viant Corporation	125	Dec. 00	17% staff reduction to refocus on media, financial services, energy, consumer goods, and technology.
Organic, Inc.	270	Dec. 00	25% of worldwide staff; closed Atlanta and Boston offices.
Breakaway Solutions	300	Dec. 00	30% of workforce
marchFirst, Inc.	550	Jan. 01	6% of remaining workforce; adapting to market conditions.

Source: Consultants News, September 2001, Kennedy Information, Inc.

Management consulting is a diverse and relatively young industry. Thousands of consultants serve businesses attempting to improve management practices. A few management-consulting firms have become large transnational corporations, employing thousands of professionals; but at the same time, almost half of the management-consulting firms employ fewer than four persons.

The term "management consulting" only entered common usage from the 1940s onward, which is when some might therefore argue the industry really started. However, modern management consulting may be traced to the beginning of "scientific management" in the 1880s as "modern business enterprise took place of market mechanisms in coordinating the activities of the economy and allocating its resources."[42] It appears that once large-scale managerial enterprise originated with the second industrial revolution in the last half of the nineteenth century, managers began seeking outside advice. Such advice was provided, typically on an ad hoc basis, by a number of professionals, including bankers, advertising agents, auditors, and engineers.

Early management-consulting pioneers, including Henry Fayol in France, Lyndall Urwick in England, Mary Parket Follet and Frank and Lillian Gilbreth in the United States, explored new methods for saving resources while maintaining that businesses operated according to universal rules. Management consulting intensified with the development of scientific management. At the end of the nineteenth century, the engineer Frederick W. Taylor (1856–1915) developed a new approach toward the management of workers on the shop floor—later extended by others to office workers—based on systematic observation followed by optimum organization of individual activities. Early management consultants that followed Taylor's approach were known as industrial engineers or "efficiency experts." Charles Bedoux introduced methods for measuring the quantity and quality of work. Arthur D. Little, eager to apply scientific ideas in business, founded in 1886 what was perhaps the first pure management consultancy. In 1914 Edwin Booz began offering "business research services" in Chicago. In 1926 James

McKinsey founded his firm to offer management consulting based on a comprehensive diagnostic approach.

The second generation of management consultancies emerged in the United States during the 1930s and came to worldwide prominence from the 1950s onward. Most of the companies founded during those years were started by former partners or employees of the pioneering consulting firms. For example, Bruce Henderson, formerly ADL, formed Boston Consulting Group in 1963. During the boom years of the 1950s and the 1960s, rapidly expanding and internationalizing firms created a growing demand for management consulting. Two salient developments during the 1960s were the entry of major accounting firms into management consulting and the creation of top-tier specialized strategy-consulting firms.

From the late 1970s onward, the large diversified corporations, increasingly facing competitive pressure, sought management consulting advice, often in consort with advice on implementing new information technology effectively, to become more efficient. The consulting arms of the large accounting firms were particularly successful in implementing assignments related to information technology, largely because auditing activities had made them familiar with the IT systems of large corporations. Large IT organizations also expanded organically or through acquisitions in offering IT consulting.

At the start of the 1990s, IT management consulting work was primarily done on custom, legacy systems. Especially prominent was the installation of enterprise resource planning systems to integrate data flow and access to information over the whole range of a company's activities. Consulting services centered on adjusting the organization to the requirements of ERP systems and train users. ERP projects very often lasted two or more years and involved large teams of consultants. In the mid-1990s ERP systems and the Y2K fear led to an overwhelming demand of IT consulting services and several specialist IT management consulting firms were formed. Several IT consulting firms went public.

In 1998 websites started springing up at companies and in 1999 e-commerce began to assume strategic significance. Netscape's IPO

(continues)

success, Amazon.com's success as an online book-seller, the success of online brokers, and the explosion of interest in on line purchases signaled major changes for firms and their advisors. A new breed of IT/Internet consultants appeared and challenged the consulting industry.

The Evolution of Consulting, 1850–2000

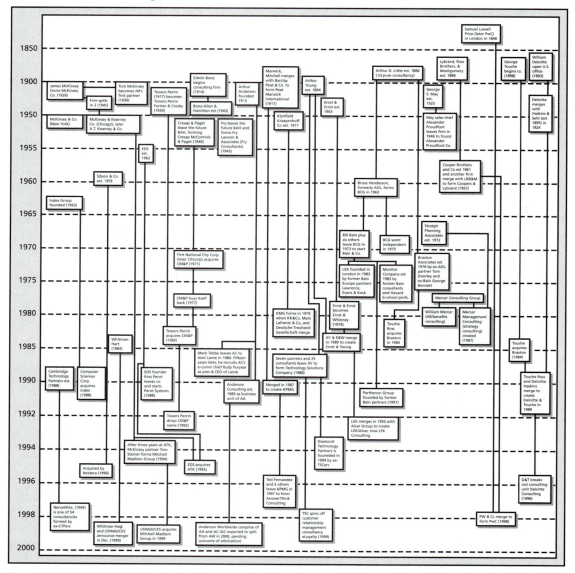

Source: Ashish Nanda, Kimberly Haddad, and Nien-hê Hsieh, "Consulting by Auditors (A)," HBS No. 902 -161, p. 20, adapted from *Consultants News,* "CN's Consulting Family Tree," January 2000.

APPENDIX II Timeline of Developments in E-Consulting (1980–2000)

	1980	1982	1985	1990	1991	1992	1993	1994	1995	1996	1997	1998	1999	2000
Economic environment			Wall Street collapse				Inflation slows bull market		Increased M&A worldwide					Nasdaq collapse
Venture capital funding number of companies	216	823								1,362	1,729	2,166	3,497	5,827
Estimated venture financing	304	2,287								7,643	11,363	18,971	57,805	16,530
Worldwide Internet-related IPO activity									9	14	12	24	248	118
Information technology developments	TCP/IP			World Wide Web			Mosaic	Netscape	Commercial Internet	IAB		Y2K	Y2K	Wireless communication
IT Services	PC introduction / Client/Server data processing			Business process reengineering					ERP			Websites	e-commerce	e-commerce
Major consulting trends	Organization rationalization					IT-based outsourcing					IT Networking/e-business/system integration			
E-consultancies founded			Rare Medium		Sapient	Breakaway	Organic	Diamond, Primix, US Interactive	Razorfish, USWeb	agency.com, e-bridge, iXL, Mainspring, Viant	Answerthink, Appnet, Scient, Xpedior	Luminant	Digitas	MarchFirst
E-consultancies IPO										Primix, Sapient, USWeb	Diamond	Answerthink, Wittman-Hart	Agency.com, Appnet, Breakaway, C-Bridge, iXL, Luminant, Proxicom, Razorfish, Scient, US Interactive, Viant, Xpedior	Digitas, Mainspring, Organic

Source: Casewriters.

References

1. "The Global Information Technology Management Consulting Marketplace: Key Data, Forecasts, & Trends 2000 Edition," Kennedy Information Research Group (KIRG).

2. Ibid.

3. *Consultants News,* June 1998.

4. Krishna Palepu, "The Role of Capital Market Intermediaries in the Dot-Com Crash of 2000," HBS No. 1010-110.

5. "Speed Kills: What Happened to Us in 2000," Webmergers.com.

6. Geoffrey Colvin, "Old Consultants Never Die: They Just Go 'e'," *Fortune,* June 12, 2000.

7. Forrester Research.

8. Colvin, "Old Consultants Never Die."

9. Ibid.

10. *Consultants News,* December 1999.

11. Forrester Research, "E-Commerce Integrators Exposed," June 2000.

12. "Global Management Consulting Mergers and Acquisitions, 1999," KIRG.

13. Estimate of Rich Legget, vice president of technology research at investment bank Friedman, Billings & Ramsey.

14. *Consultants News,* September 2000.

15. *Consultants News,* October 1999.

16. The Rodenhauser report, "Inside Consulting," April 12, 2000.

17. Peter Jordan, "Matchmaking: Between the User and the Solution Provider," *VARBusiness,* September 15, 2001.

18. Forrester Research, "E-Business Strategy Needs Help," February 2000.

19. Jupiter Executive Survey, September 1999.

20. 42 percent of Forrester's report respondents said that lack of industry knowledge was the top challenge of engaging an E-consultant as strategy provider.

21. *Consultants News,* December 1999.

22. David Witford, "Consultants Chase the Internet Express," *Fortune,* October 25, 1999, p. 4.

23. Rachel Emma Silverman, "Your Career Matters: McKinsey Tries to Outsmart Internet's Allures," *The Wall Street Journal,* April 25, 2000, p. B1

24. Elisabeth MacDonald, "PriceWaterhouse Says It Will Lay off 1,000 Employees," *The Wall Street Journal,* October 28, 1999.

25. Peter Henig, "Cash Gladly Accepted: McKinsey & Co., The Most Button-Downed of Management Consultants, Has a Plot to Accelerate E-Business. Will It Work?" *Red Herring,* February 2000.

26. *Fortune,* April 12, 1999.

27. *Cleveland Plain Dealer,* November 10, 1999.

28. "The Global Information Technology Management Consulting Marketplace: Key Data, Forecasts, & Trends 2000 Edition," Kennedy Information Research Group (KIRG).

29. Ibid.

30. Ibid.

31. Ibid.

32. Ibid.

33. Eileen Gunn, "Fast Five," *Upside Today,* September 7, 2000.

34. Michael Newman, "Dotcom Inferno: Money to Burn," November 2000.

35. J. Willoughby, "Burning Up," *Barron's,* March 20, 2000.

36. "Upshot: Upshot by Upshot Writers," *Upside Today,* January 7, 2000.

37. Chad Gallant, the U.S. regional director of Icon MediaLab International AB. Dow Jones Newswires by Ross Snel, August 27, 2001.

38. Suzanne Koudsi, "Down and Out," *Fortune,* October 2, 2000.

39. Joanne Robb, "Screeching to a Halt," *Upside Today,* March 15, 2001.

40. Koudsi, "Down and Out."

41. Information gleaned from Matthias Kipping "Trapped in the Wave: The Evolution of Management Consultancies," in *Critical Consulting: New Perspectives on the Management Advice Industry,* 2002, eds. Timothy Clark and Robin Fincham, Blackwell Business, "The Global Information Technology Management Consulting Marketplace," and *Consulting News.*

42. Alfred Chandler, *The Visible Hand,* Harvard University Press, 1977, p. 1.

External Strategy for Sustained Competitive Advantage

Every professional service firm must make strategic decisions that will have long-term implications for the viability of the enterprise. This three-case module examines various approaches to developing and sustaining strategies that center on the external domain that drive PSFs. We will see in these cases different challenges faced by the protagonists. We will observe how these professionals deal with these challenges as they confront their clients' pressing needs. We will see that clients may have a clear or murky picture of how they want to be served. However, their view of the future might be influenced by matters beyond their control. Clients may think they know what they want but have no theory or rationale for wanting to act the way they do. Often clients approach PSFs because they want guidance through the fog of indecision. Clients seek assurance that they are moving in a direction that will leverage their capabilities in a strategic way.

We have chosen to address the upper-right quadrant of the professional service model first. This is the arena in which entrepreneurs begin creating their PSFs (see

This note was prepared by Professor Thomas DeLong, Professor Ashish Nanda, Dean's Research Fellow Scot Landry, and Ying Liu (MBA 2001).

Figure 1). After developing their particular service, product, or process idea, entrepreneurs must make their ideas work within a competitive landscape. They must make them actionable. How will the creative innovator build brand? How will the brand be sustained and leveraged? How does one create an intangible service and begin the process of identifying ways to operationalize the service?

We have made the argument in Module One that PSFs exist to assist other firms in managing risk and uncertainty. Organizations experience fluctuations due to changing strategic pictures of the future and changing demands from their clients. Due to the new role technology plays in the marketplace, and because of trends toward convergence, globalization, and disintermediation, PSFs are needed more than ever to provide guidance to organizations dealing with these challenges.

This second module concerns itself with the *strategic* dynamics that influence organizations *externally*. Through these dynamics, PSFs confront their own future in the context of serving clients, with both client and PSF hoping that in some way their current work leads to future opportunities. In the same way that PSFs help client organizations assess opportunities in the context of what capabilities they bring to the marketplace, PSFs must know how their own current capabilities enhance their own future opportunities. How should PSFs balance those capabilities in the context of the changing dynamics of client expectations? How do they reinvent themselves and redefine their service concept when they believe the target market may be changing? With markets moving and firms moving in response, it is more important than ever for PSFs to be grounded in a strategic view that brings reassurance to their clients.

FIGURE 1

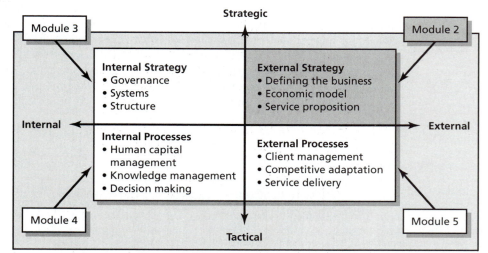

In this second module we attempt to identify some of the key dimensions in creating a professional service firm. We try to articulate the importance of being clear about the economic rationale of the PSF. We build on the research in the service management area by emphasizing the four critical dimensions of an organization that should drive the decisions in the upper-right quadrant:

1. Create a service that is unique.

2. Create an environment that is unique in which to work.

3. Create clients and professionals who are apostles.

4. Be financially successful by having good revenues, profits, and growth.

The driving principles and values in this upper-right quadrant are growth, expansion, and adaptability. We believe that being adaptive leads to creative problem solving, innovation, and change. The organizing criteria are based on vision, flexibility, external image (brand), and the economic realities of competing in the marketplace. It is also important to emphasize that uncertainty and change coupled with innovation and competition drive the activities of this domain.

THOMAS WEISEL PARTNERS

We begin this second module by introducing you to Thomas Weisel. With considerable experience in the financial services marketplace (having run Montgomery Securities for over two decades), Weisel saw a marketplace vacuum of firms focused solely on growth companies. He saw how all the former HARMs had sold out (including himself) because they believed in the benefits of scale.[1] As Montgomery Securities matured, Montgomery's clients also matured. This drives Weisel to sell to NationsBank to better meet the needs of Montgomery's clients.

But Weisel also experienced, firsthand, how a merger can alter a culture dramatically. He quickly realizes that the strong boutique culture of Montgomery has been swallowed up by the larger and more bureaucratic NationsBancMontgomery. Many of Montgomery's former employees become more and more disillusioned as the weeks progressed after the merger. Weisel understands that the most critical asset PSFs have is talented professionals. He believes that if he launches a boutique firm with a strong culture and unique strategy, those eager professionals will soon flock to it.

Weisel launches TWP with excellent timing. There is demand from new start-ups for a boutique focused on the industries TWP calls its "tailwinds." There is also the demand from professionals to work for a new boutique that looks and feels more like a merchant bank. The challenge for Weisel is to start TWP on the right track quickly. By relying on many of the qualities we will discuss in

---

[1] The four HARMs are Hambrecht & Quist, Alex. Brown, Robertson Stephens, and Montgomery Securities.

Module Five (client relationship management), Weisel recruits key professionals and clients quickly. TWP immediately becomes one of the firms most in demand for high-growth clients.

WOODLAND PARTNERS: FIELD OF DREAMS?

In Woodland Partners, we turn to study two of the most basic entrepreneurial questions: (1) Should the entrepreneurs even launch a firm? and (2) If so, what should the firm's business model be? Beth Lilly has always sought to create an investment management firm. She has found support and a potential future partner in Rick Rinkoff. But both know that they need someone like Dick Jensen, with marketing and client relationship management expertise to complement their investment management knowledge.

One of the first lessons this case suggests is that the human dimension is critical to start-up (and PSF) success. Within the context of entrepreneurial PSFs, partnerships complicate the decision-making process. Not only must Lilly and Rinkoff recruit someone with external appeal (to clients and investors), but they must also attract someone who they work well with, respect, and share similar goals. All entrepreneurial PSFs face the question of what makes a good partner. What are the criteria that one should use to answer this question? Where is it that partnerships go wrong?

Another key lesson is that firm positioning and self-definition are critical to winning the war for talent and clients. In this case, talent comes first. Dick Jensen refuses to join until the firm agrees on a positioning that he is comfortable with and that he believes will be attractive in the marketplace (in the product, capital, and talent markets). At Jensen's home, the three founders struggled to attain a clarity of purpose that would define them externally. This external strategy subsequently impacts the firm's organizational strategy.

Once Jensen, Rinkoff, and Lilly decide to exit First Bank, the question then turns to the best way to exit the firm to minimize professional and organizational risk. They do not want First Bank to tie them up in court and hold up the launch of Woodland Partners. What is the best method of giving their notice? Should they do it individually or collectively? Should they expect to be shown the door immediately? Should they contact their clients to try to bring them to Woodland, or should they not contact their clients at all?

This case also provides a lens into the war for talent—another perspective critical to PSFs (which will be covered in more detail in Modules Four and Seven). What should First Bank, or any PSF, do to keep their prized employees? What can they say in the moment of resignation to get them to reconsider? Before the moment of resignation, what can PSFs do to provide star employees the challenge, flexibility, responsibility, and excitement they seek?

The Woodland case is unique in many ways. First, it is one of the few cases that focus on the possibility of pursuing a no-growth strategy. This has incredible implications on Woodland's internal and external organization. Should more firms consider it? Second, Woodland is a case when a firms' owners, managers, and professionals are the same individuals. What are the implications of this on personal and professional development and satisfaction?

SHOULDICE HOSPITAL LIMITED

We included the Shouldice Hospital case in this module to highlight the importance of defining clear value proposition to clients by a professional service organization. For a family business with limited resources and capacity, such as Shouldice Hospital, it is critical to clarify in its service offerings to clients what are the must-haves, the should-haves, and the nice-to-haves.

Unlike most hospitals, Shouldice Hospital chose to specialize only in hernia operations—its value proposition. Over the years, Shouldice Hospital had built its reputation because its patients are treated with special care and have shorter recuperation time and lower recurrence rates.

Shouldice hospital had developed internal processes and strategy to complement its value proposition. It hired doctors and nurses who would enjoy the work environment and the time for personal lives outside work. Shouldice focused on employee satisfaction, which has led to excellent client service and low turnover. The hospital administration implemented a cost-effective system to deliver high-quality medical services that emphasize both the efficient process and the social environment.

Shouldice's reputation has put constraints on the hospital's capacity. Dr. Shouldice will have to decide whether to increase capacity, and if so, how to increase capacity while maintaining the quality of services delivered. If the hospital chooses to expand, it can add more beds to the existing facility, or add Saturday shifts, or build a new facility, or develop new procedures. However, all of these options will potentially destroy the social atmosphere for patients, the work environment for doctors and nurses, the quality and control by the hospital, and the perception by clients, not to mention the complexity of government regulations. The expansion plan will force the hospital administration to identify the cores of the Shouldice value proposition and how to duplicate its past success.

If the hospital remains status quo, it might still be able to meet and exceed client expectations, and be successful as long as it delivers on the promises it makes to clients. As Dr. Shouldice ponders the external strategy for the hospital, he must define clearly the following: who, what, how, why. (1) Who does Shouldice hospital serve? Who does it not serve? (2) What services does the hospital provide? (3) How does Shouldice provide the service, especially the core service? How does Shouldice deliver its service as an experience so that clients stay satisfied throughout the entire experience and professionals feel satisfied with their own job experience? How does a PSF balance its capacity with client experience? (4) Why does the Shouldice business exist? What is its mission?

SUMMARY

The subject of a PSF's external strategy is far too broad to cover in just three cases. Our goal has been to focus on critical decisions in the definition of a firm's future. (1) Should a group of professionals launch a given firm? (2) How should the firm define what service promises/areas it will make and which it will not? How should it determine what its brand equity is? (3) How should a firm balance its current core strengths with its future opportunities? (4) How should professionals within a PSF persuade other partners to join, adopt a new business model, or stay within the firm? (5) How should an established firm remain entrepreneurial and innovative to stay ahead of its competitors?

Many PSFs, particularly young firms, define themselves more by what they do *not* do versus what they will do. When should a PSF say yes versus no to a future opportunity? In the second case in Module One, AGENCY.COM, Chan Suh and Kyle Shannon chose not to submit the RFP to General Electric because they believed it would change the firm too much and take the firm in a direction that the founders did not want to go, at least yet. Thom Weisel set up TWP to focus only on the "tailwinds," so that clients would hopefully see TWP as the experts in those areas. In the Woodland case, we see Dick Jensen, who clearly understands this concept, waiting until the three founders determine a business model that is clear and well defined. Woodland's choice of a no-growth strategy came with the understanding of the external and internal implications. Shouldice Hospital must choose whether or not to expand and risk diluting its brand and losing quality control of services delivered. The hospital administration needs to decide who their clients are and who are not.

Partnership is another important element in PSF innovation. In AGENCY.COM, Suh and Shannon first found out that they worked well together and liked each other. The partnership in the Woodland case is fairly unique and fascinating because the three founders were of different generations. Because of the generational and life-stage differences, it took a longer time for the Woodland protagonists to pull the trigger on their idea. In each of these partnerships, diversity of background, interests, and expertise is obvious. To leverage this diversity, PSF partners must have a high degree of compatibility on a personal level.

We begin the module by studying Thom Weisel at Thomas Weisel Partners. TWP managed to make a sudden impact within the financial services arena. The case highlights how important recruiting talent is to the start of a PSF. Weisel saw demand on the behalf of former employees of the HARMs for a new boutique. He knew they would be attracted by his culture and the opportunity to focus on the tailwinds versus the organizational politics of the larger acquiring banks. The case also points to the importance of timing to success in PSFs. TWP got into the market at the time that funding for start-ups exploded in 1999.

Woodland Partners brings to the forefront the pros and cons of pursuing different growth strategies. The partners were clear about their service model and yet they had great concern about whether they could be true to their internal structural challenges. The case discussion highlights the need to link external strategy with the internal organization.

The Shouldice Hospital case emphasizes the importance of value proposition to clients. A PSF's strong brand can generate more repeat and referral businesses. At the same time, imprudent expansion might dilute a PSF's brand and quality of services. In addition, a PSF's existing strategy and processes might not suit rapid growth. As Shouldice Hospital decides whether or not to expand and revisits its value proposition to clients, Dr. Shouldice faces the challenge of protecting what the brand represents and what the family business's mission is.

QUESTIONS ARISING FROM THE CASES IN THIS MODULE

Some of the questions that emerge when we focus on the external strategic component of the professional services model are

- What are the best ways to assess the future needs of a market?

- What trends have impacted a given market for professional services? What future trends may impact the market? Is the firm prepared for these changes?

- Have there been any changes in the demand for the PSF's services (number of clients or the intensity of the demand)? In the supply of talented recruits? In the number of firms competitive in the space?

- How has the firm defined its target customer? Is this target still appropriate? What are the threats to this type of target? Should the firm refocus? Have a broader focus? Have a narrower focus? Have a different focus entirely?

- What do a PSF's current clients want? Where do they expect the market to go? What do the newest firms in a market want? Do they see the future market differently? Where do the brightest "futurists" within the firm think the market is going? Is the firm prepared?

- In launching a PSF firm, what should its business model be? To ensure high profitability? To ensure a steady stream of clients? To ensure a steady stream of talented employees?

- In dealing with rapid entrepreneurial growth, how can the PSF remain innovative and flexible yet instill enough structure to help the organization meet its current demands effectively and efficiently?

- How much and how fast should a given PSF grow? How can it control growth?

- Is the given firm's strategy aligned with its internal capabilities?

- How much of a given organization's focus should be on future opportunities (versus focusing on current clients)? What are the drivers that affect this?

- What are the benefits of scale in a PSF (for clients, for personnel within the firm, for investors, for other stakeholders)? What are the drawbacks?

- What are the signs that a PSF's strategy, positioning, and focus are on track? What are the signs when the PSF is off track?

- In a PSF merger, how should the merged firms unite two different cultures? How can strong investment banking cultures thrive when the investment bank is brought under the control of a commercial bank?

- How should an established PSF deal with innovation and entrepreneurship within the context of the current mission and focus of the business? What criteria should it use to decide?

- What makes a good PSF start-up team? What are some of the tactics for persuading people to join a PSF start-up? What are some of the tactics a firm can use to retain its stars who want to leave?

- What are the pluses and minuses of a no-growth strategy?

Thomas Weisel Partners (A)

> I love this. The passion is still there for me to work with these young entrepreneurial companies.[1]
>
> *Thomas Weisel, chairman and CEO, Thomas Weisel Partners*

New Year's Eve, December 1998, found Thomas Weisel particularly excited. The next morning, his firm would move into its new facilities and prepare to open for business February 1. Weisel had been through an eventful 18 months, first selling Montgomery Securities, the firm he had built up over 20-plus years, to NationsBank, then directing the NationsBanc Montgomery Securities unit for one year, then exiting the firm after a brief, heated battle for control of the capital markets division in September 1998. He looked forward to re-entering the competition for deals, clients, and human capital as head of Thomas Weisel Partners (TWP).

Weisel was convinced that his new mid-sized merchant bank would be able to exploit an attractive market niche. He was aware that many industry observers considered his firm to be the wrong size at the wrong time, swimming against the tide of an entire banking industry bent on increasing scale and adding services. But he had high hopes and expected to generate substantial returns for investors by focusing on investment banking, research, institutional brokerage, and private equity within key growth sectors of the economy.

Weisel was aware that his legacy would now be not his previous accomplishments but the success or failure of TWP. Although convinced that the firm's business plan, strategy, and team would deliver top performance, Weisel reflected on the questions that had been put to him over the previous three months.

> Can you really succeed as an independent merchant bank in a rapidly consolidating banking environment? Without a strong asset management business, will you be able to generate adequate returns? Will your focus on specific growth sectors limit your reach and leave you too vulnerable to a downturn in any one sector? Why will established and talented bankers leave their firms to join you? Do you really think you have the expertise or resources to succeed in an increasingly competitive private equity market? Given that you sold Montgomery Securities because you believed scale was necessary to compete, can a niche bank like TWP compete and win in this space?

THOMAS WEISEL

A surgeon's son, Weisel had been born in suburban Milwaukee in 1941. Actively competitive in many

Entrepreneurial Studies Fellow Mat Lieb, Dean's Research Fellow Scot Landry, and doctoral student Boris Groysberg prepared this case under the supervisions of Professors Thomas Delong and Ashish Nanda. HBS cases are developed solely as the basis for class discussion. Cases are not intended to serve as endorsements, sources of primary data, or illustrations of effective or ineffective management.

sports, he had become a five-time national speed-skating champion as a teenager. While attending Stanford University, in which he majored in economics, he took a winter semester off to train for the olympics.*

In 1964 Weisel headed east to Harvard Business School. Upon graduating, he joined FMC Corp's planning department, then in 1967 became the only nonpartner founding member of San Francisco–based institutional brokerage firm William Hutchinson & Co., serving as a forest products analyst and salesman. "Other guys who graduated from business school had goals like making $1 million by the time they were 30," explained Weisel. "My goal was to live in San Francisco."[2]

Unable to persuade its leaders to grow the firm more rapidly, Weisel joined Robertson Coleman & Siebel in 1971 as an equal partner, founding and building the institutional business, which specialized in technology companies, many incubated in burgeoning Silicon Valley. "We came out of the box flying," he remarked, recalling lead roles of the firm, renamed Robertson Coleman Siebel & Weisel, on early IPOs for Rolm, Applied Materials, and Tandem Computers, among others.[3]

However, the bear market of 1973–1974, followed by the advent of negotiated commissions in 1975, hurt small institutional firms. Weisel responded by building a competitive institutional business, even though investment banking remained painfully slow. By 1978 the other three name partners had left owing to differences of opinion about approaches to the business. Sanford Robertson and Robert Coleman subsequently formed Robertson Coleman Stephens and Woodman, the predecessor of Robertson Stephens & Co.[4] Weisel retained the partnership and the firm's seat on the New York Stock Exchange. He re-named the firm Montgomery Securities after J. B. Montgomery, a naval officer who had helped liberate California a century earlier, whose name was given to the street on which the firm was located.[5]

Building Montgomery Securities

Montgomery Securities' driving, aggressive style under Weisel's leadership led some to refer to it as a "jock" shop. Explained 20-year Montgomery veteran Richard Fredericks: "Tom's personality and drive formed the character of Montgomery. I saw his energy flow into this place."[6] This energy was most evident on the trading floor, Montgomery's nerve center. "The intensity level of the room is absolutely intimidating," remarked a former trader. [Chief traders] are constantly screaming at you, second-guessing you, screaming at you to get on the phones. No matter how much business you do, you're always uncomfortable about your job. Their way is the right way." On bad days chief trader Jerry Markowitz, characterized as charming outside of the office, had been known, according to one trader, to "take a phone and slam it down so hard it shatters. That kind of thing happens all over Wall Street," the trader added, "but it seems to happen a lot more at Montgomery."[7]

Despite this drive, the 1980s were a frustrating period at Montgomery. Financially engineered transactions and the need for huge, leveraged balance sheets played to the strengths of capital-rich Wall Street firms. Although Montgomery's revenues grew tenfold during the 1980s, the firm remained a relatively small operation focused on the emerging growth sector. It did no proprietary trading and virtually no debt underwriting.[8] By 1989, having slowly built up its research, corporate finance, and trading capabilities, the firm ranked nineteenth in equity underwriting.

---

* Weisel continued his interest in competitive athletics, reflected in his status as a bronze medal winner in national master skiing, a three-time world and five-time national masters cycling champion, a sponsor of the U.S. cycling team, and a former chairman of the U.S. ski team.

Montgomery experienced great prosperity in the 1990s, its revenues leaping more than sevenfold, from $94 million in 1990 to $705 million in 1997 (see Figure 1). The firm made the bulk of its money underwriting and trading shares of smaller, fast-growing companies, particularly in health care and technology. Montgomery ranked competitively with most of the larger well-established full-service firms in every category in which it competed. (Exhibit 1 presents a statistical summary of Montgomery's industry position.)

Wanting to ride "the power of growth" beyond Montgomery's traditional small-company base to challenge Wall Street's biggest firms, Weisel opened outposts in New York and Boston in 1996. He also sought to reduce the firm's dependence on small caps by substantially increasing its portion of the high-yield (junk bond) market and landing more business from larger companies. Weisel believed that crucial to the health of Montgomery's core business—corporate finance—were building a junk bond operation, a more organized financial buyer calling effort, and principal investing capability.[9]

FIGURE 1

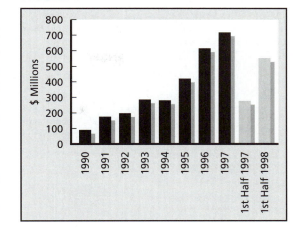

With competition intense in a junk bond market hovering near record levels, Montgomery had difficulty getting into the high-yield business. But Weisel was confident that Montgomery could make inroads despite the rugged environment.[10] "Our clients are getting bigger," he observed, "and

EXHIBIT 1   Montgomery Securities: Performance through the 1990s

Equity Offering Rankings, 1990—Third Quarter 1998				
By Number of Issues		**By Dollar Volume**		
				Proceeds[b]
Firm	Issues	Firm		($ millions)
1 Merrill Lynch	864	1 Goldman, Sachs		$209,129
2 Salomon Smith Barney	801	2 Merrill Lynch		165,014
3 Goldman, Sachs	634	3 Morgan Stanley Dean Witter		136,502
4 Morgan Stanley Dean Witter	586	4 CS First Boston		90,510
5 BT Alex Brown	477	5 Salomon Smith Barney		85,119
6 Lehman Brothers	470	6 Lehman Brothers		58,334
7 Montgomery	**400**	7 Donaldson, Lufkin & Jenrette		49,755
		8 BT Alex Brown		32,676
		9 PaineWebber		23,987
		10 Montgomery		**23,610**

(continues)

EXHIBIT 1 Montgomery Securities: Performance through the 1990s *(continued)*

Initial Public Offering Rankings, 1990—Third Quarter 1998[a]

By Number of Issues

Firm	Issues
1 Salomon Smith Barney	265
2 Morgan Stanley Dean Witter	252
3 Goldman, Sachs	246
4 BT Alex Brown	233
5 Merrill Lynch	210
6 Montgomery	**173**

By Dollar Volume

Firm	Proceeds[b] ($ millions)
1 Goldman, Sachs	$89,022
2 Merrill Lynch	44,189
3 Morgan Stanley Dean Witter	40,708
4 CS First Boston	33,457
5 Salomon Smith Barney	27,291
6 Lehman Brothers	17,813
7 Donaldson, Lufkin & Jenrette	16,204
8 BT Alex Brown	10,784
9 PaineWebber	8,901
10 JP Morgan	7,414
11 Montgomery	**7,164**

Equity Underwriting, 1990—Third Quarter 1998[c]

Sector	Issues	Rank	Proceeds[b] ($ billions)
Consumer	288	2	27
Technology	240	4	17
Health care	138	5	7
Financial services	74	4	9
Business services	87	2	7
Media and communications	37	10	10
Real estate	72	12	8
Other	2	—	1
Total	**941**		**86**

[a] Rank based on dollar volume, full credit to book manager. If full credit were given to each manager, Montgomery would be ranked twelfth in equity offering (by $ volume) and fourteenth in IPO rankings (by $ volume).
[b] Proceeds exclude closed-end funds, ADRs, and rights offerings; include domestic equity private placements.
[c] Rank based on dollar volume, full credit to each manager.
Source: Securities Data Corporation.

we need to grow with them."[11] Conceding that Wall Street's "Big Three"—Merrill Lynch, Goldman Sachs, and Morgan Stanley—were well beyond Montgomery's reach, Weisel nevertheless insisted that "there is no reason we can't rank fourth or fifth as long as we execute."[12] But Montgomery faced mounting competition from larger, better-capitalized firms.

BANKING INDUSTRY CONSOLIDATION IN THE MID-1990S

The financial services industry underwent a radical transformation during the second half of the 1990's. The Federal Reserve Board's relaxation of restrictions set forth in the 1933 Glass-Steagall Act eliminated the firewall between securities and banking, allowing debt underwriters to issue equity and equity underwriters to make loans.* To capitalize on these changes, banks and securities firms needed to add services to their existing operations either by developing them internally or by acquiring firms that already offered them. The goal for many financial services firms became the provision of one-stop shopping for companies in need of financing.

Facing slow growth and decreasing margins in their core commercial lending business, commercial banks were eager to exploit these regulatory changes and enter investment banking. Investment banks looked to the scale of commercial banks' lending as a means to keeping pace with client growth.[13] "Many of the stand-alone investment banks will have to act boldly to survive," observed CS First Boston president Allen Wheat. "Many will either have to shrink themselves by focusing on fewer products and markets, or they will have to become affiliated in some way, like it or not, with powerful commercial banks."[14]

Major acquisitions began to occur in early 1997 shortly after Wheat's prediction. In April, Bankers Trust purchased Alex. Brown & Sons, the nation's oldest brokerage firm, for $1.7 billion, approximately 2.7 times book value.[15] That left only three independent players among the group of mid-sized investment banks known on Wall Street as the "HARMs" (Hambrecht and Quist, Alex. Brown, Robertson Stephens & Co., and Montgomery Securities). The following month, SBC Warburg announced its purchase of the investment bank Dillon Read & Co for $600 million, approximately three times book value.[16] Then June, BankAmerica Corp. announced the $540 million purchase of Robertson Stephens. Although on paper these mergers made sense, analysts wondered about the challenge of blending the distinct cultures of commercial and investment banks.[17] (Exhibit 2 identifies some of the merger and acquisition activity for 1997.)

Montgomery Seeks a Partner

Weisel anticipated that despite its prosperity Montgomery Securities might need to follow the route taken by fellow HARMs Alex. Brown and Robertson Stephens. Not only was the industry consolidating, but the giants of Wall Street, awak-

EXHIBIT 2   **Selected Financial Industry Consolidation in 1997**

- Morgan Stanley and Dean Witter merge—$10 billion
- Salomon Inc. and Travelers Group Inc. merge—$9 billion
- Bankers Trust New York Corp acquires Alex. Brown Inc.—$1.7 billion
- Fleet Financial Group Inc. purchases Quick & Reilly Group Inc.—$1.6 billion
- NationsBank Corp. acquires Montgomery Securities—$1.2 billion
- SBC Warburg Inc. acquires Dillon Read & Co.—$600 million
- ING Group NV acquires Furman Selz Inc.—$600 million
- BankAmerica Corp. acquires Robertson Stephens & Co.—$540 million
- Canadian Imperial Bank of Commerce acquires Oppenheimer & Co.—$525 million
- First Union Corp. acquires Wheat First Butcher Singer Inc.—$480 million

Source: "Year Recap of Securities Industry Deals," *Dow Jones News Service,* September 24, 1997.

* The Glass-Steagall legislation segregated commercial and investment banking to protect depositors from the risks associated with securities and prevent a collapse of the U.S. banking system such as had occurred during the Great Depression. In 1996 the Federal Reserve Board raised the limit on bank affiliates' underwriting business from 10 percent to 25 percent of revenues.

ening to West Coast opportunities facing investment banks, had begun aggressively investing human capital into the region. "The competitive landscape was shifting very quickly," Weisel recalled. "We needed considerably more capital to realize our growth potential, and we needed to expand to the debt arena to stay competitive and not lose our clients. I also saw an attractive opportunity to develop a solid private equity practice, but that, too, would take a lot of money."

Undercapitalization had become a significant problem as Montgomery's client base had prospered, requiring ever-increasing amounts of financing. When longtime Montgomery client Doubletree Hotels found itself in need of a $600 million commitment, Montgomery, which had never executed a single trade greater than $215 million, was left to watch from the sidelines as the client turned to investment banking giant Morgan Stanley. "We were clearly getting beaten out," observed Weisel. "If we said, 'We'll put a syndicate together,' and someone else said, 'We'll take the whole thing,' who do you think got the business?"[18]

NATIONSBANC MONTGOMERY SECURITIES

On June 30, 1997, NationsBank Corporation of Charlotte, N.C., announced that it was acquiring Montgomery for approximately $1.3 billion, believing that the combination would create one of the nation's top full-service investment banks. The acquisition price was about 15 times the firm's earnings and 13 times its book value.

Hugh McColl and NationsBank

With 63,000 employees and net income of $2.4 billion in 1996, NationsBank had grown spectacularly, gobbling up approximately 60 banks since 1983, when McColl had taken charge as chairman and CEO. McColl, a former marine, had roiled the courtly world of banking with his aggressive demeanor and military metaphors. McColl had per-

fected an approach of buying smaller targets, replacing their top management, and cutting costs ruthlessly. Although characterized variously as a "slash and burn" approach followed by a "barbarian conqueror," the aggressive acquisition process had catapulted NationsBank from a small, regional player into a national giant.[19]

The Merger Agreement

At a June 10 meeting in New York, the first between Weisel and McColl, the latter had insisted that compensation issues be resolved, disagreements over compensation having killed a NationsBank–DLJ deal two years earlier. McColl and Weisel agreed that Montgomery's 68 partners would receive $840 million in cash upfront ($120 million to Weisel directly), $360 million to be distributed in NationsBank stock over three years. In addition, some 100 key Montgomery professionals would share a $100 million incentive pool (50 percent in options and 50 percent in cash) to be paid out over three years.

The Montgomery team was promised considerable autonomy. Under the terms of the deal, Montgomery was to become a subsidiary in NationsBank's capital markets division, with Weisel serving as division chairman and CEO of NationsBanc Montgomery Securities Inc.[20] NationsBanc Montgomery's performance would be reflected in its own profit-and-loss statement. Montgomery executives were to remain in San Francisco to oversee the investment banking, high-yield debt, financial buyers coverage, and brokerage businesses. Additionally, McColl agreed to fund at the level of $600 million a private equity group to be run by former Montgomery executives. (Exhibit 3 relates the terms of the deal.)

Weisel was optimistic about future prospects. "The combination of our two companies is a great fit," he stated,

and will allow us to reach our goal of providing one-stop shopping to our clients. Culturally, we are both extremely performance driven and team oriented. There also is a

EXHIBIT 3 **NationsBank Corp./Montgomery Securities: Terms of Transaction**

Deal Price and Terms

- $1.2 billion
- Montgomery's assets purchased and liabilities assumed by NationsBank
- Seventy percent up front cash; 30 percent NationsBank stock in escrow account to be paid out over three years; principals to participate in retention pool of $100 million
- Competitive compensation and long-term incentive plan to retain key employees

Management Structure

- Montgomery Securities to remain autonomous; name to be retained
- Montgomery to become a division of NationsBank Section 20 subsidiary
- Thomas Weisel to serve as chairman of NationsBank Section 20 subsidiary
- Montgomery to continue to be managed by current executive committee

Source: "NationsBank Corporation and Montgomery Securities Announce Merger Agreement," *PR Newswire,* June 30, 1997.

great synergy between our businesses. The breadth of the NationsBank corporate client base with our investment banking, research, and advisory capabilities will create a formidable player in the investment banking arena.[21]

McColl was similarly excited by the prospects for attracting and retaining clients. Prior to the acquisition, a number of clients that had engaged NationsBank's to co-manage debt offerings had turned to competitors for equity offerings. McColl chose the acquisition route to break this pattern. "My own judgments," McColl said of the needed capability,

> were that we could never build it [internally]. You would hire the people and you could have the skill, but where would you get the credibility from? You would have the same problem you have building anything, which is all expenses on the front end and the revenues come at a very slow pace. We thought it'd take too long to get profitable. But forget profitable, we weren't sure that we could deliver our customers to a machine that we built. It's far more important to us as a tool and a product than for its profits, $35 million to $50 million next year. It'll make a week's worth of earnings for us.[22]

NationsBank vice chairman and chief financial officer James Hance explained the synergies and overlaps between the two firms. "This combination makes good sense on several levels," he noted in the deal's press release.

> We share an interest and expertise in many of the same industry specialties, such as telecommunications, financial services, health care, and technology. Additionally, our businesses are very complementary. We bring capabilities such as syndicated lending, structured finance, high grade, and risk management to the table while Montgomery brings equity distribution and research. At the same time we each have strong capabilities in high yield, fixed-income research, institutional sales, and mergers and acquisitions advisory services, which will be greatly enhanced through the merger.[23]

NationsBanc Montgomery Securities would pursue an aggressive growth strategy of establishing new investment banking teams in energy, food and beverages, and textiles and apparel, sectors in which the parent company was a major lender. The parent's balance sheet would be used to move into areas such as derivatives and convertible securities (both required $1 billion of regulatory capital and $12 billion on the bank's balance sheet).[24]

Marriage Turns Sour

The early success of the NationsBank Montgomery merger notwithstanding, tensions began to emerge between the two entities. Weisel had noticed difficulties meshing the organizations' cultures shortly after the acquisition was completed.

> During the due diligence process for the acquisition, it seemed as though this would be a great match both strategically and culturally. But once we started working together in earnest, I began to notice some things that concerned me. Areas where former Montgomery people were supposed to be in charge suddenly had "co-heads" and I sensed a "fiefdom" rather than meritocratic approach to business among many of the NationsBank executives. It was subtle at first, but things progressed to the point where Montgomery veterans were consistently at loggerheads with the NationsBank people.

By the summer of 1998, the relationship between Montgomery's investment bankers and the parent company's had soured. NationsBankers irked Montgomery professionals by tagging along on sales calls and trying, unsuccessfully, to trim 5 percent off the firm's $400 million annual-pay kitty.[25]

In April 1998 NationsBank had begun to pursue a merger with Bank of America, which raised the prospect of bringing together their respective investment banking subsidiaries, Montgomery Securities and Robertson Stephens, and reuniting their chairmen, Sandy Robertson and Thomas Weisel. Although the firms were similar in size, product mix, and market shares, industry insiders drew a sharp distinction between Montgomery's culture, which they likened to the fast-paced, innovative trading approaches of Drexel Burnham Lambert, and Robertson Stephens', which they felt reflected "the buttoned-down, blue-blood style of Morgan Stanley."[26] Speculation about how the units might be merged ended in August 1998 when BankAmerica announced the sale of Robertson Stephens to BankBoston. Sixteen days after the NationsBank–BankAmerica merger, McColl fired the second-ranking executive in the merged firm, BankAmerica's ex-chief executive David Coulter, blaming him for a $372 million loss in a risky investment fund.[27]

In the wake of the NationsBank/Bank of America merger, control of the investment banking and high-yield units was shifted from Weisel and former Montgomery Securities executives to NationsBank veterans. The high-yield units of NationsBank and Montgomery Securities were merged under NationsBank's Thomas White rather than Montgomery Securities partner Jerome Markowitz. BankAmerica's Bob Griffin was named to head the high-yield unit, reporting directly to a McColl lieutenant.[28]

To Weisel, these moves contradicted the acquisition agreement that specified that Montgomery would retain autonomy and control over its operations. Weisel regarded the high-yield business and financial buyers' relationships as key components in helping small companies get access to financing through high-yield, an integral part of Montgomery's forte in the industry.[29] When Weisel called McColl in August in an effort to reclaim the businesses he believed were rightfully the domain of Montgomery executives, McColl rebuffed him. "Thom, I don't understand," McColl told him. "I thought we bought you."[30]

Weisel tendered his resignation on September 21, 1998. In his only public comment that day, he remarked that "the reason that I've resigned is that we just have a difference over vision and strategy for the organization."[31] NationsBank accelerated disbursements of $480 million (part of the original acquisition price) to all former Montgomery Securities employees then on the NationsBank payroll. McColl was quoted as saying, "I'd rather run through fire than walk through it anytime."[32]

"There were some very clear parameters that they bought off on in the sale and were violated soon thereafter," recalled Weisel, reflecting on his resignation.

When every principle I thought was important was violated, there was absolutely no way that I was going to stay there. It was terrible. I really went into the deal thinking it was the best thing for the business and for our employees. The most difficult part about all of this was seeing the unhappiness of many of the former Montgomery people who had followed my lead to NationsBank. I really felt like I had let down a lot of loyal people who had trusted my judgment. If I had the chance to do it all again I wouldn't do the merger.

THOMAS WEISEL PARTNERS

During his final months at NationsBank, Weisel had come to see many of the inherent shortcomings of the existing investment banking model, the most notable to him, having to do with the management of people. Banking had lost much of its appeal by essentially forcing outstanding performers to cover mature and seemingly less exciting industries. Talented bankers became bored doing the same types of deals over and over. Over time, they began to see themselves as processors rather than as investment bankers. Most large banks, Weisel believed, had become too bureaucratic, stodgy, inflexible, and lethargic, lacking in the entrepreneurial spirit that talented individuals looked for in their work. Moreover, most banks' compensation structures did not afford bankers an opportunity to earn a "carry" in the firms' investments.

Weisel subsequently drew up plans for a new full-service merchant bank called Thomas Weisel Partners (TWP).* Weisel believed that an entrepreneurial bank that catered to entrepreneurial companies could attract highly talented bankers who would welcome the competition against estab-

lished top banks. His strategy for creating a dynamic firm that attracted the best and the brightest was to establish a "research-driven" merchant bank focused on the new economy that was transforming key growth sectors, technology, consumer and business services, media and communications, health care, and financial services.† Weisel intended TWP analysts to be the foundation upon which the firm's core business lines—investment banking, institutional brokerage, private client services, and private and public equity investing—would be built. (TWP's equity research mission statement is presented in Exhibit 4.)

Weisel structured TWP around the concept of "tailwinds," currents or vectors that, moving faster than the rest of the economy, act as agents of change and power future growth. (See Exhibit 5 and Exhibit 6 for descriptions of TWP's six tailwinds.) An example of a tailwind circa 1999 was the Internet, which, when it intersected the shopping mall, restructured its established, brick-and-mortar model of retailing and gave birth to e-tailing. Weisel believed that the tailwind structure would afford TWP a significant advantage over competitors that tended to view the world through vertical industry lenses. "Our tailwind structure will allow us to leverage our knowledge of investment themes across a number of sectors," Weisel affirmed. "People will not be stuck in organizational 'silos' where they are expected to work with the same industry doing the same thing day after day. In my mind, this structure fosters more creativity and teamwork than the traditional investment-banking model."

Market Opportunity

Creating a fully integrated merchant bank focused only on growth companies was, on the surface, counterintuitive in the "bigger is better"

---

* Weisel was joined in this process by William Bunting, Frank Dunleavy, Derek Lemke-von Ammon, Alan Menkes, and Sanford Miller. All but Miller had worked together closely at Montgomery.
† Merchant banks used their own capital as principals to fund customers' activities; investment banks acted as agents for customer deals, using outside capital raised in the public or private markets.

EXHIBIT 4 **Extracts from TWP's Equity Research Mission Statement**

The Pitfalls of Today's Sell-Side Research

In our view, today's sell-side research product is being distorted by brokerage firm efforts to chase research poll rankings.

- **Overcovered Large Cap Focus.** Because the votes are weighted by the size of assets under management, vote seekers tend to focus on large capitalization names that are important to the large institutions, but are generally well-researched and have varying levels of investment appeal. . . . [T]he collective effort of 20 analysts providing such analysis is clearly disproportionate to the utility of the information.
- **Excessive Client Contact Requirements.** To increase visibility with voting accounts, many brokerage firms require analysts to visit clients 35–40 days per year and to make 100+ client telephone calls per month. Such efforts account for at least 25% of the total analyst working time, a requirement that appears excessive if the goal is to perform actual research.
- **Diminished Availability and Value of Proprietary Information.** Strict interpretation of disclosure rules has made obtaining meaningful and proprietary information from company management increasingly difficult. Additionally, the extensive use of conference calls, even by very small companies, to disseminate information to the Street simultaneously has made such information more commodity-like.

In our view, in order for analysts to dig deep to provide our clients value-added information, they must be free to perform primary research and reduce their focus on participating in "the rankings game."

At TWP, Primary Research Will Be a Key Focus

While important long-term trends and "big picture" growth opportunities will be a prominent focus, we will also place considerable effort on an area that Wall Street seems to be ignoring at its own peril: balance sheet/cash flow statement analysis and financial statement footnotes. We expect our senior analysts to be actively involved in analyzing the financial statements as well as to be actively involved in talking to and visiting non-traditional sources of information. It is our belief that other firms often delegate such important tasks to younger research associates while the senior analysts are preoccupied with "marketing."

We also expect our senior analysts to be accessible and available to our institutional clients. . . . Such dialogue can encourage our analysts to challenge and continually evaluate their own opinions and can provide them with a better sense of investor perception. . . . [W]e want our visibility to be developed from the quality of research analysts and their research product rather than rankings, per se.

In order for our analysts to manage time effectively and accomplish our key objectives, there are certain things they will not be able to do. First, we will generally not spend considerable time on mature, less interesting companies simply because they are widely owned. We will be familiar with such companies and their strategies if they are important competitors in the segments in which we focus. However, it is not our goal to be the most important source of information on these companies. . . . Second, we will not spend considerable time trying to guess whether the next quarter's EPS will be $0.26 or $0.25, especially if non-relevant items are the cause. Third, we will not generally issue a detailed report dissecting a given company's income statement following an "in-line" quarter. Finally, we will not feel compelled to issue "earnings previews" and "earnings reviews" for entire groups of companies before and after quarterly results are released, especially when nothing unusual is expected to occur.

Source: Thomas Weisel Partners.

EXHIBIT 5   TWP's Tailwind Structure—Key Growth Sectors

Internet   We believe the Internet will prove to be a medium for continued rapid growth of the technology sector, driving structural changes across all growth sectors of the economy and providing new opportunities for retail and commerce, financial services, health care, media, and business services. Potential applications will evolve daily, rendering time-honored approaches obsolete, changing cost structures, speeding product delivery cycle changes, and creating significant new opportunities for investors.

Bandwidth   The tremendous growth in the Internet and private corporate enterprise networks has driven an explosive demand for bandwidth throughout networks. A fundamental shift to packet-switching transmission technologies will drive demand for enhanced switching and routing capabilities as service providers attempt to cope with the explosive growth in the Internet and its related technologies. Today, usage on the Internet is doubling every three months. As a result, a significant opportunity exists to invest in a broad variety of companies from those that are building key components of tomorrow's networks to enhanced network service providers. In addition, more bandwidth will enable a new generation of e-commerce and Internet information service providers who will consume available bandwidth to provide enhanced service, thus creating an unending demand for more bandwidth.

Outsourcing   Managing for greater profitability and growth has compelled companies to focus on their core skills and limit investments in activities that do not contribute to their strategic goals. This trend has led to outsourcing of both assets and activities that range from manufacturing and inventory management to human resources, staffing, and sales management. This trend will continue to generate opportunities for new businesses in every growth sector as companies look to redeploy capital and resources to increase value.

Consolidation   In the face of limited pricing flexibility, many industry sectors are experiencing the need to increase economies of scale in order to improve profitability. In addition, with the aging population and increase in education levels, small, private businesses are no longer being passed on to the next generation. These trends have increased consolidation opportunities in virtually every industry, creating larger, less fragmented businesses that possess geographic coverage and scale to compete. Opportunities for consolidation will continue into the next century.

Education   The transition to a knowledge-based economy and need for quality elementary/secondary education continue to be key issues in our society.

Demographics   The aging of the baby boom population and increased levels of affluence will create unique opportunities across many of the growth sectors. The consumer industries will experience greater buying power and demand both as a consequence of improved ease of purchase via new channels and greater levels of affluence. The leisure industry will continue its rapid growth as the level of retired and semiretired people seeking new and exciting ways to spend their time increases. The health care industry will experience opportunities for growth as it addresses the needs of an aging population that possesses changing views on maintaining their health and aging. Many opportunities will be created as changing demographics cross industry sectors. Maintaining a deep knowledge base of each industry sector will enable the firm to take advantage of shifting trends and create new opportunities.

Source: Thomas Weisel Partners.

EXHIBIT 6   Thomas Weisel Partners: Tailwind Structure

Industry Sectors

Investment Themes	Technology	Business Services	Consumer	Telecom	Media	Financial Services	Health Care
Internet	Web-Based Applications	Web Consulting Services	E-Retailing	Web-Based Phones	Web Broadcasting	Internet Financial Services	Web-Based Diagnostics
Outsourcing	Electronics Manufacturing Services	Human Capital Services	Business Management	Towers Management	Syndication	Transaction Processing	Neo-Natal Care
Consolidation	Data Networking	Service Provider Consolidators	Brand Consolidations	CLECs	Outdoor Advertising	Sub-Prime Lending	Information Services and Distribution
Bandwidth	Optical Networking	Distance Learning	Streaming Video	Data/Video/Voice	Broadband	On-Line Trading	Tele-Medicine
Education	Infomediaries	Business Trading	Post-Secondary Education	Interactive On-Line Education	Distributed Learning	Financial Planning	Medical Training
Demographics	Community Web Sites	Education	Travel and Hospitality	PCS ESMR	Leisure	Asset Management	Elder Care

EXHIBIT 6 Thomas Weisel Partners: Tailwind Structure, Representative Firms on the Industry Sectors/Investment Themes Matrix *(continued)*

Industry Sectors →

Investment Themes	Technology	Business Services	Consumer	Telecom	Media	Financial Services	Health Care
Internet	Siebel	Scient	Amazon.com	WorldCom	Yahoo!	Nextcard	Healtheon
Outsourcing	Jabil	Interim Services	Staples	American Tower	Westwood One	First Data	Pediatrix
Consolidation	Lucent	RCM Tech	Chatten	Nextlink	Outdoor Systems	NCO Group	HBO/McKesson
Bandwidth	Cisco	Jones Interactive	MPATH	Rhythms	@Home	E*Trade	IDX Systems
Education	SmarterKids	GP Strategies	Apollo Group	One-Touch	Channel 1	Strategic Management	On-Line Learning
Demographics →	iVillage	Bright Family Solutions	Travelocity	Nextel	Heftel	Schwab	Genesis

banking environment. Weisel, however, saw the consolidation wave as an opportunity to concentrate on the smaller growth companies that were not big enough to garner the full attention of the large banks. Weisel described the opportunity:

> Growth companies used to be able to turn to a variety of small, focused investment banks that really understood and catered to their needs. Alex. Brown, Robertson Stephens, Cowen, Piper Jaffray, Furman Selz, Oppenheimer, and Montgomery were all excellent options for promising growth companies. All of these firms have now been absorbed by larger banks and their cultures have really suffered.
>
> The large institutions lack the creative, entrepreneurial approach required to establish, develop, and capitalize on relationships with growth companies. Most of these enormous banks are spending the lion's share of their time on integration issues, cross selling, and combining calling officers. Much of their resources are being devoted to servicing larger companies that tend to execute larger transactions. The time is just right for a new merchant bank to arrive on the scene.

SUCCESS FACTORS

Although Weisel had demonstrated with Montgomery his ability to build a bank that could successfully service emerging growth companies, investors questioned whether a repeat performance was possible in the face of the intensified, well-established competition in the current banking industry. Weisel believed that TWP's success would be determined by how effectively it responded to the following questions.

Was There a Market Vacuum? If So, Could TWP Fill It?

Weisel believed that the wave of consolidations had resulted in a lack of focused service providers skilled at identifying undervalued growth invest-

ment opportunities. "There's just a huge opportunity," enthused Weisel. "The space has been vacated by most or all the major players."[33] Institutional investors interested in small capitalization growth companies had few sources of high-quality, sector-specific information and services. Weisel believed that being the first independent bank to fill the vacuum created by consolidation, TWP could capture a large share of the institutional brokerage and equity underwriting market for emerging growth companies.

Could TWP Attract the Best Professionals?

Weisel believed that a successful bank could only emerge from a model that was attractive to professionals. He emphasized:

> There are a lot of disgruntled bankers out there who are looking for more interesting and exciting work, especially work with high-growth companies. If you create a business that provides talented people with an opportunity to challenge themselves, you will end up with something really special. We are offering people the chance to work with fast growing companies, to participate in the upside of the firm, and to be involved in private equity investing. Almost any banker will tell you that if you can deliver on those three aspects of the job, you will be able to recruit some of the best people.

Could TWP Quickly Develop the Required Skills and Provide the Required Services?

Weisel believed that TWP's success would be grounded in world-class research capabilities. TWP's research team would be responsible for evaluating economic trends and identifying transforming growth industries and sectors. Weisel expected TWP to generate through its research team's relationships with top growth companies substantial "deal flow" for its private equity fund.

TWP's private equity fund, expected to be $500 million to $1 billion in size, would be used to invest both in companies not yet ready to go public and in leveraged buyouts (LBOs). Weisel expected TWP's research analysts and investment bankers to provide proprietary deal flow and participate in the due diligence associated with these investments, thereby gaining exposure to private companies otherwise unavailable for scrutiny.

Weisel intended to provide additional expertise, capital, and services to TWP clients through partnerships. He anticipated using strategic partners as preferred providers of senior debt, high-yield debt, and other forms of financing in connection with TWP's strategic advisory and private equity transactions. Additionally, these partners might be co-investors in private equity investments. Strategic partners would be privy to TWP research, capital markets, and corporate finance thinking and participate periodically in the firm's meetings. (Exhibit 7 identifies TWP's strategic partners.)

Many of TWP's competitors remained unconvinced that Weisel would succeed. "There's always room for a very high quality player," conceded

EXHIBIT 7   **Thomas Weisel Partners: Strategic Partners and Board of Advisors**

Strategic Partners

Venture Capital	Private Equity	Financial Institutions
Bessemer Ventures	Bessemer Group	GE Investments
Brentwood Venture Capital	Charlesbank Partners	Investor AB
Institutional Venture Partners	Chase Capital Partners	James Richardson & Sons, Ltd.
Mayfield Fund	Citicorp Venture Capital	Queen Emma Trust
New Enterprise Associates	Freeman Spogli & Company	Sun America
Oak Investment Partners	J. H. Whitney	
Trident Capital	Madison Dearborn	
	Saunders, Karp & Megrue	
	TA Associates	
	Welsh, Carson, Anderson & Stowe	
	Weston Presidio	

Board of Advisors

Erik Borgen	Former CEO & owner, Founders Mutual Funds, president of Borgen Investment Group
Michael Brown	Chairman of Nasdaq, former chief financial officer, Microsoft
Michael Dolan	Vice chairman and chief financial officer, Young & Rubicam
Barry Gondor	Senior investment officer, CalPERS
B. Kipling Hagopian	Co-founder Brentwood Associates
Jack Kemp	Co-director, Empower America
Tim Koogle	Chairman and chief executive officer, Yahoo!
Jerry Markowitz	Former director of capital markets, Montgomery Securities
Philip Quigley	Former chairman and CEO, Pacific Telesis
Tom Siebel	Chairman and CEO, Siebel Systems
Larry Sonsini	Chairman Wilson Sonsini, Goodrich & Rosati
The Honorable Pete Wilson	Former governor of California
Jay Wintrob	Vice chairman and chief operating officer, SunAmerica, Inc.; boardmember of AIG

BancBoston Robertson Stephens chief executive Michael McCaffery. "But to duplicate the success he had at Montgomery, [Weisel] has to have a much larger organization with much more capital and much greater ability to sell stock to institutional investors. It is not an advantage to be as small as he is in servicing this market."[34] Carter McClelland, co-head of investment banking at NationsBanc Montgomery, questioned whether TWP could be profitable focusing exclusively on small companies and small transactions.[35]

LAUNCH

Weisel was confident that TWP was in for a big 1999. Outside investors had committed $35 million for 7 percent of the firm. (See Exhibit 8 for TWP's equity structure and pro-forma financials.) Talented professionals were approaching TWP management to join the firm. Of the 40 professionals who had been hired, 10 were former Montgomery partners.

As the countdown to 1999 began, Weisel wondered how quickly TWP would be able to execute his plans and how the marketplace would react.

EXHIBIT 8 Thomas Weisel Partners: Pro Forma Capitalization Table

Investment	Participant	Amount Invested	Shares	Post $ Ownership
Class A shares—First Tranche[a]	Founders	$ 7,500,000	7,500,000	27.9%
	Existing employees	14,083,333	14,083,333	52.4
	Issued and reserved for new employees	3,416,667[b]	3,416,667	12.7
	Total class A shares	$25,000,000[c]	25,000,000	93.0%
Class A shares—Second Tranche	Founders	1,500,000	1,500,000	—
	Existing employees	2,816,667	2,816,667	—
	Issued and reserved for new employees	683,333[b]	683,333	—
	Total class A shares	$ 5,000,000[c]	5,000,000	—
Class B shares	Employee shareholders	$ 0	25,000,000[d]	—
Class C preference shares	Weston Presidio Capital	1,500,000	80,645	0.3
	Accel Investors	1,500,000	80,645	0.3
	Bessemer Holdings	1,500,000	80,645	0.3
	Brentwood Associates	750,007	40,323	0.2
	Freeman Spogli	1,500,000	80,645	0.3
	IVP Investment Partners	1,515,060	81,455	0.3
	Oak Investment Partners	1,500,000	80,645	0.3
	Madison Dearborn Partners	1,500,000	80,645	0.3
	Mayfield Fund (individuals)	850,000	45,699	0.2
	New Enterprise Associates (individuals)	1,116,991	60,053	0.2
	Saunders Karp & Mergue Partners	1,000,000	53,763	0.2
	TA Associates	1,500,000	80,645	0.3
	Welsh, Carson, Anderson & Stowe (individuals)	1,800,000	96,774	0.4
	Citicorp Venture Capital	1,500,000	80,645	0.3
	Other	15,967,942	858,492	3.2
	Total class C preference shares	$35,000,000	1,881,720[e]	7.0%
Total		$65,000,000	26,881,720[e]	100.0%

[a] The company issued 30 million series A shares in two tranches. The first tranche participates in all liquidating proceeds; the second tranche receives no proceeds in a liquidation event.
[b] Founders contributed $4.1 million to reserve series A shares for future employees.
[c] The general partners of TWP have committed an additional $20 million for necessary regulatory capital or expansion into new business lines.
[d] The company issued 25 million class B shares. The class B shares were issued at no cost and participate in operating profits only.
[e] Represents ownership claims on liquidating proceeds only. Total, therefore, excludes second tranche series A shares and class B shares.
Source: Thomas Weisel Partners LLC Final Investment Memorandum.

EXHIBIT 8 Thomas Weisel Partners: Pro Forma Financial Statements *(continued)*

Proforma Income Statements ($ millions)

	1999	2000	2001	2002	2003
Revenue					
Investment Banking					
Strategic advisory	$35	$110	$151	$181	$212
Equity underwriting	20	67	91	108	126
Institutional Brokerage					
Listed	12	30	41	51	60
Over-the-counter	18	45	62	76	90
Private Equity					
Management fees	10	15	15	29	29
Carried interest	0	4	13	32	52
Other	1	1	1	1	1
Total revenue	$96	$272	$375	$478	$569
Net interest income	(1)	(1)	(1)	(1)	(1)
Total net revenue	$95	$271	$373	$476	$568
Expenses					
Compensation and benefits	30	65	87	107	126
Data processing, communications, and quotation services	5	14	19	24	28
Research, printing, and promotion	1	3	4	5	6
Occupancy	6	8	11	12	15
Professional services	2	3	4	5	6
Floor brokerage and clearance	3	8	11	14	17
Other	9	19	25	29	34
Total Expenses	$56	$120	$161	$195	$231
Operating Income (Loss)	$39	$151	$212	$281	$337

Proforma Balance Sheets ($ millions)

	1999	2000	2001	2002	2003
Assets					
Cash and equivalents	$37	$32	$45	$55	$54
Fixed assets, net	10	11	11	9	8
Other assets	4	9	13	16	20
Total assets	$52	$53	$69	$80	$81
Liabilities and equity					
Total liabilities	$ 2	$ 3	$ 4	$ 5	$ 6
Equity					
Employee capital	25	25	40	50	50
Outside investor capital	25	25	25	25	25
Total liabilities and equity	$52	$53	$69	$80	$81

References

1. Debora Vrana, "Cutting Edge California Dealin': Two Investment Banking Veterans Dive into New Ventures," *Los Angeles Times,* March 1, 1999, p. C1.

2. Scott McMurray, "What Makes Montgomery Run?" *Institutional Investor,* February 1997.

3. Ibid.

4. Arthur Louis, "Deal Will Marry Longtime Rivals Robertson Stephens, Montgomery Together Again," *San Francisco Chronicle,* April 14, 1998, p. B1.

5. McMurray.

6. Ibid.

7. David Dietz and Herb Greenberg, "A Firm's Go-Go Culture Pays Off, but at a Price," *San Francisco Chronicle,* September 27, 1994, p. A1.

8. McMurray.

9. Barry Henderson, "Why Montgomery Is Exiting Asset Management," *Barron's,* March 31, 1997, p. 49.

10. Ibid.

11. McMurray.

12. Ibid.

13. "Bank Buyouts Could Pinch Small Start-Ups," *San Jose Mercury News,* July 6, 1997.

14. Allen Wheat, "Glass-Steagall versus the Market: The Market Wins," *Investment Dealers' Digest,* May 22, 1995, p. 21–22.

15. "Swiss Bank Unit to Buy Dillon Read," *The Wall Street Journal,* May 15, 1997.

16. Ibid.

17. Nicole Tempest and Thomas DeLong, "Hambrecht & Quist," HBS Case No. 898-161.

18. Peter Sinton, "A Merger to Bank On," *San Francisco Chronicle,* September 23, 1997, p. C1.

19. Eleena de Lisser, "Some Skeptics Wonder Whether NationsBank Is into One Deal Too Many in Seeking Barnett," *The Wall Street Journal,* September 9, 1997, p. C4; Bernard Condon, "Who's Minding the Branches at BofA?" *Forbes,* September 6, 1999, p. 58; Erick Schonfeld, "Married with children," *Fortune,* May 11, 1998, pp. 82–83; Nikhil Deogun and Martha Brannigan, "NationsBank's McColl Masters the Soft Sell," *The Wall Street Journal,* September 2, 1997, p. B1.

20. "NationsBank Corporation and Montgomery Securities Announce Merger Agreement," *PR Newswire,* June 30, 1997.

21. Ibid.

22. Pamela Moore, *The Charlotte Observer,* June 30, 1997.

23. "NationsBank Corporation and Montgomery Securities Announce Merger Agreement."

24. Jed Horowitz, "Montgomery Explodes with Expansion Plans: NationsBank Fuels Moves into Derivatives, Energy, Lots More," *Investment Dealers' Digest,* January 12, 1998, p. 5.

25. Larry Light, "The Best Revenge? More Competition," *Business Week,* October 12, 1998, p. 6.

26. Peter Truell, "Upheaval in Banking: The Potential Clash," *New York Times,* April 14, 1998, p. 11.

27. Sam Zuckerman, "Breaking the Bank: The Untold Story of How David Coulter Lost BofA," *San Francisco Chronicle,* p. A1.

28. Alex Tarquinio, "NationsBank Expecting Montgomery Chief to Quit," *The American Banker,* September 17, 1998, p. 29.

29. Kimberly Seals McDonald, "Montgomery Founder and CEO Leaving Firm," *New York Post,* September 18, 1998, p. 32.

30. Dean Foust, "A Megabank in the Making," *Business Week,* September 13, 1999, p. 144.

31. Peter Truell, "Montgomery Chief Quits in Dispute with NationsBank Parent," *New York Times,* September 22, 1998, p. 4.

32. Foust, p. 144.

33. Sam Zuckerman, "Tycoon Trying Again: Investment Banker Hopes to Repeat Success of Montgomery Securities," *San Francisco Chronicle,* January 19, 1999, p. C1.

34. Ibid.

35. Lisa Bransten, "Montgomery Securities Founder Starts Rival Investment Bank Aimed at Giants," *The Wall Street Journal,* January 19, 1999, p. B5.

Woodland Partners:
Field of Dreams?[1]

Elizabeth Lilly wondered, as she drove off one warm fall day in 1995 after meeting with Richard Rinkoff and Richard Jensen, if her goal of creating an investment management firm, a dream that had never been far from her mind, might finally be close to becoming a reality.

BIRTH OF A GAME PLAN

Frustrated by the corporate bureaucracy of First Bank, the large, diversified financial institution for which she had managed money for the past four years, Lilly had informed Rinkoff, a colleague and friend, in July that she was leaving to start an investment firm. His 19-year tenure and successful record managing the bank's small stock fund notwithstanding, Rinkoff, sensing unfavorable changes in the air, had expressed an interest in joining Lilly.

Lilly and Rinkoff recognized that they would need someone with marketing and client management experience to complete their team. They approached 30-year bank veteran Jensen, despite doubts whether he would leave the company. Rinkoff had asked Jensen bluntly: "How committed are you to this place?" After some clarification by Rinkoff, Jensen, surprisingly, did not dismiss the plan outright. The three subsequently began to meet on Saturdays in Jensen's home to ponder the business venture.

During six months of weekend meetings, the three discussed a variety of business plans for managing a single fund, a limited series of funds, or a broad array of funds with attendant variations in staffing requirements and risks and rewards. Having taken their practice swings, was it time to step up to the plate and swing the bat? Which model should they pursue in launching their firm? Lilly and her partners pondered these questions.

THE ROSTER

Beth Lilly

Lilly, age 34, had wanted to create her own firm since her earliest days in the investment business. She had gained experience researching companies at Goldman Sachs and learned the art of value investing at Fund American companies. (Exhibit 1 provides short biographies of Lilly, Rinkoff, and Jensen.) While at Fund American, she had benefited from lunches with legendary investor Warren Buffett and learned from her mentor and teacher, Robert Bruce. "Bob always said," she reflected, "that when I left Fund American I would be prepared to start my own firm, and he encouraged me to do so. I was fascinated with the idea and compiled a folder of articles and notes over the years detailing how I would realize this dream."

Lilly had moved back to the Midwest and joined First Bank in 1992. With $30 billion in as-

Ted Seides, HBS MBA '99, prepared this case with the assistance of Dean's Research Fellow Scot Landry and under the guidance of Professors Thomas DeLong and Ashish Nanda as the basis for class discussion rather than to illustrate either effective or ineffective handling of an administrative situation.

[1] *Field of Dreams* was a movie nominated for the Academy Award for best picture in 1989. In the film, an Iowa-based farmer jeopardizes his livelihood to heed a "voice" that instructs him to build a baseball diamond in his cornfields.

EXHIBIT 1 Biographies

Richard W. Jensen, CFA was a founder and senior managing director of First Asset Management, the asset management unit of First Bank. In addition to handling major institutional accounts and firm management, he served on the core value management team and the asset allocation committee. The past president of the Twin City Society of Securities Analysts, he began his investment career with the Irving Trust Company in 1963 and served with Merrill Lynch before joining First Bank in 1967. Jensen held a BA in economics from the University of Minnesota.

Elizabeth M. Lilly, CFA spent two years managing First Asset Management's regional small-cap value portfolios with Rick Rinkoff and four years as manager/analyst for FAM's core value portfolios. Lilly began her investment career with Goldman Sachs and Co. in 1985. She subsequently worked for Fund American Companies and St. Paul Companies before joining FAM in 1992. She held a BA in economics with high honors from Hobart/William Smith College.

Richard J. Rinkoff, CFA had managed First Asset Management's regional small-cap value portfolios for 15 years, the last two years with Beth Lilly. Concurrently, he spent nine years managing FAM and First Bank System venture capital portfolios and 19 years as manager/analyst of FAM's Core Value portfolios. Rinkoff had entered the investment business in 1975 as an analyst with Pittsburgh National Bank. He held a BS in mathematics and an MBA from Carnegie Mellon University.

sets and 10,000 employees, First Bank dealt in commercial and retail banking and asset management. Lilly had worked in First Asset Management, the asset management division, researching and picking stocks for its large- and small-cap funds.[2] Almost immediately, she had felt frustrated dealing with the large company bureaucracy. "The red tape and too many group meetings tended to impede stock research," she complained.

> Even the process to gain approval for visiting companies that were potential investments was lengthy and laborious. By July 1995, I was convinced that the time had arrived to launch my own firm. I had confidence in my stock-picking ability; however, I did not have a track record to prove it.

Rick Rinkoff

Rinkoff, 44, had entered the investment business after graduating from Carnegie Mellon Business School in 1975. He had moved to First Bank in 1977. For 14 years, Rinkoff managed the institution's best-performing small-cap fund, which he had grown from infancy to nearly $500 million in assets.

But despite his long and successful tenure, Rinkoff had become uneasy. Since a new CEO had resurrected First Bank from near collapse in 1990, the company had pursued cost cuts everywhere, including the asset management division. Cutbacks through layoffs and staff reassignments, initially limited to regional satellite offices, had, by 1995, reached the central office. Rinkoff's stellar performance had led to unique pressures on him. "I had an easily marketable track record," he recalled.

> So I was asked to manage increasingly greater amounts of money. Awash in fresh capital, I had struggled to find enough new ideas to utilize all the funds on high potential opportunities. As the size of the fund grew, I worried that we would no longer generate superior investment returns.

---

[2] A stock's market capitalization ("cap") is the size of the underlying business as valued by the stock market, measured by the product of the stock price and number of shares outstanding.

Despite his performance, Rinkoff was not immune to the pressures caused by the cost cuts. "The cost cuts had reduced our access to research assistance and travel," he recalled. "More disturbing, I was irked by the lack of loyalty First Bank showed its employees. The wave of layoffs was very top-down driven and highly impersonal."

As his friends departed unceremoniously, Rinkoff wondered whether the bank would become a less congenial place to work. Despite his reservations, however, he felt little urgency to test the free agent market. His top-performing fund ensured a stable, highly respected position at First Bank. Although he questioned its continuing loyalty, First Bank had afforded him the opportunity to learn the business and the product with which to build his reputation over the past 19 years.

Dick Jensen

Jensen, 54, had spent almost his entire working career at First Bank. Over 30 years he had worked his way up the ranks from analyst to a founder of First Asset Management. Of the many roles he had played for the institution, Jensen had found his niche as the point person for major institutional accounts and an important internal decision maker. He had developed a sterling reputation in the financial community and a deep knowledge of the investment business. "By 1995," he reflected,

> I had lots of freedom and had reached a "free rein" age. I loved my work and enjoyed the people around me. In a few months I was looking forward to pulling the early retirement "rip cord," an event made more alluring as a result of the bank restructuring.

INVESTMENT MANAGEMENT INDUSTRY[3]

The mutual fund industry comprised companies that pooled the assets of individuals and institutions (e.g., pension funds, endowments, and charitable organizations) to invest in the capital markets. Fund investors sent money to fund providers who picked stocks that were expected to grow investor assets. By commingling their assets, investors derived cost benefits from record keeping and trading divisibility and investment benefits from diversification and professional expertise.[4]

Since the 1980s the mutual fund industry had been among the most dynamic of industries. Mutual fund assets under management had grown to nearly $5 trillion in 1998, a 16-fold increase since 1982. Long-term mutual funds' share of household financial assets had grown from 1.0 percent to 10.8 percent during the same period. Times could not have been better for both fund providers and fund investors.

The economics of the mutual fund industry were extremely lucrative. Fund providers' annual compensation was a percentage of the amount of assets under management. For example, the provider of a $10 billion fund with fees of 1.0 percent per annum would earn $100 million annually from investing clients. Additionally, investors paid providers' operating expenses and sometimes paid fees for entering and exiting funds.[5]

With an annuity revenue stream and low operating expenses, fund management was highly profitable and competition for investor assets, consequently, was intense. New funds were introduced daily. In fact, fund investors could choose from more mutual funds than stocks listed on U.S. security ex-

---

[3] This section draws upon Andre F. Perold, "The Vanguard Group, Inc. (1998)," Harvard Business School No. 299-002.
[4] Zvi Bodie, Alex Kane, and Alan J. Marcus, *Investments*, 4th ed. (Boston: Irwin/McGraw-Hill, 1999), p. 102.
[5] In their offering memorandum, fund providers chose whether to charge fund investors front-end loads (entry fees), back-end loads (exit fees), and 12 b-1 fees (marketing expenses to pay distributors). These fees were automatically withdrawn from investor assets held in the funds.

changes. In order to sort through the many diversified funds consultants classified them according to size and types of stocks that comprised the funds (see Figure 1).[6]

The largest fund provider, Fidelity Investors in Boston, managed $426 billion across hundreds of funds in 1995.[7] A "one-stop shop," Fidelity offered funds with stocks in one style box (e.g., Fidelity Growth—Large Cap), funds with stocks in more than one style box (e.g., Fidelity Mid Cap), funds holding stocks in a specific industry (e.g., Fidelity Select Technology), and funds with just about every subset imaginable. Hundreds of fund providers offered a similar "family of funds." Hundreds of other funds took a more focused approach, offering one or a few funds in a single style box.

FIGURE 1

Capitalization of Invested Stocks	Value	Blend	Growth
Large	Large-cap value	Large-cap blend	Large-cap growth
Mid	Mid-cap value	Mid-cap blend	Mid-cap growth
Small	Small-cap value	Small-cap blend	Small-cap growth

Investment Objective

THE GAME PLAN

Lilly Initiates

From 1993 to 1995 Lilly had spent a portion of her time assisting in the management of the small-cap value fund. "On a number of occasions while on the road visiting potential investments," Lilly recalled,

> Rick and I discussed starting an investment firm together. Rick seemed comfortable with the support offered by First Bank, but I knew my own firm was now a necessity. My time had come to leave. I walked into Rick's office and said "Rick, it's time for me to move on."

Rinkoff Responds

"It didn't take me long to answer Beth," Rinkoff recalled.

> I had observed her ability as she worked on several small-cap ideas. Based on her classical training, rigorous discipline, and extraordinary stock-picking ability she was clearly very talented. In fact, she was the "heart and soul" of First Bank's hugely successful large-cap value product. Were she to leave I would lose an outstanding research assistant on this fund. Faced with my uncertainty about the bank and the loss of Beth, I was ready to run. I knew that I owned the track record, so I responded, "You are not leaving without me."

Rinkoff, given his background in the venture capital industry, tended to stress a company's growth outlook when researching stocks. Lilly, in contrast, was trained in Graham and Dodd's principles of fundamental analysis and business valuation.[8] The two melded their approaches to improve their stock selection ability. As Lilly put it: "Rick is strong at looking at the big picture; my skill is in deciphering financial statements and valuing businesses."

As they began to develop a business model, the need for someone with experience in client rela-

[6] "Growth stocks" were those in the top one-third of a capitalization range as ranked by measures of growth such as years projected earnings growth. "Value stocks" were those in the top one-third of a capitalization range as ranked by measures of value, such as price/earnings and price/book ratios.

[7] "America's Top 300 Money Managers," *Institutional Investor,* July 1996.

[8] Benjamin Graham, *Graham and Dodd's Security Analysis,* 5th ed. (New York: McGraw-Hill, 1988).

tionships became increasingly apparent. "I had spent time with my long-standing clients reviewing their portfolios and conducting administrative matters," Rinkoff explained.

> However, I was not strong at developing new relationships and the client management function detracted from the time I could spend picking stocks. Beth and I had the investment skills and a great product, but we didn't have the critical client relationship experience.

Both agreed that, in terms of client skills, Dick Jensen stood head and shoulders above others they could consider for the position. Years of experience had made Jensen a superb client manager. Of course, Lilly and Rinkoff didn't expect a star, who seemed wedded to First Bank, to sign easily; getting him to join the discussion, they had joked, would be more difficult than hitting a Nolan Ryan fastball.[9] "Fortunately," observed Rinkoff, "Jensen was a trusted friend who would not betray our confidence if he was not interested." With little to lose, they stepped out of the on-deck circle and took a swing. Having known Jensen far longer than Lilly, Rinkoff walked into his office and asked: "How committed are you to First Bank?"

Jensen Deliberates

"When Rick posed his fateful question," Jensen recalled, "I reared back in my chair, chuckled, and responded 'What do you mean?' From there, he articulated the vision of forming an investment firm. Though I was far from signing on with Rick and Beth, I was intrigued."

Jensen thought the new venture could be an exciting way to continue to learn and grow in the business he loved. He was not sure, however, that he wanted to jeopardize his reputation and relationships. With only a few months until he could commence early retirement, he wondered if even

entertaining thoughts of a new venture was worth the risk. Despite his obvious reservations, however, Jensen agreed to further discuss a business model. "I figured," he explained,

> that we could iron out prerequisites such as the firm's investment philosophy, business model, potential clients, and staffing before I would need to commit. If any one thing blew up, it would all blow up before it started.

The three subsequently met on Saturdays at Jensen's Woodland Road home from 8:30 A.M. until early afternoon to develop business plan models.

BUSINESS MODEL

Starting Lineup

Lilly, Rinkoff, and Jensen agreed on a name for the prospective firm—Woodland Partners—and its initial product—to be modeled on the fund Lilly and Rinkoff were managing for First Bank. The fund would focus on picking small-company stocks that satisfied four criteria: (a) undergoing identifiable change; (b) inexpensively valued; (c) managed in the interest of shareholders; and (d) not well understood by Wall Street. They would evaluate corporate management firsthand, conducting in-depth "field research" besides running detailed valuation models. Since they were currently employed by First Bank, they could not even broach with their clients the possibility of their splitting off. But they were hopeful that several of their clients, particularly institutional but also individual, would "walk" with them.

From January 1981 through December 1995, the First Bank small-cap fund had returned 17.1 percent annually, as compared to the 12.4 percent return of its benchmark (see Exhibit 2). Woodland would start with the successful small-cap fund as

---

[9] Hall of Fame pitcher Nolan Ryan hurled more career strikeouts than anyone in the history of baseball. His fastball averaged nearly 100 miles per hour.

EXHIBIT 2   **Performance Record of Accounts Managed by Beth Lilly and Rick Rinkoff**

Year	Account Return	Russell 2000 Return	Difference
1995	51.0%	28.4%	+22.6%
1994	2.3	-1.8	4.1
1993	23.1	18.9	4.2
1992	12.9	18.4	-5.5
1991	64.2	46.1	18.1
1990	-2.9	-19.5	16.6
1989	21.3	16.2	5.1
1988	17.5	24.9	-7.4
1987	-4.2	-8.8	4.6
1986	7.2	5.7	1.5
1985	26.9	31.0	-4.1
1984	2.7	-7.3	10.0
1983	18.6	29.1	-10.5
Annualized	17.1%	12.4%	+4.7%

a platform. However, it was important to be explicit right from the beginning about the firm's long-term fund strategy. There were three options for developing business going forward. Woodland could manage only the one product, introduce a number of similar funds, or create a family of diverse mutual funds. Each of these options would have different managerial and organizational implications. Lilly dug into her file to put her 10-year compilation of notes to use.

Leading Off: One Product, No Growth

Rinkoff described the problems he had faced with growth in the First Bank fund he had managed:

> Managing too much money at First Bank has compelled us either to take larger, less liquid positions in our best ideas or to dilute our best ideas by increasing the number of stocks in our portfolios. Either way, our clients can't get our best efforts.

He used an example to illustrate the problem with asset growth. Suppose a fund provider is managing a $100 million portfolio holding $10 million of each of 10 stocks. In addition, suppose the $10 million stake represents 5 percent of the company (market cap = $200 million). Were the fund investors to double the fund size to $200 million, the fund provider would be compelled to either (1) double the position sizes, owning 10 percent of each company, to maintain the same portfolio, or (2) add 10 new stocks of the same market cap to maintain ownership of no more than 5 percent of any one company, or (3) find bigger stocks in which it could invest in 10 positions and maintain 5 percent stakes (market cap = $400 million).

Woodland could rectify this problem by offering only its core, small-cap value product and restricting the size of assets in the fund. It would consequently devote all of its resources to researching the best investment ideas for its one product. By limiting asset size, Woodland would concentrate its portfolio positions in the best ideas and thereby maximize the fund's performance.

Although it might generate Woodland's best single product, the "no growth" strategy would also create a fragile business model. Capping asset size would limit revenues and number of potential clients, any of whom could leave on a moment's notice. Moreover, scale-intensive activities such as marketing efforts would be swamped by the activities of large fund families.

The "no growth" model would also require that Woodland work with only a limited number of investors willing to entrust a portion of their assets to the firm's management. Ideally, Woodland would enter into enduring relationships with clients who intimately understood its investment process. When Woodland reached a predetermined size of assets under management, it could close its doors to new clients and grow by market appreciation.

Having identified Karen Bergstrom, a longtime administrative professional, Woodland would not need to add further to its team. The need for continued internal cohesion would be intense. Personal conflicts would surface quickly and need to be resolved immediately.

Batting Second: Focused Product Line

Woodland could leverage its product's track record to introduce a focused series of funds. By adding mid- and large-cap value funds to the core small-cap value product, it could manage more assets without being concerned about liquidity or concentration in the small-cap fund.

A focused series of funds could afford Woodland competitive products and a more profitable and stable business. Managing more assets could generate a larger revenue stream across a more diverse client base with a minimal increase in operating expenses. As a more profitable business, Woodland would have greater flexibility to compete for client assets.

To secure a larger asset base Woodland would have to attract more clients. Although the demands on client acquisition and retention would increase, the additional clients would reduce the impact of loss of any one client.

The focused product line, unlike the "no growth" model, could strain Woodland's internal capacity. The focused product line would necessi-

tate spreading their own efforts across funds, or adding new staff to manage the additional products. Jensen might also need assistance to nurture client relationships to his satisfaction. Lilly and Rinkoff believed the number of proficient people that they could employ to be extremely limited.

Power Hitter: Family of Funds

Starting with the small-cap product, Woodland could gradually introduce a full family of funds covering several of the nine style boxes (Figure 1). Adding staff and broadening its product offering could enable Woodland to develop the financial resources to muster a serious marketing effort and compete with large fund families.

Although economically lucrative, creating a family of funds was a fundamentally different business from managing a single fund. A single fund's professional investor sought solely to maximize investment returns for its clients. Managers of a fund family, on the other hand, were primarily asset gatherers who marketed their products effectively and generated sufficient performance to retain client assets.

Woodland would consider developing a family of funds only if it could build a collection of professional investors across different style boxes. To accomplish this, it would have to build the business over time to ensure that each product was managed effectively. Growth would be contingent on early funds delivering excellent investment returns. Successful investment performance would attract greater client assets, enabling Woodland to attract talent and roll out additional products. Scale economies would improve with each additional successful product. Increased marketing would bring in more funds, further reducing the cost of marketing and increasing returns.

CUTTING THE CORN FIELD

As the summer of 1995 gave way to fall, the Woodland vision was becoming increasingly tangible. Meeting one warm fall day, Lilly, Rinkoff, and Jensen discussed their commitment to the business idea. Lilly and Rinkoff were close to taking the plunge. Jensen wanted more time.

Lilly's Perspective

Jensen's methodical approach forced Lilly to think through her basic premises. Was this the right opportunity to make her dream a reality? Were these the right people with whom to join forces? If Rinkoff and she could not convince Jensen to complete the partnership, should they give it a go on their own the principle of "if we build it, they [other 'Jensens,' as well as clients] will come," or should they first find someone to replace him?

If they decided to open shop, how would First Bank respond to their departure? Would they be offered alluring inducements to stay but be saddled with a "win the battle, lose the war" environment in the bank? Or would the three immediately be escorted out of the bank with threats of a lawsuit if they pursued their plan?

If they were to make the leap, she wanted to be certain that the partnership would work because her reputation would be at risk if the venture failed. Jensen and Rinkoff certainly seemed like ideal partners on paper, but would three distinct personalities come together harmoniously? They had spent six months discussing the prerequisites without as much as a blip. How much longer should they wait?

Rinkoff's Viewpoint

Lilly's timing had been propitious for Rinkoff. He had established a marketable track record, but was worried that change at First Bank might cause his product and life to suffer. Lilly's proposition represented an opportunity to pursue the business he loved in an atmosphere he could influence and enjoy.

If Jensen could be enlisted, Rinkoff was ready to begin right away. With Jensen on board to concentrate on the firm's business development and client relations, he and Lilly could dedicate the majority of their time to picking stocks. Although he had known his colleague for 20 years, Rinkoff could not read Jensen's mind. What could he say to make Jensen pull the trigger? Should he take the risk if Jensen wouldn't? Would clients trust Woodland Partners to manage their assets as much as they trusted First Bank? At the core, he wondered, was he interested simply because the timing of the proposition had matched his mood, or was there intrinsic merit in the idea as well?

Jensen's Dilemma

As Rinkoff and Lilly walked out the door after the meeting, Jensen continued to ponder the opportunity. Was he ready? Of the three, he felt "both least at risk and most at risk." He was financially secure and had developed a strong reputation. With much of the initial responsibility for business development on his shoulders, the business would be both challenging and attractive. But walking out the door and leaving friends of 30 years would not be easy. Why take a risk now? Why hazard a potential fallout with his friends and jeopardize attractive monetary rewards yet to come?

TO BE OR NOT TO BE

Was the time and environment right for Lilly, Rinkoff, and Jensen to make major, career-altering changes? The three were from different generations. Could they co-exist? Could they continue to attract and retain clients? Could they continue their sterling performance? Was Woodland an alluring trap or a compelling opportunity?

Shouldice Hospital Limited

Two shadowy figures, enrobed and in slippers, walked slowly down the semidarkened hall of the Shouldice Hospital. They didn't notice Alan O'Dell, the hospital administrator, and his guest, who had just emerged from the basement boiler room on a tour of the facility. Once they were out of earshot, O'Dell remarked good naturedly, "By the way they act, you'd think our patients own this place. And while they're here, in a way they do."

Following a visit to the five operating rooms, also located on the first of three levels, O'Dell and his visitor once again encountered the same pair of patients still engrossed in discussing their hernia operations, which had been performed the previous morning.

HISTORY

Born on a farm in Bruce County, Ontario, Dr. Earle Shouldice, who was to found the hospital bearing his name, first displayed his interest in medical research at the age of 12. He performed a postmortem on a calf that, he discovered, had died from an intestinal obstruction. After a year of following the wishes of his parents that he study for the ministry, Shouldice persuaded them to let him enroll in medicine at the University of Toronto.

An attractive brochure that was recently printed, although neither dated nor distributed to prospective patients, described Earle Shouldice as follows:

While carrying on a private medical and surgical practice in the years between the two World Wars and holding a post as lecturer in anatomy at the University of Toronto, Dr. Shouldice continued to pursue his interest in research. He did pioneer work towards the cure of pernicious anemia, intestinal obstruction, hydrocephalic cases and other areas of advancing medical knowledge.

His interest in early ambulation stemmed, in part, from an operation he performed in 1932 to remove the appendix from a seven-year-old girl and the girl's subsequent refusal to stay quietly in bed. In spite of her activity, no harm was done, and the experience recalled to the doctor the postoperative actions of animals upon which he had performed surgery. They had all moved about freely with no ill effects. Four years later he was reminded of the child when he allowed washroom privileges immediately following the operations to four men recovering from hernia. All had trouble-free recovery.

By the outset of the Second World War in 1940, Shouldice had given extensive thought to several factors that contributed to early ambulation following surgery. Among them were the use of a local anesthetic, the nature of the surgical procedure itself, the design of a facility to encourage movement without unnecessarily causing discomfort, and the postoperative regimen designed and communicated by the medical team. With all of these things in mind, he had begun to develop a surgical technique for repairing hernias[1] that was superior to others. He offered his services in correcting hernias for army inductees who otherwise would not qualify for service. Because hospital beds often were not available, sometimes the surgery took place in the emergency department of the Toronto General Hospital, and the patients were transported later in the day to a medical fraternity where they were cared for by medical students for two or three days.

By the war's end, word of the Shouldice technique had spread sufficiently that 200 civilians had contacted the doctor and were awaiting surgery upon his discharge from the army. Because of the scarcity of hospital beds, particularly for an operation that was considered elective and of relatively low priority, he started his own hospital. Dr. Shouldice's medical license permitted him to operate anywhere, even on a kitchen table, and consequently he received authorization from the provincial government to open his first hospital in a six-room nursing home in downtown Toronto in July 1945. As more and more patients requested operations, Dr. Shouldice extended his facilities by buying a rambling 130-acre estate with a 17,000-square foot main house in the suburb of Thornhill, 15 miles north of downtown Toronto. Initially, a 36-bed capacity was created in Thornhill, but after some years of planning, a large wing was added to the house to provide a total capacity of 89 beds.

At the time of his death in 1965, Dr. Shouldice's long-time associate, Dr. Nicholas Obney, was named surgeon-in-chief and chairman of the board of Shouldice Hospital Limited, the corporation formed to operate both the hospital and clinical facilities. Under Dr. Obney's leadership, the volume of activity continued to increase, reaching a total of 6,850 operations in the 1982 calendar year.

THE SHOULDICE METHOD

Only external types of abdominal hernias were repaired at Shouldice Hospital. Internal types, such as hiatus (or diaphragmatic) hernias, were not treated. As a result, most first-time repairs (called primaries) involved straightforward operating procedures that required about 45 minutes. Primaries represented approximately 82 percent of all operations performed at Shouldice in 1982. The remaining 18 percent involved patients suffering recurrences of hernias previously repaired elsewhere.[2]

In the Shouldice method, the muscles of the abdominal wall were arranged in three distinct layers, and the opening was repaired—each layer in turn—by overlapping its margins in much the same manner as the edges of a coat might be overlapped when buttoned. The end result was to reinforce the muscular wall of the abdomen with six rows of sutures (stitches) under the skin cover, which was then closed with clamps that were removed within 48 hours after the operation. (Other methods might not separate muscle layers, often involved fewer rows of sutures, and sometimes involved the insertion of screens or meshes under the skin.)

The typical first-time repair could be completed with the use of preoperative sedation (sleeping

[1] Most hernias, known as external abdominal hernias, were protrusions of some part of the abdominal contents through a hole or slit in the muscular layers of the abdominal wall which was supposed to contain them. Well over 90 percent of these hernias occurred in the groin area. Of these, by far the most common were inguinal hernias, many of which were caused by a slight weakness in the muscle layers brought about by the passage of the testicle in male babies through the groin area shortly before birth. Aging also caused inguinal hernias to develop. The other, much less common, external hernias were called "femoral," in which a protrusion appeared in the top inch or so of the thigh. Because of the cause of the affliction, 85 percent of all hernias occurred in males.

[2] Based on a careful tracking of its patients over more than 30 years, it was estimated that the gross recurrence rate for all operations performed at Shouldice was 0.8 percent. Recurrence rates reported in the literature for these types of hernia varied greatly. However, one text published around that time stated, "In the United States the gross rate of recurrence for groin hernias approaches 10 percent."

pill) and analgesic (pain killer) plus a local anesthetic, an injection of Novocain in the region of the incision. This allowed immediate patient ambulation and facilitated rapid recovery. Many of the recurrences and the very difficult hernia repairs, being more complex, could require up to 90 minutes and more. In some circumstances, a general anesthetic was administered.

THE PATIENTS' EXPERIENCE

It was thought that most potential Shouldice patients learned about the hospital and its methods from past patients who had already experienced them. Although over 1,000 doctors had referred patients, doctors were less likely to recommend Shouldice because of the generally regarded simplicity of the surgery, often considered a "bread and butter" operation. Typically, many patients had their problem diagnosed by a personal physician and then took the initiative to contact Shouldice. Many more made this diagnosis themselves and contacted the hospital directly.

The process experienced by Shouldice patients depended on whether or not they lived close enough to the hospital to visit the facility to obtain a diagnosis. Approximately 42 percent of all Shouldice patients came from the United States. Another 2 percent originated from provinces other than Ontario and from European countries. These out-of-town patients often were diagnosed by mail, using the Medical Information questionnaire shown in Exhibit 1.

Of every eight questionnaires sent, seven were returned to the hospital in completed form. Based on information in the questionnaire, a Shouldice surgeon would determine the type of hernia the respondent had and whether there were signs that some risk might be associated with surgery (for example, an overweight or heart condition, or a patient who had suffered a heart attack or a stroke in the past six months to a year, or whether a general or local anesthetic was required). At this point, a patient was given an operating date, the medical information was logged into a computerized database, and the patient was sent a confirmation card; if necessary, a sheet outlining a weight loss program prior to surgery and a brochure describing the hospital and the Shouldice method were also sent. A small proportion was refused treatment, either because they were too fat, represented an undue medical risk, or because it was determined that they did not have a hernia.

If confirmation cards were not returned by the patient three days or more prior to the scheduled operation, that patient was contacted by phone. Upon confirmation, the patient's folder was sent to the reception desk to await his or her arrival.[3]

Arriving at the clinic between 1:00 P.M. and 3:00 P.M. the day before the operation, a patient might join up with 30 to 34 other patients and their friends and families in the waiting room. After a typical wait of about 20 minutes—depending on the availability of surgeons—a patient was examined in one of six examination rooms staffed by surgeons who had completed their operating schedules for the day. This examination required no more than 15 to 20 minutes, unless the patient needed reassurance. (Patients typically exhibited a moderate level of anxiety until their operation was completed.) At this point it occasionally was dis-

---

[3] Patients living within 50 miles from the hospital (about 40 percent of all patients) were encouraged to come to the clinic on a walk-in basis for an examination, usually requiring no more than 15 or 20 minutes for the physical and completion of an information questionnaire. If the doctor performing the examination diagnosed the problem as an external hernia, the individual could obtain immediately a future booking for the operation. On occasion, when a previously booked patient canceled at the last minute, a walk-in patient, or one selected from a special waiting list, could be scheduled for the next day. At the time of booking, the potential patient was given a specific date for the operation, a letter estimating the total cost of the operation (as required by the Ontario provincial government for all Ontario residents), and information supplied to out-of-province patients.

EXHIBIT 1 Medical Information Questionnaire

FAMILY NAME (Last Name)	FIRST NAME	MIDDLE NAME

STREET & NUMBER (or Rural Route or P.O. Box)	Town/City	Province/State

County	Township	Zip or Postal Code	Birthdate: Month	Day	Year

Telephone
Home .... If none, give
Work .... neighbour's number ....

Married or Single | Religion

NEXT OF KIN: Name | Address | Telephone #

SHOULDICE HOSPITAL

7750 Bayview Avenue
Box 370, Thornhill, Ontario L3T 4A3 Canada
Phone (416) 889-1125

(Thornhill - One Mile North Metro Toronto)

MEDICAL

INFORMATION

Patients who live at a distance often prefer their examination, admission and operation to be arranged all on a single visit — to save making two lengthy journeys. The whole purpose of this questionnaire is to make such arrangements possible, although, of course, it cannot replace the examination in any way. Its completion and return will not put you under any obligation.

INSURANCE INFORMATION: Please give name of Insurance Company and Numbers. | Date form completed

HOSPITAL INSURANCE: (Please bring hospital certificates) | OTHER HOSPITAL INSURANCE
O.H.I.P.   BLUE CROSS | Company Name _____
Number ___   Number ___ | Policy Number _____

SURGICAL INSURANCE:(Please bring insurance certificates) | OTHER SURGICAL INSURANCE
O.H.I.P.   BLUE SHIELD | Company Name _____
Number ___   Number ___ | Policy Number _____

WORKMEN'S COMPENSATION BOARD | Approved | Social Insurance (Security) Number
Claim No. | Yes   No

Occupation | Name of Business | Are you the Owner? If Retired — Former Occupation
 | | Yes   No

How did you hear about Shouldice Hospital? (If referred by a doctor, give name & address)

Are you a former patient of Shouldice Hospital?   Yes   No   Do you smoke?   Yes   No

Have you ever written to Shouldice Hospital in the past?   Yes   No

What is your preferred admission date? (Please give as much advance notice as possible)
No admissions Friday, Saturday or Sunday.

Please be sure to fill in both sides.

FOR OFFICE USE ONLY

Date Received | Type of Hernia | Weight Loss
 | | lbs.

Consent to Operate ☐ | Special Instructions | Approved
Heart Report ☐

Referring Doctor Notified | | Operation Date

This information will be treated as confidential.

(continued on next page)

covered that a patient had not corrected his or her weight problem; others might be found not to have a hernia after all. In either case, the patient was sent home.

Following his or her examination, a patient might experience a wait of 5 to 15 minutes to see one of two admitting personnel in the accounting office. Here, health insurance coverage was checked, and various details were discussed in a procedure that usually lasted no more than 10 minutes. Patients sometimes exhibited their nervousness by asking many questions at this point, requiring more time of the receptionist.

Patients next were sent to one of two nurses' stations where, in 5 to 10 minutes and with little wait, their hemoglobin (blood) and urine were checked. At this point, about an hour after arriving at the hospital, a patient was directed to the room number shown on his or her wrist band. Throughout the process, patients were asked to keep their luggage (usually light and containing only a few items suggested by the hospital) with them.

All patient rooms at the hospital were semiprivate, containing two beds. Patients with similar jobs, backgrounds, or interests were assigned to the same room to the extent possible. Upon reaching their rooms, patients busied themselves unpacking, getting acquainted with roommates, changing into pajamas, "prepping" themselves

EXHIBIT 1 (continued)

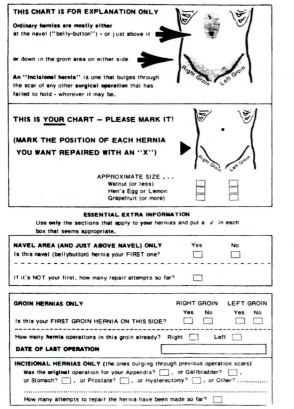

THIS CHART IS FOR EXPLANATION ONLY

Ordinary hernias are mostly either
at the navel ("belly-button") - or just above it

or down in the groin area on either side

An "Incisional hernia" is one that bulges through
the scar of any other surgical operation that has
failed to hold - wherever it may be.

THIS IS YOUR CHART — PLEASE MARK IT!

(MARK THE POSITION OF EACH HERNIA
YOU WANT REPAIRED WITH AN "X")

APPROXIMATE SIZE . . .
Walnut (or less)
Hen's Egg or Lemon
Grapefruit (or more)

ESSENTIAL EXTRA INFORMATION
Use only the sections that apply to your hernias and put a ✓ in each
box that seems appropriate.

NAVEL AREA (AND JUST ABOVE NAVEL) ONLY   Yes   No

Is this navel (bellybutton) hernia your FIRST one?

If it's NOT your first, how many repair attempts so far?

GROIN HERNIAS ONLY   RIGHT GROIN   LEFT GROIN
                                       Yes   No   Yes   No
Is this your FIRST GROIN HERNIA ON THIS SIDE?

How many hernia operations in this groin already?   Right ☐   Left ☐

DATE OF LAST OPERATION

INCISIONAL HERNIAS ONLY (the ones bulging through previous operation scars)
Was the original operation for your Appendix? ☐ , or Gallbladder? ☐ ,
or Stomach? ☐ , or Prostate? ☐ , or Hysterectomy? ☐ , or Other? ....
....
How many attempts to repair the hernia have been made so far? ☐

Exhibit 1 (continued)
PLEASE BE ACCURATE!: Misleading figures, when checked on a
admission day, could mean postponement of your operation till your weight
is suitable.

HEIGHT ...... ft......... ins.   WEIGHT ...... lbs. Nude   Recent gain? ...... lbs.
                                  or just pyjamas   Recent loss? ...... lbs

Waist (muscles relaxed) .... ins.   Chest (not expanded) ....ins.

GENERAL HEALTH

Age .... years   Is your health now GOOD ☐ ,   FAIR ☐ , or POOR ☐

Please mention briefly any severe past illness — such as a
"heart attack" or a "stroke", for example, from which you
have now recovered (and its approximate date) ....
....

We need to know about other present conditions, even though your admission is
NOT likely to be refused because of them.

Please tick ☑ any condition for which you are having regular treatment:		Name of any prescribed pills, tablets or capsules you take regularly: —
Blood Pressure	☐	
Excess body fluids	☐	
Chest pain ("angina")	☐	
Irregular Heartbeat	☐	
Diabetes	☐	
Asthma & Bronchitis	☐	
Ulcers	☐	
Anticoagulants (to delay blood-clotting or to "thin the blood")	☐	
Other		

Did you remember to MARK AN "X" on your body chart to show us where
each of your hernias is located?

(shaving themselves in the area of the operation), and providing a urine sample.

At 5:00 P.M. a nurse's orientation provided the group of incoming patients with information about what to expect, the drugs to be administered, the need for exercise after the operation, the facility, and the daily routine. According to Alan O'Dell, "Half are so nervous they don't remember much from the orientation." Dinner was served from 5:30 to 6:00 P.M. in a 100-seat dining room on a first-come, first-served basis. Following further recreation, tea and cookies were served at 9:00 P.M. in the lounge area. Nurses emphasized the importance of attendance at that time because it provided an opportunity for preoperative patients to talk with those whose operations had been completed earlier that same day. Nearly all new patients were "tucked into bed" between 9:30 and 10:00 P.M. in preparation for an early awakening prior to their operations.

Patients to be operated on early in the day were awakened at 5:30 A.M. to be given preop sedation and to be dressed in an O.R. (operating room) gown. An attempt was made to schedule operations for roommates at approximately the same time. Patients were taken to the preoperating room where the circulating nurse administered Demerol, an analgesic, 45 minutes before surgery. A few minutes prior to the first operation at 7:30 A.M., the surgeon assigned to each patient administered

Novocain, a local anesthetic. During the operation, it was the responsibility of the circulating nurse to monitor the patient's comfort, to note times at which the Novocain was administered and the operation begun, and to arrange for the administration of Demerol to the patient scheduled next on the operating table, depending on the progress of the surgery under way. This was in contrast to the typical hospital procedure in which patients were sedated in their rooms prior to being taken to the operating rooms.

Upon the completion of the operation, during which a few patients were "chatty" and fully aware of what was going on, patients were invited to get off the operating table and walk to the postoperating room with the help of their surgeons. According to Ursula Verstraete, director of nursing:

> Ninety-nine percent accept the surgeon's invitation. While we put them in wheelchairs to return them to their rooms, the walk from the operating table is for psychological as well as physiological [blood pressure, respiratory] reasons. Patients prove to themselves that they can do it, and they start their all-important exercise immediately.

Throughout the day after their operation, patients were encouraged to exercise by nurses and housekeepers alike. By 9:00 P.M. on the day of their operations, all patients were ready and able to walk down to the dining room for tea and cookies, even if it meant climbing stairs, to help indoctrinate the new "class" admitted that day.

Patients in their second or third day of recovery were awakened before 6:00 A.M. so they could loosen up for breakfast, which was served between 7:45 and 8:15 A.M. in the dining room. Good posture and exercise were thought to aid digestion and deter the buildup of gas that could prove painful. After breakfast on the first day after surgery, all of the skin clips (resembling staples) holding the skin together over the incision were loosened and some removed. The remainder were removed the next day. On the fourth morning, patients were ready for discharge.

During their stay, patients were encouraged to take advantage of the opportunity to explore the premises and make new friends. Some members of the staff felt that the patients and their attitudes were the most important element of the Shouldice program. According to Dr. Byrnes Shouldice, the 53-year-old son of the founder and vice president of the corporation—a surgeon on the staff and a 50 percent owner of the hospital:

> Patients sometimes ask to stay an extra day. Why? Well, think about it. They are basically well to begin with. But they arrive with a problem and a certain amount of nervousness, tension, and anxiety about their surgery. Their first morning here they're operated on and experience a sense of relief from something that's been bothering them for a long time. They are immediately able to get around, and they've got a three-day holiday ahead of them with a perfectly good reason to be away from work with no sense of guilt. They share experiences with other patients, make friends easily, and have the run of the hospital. In summer, the most common after-effect from the surgery is sunburn. They kid with the staff and make this a positive experience for all of us.

The average patient stay for comparable operations at other hospitals was thought to be five to seven or eight days, but it had been declining because of a shortage of beds and the tendency to give elective surgery a low priority for beds. Shouldice patients with jobs involving light exercise could return to work within a week after their operations, but those involved in more strenuous work, whose benefits were insured, received four weeks of benefits and recuperation. All self-employed persons returned to work much earlier. In general, typical times for recuperation from similar operations at other hospitals were two weeks for those in jobs requiring light exercise and eight weeks for those in more strenuous jobs, due largely to long-established treatment regimens.

THE NURSES' EXPERIENCE

The nursing staff comprised 22 full-time and 18 part-time members. They were divided into four groups (as shown in Exhibit 2), with supervisors for the hospital, operating room, laboratory, and central supply reporting to Ursula Verstraete, the director of nursing.

While the operating rooms were fully staffed from about 7 A.M. through the last operation ending in the mid- to late afternoon, the hospital was staffed with three shifts beginning at 7 A.M., 3 P.M., and 11 P.M. Even so, minimal patient needs for physical assistance allowed Shouldice to operate with a much lower nurse-to-patient ratio than the typical hospital. Shouldice nurses spent an unusually large proportion of their time in counseling activities. As one supervisor commented, "We don't use bedpans." In a typical year, Verstraete estimated that she might experience a turnover of four nurses.

THE DOCTORS' EXPERIENCE

The hospital employed 12 full-time surgeons, 7 part-time assistant surgeons, and one anesthetist. Each operating team required a surgeon, an assistant surgeon, a scrub nurse, and a circulating nurse. The operating load varied from 30 to 36 operations per day. As a result, each surgeon typically performed three or four operations each day.

A typical surgeon's day started with a *scrubbing* shortly before the first scheduled operation at 7:30 A.M. If the first operation was routine, it usually was completed by 8:15 A.M. At its conclusion, the surgical team helped the patient walk from the room and summoned the next patient. While the patient was being prepared and awaiting the full effects of the Demerol to set in, the surgeon completed the previous patient's file by dictating five or so minutes of comments concerning the operation. Postoperative instructions were routine unless specific instructions were issued by the sur-

geon. After scrubbing, the surgeon could be ready to operate again at 8:30 A.M.

Surgeons were advised to take a coffee break after their second or third operation. Even so, a surgeon could complete three routine operations and a fourth involving a recurrence (a 60- to 90-minute procedure) and still be finished in time for a 12:30 P.M. lunch in the staff dining room.

Upon finishing lunch, as many as six of the surgeons not scheduled to operate in the afternoon moved upstairs to examine incoming patients between 1:00 and 3:00 P.M. A surgeon's day ended by 4:00 P.M. In addition, a surgeon could expect to be on call one weekday night in ten and one weekend in ten. Alan O'Dell commented that the position appealed to doctors who "want to watch their children grow up. A doctor on call is rarely called to the hospital and has regular hours."

According to Dr. Obney, chief surgeon:

When I interview prospective surgeons, I look for experience and a good education. I try to gain some insight into their domestic situation and personal interests and habits. Naturally, as in any field, we try to avoid anyone with a drinking or drug problem. Oftentimes these people can hide their illness very well and it can take a while before it is detected. Here, sometimes, recommendations can be of great help. I also try to find out why a surgeon wants to switch positions. And I try to determine if he's willing to perform the repair exactly as he's told. This is no place for prima donnas.

Dr. Shouldice added:

Our surgeons enjoy operating, but sometimes are less interested in the more mundane office routines that all vocations have. Traditionally a hernia is often the first operation that a junior resident in surgery performs. Hernia repair is regarded as a relatively simple operation compared to other major operations. This is quite wrong, as is borne out by the resulting high recurrence

EXHIBIT 2 Organization Chart

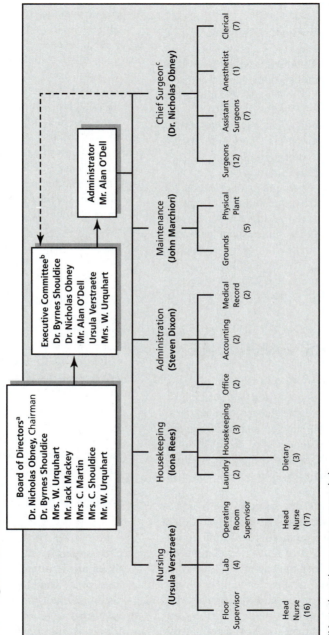

aMeets three times a year or as needed.
bMeets as needed (usually twice a month).
cInformally reports to Executive Committee.

rate. It is a tricky anatomical area and occasionally very complicated, especially to the novice or those doing very few hernia repairs each year. But at Shouldice Hospital a surgeon learns the Shouldice technique over a period of several months. He learns when he can go fast and when he must go slow. He develops a pace and a touch. If he encounters something unusual, he is encouraged to consult immediately with other surgeons. We teach each other and try to encourage a group effort. And he learns not to take risks to achieve absolute perfection. Excellence is the enemy of good.

Dr. Obney assigned surgeons to an operating room on a daily basis by noon of the preceding day. This allowed surgeons to examine the specific patients that they were to operate on. Surgeons and assistants were rotated every few days. Scrub nurses and circulating nurses were assigned to a new operating room every two weeks and four weeks, respectively. Unless patients requested specific doctors, cases were assigned to give doctors a nonroutine operation (often involving a recurrence) several times a week. More complex procedures were assigned to more senior and experienced members of the staff, including Dr. Obney himself. Where possible, former Shouldice patients suffering recurrences were assigned to the doctor who performed the first operation "to allow the doctor to learn from his mistake."

As Dr. Obney commented:

> If something goes wrong, we want to make sure that we have an experienced surgeon in charge, and we don't like surgeons who work too fast. Experience is most important. The typical general surgeon may perform 25 to 50 hernia operations per year. Ours perform 600 or more.

The 12 full-time surgeons were paid a straight salary. A typical starting salary at that time for someone with 5 to 10 years of experience was $50,000. In addition, bonuses to doctors were voted by the board of directors twice a year, depending on profit and performance. The total bonus pool paid to the surgeons in a recent year was approximately $500,000. Assisting surgeons were part-time, and they received 51 percent of the $60 fee that was charged to patients who received their services.

The anesthetist was hired for $300 per day from a nearby partnership. Only one was required to be on duty on any given day and could supervise all five operating rooms in addition to administering an occasional general anesthetic to a patient with a complex case or to a child.

Training in the Shouldice technique was important because the procedure could not be varied. It was accomplished through direct supervision by one or more of the senior surgeons. The rotation of teams and frequent consultations allowed for an ongoing opportunity to appraise performance and take corrective action.

According to Dr. Obney:

> We haven't had to let anyone go because they couldn't learn, or continue to adhere to, the method. However, a doctor must decide after several years whether he wants to do this for the rest of his life because, just as in other specialties—for example, radiology—he loses touch with other medical disciplines. If he stays for five years, he doesn't leave. Even among younger doctors, few elect to leave.

THE FACILITY

A tour of the facility with Alan O'Dell yielded some interesting information. The Shouldice Hospital comprised two basic facilities in one building—the hospital and the clinic.

On the first-level opening to grade at the back of the building, the hospital contained the kitchen and dining rooms as well as the office of the supervisor of housekeeping. The second level, also opening to grade but at the front of the building, contained a large, open lounge area, the admissions offices, patient rooms, and a spacious glass-covered Florida room. The third level had additional patient rooms, a large lounge, and a recreational area.

Throughout the tour, patients could be seen visiting in each others' rooms, walking up and down hallways, lounging in the sunroom, and making use of light recreational facilities ranging from a pool table to an exercycle.

Alan O'Dell pointed out some of the features of the hospital:

The rooms contain no telephones or television sets. If a patient needs to make a call or wants to watch television, he or she has to take a walk. The steps are designed specially with a small rise to allow patients recently operated on to negotiate the stairs without undue discomfort. Every square foot of the hospital is carpeted to reduce the hospital feeling and the possibility of a fall. Carpeting also gives the place a smell other than that of disinfectant.

This facility was designed by Dr. Byrnes Shouldice. He thought about it for years and made many changes in the plan before the first concrete was poured. A number of unique policies were also instituted. Because Dr. Shouldice started out to be a minister, ministers are treated gratis. And you see that mother and child in the next room? Parents accompanying children here for an operation stay free. You may wonder why we can do it, but we learned that we save more in nursing costs than we spend for the patient's room and board. Children may present difficulties in a hospital environment, but when accompanied by a parent, the parent is happier and so is the child.

While patients and staff were served food prepared in the same kitchen, the staff was required to pick up its food from a cafeteria line placed in the very center of the kitchen. This provided an opportunity for everyone to chat with the kitchen staff several times a day as they picked up a meal or stopped for coffee. Patients were served in the adjoining patient dining room.

According to O'Dell:

We use all fresh ingredients and prepare the food from scratch in the kitchen. Our kitchen staff of three prepares about 100 breakfasts, 200 lunches, and 100 dinners each day at an average raw food cost of $1.10 per meal.

Iona Rees, director of housekeeping, pointed out:

We do all of our own laundry in the building with two full-time employees. And I have only three on my housekeeping staff for the entire facility. One of the reasons for so few housekeepers is that we don't need to change linens during a patient's four-day stay. They are basically well, so there is no soiling of bed linens. Also, the medical staff doesn't want the patients in bed all day. They want the nurses to encourage the patients to be up socializing, comparing notes [for confidence], encouraging each other, and walking around, getting exercise.

Of course, we're in the rooms straightening up throughout the day. This gives the housekeepers a chance to josh with the patients and to encourage them to exercise.

The bottom level of the clinic housed five operating rooms, a laboratory, the patient-recovery room, and a central supply area where surgical instruments were cleaned and sterilized. This was the only area of the entire facility that was not carpeted, to prevent static electricity from forming in areas where potentially explosive anesthetics might be used. In total, the estimated cost to furnish an operating room was no more than $30,000. This was considerably less than for other hospitals requiring a bank of equipment with which to administer anesthetics for each room. At Shouldice, two mobile units were used by the anesthetist when needed. In addition, the complex had one "crash cart" per floor for use if a patient should suffer a heart attack or stroke during his or her hospital stay.

The first floor of the clinic contained admissions and accounting offices, a large waiting room with a capacity for as many as 50 people, and six examination rooms. On the second floor of the clinic, situated in much of what was the original house, was found the administrative offices. A third floor contained 14 additional hostel rooms where patients could be held overnight awaiting the assignment of a room and their operations. At such times when the hospital was particularly crowded, doctors were asked to identify those postoperative patients who could be released a day early. Often these were local residents or children.

ADMINISTRATION

Alan O'Dell, while he walked, described his job:

I'm responsible for a little of everything around here. We try to meet people's needs and make this as good a place to work as possible. My door is always open. And members of our staff will come in to seek advice about everything from medical to marital problems. There is a strong concern for employees here. Nobody is fired. [This was later reinforced by Dr. Shouldice, who described a situation involving two employees who confessed to theft in the hospital. They agreed to seek psychiatric help and were allowed to remain on the job.] As a result, turnover is low.

We don't have a union, but we try to maintain a pay scale higher than the union scale for comparable jobs in the area. For example, our nurses receive from $15,000 to $25,000 per year, depending on the number of years' experience. We have a profit-sharing plan that is separate from the doctors'. Last year the employees divided up $65,000.

If work needs to be done, people pitch in to help each other. A unique aspect of our administration is that I insist that each secretary is trained to do another's work and in an emergency is able to switch to another function immediately and enable the more vital workload to proceed uninterrupted. With the exception of the accounting staff, every secretary, regardless of her or his position in the hospital, is trained to handle the hospital switchboard and work at the reception desk. If necessary, I'll go downstairs and type billings if they're behind. We don't have an organization chart. A chart tends to make people think they're boxed into jobs.[4]

In addition to other activities, I try to stay here one night a week having dinner and listening to the patients to find out how things are really going around here.

Administrative Structure

The hospital was operated on a nonprofit basis and the clinic on a for-profit basis. Dr. Shouldice and Mrs. W. Urquhart, his sister, each owned 50 percent of each.

O'Dell, as administrator of the hospital, was responsible for all of its five departments: surgery, nursing, administration, maintenance, and housekeeping. Medical matters were the domain of Dr. Obney, the chief surgeon. Both Alan O'Dell and Dr. Obney reported directly to an executive committee composed of Drs. Shouldice and Obney, Alan O'Dell, Ursula Verstraete (director of nursing), and Mrs. Urquhart. The executive committee met as needed, usually twice a month, and in turn reported to an inside board (as shown in Exhibit 2). In addition to executive committee members (except Ursula Verstraete), the board included the spouses of Dr. Shouldice and Mrs. Urquhart, two former longtime employees, and Jack MacKay. The board met three times per year, or when necessary.

---

[4] The chart in Exhibit 2 was prepared by the casewriter, based on conversations with hospital personnel.

Operating Costs

It was estimated by the casewriter that the 1983 budgets for the hospital and clinic were close to $2.8 million and $2 million, respectively.[5]

THE MARKET

Hernia operations were among the most common performed on males. In 1979, for example, it was estimated that 600,000 such operations were performed in the United States alone. Only in the early 1980s had the hospital begun to organize information about either its client base of 140,000 "alumni" or the market in general.

According to Dr. Shouldice:

> When our backlog of scheduled operations gets too large, we begin to wonder how many people decide instead to have their local doctor perform the operation. Every time we have expanded our capacity, the backlog has declined briefly, only to climb once again. Right now, at 1,200, it is larger than it has ever been at this time of year [January].

The hospital relied entirely on word-of-mouth advertising, the importance of which was suggested by the results of a poll carried out by students of DePaul University as part of a project (Exhibit 3 shows a portion of these results). Although little systematic data about patients had been collected, Alan O'Dell remarked that "if we had to rely on wealthy patients only, our practice would be much smaller."

Patients were attracted to the hospital, in part, by its reasonable rates. For example, charges for a typical operation were four days of hospital stay at $111 per day, a $450 surgical fee for a primary inguinal (the most common hernia) operation, and a $60 fee for the assistant surgeon.[6] If a general anesthetic was required, an additional fee of $75 was assessed. These were the charges that compared with total costs of $2,000 to $4,000 for operations performed elsewhere.

Round-trip fares for travel to Toronto from various major cities on the North American continent ranged from roughly $200 to $600.

In addition to providing free services to the clergy and to parents of hospitalized children, the hospital also provided annual checkups to its alumni, free of charge. Many of them occurred at the time of the annual reunion. The most recent reunion, featuring dinner and a floor show, was held at a first-class hotel in downtown Toronto and was attended by 1,400 former patients, many of them from outside Canada.

The reunion was scheduled to coincide with the mid-January decline in activity at the hospital, when an average of only 145 operations per week were performed. This was comparable to a similar lull in late summer and contrasted with the peak of activity in September, when as many as 165 operations per week might be performed.

It was thought that patients from outside Canada were discouraged from coming to Toronto in midwinter by often misleading weather reports. Vacations interfered with plans in late summer. For many of the same reasons, the hospital closed for two weeks late in December each year. This allowed time for major maintenance work to be performed. Throughout the year, no operations were scheduled for Saturdays or Sundays, although patients whose operations were scheduled late in the week remained in the hospital over the weekend.

PROBLEMS AND PLANS

When asked about major questions confronting the management of the hospital, Dr. Shouldice cited a desire to seek ways of increasing the hos-

---

[5] The latter figure included the bonus pool for doctors.
[6] At the time this case was written, a Canadian dollar was worth about 80 percent of an American dollar.

pital's capacity while at the same time maintaining control over the quality of the service delivered, the future role of government in the operations of the hospital, the use of the Shouldice name by potential competitors, and the selection of the next chief surgeon.

As Dr. Shouldice put it:

I'm a doctor first and an entrepreneur second. For example, we could refuse permission to other doctors who want to visit the hospital. They may copy our technique and misapply it or misinform their patients about the use of it. This results in failure, and we are concerned that the technique will be

---

EXHIBIT 3 **Shouldice Hospital Annual Patient Reunion, January 15, 1983**

Direction: For each question, please place a check mark as it applies to you.

1. Sex   Male _41_ 95.34%
          Female _2_ 4.65%

2. Age   20 or less ___
          21–40 _4_ 9.30%
          41–60 _17_ 39.54%
          61 or more _22_ 51.16%

3. Nationality

    Directions: Please place a check mark in nation you represent and please write in your province, state or country where it applies.

    Canada _38_ Province 88.37%
    America _5_ State 11.63%
    Europe ___ Country _____
    Other ___ _____

4. Education level

    Elementary _5_ 11.63%
    High School _18_ 41.86%
    College _13_ 30.23%
    Graduate work _7_ 16.28%

5. Occupation _____

6. Have you been overnight in a hospital other than Shouldice before your operation?
    Yes _31_
    No _12_

7. What brought Shouldice Hospital to your attention?

    Friend _23_ Doctor _9_ Relative _7_ Article ___ Other _4_
          53.49%   20.93%   16.28%   (Please explain) 9.30 %

8. Did you have a single _25_ or double _18_ hernia operation?
                        58.14%   41.86%

9. Is this your first Annual Reunion? Yes _20_ No _23_   (2-5 reunions -11 47.83%
                                           46.51%   53.49%   (6-10 reunions - 5 21.73%
    If no, how many reunions have you attended? ___   11-20 reunions - 4 17.39%
                                                          21-36 reunions - 3 13.05%

10. Do you feel that Shouldice Hospital cared for you as a person?

     Most definitely _37_ Definitely _6_ Very little ___ Not at all ___
                   86.05%   13.95%

(continues)

EXHIBIT 3   Shouldice Hospital Annual Patient Reunion, January 15, 1983 (continued)

11.   What impressed you the most about your stay at Shouldice? Please check one answer for each of the following.

A.   Fees charged for operation and hospital stay
Very Important _10_   Important _3_   Somewhat Important _6_   Not Important _24_

B.   Operation Procedure
Very Important _33_   Important _9_   Somewhat Important _1_   Not Important ____
76.74%   20.93%   2.33%

C.   Physician's Care
Very Important _31_   Important _12_   Somewhat Important _—_   Not Important _—_
72.10%   27.90%

D.   Nursing Care
Very Important _28_   Important _14_   Somewhat Important _1_   Not Important ____
65.12%   32.56%   2.33%

E.   Food Service
Very Important _23_   Important _11_   Somewhat Important _7_   Not Important _2_
53.48%   25.59%   16.28%   4.65%

F.   Shortness of Hospital Stay
Very Important _17_   Important _15_   Somewhat Important _8_   Not Important _3_
39.53%   34.88%   18.60%   6.98%

G.   Exercise; Recreational Activities
Very Important _17_   Important _14_   Somewhat Important _12_   Not Important _—_
39.53%   32.56%   27.91%

H.   Friendships with Patients
Very Important _25_   Important _10_   Somewhat Important _5_   Not Important _3_
58.15%   23.25%   11.63%   6.98%

I.   "Shouldice Hospital hardly seemed like a hospital at all."
Very Important _25_   Important _13_   Somewhat Important _5_   Not Important ____
58.14%   30.23%   11.63%

12.   In a few words, give the MAIN REASON why you returned for this annual reunion.

blamed for the recurrences. But we're doctors, and it is our obligation to help other surgeons learn. On the other hand, it's quite clear that others are trying to emulate us. Look at this ad. [The advertisement is shown in Exhibit 4.]

This makes me believe that we should add to our capacity, either here or elsewhere. Here, for example, we could go to Saturday operations and increase our capacity by 20 percent or, with an investment of perhaps $2 million and permission from the provincial

EXHIBIT 4   **Advertisement by a Shouldice Competitor**

government, we could add another floor of rooms to the hospital, expand our number of beds by 50 percent, and schedule the operating rooms more heavily.

On the other hand, with government regulation being what it is, do we want to invest more money in Toronto? Or should we establish another hospital with similar design outside Canada? I have under consideration a couple of sites in the United States where private hospital operations are more common. Then, too, there is the possibility that we could diversify at other locations into other specialties offering similar opportunities such as eye surgery, varicose veins, or hemorrhoids.

For now, I have my hands full thinking about the selection of someone to succeed Dr. Obney when he retires. He's 65, you know. And for good reason, he's resisted changing certain successful procedures that I think we could improve on. We had quite a

time changing the schedule for the administration of Demerol to patients to increase their comfort level during the operation. Dr. Obney has opposed a Saturday operating program on the premise that he won't be here and won't be able to maintain proper control.

Alan O'Dell added his own concerns:

How should we be marketing our services? Right now, we don't. We're even afraid to send out this new brochure we've put together for fear it will generate too much demand. We know that both patients and doctors believe in what we do. Our records show that just under 1 percent of our patients are medical doctors, a significantly high percentage. How should we capitalize on that? And should we try to control the misuse of the hospital's name by physicians who say they use our techniques but don't achieve good results? We know it's going on, because we get letters from patients of other doctors claiming that our method didn't work.

On the other hand, I'm concerned about this talk of Saturday operations. We are already getting good utilization of this facility. And if we expand further, it will be very difficult to maintain the same kind of working relationships and attitudes. Already there are rumors floating around among the staff about it. And the staff is not pleased.

We still have some improvements to make in our systems. With more extensive computerization, for example, we could improve our admitting procedures.

The matter of Saturday operations had been a topic of conversation among the doctors as well. Four of the older doctors were opposed to it. While most of the younger doctors were indifferent or supportive, at least two who had been at the hospital for some time were particularly concerned about the possibility that the issue would drive a wedge between the two groups. As one put it, "I'd hate to see the practice split over the issue."

Internal Strategy of Organizational Design

Internal strategy relates to the deployment and administration of mutually consistent governance mechanisms, formal and informal structures, and various systems that are designed to create the alignment required to achieve competitive advantage. When we speak and write about organization we use the term as a verb not a noun because we want to underscore the complexity and dynamic nature of PSFs as systems. We have attempted to illustrate through this module's six cases how to create a professional services firm that leverages the two key forms of capital: human and financial. We have emphasized the importance of partnerships in building these firms and we have noted how those partnerships are driven and organized around certain governing principles.

This seven-session module focuses on the second quadrant of internal strategy and opens with the observation that, whereas in product firms owners, managers, and employees tend to be different groups of people, in professional service firms these groups tend to overlap (Figure 1). This overlap demands careful attention to organizational governance, structure, and systems since they simultaneously impact on all three key resource providers. Only through alignment of its systems, structure, and governance can a PSF sustain its competitive advantage.

This note was prepared by Professor Thomas DeLong, Professor Ashish Nanda, Dean's Research Fellow Scot Landry, and Ying Liu (MBA 2001).

FIGURE 1

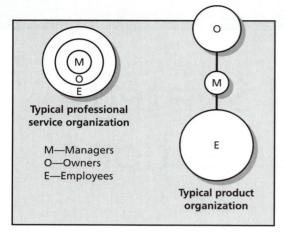

Typical professional
service organization

M—Managers
O—Owners
E—Employees

Typical product
organization

We emphasize throughout this module that the way in which PSFs organize themselves to leverage strategic capabilities is imperative in achieving high performance. This is consistent with our belief that effective PSFs must balance the four quadrants, placing emphasis on one quadrant, both quadrants, one side, or all of the quadrants, depending on the pressures and demands facing the firm. Yet we know through the focus on Diamond Technologies, Morgan Stanley Dean Witter Private Client Services, and the other cases that the governance decisions, coupled with the systems and structures created to operationalize the values of the firm, are critical for the success of PSFs.

Most important, the business model must follow the values that motivate and drive the leaders of the firm. We know that it is imperative to create compensation, succession, promotion, benefit, and evaluation systems that are linked and connected by the values and behaviors of the professionals. These internal strategies must also be linked to a firm's external strategy (Figure 2).

PROFITABILITY AND INCENTIVES

We will learn in this module that three levers drive PSF profit-per-partner: leverage, productivity, and margin. David Maister, in *Managing Professional Service Firms,* developed a model that illustrates these levers (Figure 3).

FIGURE 2

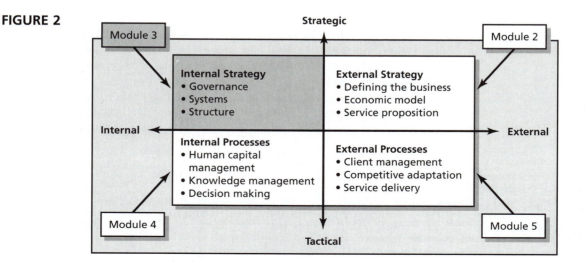

FIGURE 3

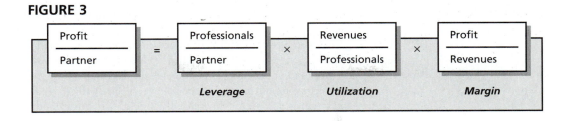

$$\frac{Profit}{Partner} = \frac{Professionals}{Partner} \times \frac{Revenues}{Professionals} \times \frac{Profit}{Revenues}$$

Leverage   *Utilization*   *Margin*

We will also discuss how the governance decisions regarding (1) how broadly to share ownership, and (2) whether to be public or private greatly affect a PSFs ability to recruit and retain talent (Figure 4). Privately held firms with broad shareholding motivate junior employees to try to make partner, at which level the financial rewards are substantial. On the other hand, privately held firms that prefer not to share ownership broadly need to attract employees with a different incentive equation. These firms often have retention issues, as there is no "brass ring" at the end of a period of intense work at the junior levels of a firm.

Firms that plan to go public that share stock (or options) broadly with employees create huge incentives for the employees to stay. However, post-IPO employee motivation to remain at this firm (after their stock vests) is lower. Also, unless the stock price is expected to appreciate rapidly, it is often much harder post-IPO to recruit new employees to join the firm, as is the desire of recruits to join the firm. On the other hand, firms that plan to go public that prefer not to share stock broadly often find that employees often act to build up personal skills rather than firm-specific skills. Employees will not act like owners.

FIGURE 4

	Financial Model	
Broad Shareholdings	**Brass Ring** • McKinsey • BCG • Top law firms	**Windfall** • Diamond • AGENCY.COM
Narrow Shareholdings	**Great Base Comp** • Family firms • Woodland (if it hired others)	**Fun Startup** • Eggrock
	Desire Private Ownership	**Desire Public Ownership**

MORGAN STANLEY DEAN WITTER PRIVATE CLIENT SERVICES

By discussing the challenge of postmerger integration, the Morgan Stanley Dean Witter Private Client Services (MSDW PCS) case illustrates the links between internal cohesion and market success (or challenges). It highlights how market innovation and entrepreneurship must concentrate on aligning firm organization, governance, and systems. If a system is out of alignment, firm governance and external performance is influenced dramatically. The more speed-to-market is valued, the more important internal alignment is in impacting the marketplace of professional services.

After the merger of the investment banking and retail powerhouses, Morgan Stanley and Dean Witter executives confronted the immediate issue of integration. Robert Sculthorpe, recently selected to merge the Private Client Services area with the vast retail distribution channel of Dean Witter, had to assess the correct market segmentation for each group of professionals. He had to analyze the prospecting system interface of Morgan Stanley with the lead management process of Dean Witter. He had to worry about the sales force synergies and how clients would be impacted by his given alternatives. He had to consider organizational positioning and the structure of the groups both functionally and geographically. He needed to confront the fact that the recruiting, retention, and training systems were different for both groups. He had to figure out the technology and operations that supported the two processes. Finally, he needed to confront

FIGURE 5

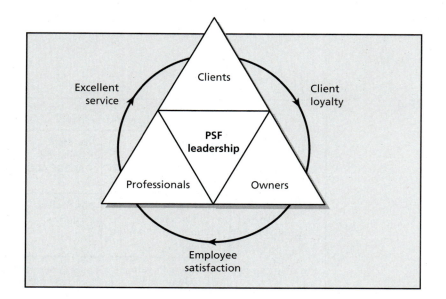

the branding challenges that faced MSDW PCS in the future in order to leverage the brand assets in the joined firm to make the merger work.

Our discussion focuses on the characteristics of the PSF economic pyramid and the need to have symmetry between client, professional, and firm (Figure 5). We highlight how leaders must try and understand how a merger would impact all stakeholders and how the interests of stakeholders become highlighted through the process of attempting a merger. We focus on the importance of how defining a target client creates internal strategic decisions that influence the whole organizational context and system. We also underscore the importance of viewing internal structures and systems strategically. Most important, we see the struggle organizations have in attempting to define and articulate who "owns" the client and then finding ways to operationalize this definition in ways that leverage the firm's strengths.

DIAMOND IN THE ROUGH

The Diamond in the Rough case bridges the second and third modules, focusing on the vision of Mel Bergstein, a mid-career entrepreneur and founder of Diamond Technology Partners (DTP). It explores the benefits and risks of pursuing Bergstein's chosen approach of focusing first on organization building and only later on market opportunities. In a similar way to the Woodland Partners case, Bergstein created a firm from scratch with a specific focus on the importance of confronting the internal challenges before addressing both external challenges and opportunities. Bergstein is an experienced mid-career professional who wanted to leverage the learning he gained as an observer and participant in a number of PSFs. He sought to create a new organization that embodied the values he always thought were lacking in his previous organizational experiences.

From an external strategic point of view, DTP was created to fill a consulting niche—a firm that bridges the gap between information technology consulting and strategy consulting. Thus, he created the world of digital strategy consulting. However, DTP's external market opportunities were the lag variable. Bergstein knew if he created a firm that professionals would love to work in, that clients would flock to his firm once he built his team. Bergstein focused on internal processes and systems for the first two years.

Bergstein chose the internal approach for two reasons. First, he wanted to build the organization around the principles he believes must be followed in order to thrive long term. Second, he did not want to be categorized and stereotyped by competitors, clients, and prospective professionals as being solely either a strategy consulting firm or an IT consulting firm. Bergstein shows remarkable patience, waiting for his firm to slowly evolve over time and allowing its strategic vision to take hold in this new consulting channel.

It is also important to note that Bergstein did create guiding principles that focused on the firm's external world (client focus). These principles became DTP's espoused theory for how to serve clients. Bergstein's emphasis on internal issues was intended to build alignment and bring DTP's theory-in-use (i.e., actual practice) to be consistent with this espoused theory.

The Diamond in the Rough case addresses the hypothesis that there are organizing principles that drive those organizations that achieve high performance and exceed client expectations. However, those principles are based on ensuring that the internal processes of the firm (1) function at a consistent and high level, (2) build on sound foundations, (3) maintain a strong connection between people and processes, and (4) have economics that ensure a sustainable value proposition.

THE GOLDMAN SACHS IPO

The Goldman Sachs IPO decision process allows us to study the comparative benefits of a private versus public ownership structure and how different incentives influence the two governance mechanisms. More important, the case also illustrates (better than any other case in the book) the links between three markets: product, labor, and capital markets. We highlight the link between capital markets and organizational structure through Goldman's effort of becoming a public company. We explore the advantages of remaining a private entity and the ramifications of such a move in light of the competition. Through their own experiences, readers can reflect on the nature of mergers and how they influence individual actors on many levels.

We also delve into a study of the nature of partnership structures and how we define that structure regardless of firm size. We explore whether there is a limit to how big a true partnership can be based on simple additive principles. Just how unique is a partnership if there are 500 partners? With a partnership this large, how does the firm's governance and structure influence the individual professional each day in producing work? Does the allure of becoming a partner lose its appeal when it is no longer exclusive—that is, does the "brass ring" incentive get diminished? Goldman was able to learn from its competitor Morgan Stanley, which went public more than 10 years prior and continued to deal with postmerger residue in the early 1990s. How can Goldman learn and not repeat those mistakes? How does a firm become a corporation and yet act like a partnership?

FAMILY FEUD: ANDERSEN VERSUS ANDERSEN

The Family Feud: Andersen versus Andersen case allows us to explore the internal tensions that can occur as a firm broadens its scope of PSF activities. The internal conflict within Andersen Worldwide between the accounting and consulting units had been going on for years, only to erupt in the mid-1990s when the consulting revenues and profits became larger than those of the accounting unit. When the consultants expected a corresponding shift in organizational control, the accounting partners rebuffed them. Could anything have prevented this split?

An important element of the division between the units is the cultural division. This raises an important question: How should a multidisciplinary PSF define its culture? Is it feasible to have a one-culture firm when members of the units have such different backgrounds, career prospects, and goals? Or should the parent organization allow strong cultures within each of the professional subunits? What are the benefits and drawbacks of each approach? If the latter is allowed, how can the parent organization maintain control and unity over the subunits?

We also see in this case how decisions around partnership, governance, and structure influence the outcome of organizational identity. Clearly, Judge Gamba has heard compelling arguments by both Arthur Andersen and Andersen Consulting. However, both organizations found themselves backed into corners as a result of not understanding how and in what ways multidisciplinary practices can eliminate wedges between core businesses.

All PSFs fear that strong professionals will create sub-units that may eventually break away and begin their own firms. PSFs must create partnerships and practices that support individual entrepreneurship and yet create a culture that has common norms. The challenges of managing globally come into play as we wrestle with how to create organizations that support the individual but also build commitments that transcend organizational boundaries and geographic borders.

THE SAGA OF PRINCE JEFRI AND KPMG

The Prince Jefri case gives us the opportunity to view the challenges inherent in organizations that have multidisciplinary practices. We see through the struggles of KPMG a picture into the future of what many experts predict will face PSFs that branch out and expand their business. The process of managing conflicts of interest within its multidisciplinary firm was at the core of how KPMG conducted its business on an everyday level.

This case allows us to study the critical concept of "Chinese walls," which are part of nearly every large PSF. Are Chinese Walls enough to protect clients from risk of sensitive information getting into the wrong hands. What are the benefits and limitations of Chinese Walls? Were KPMG's Chinese walls enough to protect Prince Jefri's interests?

PSFs are colliding more than ever internally as professions are encroaching on each other's space. Large PSFs, when unimpeded by government regulation, seem to want to assume greater competence in more and more arenas of technical expertise. While there are many benefits for PSFs to take this approach, competition within the firm's organizational boundaries can create the possibility for organizational disequilibria (as in the Family Feud case). Each firm through its strategic decision-making process must decide on how broadly or narrowly to define its divisional boundaries. These divisional definitions often impact the way the firm defines its purposes and functions. Firms also begin to confront ethical considerations as lines between operating units become murkier.

More than any other case in the book, the Prince Jefri case allows us to see the competition between many professional disciplines within organizational systems. Other than national governments, who will determine the set of rules firms will adhere to while integrating accounting, consulting, law, and investment firms under one roof? Should there be restrictions on how firms define themselves and how they provide service to their clients? Does the client define for PSFs what business(es) firms should be in? If clients truly want one-stop shopping, is it anticompetitive for governments or other organizations to not allow it? Or is the role of governing agencies to help protect clients from conflicts of interest?

INTERNATIONAL PROFIT ASSOCIATES

The International Profit Associates (IPA) case introduces the 7-S model for organizational alignment in a PSF,[1] which echoes with the observation that interactions among internal systems, such as the compensation system, the recruiting and training system, and the work environment, drive the success of a PSF. Revolving around the strategy of making profits while serving small business clients, IPA designed a nonhierarchical structure with a direct reporting system, measurement-linked internal systems (compensation, recruiting, and training systems), and a fluid staffing system.

The IPA case also explores the performance measurement systems in motivating professionals in a unique mass-market-oriented PSF. IPA used a micromanagement style of accountability. The work environment favors stars, and professionals self-select to stay with or leave IPA. Is this the best way to motivate employees? Are there nonmonetary rewards IPA could have used?

This case allows readers to challenge the sustainability of a business model, such as IPA's. The IPA model created high turnover among employees and offered little incentives to get repeat businesses. Why didn't IPA worry about high turnover? Will employees working under such a stressful environment burn out? Are repeat businesses important for IPA's business model? Should IPA change their client mix? Can IPA replicate its success at its high growth rate? What challenges will rapid growth bring in?

SUMMARY

High performance is the end goal in PSFs. Leveraging financial and human capital in ways that are strategic and aligned with organizational purpose is key to success. The way in which PSFs govern and structure themselves is crucial in achieving excellence. The systems we use to support structure assist the organization to achieve alignment with purpose. Through the creation of a firm or a new office, through a merger, through the process of going public, and through exter-

[1] The description of the 7-S model was presented in R.H. Waterman, T.J. Peters, and J.R. Phillips, "Structure Is Not Organization," *Business Horizons,* 1980.

nal and internal competition, we have touched upon how and why we need to focus on this quadrant. It becomes the glue that connects the strategies with the processes and people that we cover in Module Four.

The only way for a PSF to achieve its desired outcome by helping organizations reduce risk and leverage capabilities is to have leaders who know that they cannot deliver on promises made to clients unless their internal systems and structures have internal consistency. There must be common themes and principles that form the skeleton of the systems and structures. Internal consistency will be more crucial to PSFs as they are required to comfort their clients in dealing with ever-increasing risk, uncertainty, and global challenges.

We illustrate six organizations at different organizational stages that must confront turbulence and velocity as they serve their clients. After all, PSFs were created in the beginning to serve clients in pain. PSFs must deal with their own internal pain through insightful governance decisions along the organizational journey. Organizational structure and systems must receive ongoing attention throughout the journey. They must be in alignment with not only governance processes but with the concepts described in the second module centered on purpose and the future. Module Four will highlight the role processes and people play in the dynamic world of PSFs.

QUESTIONS ARISING FROM THE CASES IN THIS MODULE

These are some of the many questions that were raised in our study of the internal organizational strategy of PSFs:

- How should PSFs separate the roles that professionals play as owners, managers, and employees?

- How should PSFs focus on external pressures simultaneously with internal pressures?

- What impact does a firm's governance and structure have on the way it serves clients?

- How do PSFs find capable professionals with both marketable expertise and an interest in focusing on internal strategic issues?

- How can PSF leaders be confident that greater internal alignment will attract clients? Should client organizations care about what happens within the provider's organization as long as the product is delivered?

- How can PSF leaders create working environments where professionals are more loyal to the firm than their clients? What systems can be created that will ensure employee loyalty and longevity to the firm?

- How can PSF leaders develop professionals that grow and develop yet remain committed to the firm?

- How can PSFs structure client relationships so that the primary relationship clients have is to the firm and not to the professional that serves them?

- How quickly should PSFs integrate the structure of merged or acquired units to optimize performance?

- Is it ethical for a PSF's current partners to reap the full market value of the firms' worth for themselves in an IPO when the many generations of partners that helped build up the equity cashed out at book value?

- How do a firm's utilization, margin, and leverage impact a PSF's profits? How do these different profitability levers affect professional career paths?

- How does a firm's financial model impact the incentives and motivation of its professionals to remain at the firm?

- How do incentives differ for employees in public and private PSFs? In firms that broadly share ownership versus ones that narrowly share ownership?

- What are the benefits and limitations of Chinese walls? Do Chinese walls within large PSFs sufficiently protect clients against conflict of interest? What role should regulatory and governmental agencies have in this debate?

- From a client's perspective, what are the pros and cons of multidisciplinary PSFs? From a junior professional's perspective?

- What professional norms should multidisciplinary firms be required to adhere to? How should norms of the different professions be integrated in a large firm?

- Should a PSF integrate the cultures of its different professional subunits or let each subunit develop its own culture?

- How should a PSF determine control and compensation among its different professional subunits?

- How can a PSF align its strategy, structure, systems, staffing, skills, style, and shared values?

- How can a PSF determine whether its business model is sustainable? How important is internal alignment?

- Before a PSF expands overseas, how important is it to know what the firm can copy from its existing practices and what will be developed locally?

- How can a PSF manage changes or develop new initiatives under capital and resource constraints?

Morgan Stanley Dean Witter Private Client Services

Almost a year had passed since the 1997 merger of retail giant Dean Witter (DW) and bulge-bracket investment bank Morgan Stanley (MS). The combination had stunned Wall Street and prompted predictions of grand failure in the attempt to integrate the cultures of two vastly different entities. One headline at the time of the merger was indicative of the consensus attitude: "Upscale Morgan Stanley and downscale Dean Witter have radically different cultures: The Four Seasons meets Burger King."[1] Robert B. Sculthorpe, director of Private Client Services (PCS), sat at his desk and reread the announcement from Phil Purcell, CEO, and John Mack, president, dated February 19, 1998: In an effort to create a single, global brand, the use of the Morgan Stanley Dean Witter (MSDW) name would be used throughout the firm's individual, institutional, and proprietary asset management businesses.

For the DW retail salesforce, this meant that the Morgan Stanley Dean Witter name would appear outside their offices and on their business cards. In prospecting for new clients, the new name gave the former Dean Witter brokers greater credibility with wealthier prospects and clients. The Dean Witter brokers also hoped to gain access to more of the services available to Morgan Stanley PCS investment representatives, including firm-sourced referrals, proprietary investment products, high-end services such as restricted stock sales and asset allocation, and senior-level management focus. In

the minds of the Morgan Stanley PCS brokers, however, the proposal risked a dilution of the brand equity of the Morgan Stanley name that had opened so many doors to high net worth (HNW) investors in the past. Instead of being one of 260 elite professionals worldwide who were "MS investment representatives," they were suddenly, in name, one of over 10,000 "MSDW brokers."

Sculthorpe, formerly director of Dean Witter's Institutional Equity Division, with responsibilities for Dean Witter's sales, trading, and research businesses, was appointed as director of Morgan Stanley's Private Client Services division in January 1998. Prior to the merger, PCS reported jointly to Morgan Stanley's Institutional Equity (IED) and Asset Management (MSAM) divisions. As part of the subsequent reorganization of businesses after the merger, PCS was now under the Dean Witter Securities division umbrella. Sculthorpe's mandate was to run the department under its new reporting lines, expand the HNW business, and integrate some of the overlapping functions between the PCS and DW salesforces.

Upon assuming his new responsibilities, Sculthorpe spent several weeks visiting with PCS sales teams in New York and in the 10 PCS branch offices worldwide. His initial inclination was to continue to keep PCS separate and distinct from DW, reflecting their different business models, organizational structures, hiring sources, client bases, cultures, and services. Sculthorpe was pleased that

David M. Darst (MBA '71), Ann Kelsey Rusher (MBA '00), and Research Associate Catherine Conneely prepared this case under the supervision of Professor Thomas DeLong as the basis for class discussion rather than to illustrate either effective or ineffective handling of an administrative situation.

[1] Leah N. Spiro, "Class Meet Mass on Wall Street," *Business Week,* February 17, 1997.

senior management was addressing the branding of Morgan Stanley Dean Witter's full-service brokerage capabilities, but he wondered what exactly the name change meant to the brokers and clients of Morgan Stanley PCS and DW. The firm was still operating under two separate broker-dealer licenses and there had been no satisfactory resolution to the dilemma facing the leaders of the retail securities division of MSDW: where did Morgan Stanley PCS and its high net worth focus fit into the retail/investment banking giant? Should Morgan Stanley PCS be merged with the 10,000 account executives of DW? Feedback from PCS professionals indicated that they believed their position as an elite group of financial advisors for the ultra-wealthy would be weakened by their association with the DW account executives. Would the highly compensated MS PCS brokers stay in an integrated brokerage unit? Client retention could also be a problem if the two salesforces were merged in a manner inconsistent with the branding of either.

Sculthorpe realized that he needed to develop a solution that would improve the business model, service level, and scalability of the PCS business, possibly by using tools and strategies developed by the Dean Witter organization. At the same time, he had committed to senior MSDW management to grow the PCS salesforce to compete globally with the traditional HNW-focused offerings of several major competitors in the investing services business. These competitors included (i) the bulge-bracket investment banks such as Goldman Sachs, J.P. Morgan, Merrill Lynch, and Salomon Smith Barney; (ii) trust companies like U.S. Trust, Northern Trust, Mellon Bank, and Bessemer Trust; and (iii) the largest Swiss banks, such as UBS, Credit Suisse First Boston, Julius Baer, and Pictet & Cie; (iv) financial consultants such as Cambridge Associates and Frank Russell; (v) family office organizations such as TAG and the Family Office Exchange; and (vi) investment management boutiques. Lehman Brothers and DLJ Se-

curities had also built up competitive PCS initiatives. With several key PCS investment professionals in various stages of considering whether to leave for competitors, he knew that he must act quickly and decisively.

GENERAL BACKGROUND

The financial services industry encompassed several diverse lines of business, including investment banking, institutional sales, trading, and research, and retail brokerage. As a result of the favorable economic environment throughout a significant portion of the 1980s and 1990s, major participants in the investment banking industry experienced a period of unprecedented prosperity. In contrast, stock prices of firms catering to mainstream individual investors were not as highly valued and did not produce the same returns. Average return on equity (ROE) for full-line investment banks ranged from 50 percent in 1981 to about 20 percent in the 1990s, due in part to overcapacity in the investment banking business. On the other hand, as individual investors contributed in greater numbers to equity mutual funds through their 401(k) plans and other retirement vehicles, investing over $235 billion in 1996, up from $22 billion in 1990, the average ROE for retail brokerage firms rose steadily to 20 percent by 1997.[2] With these increasing returns on equity and the newfound attractiveness of the individual investor, investment banks re-evaluated the retail distribution business. In 1997 the investment banks Morgan Stanley and J.P. Morgan each had a pretax return on equity of approximately 22.0 percent and 13.4 percent, respectively. On the other hand, Merrill Lynch, which had built a strong institutional presence to match its existing retail strengths, generated a pretax return on equity of 26.8 percent in 1997. It became evident that pure investment banks faced inevitable consolidation, and the once-shunned retail firms began to look more attractive.

---

[2] Floyd Norris, "A Deal Reaffirms the Strength of the Individual Investor," *New York Times,* February 7, 1997.

Changes in technology and financial innovation had also brought retail brokerages to the forefront of financial services. With reduced transaction costs, investments could be packaged and sold efficiently to a very broad base of individual investing clients. Decreased processing costs, the standardization of financial products, national branding, and technology-assisted distribution offered major profit opportunities to firms that could effectively penetrate the broad retail marketplace. The increasing penetration of touch-tone telephone-based, on-line, and Internet-based securities brokerage in the late 1990s reinforced downward pressure on pricing and margins.

Economic and financial deregulation also added to the expansion in financial services in the 1990s. In March 1997, the Federal Reserve further reduced the scope of the Glass-Steagall Act, allowing greater integration between commercial and investment banks. This trend was evidenced by commercial banks' purchases of investment banking firms. Firms in the financial services industry began to see the benefits of providing a single service platform for clients, offering many services, from securities brokerage and asset management, to credit cards and mortgages, to investment banking advice.

FINANCIAL SERVICES INDUSTRY BACKGROUND AND ENVIRONMENT

The February 5, 1997, merger between Morgan Stanley and Dean Witter, Discover & Co. was part of a wave of international mergers in the financial services industry. One prominent merger in 1989, Deutsche Bank's purchase of the London-based investment firm, Morgan Grenfell, creating Deutsche Morgan Grenfell, sparked further securities industry consolidation throughout the 1990s. The merger of Merrill Lynch & Co. and UK broker Smith New Court took place in 1995 as part of

Merrill Lynch's widely publicized globalization initiative, and was reinforced in 1997 by Merrill's $4.1 billion purchase of another London firm, Mercury Asset Management.

By 1997, it had become clear that to compete in the global financial arena, securities firms and banks would need to offer a wider range of services and have a larger geographical reach. A new wave of mergers began: (i) Swiss Bank Corp. (SBC Warburg) acquired the New York investment firm, Dillon Read & Co. in 1997 for $600 million. [SBC itself bought out Union Bank of Switzerland in early 1998 for $20 billion]; (ii) BankAmerica Corp., the nation's third-largest bank, bought Robertson Stephens & Co., an investment firm, in June 1997 for $540 million; (iii) Bankers Trust took over Alex. Brown, the Baltimore investment bank, in 1997 for $2.8 billion; (iv) NationsBank, a North Carolina–based bank with $290 billion in assets, paid $1.2 billion for the California-based investment bank and regional brokerage firm, Montgomery Securities [When NationsBank and BankAmerica merged, creating some degree of overlap between each firm's newly acquired securities affiliate, Montgomery Securities was retained and Robertson Stephens was sold in 1998 to Bank Boston for $1.0 billion]; and (v) Fleet Financial Group, the eleventh-largest bank in the United States, announced in September 1997 that it was buying the 117 offices of the discount brokerage firm Quick & Reilly for $1.6 billion in stock. (Exhibit 1 is a list of selected financial industry consolidation in 1997.)

RUMORS OF OTHER IMPENDING MERGERS

If you believe consolidation is inevitable, it makes sense to pick your partner.

Dick Fisher, chairman of Morgan Stanley & Co. Incorporated[3]

---

[3] Spiro.

EXHIBIT 1 Selected Financial Industry Consolidation in 1997

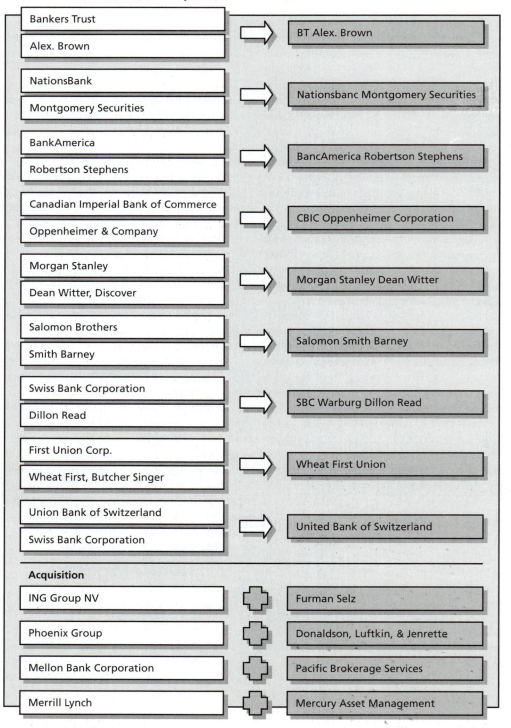

Bankers Trust / Alex. Brown	→	BT Alex. Brown
NationsBank / Montgomery Securities	→	Nationsbanc Montgomery Securities
BankAmerica / Robertson Stephens	→	BancAmerica Robertson Stephens
Canadian Imperial Bank of Commerce / Oppenheimer & Company	→	CBIC Oppenheimer Corporation
Morgan Stanley / Dean Witter, Discover	→	Morgan Stanley Dean Witter
Salomon Brothers / Smith Barney	→	Salomon Smith Barney
Swiss Bank Corporation / Dillon Read	→	SBC Warburg Dillon Read
First Union Corp. / Wheat First, Butcher Singer	→	Wheat First Union
Union Bank of Switzerland / Swiss Bank Corporation	→	United Bank of Switzerland

Acquisition

ING Group NV	+	Furman Selz
Phoenix Group	+	Donaldson, Luftkin, & Jenrette
Mellon Bank Corporation	+	Pacific Brokerage Services
Merrill Lynch	+	Mercury Asset Management

Source: Morgan Stanley Dean Witter.

With Morgan Stanley merging with Dean Witter, rumors spread of other potential merger combinations. Analysts, investors, and employees began to look at who was left and what other combinations made sense. One rumor became reality in October 1997, when Travelers Group purchased the investment banking firm Salomon Inc. in a $9 billion all-stock swap, creating one of the largest securities and investment banking firms in the world. Salomon was merged into Travelers' subsidiary Smith Barney Holdings to create Salomon Smith Barney Holdings Inc.

Among the perpetual *marriage partners* of Wall Street, Lehman Brothers had long been ticketed as a potential acquisition target. With a $3.8 billion market capitalization in 1997, its size and fixed-income focus made it difficult to integrate for a prospective partner or purchaser. PaineWebber, a retail brokerage which had acquired Kidder, Peabody & Company from General Electric Capital Corporation in 1994, was perpetually on the short list for takeovers and had even been a rumored target for Morgan Stanley just prior to its Dean Witter merger announcement. While acquiring PaineWebber would be expensive, its large number of brokers would add necessary size and distribution strength to likely partners. Hambrecht & Quist, a San Francisco investment bank specializing in high-technology companies, was also the target in takeover talks with Merrill Lynch, which were later called off due to changing market valuations.

Two even larger potential *takeover candidates* or *merger partners* were the investment banks Goldman Sachs and Merrill Lynch. Morgan Stanley had traditionally considered Goldman Sachs and Merrill Lynch its primary competitors. However, Morgan Stanley's merger with Dean Witter launched it into a smaller subset of its bulge-bracket peer group, with size, revenue streams, client profile, and services more resembling Merrill Lynch than any other securities firm. This put pressure on the private partnership of Goldman Sachs to grow as aggressively as its publicly held peers on Wall Street.

Repeatedly rumored *acquirers* in the financial services industry worldwide included AIG, a New York–based global insurer and underwriter; Citicorp (which announced its then-valued $81 billion merger with Travelers Group in April 1998); GE Capital; Deutsche Bank; and Fidelity Investments.

MORGAN STANLEY BACKGROUND AND CULTURE

Morgan Stanley & Co. was established on September 16, 1935, by several young partners of J.P. Morgan & Co., of New York, and Drexel & Co., of Philadelphia, after the Banking Act of 1933, the Glass-Steagall Act, forced commercial banks to split their lending and securities underwriting businesses.[4] Morgan Stanley was named for two of the seven officers that made up its founding group, Henry Sturgis Morgan, grandson of J. Pierpont Morgan, and Harold Stanley, its president.[5]

From the storied banking house of J.P. Morgan, Morgan Stanley derived not only its initial capitalization of $6.6 million, but also a gilt-edged client list and a culture of exclusivity.[6] In its first year, the firm lead-managed over $1 billion in public offerings and private placements, commanding a 24 percent market share. From the start, Morgan Stanley focused on building enduring relationships with blue-chip corporate clients, doing, in J.P. Morgan's words, "only first-class business in a first-class way." J.P. Morgan's persona and philosophy were essential elements in the development of Morgan Stanley's culture, and continued to define the firm in part late into the 1990s.

Within a short time, Morgan Stanley became the world's premier underwriter of corporate securities, "so powerful that it could and did demand

[4] *Morgan Stanley: The First Fifty Years,* published privately in 1985 by Morgan Stanley & Co. Incorporated.
[5] Morgan Stanley website homepage: www.ms.com.
[6] Harvard Business School case no. 897-082.

that it be sole lead-manager before it would underwrite a deal."[7] The firm neither traded nor distributed securities at the retail level, believing that these activities were better left to other firms, whose underwriting activities were directed in Morgan Stanley–led syndicates. By the late 1960s, a complacent Morgan Stanley began to see increased competition from firms like Salomon Brothers and Goldman Sachs, which had concentrated on building strong institutional sales, trading, operations, and research capabilities.[8]

In 1970, Chairman Robert Baldwin engineered a major restructuring, converting Morgan Stanley from a partnership to a corporation. Top-level employees changed from being partners to managing directors. At the time, Baldwin was quoted as saying, "As we look to the future, it is clear that change will be constant and that financial organizations must adapt or perish." Morgan Stanley applied this philosophy in making many of its strategic decisions over the next 28 years, focusing on long-term goals and investing in its franchise even during periods of market volatility.[9]

For Morgan Stanley, the 1980s witnessed (i) increasing international expansion driven from its regional headquarters in London and Tokyo; (ii) the expansion of its institutional asset management arm, Morgan Stanley Asset Management; (iii) the founding of its Fixed Income division and Institutional Equities division in 1983; (iv) successful investing in several principal investments in the textiles and first product industries; and perhaps most significantly, (v) transformation to public ownership through an initial public offering of 20 percent of Morgan Stanley's equity on September 16, 1986. Total employment grew from 1,700 in 1980 to 4,300 in 1990, with year-end 1990 capital of $1.0 billion.

Initially, with the 1996 Van Kampen acquisition, and later, with the 1997 Dean Witter merger, Morgan Stanley's senior management made a clear strategic choice to move into the retail realm in the 1990s, realizing the profound advantages that a powerful brand and a strong retail distribution network would hold for underwriters in the future. Investment banks that had their own distribution capabilities would be positioned to place new issues of securities with a wide variety of investors diversified as to type, geographical location, and asset size, a capability that many corporate clients had begun to demand from their lead underwriters. In addition, it was anticipated that the steady income stream from the sales and management of retail mutual funds and credit cards would aid Morgan Stanley in a market downturn.

Despite the Van Kampen experience and the potential synergies of the Morgan Stanley Dean Witter combination, on January 9, 1997, when Morgan Stanley and Dean Witter Discover announced their $10 billion "merger of equals," the fate of the Morgan Stanley Private Client Services group was most unclear.

DEAN WITTER BACKGROUND AND CULTURE

We serve more than three million individual investors throughout the country. Our customers benefit from the close attention and advice of our nationwide network of professional account executives. These account executives are the heart of our business. They remain in close contact with customers, carefully manage their assets, and create new customer relationships. Our greatest strength is our ability to serve traditional clients through our professional account executives.

Philip J. Purcell, chairman and CEO[10]

---

[7] *Morgan Stanley: The First Fifty Years.*
[8] Ibid.
[9] Ibid.
[10] Dean Witter marketing materials.

Dean Witter, a securities brokerage firm with a nationwide network of small investors, catered to typically middle-class investors described as "Middle America personified." DW's close to four million individual investors bought equities, fixed income securities, mutual funds, insurance products, and variable annuities from a network of brokers. Over 39 million individuals also held DW's Discover credit card, launched in 1986. The DW motto, "We measure success one investor at a time," was part of a culture that had helped the company become the third-largest sales organization in domestic securities. Almost 10,000 account executives (AEs) served more than 3.9 million clients, with products and services ranging from retirement planning to internal and external money management. In January 1997, Dean Witter acquired Lombard Brokerage, Inc., an on-line equities brokerage company, and renamed it Discover Brokerage Direct. Coincidentally, Morgan Stanley's investment bankers had advised DW on this purchase. Dean Witter opened a net total of 33 new branch offices in the 1994–1996 period, and had over $280 billion in assets under management by year-end 1997.[11]

The culture at DW was built on economies of scale, a highly disciplined approach to all elements of the investment process, tight financial and compliance controls, and a well-organized system of branch offices reporting to its New York headquarters through seven regions.

Dean Witter's approach to recruiting and training account executives differed substantially from the PCS graduate school–oriented and professional lateral recruitment practices of bulge-bracket firms. DW new account executive recruiting took place via career nights, through newspaper advertisements and articles, and through referrals. Experienced brokers from other firms were recruited and hired laterally by the DW Regional and Branch Managers. Dean Witter, like other retail firms, often had to compensate lateral hires for the deferred reward packages they left behind at their former employers. As a result, less than 20 percent of Dean Witter account executives were hired laterally from other retail firms.

Dean Witter's salesforce focused on selling in-house products such as internally managed mutual funds. According to the *Wall Street Journal,* most retail-oriented firms sold approximately 50 percent internally managed mutual funds and 50 percent externally managed mutual funds, whereas at DW, its in-house InterCapital funds made up 75 percent of mutual fund sales. Past complaints by investors and certain DW brokers about the narrow range of product offerings and the relative performance of many InterCapital mutual funds would be rectified with the Morgan Stanley merger, as Dean Witter AEs gained access to Van Kampen, MS Asset Management, and Miller Anderson & Sherrerd funds, and MSDW underwritings.

With 10,000 account executives, Dean Witter ranked behind Merrill Lynch and Salomon Smith Barney in salesforce size. Furthermore, with productivity of $293,000 per AE in annual commissions and fees, DW ranked fifth among nationally oriented firms, as shown below:[12]

Retail Broker Productivity (as of June 1997)	
Firm	Annual Broker Productivity
Merrill Lynch	$440,000
PaineWebber	429,000
Smith Barney	375,000
Prudential Securities	331,000
Dean Witter	293,000
A.G. Edwards	257,000

Source: Company Reports, SIA Survey.

[11] Erima Karim, Carol Dean, and Yang Wai Wai, "Merging Market Muscle," *IFR Review of the Year,* December 20, 1997.
[12] Anita Ragavan and Patrick McGeehan, "Brokerage Giant Created by Dean Witter Merger," *The Wall Street Journal,* June 25, 1997.

DW was considered to be the fastest-growing U.S. brokerage firm, adding 500 new AEs in 1996 and close to 1,000 each in 1997 and 1998. DW operated as a profit center, relying on financial tools and workstation-based software to increase productivity among its brokers. This centralized platform offered substantial opportunity for leveraging more sophisticated investment products and research through the DW salesforce.

DEAN WITTER INVESTMENT CONSULTING SERVICES

Dean Witter's Investment Consulting Services department (ICS) was started in 1989. ICS concentrated on providing professional asset management services not typically available to retail investors. In 1997, Dean Witter Investment Consulting Services ("wrap") fees represented $114.7 million, or 11.4 percent of total asset management and administration fees.

At the end of 1997, there were 300 ICS senior consultants out of a 10,000-person DW salesforce who had graduated from a special program, developed in conjunction with the Wharton School, on asset allocation and portfolio theory. ICS professionals, drawn from the ranks of the top-producing retail salespeople at Dean Witter, collected assets for DW that were then placed with several different outside managers in separately managed accounts custodied with and traded through DW. In addition to the Wharton program, ICS senior consultants had successfully completed the Investment Manager Certification Association (CIMA)

certification process. A number of ICS senior consultants were also pursuing the CFA designation. As a result of this training, ICS consultants were well versed in asset allocation software and techniques, including specialized software packages created by Ibbotson Associates and Frontier Analytics.

At Morgan Stanley, PCS management had traditionally encouraged PCS IRs to gather HNW assets to be managed by MS Asset Management and PCS on a discretionary basis in the form of pooled vehicles and/or separate accounts. Conversely, Dean Witter ICS consultants gathered assets to be managed by external managers and were not allowed to exercise any discretionary authority. Through DW workstation-based technology, in one meeting, ICS senior consultants could interview a client, complete a personalized Investment Policy Statement, select external managers, and print client account opening documents. The same process, through Morgan Stanley Private Client Services for a HNW individual, was more highly tailored and typically took a week to complete.

Dean Witter had always maintained a Chinese wall between internal and external investment management programs, offering asset allocation programs that incorporated either (i) all externally managed separate accounts; or (ii) all Dean Witter InterCapital separate accounts, but not both. In fact, Dean Witter ICS and Morgan Stanley PCS offered similar products, with the primary differences in the degree of the customization and sophistication, based on the investor's asset size and investment knowledge:

Asset Allocation Program Type	Morgan Stanley PCS Program Name		Dean Witter ICS Program Name	
	MSAM/MAS	**External**	**InterCapital**	**External**
Asset allocation; mutual fund management, custody, and reporting; wrap fee program	Total Funds Management ($1MM min)	Not broadly available through 1997	Portfolio Architect	Fund Solution ($200,000 min)
Asset allocation; separate account management, custody, and reporting; wrap fee program	Wealth Management Services ($10MM min)		Investment Management Services	Access
Asset allocation; separate account management, custody, and reporting; priced á la carte	Wealth Management Services ($10MM min)		Custom	Vision

In February 1998, at the annual ICS Senior Consultants Conference in Palm Springs, CA, the ICS consultants expressed enthusiasm about using the Morgan Stanley Dean Witter name in their activity to prospect for and obtain high net worth clients. When discussing the HNW market and potential synergies between PCS investment representatives and ICS senior consultants, there was only a low level of understanding by both parties about each other's respective functions and capabilities. The ICS consultants were particularly interested in incorporating PCS resources into their own sales practices, but at the same time, they did not want to pay for access to the PCS product support groups through any form of revenue-sharing arrangement.

MORGAN STANLEY/DEAN WITTER MERGER

We're trying to capitalize on these great franchises by putting them together. We're not underestimating the degree of difficulty. We're not going to mess up these franchises. We're going to run them separately in very large measure.

It's not an easy decision to try a merger of equals.

Philip J. Purcell, chairman and CEO[13]

Talks between Morgan Stanley and Dean Witter started in 1996. Morgan Stanley's senior management was already intimately familiar with Dean Witter's management team, having engineered the spin-off of DW from Sears and the subsequent DW IPO on March 1, 1993. The idea of combining Morgan Stanley's investment banking business with Dean Witter's retail distribution capability was extremely attractive to both parties. It would dramatically increase market share and revenues. It also meant that, as the world's largest securities firm, large corporate clients would want to include Morgan Stanley Dean Witter not only in such roles as M&A advisor in their corporate strategic plans, but also as an underwriter of their equity and debt securities. The investment community appeared to agree, with Morgan Stanley's stock rising $7.875

[13] Peter Truell, "A Cross-Cultural Match in the Financial World," *New York Times,* February 8, 1997.

on February 5, 1997, the day the merger was announced.

Morgan Stanley and Dean Witter together created a global franchise with strong origination and distribution skills and a healthy balance between institutional and individual investor revenue sources. As of February 1997, the new company had a market capitalization of $21 billion and over 45,000 employees in 409 offices in 22 countries worldwide.

The merger had several other benefits: (i) it increased Morgan Stanley's total assets under management to $270 billion, and offered broader access to individual mutual fund investors, with MSDW owner of the fourth-largest mutual fund business in the United States; (ii) the more predictable, less volatile fee-based income from asset management and credit cards helped offset the greater variability in income typical of Morgan Stanley's securities businesses; (iii) the retail distribution network increased the firm's ability to win underwriting mandates; (iv) the use of the Morgan Stanley name gave Dean Witter's brokerage force additional credibility with wealthy investors; (v) the combined platform offered DW brokers a broader, more diversified product base; (vi) it enhanced MSDW's ability to attract and retain retail brokers; and (vii) it allowed Morgan Stanley and Dean Witter to each choose their partner rather than be acquired by a large U.S. or foreign commercial bank.

Among other factors, the union with Morgan Stanley and greater diversity of products enabled Dean Witter account executives to open 700,000 new accounts in 1997 (compared to 615,000 in 1996).[14] In turn, Dean Witter's 10,000 account executives and favorable securities markets significantly increased the firm's funds under management, to $338 billion at the end of November. One example of the powerful force of the MSDW combination was the offering of MSDW's research product, *The Competitive Edge,* as a Unit Trust. Within 18 days, the DW salesforce raised $1.3 billion in assets for the Morgan Stanley Dean Witter Competitive Edge Best Ideas Portfolio from its initial launch in January 1998.

Despite the obvious synergies between the two businesses, the management of MSDW had to contend with major cultural barriers between the two firms, particularly between the 10,000-person DW salesforce and the 260 Morgan Stanley PCS investment representatives. Many of the PCS IRs were highly educated, highly paid, and accustomed to advising on the private investment activities of the world's corporate and government elite. Dean Witter's salesforce was dispersed throughout the United States in cities and towns of all sizes. A significant percentage did not have graduate degrees, their average annual earnings were more modest by investment banking standards, their clients were mass-market consumers, and their products were mainly stocks, bonds, and mutual funds.

PRIVATE CLIENT SERVICES BACKGROUND AND CULTURE

MS's 250+ private client brokers—who deal only with the very rich—are not pleased that [10,000] brokers can now say they are from MSDW. Rivals say there have been several departures of disgruntled brokers, but MS says only one senior person has left.[15]

Morgan Stanley Private Client Services was established in 1977 as a financial advisory group to provide comprehensive wealth management services to individuals, families, closely held corporations, and foundations controlling significant

[14] Interview with John Mack, *Le Monde,* February 6, 1998.
[15] Ibid.

private pools of investment capital. These services included access to Morgan Stanley's institutional research, conventional and specialized investment instruments, asset management products, and custody, financing, and reporting. In 1997, PCS operated from a total of 11 branch offices worldwide and employed 622 people, including 261 Investment Representatives. The primary mission of PCS was to initiate and manage key generation-spanning relationships with high net worth individuals and family groups.

PCS clients ranged from individuals with substantial inherited wealth to entrepreneurs and business owners who had recently experienced a liquidity event, such as their company being sold or going public. The proceeds from these change-of-circumstance situations ranged from $5 million to $1 billion or more. Under the PCS business development model, the investor met with a representative of PCS Management and/or of the Client Advisory Group to discuss the assets that they had received or were about to receive as a result of a transaction which may or may not have been Morgan Stanley–advised. PCS Management then appointed a PCS client relationship team to act as the HNW investor's point of access to the services of the firm. The PCS investment representative, much like a Corporate Finance coverage officer, then employed resources as needed from various product groups to meet the needs of the HNW investor.

Ongoing client relationship management was typically comprised of professional teams of three to four investment professionals that provided business development, asset allocation, money management expertise, and traditional securities brokerage services, including equity, fixed income, restricted stock, and hedging and monetization activity.

On January 22, 1998, Phil Purcell and John Mack announced that, in an effort to advance and leverage Morgan Stanley Dean Witter's global positioning, Jeff Salzman, the then head of Private Client Services, would report to them directly, with responsibility for developing MSDW's individual client business throughout Europe, Asia,

and Latin America. To replace him, Purcell and Mack appointed a Dean Witter management veteran, Robert B. Sculthorpe, executive vice president and director of the Dean Witter Equity division, as director of Private Client Services. (Exhibit 2 shows these organizational changes.)

ISSUES FACING BOB SCULTHORPE

As he reflected on the challenges and opportunities in his new assignment, Sculthorpe recalled the series of meetings between PCS and DW management that had taken place during the final months of 1997. Aside from the normal topics that had been discussed in these sessions, relating to each firm's accounting systems, internal transfer pricing, profitability measurement, technology and client reporting platform, and geographical organizational structure, Sculthorpe sensed a more philosophical gap that needed to be addressed.

In short, many Morgan Stanley PCS managers and professionals viewed Dean Witter as having a different business approach and culture. The Dean Witter professionals viewed the Morgan Stanley PCS organization and strategy as not that different from their own.

Sculthorpe took a legal pad out of his drawer and listed several of the questions he wanted to think about and discuss with other members of senior management in the Morgan Stanley and Dean Witter organizations:

Market Segmentation   Should there be any size-based distinction between the prospects that can be called on by members of the PCS and DW salesforces? What is the definition of a high net worth client? How should the current PCS prospecting system interface with the lead management process at DW? (Exhibits 3 and 4 show the core PCS products, services, and market segments.)

PCS and DW Salesforce Synergies   What means are available to ensure delivery of high-touch, cus-

EXHIBIT 2 PCS Organizational Structure

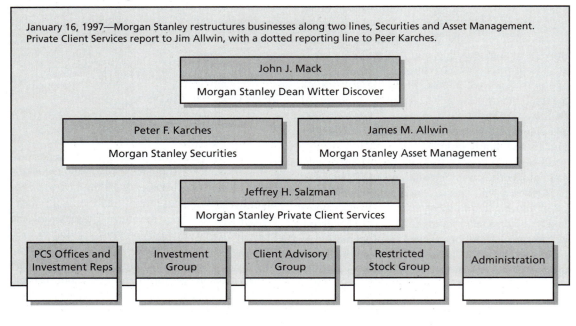

January 16, 1997—Morgan Stanley restructures businesses along two lines, Securities and Asset Management. Private Client Services report to Jim Allwin, with a dotted reporting line to Peer Karches.

John J. Mack
Morgan Stanley Dean Witter Discover

Peter F. Karches	James M. Allwin
Morgan Stanley Securities	Morgan Stanley Asset Management

Jeffrey H. Salzman
Morgan Stanley Private Client Services

PCS Offices and Investment Reps	Investment Group	Client Advisory Group	Restricted Stock Group	Administration

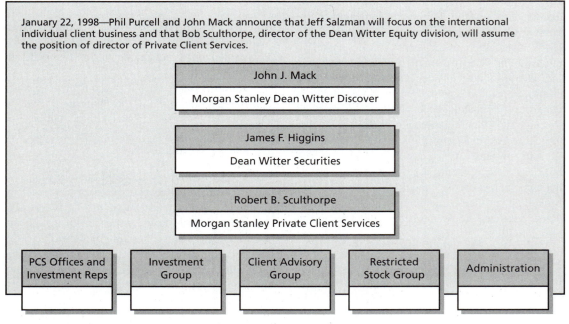

January 22, 1998—Phil Purcell and John Mack announce that Jeff Salzman will focus on the international individual client business and that Bob Sculthorpe, director of the Dean Witter Equity division, will assume the position of director of Private Client Services.

John J. Mack
Morgan Stanley Dean Witter Discover

James F. Higgins
Dean Witter Securities

Robert B. Sculthorpe
Morgan Stanley Private Client Services

PCS Offices and Investment Reps	Investment Group	Client Advisory Group	Restricted Stock Group	Administration

Source: Morgan Stanley Dean Witter.

EXHIBIT 3 Increasing Salesforce Effectiveness

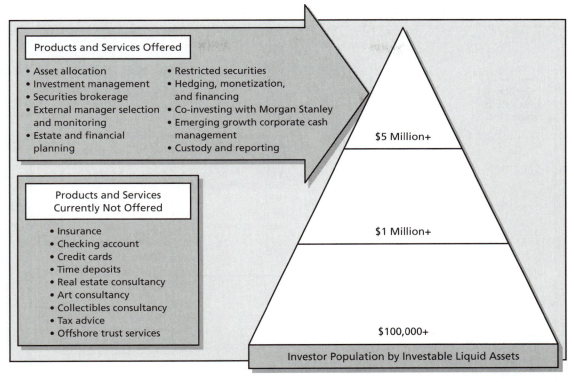

Source: Morgan Stanley Dean Witter.

tomized service to the wealthiest family groups? What PCS products and services might be primary candidates to be leveraged over the broader DW client base? Should there be any form of revenue-sharing for referrals introduced from PCS to DW and vice versa? (Exhibits 5 and 6 address strategies for increasing salesforce effectiveness and maximizing firm, client, and investment representative relationships.)

Organizational Positioning Should the PCS branch system be integrated into the DW regional reporting structure? What are the key differences in PCS branch managers' job responsibilities, performance evaluation criteria, and compensation methodology compared with DW office managers? Will regional integrity of PCS sales coverage be mandated going forward (for instance, will San Francisco–based PCS professionals be allowed to prospect in Texas?)

Recruiting, Compensation, and Training What entry and first two-year compensation levels should be offered to PCS new hires from graduate business schools? Should separate recruiting channels, compensation systems, and career opportunities be maintained to attract bright entrepreneurially oriented MBAs? How essential are MBAs in the competitive marketplace to offer comprehensive, sophisticated services to high net

EXHIBIT 4 Market Segmentation

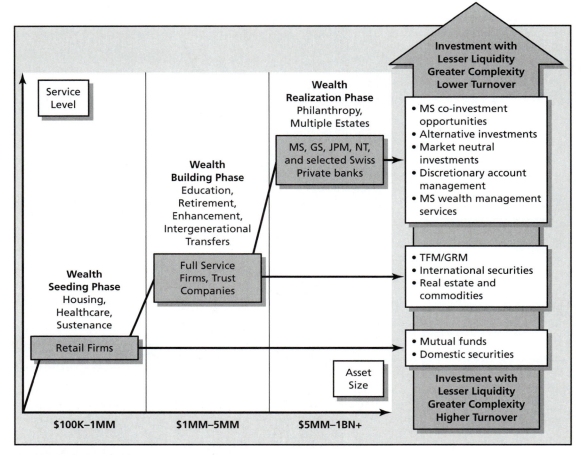

Source: Morgan Stanley Dean Witter.

worth investors with $50 million or more of investible assets?

Operations and Technology Should the PCS Operations and IT groups, or their DW counterparts, support the PCS portfolio reporting system and client technology platform? Is it feasible and cost-effective to deliver the MS client statements and trade confirms on the DW technology platform?

Branding Should PCS maintain its distinct identity within the MSDW organization? How real, valuable, and long-lasting are the differences between the DW and PCS cultures, target market segments, revenue sources, and client acquisition strategies?

As Sculthorpe reflected, he was not sure where to start but he knew his leadership team and the many professionals he managed were looking for answers.

EXHIBIT 5

PCS Core Products, Services, and Market Segments

Source: Morgan Stanley Dean Witter.

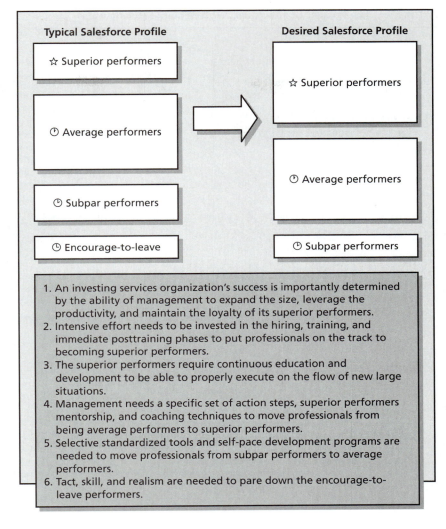

Typical Salesforce Profile	Desired Salesforce Profile
☆ Superior performers	☆ Superior performers
🕐 Average performers	🕐 Average performers
🕐 Subpar performers	🕐 Subpar performers
🕐 Encourage-to-leave	

1. An investing services organization's success is importantly determined by the ability of management to expand the size, leverage the productivity, and maintain the loyalty of its superior performers.
2. Intensive effort needs to be invested in the hiring, training, and immediate posttraining phases to put professionals on the track to becoming superior performers.
3. The superior performers require continuous education and development to be able to properly execute on the flow of new large situations.
4. Management needs a specific set of action steps, superior performers mentorship, and coaching techniques to move professionals from being average performers to superior performers.
5. Selective standardized tools and self-pace development programs are needed to move professionals from subpar performers to average performers.
6. Tact, skill, and realism are needed to pare down the encourage-to-leave performers.

EXHIBIT 6   The Triangle of Firm/Client/Representative Relationships

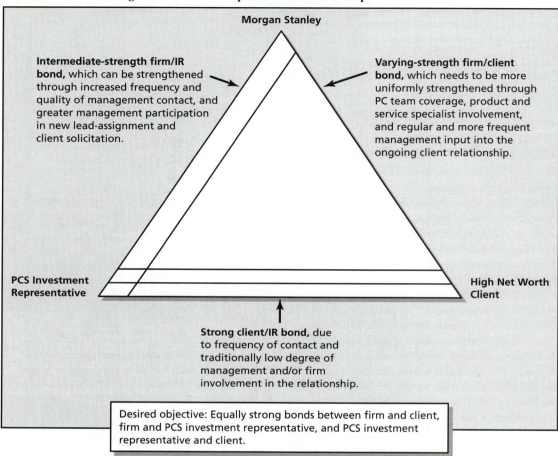

Morgan Stanley

Intermediate-strength firm/IR bond, which can be strengthened through increased frequency and quality of management contact, and greater management participation in new lead-assignment and client solicitation.

Varying-strength firm/client bond, which needs to be more uniformly strengthened through PC team coverage, product and service specialist involvement, and regular and more frequent management input into the ongoing client relationship.

PCS Investment Representative

High Net Worth Client

Strong client/IR bond, due to frequency of contact and traditionally low degree of management and/or firm involvement in the relationship.

Desired objective: Equally strong bonds between firm and client, firm and PCS investment representative, and PCS investment representative and client.

Diamond in the Rough (A)

One evening in July 1996, Mel Bergstein and Chris Moffitt sat talking, smoking, and worrying in a glass-walled office 30 stories above Lake Michigan. Bergstein was CEO of Diamond Technology Partners, a two-year-old strategy and technology consultancy, Moffitt his co-founder. Old colleagues and friends, they had doubled Diamond in each of its first two years from nothing to $12.8 million in 1994 to $26.3 in 1995. Earlier in 1996 they had planned to double again. The information technology consulting and systems integration market was huge and rapidly growing. Industry analysts estimated it at $100 billion and growing at 25 percent to 35 percent per year. The largest firms in this industry, such as Andersen Consulting, IBM, and so on, were about $1 billion to $2 billion in size and growing at the rate of the market or faster. Bergstein and Moffitt, having been part of this industry for decades, believed there was a need for an independent and objective voice that could assess the needs of a digital strategy without being biased toward trying to sell a big outsourcing or systems integration job. They estimated that this independent advice market was approximately 10 percent of the total market, or $10 billion. Furthermore, this market was growing faster and had higher margins than the total market, thus providing an enormous opportunity for Diamond.

In April at the beginning of Diamond's third fiscal year, two major clients, representing 50 percent of the prior quarter's revenues, had pulled out of deals. All of the partners had hunted up projects to cover these losses, but their heroic efforts produced only damage control. Having lost $0.7 million in the past quarter, Diamond was now operating below break-even. To add to the seriousness of the situation, a long-planned IPO was imminent; Diamond had recently offered jobs with signing bonuses of $20,000 to $30,000 each to 50 MBAs, 28 of whom had accepted; and staff and employees were expecting their standard year-end bonuses (which were budgeted between $1.5 million and $2 million). Now, all this was on hold, and tomorrow Bergstein would have to host the monthly All Hands Meeting—a gathering of the whole firm, known as an occasion for open communication and collegiality. Most of these meetings had been high-spirited events. Bergstein and Moffitt had dressed up as the Blues Brothers to kick off the first one in early 1994. Now celebration was far from their minds. The question was how to break the bad news to their talented, hardworking staff. Bergstein exhaled a big puff of smoke and stubbed out his cigarette.

MEL BERGSTEIN

Bergstein's business experience extended back to 1968, when he started in the consulting division of Arthur Andersen & Co. (now Andersen Consulting). After rising through the ranks to partner (1977–1989), managing director of worldwide technology, and member of the board (1985–1989), he also chaired the firm's Consulting

Research Associate Catherine Conneely prepared this case under the supervision of Professor Thomas DeLong as the basis for class discussion rather than to illustrate either effective or ineffective handling of an administrative situation.

Oversight Committee. Then he left Andersen to become senior vice president of Computer Sciences Corporation and made another move, in 1991, to become president, co-CEO, and a member of the board of directors of Technology Solutions Company (TSC), a publicly traded Chicago-based systems integrator. At TSC, his function was to balance the founder-CEO's creative influence. When TSC went through a period of internal strife in 1993, the board forced the founder-CEO to leave. As part of a compromise between the board and the founder's family, Bergstein also lost his job.

Bergstein commented: "One of the lessons I learned from being fired was that I never again wanted to be in a position where outsiders controlled the firm."

CHRIS MOFFITT

Chris Moffitt met Mel Bergstein at TSC, which Moffitt had helped found in 1988. When Bergstein left, Moffitt resigned in protest against the board's treatment of the CEO. Moffitt had a strong background in information systems. In 1974, he began as a systems engineer and account manager at Electronic Data Systems. Then he became director of information systems for Neiman Marcus (1981–1986), and moved to the Management Consulting Group of Arthur Young (now Ernst & Young). There he advanced to principal and, later, partner (1986–1988), before leaving to help establish TSC. He served as TSC's senior vice president until his departure in protest in 1993.

Moffitt, too, learned from the experience at TSC:

Starting TSC had shown me that I really enjoyed the thrill of establishing and running my own business. I said to Mel, "We have to write a plan together or I'm going to go start a company on my own." I was convinced [our] new company would be four times the size of anything I could do personally if I could persuade Mel to take a stake in the

foundation. With over 20 years' experience in the IT/consulting business, Mel had a name in the industry. I also thought that Mel had a clearer notion of where the market was going.

THE BUSINESS PLAN

Bergstein recollected:

After I left TSC, Chris would not stop badgering me to start a company. I was still licking my wounds and trying to decide what I wanted to do—talking to friends in the industry and listening to potential job offers at big companies and so on. Eventually I concluded that Chris was right. We could have started a company with our own money. We had enough to do it. But we concluded that we needed outside funding for several reasons. First, we did not think we could do really important work for our clients if we could not show financial stability. Second, we did not think we could attract real talent if there was very significant financial risk. Third, we did not want to do work simply to pay the payroll, as we had a very specific scope of practice and a very specific client base in mind. Lastly, we decided that sleeping at night was a good thing.

They found potential investors reluctant to provide capital for a proposed business with no concrete outline or detailed financial forecasts. Moffitt told Bergstein, "We have to have a business plan." Bergstein decided to work on one while searching for a new position. In October 1993, they both started work on what Bergstein called the "blue book."

Bergstein reported:

We put together a business plan in an empty office borrowed from our attorneys. A lot of cigarettes and a lot of late nights went into it. It seems to me that it came together at the beginning of November 1993. A lot of what we did was in reaction to our experiences at different companies. For example, we wanted to prevent any possibility of "founderitis." My son, an analyst at Morgan Stanley, helped us put together the financial models, and Chris's father, a retired editor, flew to Chicago to polish the final document. We ended up with a business plan that many folks considered one of the best they had seen. (See Exhibit 1.)

Bergstein and Moffitt agreed to call the venture Diamond Technology Partners because of the "diamond" team and partnership structures they planned to use.[1] They both wanted a particular kind of corporate culture, driven by a set of guiding principles:

- to deliver for clients the highest quality economic results achievable through the creative application of technology;

- to place clients' interests ahead of their own;

- to hold clients' confidences sacred;

- to communicate the truth to clients, even if it challenged their own positions;

- to agree to do only work that would achieve superior economic benefits for clients.

Instead of keeping ownership for themselves, they decided to require partners to put in personal funds—as Bergstein and Moffitt would—at the same price as external investors. They agreed that the firm would deploy small, multidisciplinary teams on which business strategists and technologists worked in concert. And they allowed for a steady pace of growth. (In initial discussions with investors, the founders predicted an eventual growth rate between 25 and 35 percent per annum. Growth rates were built from general expectations about the growth of the client/server and reengineering markets coupled with Bergstein's and Moffitt's judgments about the firm's capacity to absorb and assimilate new staff.)

Early in the design process they decided to plan for Diamond to go public. Bergstein explained, "We felt the wealth creation opportunity in public firms was much greater than in private firms. By going public we could attract and reward higher-quality people." By sharing equity in the new company, Bergstein ensured talented professional staff whose interests, as shareholders, would be aligned with the market.

EXHIBIT 1 Diamond Technology Partners, Financial Projections for Fiscal Years 1994–1998 ($ millions)

	1994	1995	1996	1997	1998
Net revenue	$10.7	$28.7	$43.3	$53.2	$63.8
Gross margin	0.8	10.9	18.2	22.3	26.5
Gross margin	5.6%	40.0%	42.0%	42.0%	41.5%
PBT	(3.3)	4.0	10.1	12.5	15.1
PBT margin	(30.8%)	13.9%	23.3%	23.5%	23.7%
Net income	$(3.3)	$2.4	$6.0	$7.5	$9.1
Net income margin	(30.8%)	8.4%	13.9%	14.1%	14.3%

Source: Diamond Technology Partners Business Plan, November 1993.

[1] The "Diamond approach" consisted of a team of 5 to 10 people who held the key positions in implementing the project. A partner headed up the team of 5 to 6 principals and associates, and 1 to 2 analysts, in contrast to other consulting firms which used pyramidlike team structures and kept most systems building in-house. (See Exhibit 2.)

EXHIBIT 2 "The Diamond Approach" Service Delivery Model

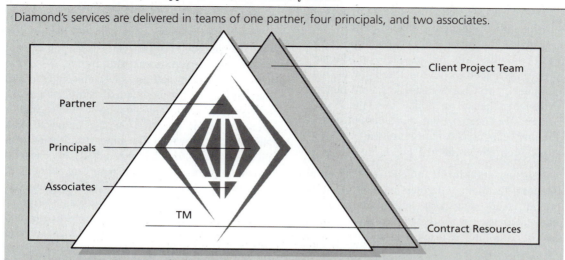

Diamond's services are delivered in teams of one partner, four principals, and two associates.

Partner
Principals
Associates
TM
Client Project Team
Contract Resources

Conventional systems implementation teams resemble a pyramid with an experienced leader plus a few capable specialists at the top, supervising a large number of relatively less experienced staff. The Diamond service model, in contrast, delivers a greater concentration of experience and greater depth of specialized skills. If a project requires general purpose programmer or analyst skills—typically the lower levels of implementation—Diamond will complement the team with lower cost contract resources to maintain the overall cost effectiveness of the solution. . . .

From *Managing Complexity Strategy, Process, Technology, and Organization.*
Contemporary Solutions for Contemporary Problems

Diamond delivers its services in small, experienced and focused teams. We build trust in our clients by demonstrating—and more importantly, by sharing—our industry, program management and technical experience. With Diamond, [staff] work closely with clients to help them set the right goals, initiate the right programs and make the appropriate investments to translate their strategy into concrete business solutions.

Active involvement by our clients helps them build the foundation for lasting organizational change. For our people, this collaborative method means we are continuously teaching our clients what we know. This, in turn, offers—in fact, demands—continual professional growth and development as we force ourselves to stay ahead of the curve.

From *Diamond: Breaking the Traditional Barriers, Experience Consulting with a Personal Focus*

Source: Company documents.

OTHER FOUNDING PARTNERS JOIN

Mike Mikolajczyk *(Mik-o-lay-chick)* met Bergstein and Moffitt at TSC. There, Mikolajczyk was senior vice president of finance and administration and CFO from 1993–1994. A Harvard MBA, he had previously worked with MCI Telecommunications Corporation as vice president of various departments. He joined Bergstein and Moffitt because of his interest in the kind of company they were building and enthusiasm about the financial projections in their business plan.

Another founding partner commented, "To me, the critical thing we did early on was to assemble a nucleus of people who shared the core principles and values of the business plan." (See Exhibit 3 for more founders' and partners' information.)

POSITIONING THE COMPANY

In discussions with other founding partners, Bergstein saw a real opportunity to fill a gap in the consulting industry by uniting information technology (IT) with business strategy. (See Exhibit 4.)

He and Moffitt estimated the domestic (U.S.) market in which Diamond would compete at $37 billion in 1993. Some forecasts for the total U.S. consulting and systems integration market suggested that it could reach $60 billion by 2000.[2] Diamond had the potential to become a player in a market with annual growth of nearly 15 percent.[3]

EXHIBIT 3   **Diamond's Founding Professionals (ages in February 1994)**

Founding Partners

- Mel Bergstein (51), formerly TSC, Andersen Consulting.
- Chris Moffitt (39), formerly TSC.
- Mike Mikolajczyk (43), formerly TSC, MCI.
- Jim McGee (40), formerly Andersen Consulting. Knowledge Architect.
- Kirk Siefkas (37), formerly TSC. Strength in program/project management, IT strategy.
- Mike Palmer (41), formerly TSC, James Martin Associates, Andersen Consulting. Strength in program management, data warehouse.
- Woody Forsythe (46), formerly TSC, CIO of Fingerhut. Strength in program management, IT management.
- Adam Gutstein (31), formerly TSC, Andersen Consulting. Strength in program management.
- Karl Bupp (31), formerly TSC, MCI. Head of internal planning.
- Bruce Quade (36), formerly Booz Allen, Andersen Consulting. Strength in reengineering, operations improvement.

Founders Who Were Later Promoted to Partner

- Alan Matsumura (36), formerly TSC, industry. Knowledge leader in data warehouse, data management.
- Mark Sieferston (34), formerly TSC, EDS. Knowledge leader in technology architecture, head of Technology group.
- Brent Lohrmann (38), formerly TSC, industry. Strength in program management, IT operations, management.

Source: Company documents.

[2] IDC Research 1996.
[3] Tucker Anthony Equity Research, April 29, 1997.

EXHIBIT 4   Diamond's Market Positioning in the Consulting Industry: Digital Strategy

(a) The Consulting Industry

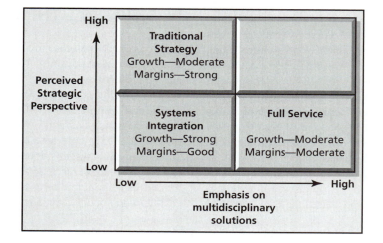

(b) Digital Strategy Market Attributes

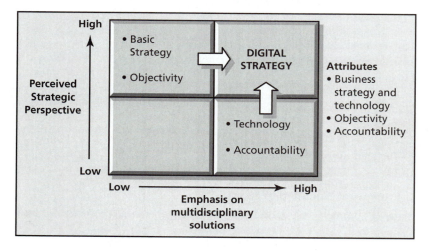

(c) Diamond's Competitive Position

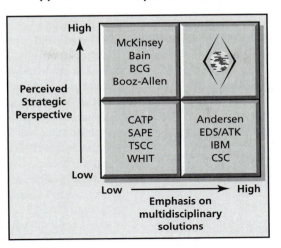

Note: CATP—Cambridge Technology Partners (Cambridge, MA); SAPE—Sapient Corporation (Cambridge, MA); TSCC—Technology Solutions, Inc. (Chicago, IL); WHIT—Whittman-Hart, Inc. (Chicago, IL).
Source: Company documents.

GETTING START-UP FUNDING

With business plan in hand, Bergstein and Moffitt began to meet with potential investors. A headhunter friend told Bergstein about a Pennsylvania-based firm that invested in high-tech start-ups and brought firms public through a rights-offering process.[4] The firm was called Safeguard Scientifics, Inc.

Bergstein remembered:

At first I was reluctant to meet the Safeguard team because one of their investments was a Massachusetts-based systems integrator, which had just completed an IPO. I thought they were going to see a conflict there and I didn't really want to waste their time or mine. When I talked to Pete Musser, the CEO of Safeguard, in early December 1993, he assured me that an industry that would eventually be worth one hundred billion dol-

lars would have room for Diamond and another firm.

Bergstein went on:

Chris and I met with the Safeguard team the following week and were invited back to the table on January 6, 1994. They offered us a term sheet over dinner that night. They had brought along Safeguard sweatshirts to give us if we signed the deal. We were very disappointed in the deal for three reasons. We thought the standstill period could be shorter for Diamond. We did not like outside investors having too much equity—the maximum we wanted to give them was 50 percent. And . . . I can't remember the third reason now.

Bergstein and Moffitt rejected Safeguard's terms but took the sweatshirts anyway. They ex-

---

[4] A rights-offering allowed holders of Safeguard Scientifics stock to acquire shares of the company going public, relative to the amount of Safeguard stock they held. The rights usually traded on NASDAQ and could be bought or sold during the offering period.

pected to fly out of Philadelphia the next day, but an ice storm hit the city overnight. Over breakfast the next morning they decided to call the Safeguard team again. They contacted the president, Don Caldwell, and arranged to meet him at the Safeguard offices.

Bergstein recounted what happened next:

> Over dinner the previous night, the Safeguard team told a story about a watchman in one of their facilities hitting a guy in the head with an ax—and the guy showing up for work two days later. We wore the Safeguard sweatshirts the CEO had given us, and, on the way to the Safeguard offices, we bought a big ax. The offices were dark because of the ice storm. Nobody was there but the president. We showed up wearing the shirts, carrying the ax, and saying, "We've come to make the deal." Then we sat down and made the deal. It wouldn't have happened if there hadn't been an ice storm.

THE START-UP (FEBRUARY–MAY, 1994)

Bergstein and Moffitt each put $250,000 into the company and started work with 11 employees, including 5 partners, in February 1994. Their first client was a former TSC client. (Bergstein observed that clients and employees initially came to Diamond because of prior business connections.) Mike Mikolajczyk, who decided to join Diamond after working as a consultant, put in his tranche early in March. Safeguard's $3 million investment in Diamond was completed on March 22, 1994. The other founding partners, 13 in all, put in their investment in May 1994. By June, there were 37 people on the payroll.[5]

Bergstein and Moffitt established a system of governance meant to see the company through the IPO and beyond.

Bergstein said:

> We sat down and wrote a governance agreement, which we now call the Partners' Operating Agreement. We had some basic rules about how we were going to run the place. One was that we, the partners, were going to manage internally as a group of partners. At the same time, as majority shareholders we wanted a clear boundary between internal operations and our responsibilities as a public entity. At TSC, we had seen the troubles that happened when that boundary wasn't clear. Our solution was the CEO proxy. All partners grant a proxy to the incumbent CEO for their shares. That gives us a single voice in the market as majority shareholders. Our internal governance processes then ensure that the CEO has the support of the partners as a group.
>
> Second, we shared the equity broadly. When the partners started coming up with money, I did not have any more cash, so Chris said to me, "Take options. You're the franchise here. We'll give you a ton of options." But we had employees coming in who had an opportunity to buy into the firm, and I was concerned about taking options. We agreed that no one in the firm would take options—everyone would buy in at the same price. If people want to be here, they must buy shares. But only a limited amount of stock could be held by any one person. We gave Safeguard 40 percent and of the remaining 60 percent, I took 6 percent, Chris took 5 percent, and Mike took 4 per-

---

[5] According to Jim McGee: "The initial shares were priced at $1.50/share. The company authorized a total of 5,000,000 shares of which Safeguard bought 2,000,000 shares for their initial $3 million investment. Bergstein, Moffitt, and Mikolajczyk each put in an initial $250,000 for the spring 1994 launch. Bergstein, in common with many other early partners, got his cash by taking a second mortgage on his house. Bergstein and the others put in additional amounts (which account for the differences in their holdings) when the initial round of financing closed in May."

cent. The employees held 45 percent of the company.

Third, the firm was organized around four committees: management, nomination, compensation, and CEO succession. The management committee is appointed at the discretion of the CEO and consists of four members. The nomination committee and compensation committee are elected by the partners and partners on these committees are limited to three-year terms. The nominating committee identifies and performs due diligence for internal or external candidates to become partners at Diamond. The compensation committee prepares the compensation plan for the organization as a whole including partner compensation. Seventy percent of the partnership must approve the plan for it to pass. If the partners vote down the plan, then the CEO succession process is triggered. In that event a new CEO would be elected and the CEO proxy transfers to the CEO-elect. The CEO thus undergoes an annual vote of confidence in his or her leadership.

As the firm operated, Bergstein and the other partners tried to create a unique culture. This goal included everything, from communication and training policies to the office layout. They offered employees attractive benefits, such as equity and widespread ownership of the company; downtime between assignments; and light workloads on weekends.

DIAMOND'S SERVICE MODEL

Bergstein and Moffitt saw other consulting firms using project teams that resembled a pyramid, with an experienced leader supervising numerous relatively inexperienced consulting associates. At Diamond, partners managed projects as well as client relationships.

Principals were responsible for helping partners complete engagements successfully. Senior principals worked on client engagements, extended client relationships to get extra work, and mentored new staff members. Associates and analysts supported teams during the client engagement. Promotion to senior principal, and then partner, went relatively fast at Diamond.

According to Bergstein:

The strength of Diamond's service model is that clients see the partners as the most senior team members and a very important part of each team. Having partners involved day-to-day, on the ground, three to five days a week adds to the quality of our results for clients. It also gives younger consultants interactive time with very senior people and opportunities to learn from them. This is important to our current capabilities and long-term health.

Diamond kept consulting teams small for practical reasons. Bergstein explained:

Part of the value of a collaboration lies in not disrupting the client. Small teams can collaborate smoothly with clients and enhance the client's knowledge base, particularly about issues of long-term economic value to the client.

Diamond's projects included an informal transfer of knowledge throughout the whole process of finding and implementing strategies. The goal was to make clients self-reliant.

Diamond's teams were interdisciplinary because Bergstein and Moffitt felt that no individual could have all the skills necessary for consulting—there is no such thing as the "renaissance consultant." There was no bias at Diamond in favor of either the business strategy or technology side of consulting. Salary rates were the same for all partners and staff at particular levels, and all projects had the same billing rates. (See Exhibit 5 for a comparison of revenues per consultant at Diamond and its main competitors.)

EXHIBIT 5

Revenues per Consultant: Diamond Technology Partners and Competitors, 1996

Source: Company documents; *Consultants News,* March 1997.

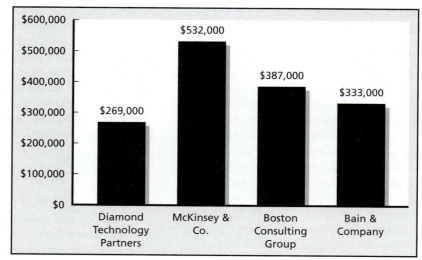

CLIENT RELATIONSHIPS

To Diamond's staff, Bergstein emphasized the great importance of staying focused on the clients' needs—even if this should mean ignoring what was best for Diamond. He also believed that the company should take on projects only if a Diamond team could genuinely add value to the client's business. If not, he considered it important to have the courage to turn down a project.

EARLY GROWTH

By June 1994, four months after going into business, Diamond had eight clients. (Seven had developed from the partners' previous business relationships.) By this time there were 37 employees. The partners put minimal effort into marketing because they did not want to risk generating demand they could not fill. Also they feared that Bergstein and Moffitt's reputations would tag Diamond as a technology firm, and they intended to be known as much more than an IT/systems integration company.

Bergstein instituted the tradition of monthly All Hands Meetings as a way for Diamond's staff to stay connected by coming in from client sites to meet and discuss issues with peers. His policy of openness with staff led to wide-ranging discussions at the meetings. Even the office layout at Diamond headquarters, in the Hancock Tower in Chicago, was designed to promote a feeling of equality. Teams, not partners, had the corner offices. All partners' offices were the same size, and all had glass walls so that private meetings could be seen, if not heard. Outside walls included as much glass as possible. Everyone walking around the office could enjoy the spectacular 30-story views of Lake Michigan.

THE INVESTMENT PHASE: YEAR TWO, 1995, TWENTY-THREE-AND-A-HALF-YEAR PLAN

Bergstein and Moffitt had seen too many companies fail after a successful IPO for the simple reason that they had not adequately prepared to go public. Late in 1994, they drew a graph to represent a 23½-year plan that included an IPO. (See Exhibit 6.) The point of the diagram was to emphasize that Diamond's goal was to create an organization that could grow sustainably for 20 years, not to do an IPO. They accompanied the graph with a short list of goals to explain what the partners were trying to accomplish over time. Their original business plan had not explicitly identified an investment stage. Bergstein and Moffitt articulated this stage to clarify priorities as Diamond entered its second year of business. They showed their graph to recruits and potential clients to underscore Diamond's long-term aspirations and perspective.

According to the plan, once the investment stage was complete, management would look for four or more quarters of good growth, with positive cash-flow, and then embark on the IPO. Early investment in human resources, training, development, and operations policies were meant to build an infrastructure that would not need constant reworking as the company grew and went public.

YEAR THREE: 1996

In April 1996, after completing two years of operation, Diamond had a staff of 138, with projects running for 17 clients. The firm's consultants were now becoming known for "digital strategy" and consulting teams whose members understood both technology and business strategy in depth (as the founders had hoped). Diamond's projects ended not only with strategy reports, but also with tangible assurance that the client had achieved beneficial results.

In order to create equality within the partnership, Bergstein and Moffitt went to great lengths to avoid dominating junior partners. For example, the first time partners were elected, a process was put in place whereby partners spoke in order of reverse seniority, with Bergstein and Moffitt speaking last, so as not to influence junior partners' decisions.

The organizational structure of Diamond had also now reached some stability. Diamond's management committee consisted of Bergstein, Moffitt, Mikolajczyk, and a fourth partner, James Spira. Each member of the management commit-

EXHIBIT 6

Diamond's 23½-Year Plan, Showing Investment Phase

Source: Company documents.

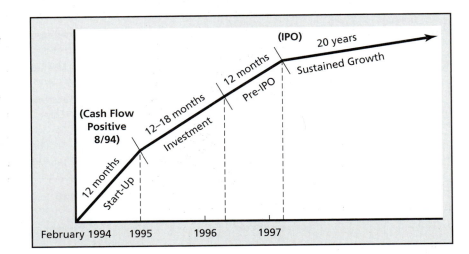

tee had specific responsibilities. Mikolajczyk, as CFO, owned the back office. Moffitt was in charge of the bulk of the organization—line consultants and clients. Bergstein spent the majority of his time externally and Spira was in charge of marketing the company. (See Exhibit 7.) This was the company the partners now felt ready to start marketing.

The consultants were organized by industry, in a series of groups vertically aligned within the organization. The partners and senior principals each belonged to one of four market- and industry-focused vertical teams: banking and finance; product-oriented businesses; services; or telecommunications and insurance. In addition, the company included staff teams—groups of 12 to 15 associates and principals, each managed by a partner. Staff teams were filled with an intentional mix of individuals from each core competency. Staff team partners managed the staffing process and employees' career development.

By now the partners had identified a further core competency—speed—to accompany technology and strategy. On the down side, in this two-year-old company, most of the staff were relatively new and not everyone knew where they fit in the industry groups or the competencies. On the positive side, Diamond's attractiveness for talented recruits increased. New employees felt encouraged to develop skills and talents in many areas. The

EXHIBIT 7 **Organizational Chart of Diamond Technology Partners**

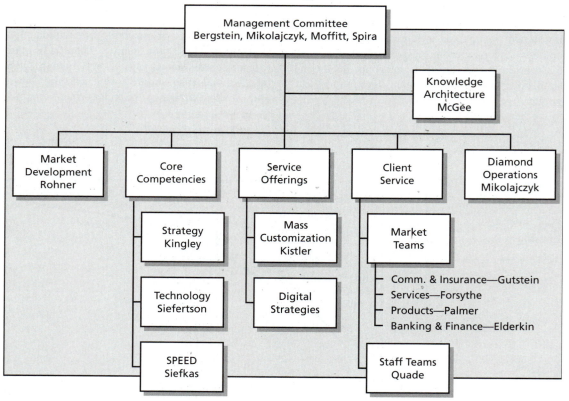

Source: Company documents.

multidisciplinary structure did not force them into rigid categories.

Diamond was now growing at more than 100 percent per annum. The partners had just developed a plan based on the assumption that the firm was ready to do over $50 million worth of business in the next 12 months. Bergstein and the partners set the plan at $50 million to achieve a critical mass for the company as quickly as possible. All were concerned about revenue concentration with a few major clients and wanted to grow to a point where no project team, or "diamond," represented more than 5 percent of revenues. (This worked out to around $100 million in revenue assuming 20 diamonds of seven professionals generating $5 million in fees each.) The company's revenues had doubled in each of the first two years; the partners were convinced that they could do it again.

By April, staff compensation plans had been decided; people were looking forward to substantial year-end bonuses. In the previous six months, Diamond had offered positions to 50 MBAs, 28 of whom expected to join the company over the summer. Diamond had also expanded physically: its Cleveland office was scheduled to open at the beginning of August.

In April 1996, the partners were pondering a number of issues. Marketing had now become a major priority. Two initiatives formed the core of the initial marketing plans. Diamond Network was designed to be "a 'virtual organization' of world-class experts that can provide clients with a broad range of perspectives during an engagement." Members of the network were granted stock options, and consulting arrangements were defined in advance. Exhibit 8 identifies the members of the Diamond Network. Diamond Exchange was planned as a forum to bring together senior executives from clients and prospective clients, the Diamond Network, and consultants from Diamond. Deliberately designed to be a small group of less than 50, the Exchange intended to focus on helping organizations cope with the changes brought on by a digital world.

The company's growth meant that many new employees were operating in a structure initially created for only 50. Bergstein worried about keeping staff feeling connected to the firm. Another issue was keeping Diamond's professionals abreast of technological advances; in this culture, knowledge and intellectual capital development were as important as training for client engagements. In addition, the long-range plan called for

EXHIBIT 8 **Members of the Diamond Network**

John Perry Barlow	Co-founder and vice chairman, Electronic Frontier Foundation
Gordon Bell	Senior researcher, Microsoft Bay Area Research Center
Leonard L. Berry	Professor of Marketing at Lowry Mays College and Graduate School of Business
Larry Downes	Consultant and author, Digital Strategies
Tim Gallwey	Author and consultant on learning
James H. Gilmore	Co-founder, Strategic Horizons LLP
Alan Kay	Disney fellow and VP of research and development, Walt Disney Imagineering
Andrew Lippman	Associate director and founding member, MIT Media Lab
B. Joseph Pine II	Founder, Strategic Horizons LLP
David P. Reed	Information architect and independent entrepreneur
John J. Sviokla	Associate professor, Harvard Business School
Richard Y. Wang	Associate professor, MIT Sloan School of Management
Marvin Zonis	Professor, International Economics, University of Chicago Graduate School of Business

Source: Company documents.

EXHIBIT 9   Balance Sheet of Diamond Technology Partners for Fiscal Years Ended March 31, 1995 and 1996 ($000s except share data)

	1995	1996
Assets		
Current Assets:		
Cash and cash equivalents	$4,690	$4,635
Cash in escrow from subscribed stock		
Accounts receiveable, net of allowance of $512, $270 and $566 as of March 31, 1995, 1996 and 1997, respectively	1,435	3,304
Prepaid expenses	320	1,180
Notes receivable from stockholder	163	226
Deferred income taxes	119	99
Total current assets	$6,727	$9,444
Computers, equipment, and training software, net	573	2,010
Other Assets:		
Deferred organization costs, net	213	161
Total Assets	$7,513	$11,615
Liabilities and Stockholders' Equity		
Current Liabilities:		
Notes payable	$150	$125
Accounts payable	557	1,155
Accrued compensation	160	1,089
Deferred compensation	622	1,452
Income taxes payable	119	83
Deferred revenue	612	
Accrued stock issuance costs	106	
Other accrued liabilities		1,143
Total current liabilities	$2,326	$5,047
Stockholders' Equity:		
Preferred stock, $1.00 par value, 2,000,000 shares authorized, no shares issued		
Class A common stock, $.001 par value, 40,000,000 shares authorized, 3,320,625 issued in 1995, 3,370,125 issued in 1996 and 4,594 issued in 1997	3	3
Class B common stock, $.001 par value, 20,000,000 shares authorized, 4,392,092 issued in 1995, 4,505,119 issued in 1996 and 4,967 issued in 1997	4	4
Class A common stock subscribed, 1,755 shares		
Additional paid-in capital	6,533	6,844
Notes receivable from sale of common stock	(91)	(257)
Retain earnings (deficit)	(1,263)	(26)
Total stockholders' equity	$5,187	$6,568
Total liabilities and stockholders' equity	$7,513	$11,615

Source: Company documents.

beginning the IPO within 12 months. (See Exhibits 9 and 10 for financial information.)

BAD NEWS IN APRIL

Two clients canceled projects in April 1996, the beginning of the first quarter of fiscal 1997. One canceled because of the acquisition of a business that eliminated the need for Diamond's services. The other canceled the business initiative for which it had retained Diamond. These two clients represented 50 percent of revenues in the January–March quarter of 1996, that is, the last quarter of the fiscal year.

Bergstein's immediate response was to ensure that all professionals had something to work on. Diamond put staff on projects for free to keep them employed. The partners went into high gear to find extra business and managed to bring in the first quarter at just over the previous quarter's revenue. Many of the partners believed they could turn things around without cutting any expendi-

tures for the year. Diamond's second quarter, however, had been one of the slowest for closing new work. The partners were running out of untapped names in their rolodexes.

Bergstein and his management committee held intense discussions as they tried to form a plan of action. The issue of hiring so many MBAs was divisive. Some partners questioned the practice of paying competitive signing bonuses to new recruits and pointed out that the total amount of these bonuses could have covered employee bonuses at year-end. Some worried about reneging on commitments. Others pointed out that the MBAs came from Kellogg, Wharton, and Chicago, so the firm could withdraw on its offers to them and recruit at new business schools the following year.

Fundamental questions were raised: How would Diamond deal with the loss of revenue in light of its espoused long-term strategy? How would Diamond grow without more contacts? Would lack of growth change the basic philoso-

EXHIBIT 10   **Statement of Operations, Fiscal Years Ended March 31, 1994, 1995, and 1996**
($000s except per share data)

	1994	1995	1996
Net Revenues	**$261**	**$12,843**	**$26,339**
Operating Expenses:			
Project personnel and related expenses	633	8,351	15,312
Professional development and recruiting	106	1,395	4,587
Marketing and sales	94	451	606
Management and administrative support	317	3,108	4,460
Total Operating Expenses	$1,150	$13,305	$24,965
Income (loss) from operations	$(889)	$(462)	$1,374
Interest income	3	136	251
Interest expense		(51)	(87)
Income (loss) before taxes	$(886)	$(377)	$1,538
Income taxes			(302)
Net Income (loss)	$(886)	$(377)	1,236
Net Income (loss) per share of common stock	(0.35)	(0.05)	0.13
Shares used in computing net (income) loss per share of common stock	2,511	8,272	9,824

Source: Company documents.

phies on which Diamond was built? Most important, would Diamond still exist in a year?

Eventually the management committee came up with two options. Either the partners would take a significant pay cut or Diamond would have to renege on its job offers to MBAs. The partners had all invested financial and sweat equity in growing Diamond to $26.3 million in revenue in two years. It would be painful to tell them their bonuses were gone. Even more galling would be announcing that the long-anticipated IPO was now on hold. Bergstein and Moffitt agonized over how to present the news to the partners and the rest of the organization. The fate of Diamond—and, ultimately, its founders' professional and economic futures—rode on what Bergstein would say at the next day's All Hands Meeting.

The Goldman Sachs IPO (A)

[Y]ou can't run a multinational global business on partnership capital.

Former Goldman Sachs partner[1]

If it ain't broke, don't fix it.

John Whitehead and John Weinberg, former co-chairmen of Goldman[2]

INTRODUCTION

In August 1998, the 188 partners of Goldman Sachs met to decide whether to sell a portion of their firm to the investing public. The IPO idea had been proposed, and rejected, six times before. Goldman was doing just fine—the first half of 1998 had brought in record profits—leading several partners to argue that the firm should remain as a private partnership. (Exhibit 1 presents a summary of recent financial data.) The firm was a major player in almost every major industry category. (For industry rankings based on various investment banking activities, see Exhibit 2.)

But others, concerned about the size and capabilities of the financial behemoths created by recent mergers among several of Goldman's rivals, argued that management would need publicly traded shares to expand and achieve global prominence via acquisitions. Was IPO the right decision for Goldman?

FIRM HERITAGE, 1869–1994[3]

M. Goldman and Sachs

In 1869, Marcus Goldman, a German immigrant, opened shop on Pine Street in lower Manhattan as a broker of promissory notes, precursors to commercial paper. By 1880, with $100,000 accumulated in capital, Goldman was turning over $30 million worth of paper. Two years later, he invited his son-in-law, Sam Sachs, to join him, and the firm's name was changed to M. Goldman and Sachs. The company's named changed again, in 1885, to Goldman Sachs & Co., and in 1896, it joined the New York Stock Exchange (NYSE). By the turn of the century, the partners' capital had grown to $2.5 million.

The relationships that grew out of the commercial paper business provided the foundation for a new line of business, underwriting. In 1906, Goldman Sachs underwrote its first public offering for the United Cigar Manufacturers. A steady stream of underwritings followed, transforming Goldman Sachs into an investment bank.

In 1928, Waddill Catchings, the leader of the firm in the late 1920s, established an investment trust, named Goldman Sachs Trading Corporation, an early version of what is now called a mutual fund. Catchings was praised for his business genius when, by October 1929, shares in the Trading Corporation were trading at $326. The following month, the share's price plunged to $1.75, taking Catchings' and Goldman's reputation with it.[4] Catchings was replaced as Goldman's chairman by Sidney Weinberg.

Doctoral student Boris Groysberg, Research Associate Sarah Matthews, Professor Ashish Nanda, and Professor Malcolm Salter prepared this case from published sources as the basis for class discussion rather than to illustrate either effective or ineffective handling of an administrative situation.

EXHIBIT 1   Goldman Sachs Group, Inc.—Annual Results ($ billions)

($ million)	1994	1995	1996	1997	1998E
Revenue:					
Advisory			$931	$1,184	$1,774
Underwriting			1,182	1,403	1,594
Investment banking			2,113	2,587	3,368
FICC			1,210	954	386
Equities			730	563	795
Principal investments			214	298	146
Principal transactions			2,154	1,825	1,327
Asset management			242	458	675
Securities services			354	487	730
Commissions			727	989	1,368
Asset management and securities services			1,323	1,934	2,773
Net interest revenue			539	1,101	1,052
Net revenue	$3,537	$4,483	6,129	7,447	8,520
Expenses:					
Compensation			2,421	3,097	3,838
Noncompensation expense			1,102	1,336	1,761
Operating expense	3,029	3,115	3,523	4,433	5,599
Pretax income before partners' compensation	508	1,368	2,606	3,014	2,921
($ billion)					
Total assets	95.3	100.0	132.6[a]	178.4	
Partners' capital	4.8	4.9	5.2[a]	6.5	
Outside capital	1.9	1.8	1.9[a]	2.1	
Return on equity	10.5	28.3	NA	46.1	

E: estimated; NA: Not available.

[a] As of May 31, 1996.

Source: Raphael Soifer and Hitami Asada, Brown Brothers Harriman & Co., May 5, 1999.

The Weinberg Era, 1930–1969

Sidney Weinberg began his Goldman career in 1907 as a janitor's assistant for $3 per week, became a partner 20 years later, and was named chairman in 1930. His ascension came at a particularly low point—the depression of the 1930s yielded little business and virtually no profits for the firm. But Weinberg had a clear vision for Goldman. He saw that the cornerstone of future profitability and reputation would lie in the firm's ability to cultivate a first-rate client list, composed of the top corporations in the United States.

Weinberg built this list by serving as Goldman's "ambassador." Sitting on the boards of more than 30 corporations, he attended an average of 250 board or corporate committee meetings per year for more than 20 years, and in so doing built lucrative business relationships for the firm. One relationship in particular would ensure Goldman's, and Weinberg's, place in the history books.

In 1947, Weinberg met Henry Ford II, CEO of Ford Motor Company (FMC), the largest company in the United States at the time. Ford wanted to take FMC public, but did not want to make this

EXHIBIT 2   Selected Industry Rankings, 1997

Category	1997 Ranking	Advisors/Managers	Total Proceeds ($ billions)	Number of Deals/Issues
M&A advisors	1	**Goldman Sachs & Co.**	$326.0	353
	2	Morgan Stanley Dean Witter	324.5	307
	3	Merrill Lynch & Co.	279.3	301
	4	Lazard Houses	201.3	178
	5	Salomon Smith Barney	195.8	302
Debt and equity underwriters	1	Merrill Lynch	$342.0	2,445
	2	**Goldman Sachs & Co.**	265.3	1,482
	3	Salomon Smith Barney	259.8	1,595
	4	Morgan Stanley Dean Witter	257.3	1,907
	5	Lehman Brothers	181.3	1,272
IPO underwriters	1	**Goldman Sachs & Co.**	29.8	64
	2	ABN AMRO	22.8	14
	3	Merrill Lynch & Co.	18.7	69
	4	Cazenove & Co.	17.6	—
	5	Morgan Stanley Dean Witter	15.0	72
Common share offering underwriters	1	**Goldman Sachs & Co.**	$67.2	154
	2	Morgan Stanley Dean Witter	59.3	171
	3	Merrill Lynch & Co.	48.4	195
	4	Warburg Dillon Read	25.8	87
	5	ABN AMRO	25.1	28

Source: Securities Data Company.

known until he had figured out the best possible way to restructure the company. Weinberg took charge of the project in 1954, and for two years worked with Ford in secret to come up with a plan. Ford's announcement, in January 1956, that $650 million of FMC stock was to be made available constituted the largest IPO to date. The deal secured Weinberg's reputation as "the best-known business man in America."[5]

The Levy Era, 1969–1976

After nearly 40 years of stewardship, Weinberg was succeeded by Gus Levy, who was selected primarily because he was Goldman's number two profit maker, topped only by Weinberg himself. Shortly before he died in 1969, Weinberg had established a six-member Management Committee composed of his peers—primarily older partners

from the banking side—that met every Monday morning from 8:00 to 9:00 A.M. Although it had been formed to oversee his strategic and budgetary decisions, the committee's scope was restricted over time by Levy, who limited the meetings to fifteen minutes.

Unlike Weinberg, who had been a conservative banker, Levy was a risk-taking trader. Upon taking charge, he instituted new measures to prepare the firm to assume greater trading risk, his area of expertise. One of his most significant initiatives, an innovative new method of buying and selling large stock holdings, termed "block trading," revolutionized the trading business.

When recession hit hard in the 1970s and one of its commercial paper clients, Penn Central Railroad, went bankrupt, Goldman was censured by the Securities and Exchange Commission for not disclosing the client's financial condition to its commercial paper customers. The railroad's default on $87 million worth of commercial paper led to Goldman being named in 45 lawsuits, subjecting its 45 partners to unlimited liability. Although Goldman settled out of court without admitting liability, the incident seriously damaged the firm's finances and tarnished its reputation.

The Two Johns, 1976–1990

When Levy died in 1976, he left no clear successor. The two front-runners, John Weinberg and John Whitehead, had both attended Harvard Business School (classes of 1950 and 1947, respectively) and made partner at Goldman in 1956. As of 1976 they had worked together for 25 years. Whitehead, slightly older and more experienced, was considered a strategist and a visionary. Weinberg, son of Sidney Weinberg and the "soul of the firm" to many, had inherited his father's knack for business development.

When Levy was on his deathbed, the two Johns, as they would later become known, met privately and decided to share Goldman's top job. When presented with the idea, the Management Committee made no objections. Interestingly, at the reading of Levy's will, it was discovered that the former head of the firm had named the two Johns the joint executors of his estate—the closest thing to a validation of their new role as co-heads of Goldman Sachs.

Weinberg and Whitehead ran the firm together over the next eight years. Among the first changes the two Johns made was to reinstate the Management Committee's former role. The committee was expanded to eight partners and in-depth discussions on strategic issues were resumed at the Monday morning meetings. While consensus was the ultimate goal in reaching a decision, the views of the two Johns carried significant weight.

Whitehead, taking charge of the firm's long-term direction, oversaw its business objectives and budget. Weinberg, continuing his father's legacy, focused on bringing in new clients and maintaining strong client relations. "I didn't think a dual chief executive was possible," acknowledged Citicorp chairman Walter Wriston, "but [the Weinberg-Whitehead partnership] ran like a clock."[6]

The two Johns rededicated themselves to Sidney Weinberg's legacy: that short-term profits never be earned at the expense of long-term relationships and that reckless risk-taking be replaced by cautious business development. The two Johns forbade Goldman from making bridge loans, buying junk bonds, and putting capital in takeovers, activities that led to the demise during the 1980s of several of Goldman's competitors including First Boston, Shearson Lehman Brothers, and Drexel. "We watch our eggs very carefully," said Weinberg, "because they are everything we have."[7]

Whitehead circulated a document that emphasized Goldman's values of teamwork, long-term client relationships, integrity, honesty, and reputation. "When Whitehead drew up a list of business principles by which the employees of the firm would abide, he came up with four more than God gave Moses to codify earthly morality," remarked *Institutional Investor* of the document. "Nowhere else on Wall Street has a firm attempted to institutionalize something as intangible as a corporate ethic."[8] These "Fourteen Commandments" came to be routinely read aloud at Goldman events and were often referenced when making judgment calls.

The Goldman Work Environment

Goldman employees were proud of the quality of the firm's talent. In hiring new employees, the firm asserted, "Although our activities are measured in billions of dollars, we select our people one by one. In a service business we know that without the best people we cannot be the best firm."[9]

"They're the tops," affirmed New York University professor of finance Ernest Bloch. "You meet them for five minutes and know that they're the smartest people you've ever met."[10] Opined Cecil of Lehman Brothers: "When people think about Goldman Sachs . . . they think about the quality of [its] people."[11]

Goldman traditionally promoted talent from within its own ranks. Lateral hires not "raised" in Goldman were viewed as corrosive to the firm's cultural foundation. Attracted by the challenges and rewards associated with working on tough and important projects, MBA graduates universally considered a position as a Goldman associate as one of the best job opportunities.[12] The exhilaration and rewards from working on interesting and consequential deals kept Goldman's employee turnover at one of the lowest on Wall Street.

Goldman employees were renowned for working long hours, even by Wall Street's exacting standards. These top-quality professionals saw the first 10 years of 14- to 18-hour days at salaries often lower than they could earn at rival publicly held firms as investment that might one day translate into "the elusive prize of a partnership" that brought with it not only the cachet of belonging to an exclusive club but also eight-figure compensation.[13] This figure came from the annual base salary, which for a partner inducted in 1995 started at $200,000, and the lucrative profit-share and interest draw (8 percent in 1995) on partners' capital investments. Even a half-percent ownership of the firm could translate into an annual income of $2 million. (Exhibit 3 lists compensation for Goldman employees as of 1999.) A significant fraction of the income was reinvested by new partners into partnership capital, making these new partners "asset-rich but relatively cash-poor" in their first few years.[14] Over the course of their careers, Goldman Sachs partners could expect to earn at least $25 million.[15]

Partners were chosen at Goldman once every two years. Weinberg remarked: "The process is so elaborate [and] excruciating . . . for everybody [that] we wouldn't want to go through it every year."[16] Only a select group was considered, and within the group, not all nominees made the final cut the first time around, or sometimes even the second time around.

A partner could recommend to the Management Committee for partnership any executive who had worked for Goldman for 8 to 10 years. Although other partners could submit letters of recommendation on a nominee's behalf, "overt campaigning" was perceived to be "the best way to ruin one's chances."[17] The partners then thoroughly reviewed each nominee at one or more formal meetings, and a vote was taken.[a] Although some believed that connections played a significant role, management insisted that the process was "honest" and that merit outweighed connections in the final decision.

The firm had historically based partner compensation on seniority, not performance. Tying employees' compensation directly to personally generated profitability risked contradicting Goldman's eighth commandment: "While individual

EXHIBIT 3 **Compensation of Goldman Sachs Employees**

Analyst:	First year: $45,000 (base salary), $15,000 to $25,000 (bonus)
Associate:	First year: $75,000 (base salary), $25,000 (signing bonus), $40,000 to $50,000 (end of year bonus)
Vice president:	$400,000 to $700,000 (salary and bonus)
Partners:	$200,000 (base salary), a stake in the company that is raised every two years, and returns on partners' stakes average $3 to $6 million annually.

Source: Vault Reports, Inc., 1999.

[a] Initially, all partners reviewed each nominee, but as the firm (and, hence, number of partners) grew, this responsibility was transferred to the partners named to the Partnership Committee.

creativity is always encouraged, we have found that team effort often produces the best results. We have no room for those who put their personal interests ahead of the interests of the firm and its clients."[18] In the words of one senior Goldman banker, "We're like Penn State. Simple uniforms, no insignia, no names, just a number."[19] Management believed that individual performance-based compensation encouraged "plunging," incurring excessive risk for marginal increases in returns, while discouraging teamwork and loyalty. One bond trader, who would write "I did this trade" on each of her transactions, was reminded by Whitehead, "At Goldman Sachs, we say 'we.' We never say 'I.'"[20]

Merger and Acquisition's Rapid Growth

In contrast to Goldman's other departments, which experienced measured success, the mergers and acquisitions (M&A) department enjoyed tremendous growth. Begun in 1976 as a small subsection of the investment banking department, its initial revenues of $600,000 jumped to $90 million in 1980, and nearly quadrupled to $350 million in 1989.

Outsiders attributed the department's success largely to its refusing to assist clients in pursuing hostile deals. Prior to the 1970s, in a world in which deals were sealed with handshakes, hostile bids were all but unheard of and considered almost immoral. But in 1974, Morgan Stanley broke ranks with other investment banks by representing International Nickel (INCO) when it raided Electric Storage Battery (ESB). ESB turned to Goldman for help. Goldman's white knight strategy (a friendly bidder brought in by the target company) succeeded; the entrance of United Aircraft as a potential buyer drove ESB's stock price up and its shareholders earned a 100 percent premium.

Even as other investment banks began to represent hostile bidders, Goldman stuck firm to its policy of not representing hostile bids. In the environment of mistrust among CEOs toward investment bankers, Goldman came to be viewed as a trustworthy partner. The result, according to John Thornton, head of M&A in Goldman's London office in the mid-1980s, was that "while [other] banks had about a one in six chance of getting work by the bidder, we were the only one who fought for the other side."[21] The firm was able to corner the market on representing firms targeted by hostile suitors.

The First IPO Debate

In 1986, after the firm had negotiated with outside investors, a $500 million investment that had grown its capital by one-third, an idea surfaced within Goldman that the firm go public. Donaldson, Lufkin & Jenrette was one of the first to start this trend among Goldman's competitors when it went public in the early 1970s. Bear Stearns and Morgan Stanley followed suit in 1985 and 1986, respectively.

The Goldman partnership commissioned a study (called "Pegasus") to evaluate the merits of an IPO. That fall, Goldman's Management Committee proposed for the first time in the history of the 117-year-old partnership that it consider going public. The reason given in favor of an IPO was the same as had been advanced by Morgan Stanley when it had gone public earlier that year: the need to have more capital in order to successfully compete in a new, fiercer, globalized environment.

Others, however, believed that Goldman's partnership arrangement constituted the foundation of its culture, which, in turn, was responsible for much of the firm's success. Principal among those skeptical of the IPO proposal was Weinberg. Were Goldman to have gone public in 1986 at the valuations of Morgan Stanley, Weinberg's share, estimated at between 4 and 5 percent of the company, would have been worth more than $100 million. But Weinberg believed that the firm did not need to follow the rest of Wall Street. "The challenge is keeping our culture, our profitability, and our growth," he reminded his partners. "It's human nature not to tinker with a good thing."[22]

One key concern of the skeptics was that elimination of partnership would diminish the firm's employee retention power. "You'd have the head-hunters all over this place if we announced the end [of our partnership]," insisted H. Frederick Krimendahl, who had been in charge of operations and administration while a partner at Goldman.[23] Partnership, according to John Cecil, chief administrative officer of Lehman Brothers, contributed to the long-term employment relationships that characterized Goldman. "When do you become a partner?" he mused. "In 10 to 12 years, maybe. You don't quit when you become a partner. So you stay there for 5 to 10 more years."[24] Lehman Brothers had recently gone through the experience of moving away from a partnership structure. Several employees left the firm after it was acquired by American Express in 1984. "I joined Lehman because it was a partnership," remarked a departing Lehman executive, who had moved on to a small partnership firm. "And I was willing to put in 100-hour weeks for a shot at the brass ring. They took that away."[25]

The partners meeting called upon to deliberate the IPO option generated a great deal of controversy. Many of the partners were said to have been very upset. After heated debates on the merits of the IPO proposal in relation to the firm's optimum size, ability to generate capital, and culture and values, the proposal was shelved.

THE FRIEDMAN AND RUBIN ERA, 1990–1994

Succession

In late 1985, a year following Whitehead's departure to join the Reagan administration as Deputy Secretary of State, Weinberg named Stephen Friedman and Bob Rubin as co-heads of the fixed-income division to test them as potential successors. "The big question," he recalled, "was to decide whether [they] would be able to do what John Whitehead and I did."[26] The question was answered to Weinberg's satisfaction; in 1990, Friedman and Rubin were named Goldman's co-chairmen.

Friedman and Rubin had joined Goldman in 1966 and made partner in 1971 and 1973, respectively. An investment banker by training, Friedman was the motivating force behind the development of the mergers and acquisitions department; Rubin, a trader, carried on the development of the risk-arbitrage business created by Gus Levy.

The two had remarkably compatible management styles. "Our minds work in similar ways and we will tend to see things in relatively similar ways," remarked Friedman. Added Rubin: "Neither of us has an ego invested in doing it my way or . . . your way. If we had egos invested in it, this thing could never work."[27]

Fighting the War for Talent

Friedman and Rubin took charge of a firm with a hallowed tradition but experiencing a significant drain of talent. During the late 1980s and early 1990s, a number of hedge funds had begun to offer compensation schemes that paid generously according to formulae based on individually generated profits. This pay structure attracted many capable traders from established firms, including Goldman.

Many experienced and high-performing traders and economists left Goldman for hedge funds during this period, complaining that the firm's compensation package was no longer competitive by market standards. Unable to turn a blind eye to the steady loss of key people and feeling that new blood was needed to propel the business further, Friedman and Rubin broke from the tradition of no lateral hiring and announced that henceforth the firm would recruit experienced traders from other firms and people who had achieved success in areas unfamiliar to the firm such as the fixed income business.

In 1990, management decided to divide each partnership class into thirds based on an annual assessment of the partners' contributions to the firm. In the words of one partner, differentiation would help "clear out the mezzanine layer"—partners who held large stakes in the firm due to seniority, but failed to pull their weight—by redistributing shares from underperforming senior members to high-performing junior members. "Grading" would also help rectify selection errors and nudge out those not performing up to par. New partners would be given four to six years to prove themselves. Failure to perform could lead first to a reduction in percentage of ownership, and ultimately to a nod toward the door. But since the firm had always championed collegiality and teamwork, the new system exacted an emotional toll.

To retain its top talent, Goldman management decided in 1993 to tie compensation more tightly to individual performance so as to pay successful traders at higher levels. The firm introduced a "360-degree review" whereby superiors, subordinates, and peers all submitted employee evaluations that were used as a basis for differentially rewarding partners.[b]

Assuming Greater Risk for Higher Return

Following Rubin's philosophy of "no risk, no profit," Goldman began to venture beyond its traditional role of client agent to become increasingly involved in principal transactions, risking its own capital in exchange for high returns. The old trading approach of seeking steady profits was superceded by a more aggressive style that accepted the risk of substantial losses as the price for even greater gains.

These initiatives brought financial success in the early 1990s. Firm profits totaled $886 million in 1990, passed the $1 billion mark ($1.15 billion) one year later, and by Thanksgiving 1992 had reached $1.46 billion. Return on equity in excess of 35 percent that year dwarfed that of its competitors. This success provided Goldman resources to invest in new businesses and open offices in financial centers around the world.

WATERSHED[28]

A Disastrous Year

In 1994, Goldman suffered substantial financial losses caused, according to industry experts, by the firm's extravagance—annual expenses had risen to $3.6 billion, twice the level for 1990—and high-risk trading activity that coupled a short-term mentality with poor risk management. The losses triggered a precipitous decline in partner confidence, leading to the departure, by late November 1994, of 30 percent of the partnership that had signed the last partnership agreement in 1992.[c] "1994 was a time for humility," reflected Friedman,[29] who had been running the firm solo since Rubin had joined the Clinton administration as Assistant to the President for Economic Policy in 1992.

The fickleness of partner commitment was cited by some as exacerbating the travails of 1994. The departure, between 1992 and 1994, of more than 40 partners not only devastated employee morale and sundered the collegiality that had bound the firm together but also weakened partnership capital, since the departing partners took with them a substantial portion of the firm's capital. Even though Goldman's assets at the end of 1994 were $95 billion, down from $115 billion at the end of 1993, its capital-to-assets ratio had halved since 1990.

---

[b] In contrast to the traditional performance appraisal format wherein one person, generally a manager, is responsible for reviewing all employees under his or her supervision, the 360-degree appraisal incorporates evaluations from supervisors, subordinates, co-workers, and sometimes even clients. Supporters of the 360-degree appraisal system claimed that it generated a more accurate picture of an employee's performance and development needs and provided more thorough and helpful feedback than the traditional "one-sided" appraisal system. In a 1993 memo that discussed "the necessity of thoughtful reviews and mentoring by managers in order to improve employee performance and career development," Friedman cited the 360-degree review approach as superior to "mechanistic formulas, which do not encourage people to cooperate or focus on the firm's broader interests." [Endlich, p. 188.]

[c] Current partners renewed their partnership agreements, along with newly elected partners, every two years.

"1994 was a watershed year for Goldman Sachs. The firm's mentality changed forever," recalled a former partner. "They saw that you can't run a multinational global business on partnership capital . . . a risky business on top of a risky capital structure."[30] Others believed that the partnership structure had in fact helped Goldman weather difficult times. Goldman's small group of partners-cum-employees, they reasoned, had been far more tolerant of the substantial trading losses it had suffered than would have been public shareholders seeking predictable recurring earnings.

Changes in Capital Structure

General and limited partners were once the firm's two sources of equity. In 1985 they claimed ownership in excess of 80 percent. The addition of other equity holders had halved the partners' share in Goldman's equity to 40 percent ($2 billion of the firm's $5 billion in equity) by 1993, and to 28 percent (just over $1.3 billion of the firm's $5 billion in equity) the following year. Despite this decline in proportional ownership, Goldman partners retained full control of voting rights.

At the end of 1994, with almost $5 billion in equity, Goldman had amassed $14 billion in long-term debt. These capital injections by outsiders created new pressures for growth in firm profits. (For a breakdown of how the ownership structure would look by 1997, see Figure A.) Additionally, as the firm's ambitions grew, so did the partnership, necessitating commensurate growth in firm profits to maintain the income levels of existing partners. (See Figure B.)

New Leadership

Citing physical exhaustion after years of grueling hours and pressure, Friedman announced his retirement in December 1994—a decision criticized by some as abandoning his troops when they needed him most.

The Management Committee's consensus preference for Friedman's successor was Jon Corzine, a trader who had for years been the firm's CFO. Friedman, however, favored continuing the joint-leadership formula that had worked so well for him and Rubin, and for Weinberg and Whitehead before them. He wanted Hank Paulson, who was head of the investment banking department and had shared leadership of the Principal Investment Area with Friedman since 1990, to share the chief executive's post. The Management Committee decided to name Corzine chairman and Paulson vice chairman.[d] But Corzine and Paulson, unlike the previous duos, were relative strangers thrown together in the wake of Friedman's abrupt departure.

Handing over charge to Corzine and Paulson, Friedman described the opportunity and challenge that they faced: "[T]he firm's profits have been disappointing, particularly as a result of trading results in some of the same businesses which performed extraordinarily well in the last few years. . . . I believe that Goldman Sachs, and in my opinion our entire industry, has to come to grips with the proper pacing and prioritization of our expansion and with addressing our cost structure better."[31]

A study in contrasts, Corzine and Paulson rose up through the ranks of Goldman Sachs from the trading and investment banking sides, respectively. With bond trading becoming more prominent in the industry, Corzine, a former co-head of Goldman's bond group, had increased its role within the firm. (By mid-1998, the firm would make nearly half of its revenue from trading.)[32] Loyal to his trading roots, Corzine did not shy away from risk-taking activities as a means to swiftly fuel growth. Paulson, on the other hand, exemplified the staid, conservative persona of the Goldman investment banker. He was well aware that stable revenues, principally in the form of investment banking fees, yielded a steadier formula for long-term growth than high-risk trading, even though

---

[d] Paulson was promoted to the newly created position of president in 1997.

FIGURE A   **Estimated Breakdown of Goldman Sachs' Ownership Structure, 1997**

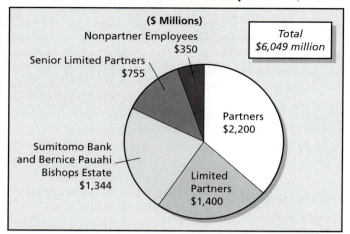

Partners (only group with voting rights) owned 100 percent of the firm. They received 76 percent of the annual profits or losses, and were constrained to keep their money in the firm. Stakes for each of the 190 partners ranged from 0.25 to 1 percent. They also received $300,000 annually in salary and a fixed rate of return on their capital investment.

Limited partners (nonvoting, retired partners who had to keep the bulk of their accumulated earnings in the firm for up to 14 years) received a fixed rate of interest on their capital.

Sumitomo Bank and Bernice Pauahi Bishops Estate (nonvoting) received about 20 percent of annual earnings or losses.

Senior limited partners (nonvoting institutional investors, mainly insurance companies) received a fixed rate of return on preferred equity that would begin to mature in 2001.

Nonpartner employees (nonvoting) enjoyed a profit-sharing plan with no fixed interest rate that received approximately 4 percent of the firm's annual profits or losses.

Sources: Leah Nathans Spiro and Stanley Reed, "Inside the Money Machine," *Business Week,* December 22, 1997, p. 86; DATA: *Business Week,* Moody's Investors Service.

FIGURE B

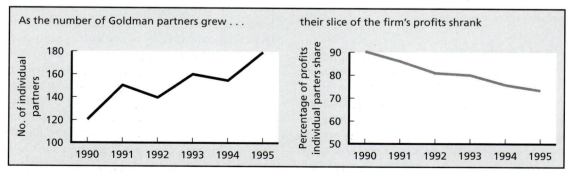

Source: Michael Carroll, "Which Way Out?" *Institutional Investor,* September 1995, p. 65.

Goldman's earnings from proprietary trading outpaced those from investment banking.[33] (By mid-1998, only one third of the firm's revenue would come from investment banking.)[34]

THE CORZINE-PAULSON ERA, 1995–1998[35]

Improving the Bottom Line

One of Corzine's first initiatives as chairman was to reduce costs partly through large-scale layoffs; 10 percent of the firm was asked to leave during the early part of the Corzine-Paulson reign. Those who stayed were not spared either. Professional staff's pay was cut by 40–60 percent, and the year-end bonus for nonprofessional staff plummeted from 30 to 8 percent of salary, the lowest level since the 1970s.

These changes helped improve the firm's operating results, which enabled it to grow equity through profits and capital infusions from a number of investors. By 1995, the firm was back on track, competing aggressively in all of its major business segments. One survey of CFOs ranked Goldman Sachs as the most trusted firm in investment banking by a margin of over 4:1 over the runner-up.[36]

Changes in Governance and Personnel Practices

Some of the 172 Goldman partners were concerned that a small Management Committee (which had grown from 8 persons in 1976 to 12 in 1995) was insufficient to represent all the partners' interests in governance; others felt that deferring strategic decisions to a 12-member committee slowed down decision-making within the firm. To ensure that all product lines, not just the top six, were represented at the managerial level without compromising efficient decision-making, Corzine and Paulson decided to streamline the governance structure.

They replaced the Management Committee with a six-member Executive Committee that would re-semble "an office of the chairman."[37] Except for matters that required a vote of the partnership or the consent of the individual affected partner, the Executive Committee would be the firm's final decision-making body.

In an effort to "broaden the firm's governing base" by allowing a greater number of partners from the different product lines to participate in the decision-making process, two new committees were formed: the Partnership Committee (initially chaired by Corzine) and the Operating Committee (initially chaired by Paulson). Each committee was to be composed of 18 partners (including selected members of the Executive Committee) and would report to the Executive Committee. Corzine and Paulson were concerned that "[a]s we expand globally, we are an increasingly diverse community, and it is particularly important that we commit to strengthen our culture of cooperation and teamwork."[38] They hoped that bringing a larger group of partners into upper management would have the added effect of more thoroughly spreading the firm's culture. (Exhibit 4 identifies the members of the committees in 1995.)

Corzine also introduced important changes in personnel practices. The title "partner" was replaced by "managing director," the equivalent title at rival public firms. The "managing director" title was bestowed, however, not only on partners, but on several nonpartner vice presidents as well. Senior vice presidents at Goldman had long complained that the title of vice president at Goldman lacked distinction; a significant number of associates who had been with the firm for four years earned it. The select vice presidents who were named managing directors would earn higher salaries, be provided with office space equivalent to that provided to partners, and have access to the former partners', now managing directors', dining and meeting rooms. With these changes, the new titles, management believed, more accurately reflected the status and level of responsibility of vice presidents who had made exceptional contributions to the firm.

Adding a "rank" equivalent to that in place at rival firms would also put Goldman in a more

EXHIBIT 4 **Goldman Sachs' New Management Structure**

EXECUTIVE COMMITTEE
The Senior Governing Body

Jon Corzine, Chairman	David Silfen
Henry Paulson, Jr., Vice Chairman	Robert Hurst
Roy Zuckerberg	John Thain

PARTNERSHIP COMMITTEE
Oversight of partnership practices, policies, selection; review and oversight of capital structure

Jon Corzine, Chairman	Philip Murphy
David Ford	Daniel Neidich
Frederic Garonzik	Donald Opatmy, Jr.
Richard Hayden	James Riley, Jr.
Steven Heller	J. David Rogers
Stephen Hendel	Mark Schwartz
Robert Kaplan	Patrick Ward
Robert Katz	Jon Winkelreid
Keven Kennedy	Roy Zuckerberg

Robin Neustein, *ex officio*

OPERATING COMMITTEE
Promote strategic cohesion; coordinate operations; facilitate communication between partners and business lines

Henry Paulson, Jr., Chairman	John McNulty
Lloyd Blankfein	Michael Mortara
Eric Dobkin	Gregory Palm
Steven Einhorn	David Silfen
W. Mark Evans	Robert Steel
Richard Friedman	Peter Sutherland
Jacob Goldfield	John Thain
Robert Hurst	John Thornton
Hideo Ishihara	Leslie Tortora

Robin Neustein, *ex officio*

Source: Philip Maher and Anne Schwimmer, "Goldman Sachs Revamps Its Governance Structure," *Investment Dealers' Digest,* November 27, 1995, p. 3.

competitive position to make lateral hires. Goldman's public rivals had lured away some of its high-performing vice presidents by offering managing director positions with guaranteed bonuses and stock options. When Goldman had made lateral hires, it could only offer the partner title, not vice president, since that would be a step down for managing directors.

Some partners complained, however, that the close-knit, collegial atmosphere of Goldman, traditionally known for its horizontal management structure, was giving way to a more vertical management structure.

Impact of Industry Dynamics on Goldman's Strategy

Asked in 1995 to predict the future of investment banking in 2000, Corzine emphasized three industry trends—globalization of finance, diversification of product and services, and consolidation in international banking—to which every major investment bank would have to respond effectively to survive and prosper. "[H]eightened competition," he observed,

> will put a premium on cutting-edge technology, up-to-the-moment intelligence on global market opportunities, the development of innovative products and services, and a redoubled dedication to the customer. Competition will also require a renewed emphasis on risk-management and financial soundness if firms are to survive the inevitable cyclical downturns like the one from which the industry is even now emerging. Striking the right balance between entrepreneurial initiative and financial prudence will be the fundamental test of success.[39]

Corzine's analysis resonated with an increasingly strongly held belief on Wall Street during the late 1990s that size was necessary to compete in the global financial services market. Remarked Donald McNees, director of Towers Perrin's New York Financial Institutions practice: "During the next year, a few players will emerge as major global investment management brands, a position that will ensure huge future opportunities."[40] (For performance of major industry players, see Exhibit 5.) Corzine spent the next three years positioning Goldman to face industry challenges effectively and establish itself as a leading global bank.

Merger Mania

In 1997, Morgan Stanley and Dean Witter merged, combining a successful investment bank with a distribution powerhouse, and Travelers and Salomon Brothers merged to create one of the most well-capitalized Wall Street institutions. Subsequent mega-deals—the 1997 Union Bank of Switzerland-Swiss Bank Corp. merger and the 1998 Travelers-Citicorp merger—capped a wave of increasing consolidation in investing banking.

Mergers and alliances were not restricted to blockbuster deals, however; the entire industry experienced frenetic acquisition and alliance activity during 1995 to 1997.

These mega-mergers prompted Wall Street analysts to question whether Goldman Sachs had what it took to survive in a more global, consolidated industry—specifically, whether its capital structure was sufficient to weather another downturn of the cyclical security industry. Salomon Brothers had not been the number one acquisition target for Travelers Group chief executive Sanford I. Weill. Weill had wanted Goldman Sachs. Two months before the Salomon deal, he had declared that a deal with Goldman would be a "match made in heaven." Weill met with Corzine to test the waters about a possible buyout of Goldman. Half hour after it had started, the meeting ended with no deal. The Travelers CEO was informed that Goldman was doing great without needing anyone else. "I see no reason to turn over our franchise—our reason to be—to a larger organization," explained Corzine, adding: "We have to be able to control the cultural character of the place."[41]

Seeking Stable Revenues through Asset Management

The acquisition spree in the industry was fueled partly by the headlong rush of investment banks into asset management. Declining fees and high volatility in their traditional businesses led investment banks in the late 1990s to reevaluate their attitudes towards asset management, a relatively unglamorous business serviced primarily by brokerages and mutual fund companies. But as understanding developed of asset management's economies of scale ("[O]nce all fixed costs are covered, it can realize up to 80 percent in margins on each dollar of revenue," observed Richard Forte, a partner at Berkshire Capital Corp., a money management firm[42]), the steady, attractive margins it offered, and the worldwide explosion of demand for asset management, investment banks began to rush into the business.

EXHIBIT 5 Comparative Performance of Security Industry Firms

Financial and Stock Market Performance

	FY	Earnings per Share					Return on Common Equity (%)				Price/ Earnings 1998E	Price/Book Ranges (1981–1997)	
		1994	1995	1996	1997	1998E	1994	1995	1996	1997		High	Low
Bear Stearns[a]	Jun.	$2.50	$2.42	$3.90	$4.51	$4.60	12.1%	20.1%	23.5%	26.0%	11.7x	2.73	0.79
Donaldson, Lufkin & Jenrette	Dec.	1.98	3.08	4.59	3.16	3.60	13.1	17.1	20.6	24.1	12.2	2.80	1.13
Lehman Brothers	Nov.	0.69	1.76	3.24	4.72	5.50	6.2	7.5	13.9	15.6	13.1	2.80	1.13
Merrill Lynch	Dec.	2.37	2.71	4.11	4.83	4.90	18.6	20.1	26.8	26.8	17.3	3.30	0.54
Morgan Stanley	Nov.		2.22	3.14	4.15	4.60	8.8	16.2	21.5	21.0	16.5	2.71	0.82
PaineWebber[c]	Dec.	0.27	0.35[b]	2.25	2.56	2.85	7.9	12.7	21.9	22.3	14.6	3.53	0.44

[a] Bear Stearns calendar year estimates.
[b] PaineWebber 1995 EPS includes $230 million pretax litigation charges; excluding these charges, EPS was $1.90.
[c] PaineWebber adjusted for November 1997 three-to-two stock split.
Source: James P. Hanbury and Lina F. Chou, "Brokerage Industry," Schroderes & Co. Inc., March 3, 1998, and November 16, 1998.

Number of Offices, Customer Accounts, Capital Structure, and Sales Force

	Year Founded	Number of Locations		Customer Accounts (000s)	January 1, 1998			January 1, 1997	Employees No. (000s)
		Domestic	Foreign		Long-Term Borrowings ($ billions)	Ownership Equity ($ billions)	Capital[d] ($ billions)	Capital ($ billions)	
Merrill Lynch & Co., Inc.	1885	695	50	9,000	43.1	8.3	51.4	33.0	57
Morgan Stanley Dean Witter & Co.[a]	1924	420	28	3,600	25.8	14.0	39.7	21.9	47
Salomon Smith Barney Holding, Inc.	1910	442	41	5,000	19.1	8.5	27.6	19.0	34
Lehman Brothers Holdings, Inc.[a]	1850	16	24	NA	20.3	4.5	24.8	19.8	8
The Goldman Sachs Group, L.P.	1869	15	33	267	15.7	6.1	21.8	17.7	11
The Bear Stearns Companies, Inc.	1923	8	12	NA	10.9	3.9	14.8	9.5	9
Paine Webber Group, Inc.	1879	292	7	2,917	4.0	1.9	5.9	4.9	17
Donaldson, Lufkin & Jenrette	1959	12	11	1,000	2.3	2.3	4.5	3.4	8
Credit Suisse First Boston[b]	1975	9	50	120	2.6	1.2	3.7	2.8	12
BT Alex. Brown, Inc.[c]	1800	23	1	243	1.2	1.2	2.40	0.6	4

NA = Not available
[a] Morgan Stanley Dean Witter and Lehman Brothers data are as of 11/30/97 and 11/30/96.
[b] First Boston was founded before 1975.
[c] BT Alex. Brown customer accounts comprised 233,096 retail and 9,745 institutional accounts.
[d] Firm capital is the sum of long-term borrowings and ownership equity.
Source: SIA Data 1999.

Merrill Lynch's $5.2 billion purchase of Mercury Asset Management ($177 billion of assets under management) in 1997 allowed the firm in one transaction to double the assets under its management and become one of the dominant players in the United Kingdom. Thereafter, acquisitions intensified from 62 in 1994 to 86 in 1995, 96 in 1996, and 100 in 1997.[43] "It's been a frenzy out there," remarked Booz Allen & Hamilton partner Peter Davis. "The deals have gone up progressively in dollar volume and in number of transactions."[44]

Usually cautious when it moved into a new business area, Goldman Sachs had been late in the past in entering newer, growing businesses such as mortgage-backed securities and international investment banking. It was a late entrant in asset management as well, establishing in 1989 Goldman Sachs Asset Management (GSAM) to manage the portfolios of high-wealth individuals. During the late 1990s, the firm supplemented internal growth with acquisitions focused primarily on smaller, more specialized asset management firms. It acquired Liberty Asset Management, a firm with approximately $5 billion in assets and a solid track record, in 1996; U.K. Cinman, a firm with $23 billion of assets in Asia and Europe, in 1996; and Commodities Corporation, an institutional trading firm specializing in commodities, in 1997. Between 1997 and 1998 Goldman also augmented its salesforce from 2 persons to 40 to gain greater access to third-party retailers who would sell the firm's products to the "masses." Consequently, assets under its management increased threefold, from around $40 billion in 1993 to $125 billion in 1997, and the number of institutional clients increased twofold, from 95 in 1993 to 204 in 1997.[45] In 1997 Goldman ranked fifth in asset management, after J.P. Morgan, Merrill Lynch, Morgan Stanley, and Smith Barney.[46]

The IPO Debate Rekindled

During the 1980s and 1990s, the idea of going public periodically surfaced within Goldman. In the tradition of the 1986 Pegasus study, commissioned by the partnership to evaluate the merits of an IPO, Pegasus II and III were conducted in 1991 and 1993, respectively. Even as the debate continued internally, Goldman watched all of its major competitors become, or merge with, public corporations.

The IPO debate resurfaced in 1996. With 1995 profits at $1.37 billion, not outstanding but certainly solid, Goldman Sachs was back on track. Morale, too, was recovering. Returning the focus to steadier, long-term growth had played a major role in restoring the firm's health. But the 1994 crisis had provoked the question: was a private partnership, with unlimited liability and inherently unstable capital, an outmoded form of ownership for a modern investment bank? "Goldman's capital structure is inappropriate," asserted an employee at a competitor. "You have to have permanent equity. Goldman would never allow a client to have that capital structure."[47]

Goldman had approached the 1986 debate from a position of strength—the firm was growing rapidly and management's primary concern was whether it would have sufficient capital to finance its expansion needs. But as of 1994, "unlimited liability partnership" was no longer a vague, legal concept; Goldman had felt the full weight of its meaning with partners taking big hits from trading losses and many reacting by exiting the firm along with their capital.

Corzine wanted to establish a more secure capital structure "rather than remaining hostage to fickle capital that partners could withdraw," with less personal exposure than offered by a partnership.[48] Hence, despite protests from the Partnership and Operating Committees, which favored maintaining the partnership to preserve Goldman's unique culture, he reignited the IPO proposition. The six-member Executive Committee was evenly divided for and against Goldman going public. Corzine, Roy Zuckerberg, and Robert Hurst were in favor; Paulson and co-heads of Goldman's European business John Thain and John Thornton (who had replaced David Silfen on the committee) were opposed. Pegasus IV was thus initiated.

The issues considered in January 1996 were much the same as those raised in previous debates. Those who supported the IPO spoke to economic parameters, those opposed emphasized pride in ownership of the firm. Ultimately, the IPO proposal was again rejected, premised on the loss of uniqueness that would result and the grounds that the firm was undervalued due to prevailing market conditions.

Corzine acknowledged the importance of maintaining Goldman's culture, but was nevertheless disappointed by the rejection of the IPO option. "I don't think our culture has to go away [with an IPO]," he reflected:

> It's subject to the style and character of leadership. If you lead with that in mind I think you can carry through the cultural instincts that have always been at the heart of the firm. In a public company your choices with regard to governance, how you set strategy and choose leadership, how you reward people and whom you choose to reward will set the cultural reality.[49]

Although convinced that an IPO would stabilize capital and maintain the talented pool of partners without seriously eroding the firm's culture, Corzine was not willing to go against the consensus. But he did introduce structural changes that left no doubt as to the direction in which he wanted the firm to go. Rules governing the withdrawal of partners' capital were made more restrictive. Goldman's partnership structure in which the individual partners had unlimited liability was replaced by one in which the corporation became the general partner and individual partners (as well as other equity holders Sumitomo, Bishops Estate, and senior limited partners) became limited partners. The new liability structure protected senior partners' exposure as well as individual partners' private assets such as bank accounts and homes. According to Corzine, most individual partners had invested about 90 percent of their net worth with the firm, so although the new structure might have offered them some peace of mind, it made little difference materially.

TO BE, OR NOT TO BE (PUBLIC)[50]

1997 was a stellar year for Goldman: profits of more than $3 billion and return on equity of 51 percent, well above the industry average of 36 percent. The firm had participated in some of the most important financing deals in the world, including the largest IPO to date (the $13 billion privatization of Deutsche Telekom); the largest industrial merger to date (the $38 billion merger of Daimler-Benz and Chrysler Corporation); the first privatization in China (of China Telecom); and the largest sovereign debt deal in Asia (a $4 billion bond offering for South Korea).

But the firm's leaders were ambivalent toward an IPO. "If we thought we couldn't withstand a cyclic downturn at least as well as our public competitors, we'd be public," maintained Paulson. "This isn't the 11th Commandment around here: 'Thou shalt be private.'"[51] However, he valued the benefits that the partnership structure brought and was skeptical of the potential benefits of scale. "We have something unique, and it's a competitive weapon," insisted Paulson.[52] "Size alone is not a competitive advantage," concurred Executive Committee member John Thain. Even Corzine acknowledged that Goldman's partnership structure helped the firm retain its superstars and maintain its aggressive "we're going to win" culture. Both Corzine and Paulson rejected the reason advanced by some proponents of an IPO that substantial capital would be needed to build a powerful Goldman presence in asset management. They believed that an asset management business could be built internally with some small, highly specialized acquisitions to fill gaps in product offerings. "I find it a bunch of malarkey that we couldn't make an acquisition," remarked Corzine. "We can figure out a lot of ways to do a lot of different things if we so choose."[53]

In March 1998, a subcommittee of the Operating Committee was established to review the firm's strategy and again weigh the merits of an IPO. The committee was to report to the Executive

Committee in mid-May and to the entire partnership (the managing directors who owned a piece of the firm) in June.

The Subcommittee's Deliberations

The subcommittee carefully examined whether an IPO had economic, strategic, and cultural merit. The score on economic merit was clear; the financial rewards of an IPO would be overwhelming. The media had a field day with the numbers an IPO was expected to yield and was quick to cite greed as the motivating factor behind the potential offering. "You can't tell me this isn't about money. In this business, everything is about money," commented a Wall Street banker.[54] Even Whitehead acknowledged that he didn't "find anyone who denie[d] that the decision of many of the partners, particularly the younger [ones], was based more on the dazzling amounts to be deposited in their capital accounts than on what they felt would be good for the future of Goldman Sachs."[55] "For me," countered Corzine, "an economic system in which 1.5 to 1.75 percent of the people capture a high percentage of the upside in good times and adjust the other 98 percent of the participants' compensation and jobs on the downside is selfish."[56] Goldman had downsized six times between 1987 and 1994 in response to poor earnings, and the employees, not the partners, had suffered the consequences. Perhaps, suggested Corzine, a public Goldman would be less greedy in good and less severe in bad times.

An IPO scored high on strategic merit as well. Although some went so far as to speculate that Goldman might partner with retail powerhouses such as J. P. Morgan or Chase Manhattan Bank, the subcommittee judged the enormous overhead of retail excessively risky. Instead, the subcommittee determined that the firm could best retain its unique edge by continuing to provide wholesale investment banking services. An IPO would allow Goldman access to public funds to expand rapidly and face its giant competitors as well as substantially reduce partners' liability. Going public during the bull market of the late 1990s would help Gold-

man raise these funds at high valuations, thus minimizing dilution.

But how did an IPO score on cultural merit? Would an IPO dissolve the partnership, destroy the legacy and intangible value that made Goldman Sachs unique? Reflecting this argument against going public, Jeffrey Hookey, author of *Security Analysis on Wall Street,* remarked: "As a public entity Goldman will lose some of its prestige. They still have the Goldman reputation and history, but they will not be unique anymore. . . . [Morgan Stanley] was the ultimate white-shoe firm [during the 1980s]. But after it went public, they lost something in the translation. It's still a fine bank, but it has lost some of its aura."[57]

The Partners Decide

On June 12, 1998, the 190 partners of Goldman Sachs assembled at the IBM Palisades Executive Conference Center in New York for a weekend meeting. The vantage point for this group was much different than it had been in 1996, or even in 1986. During the 1986 debate, the newest partnership class had been elected only six days prior and had virtually no equity in the firm. When the debate resurfaced in 1996, a weak 1995 had left the most recent partnership class (elected in 1994) with only a nominal equity stake. But in 1998, the newest partners, brought in two years prior, had already gained from one record year and the follow-up year looked very promising. Having earned more than $1 billion in each of the first two quarters, Goldman was rumored in mid-1998 to be worth 3.5–4.0 times its book value.

Paulson, who in 1998 had been named co-chair and co-CEO of the firm with Corzine, made persuasive presentations at the conference, summarizing the polar viewpoints for the "going public" and "staying private" camps.[58] He urged the partners to make their decision based on the long-term interests of the firm and not "on the basis of how much money you are going to make."[59]

In the ensuing debate, those who favored staying private emphasized that the partnership was Goldman's mark of distinction. They feared that going public would destroy the teamwork that was a defining characteristic of the partnership and set Goldman apart from its competitors. They emphasized the recruiting strength of the partnership, that those who came to Goldman did so with an eye on the partnership, not on stock options. Some opponents, particularly those from the investment banking side, were also concerned about positioning the firm in the stock market, given that it derived a large portion of its profits from the volatile proprietary trading business. Even the two Johns became involved, warning via a letter read by Corzine: "If it ain't broke, don't fix it."[60]

Those who supported an IPO argued that a firm that wanted to become a major international player could not rely on an insecure capital base and certainly could not grow and make major acquisitions without stock. They contended that the firm was in danger of being reduced to a niche player, unable to compete for the top businesses. Going public, moreover, would reduce the high level of liability to which individual partners were exposed. Arguments such as these provoked criticism from Goldman's competitors; remarked Donaldson, Lufkin & Jenrette's CEO Joe Roby: "I wish I could find a business where Goldman is capital constrained."[61] Even Thain, who opposed an IPO, emphasized to fellow committee members that "we have all the capital we need."[62] Finally, John Thornton had suggested that if access to publicly traded stock was the goal for making acquisitions, perhaps the best route would be to merge with a public company.

At the end of the weekend each partner was asked to answer two questions on an anonymous questionnaire: which format (public or private) do you prefer and why? The partners had by this time heard many arguments for and against each, but it was not enough to simply choose one format; they had to justify their decisions with solid reasoning. Corzine and Paulson wanted a carefully weighed decision, not just a snap judgement.

The Proposal

After reviewing the survey results, the Executive Committee decided unanimously to prepare a de-

tailed proposal to sell a portion of the firm to the investing public. The proposal would be submitted to the partnership for a vote later in the summer. The dimensions of the plan were as follows: of 467 million shares outstanding, 69 million (or 14 percent) would be sold in the IPO. Of the 398 million shares left over, 265 million (70 percent) would go to the managing directors, and the remaining 132 million would be divided roughly equally between the limited partners (47 million), Sumitomo and Bishops Estates (43 million), and employee bonus and benefit plans (42 million). According to the proposed shareholders' agreement, both Sumitomo and Bishops Estates would be asked to agree to vote their shares of common stock in the same manner as a majority of the shares held by the managing directors of Goldman Sachs.

Although official figures were not released, many believed that the pay-outs to the general partners would amount to $5–6 billion. Many individuals would see their wealth increase by anywhere from $50–75 million and senior partners would potentially realize upward of $100 million. Nonpartner employees would take home 50 percent of their 1997 or 1998 compensation in addition to a bonus for each year of service. Limited partners would be paid a premium over the book value of their investment—anywhere from 25–55 percent depending on whether they chose cash or stock. As a safeguard against another mass exodus of people and funds, sales of shares distributed through the offering were not to be permitted for three to five years. In an attempt to preserve a teamwork mentality, a "partnership pool" was proposed to tie the compensation of managing directors to the firm's overall performance.

On August 10, 1998, the partnership reconvened and was asked to vote on two separate questions: Are you in favor of proceeding with the plan as outlined? If it proceeds, would you wish to participate? With a valuation of $20–35 billion, partners who supported the IPO were eagerly anticipating the prospect of going public.

References

1. Michael Carroll, "Which Way Out?" *Institutional Investor,* September 1995, p. 63.

2. Anita Raghavan, "Seeking to Go Public? It's a Capital Question," *Wall Street Journal,* August 7, 1998, p. A1.

3. This section draws information from R. Bennett, "Can Mighty Goldman Stay Private?" *New York Times,* April 13, 1986, section 3, p. 1; L. Endlich, *Goldman Sachs: The Culture of Success* (New York: Knopf, 1999), pp. 32–33, 49–59, 63–73, 75, 81, 82, 127–29, 132, and 176; and L. Spiro and S. Reed, "Inside the Money Machine," *Business Week,* December 22, 1997, p. 86.

4. John Cassidy, "The Firm," *The New Yorker,* March 8, 1999, p. 28.

5. John Whitehead, quoted in Endlich, p. 60.

6. Bennett.

7. "Goldman Sachs: Wall Street's Shining Maiden," *The Economist,* September 29, 1990.

8. Beth Selby, "The Steve and Bob Show," *Institutional Investor,* December 1990, p. 70.

9. "Business Principles of Goldman Sachs," Goldman Sachs website, www.gs.com.

10. Bennett.

11. Robert Clow, "Fuld's Gold," *Institutional Investor,* July 1998, p. 47.

12. Vault Reports, Inc., 1999.

13. Bethany McLean and Andrew Serwer, "Goldman Sachs: After the Fall," *Fortune,* November 9, 1998, p. 128.

14. Carroll, p. 65.

15. Vault Reports, Inc., 1999.

16. Ibid.

17. Ibid.

18. "Business Principles of Goldman Sachs," Goldman Sachs website, www.gs.com.

19. Cassidy, p. 30.

20. Ibid.

21. Endlich, p. 84.

22. Bennett.

23. Henry Sender, "Too Big for Their Own Good," *Institutional Investor,* February 1987.

24. Clow, p. 51.

25. Selby, p. 58.

26. Ibid., p. 73.

27. Ibid., p. 70.

28. This section draws information from Carroll, p. 73; Endlich, pp. 174–75, 203–4, and 209; and Spiro and Reed.

29. Endlich, p. 195.

30. Carroll, p. 63.

31. "Goldman Sachs Announces Management," *PR Newswire,* September 13, 1994.

32. Amanda Lang, "Goldman Sachs' Bankable Mystique," *National Post,* January 20, 1999, p. C13.

33. Leah Nathans Spiro, Gary Silverman, and Stanley Reed, "The Coup at Goldman," *Business Week,* January 25, 1999.

34. Lang, p. C13.

35. This section draws information from Bennett; Rose Darby, "Courting Stability," *Investment Dealers' Digest,* September 7, 1998, pp. 18–23; Endlich, pp. 234–37; and Philip Maher

and Anne Schwimmer, "Goldman Sachs Revamps its Governance Structure," *Institutional Dealers' Digest,* November 27, 1995, p. 3.

36. "What CFOs Really Think about Investment Bankers," *Investment Dealers' Digest,* February 6, 1995, p. 16.

37. Maher and Schwimmer.

38. "Goldman Sachs Announces Management," *PR Newswire,* September 13, 1994.

39. Jon S. Corzine, "Looking Towards the Year 2000: The Future of Investment Banking," *Investment Dealers' Digest,* May 22, 1995, supplement on "The New Wall Street," p. 16.

40. Patricia Coate, "Will banks exit the proprietary fund business?" *Source Bank Marketing,* 29(10), 1997 October, p. 21.

41. Spiro and Reed.

42. Ibid.

43. Investment Counseling, Inc.

44. Darby.

45. Nelson's Investment Manager Database and Nelson's *Directory of Investment Managers— 1998.*

46. *Investor Dealers Digest,* September 7, 1998.

47. Spiro and Reed.

48. Ibid.

49. Michael Carroll, "Goldman's Public Deliberations," *Institutional Investor,* July 1998, p. 11.

50. This section draws information from Endlich, pp. 238-239; Lang, p. C13; and Anita Raghavan, "Seeking to Go Public? It's a Capital Question," *Wall Street Journal,* August 7, 1998, p. A1.

51. Ibid.

52. Spiro and Reed.

53. Ibid.

54. Cassidy, p. 35–36.

55. McLean and Serwer.

56. Raghavan.

57. Lang.

58. Leah Nathens Spiro, "The Coup at Goldman: How the Fight over Going Public and a Banker-Trader Clash Helped Topple Jon Corzine," *Business Week,* January 25, 1999; and "Goldman Sachs: Palace Coup," *The Economist,* January 16, 1999.

59. Raghavan.

60. Ibid.

61. McLean and Serwer.

62. Raghavan.

Family Feud (A): Andersen versus Andersen

In early 1998 Andersen Worldwide (AW) was scouring the globe for an adjudicator from a country in which it had no business operations or clients, a challenging task for the world's largest consulting and accounting practice. The firm needed an arbitrator to resolve a dispute between its consulting (Andersen Consulting) and accounting (Arthur Andersen) business units. Its only two options were "Colombia or Antarctica. Since penguins don't make good judges," AW engaged Harvard-educated Colombian lawyer Guillermo Gamba.[1]

Andersen Consulting (AC) had filed for arbitration in December 1997, seeking to sever its ties with Arthur Andersen (AA) and its parent company AW. AC alleged that AA had breached a 1989 agreement not to compete with AC for consulting business. AA responded that if AC wanted to secede, it was required to pay AW, per its partnership agreement, $10 billion in compensation.

The roots of the AA-AC dispute lay much deeper than the fracas over market competition. Long-standing battles over partner compensation and organizational control had deepened the existing cultural division between the consulting and accounting partners, leading, in 1997, to their inability to ratify either AA's Jim Wadia or AC's George Shaheen as the new CEO of the parent company. Considering the history of bad blood between the parties, together with the complexity of the issues involved, Gamba faced a monumental challenge.

ARTHUR ANDERSEN'S HERITAGE

Origins and Early Growth[2]

In 1908, after becoming, at age 23, Illinois' youngest CPA, Arthur Andersen began teaching accounting at Northwestern University. Recognizing that the creation of the Federal Reserve and the levying of federal income tax in 1913 would greatly increase the demand for accounting services, he partnered on December 1 of that year with fellow accountant Clarence DeLany to form the public accounting firm Andersen, DeLany & Company. Early clients of the newly formed firm included ITT, Colgate Palmolive, and Parker Pen. DeLany departed in 1918, whereupon the firm was renamed Arthur Andersen & Co. (See Exhibit 1 for a timeline of key events.)

Convinced that an advanced understanding of business operations was worth the extra cost, Andersen became the first provider of accounting services to hire only college graduates. Responding to Andersen's emphasis on the need for these bright professionals to speak as "one firm," AA established in 1929 the Committee on Technique to standardize practices and procedures. "If we fail to speak consistently with one voice," Andersen maintained, "we will confuse clients and undermine the credibility that is crucial to an auditor's

Dean's Research Fellow Scot Landry and Professor Ashish Nanda prepared this case entirely from published sources as the basis for class discussion rather than to illustrate either effective or ineffective handling of an administrative situation. It draws upon "Andersen vs. Andersen," a paper written by Dan Hays (HBS MBA'99), under the supervision of Professor Ashish Nanda.

EXHIBIT 1 Timeline of Key Events

1913	• Arthur Andersen forms public accounting firm, Andersen, DeLany & Company, with Clarence DeLany.
1918	• DeLany departs and firm becomes know as Arthur Andersen & Co.
1929	• Andersen launches Committee on Technique, emphasizing "one firm" approach.
1947	• Arthur Andersen dies. Leonard Spacek succeeds him as CEO.
1954	• Andersen begins official consulting operations, performing a systems-integration project on a mainframe computer for GE.
1971	• Andersen establishes a permanent Center for Professional Education in St. Charles Illinois.
1987—June	• Executive recruiter Stephen Page tries to recruit consulting partners from Big Five firms.
1987—September	• Andersen reorganizes consulting operations in the U.S. and Canada, separating consultants from traditional office reporting structure. Global and regional chiefs of consulting are named.
1988—May	• Lead consulting partner Gresham Brebach is relieved of duties for allegedly planning to leave and take consulting operations with him.
1988—October	• Six AC partners leave to form International Consulting Group.
	• Andersen Worldwide agrees to allow consulting partners to develop a unique identity as Andersen Consulting.
1988—November	• Andersen Worldwide decides to separate Andersen Consulting from Arthur Andersen.
	• New partner compensation plan established based on "performance."
1989—January	• "Florida accords" signed.
	• Andersen Consulting formally created as separate operating unit with George Shaheen as managing partner.
1989—March	• Lawrence Weinbach replaces Duane Kullberg as Andersen CEO.
1994—December	• Arthur Andersen formally launches consulting business.
1997—February	• Weinbach tenders resignation effective August 31, 1997.
1997—May	• The 12-person nominating committee names Shaheen to succeed Weinbach.
	• Board asks both Wadia and Shaheen to speak to partners.
1997—June	• Wadia, then Shaheen, fail to win two-thirds majority of partners.
	• Chairman of Andersen's board of partners W. Robert Grafton is named acting CEO.
1997—July	• Wadia named managing director of Arthur Andersen, replacing Richard Measelle.
1997—December	• Wadia calls for "free competition" between Andersen Consulting and Arthur Andersen consulting practices, and a $150 million transfer payment from Andersen Consulting to Arthur Andersen "in perpetuity."
	• Andersen Consulting partners vote unanimously to seek to sever ties with Arthur Andersen and Andersen Worldwide.
	• Andersen Consulting files request with international arbitration panel to break away from Andersen Worldwide.
1998	• Harvard educated Colombian attorney Guillermo Gamba is named arbitrator.

success."[3] Implicit in the "one firm" philosophy was the approach of treating all AA partners as equals, sharing the same privileges and obligations.

Accounting firms received a major boost during the 1930s with the passage of securities laws requiring public corporations to be audited on an annual basis. AA remained a small accounting firm with Arthur Andersen in firm control—retaining 50 percent of its shares and profits, the other partners splitting the remaining 50 percent—until he died. Upon Andersen's death in 1947, Leonard Spacek, at age 40, succeeded Andersen as AA's managing partner. During Spacek's tenure, which lasted until 1963, the firm grew rapidly, opening 18 new U.S. and 26 foreign offices. Despite this expansion, AA remained firmly committed to its "one firm" philosophy. New hires joined the firm immediately out of college, passed the grueling CPA exam, and stayed for life. Loyal, consistent, and unflappable under duress, AA partners were proud of the nickname they earned, "Andersen Androids."[4]

Consulting's Rapid Rise— A Business Opportunity, an Organizational Problem[5]

AA entered consulting in 1954 helping clients such as General Electric develop and integrate their first electronic information systems. Initially offered as "a subordinate aid to audit clients," over time, the consulting business developed its own clientele.[6] In the early 1960s the practice of having newly hired consultants serve as auditors for a minimum of two years was rescinded, opening, according to an outside observer, "a gap [between accounting and consulting practices] that would grow into a schism."[7] During the tenure of Harvey Kapnick, named AA's chairman in 1970, industrywide audit revenues plateaued whereas consulting's growth accelerated. AA consultants specially focused on developing a uniform methodology and linking their practice to computerization. Kapnick, famous for "ramrodding innovative and often controversial ideas" past the partners, oversaw consulting—which had quickly earned a reputation of being the "marine corps" of data processing—grow rapidly to account in 1978 for 21 percent of AA's $546 million total income (compared to 5 to 10 percent at most of its competitors).[8]

In response to a Securities and Exchange Commission (SEC) warning in 1979 that certain management advisory services offered by accountants might come under its scrutiny, Kapnick recommended to AA partners that the firm's accounting and management consulting activities be separated. Kapnick's proposal, presented at a stormy annual partner's meeting in September 1979, was scrapped in favor of a compromise resolution after most of the partners argued that the accounting and management services were complementary and thus should not be separated. The compromise called for further discussions with the SEC concerning "the extent of so-called nonaudit work that can be performed without raising questions about independence."[9] Remarked an observer: "The water was tested on that issue, and Kapnick had to back down."[10] The internal fight and his failure to win partner acceptance of his proposal led to Kapnick's resignation from leadership of the organization on October 15, 1979, citing "disagreement over the firm's future direction."[11] He was replaced as managing partner by Duane Kullberg, a "dyed-in-the-wool auditor . . . a consensus builder. The polar opposite of Kapnick, he was quiet, stable, cautious. . . ."[12]

The internal debate at Andersen was only symptomatic of an emerging tension within the profession. Accounting was becoming an increasingly competitive business. The auditors, to differentiate themselves, often went beyond just auditing clients' books to offering management advice. Addressing these tasks required broader, differently educated partners than in the past and opened the door for arguments over sharing earnings between those who were eager to play such roles and those who were not.

CONSULTING—GROWING UP, GROWING APART

Growing Dissatisfaction Among Consultants[13]

As consulting came to account for a greater share of Andersen's business—by 1984 the consulting practice was more profitable per partner than AA's traditional accounting and tax business; by 1987 it had grown to 36 percent of revenue and to 9,639 consultants—the consultants began to seek greater control over their practice's direction. AA consultants technically were "principals"; only auditors could be partners. Consultants reported to local office partners-in-charge who were typically auditors. Additionally, consultants held minority representation on the Andersen board.

AA consultants also worried that association with the accountants was diluting their identity. Consultants and accountants typically had quite different perspectives. Consultants viewed their clients' businesses in process terms, liked to conceptualize, and offered advice to improve business performance; accountants took a deep view of operations, liked to establish and test concrete rules and procedures, and offered advice on avoiding major problems. Consultants were the "go-getters," accountants the "traditionalists." Consultants were often characterized by accountants as "the suits," accountants by consultants as "bean counters."

Asserting that the consulting partners "seek equity and governance . . . more of a hand in running the business than they now have" and expressing a desire "to operate in an environment where people didn't feel threatened by my success" Andersen's top consulting partner Victor Millar left the firm in late 1986 to join Saatchi & Saatchi.[14] Millar quickly built the Saatchi practice into a top-10 consulting firm through acquisition of several small and mid-sized competitors. His offer to purchase all of Andersen's consulting practice was, however, rejected.

Shortly before Millar's departure, Kullberg, in response to the expressions of discontent among consultants, appointed a "mix of services committee" to advise management on the proper balance among the firm's activities. The committee recommended spinning off the large systems practice while retaining the rest of consulting practice within AA. The first of three meetings convened to discuss the committee's recommendations, named "Williamsburg One," was extremely contentious. Alleging that the committee, "which was dominated by auditors, was biased from the start," Gresham Brebach, Millar's successor at AA, demanded that the committee report be written. His demand was rejected.

Brebach warned Andersen partners that "if the balance of power remains with the accountants and a disparity continues between revenues consultants bring in and what they earn, you're going to see more unrest, discontent, and departures of the consultants."[15] Besides power-sharing, identity was a major concern for Andersen consultants. Brebach publicly wondered: "Are we an accounting firm with a sideline consulting practice, or a consulting firm with an accounting and auditing arm?"[16]

Consulting partners also complained that their compensation lagged market rates. AA partners were paid on a per-share basis from a pool of worldwide profits; a policy developed by Arthur Andersen himself to maintain the "one firm" culture.[a] Consulting partners protested that consulting was contributing an ever-growing proportion of those worldwide profits (emphasized Brebach: "We contribute almost twice as much as auditing and tax partners to gross profits after deducting salaries and other costs"[17]), but their compensation was not rising proportionally. A number of consulting partners began to hint that, attracted by

---

[a] Each partner "owned" shares in AA. Upon election, new partners were allowed to purchase a fixed number of shares at book value. Additional shares were allotted to partners biannually based on their performance. Retiring partners had to return their shares to AA at book value. Partners' shares determined their proportion of profits.

signing bonuses of upward of $1 million, they might leave the firm and take their business with them.

In June 1987 executive recruiter Stephen Page attempted to recruit AA's consulting leaders en masse together with top consultants from the other big accounting firms to form a "huge new consulting firm." Page invited the consultants to a secret meeting at New York's LaGuardia airport, promising them an opportunity to "attain their professional goals and . . . double or triple their current earnings."[18] His plans were foiled, though, when an AA partner showed his letter of invitation to Kullberg, who immediately alerted the heads of all the Big Eight accounting firms, quashing any potential rebellion.

In July 1987 Brebach convened a meeting of consulting partners in London to discuss the future of AA's consulting practice. "[W]here the consulting executives saw an exchange of ideas and an attempt to resolve a serious schism in the firm," Brebach recalled, "the auditors could see only treason. At a break in the meeting, a senior auditor placed an urgent call to Kullberg, telling him, 'We have a revolt on our hands. We must act to quash it! There's no time to waste!'" Brebach, and four other "ringleaders," were summoned before AA's operations committee "to air some of the issues raised at the London meeting." Brebach, however, saw this meeting as an "inquisition" at which he and his consulting colleagues were accused of insubordination.[19]

"Market Driven" Changes Fail to Quell Dissent[20]

In September 1987 AA made what Kullberg characterized as "market driven" organizational changes. "Historically," he explained, "management consulting was to be a subordinate aid to audit clients. Instead, consulting has become the fastest-growing practice at Arthur Andersen, and the great growth is in nonaudit client work." The changes were "aimed at making it easier for partners around the nation to tap into the firm's pool of consultants and to recognize consulting as an independent function."[21]

Whereas the firm had previously been organized on a geographic basis, reporting into the executive team by office, the consultants and accountants were now organized by business practice, reporting separately to Andersen's partner committee. Consulting partners were asked to report not to office managing partners, who were typically accountants, but to regional consulting heads who reported to the national head of consulting.

Organizational restructuring did little to stem dissent among the consultants, who continued to argue for increased representation and greater autonomy. They pointed out that consultants held only five of sixteen seats on AA's executive committee, even though consulting revenue was projected to account for 50 percent of firm revenue by 1993. Prospects of the consulting business would improve, they contended, by giving the consulting division greater control over its own strategy and allowing it the flexibility to engage in joint ventures with clients (prohibited by accounting conflict-of-interest rules). A clear partition would also help the consultants further boost their compensation and eliminate for them the risk of litigation that attended the audit business.

Another Mutiny?[22]

In May 1988, less than two years after Millar's departure, Brebach was relieved of his duties for allegedly planning to leave the firm and take the consulting operation with him. Brebach was apparently betrayed by one of the 11 partners who had attended a meeting he had called in April to discuss opposition to an October 1987 Board of Partners' recommendation of an amendment to Andersen's bylaws. Proposed in the wake of Millar's departure, the change would have added a one-year "noncompete" clause to partners' contracts and "shackle Andersen partners to the firm," according to Brebach.[23] The proposed amendment was withdrawn in May but, days later, Kullberg, convinced that Brebach was trying to cleave the consulting practice away from the firm, relieved him of his duties.

Maintaining that many of Andersen's consulting partners "have a major disagreement with top management over the strategic direction and philosophical approach of the firm," Brebach left the firm with five other senior consultants to form International Consulting Group (ICG), a competing business information systems firm financed in part by Saatchi & Saatchi.[24] Andersen filed a lawsuit against the new company, charging it with stealing Andersen clients and employees. ICG countersued, claiming violations of antitrust laws stemming from Andersen's attempts to prevent it from engaging in the consulting business. In July 1989 the firms settled the dispute, ICG committing "not to hire any more Andersen employees until January" and Andersen assenting "to pay the founders the capital and share of earnings they had accumulated before their departure."[25]

THE NEW ANDERSEN

Andersen consultants continued to express disenchantment with their "forced proximity" with the accountants. "You can't imagine," remarked Stanley Cornelison, Brebach's successor as head of consulting,

> how many times I sit on an airplane with a businessman next to me. We begin talking. When I say I am with Arthur Andersen, he'll say: "Oh, the public accounting firm." When I tell him that I head up the management consulting practice, the response is: "Golly, I didn't know you were in that kind of business."[26]

Instituting a Few Degrees of Separation[27]

On November 29, 1988, Andersen became the first of the large accounting firms to announce, in a set of arrangements dubbed the "Florida accords,"

that its two practices would henceforth run as separate units—Arthur Andersen and Andersen Consulting—each with its own managing director, under the umbrella of a new parent company, Andersen Worldwide. AC was to consult to large corporations, primarily in computer systems integration and business strategy, AA to continue its work in audit and tax, but would also be free to provide consulting to small and middle-market companies with annual revenues of less than $175 million, which AC would not pursue. The consulting practice, thus, achieved a new and separate identity as Andersen Consulting, a behemoth at birth with more than $1.5 billion in revenues. The consulting partners were also promised greater representation on the governance committees.

Nor would the two business units continue to pool their profits; only an annual transfer payment of 15 percent of the more profitable business unit's earnings would be siphoned off to the less profitable unit. Andersen's consulting partners were thus able to earn $50,000–100,000 more than their accounting partners, and achieve compensation approaching the level earned by partners in consulting firms such as McKinsey and Booz, Allen & Hamilton.

"Two clear lines," Kullberg averred, "gives a more direct voice to the business units."[28] Added Cornelison: "We've created two strategic business units that are equal in the eyes of the partners. . . . It's a big change."[29] Senior accounting partner James Kackley concurred: "[Andersen Consulting] is the world's largest consulting organization and it truly deserves a separate and distinct identity. The increased visibility that will come with this identity will benefit all of our practices, including tax and audit and financial consulting."[30]

Some outsiders, however, expressed reservations. David Lord, managing editor of *Consultants News,* remarked ominously: "Andersen is scrambling to keep its consulting partners happy and together, but some consulting people may still leave for greener pastures."[31] Brebach observed that Andersen's decision to set up a separate consulting unit without spinning it off "doesn't really resolve many of Andersen's problems." The changes, he remarked, neither afforded AC the "freedom to be its own master," nor "resolved how to raise capital and do joint ventures with audit clients without raising conflict-of-interest problems."[32] Although the newly autonomous AC was permitted to enter into contingency payment agreements previously forbidden by accounting regulations, as members of a unified partnership AC partners remained liable for damages awarded in negligence lawsuits brought against AA auditors. Moreover, AC's ability to finance investments in computers and software by "going public" remained constrained by the potential for conflict of interest should share ownership happen to reside with one of AW's large, institutional clients.

New Leadership for a New Organization[33]

In January 1989 George Shaheen was appointed head of AC and Richard Measelle head of AA. Two months later, AW chief operating officer Lawrence Weinbach replaced Duane Kullberg as CEO of AW (organizational charts are presented in Exhibit 2). Under Kullberg's leadership, the firm had grown from revenues of $650 million in 1980 to $2.8 billion in 1988 and from 18,000 personnel

EXHIBIT 2

Andersen Worldwide Organization

Source: Casewriters.

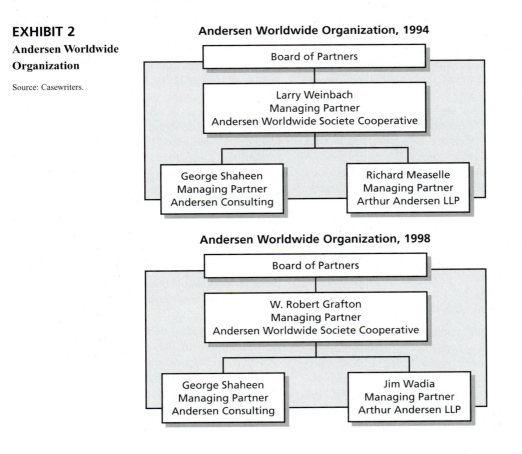

Andersen Worldwide Organization, 1994

Board of Partners

Larry Weinbach
Managing Partner
Andersen Worldwide Societe Cooperative

George Shaheen
Managing Partner
Andersen Consulting

Richard Measelle
Managing Partner
Arthur Andersen LLP

Andersen Worldwide Organization, 1998

Board of Partners

W. Robert Grafton
Managing Partner
Andersen Worldwide Societe Cooperative

George Shaheen
Managing Partner
Andersen Consulting

Jim Wadia
Managing Partner
Arthur Andersen LLP

TABLE A   AW's Revenues (1990–1993)

Year	Revenues ($ m)			% of AW's Total Revenues		Revenue Growth over Previous Year (%)	
	AA	AC	AW	AA	AC	AA	AC
1990	2,284	2,085	4,341	53	47	18	32
1991	2,692	2,341	5,033	53	47	18	14
1992	2,994	2,723	5,717	52	48	11	16
1993	3,185	2,876	6,061	53	47	6	6

Source: AA, www.arthurandersen.com, and AC, www.ac.com, websites, accessed August 5, 1999; "Arthur Andersen Worldwide Organization announces annual revenues," *Business Wire,* October 18, 1990.

to 46,000. However, the firm was facing growing rifts between its two operating units.

According to AW's press release, Weinbach's first task would be to "help implement the restructuring."[34] One of his major goals was to keep all the partners within the firm. "You can't mandate within an organization that people must remain," he reflected. "People stay because they want to, but we've created ways to solve our compensation problems and to get sufficient representation of consulting, audit and tax partners, and geographic units in separate Andersen business units."[35]

The early 1990s passed relatively quietly with little public display of animosity between the two business units. Both business units grew steadily from 1990 to 1993, contributing roughly the same relative proportions to AW's revenues (see Table A). By 1990, only its second year as an independent entity, AC had become the world's largest consulting firm with revenues in excess of $2 billion, 157 offices in 45 countries, and more than 20,000 professionals.

AC Overtakes AA[36]

Waves of reengineering, outsourcing noncore processes, installing sophisticated software to support core processes, and ensuring Y2K-compliance of legacy software that swept large firms engendered a boom in consulting during the mid-1990s. AC's "business integration" concept— "one-stop" delivery of strategic consulting, tech-

nology implementation, and change management—flourished in this business environment. Andersen's restructuring, moreover, enabled AC to offer new, innovative services, including outsourcing of entire departments such as financial administration. Under multiyear mega-contracts, AC assumed responsibility for the management of client departments with agreed-upon performance targets against hundreds of millions of dollar payments. Cost overruns and savings were shared by AC and its clients. Even though AA was experiencing healthy double-digit growth, its revenues were quickly exceeded by AC's (see Table B).

Besides Andersen, all the other "Big Five" firms were experiencing rapid increase in their consulting revenues (see Table C).

Compounding the growing differences between Andersen's two units was the increasingly greater gap between the profitability of consulting and accounting. As auditing, which constituted the bulk of accounting, became increasingly commoditized, its margins declined. With demand burgeoning, consulting was sustaining high margins with value-based pricing.

The two business units were developing divergent identities. In the marketplace AA was increasingly viewed as entrenched, stable, and mature, AC as young, growing, and brash. Internally, AC partners characterized AA partners as stolid and unimaginative, AA partners their AC counterparts as arrogant, obstinate, and selfish.

TABLE B AW's Revenues (1994–1998)

	Revenues ($ m)			% of AW's Total Revenues		Revenue Growth over Previous Year (%)	
Year	AA	AC	AW	AA	AC	AA	AC
1994	3,519	3,452	6,971	50	50	10	20
1995	4,133	4,224	8,357	49	51	17	22
1996	4,605	5,302	9,907	46	54	11	26
1997	5,191	6,647	11,838	44	56	13	25
1998	6,093	8,307	14,400	42	58	17	25

Source: AA, www.arthurandersen.com, and AC, www.ac.com, websites, accessed August 5, 1999.

TABLE C Big Five Revenues in 1997 and 1998

($ millions)	1998 Revenues (versus 1997)						
	Management Consulting $	MC % Growth	Audit, Tax, Other $	A/T/O % Growth	Total $	Total % Growth	
AW[a]	$7,740	29.1%	$6,160	16.1%	$13,900	23.0%	
Deloitte & Touche	3,000	30.4	6,000	18.2	9,000	22.0	
Ernst & Young	4,000	33.3	6,900	13.1	10,900	19.8	
KPMG	3,000	30.4	7,400	10.4	10,400	15.6	
PriceWaterhouseCoopers	3,970	41.5	11,343	13.8	15,312	19.9	
Total	$21,710	32.4%	$37,803	14.0%	$59,512	20.1%	

[a] Self-reported 1998 revenues for Andersen Consulting and Arthur Andersen (in Table B) are slightly different from the *Consultants News* estimates used in Table C.
Source: *Consultants News*, February 1999.

Pinpricks in the Marketplace: AA Enters Consulting, AC the Boardroom[37]

In December 1994, citing unmet needs of mid-sized client companies, AA's small consulting operation had crossed the limits imposed by the Florida accords that had constrained it to working with companies with annual revenues of less than $175 million. The accounting unit, according to AA's managing partner Richard Measelle, would be "focusing on the middle market, companies with $500 million to $2 billion in annual net revenue."[38] AC, which was focusing on large multinational clients, seemed initially to accommodate AA's entry. Wishing Godspeed to AA's consulting efforts, AC's Shaheen remarked: "There is enough room for everyone."[39]

AA's 1996 consulting revenues were in the neighborhood of $500 million. Rumblings of AC's frustration began to be heard after 1996, when AA became an official installer of SAP, the popular business process software, and began to compete seriously with AC for systems integration projects. AC managing partner Shaheen's expressions of concern were widely reported. "It's difficult for two brothers to date the same gal."[40] "The internal competition in the marketplace must be addressed."[41] "The amount of client confusion is severe. It's gotten worse as they've encroached on our space."[42] "It requires fixing. I think it can be fixed. I think it will be fixed."[43]

As AC's service offerings increasingly went beyond IT implementation to "business integration" solutions its reach extended beyond client companies' chief information and chief technology officers to their CFOs and CEOs, access to whom had thus far been restricted to AA's auditors. AA partners' concern that their AC brethren were challenging the exclusivity of their relationships with clients' top executives was borne out by instances of the two units pitching against each other to CEOs of potential clients.

Bad Blood and Trash Talking[44]

Marketplace competition soon degenerated into public recriminations. Remarked one AA partner: "The business consulting unit of Arthur Andersen is the fastest-growing unit in the company. Maybe that's why Andersen Consulting doesn't like us. They see us as a threat to their turf. There are some big egos involved here and most of these people have forgotten what they learned in kindergarten about sharing their toys."[45] Responded an AC partner: "The feeling within Andersen Consulting is that we are outstripping Arthur Andersen with fewer partners and employees in fewer offices. Some people feel that we bring more to the table than the number crunchers over at Arthur Andersen."[46]

As their business unit generated higher revenues and higher profits than AA, AC partners began to chafe vocally at their comparative underrepresentation (see Table D). Because they had typically been elected partners more recently than their counterparts in accounting, consulting's fewer partners also had comparatively smaller shares and lesser representation on AW's governing board. Acknowledging that only one-third of the members of AW's board of partners came from the consulting side, Weinbach conceded: "The governance is disproportionate and needs to be reviewed."[47]

With antipathy intensifying, AC partners began to question the rationale for the transfer payments established in the 1989 agreements to level partner compensation across AW. Whereas the consultants had received transfer payments from the accountants in the early 1990s, the flow, in increasingly larger amounts, had shifted in the other direction. In 1997 AC paid AA $173 million, an average of $153,000 per AC partner. AC partners began to publicly protest that the transfer payment was essentially subsidizing a competitor. Complained one AC partner: "The payment stipulated in the firms' operating agreements is based on the premise of inter-firm cooperation but has, in effect, served to finance the continued expansion of Arthur Andersen's consulting business."[48] Arguing for an end to the transfer payment, Shaheen maintained that "it doesn't make sense for Andersen Consulting to continue to send money, especially the amount of money we send to Arthur Andersen, and at the same time compete more and more in the marketplace. That is not a sustainable situation."[49]

TABLE D

AW Partners (1996–1997)

Sources: Yates, "Famous Family Thinks about a Breakup;" Elizabeth MacDonald and Joseph White, "Generation Gap: At Arthur Andersen, The Accountants Face an Unlikely Adversary" *The Wall Street Journal,* April 23, 1997.

Year	Number of Partners			% of Total Partners	
	AA	AC	AW	AA	AC
1996	1,835	965	2,800	66	34
1997	1,700	1,038	2,738	62	38

BEYOND RECONCILIATION?

Search for Weinbach's Successor[50]

The one element that had remained constant at Andersen throughout the waves of growth and change had been the firm's leadership. Under Weinbach, whose two four-year terms as worldwide managing partner had passed uncontested, Andersen had prospered as never before. In the industry analysts' reports Measelle and Shaheen often shared with Weinbach credit for the firm's stunning performance. Shaheen was especially visible in the press, which characterized him as "driven and scrappy" while also emphasizing his "arrogance and obstinacy."[51]

When Weinbach announced in February 1997 that he would step down as AW's CEO at the end of August, AW's cumbersome process for electing a CEO was set into motion. A 12-person nominating committee (six from each unit) was charged with presenting to the AW board a ranked list of nominees. The board then named a single candidate whom the partners could "approve" or "disapprove." A two-thirds vote was needed to elect a CEO. Former partner Millar described the process as "a very efficient internal system for being sure that when a candidate went up the support was adequate to make [election] happen."[52]

Andersen's partners had never rejected a nominee for CEO in the firm's 84-year history. But this was the first time since the 1989 split that the AW partners had been charged with choosing a new leader. The consulting partners immediately put forward Shaheen as a candidate. Richard Measelle announced that he would not be a candidate; in his place the accounting partners nominated Jim Wadia, AA's U.K. managing partner (see Exhibit 3 for biographies of the candidates). In Shaheen's favor was AC's track record of quintupled revenues since 1989 and sustained high profitability. Wadia enjoyed the support of the accounting partners who outnumbered the consulting partners 1,700 to 1,038 and comprised 18 of the 27-member AW board.

Shaheen and Wadia were ranked one and two, respectively, on the list the nominating committee sent to the board. The AA-dominated board refused to endorse Shaheen and fearing a "partners' rebellion," also hesitated to buck the committee's recommendation by endorsing Wadia.[53] Ultimately, the board determined that both Shaheen and Wadia should address the entire partnership at an April 1997 session of AW's worldwide meeting in Paris and the nominee selected after their addresses.

Move, Countermove . . . Stalemate?[54]

Shaheen, the first to speak during the session, proposed to consolidate the firm's consulting activities into one arm and reposition Andersen Worldwide as a "broad-based consulting firm."[55] Recalled one attendee: "George basically said, 'This firm is in crisis. Let's recognize the fact that it doesn't make sense the way that things are—so let's further segregate and separate.'"[56] Incensed accounting partners alleged that Shaheen was effectively trying to mount a takeover and change Andersen into a different company. "There was a feeling among the accounting partners that Shaheen would build a power base and split the firm," observed an AA partner. "He was hesitant to support Wadia [if Wadia won]. He implied that 'I'll do what I can to help' but not 'Yes, I'll give him my 100 percent support.'"[57] Shaheen's unwillingness to state unequivocally that he would support Wadia if the latter were elected irked several AA partners. "When confronted with a test of partnership, he didn't pass," remarked one.[58]

In contrast, Wadia's speech, which expressed confidence in Andersen's ability to work out its internal issues over time, was viewed as conciliatory. He proposed no drastic realignment, suggesting instead a one-year waiting period before making any changes at all, and appeared willing to compromise with the consulting partners on money, governance, and intra-firm competition. One supporter recalled that Wadia "put forward views that were not necessarily pure, mainstream Arthur Andersen.

EXHIBIT 3 Biographies

George Shaheen

Andersen's First Six Managing Partners	
Arthur Andersen	1913–1947
Leonard Spacek	1947–1963
Walter Oliphant	1963–1970
Harvey Kapnick	1970–1979
Duane Kullberg	1979–1989
Lawrence Weinbach	1989–1997

Jim Wadia

George Shaheen

Shaheen joined Arthur Andersen in 1967 and became a partner in 1977. From 1980 to 1985 he oversaw the consulting practice for North and South Carolina, then the San Francisco–based Northern California consulting practice. He was managing partner of the Southeast U.S. Region and North American practices and practice director for Japan and the Pacific Northwest before becoming managing partner of Andersen Consulting Worldwide.

Shaheen held a bachelor's degree in marketing and a master's degree in finance from Bradley University in Peoria, Illinois. He was on the board of trustees for Bradley University, was a member of Northwestern University's J. L. Kellogg Graduate School of Management's board of advisors and the Chairmen's Committee of the Computerworld Smithsonian Awards for technological innovation, and served on *Chief Executive* magazine's advisory board and Siebel Systems' board of directors.

Jim Wadia

Wadia was born in Bombay, India, but left the country when he was two years old. He was educated in Switzerland and emigrated to the United Kingdom in 1965. He qualified for the English Bar as a barrister (attorney) in 1969 and then as a chartered accountant (CPA) in 1973. He joined Arthur Andersen in 1977 in the tax practice, became a manager in 1978, and a partner in 1982. From 1989 to 1993 he was head of the London Tax Practice and was elected United Kingdom Managing Partner of Arthur Andersen in September 1993. Since 1993, he has served as a member of the Andersen Worldwide board of partners. In July 1997, he was named managing partner of Arthur Andersen Worldwide, succeeding Richard Measelle.

Sources: Shaheen's biography taken from Andersen Consulting website, www.ac.com, accessed August 3, 1999. Wadia's biography taken from "Arthur Andersen Names Jim Wadia Managing Partner," *Business Wire,* July 23, 1997; and Elizabeth MacDonald, "Arthur Andersen Appoints Jim Wadia to Top Post amid Corporate Tensions," *The Wall Street Journal,* July 23, 1997, p. A2. Photographs taken from Elizabeth MacDonald and Joseph B. White "Divorce Petition: How Ugly is the Split of the Andersens? Even Worse Than It Seems," *The Wall Street Journal,* February 4, 1998.

He offered a clear compromise on consulting, agreeing to pursue very distinct markets." Wadia also responded immediately and clearly that if Shaheen were elected he would support him.[59]

The board nominated Wadia. But in a May 1997 election, despite his moderate stance, Wadia garnered only 51 percent of the votes. The board then nominated Shaheen, who, in a June election, also failed to command the necessary two-thirds support, receiving only 63 percent. W. Robert Grafton, chairman of the partner's committee, was hastily appointed acting CEO as the firm sought a way around the impasse.

The December 1997 AC Partnership Meeting[60]

To try to ease tension and ameliorate fallout from the votes in May and June, the AW board appointed a high-level committee in July to address the imbalance of power in the firm, wrestle with marketplace confusion, and deal with the transfer payment issue. But no significant progress was made towards a compromise.

Momentum began to build within AC toward breaking away entirely. Shaheen called an AC partnership meeting in San Francisco for the second week of December 1997 to which he also invited Wadia (who had been named managing partner of AA in July after failing in his quest to be AW CEO) and Grafton.

Ninety-percent of AC's 1,124 partners attended the meeting. Wadia called for "free competition" by each unit in its marketplace and "free movement" of partners and staff between the two firms.[61] Wadia also suggested that rather than calculate the transfer payment each year AC pay "in perpetuity" up to a $180 million transfer payment, adjusted for inflation.[62] Shaheen described AC partners' reaction to Wadia's speech: "My partners sat there in stunned silence."[63] Grafton then spoke, asking the accounting and consulting partners to resolve their differences internally.

The next morning the AC partners voted unanimously to reject Wadia's offer. At noon Shaheen and Jon Conahan, managing partner for strategy

for AC, convened the partners and recommended that AC seek to sever its ties with AA through arbitration in the International Chamber of Commerce (ICC) in Paris, AW's officially designated method of dispute resolution. "The vision I have for Andersen Consulting," explained Shaheen,

> is that we are building the consulting firm of the future. But that vision in now in jeopardy because of these internal machinations. . . . Our intent is that arbitration will bring to an end our internal structural issues with Arthur Andersen and Andersen Worldwide. This process will allow us to reach a fair and amicable solution that will enable both Andersen Consulting and Arthur Andersen to continue successfully serving clients in their respective marketplaces.[64]

The AC partners again voted unanimously, this time in support of the proposal. AC immediately applied to ICC to arbitrate its dispute with AA.

AA Prepares to Defend

Reacting to news of AC's decision to seek arbitration, a weary Grafton said: "It's no secret we've been trying to work through a range of issues. Our organizational agreements provide for arbitration as a method to resolve disputes and, as one of our businesses has filed for arbitration, we'll now try to resolve the issues using an arbitrator."[65] Lamented Wadia:

> Arthur Andersen attempted to keep the existing structure intact. Arthur Andersen presented a proposal to Andersen Consulting that addresses concerns of both sides and keeps Arthur Andersen and Andersen Consulting under the Andersen Worldwide umbrella. We are disappointed that Andersen Consulting rejected that approach and filed for arbitration. We would have preferred to continue the dialogue and resolve this in a less confrontational way. But however this process ultimately gets resolved, the Arthur Andersen brand and business are extraordinarily strong and will continue to get even stronger.[66]

One less diplomatic AA partner threatened that the accountants would "make life miserable for Andersen Consulting."[67] At a meeting of the accountant-dominated Andersen Worldwide board on February 12, 1998, the accounting partners pushed through a resolution, over Grafton's protests, to establish an accountant-only "protection committee" charged with devising measures to "protect AW and AA."[68] The "sham resolution" outraged AC partners. Characterizing it as a "lawless exercise" intended to "hijack" the organization before the arbitration process had a chance to begin, AC sued on February 18 to compel AA to participate in the arbitration process.[69] On March 16, the court ruled that the ICC was to be the only venue for resolution of the Andersen dispute.[70]

THE ARBITRATION PROCESS

In mid-1998 Shaheen, Wadia, and the rest of Andersen's leadership team met and embarked on ICC's nine-step arbitration process (see Table E).

Gamba, who had been accepted by both AA and AC as the arbitrator, was called upon to rule on a number of complex issues.

Did AA Breach Its 1989 Agreement with AC?[71]

AC charged in its arbitration filing that AA had breached the 1989 Florida accords, which proscribed it from pursuing consulting engagements with corporations that had revenues in excess of $175 million. Market competition had led AA, AC alleged, to duplicate AC's consulting capabilities, sometimes by competitively hiring AC personnel.

Wadia responded on behalf of AA: "We have not infringed our obligations; we have not violated operating agreements."[72] AA was expected to argue that it had, since the 1994 launch of its business consulting division, openly announced, without objection from AC, its strategic intent to build a large-scale consulting practice. In any case, AA would argue that the accords were informal and applicable only in the United States.

Was Any Monetary Compensation Warranted?[73]

Many AA partners maintained that they had a justifiable claim over part of AC's profit stream, because AC had been conceived, initially staffed, and seeded by AA partners, who, together with AC

TABLE E ICC Arbitration Process

1. AC files a request with the International Chamber of Commerce's Court of Arbitration that summarizes the dispute, issues involved, and claims to be decided.
2. AA and AW have 30 days to respond to the claim and make counterclaims.
3. AC responds to the counterclaims.
4. Both parties submit arbitrator candidates—typically lawyers, retired jurists, or academics—based on a set of rules. If both sides can't agree on an acceptable person, ICC decides.
5. Arbitrator-prepared "Terms of Reference" summarizing both sides' positions is submitted.
6. Arbitrator initiates fact checking through such processes as witness statements and legal briefs.
7. Rules set a six-month time limit following approval of Terms, to decide the case (extensions permissible).
8. Arbitrator submits draft award to ICC's Court, which may offer suggestions and modifications as to form. The final award is decided solely by the arbitrator.
9. Both parties act on the final determination, including the division of costs associated with the process.

Source: *Consultants News,* January 1998, p. 1.

partners, still owned it. AC partners, on the other hand, believed that only they were entitled to reap the full reward from the income AC would produce in the future. To the question posed by AA partners, "Would AC be a $7 billion business if it didn't leverage off 85 years of Arthur Andersen's effort and the name?"[74] Shaheen responded by stating emphatically: "Could we have built this company [AC] under a totally different name? Yes, I believe we could. Absolutely we could. We made a tremendous investment in building the Andersen Consulting name. . . . No AA partner owns any piece of AC."[75]

AA partners retorted that if their counterparts at AC no longer wanted to share profits, all they needed to do was follow 20-year-old provisions that established a one-time payment of one-and-a-half times annual revenues from the seceding unit to the rest of the partnership. Based on AC's 1997 worldwide revenues of $6.6 billion, this amounted to a payment of nearly $10 billion. Wadia justified the fairness of this approach:

> You can't stop [AC if they want to leave]. . . .
> It's a people business. But we would ask the arbitrator to ensure that the contractual provisions that bind us are enforced. There are three contractual provisions. One is the return of the Andersen name; one is the return of Andersen technology, which is a broad word for methodologies and programs etc.; and the third is the financial cost of leaving the network. . . . These provisions have been in our documents since 1977, so it is not as if these provisions were suddenly created and put into our documents in the last couple of years whilst some of the tensions between AA and AC were taking place.[76]

AC partner Conahan responded that not only did the "poison pill" clause not apply to AC's impending departure because the clause was "specific to individual practice groups, not the organization as a whole,"[77] but also "any assertions that the ["poison pill"] provision would even come into play is something I believe that Andersen is putting forward to distract from the core issue—that they breached the contract by getting into consulting."[78] AC's Marketing and Communications director James Murphy echoed Conahan's statements.

> The contractual provision doesn't apply here since Andersen Consulting has not left the worldwide firm. The arbitration filing requests that the firm be excused from all further contractual obligations based on serious breaches by Arthur Andersen.[79]

"AC owes no penalty because AA violated the contract," added Shaheen, "If any money is owed, it's to AC."[80] AC filed a lawsuit for more than $500 million, seeking reimbursement for all transfer payments it had made to AA between 1994 (the time of the alleged breach of contract) and 1997, and put the projected $200 million payment for 1998 in escrow pending resolution of the issue in arbitration.

AA partners construed AC's argument in blocking transfer payments as simply an expression of AC partners' greed. Reflected one longtime AA partner: "A few years back, AA could have said the same thing [Shaheen is now]—'we want to keep what we make'—but we never did because we recognized the way it [the Andersen partnership] works."[81]

GAMBA'S CHALLENGE[82]

Despite the distractions and negative publicity generated by the arbitration proceedings, AW continued to prosper in the late 1990s. Facing mounting demand for information technology consulting, AC revenues topped $8.3 billion in 1998 and the firm hired a legion of 15,000 new consultants, increasing its worldwide staffing to 65,000 and surpassing the personnel levels of Arthur Andersen. AC remained the world's largest management consulting practice—19 percent larger than its nearest rival PriceWaterhouseCoopers (see Exhibit 4). AA also continued to expand, booking more than $6 billion

EXHIBIT 4   Top 20 Management Consulting Firms (based on 1998 revenues)

Firm	Rank	1998 Global Consulting Revenue ($ m)	Rank	1997 Global Consulting Revenue ($ m)
Andersen Consulting	1	$7,129	1	$5,726
PriceWaterhouseCoopers	2	6,000	4, 9[a]	3,800
Ernst & Young	3	3,870	3	2,680
Deloitte Consulting	4	3,240	5	2,300
CSC	5	3,000	2	3,000
KPMG	5	3,000	7	2,011
McKinsey & Company	7	2,500	6	2,200
Cap Gemini Group	8	2,261	8	1,648
Mercer Consulting Group	9	1,543	10	1,338
Arthur Andersen	10	1,368	14	953
A.T. Kearney	11	1,234	12	1,100
Towers Perrin	12	1,230	11	1,120
Booz-Allen Hamilton	13	1,204	13	1,075
IBM Consulting	14	990	16	880
American Management Systems	15	913	17	791
Keane	16	872	24	560
Hewitt Associates	17	858	18	709
Sema Group	18	836	15	888
Logica	19	790	23	570
Boston Consulting Group	20	730	20	655

[a] In 1997, prior to the Coopers and Lybrand-Price Waterhouse merger, Coopers and Lybrand was ranked fourth with $2,400 million revenue and Price Waterhouse ninth with $1,400 million revenue.
Source: "50 Largest Management Consulting Firms," *Consultants News,* June 1999, p. 6.

in revenues in its 1998 fiscal year (see Exhibits 5 and 6). Yet, partners of both firms were anxiously awaiting Gamba's momentous judgment.

Gamba surely was pondering the arguments presented by both sides in anticipation of the closed-door hearing on October 25, 1999 with AA and AC representatives. The Andersen case was one of the most complicated the ICC had ever adjudicated. Gamba must have recognized the gravity of his task and been aware that both sides wanted the dispute resolved quickly. The fate and future of the two firms, as well as a large portion of the personal wealth of the 2,800 partners, lay in his hands.

EXHIBIT 5   Andersen Consulting Growth—Revenues and Personnel

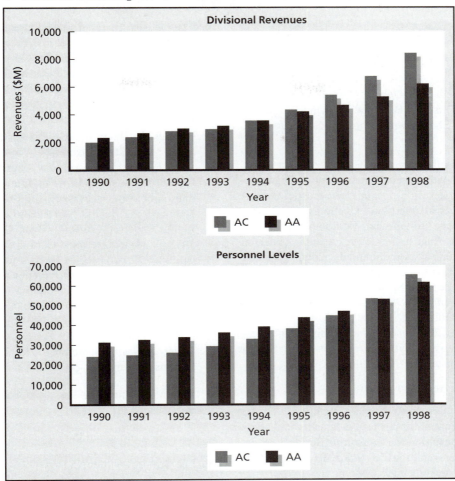

Source: Company websites www.ac.com and www.arthurandersen.com; accessed March 29, 1999.

EXHIBIT 6   Andersen Consulting and Arthur Andersen in 1998

	Andersen Consulting	Arthur Andersen
Revenues ($ million)	8,300	6,093
Employees	65,000	61,500
Major competency and practice areas	• Process • Change management • Strategic services • Technology	• Assurance and business advisory services • Business consulting • Global corporate finance • Tax, legal, and business advisory services

Note: AW and AA's fiscal years ended on August 31, AC's on December 31.
Sources: Company websites www.ac.com and www.arthurandersen.com; accessed March 29, 1999.

References

1. Dominic Walsh, "Game of Halves," *The Times of London,* July 7, 1998, section 4m2, p. 29; Elizabeth MacDonald, "Andersen Consulting's Breakup Battle with Arthur Andersen Nears Showdown," *The Wall Street Journal,* July 28, 1999, p. A2.

2. Besides the direct quotes, this section draws upon "Arthur Andersen Worldwide Organization," *Hoover's Profiles Business Descriptions,* available via OneSource Business Browser, http://globalbb.onesource.com, accessed August 3, 1999; Arthur Andersen website, www.arthurandersen.com, section "About Arthur Andersen," accessed August 3, 1999; Leonard Spacek, *The Growth of Arthur Andersen—An Oral History* (New York: Garland Publishing, 1989), pp. 9, 83; and Mark Stevens, *The Big Six: The Selling Out of America's Top Accounting Firms* (New York: Simon & Schuster, 1991), p. 106.

3. Arthur Andersen website.

4. David Whitford, "Arthur, Arthur . . . The Combination of Arthur Andersen and Andersen Consulting is a Consulting Services Giant. So Why Can't the Two Sides Get Along," *Fortune,* November 10, 1997, p. 169.

5. Besides the direct quotes, this section draws upon Andersen Consulting website, www.ac.com, section "Our History," accessed August 3, 1999; "The Palace Revolt at Arthur Andersen," *Business Week* October 29, 1979, Industrial Edition, p. 52; and Stevens, *The Big Six,* pp. 105–15.

6. Duane R. Kullberg, quoted in Sallie Gaines, "Andersen Reorganizes Consulting Operations," *Chicago Tribune,* September 16, 1987, business section, p. 5.

7. Stevens, *The Big Six,* p. 108.

8. Ibid., pp. 112, 114.

9. "The Palace Revolt at Arthur Andersen."

10. Ibid.

11. Ibid.

12. Stevens, *The Big Six,* p. 116.

13. Besides the direct quotes, this section draws upon "Andersen Consulting," *Hoover's Profiles Business Descriptions,* available via OneSource Business Browser; http://globalbb.onesource.com, accessed August 3, 1999; Kathleen A. Behof, "An Identity Crisis at Arthur Andersen," *Business Week,* October 24, 1988, p. 34; Lee Berton, "Cutting the Pie: Accounting Firms Face a Deepening Division over Consultant's Pay as Revenues in Advice Field Outrun Rises in Auditing," *The Wall Street Journal,* July 26, 1988; Lee Berton, "Arthur Andersen Weighs Restructuring to Make Consulting Practice Separate," *The Wall Street Journal,* September 29, 1988; and Stevens, *The Big Six,* pp. 117, 121–27.

14. Berton, "Cutting the Pie"; and Stevens, *The Big Six,* p. 120.

15. Berton, "Cutting the Pie."

16. Lee Berton, "Arthur Andersen's Chief of Consulting Relieved of Role," *The Wall Street Journal,* May 19, 1988.

17. Ibid.

18. Berton, "Cutting the Pie."

19. Stevens, *The Big Six,* pp. 123–24.

20. Besides the direct quotes, this section draws upon Behof, "An Identity Crisis at Arthur Andersen"; Berton, "Arthur Andersen Weighs Restructuring"; and Gaines, "Andersen Reorganizes Consulting Operations," p. 5.

21. Gaines, "Andersen Reorganizes Consulting Operations."

22. Besides the direct quotes, this section draws upon Berton, "Arthur Andersen Weighs Restructuring"; Lee Berton, "Andersen's Lawrence Weinbach Picked to Head Firm Amid Its Restructuring," *The Wall Street Journal,* March 23, 1989; Adam Bryant, "The Andersen Family Feud; 2 Units Split on New Leadership," *New York Times,* June 28, 1997, section 1, p. 35; and Stevens, *The Big Six,* pp. 131–40, 148.

23. Berton, "Arthur Andersen Weighs Restructuring."

24. Lee Berton, "Arthur Andersen's Chief of Consulting Relieved of Role."

25. Michael Skapinker, "McKinsey in Talks over ICG Acquisition, *Financial Times,* September 30, 1989, section I, 12.

26. Behof, "An Identity Crisis at Arthur Andersen."

27. Besides the direct quotes, this section draws upon Lee Berton, "Andersen Will Raise Its Consultants' Pay in an Apparent Effort to Stop Defections," *The Wall Street Journal,* November 29, 1988; Jim Kelly, "Andersen Bad Blood Spells a Difficult Path to Divorce: Dispute over Consulting Arm's Desire to Split Could Last Years," *Financial Times* (London), January 13, 1998, p. 26; Julia Flynn Siler, "Andersen Plans a Restructuring," *New York Times,* November 29, 1988, section D, p. 1; Whitford, "Arthur, Arthur"; and Ronald E. Yates, "Famous Family Thinks about a Breakup," *Chicago Tribune,* September 8, 1996, business section, p. 7.

28. Siler, "Andersen Plans a Restructuring."

29. Ibid.

30. Ibid.

31. Ibid.

32. Berton, "Andersen Will Raise Its Consultants' Pay."

33. Besides the direct quotes, this section draws upon "CBOE Appoints Kullberg as Public Director." *PR Newswire,* March 22, 1990; and United Nations Conference of Trade and Development, "Management Consulting: A Survey of the Industry and Its Largest Firms," (New York, United Nations, 1993), 41.

34. "CBOE Appoints Kullberg as Public Director."

35. Berton, "Andersen's Lawrence Weinbach Picked to Head Firm."

36. This section draws upon Thomas Hoffman, "Some Contracts Share Pain, Gain," *Computerworld.* November 25, 1996, p. 69; "Big Five Post 32.4% Consulting Growth," *Consultants News,* February 1999; and Whitford, "Arthur, Arthur."

37. Besides the direct quotes, this section draws upon Elizabeth MacDonald, "Andersen Consulting Votes to Go It Alone," *The Wall Street Journal,* December 19, 1997.

38. MacDonald and White, "Generation Gap."

39. *Consultants News,* April 1997.

40. McDonald and White, "Generation Gap."

41. Bryant, "The Andersen Family Feud."

42. *Consultants News,* February 1998, p. 3.

43. McDonald and White, "Generation Gap."

44. Besides the direct quotes, this section draws upon McDonald and White, "Generation Gap"; and "AC Seeks Divorce through Arbitration," *Consultants News,* January 1998, pp. 1–2.

45. Yates, "Famous Family Thinks about a Breakup."

46. Ibid.

47. Elizabeth MacDonald, "Arthur Andersen Appoints Jim Wadia to Top Post amid Corporate Tensions," *The Wall Street Journal,* July 23, 1997, p. A2.

48. "AC Seeks Divorce through Arbitration."

49. Kevin Merrill, "George Shaheen—Shaheen Helped Engineer Andersen Consulting's Vote to Take Dispute with Arthur Andersen to an Arbitrator," *Computer Reseller News,* November 16, 1998.

50. Besides the direct quotes, this section draws upon Bryant, "The Andersen Family Feud"; Joanne Gordon and Robert Lenzer, "The Messiahs of the Network," *Forbes,* March 8, 1999; McDonald and White, "Generation Gap"; Ravi Velloor, "Andersen's Chief 'Android'," *The Straits Times,* March 23, 1998, section Money, p. 62; and Whitford, "Arthur, Arthur."

51. Gordon and Lenzer, "The Messiahs of the Network."

52. Whitford, "Arthur, Arthur."

53. Bryant, "The Andersen Family Feud."

54. Besides the direct quotes, this section draws upon MacDonald, "Arthur Andersen Appoints Jim Wadia to Top Post amid Corporate Tensions"; and Elizabeth MacDonald and Joseph B. White "Divorce Petition: How Ugly Is the Split of the Andersens? Even Worse Than It Seems," *The Wall Street Journal,* February 4, 1998.

55. Ibid.

56. Ibid.

57. Whitford, "Arthur, Arthur"; and *Consultants News,* June 1997, p. 2.

58. Whitford, "Arthur, Arthur."

59. Ibid.

60. Besides the direct quotes, this section draws upon MacDonald, "Arthur Andersen Appoints Jim Wadia to Top Post amid Corporate Tensions"; MacDonald, "Andersen Consulting Votes to Go It Alone"; and Michael Rapoport, "Andersen Worldwide Unit Files Suit Alleging Parent Is Scuttling Arbitration," *The Wall Street Journal,* February 17, 1998.

61. "Andersen vs. Andersen," *CNNfn,* December 18, 1997; www.cnnfn.com; accessed February 24, 1999.

62. MacDonald and White "Divorce Petition."

63. MacDonald, "Andersen Consulting Votes to Go It Alone."

64. "AC Seeks Divorce through Arbitration"; and MacDonald, "Andersen Consulting Votes to Go It Alone."

65. Bryant, "The Andersen Family Feud."

66. *Consultant News,* January 1998, p. 1.

67. Rapoport, "Andersen Worldwide Unit Files Suit Alleging Parent Is Scuttling Arbitration."

68. Ibid.

69. Ibid.

70. "Judge Won't Step into Bitter Andersen vs. Andersen Dispute," *Dow Jones News Service,* March 20, 1998.

71. Besides the direct quotes, this section draws upon "AC Seeks Divorce through Arbitration"; and Kelly, "Andersen Bad Blood Spells a Difficult Path to Divorce."

72. MacDonald, "Andersen Consulting Votes to Go It Alone."

73. Besides the direct quotes, this section draws upon Whitford, "Arthur, Arthur"; and Roger O. Crockett, "Next Stop, Splitsville: What a Divorce Will Cost Andersen Consulting," *Business Week,* January 18, 1999, p. 100.

74. Robert Bruce, "A Poker Game with Billions to Play For," *The Times of London,* January 15, 1998, p. 28.

75. Whitford, "Arthur, Arthur"; and *Consultants News,* February 1998, p. 3.

76. Chris Merritt, "Andersen Groups May Still Remain Together—Leaders," *Australian Financial Review,* February 12, 1999, p. 17.

77. "AC Seeks Divorce through Arbitration."

78. "Accountants vs. Consultants," *CNNfn,* January 20, 1998; www.cnnfn.com; accessed February 24, 1999.

79. James E. Murphy, "Letter to the Editor: What Dark Cloud Over Andersen?," *Business Week,* February 1, 1999, p. 12.

80. *Consultants News,* February 1998, p. 3.

81. Whitford, "Arthur, Arthur."

82. Besides the direct quotes, this section draws upon Gordon and Lenzer, "The Messiahs of the Network"; and Jim Kelly, "Warring Andersen Sisters Keep Mum Ahead of Paris Court Case," *Financial Times (London),* May 13, 1998, p. 32.

The Saga of Prince Jefri and KPMG (A):
Mystery of the Missing Billions

Accounting and law firms around the globe were following with great interest during the fourth quarter of 1998 the progress through British courts of a lawsuit. Those familiar with the suit, filed by Prince Jefri of Brunei against the professional service firm KPMG Peat Marwick, remarked that its judgment would be "a landmark ruling with profound implications."[1] At stake was nothing less than how professional service firms conduct their business.

THE SULTANATE OF BRUNEI

A lawsuit of grave import to professional service firms the world over had originated in a location remote from the crossroads of international commerce, Brunei.

"The Abode of Peace"[2]

Borneo, the third-largest island in the world, was located in Southeast Asia and apportioned among three countries. The Indonesian state of Kalimantan occupied the southern part and the Malaysian state of Sarawak occupied the north. Surrounded by Sarawak, was Brunei Darussalam, the "Abode of Peace," occupying 2,226 lush, heavily wooded square miles (about the size of Delaware) on Borneo's northwest coast (see Exhibit 1).

Historical references have been found in Chinese and Hindu chronicles of the sixth and seventh centuries referring to Brunei as "Polo," "Puni," and "Poli." A principality since the thirteenth century, when a prince from western Borneo became its first Sultan, Brunei rose to prominence in the fifteenth and sixteenth centuries, when it controlled coastal areas of northwest Borneo, parts of Kalimantan, and the southern Philippines. Trade in camphor, pepper, and gold brought wealth and power, until the onset of European colonialism. After losing its outlying possessions to the Spanish and the Dutch, in the nineteenth century, Brunei lost most of its remaining Borneo territory to Sarawak and was split in two. Fearing absorption by Sarawak, in 1888 Brunei voluntarily became a British protectorate. A 1906 treaty with the United Kingdom assured continuation of the ruling dynasty and introduced a British resident advisor.

A written constitution adopted in 1959 gave Brunei internal self-rule (with a legislative council) under British protection. When elections in 1962 to the legislative council brought sweeping victory for a party with a long-term agenda that included his removal, the Sultan annulled the election results, sparking a rebellion that was swiftly suppressed with the help of British Gurkha troops flown in from Singapore. An emergency was declared, the legislature disbanded, and much of the country's constitution suspended.

Sultan Hassanal's Reign: Wealth in Plenty but Circumscribed Freedoms

The twenty-eighth Sultan of Brunei, Sir Omar Ali Saifuddien, abdicated in October 1967, nam-

Professor Ashish Nanda prepared this case entirely from public sources as the basis for class discussion rather than to illustrate either effective or ineffective handling of an administrative situation.

EXHIBIT 1   Brunei—Geographic Location

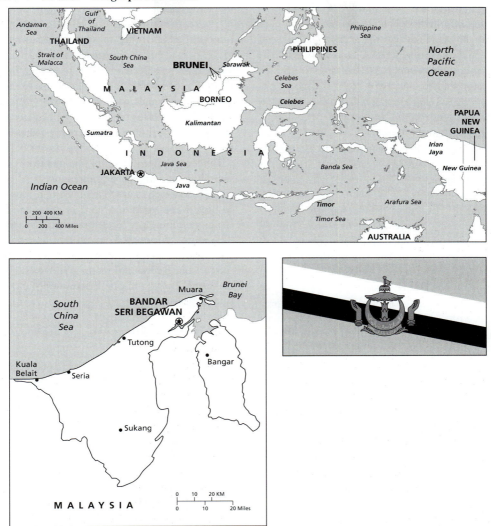

Sources: The Perry-Castañeda Library Map Collection, University of Texas at Austin, accessed May 7, 1999,
www.lib.utexas.edu/Libs/PCL/Map_collection/Map_collection.html; and the Government of Brunei Darussalam official website, accessed May 7, 1999,
www.brunei.gov.bn/about_brunei/flag.htm.

ing as successor his eldest son, 22-year-old Hassanal Bolkiah. (The elder Sultan died in 1986.) A few years after Hassanal ascended the throne, Brunei was catapulted by the oil price shock of 1974 from the ranks of developing countries into the league of newly rich oil powers. Its oil re-serves, contributing negligible revenues since their discovery in 1929, were transformed into sources of vast wealth. Brunei exploited these reserves to become one of the region's richest nations with a per capita annual income of $25,200 in 1997.

Sultan Hassanal channeled much of the country's wealth into the provision of generous benefits to its 300,000 citizens. Education and health care were free, no personal income tax was levied, and housing and pensions were subsidized. Brunei's civil service grew into the largest employer of Brunei Malays; in 1991, 68 percent of Brunei citizens and permanent residents were employed in the public sector.

Yet the sultanate remained autocratic. Even after Britain granted independence to Brunei on January 1, 1984, Sultan Hassanal continued to exercise absolute power. The Sultan was also the prime minister, defense minister, and religious head. During the mid-1990s his three-years-younger brother, Prince Mohamed, was foreign minister and nine-years-younger Prince Jefri, youngest of the three brothers, was finance minister. "In Brunei," observed a Western diplomat, "government is a family business."[3]

Brunei maintained a formidable military force equipped with U.S. and West German helicopters, British Scorpion tanks, and French Exocet missiles. A British Gurkha battalion was "rented" to protect Brunei's oil facilities. The Sultan's personal security and protection of the armed forces arsenal were entrusted to a special unit, recruited from among retired Gurkhas.

Political expression and dissent were strongly discouraged. "Brunei is somewhere in the early Tudor period, between Henry VII and Henry VIII," remarked a Western businessman familiar with Brunei politics.[4] "Brunei is an absolute monarchy with no political parties and little freedom of speech," a reporter observed. "The government is conducted in almost total secrecy. Residents say they believe their telephones are regularly tapped."[5]

There was hardly any public display of dissatisfaction. The Sultan's deployment of oil revenues appeared to have transformed Brunei into a politically sedated enclave of docile affluence that observers dubbed the "Shellfare state." Asked about the continuing state of emergency, first declared in 1962 and routinely renewed every two years, an aide to the Sultan quipped: "We haven't had any elections. So what? The people are happy."[6] (Exhibit 2 profiles Brunei.)

Grandiose Plans for a Post-Oil Economy

Desirous of building a flourishing economy before Brunei's oil ran out—proven oil reserves in the

EXHIBIT 2 **Brunei—Country Profile**

Land area	5,765 sq. km (2,226 sq. mi.)
Population (1998 estimate)	315,292 (64% Malay, 20% Chinese, 16% other communities)
Religions (1981)	Muslim (official) 63%, Buddhism 14%, Christian 8%, other 15%
Literacy	88%
Executive and legislative branches	Five councils, all appointed by the Sultan—the Religious Council, the Privy Council, the Council of Cabinet Ministers, the Legislative Council, and the Council of Succession
Labor force	144,000 (1995 estimate); engaged in government (48%); production of oil, gas, services, and construction (42%); agriculture, forestry, and fishing (4%); other (6%) (1996 estimate); about 60,000 of the labor force were temporary residents (1991 estimate)
Land use (1993 est.)	Arable land 1%; crops 1%; pastures 1%; forests and woodland 85%; other 12%
Climate	Tropical; hot, humid, rainy
Currency	Brunei dollar or ringgit (Br$)

EXHIBIT 2   Brunei—Country Profile *(continued)*

Gross Domestic Product

	1991	1992	1993	1994	1995
Total (Br$ m)					
At current prices	6,621	6,565	6,585	6,686	7,067
At 1974 prices	3,736	3,698	3,548	3,612	3,684
Real change (%)	3.6	(1.0)	(4.1)	1.8	2.0
Per head (BR$)					
At current prices	25,401	23,865	23,459	23,501	23,162
At 1974 prices	14,351	13,483	13,254	12,696	12,446
Real change (%)	(1.3)	(6.0)	(1.7)	(4.2)	(4.9)

Origins of Gross Domestic Product, 1995

Sector	% of total
Oil	35.9
Agriculture, forestry and fishing	2.7
Construction	5.7
Transport and communications	4.2
Wholesale and retail trade	10.0
Services	33.8
Miscellaneous	7.7

Main Trading Partners (US $ m)

	1992	1993	1994	1995
Exports				
Japan	1,233	1,287	1,079	1,220
U.K.	208	414	416	182
Thailand	199	206	166	263
Singapore	242	196	189	203
Others	614	259	256	216
Total	2,496	2,362	2,106	2,084
Imports				
Singapore	730	698	897	1,612
U.K.	418	495	595	444
U.S.	498	526	414	209
Malaysia	165	207	287	326
Japan	175	140	147	144
Others	444	534	784	755
Total	2,430	2,600	3,124	3,490

(continues)

EXHIBIT 2

Brunei—Country Profile *(continued)*

Sources: *Economist Intelligence Unit: Country Profile of Brunei,* 1996–97, 1998–99; CIA World Factbook, Country Profile of Brunei, accessed May 7, 1999, www.odci.gov/cia/publications/factbook/bx.html.

Foreign Trade				
	1992	**1993**	**1994**	**1995**
Key exports (Br $ m)				
Crude petroleum	2,036	1,786	1,550	1,476
Petroleum products	121	122	106	111
Natural gas	1,562	1,591	1,413	1,561
Key imports (Br $ m)				
Machinery	228	389	153	187
Motor vehicles	213	271	220	206
Electrical equipment	256	285	416	375
Iron and steel	137	105	181	203
Avg. annual exchange rate				
(B$ per US $1)	1.629	1.616	1.527	1.417

1990s were expected to last another 25 years—the royal family was attempting, under Prince Jefri's leadership, to develop industries and tourism.[a]

Prince Jefri was not only finance minister, but also chairman of Amadeo Development Corporation (ADC), which handled government construction work, and the Brunei Investment Agency (BIA), which managed the savings accumulated by the state of Brunei.[b] During the 1990s, to boost tourism in Brunei, ADC had embarked on the construction of one of the world's largest amusement parks together with a luxury hotel.[c] The amusement park—which contained cascading fountains, lush gardens, Italian-marble walkways, and state-of-the-art roller coasters—even though free to visitors, had failed to attract the anticipated patronage. The 600-room, $800 million hotel compound—which featured a saltwater lagoon, a Nicklaus golf course, eight swimming pools, nine restaurants, the world's biggest atrium, 24-karat gold-leaf detail, and gold-plated fittings in every bathroom—had, because of these luxurious details, become a white elephant even before its opening. "At $500 per night and a 90 percent occupancy rate, it would take 60 years for them to get their money back," remarked one hotel expert.[7]

The BIA, the other organization chaired by Prince Jefri, managed funds estimated in 1995 at U.S. $40 billion. Although its affairs were treated as state secrets (unapproved disclosures could lead to three-year prison terms), financiers estimated that conservative management of the funds by the BIA in association with foreign institutions[d] was generating substantial investment income by the mid-1990s, in excess of Brunei's combined oil and gas revenues. The BIA also owned properties, including the Dorchester Hotel in Park Lane, London, and Beverly Hills Hotel in California.

Over the years numerous large transfers of capital, termed "special transfers," had been made out of the BIA's core funds. Auditor KPMG was required to accept an annual representation from the BIA's board that the transfers were made on behalf of and for the benefit of the Brunei government.

[a] Only 2 percent of Brunei being arable, agriculture contributed a negligible 3 percent to the economy.
[b] In 1997 Prince Jefri resigned as finance minister in favor of his brother the Sultan in order to concentrate on his responsibilities at ADC and the BIA.
[c] ADC had also built power stations in a joint venture with Siemens and entered into a telecom venture with AT&T.
[d] The financial institutions included Morgan Guaranty, Citicorp, Morgan Grenfell, James Capel, Nomura, and Daiwa.

To outsiders, the ultimate destination of these funds was conjecture at best. "[The royal family] treat the Brunei Investment Agency and the treasury as their own private piggy bank," remarked a diplomat. "It's impossible to separate what belongs to the government and what belongs to the family."[8]

The Royal Family's Lifestyle[9]

The Brunei royal family led lavish lifestyles. ADC had built the 1,788-room royal palace spread over nearly 300 acres. The world's largest private residence, bigger even than the Vatican, it included air-conditioned quarters for 200 polo ponies and more than 50 crystal chandeliers in the main dining room. The Sultan's fiftieth birthday party, celebrated in the royal palace, was a $17 million gala event featuring three Michael Jackson concerts. The royal family's 17 aircraft included a Boeing 747 used by the Sultan for foreign trips, a 150-seat jet favored by one of his wives, and an Airbus the Sultan had presented as a gift to one of his daughters on her eighteenth birthday. The family owned 2,000 cars and was among the largest purchasers of Rolls-Royces. The $70 million Renoir the Sultan had paid for in the mid-1980s had set a world record for the price paid for a painting.

Youngest brother Prince Jefri also enjoyed living life on a grand scale.[e] He owned an Airbus jet, a Sikorsky helicopter, and a yacht valued at $35 million. When the Sultan and Prince Jefri wanted to play polo, a sport both enjoyed, the world's top players were flown in from Argentina. To learn golf, they once flew in Jack Nicklaus and, in 1994, the NFL's Joe Montana and Herschel Walker were hired to teach football to Prince Jefri's son.

Prince Jefri and his family trust owned properties across the world, including three of the world's leading hotels, the Bel Air in Beverly Hills, Palace in New York, and Plaza Athenee in Paris. Other British assets included a controlling stake in As-prey & Garrard, the Queen of England's jeweler, and a number of richly furnished mansions in Hampstead, London.

TROUBLE IN AN IDYLL

Project Lucy[10]

In July 1996 Prince Jefri instructed KPMG, auditors of the core assets since the BIA's inception in 1983, to undertake a personal assignment for him in connection with litigation at London's law courts against former friends and emissaries Bob and Rafi Manoukian. The Manoukian brothers were suing Prince Jefri for reneging on two property deals and Prince Jefri was countersuing the brothers for creaming off profits on past deals.

The assignment, code named Project Lucy, was conducted mainly by KPMG's London forensic accounting department, under the leadership of engagement partner Adam Bates. (Exhibit 3 profiles KPMG.) Litigation support provided to Prince Jefri by KPMG generated fees of £4.6 million, requiring, at various stages, the services of 12 partners, 15 directors, nine consultants, one assistant general counsel, 43 managers, five administrative and information technology managers, and 18 assistant managers, as well as other junior staff. In the course of working on Project Lucy, KPMG staff acquired extensive confidential information about Prince Jefri's assets and financial affairs.

During the hearings the Manoukian brothers' counsel shocked the court with salacious tales of Prince Jefri's alleged debauchery, accusing him of spending prodigally on wild sex parties and gambling sessions and alleging that the scale of the prince's wealth was "matched by his appetite for extravagance and self-indulgence."[11] (Subsequent to the abrupt announcement in March 1998 of a settlement on undisclosed terms, KPMG was involved in only two relatively minor assignments

[e] Prince Mohamed, unlike his brothers, was deeply religious and comparatively abstinent.

EXHIBIT 3 KPMG Profile

The Global Advisory Firm

One of the Big Five accounting firms, KPMG was a federation of national firms that billed itself as "the global advisory firm whose aim is to turn knowledge into value for the benefit of its clients, its people and its communities." KPMG claimed that it "provided services to 26.4 percent of the world's top 1,000 commercial and industrial companies." Its chairman had affirmed its commitment to building a global professional services firm that integrated "teams of the right people, with the right skills, in the right place—where their clients need them." The only Big Five firm that was bigger in Europe than in North America, KPMG was proud of its global coverage; it operated in 155 countries with more than 85,000 partners and staff worldwide. "One of the essential strengths of KPMG," the company stressed, "is the efficiency within this international network. We use the same approach and methods in every office around the world. There is a virtually seamless interaction between the industry experts, no matter where they are located."

Source: KPMG International website, accessed April 25, 1999, www.kpmg.com/home.htm.

KPMG Revenue and Personnel (1996–1998)

	1996	1997	1998
Revenue (US $)$S	8,100	9,000	10,400
Personnel (000s)	78.7	85.3	92.7

1998 Revenue and Personnel (by region)

Region	Revenue (US $ m)	Partners	Professionals	Administrative	Total Personnel
Asia Pacific	855	924	10,861	2,500	14,285
Europe	4,601	2,766	29,309	9,213	41,288
Middle East	42	73	808	246	1,127
Africa	112	247	2,321	815	3,383
North America	4,562	2,441	18,373	6,846	27,660
South America	229	268	3,668	1,029	4,965
Total	10,400	6,719	65,340	20,649	92,708

Key functional areas: Accounting and auditing, tax, management consultancy, corporate finance.
Major industry groups: Banking and finance; building and construction; energy and natural resources; government; health care and life sciences; industrial products; information, communications, and entertainment; insurance; retail and consumer products; and transportation.
Source: KPMG International website, accessed April 25, 1999, www.kpmg.com/home.htm.

Estimate Revenues of the "Big Five" (1998)

Ranking	Firm	Fee income ($ million)
1	PriceWaterhouseCoopers	15,300
2	Andersen	13,900
3	Ernst & Young	10,900
4	KPMG Peat Marwick	10,400
5	Deloitte Touche Tohmatsu	9,000

Source: *Management Consultant International*, n. 112, February 1999, p. 8.

on behalf of Prince Jefri and work on these had ceased by mid-May 1998.)

The Sexual Harassment Suit[12]

Prince Jefri's legal troubles had not been limited to the Manoukian litigation. In 1997 a former Miss USA had brought a sexual harassment suit in a California court charging the Sultan and Prince Jefri with inviting her to Brunei under false pretexts and holding her there in captivity.

Both the Sultan and Prince Jefri had sovereign immunity from prosecution by American courts. Although the case could have been settled quietly and further controversy avoided, Prince Jefri chose to fight it to forestall suits from "50 million other golddiggers." This generated, notwithstanding considerable skepticism about some of the litigant's claims, a substantial amount of tawdry publicity. (In early 1998, after the accuser admitted never having met Prince Jefri or the Sultan, the court dismissed her case.)

Denouement for Prince Jefri

1998 had begun as a turbulent year for Prince Jefri. Besides the various litigations, he was facing an economic crunch. Brunei's revenues had dropped precipitously in the wake of declining crude oil prices, necessitating belt tightening by all, especially the free-spending royal family. Their expenses were reportedly barely being covered by the dwindling oil and gas revenues. As the financial situation worsened, some of Brunei's educated citizenry appeared to grow increasingly resentful of the royal family's lifestyle.

Brunei's cash flow problem was brought home dramatically to the Sultan when he offered loans to crisis-stricken Thailand and Indonesia only to find that the BIA did not have the available cash to make good on his promise of support. Following the Asian economic crisis of 1997, the value of the BIA's investment portfolio had plummeted reportedly by 40 percent during the previous year to below $20 billion, down from a peak of $60 billion. His inability to provide promised funds to friendly countries was a "massive embarrassment" to the Sultan.[13]

Soon after this episode, in March 1998, amidst allegations that he had squandered his country's money on bad investments and a profligate lifestyle, Prince Jefri was removed as chairman of ADC and the BIA.

Just Desserts or Palace Revolt?[14]

Brunei, rife with palace gossip in the best of times ("You live in murk," a Western banker had remarked[15]), was buzzing with rumors of a sinister plot underlying Prince Jefri's downfall. The prince added fuel to these rumors by claiming, in a letter published in the French newspaper *Le Monde,* that "what is really happening in Brunei is a power struggle between different groups—one supporting an open, modern and pro-Western policy, which I represent, and the other wanting a conservative, religious regime."[16] He claimed that his support for satellite TV broadcasts into Brunei and his contribution of a Western-style school, modern hospital, and amusement park had angered religious conservatives.

Prince Jefri's supporters blamed his problems on family intrigue arising out of Prince Mohamed's resentment toward him. Explained one of his aides: "You're basically dealing with a little medieval kingdom, a little medieval court, which goes back to brother against brother, to the power struggles you've read about down the ages, whether in Florence or Venice or anywhere else. That's life. Times don't change."[17]

Insiders traced Prince Mohamed's rancor toward Prince Jefri to a 1980s feud triggered by Prince Jefri's ridicule of Prince Mohamed for investing in two failed business ventures. In the years that followed, the deeply religious Prince Mohamed came to resent, too, Prince Jefri's playboy appetites and grew jealous of his close friendship with the Sultan. Prince Mohamed reportedly began to bide his time awaiting an opportunity to exact suitable revenge against his younger brother.

In 1998 Prince Mohamed, while holding Brunei's reins in the Sultan's absence, ran a story in *The Borneo Bulletin,* a newspaper he owned, claiming that Prince Jefri's misspending had caused huge losses. The news article was followed by the withdrawal of ADC's work permits and freezing of its accounts. Chaos ensued as ADC collapsed. Contractors were left with unpaid invoices of £500 million, thousands of workers were laid off, work permits were revoked for 20,000 mostly Thai construction workers, and projects with a combined value of £1.5 billion were left unfinished.[18]

Observers believed that Prince Mohamed persuaded the Sultan, upon his return to Brunei, that Prince Jefri was responsible for the country's financial mess. ADC's assets were seized and an after-the-fact "emergency order" issued giving the Sultan the right to seize private companies. When Brunei's law minister, a friend of Prince Jefri, objected his post was abolished.

Prince Jefri was stripped of all his posts. Haji Awang Abdul Aziz, the education minister and a devout Muslim, was placed in charge of the BIA and instructed to lead an economic task force to find a way out of the crisis. Prince Jefri departed for Europe, claiming that Prince Mohamed, Haji Aziz, and foreign advisors (including 40 Iranian "teachers" and Libyan fundamentalists) had turned the Sultan against him. "[Reactionaries] are determined to crush Prince Jefri's power-base and with it the only real force for opening up Brunei to the West," lamented a spokesman for Prince Jefri. "The changes represent the tightening grip of a group of Muslim conservatives, backed by their shadowy foreign advisors, that has gained an unhealthy influence over His Majesty the Sultan."[19] The Brunei government dismissed these charges as preposterous and baseless.

The Prince in Exile

Prince Jefri's spokesman characterized as "rubbish" reports that the prince had fled Brunei after misappropriating a vast sum of money. The so-called "missing billions," the spokesman claimed, were the product not of mismanagement by Prince Jefri, but of "general extravagance by the ruling family and investment losses taken in the Asian financial crisis."[20]

Prince Jefri's Brunei assets—yachts, cars, and homes—were seized. But when Brunei authorities tried to impound his private Airbus in France, the prince successfully blocked the action.[21] "I do not seek a fight and prefer to be left alone," Prince Jefri stated. But, determined to retain control over his offshore assets, he added: "I shall, however, vigorously defend my position and interests of my family."[22] Warned the prince's spokesman:

> While the religious conservatives find it easy in Brunei to make up laws as they go along, any attempts to behave in such a cavalier fashion with the business interests of Prince Jefri's family in the rest of the world will have to deal with real laws and proper courts to enforce them.[23]

Prince Jefri declined an invitation to return to Brunei in August 1998 for Brunei's most important royal ceremony since the Sultan's coronation in 1967—the investiture of the Sultan's 24-year-old son, Prince Billah, as heir to the throne. Instead, he issued a statement that he could not return to Brunei because "there is little I can do to oppose the destructive action of reactionary forces, which are becoming increasingly entrenched at all levels of government."[24]

Privately, Prince Jefri's advisors insinuated that Prince Billah would make a less-than-convincing figurehead whose ascension conservatives such as Haji Aziz would welcome as an interim step toward installing a puppet or toppling the monarchy. "If you are looking to knock out the royal family," remarked one of Prince Jefri's aides, "Billah is your man." The Sultan's spokesman denied these rumors, stating that Prince Billah was "bright, diligent, serious," and fit to rule and Haji Aziz was "a believer in the sultanate." Some observers noted, however, that "the foundations of most republics cover the bones of monarchy" and that "Aziz has lots of influence and is building a power base."[25]

ON THE TRAIL OF BILLIONS

Investigations into "Special Transfers"[26]

The Sultan, ranked since 1987 by *Fortune* magazine as the world's richest man, was displaced from that position in 1998 by Microsoft CEO Bill Gates. "Being toppled from the perch of the richest man in the world by a computer nerd is likely to put any potentate into ill humor and have him demanding investigations," noted *The Times,* tongue-in-cheek.[27] In June 1998 the government of Brunei hired a team of investigators from Arthur Andersen to assess ADC's financial solvency and appointed a finance task force to investigate the movement of the BIA's core funds over the past 15 years. If investigators could determine that Prince Jefri had used BIA funds to finance or collateralize his purchase of foreign assets, the BIA could presumably requisition his overseas properties.

On June 16, 1998 Brunei's Ministry of Finance summoned Peter Harrison, KPMG's audit engagement partner for the BIA, to Brunei to attend a meeting with the BIA task force on June 18. Harrison explained to the task force the nature of his firm's audit of the core funds and what little KPMG as auditor knew of the "special transfers." The task force asked him to establish the position of the core funds as of May 31, 1998 and prepare a summary of the core funds' movements, including the special transfers, since the BIA's establishment in 1983. Harrison's audit team carried out the work and reported back to the task force on July 8, 1998.

Meanwhile, on the afternoon of July 2, a Brunei solicitor telephoned KPMG forensic accounting partner John Ellison to request that KPMG assist the BIA's task force with the investigation into the "final resting place of several bil-

lion dollars" worth of special transfers from the core funds.[28]

Prince Jefri's Queries and KPMG's Stonewalling

With the dissolution of the BIA board and his formal removal as chairman on July 16, Prince Jefri was growing increasingly concerned that the BIA might ask KPMG to assist in pursuing him. He worried that KPMG might use to his detriment the extensive information he had shared with Project Lucy staff while reconstructing his financial affairs over the past 14 years.

On July 24 Prince Jefri's solicitor sought confirmation from KPMG that it was not involved in any investigation concerning the prince's financial dealings. KPMG responded: "The duty of confidentiality owed to clients makes it inappropriate for this firm to give you or anybody else acting for or purporting to act for any party any information whatsoever in relation to any work we may or may not undertake for any other party."[29] On July 31 the prince's solicitor again sought assurance that KPMG would cease immediately "acting for any client who has instructed KPMG in an investigation which relates in any way to the affairs of Prince Jefri."[30] "In the absence of proper authorization from the client (or former client)," KPMG replied, "this firm is unable to discuss the affairs of any client with you or anyone else."[31] A letter of authorization from Prince Jefri forwarded by his solicitor drew the following response from KPMG: "[K]indly confirm that your letters are written in your capacity as a solicitor on behalf of Prince Jefri."[32]

Prince Jefri's solicitor reflected on KPMG's responses to the prince's inquiries. " 'Please set my mind at rest,' he asked. The answer was that we are not going to tell you anything. It was a polite and reasonable letter and they gave him the brush off."[33] Correspondence between Prince Jefri and KPMG continued until, ultimately, KPMG's solicitors, in letters dated August 18 and 20, revealed that KPMG was acting for the BIA, but was confident that it could honor the confidentiality owed to Prince Jefri.

PROJECT GEMMA

KPMG's Rationale for Joining the Hunt[34]

In seeking help to track the special transfers, the BIA had naturally turned to its longtime auditor and trusted advisor. Over the past three years, KPMG, led by engagement partner Peter Harrison, had invested more than 6,000 hours annually on BIA audits. In addition, KPMG had spent approximately 4,000 hours per year of chargeable time in associated advisory and consultancy work for the BIA.

On July 3, Harrison, forensic accounting partner John Ellison, and KPMG partner Michael Fowle had met in the presence of KPMG's solicitors to consider whether the company could accept the BIA's request to assist its task force. Prior to the meeting, Ellison had discussed the matter by telephone with Project Lucy engagement partner Adam Bates.[f] Ellison recalled what transpired at the meeting:

> It was clear to me that we did not regard Prince Jefri . . . as a continuing client, with Project Lucy having been completed some months earlier. . . . The conclusion of that meeting was that there would be no conflict, but it was recognized that KPMG owed a duty of confidentiality to Prince Jefri . . . and, in maintaining that confidentiality, appropriate information barriers would have to be set up between Project Lucy and [the new project].[35]

On July 8, 1998, the BIA formally instructed KPMG to work with the BIA's legal advisors to obtain evidence and, where appropriate, trace, se-

cure, and recover assets belonging to the BIA both in Brunei and overseas. KPMG's forensic accounting department was to undertake the assignment with Peter Harrison as lead partner. KPMG treated forensic projects as exceptionally confidential, usually assigning them code names. The BIA's assignment was code named Project Gemma.

Operating the Project behind "Chinese Walls"[36]

Under pressure from the BIA, KPMG decided not to inform Prince Jefri of its new assignment. KPMG partners held that, in the absence of a client relationship with Prince Jefri, there was no direct conflict of interest and disclosure to the prince was not necessary. For its part the BIA accepted that KPMG would not disclose any confidential information acquired by it when acting on behalf of Prince Jefri.

Having worked for the BIA for 15 years, KPMG believed that it would be well down the learning curve on Project Gemma even without accessing any confidential information that Prince Jefri might have shared with the Project Lucy team. To protect such information from being used in Project Gemma, Ellison instructed that an information barrier (popularly known as a "Chinese wall") be erected in KPMG's forensic accounting department. The wall had two components. First, staff selection for Project Gemma excluded anyone who possessed confidential information related to Prince Jefri. Second, steps were taken to preclude such information becoming available to those assigned to Project Gemma. Confidentiality rules were announced at a meeting of Project Gemma staff on July 3.

Even as KPMG rebuffed Prince Jefri's inquiries, some 50 Project Gemma staff spent more than 7,500 hours before mid-September "hot on the trail of substantial funds."[37] Most of the proj-

---

[f] On June 30, in a routine meeting related to outstanding fees, Prince Jefri's representative had explored the possibility of Adam Bates resigning as a KPMG partner to join the team being assembled to defend Prince Jefri in the dispute with his brother.

ect work was carried out in Brunei. A reporter who visited Brunei in September 1998 recalled the hotel "crawling with boyish accountants from KPMG flown in to investigate the BIA."[38] Work done in London was confined to a room with restricted access in a building separate from the building that housed the rest of the forensic accounting department. Separate computer file servers were used for Project Gemma and all electronic information related to Project Lucy was deleted from KPMG servers.

Notwithstanding the constraint of operating within the boundaries of the Chinese walls, the Project Gemma team made substantial progress. By mid-September, KPMG believed that it was close to demonstrating "for the first time that many of the withdrawals from the core funds had been used for the benefit of . . . Prince Jefri."[39]

THE PRINCE OBJECTS

On September 2, 1998, arguing that KPMG confronted an unacceptable conflict of interest, Prince Jefri moved to obtain an injunction from the London High Court restraining KPMG from working on Project Gemma. Counsel for the prince told the High Court that some of the 100 KPMG staff connected with Project Gemma might have also worked on Project Lucy, posing a real and urgent danger that private information might leak by accident.

His aides insisted on Prince Jefri's innocence. "Jefri wouldn't know how to steal," remarked an advisor. "He has no sense of what money is worth."[40] Added his spokesman: "Prince Jefri has nothing to hide. He has absolutely no objections to legitimate professionals being engaged to make these sorts of investigations, as long as they are not conflicted."[41] Privately, the prince's advisors expressed confidence that, absent sabotage, the in-

vestigators would not be able to find anything to pin specifically on him. "Those poor Western accountants won't even know where to begin," remarked one aide. "When you have no walls between what is state money and what is family money, it just gets used. . . . [W]hatever he did wasn't any different from what his brothers did."[42]

KPMG Reacts[43]

Responding to Prince Jefri's claim, KPMG emphasized that it was common for large accounting firms to provide a comprehensive range of professional services—including audit, corporate finance and tax advice, and management consultancy—to clients with competing commercial interests. These firms had gained considerable experience erecting, and developed a professional culture respectful of, information barriers to protect the confidential information of individual clients. "I am familiar with conflict issues, as they frequently arise in my department," averred a KPMG forensic accounting partner. "Our clients (and former clients) often have conflicting interests and sometimes have disputes with each other. I have never known any information leak and no one has ever complained that there has been a leak, so far as I am aware."[44]

KPMG maintained that its arrangements for isolating Project Gemma from Project Lucy information satisfied the most stringent test of ensuring client confidentiality. Consequently, there was no risk that information obtained by KPMG in the course of Project Lucy would become available to anyone engaged in Project Gemma. KPMG solicitors even collected upwards of 100 affidavits from KPMG staff working on Project Gemma affirming their lack of knowledge of Project Lucy. "[KPMG] is confident," noted a reporter, "its strict ethical rules prevent any leakage of confidential information."[45]

References

1. Jim Kelly, "Chinese Walls 'Must Not Be Created Ad Hoc,'" *Financial Times* (London), December 19, 1998, p. 7.

2. This section draws information from the Government of Brunei Darussalam official website, www.brunet.bn/homepage/intro/nbdhis.htm, accessed May 7, 1999; the *Economist Intelligence Unit: Country Profile of Brunei,* 1998–99; and Louis Kraar, "Brunei's Free-Spending Sultan of Oil," *Fortune,* October 12, 1987, p. 132.

3. Peter Koenig, "The Brunei Mystery: How the World's Richest Man Manages His Money," *Institutional Investor,* December 1985, pp. 138–48.

4. Richard Behar, "The Fairy Tale's Over for the Kingdom of Brunei," *Fortune,* February 1, 1999, pp. 90–102.

5. Garth Alexander, "Brunei's Missing Billions," *Sunday Times,* August 30, 1998.

6. Behar, "The Fairy Tale's Over for the Kingdom of Brunei."

7. Ibid.

8. Alexander, "Brunei's Missing Billions."

9. This section draws information from Behar, "The Fairy Tale's Over for the Kingdom of Brunei."

10. This section draws information from Jim Kelly, "Prince Jefri Takes KPMG to High Court," *Financial Times,* September 10, 1998, p. 9; *Prince Jefri Bolkiah v. KPMG,* Chancery Division, [1999] 1 BCLC 1; and *Prince Jefri Bolkiah v. KPMG,* House of Lords, [1999] 1 All ER 517.

11. Behar, "The Fairy Tale's Over for the Kingdom of Brunei."

12. This section draws information from Alexander, "Brunei's Missing Billions."

13. Alexander, "Brunei's Missing Billions."

14. This section draws information from Alexander, "Brunei's Missing Billions"; and Behar, "The Fairy Tale's Over for the Kingdom of Brunei."

15. Koenig, "The Brunei Mystery: How the World's Richest Man Manages His Money."

16. Alexander, "Brunei's Missing Billions."

17. Behar, "The Fairy Tale's Over for the Kingdom of Brunei."

18. This paragraph draws information from Alexander, "Brunei's Missing Billions"; and Behar, "The Fairy Tale's Over for the Kingdom of Brunei."

19. Alexander, "Brunei's Missing Billions."

20. John Jay, "Sultan Pulls Billions Out of Market," *Sunday Times,* August 30, 1998.

21. Jon Ashworth, "Pressure Mounts on the Playboy Prince," *The Times,* September 19, 1998.

22. Mark Landler, "The Royal Treatment," *New York Times,* August 27, 1998.

23. Alexander, "Brunei's Missing Billions."

24. Landler, "The Royal Treatment."

25. Behar, "The Fairy Tale's Over for the Kingdom of Brunei."

26. This section draws information from Alexander, "Brunei's Missing Billions"; *Prince Jefri Bolkiah v. KPMG,* Court of Appeal, [1999] 1 BCLC 1; and *Prince Jefri Bolkiah v. KPMG,* House of Lords, [1999] 1 All ER 517.

27. "Undermining Chinese Walls," *The Times,* September 16, 1998.

28. *Prince Jefri Bolkiah v. KPMG,* Court of Appeal, [1999] 1 BCLC 1; *Prince Jefri Bolkiah v. KPMG,* House of Lords, [1999] 1 All ER 517; "Secrets at Stake," *Financial Times* (London), October 1, 1998, p. 34.

29. *Prince Jefri Bolkiah v. KPMG,* Chancery Division, [1999] 1 BCLC 1.

30. Ibid.

31. Ibid.

32. Ibid.

33. Jim Kelly, "Prince Jefri and KPMG Court Case Opens," *Financial Times* (London), September 10, 1998, p. 10.

34. This section draws information from *Prince Jefri Bolkiah v. KPMG,* Chancery Division, [1999] 1 BCLC 1; *Prince Jefri Bolkiah v. KPMG,* Court of Appeal, [1999] 1 BCLC 1; and *Prince Jefri Bolkiah v. KPMG,* House of Lords, [1999] 1 All ER 517.

35. *Prince Jefri Bolkiah v. KPMG,* Chancery Division, [1999] 1 BCLC 1.

36. This section draws information from *Prince Jefri Bolkiah v. KPMG,* Chancery Division, [1999] 1 BCLC 1; *Prince Jefri Bolkiah v. KPMG,* Court of Appeal, [1999] 1 BCLC 1; *Prince Jefri Bolkiah v. KPMG,* House of Lords, [1999] 1 All ER 517; Jim Kelly, "Judge Rules that Chinese Walls Could Whisper," *Financial Times* (London), September 16, 1998,

p. 10; and Kelly, "Prince Jefri Takes KPMG to High Court."

37. *Prince Jefri Bolkiah v. KPMG,* House of Lords, [1999] 1 All ER 517.

38. Behar, "The Fairy Tale's Over for the Kingdom of Brunei."

39. *Prince Jefri Bolkiah v. KPMG,* Court of Appeal, [1999] 1 BCLC 1.

40. Behar, "The Fairy Tale's Over for the Kingdom of Brunei."

41. "Prince and KPMG Meet in Court," *The Independent,* September 2, 1998, p. 14.

42. Behar, "The Fairy Tale's Over for the Kingdom of Brunei."

43. This section draws information from *Prince Jefri Bolkiah v. KPMG,* Chancery Division, [1999] 1 BCLC 1 and *Prince Jefri Bolkiah v. KPMG,* House of Lords, [1999] 1 All ER 517.

44. *Prince Jefri Bolkiah v. KPMG,* Chancery Division, [1999] 1 BCLC 1.

45. Jim Kelly, "Brunei's Prince Jefri Seeks Court Order on KPMG Confidentiality," *Financial Times,* August 28, 1998, p. 16.

International Profit Associates

As the largest management consulting firm for small businesses in the United States, our mission is to give our clients the basic, but required, business skills to succeed."

John Burgess, CEO of International Profit Associates

At 4:45 P.M. one Friday in December 2000, International Profit Associates (IPA) analyst Ken Breeman received from his senior executive Richard Egan instructions on his Monday assignment. He was to visit Charlie's, a Remote, Massachusetts–based small business (2000 revenues of approximately $1.5 million) specializing in the construction and maintenance of septic tanks and equally owned by Stan Bennett and Phil Sutton. Bennett and Sutton were brothers-in-law whose wives were sisters.

TWO DAYS IN THE LIFE OF AN IPA ANALYST

Day One

Breeman left his home in Atkinson, New Hampshire, at 5:00 A.M. on Monday morning and reached Remote, Massachusetts, at 8:45 A.M., in time for his 9 A.M. appointment at Charlie's. A small sign, "Charlie's," hung over the door of a simple two-room structure located on a residential farm on the one main road of the town.

Breeman was greeted first by Jasper, a golden retriever, and then by Martha Graham, the receptionist-cum-bookkeeper. Karen directed him around the back to the "guys' office." Breeman walked along the muddy driveway filled with deep ruts, passed three parked utility trucks, and climbed the steps along side of the back office. Bennett and Sutton, both wearing construction attire, welcomed Breeman into the office. As they sat at a small round table in Bennett's fake-wood paneled office, Breeman introduced himself: "Over the next two days, I am going to perform a thorough physical of your business, just as a general practitioner does with people. I will need your help to explore over 300 aspects of your business." Breeman next reviewed the confidentiality agreement between IPA and Charlie's and continued:

> On Tuesday afternoon, we will have a "findings meeting," where I will provide you with a diagnosis of your business. I will identify Charlie's problem areas, propose solutions, and calculate the cost versus benefit of those solutions. Then I will outline your options, which will include inviting an IPA consulting team to help you implement the solutions.

After receiving Bennett and Sutton's agreement, Breeman pulled out an IPA binder and began using it as a guide to learn about the history, goals, employees, performance, and financial practices of Charlie's. Charlie's was named after Bennett and Sutton's father-in-law, who had started the business in 1958. Bennett had started

Research Associate Monica Mullick, Professor Ashish Nanda, and Professor Thomas DeLong prepared this case as the basis for class discussion rather than to illustrate either effective or ineffective handling of an administrative situation.

working at Charlie's one year out of high school in 1974. Sutton started working at Charlie's in 1977. Bennett and Sutton purchased the business from Charlie in 1978 for $100,000. "I'm not sure how we determined how much the business was worth," noted Sutton. In 1986 Sutton and his wife also purchased the property where the business resided for $150,000—a 17-acre farm where Charlie had raised his family.

By lunch, it had become obvious to Breeman that Bennett's and Sutton's business goals were polar opposite. Bennett, the manager of Charlie's septic tank construction services, wanted to "sit on a dozer" until he died. Sutton wanted to grow the business, enter other markets, and in 10 years make enough money to fund his dream of starting a bed and breakfast in Vermont. Bennett's philosophy of running the business was, "How do I price to cover my costs?" whereas Sutton's was, "How else can we make money?" Breeman sensed a well of resentment between the partners.

By the end of the first day, Breeman learned that Charlie's had a three-to-six month backlog of work because of its reputation of good service in the community, but the financials of the firm were weak. Over a four-year period, although sales volume had steadily increased, profit margins had declined. In 2000, Bennett and Sutton had each taken pay cuts in their salaries and bonuses to keep the business healthy.

By 7:30 P.M., Breeman was done with the interviews for the day. First, he faxed in his qualitative and quantitative data to his senior executive Egan, who was at IPA headquarters, Buffalo Grove, Illinois. Next, he inputted the data he had collected into IPA's "field analyst computer system program" on his laptop. The program generated an output that projected four-year trends for the business.

Day Two

Breeman called Egan at 7:30 A.M. on Tuesday morning to discuss the outputs, learn the industry comparisons (Egan had reviewed overnight comparative statistics using the Dun & Bradstreet industry norms and ratios database), and seek advice on next steps. At 8 A.M., Breeman returned to Charlie's to interview other employees and review company systems and procedures. He spent most of his time with Graham to review her activities as Charlie's bookkeeper. Graham, a longtime employee of Charlie's, was defensive at first, but after she realized Breeman was sincere and had come to help, she warmed up. Breeman discussed with her how she could produce a profit/loss statement, which she had never done before. Breeman also talked with Bennett's and Sutton's wives, who performed administrative roles in the firm.

By 4 P.M. on Tuesday afternoon, Breeman had completed his survey of Charlie's. He called Egan to relay progress and review findings. At 4:30 P.M., Breeman began the findings meeting with Bennett and Sutton. Breeman later reflected on the meeting:

> First we reviewed the short- and long-term objectives of Charlie's from both Stan's and Phil's perspectives. This in itself was a breakthrough for them because they had never really talked about their goals with each other. They had just kept their heads in the sand for over 20 years and kept on doing what they had been doing. Then we reviewed financials. Even with a three- to six-month backlog of work, Charlie's was operating below industry standard and below their personal and family needs. Some of the causes were their pricing strategies, their low efficiency, and their lack of planning, organization and controls. Then we reviewed infrastructure. Charlie's had outgrown their location and Phil's wife was sick of utility trucks digging up her driveway. And Stan was embittered because part of their earnings went to Phil for "rent." It was time for Charlie's to move off the farm.

Breeman outlined Charlie's options. One, Bennett and Sutton could dissolve the business to which the owners immediately said no. Two, they could sell the business. Again, Bennett and Sutton said no. Three, they could merge with another company. They both said no, because they felt that "more partners would mean more problems." Four, they could downsize so that Sutton could handle all the service needs and Bennett cut his team of workers from three to two. But Bennett wanted to expand. Five, they could remain at status quo. Bennett was vehemently opposed to this option as well. Six, they could hire IPA to fix the organization by introducing systems and controls so that they could expand over time. Bennett and Sutton chose the last option.

"We need your help," they said. "Are you committed?" asked Breeman. "Yes," they replied. "One hundred percent?" "Yes," they replied. "Are you committed to your partner?" asked Breeman. "Yes," they replied. "You brought us closer together than we have been in 22 years." Breeman calculated the scope of the project, priced it, and then turned to Bennett and Sutton.

> Your firm has a potential for $197,000 improvement in annual profits. A moderate scenario would yield half that level of savings—$100,000. I would recommend a 177-hour project for $195 per hour totaling $35,000, involving a team of one consultant and one project manager. The potential improvement is almost six times the cost of the project. Even if improvement is moderate, you are almost guaranteed a return within the first year of about three times the cost of the project.

By 5:30 P.M., Bennett and Sutton had signed the agreement and Breeman had faxed it to Egan. At 7:30 A.M. on Wednesday, Breeman received from Egan instructions for his next assignment, a carpentry and contracting business in Kentucky. At 8:30 A.M., a two-person consulting team from IPA arrived in Remote, Massachusetts, to meet with Breeman and capture his insights and learnings over breakfast. Breeman introduced the consulting team to Bennett and Sutton and bade goodbye. He drove to Logan airport, Boston from where he

would be taking a flight later that afternoon to Louisville, Kentucky.

AT IPA HEADQUARTERS

At about 4:30 P.M. central time, Egan received a fax of the signed agreement from Breeman, he added a tally mark on the sheet on his desk, made two copies of the fax, and walked one copy over to the office of director of survey services Valerie Ramsdell. Ramsdell reviewed the fax and went to the dry erase board, which lined one of her office walls from floor to ceiling, erased "16" and wrote "17" in the column that maintained a running tally of the number of consulting projects achieved so far that day.

Egan walked the second copy of the fax over to the office of director of management services Ken Sweet. Sweet immediately began the process of identifying the consultant and project manager for the project. Within 10 minutes, he had called a project manager and assigned the project. Sweet looked at his watch. It was five minutes to five, almost time for IPA's management team "huddle" with CEO John Burgess to review the day's progress since their last huddle at noon. He walked over to Burgess's office. Ramsdell was already there. A few minutes later business coordination director Tyler Burgess and sales and marketing director Dan Drugan joined the huddle.

Burgess reviewed with his management team the afternoon sales numbers, and even though they had dramatically improved from the morning, progress, according to Burgess, had still been "poor." "We'll never make our week's target at this rate, folks," Burgess thundered in his gravelly voice. "You have to drive up the numbers. Keep driving up the numbers."

That day's rhythm of work was typical of how IPA management had been conducting business over the past several years. This rhythm of work had led IPA, based in the Chicago suburb of Buffalo Grove, Illinois, to realize remarkable growth since its inception in 1991, catapulting it among the top 10 fastest growing privately held companies in the United States according to Inc. magazine's 1996 and 1997 surveys. In 2000 IPA had over 1,500 employees on its payroll (250 in Buffalo Grove and the rest distributed across the United States and Canada). The firm had managed 6,090 consulting projects that year, generating revenues of $132 million (see Exhibit 1).

THE TYPICAL IPA CLIENT: "JOE THE ELECTRICIAN"

IPA targeted primarily small businesses with annual revenues between $500,000 and $10 million across the United States and Canada. IPA consultants typically helped their clients understand and overcome "the small business person's dilemma." CEO John Burgess described the dilemma:

> Joe the electrician starts a business in his garage and, after two years of hard work, is generating annual revenue of $250,000. He runs the entire business himself. Overhead is low, he knows every client, and so receivables are very low. He is making a significant amount of money, compared to the $45,000 per year he was earning as a union employee. Joe decides that it is time to expand operations, which requires renting a space and buying a truck and some specialty equipment. He needs to hire people to run his expanded facility, which means that he has to pay salary and benefits. Joe gets a $200,000 loan from the bank against personal collateral.
>
> In two years, Joe's annual revenue has jumped from $250,000 to $750,000, but receivables have also gone up so that one-seventh of his revenue is tied up in receivables. His inventories are also up to $150,000. Joe has used up his entire credit line at the bank. Joe raises more money from the bank by mortgaging his business.
>
> Joe's reputation is spreading and business is growing. But the workers he has hired don't work as hard as he does, and he can't continue working and overseeing the whole business. So he hires a foreman who has to be paid $60,000 per year including benefits. His costs have increased—receivables are up, inventories are substantial, and he has a foreman. He raises prices to cover costs, but now his bid/award ratio gets slashed from 20 percent to 10 percent. Suddenly, he discovers that his employees are not being used at full capacity. So he sharpens his pencil and cuts prices but his costs are not curtailed. He goes through cycles of raising prices, losing business, then cutting prices again, but making losses.
>
> All this happens while Joe has been working hard as ever and business has grown dramatically. Revenues have become huge, he has many customers, and several people work for him. Yet, he is earning less money than he was as a solo operator. Joe can't understand what he is doing wrong!
>
> Most of our prospective clients are like Joe the electrician—excellent in their crafts but lacking an understanding of the basic tenets of business. They try to fund the working capital needs of their businesses through payables. But they don't realize that for every dollar increase in working capital needs—cash, inventory, and receivables—payables increase only by 35 cents. They end up running growing but increasingly cash-starved operations. Life becomes too complicated to handle as they find it more and more difficult to "play the float." Last year, about 50 percent of our clients paid more on penalties to the federal government than they earned in personal income. We help people such as Joe understand the basics of running a business.

IPA'S FOUR-STEP APPROACH: CALL, VISIT, ANALYZE, ADVISE

IPA had perfected a step-by-step approach to providing advice to small business owners.

EXHIBIT 1 IPA Revenues and Competitive Position

IPA Revenues, 1991–2001

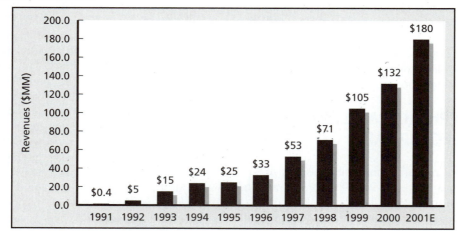

E: expected.
Source: IPA.

George S. May Revenues, 1999–2000	
Year	**Revenue ($ m)**
1999	116
2000E	130

E: estimated.

IPA Consulting Services by Sector (in revenue terms, 2000)

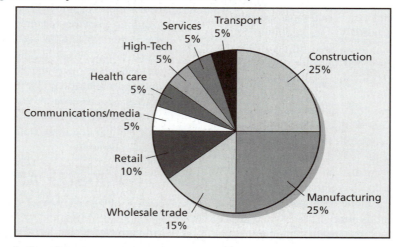

Source: Kennedy Information Research Group.

EXHIBIT 1 IPA Revenues and Competitive Position *(continued)*

Top Management Consulting Practices, 1999

Firm	Revenue ($m)			Firm	Revenue ($m)		
	Total (U.S.)	Strategy (Global)	Operations (Global)		Total (U.S.)	Strategy (Global)	Operations (Global)
Andersen Consulting	4,392	1,028	1,879	Tata Consultancy	230	NA	NA
Pricewaterhouse Coopers	3,900	932	1,444	Horwath International	224	NA	NA
Deloitte Consulting	3,076	1,111	909	Arthur D. Little	223	145	300
Cap Gemini Ernst & Young	2,884	503	759	First Consulting Group	217	NA	23
IBM Global Services	2,653	NA	NA	Perot Systems	190	NA	NA
CSC	2,293	728	692	Hagler Bailly	150	87	87
KPMG Consulting	2,201	431	497	Nextera Enterprises	140	51	NA
Booz-Allen & Hamilton	1,260	480	411	Diamond Technology	136	NA	29
AMS	1,240	NA	267	Moores Rowland	124	NA	NA
McKinsey & Co.	1,210	1,450	1,073	Monitor Company	120	182	26
Mercer Consulting	1,033	390	NA	Abt Associates	120	56	56
Hewitt Associates	999	NA	NA	PRTM	119	35	84
Towers Perrin	993	NA	NA	DMR Consulting Group	115	NA	151
Arthur Andersen	824	140	700	The Segal Company	111	NA	NA
Keane, Inc.	777	125	166	Kurt Salmon	107	NA	68
CIBER Inc.	731	NA	NA	CTG	106	NA	NA
A.T. Kearney	716	466	333	**IPA**	**105**	**32**	**63**
Watson Wyatt	476	39	NA	Hay Group	103	NA	NA
Aan Consulting	405	NA	NA	RSM McGladrey	102	55	47
Cambridge Technology Partners	395	31	124	Grant Thornton	100	NA	14
Interim Technology	391	NA	36	ICF Consulting	100	NA	62
Navigant	378	168	NA	Scient	99	NA	NA
CBSI	333	55	111	Roland Berger	96	379	NA
Bain & Co.	316	604	140	Logica	95	NA	87
Telcordia Technologies	308	55	228	Gartner Group Consulting	92	48	NA
Boston Consulting Group	293	806	142	Luminant	92	NA	NA
Buck Consultants	285	NA	NA	AG Consulting	85	NA	NA
Sapient	277	NA	NA	Crowe Chizek	81	NA	NA
Milliman & Robertson	270	NA	NA	Marakon Associates	60	105	NA
AnswerThink	247	NA	NA	Plaut	58	46	197

NA: Information not available.
Sources: IPA; *Management Consultant International*, September 2000, pp. 2–3; *Consultants News*, June 2000, p. 4; and *Consultants News*, July 2000, p. 4.

Telemarketing

IPA's selling process began with its in-house tele-marketing team, called business coordination, located at Buffalo Grove. Each day, these 285 individuals, called business coordinators (BCs), cold-called an average of 13,200 small business owners across the United States and Canada and generated an average of 1,500 appointments. (See Exhibit 2 for BCs' pitch.) At the end of every business day, all appointments were faxed to IPA salespersons, who would confirm with the business owners that they would be visiting them the next day. On average, approximately 1,350 "leads," 90 percent of the 1,500 appointments, were confirmed daily.

Field Visit

The second step of the selling process was driven by IPA's 300 field sales representatives (FSRs), who operated out of their homes across the United States and Canada. The FSRs' first objective was to translate leads into actual meetings, called "sits," with business owners or other key decision makers. On average, approximately 630 of the 1,350 confirmed leads were converted to sits on a given day.

The FSRs' second objective was to convert sits into "surveys" by convincing business owners to buy the services of IPA analysts. The analysts would perform a two-day diagnosis of the businesses. On average, approximately 130 of the 630 daily sits were converted into surveys.

Survey

The next stage of the selling process was led by a team of 210 analysts, who operated out of their homes. On average, about one-third of the "surveys sold" were canceled by business owners before the analysts even began the surveys. For the remaining clients, over a two- to three-day period, analysts met with business owners and their employees and used a comprehensive questionnaire created by IPA to diagnose the state of the businesses, all for an average price of $890. At the end of the surveys, the analysts shared with the business owners their findings, which included an evaluation of the businesses' key strengths and weaknesses as well as improvement plans with quantified annual cost savings. At that stage, the analysts encouraged the business owners to engage IPA consultants to help implement the improvement plans. On average, 50 percent of the survey clients agreed to engage IPA for consulting services.

Management Services

Consulting constituted "the end of the IPA food chain," according to Sweet. IPA charged $195 per hour for these projects. The minimum engagement size for a consulting project was 100 hours, spread over two weeks. An average IPA consulting project was $27,500, requiring 140 hours of consulting—three weeks with one consultant or two weeks with an average of 1.6 consultants.

EXHIBIT 2   **The Telemarketers' Pitch**

This is [BC's name]. I am calling for my boss/partner [FSR's name] who is making sure business owners know about our company. May I please speak with [business owner's specific name]. We offer a full complement of business services that include getting, keeping and maintaining quality employees, increasing productivity using profit-based incentives, improving operational systems, market share, and cash flow. We also handle mergers, acquisitions, business valuations, and we have a tax division, and things of that nature.

(Sales rep's first name) would like to meet with you briefly tomorrow to give you a brief overview of what we do. He/she can see you tomorrow at _____ unless just before lunch works better for you.

Consulting charges did not include expenses, which typically amounted to 17 percent of the consulting charges. Burgess commented on consulting fees.

> Our fees are non-negotiable. We don't give discounts. Since many of our clients are cash poor, we may take terms, such as accepting postdated checks. All such exceptions have to be approved by me. This year we collected $1.5 million in postdated checks. Ninety-seven percent of our fees were collected in 2000; 95 percent by us and 2 percent by collection agencies.

Service Quality

Management was proud of IPA's reputation among clients, the vast majority of who, according to Burgess, were "highly satisfied by IPA's services, because we guarantee satisfaction." IPA asked for, and received, customer letters at the conclusion of a consulting project evaluating IPA's work. Burgess personally read all the letters that arrived. "We get very few complaints," he averred. His folder of customer letters was filled with effusive praise from satisfied customers.

There were dissenters, however, who questioned the quality of IPA's customer relationships. *Inc.* magazine, for example, reported receiving "scalding complaints" from aggrieved former IPA clients after it had anointed IPA as one of the fastest-growing privately held companies in the United States. Over the three years ending December 1999, 47 complaints had been filed by dissatisfied IPA clients with the Better Business Bureau of Chicago and Illinois. (IPA had a "satisfactory" rating with the bureau because all but three of the cases had been resolved.) This number represented less than 0.4 percent of the firm's total clients during that period. Most of the complaints, observed Burgess, "are people who didn't pay us."[1]

INSIDE THE ORGANIZATION

Business Coordination

Recognized within IPA as the firm's "business production engines," the BCs cold-called small business owners using databases on approximately 1.7 million small businesses. IPA paid an annual fee of $250,000 to Dun & Bradstreet and other database suppliers plus $50,000 per year for "washing" the databases to suit IPA needs.

Located in one large open room and working intensely in two shifts—from 7 A.M. to 12:30 P.M. and 12:30 to 6 P.M.—about 175 of the 285 telemarketers would be lined along the perimeter walls or clustered in groups of four in the middle. Above each telemarketer's two-and-a-half foot desk space hung a sign indicating which of the eight geographical regions the BC was covering. The BCs covering the same region were seated together. (See Exhibit 3 for IPA's organization chart.) The BCs reported to zone managers, who sat in the same room facing their BCs.

With sounds of dialing, ringing, yelling, and bustling, the atmosphere of the room reminded the casewriters of an investment bank trading floor. There was constant movement in the room as BCs whizzed over to report new leads to their zone managers. Every hour, the number of leads generated in each region was tallied, provided to Tyler Burgess and conveyed to John Burgess. "Every hour, everyone knows how much progress we have made during the day," observed Tyler Burgess. "If we are having a bad day, we do not have to wait till the end of the day to find that out. We find that out in real time and can take corrective action, if required."

Sales and Marketing

Business coordination zone managers were responsible for assigning the leads generated by the BCs to the field sales representatives (FSRs) in their regions such that each of the 300 FSRs received an average of three leads per day within a 50-mile radius of their homes. "We buy fax ma-

EXHIBIT 3   **IPA Organization Chart**

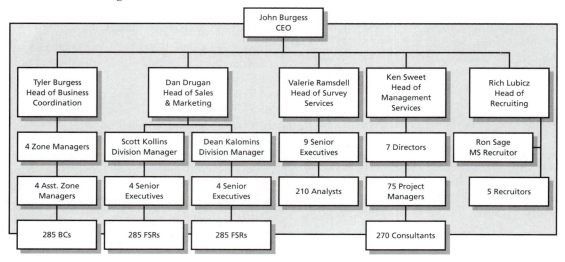

Source: IPA.

chines and lend them to our FSRs," said Burgess. "Every evening, every one of our FSRs gets a fax listing their leads for the next day." FSRs were grouped, like the BCs, in eight regions. Often the FSRs were paired with specific BCs covering their regions. Drugan explained the strategy behind this teaming of FSRs with designated BCs: "We try to pair top FSRs with top BCs. Eighty percent of the work gets done by placing the best with the best. And everybody stays motivated." Added Tyler Burgess: "The FSRs put more pressure on the BCs to generate leads than even BCs' zone managers can."

"Following a lead" required that an FSR meet with the business owner on site for an appointment already scheduled by the BC. About 30 percent of all confirmed appointments were canceled. At the meeting, the FSR tried to obtain a snapshot of the owner's business goals and concerns and give a 30-minute pitch of the IPA survey which explained how IPA had helped similar businesses run more efficiently and more profitably. On average, 325 such **direct sales** were closed every month. If a survey was sold, the FSR immediately notified the

FSR's senior executive. This information triggered three activities: (1) the terms of the sale were confirmed with the client; (2) the process of allocating an analyst to the survey was initiated; and (3) the "score" of survey sales was updated.

In addition to normal sales, FSRs could be involved in two other types of sales. If an FSR had visited the company, presented the IPA pitch, and found the business owner somewhat receptive, but for some reason had been unable to close the sale, the FSR would call or fax a summary of the meeting to the FSR's senior executive who would make a follow-up call to the business owner. If the senior executive succeeded in closing the sale, it would be called a **three-way sale.** On average, 575 three-way sales were consummated every month.

To encourage FSRs to create their own leads, Drugan had created another category of sale. The FSR might cold-call a small business by walking in, giving a short introduction of IPA, and trading business cards. The FSR would fax the pertinent information to the corresponding BC and follow up with the client. If this "warmer lead" closed in a sale, it would be called a **hybrid sale.** On average, 600 hybrid sales were closed every month.

Some low-density areas, such as Fairbanks, Alaska, could not generate enough leads to sustain FSRs dedicated to those territories. To ensure coverage of these territories, IPA had identified 10 FSRs, called "blitzers," who would be stationed temporarily in the low-density territories. After spending a few weeks in one particular territory, the blitzers would move on to another low-density territory.

Besides the 300 FSRs, IPA employed 40 headquarters-based inside sales representatives (ISRs). The ISRs made IPA's last-ditch sales effort by tracking relinquished leads in IPA's central database and following up on "cold leads" that were more than 14 days old. ISRs would "smile and dial" the cold leads and offer surveys at discounted fees in the hope that some of the leads would respond favorably. An ex-IPA ISR described her pitch: "I would say [to the cold leads], 'We just happen to have an analyst in the area. A project fell through; we can reduce your price.'"[2] On average, 1 out of 20 such calls came through, and the ISRs closed 50 sales per day at an average price of approximately $350 per survey.

Survey Services

Every Wednesday and Friday evening, analysts called in to their senior executives (one senior executive to 20–25 analysts) at IPA's headquarters for their next assignments, which could be anywhere in the United States or Canada. Analyst assignments were based on the fit between business owner needs and analyst skills, not geographical proximity. Burgess himself allocated analysts to specific surveys that he believed were "key to business."

Surveys began on Mondays and Thursdays. IPA tried to minimize the time lapse between an FSR selling a survey and an analyst conducting it. If a survey was sold on Monday by an FSR, an analyst would receive the assignment on Wednesday,

travel by car or plane that evening to the business site, and begin the survey on Thursday. Analysts left their homes on Sunday evenings for their Monday surveys, traveled on Wednesday evenings for their Thursday surveys, and returned home Friday nights. After a detailed two-day survey on site, the analyst convened a "findings meeting" with the client to review the business's key strengths and weaknesses as well as an improvement plan with quantified benefits. The client was then given the option of hiring IPA consultants to implement the plan.

On occasion, analysts did not offer clients the option of IPA consulting services because the clients were on the brink of bankruptcy with little hope of turning things around or because the clients were involved in illegal practices. "IPA declines 28 percent of potential business," noted Burgess, "because a prospective client either cannot afford to pay or is not rational in what he or she expects the company to accomplish."[3] In addition, analysts were encouraged to sell management services to clients only if they had clearly identified a problem that they knew consulting services would remedy. "No recommendation will be made for consulting services unless I am able to substantiate a three-to-one return for every dollar invested," read a talking point in the analyst's sales pitch. Former IPA analysts had complained, however, about intense pressure exerted by their supervisors to sign clients to management services. Recalled an ex-IPA analyst: "They [the supervisors] thought you should make a sale on every call, and they'd really ride you if you didn't."[4] On average, analysts in their first year at IPA converted 38 percent of the surveys into consulting projects. In their second year, the conversion rate increased to approximately 50 percent. Top-ranked analysts achieved a conversion rate of about 75 percent.

"Analysts have to learn to deal with long hours, prohibitive travel, and high pressure," said Ramsdell, describing the challenges of the analysts' job:

Often, they have to work with somewhat closed-minded people and confront racism, sexism, and ageism. If they are successful in building rapport, then they face the next hurdle—they have to make the small business owners take a hard look at their practices, and often this exercise is disheartening to the business owners. Even if they do everything right, our analysts have to learn to manage rejection, not because they are wrong, but because some small business owners can't face the truth.

Even though senior executives keep in frequent phone contact with the analysts, and our analysts attend regular retraining programs at IPA, they operate *alone* in the field. I tell them, "You are your own business out there." The good news is that once an analyst gets over the three-month hurdle and survives, job satisfaction is high because, by and large, analysts are helping hardworking people who are "salt of the earth" obtain a better living for themselves and their families.

Management Services

Consultants were assigned to projects by Sweet as soon as analysts closed sales on consulting services. "I try to match knowledge, chemistry, and geography in assigning consultants to projects," reflected Sweet. Consultants traveled to the business sites, absorbed key learnings from the analysts, and began the consulting project, all within 24 hours of the consulting project sale. "We show up the very next day after the analyst closes," explained Sweet,

because we don't want buyer's remorse to set in. More important, it is cost effective for the client to have us fixing the problems that the analysts have identified before the situation changes very much. Also, by entering soon after the analysts, our consultants are able to build on the momentum our analysts have created at the client sites.

The 270 consultants were supervised in each of their consulting projects by one of IPA's 74 project managers (PMs). Consultants and their PMs opened all projects by jointly visiting with the clients and reviewing with them the analysts' findings and client expectations of the consulting projects. The PMs stayed on client sites for the first two days to ensure the projects had been launched on the correct trajectory. Thereafter, the consultants were expected to work continuously at client sites until project completion.

PMs managed the projects' progress remotely, communicating with the consultants at least twice every day. PMs oversaw between 4 and 18 projects at any given time and were ultimately responsible for delivering the consulting services that had been promised to the clients. IPA promised to continue working with clients that were not satisfied at the completion of consulting projects on a nonbillable basis until the clients were satisfied. In 2000 such a situation had arisen in less than 1 percent of the projects.

Although IPA's website listed, and in conversations with small business owners the consultants mentioned, the firm's "10 rules for growing your business" (see Exhibit 4), Sweet emphasized, "We don't have a one-size-fits-all mentality; we offer advice that fits specific client needs." He distinguished IPA's management services from other professional services that were offered to small business owners:

Our objective is to provide cures for our clients—not maintenance dosages like attorneys, accountants, and other handholding consultants. When our consultants complete their projects, they leave knowing that their clients have learned how to implement the tools needed to grow a successful business.

Consultants followed a challenging schedule involving extensive travel and on-site work. But they were rewarded, Sweet opined, by the response they evoked from the clients. "Our consultants experience tremendous ego gratification," he observed,

because they are seen as "knights in shining armor." Walking into a difficult business sit-

EXHIBIT 4   IPA's 10 Rules for Growing Your Business

1. Create a strategic plan for growing your business, establish benchmarks for performance, and hold your managers accountable for the numbers.
2. Don't wait for annual reviews to make adjustments to your business plan. Markets don't wait for annual planning reviews, nor should you.
3. Every business owner must make a personal transformation from technical expert to master strategist for the enterprise.
4. Adopt the three cardinal principles of business growth: Drive the numbers higher today; drive the numbers higher tomorrow; and drive the numbers higher this week. If you focus on growing your business in the short term, you won't have to worry about growth over the long run.
5. Develop a financial and operational reporting system that allows you to track all your critical numbers. If you don't measure it, you can't manage it.
6. Hold a daily management "huddle" with all department heads to go over the numbers, and make adjustments to daily action plans.
7. Control your costs when growing your business by budgeting percentages rather than dollars.
8. Identify all the key people who are driving your business and create incentives for each of them to grow your business for you.
9. Throw out the old management model you started your business with and create a new one. Innovation in management systems is the key to outdistancing your competitors in the race to the top.
10. Growing a business is like competing in championship sport: Play the game the way a championship athlete plays: Play to win instead of playing not to lose. And enjoy the game.

Source: IPA.

uation and improving it gives a feeling of tremendous power. What they do has an immediate and lasting effect on the quality of life of the business owners. Plus, this is the only position at IPA, besides management, where there is no pressure to sell.

In 2000, 7 percent of IPA's consulting clients were repeat customers compared to 1 percent in 1995. The increase in repeat business was primarily because of three programs that management services had introduced to foster long-term client relationships. Offered to IPA clients upon completion of traditional consulting projects, the retainer program included a two-day visit by IPA consultants every quarter for one year. Clients were charged a reduced rate of $127.50 per hour for retainer consulting service. A slightly more in-depth version of the retainer program, the **business partners program** included week-long

visits at quarterly intervals by one or two IPA consultants. Clients were charged a reduced rate of $127.50 per hour. More flexible than the other two add-on programs, the **term contract program** stipulated that, upon completion of the traditional consulting engagement, IPA would provide the client with a consultant for four weeks to four months to temporarily fill a key position within the client's business to launch a new project or practice. The client was billed $145 per hour.

On occasions, clients wanted to recruit particular IPA consultants for permanent employment. "We are not in the executive placement business. We prevent talent-poaching by having our clients sign a two-year nonhiring provision in their contracts with IPA," noted Sweet. "However, if a client desperately needs an individual and the consultant is eager to go, we allow such moves for a nominal finder's fee. Usually, such people come back to us in six months or so, bored by the monotony of what they are doing. We hire them back."

WORK ENVIRONMENT

During their visit to IPA's Buffalo Grove headquarters, the casewriters were struck by the expression "playing the IPA game" employed by Burgess and his colleagues. Burgess's office was dubbed Grand Central Station because of the frequent visits of executives and the frenetic pace of activities. Besides those who came to inform or seek direction from Burgess—rarely did anyone escape from the office without being subjected to rapid-fire questions, caustic remarks, or exhortations from Burgess—other employees came, like clockwork, on the hour, to update on the two large dry erase boards that lined his office walls scores for the day on leads generated, leads converted to sits, sits converted to surveys, and surveys converted to consulting projects. "I don't manage this machine week by week, or even day by day," remarked Burgess. "I manage it hour by hour."

The metaphor of "playing the game" was echoed throughout the organization as division heads recorded on an hourly basis the "scores" on key variables within their divisions on dry erase scoreboards that lined their office walls. An IPA executive emphasized the importance of these scores by intoning the firm's motto: "If you don't measure it, you can't manage it."

Burgess came to the office at 5:30 A.M. and left at 6:00 P.M. His hands-on approach to work characterized IPA's work ethic. His son Tyler Burgess, who was also business coordination director, remarked: "He expects a lot from everyone around him, especially from me. He beats me up even as he pushes me forward. My father has instilled in me the principle that hard work is the key to success. Everything depends on your spirit toward work." "The day starts at 7 A.M. and ends after 6 P.M.," noted one employee. "We have no formal lunch break. People just sneak away whenever they can to the lunch truck that is usually parked outside our building to buy sandwiches and bring them back to their desks." Despite the long hours, the employees generally reported being satisfied that they were working in an active, successful business. "I'll do this forever," said an analyst. "Here, you're providing somebody something he needs at the time he needs it."[5] Several of IPA's ex-employees, however, complained about the work atmosphere. Remarked an ex-analyst who accused the firm of withholding back-pay: "They treat their employees terribly." Burgess responded that such complaints were primarily a case of sour grapes. "They come here and see other folks being eminently successful financially and professionally," he said. "They then fail. They get distraught with that."[6]

RECRUITMENT AND TRAINING

Business Coordinators

The BCs ran the gamut on a number of dimensions: age (from 18 to 65), education, ethnicity, and socio-economic backgrounds. "One of my best BCs is an intense and eccentric individual," remarked Tyler Burgess. "He cuts his hair Mohawk style and colors it purple. But he is just great at what he does—convincing business owners over the phone to have our sales representatives visit them."

Every week, IPA received over 200 responses to advertisements for the BC position placed in Chicago-area publications and radio stations. The respondents' educational backgrounds varied from GEDs to college degrees. Fifty percent of the applicants were invited for an interview during which characteristics such as work ethic, attitude, and fit were assessed. Sixty percent of the candidates interviewed were selected to attend the two-day business coordination training seminar offered weekly at IPA headquarters in Buffalo Grove, Illinois. (In 2000 IPA spent close to $2 million on advertising and $2 million on training.) Recruiting director Rich Lubicz explained the theory behind the training:

We try to weed out people who would end up quitting anyway by exposing the trainees to the harsh reality of the BCs' job. We tell them, "Out of every 40 phone calls you will make in an hour, only in seven cases will business owners talk to you. You will be lucky if you make an appointment with one of those seven. Do you have the determination and persistence the job requires?" If 60 people attend a training seminar, we lose 12 by the end of training. Of the remaining 48 that show up for work, about 10 stay beyond the first month. But those 10 are going to be good BCs and we can count on them staying with us for at least one year. Of our 285 BCs, only about 50 make up the core, that is, have tenure of two or more years, and only 10 of those have been with us for five years or more.

Sales Representatives

FSRs ranged in age from 30 to 50 years. A typical FSR would be a college graduate with small business experience and a self-starter mentality. One-tenth of the FSRs were women. Of the 300 FSRs, about 60 constituted the "core," in Lubicz's terminology—FSRs with tenure of two years or more.

FSRs were recruited on a national scale through newspaper advertisements. Three full-time IPA recruiters traveled throughout the United States and Canada to interview prospective FSRs, together visiting, on average, 15 cities per week. Applicants with five or more years of experience in selling services were interviewed. Every day, each recruiter invited eight applicants for in-person interviews to screen for work ethic and self-starter mentality. Of every eight interviews scheduled, roughly five candidates showed up. Of those, approximately two were invited to attend the four-day FSR training offered weekly at IPA headquarters. On average, 30 new FSRs attended the training seminar. Of these, between five and eight stayed at IPA beyond their first 30 days.

Analysts

Analysts were typically in their 30s, 40s, or 50s and had undergraduate degrees and five to ten years of business experience. Although there was "no unique ideal profile," according to Ramsdell, successful analysts

> possess analytical skills, a strong work ethic, stamina, and adaptability. Analysts who are excellent at crunching numbers do not always sell the consulting services. This is very much a people business. Good analysts can do the analysis well, but also connect well with people.

Analysts, like FSRs, were recruited nationally by two full-time recruiters who together visited 10 cities per week. Each week the recruiters screened an average of 250 resumes for the analyst position and invited approximately 70 candidates for interview. Each recruiter scheduled an average of eight interviews every day. Of the eight candidates invited, approximately seven showed up, and of these seven, two were invited to attend the headquarters-based week-long analyst training, which commenced every alternate week. Of the 40 analysts who attended training, only five stayed at IPA beyond their first 30 days. Of the five, only one or two stayed for a whole year.

Besides induction training for new analysts, IPA conducted quarterly weekend "retraining" sessions in Buffalo Grove that seasoned analysts were required to attend. Lubicz explained:

> Analysts have to attend four weekends of retraining every year to brush up on skills and learn new ones. Retrainings not only make good analysts better, but they also build company loyalty and establish a strong network of support, knowledge, and cohesiveness around the analysts.

Consultants

IPA consultants had a minimum of 10 years of hands-on middle-to-senior level management experience. All consultants were expected to have bachelor's degrees; many were equipped with master's degrees and professional certifications such as JDs, CPAs, and PhDs. "Although the percentage of consultants in their 30s has increased from 5 percent to 15 percent during the last two years, largely to develop expertise in the technology sector," noted Sweet, "in areas such as retail and distribution, we continue to hire seasoned managers to our consulting practice." The average age of IPA consultants was 52 years.

Recruiting coordinator Ron Sage directed the recruiting effort for consultants. Based on need, Sage ran newspaper advertisements every few weeks in major cities throughout the United States and Canada. Sage received an average of 150 resumes in a two-week period. Approximately half of the applicants met the preliminary qualifications of an IPA consultant—10 years of hands-on middle-to-upper management experience. Sage conducted phone interviews with these candidates to screen for industry expertise, commitment level, and willingness to travel. About 35 candidates were short-listed after the initial interview and sent a preliminary computer and financial exam as well as details of the compensation schedule and required travel. Sage followed this with another phone conversation to discuss questions and concerns to further weed out the uncommitted. Only about 7 of the 35 were eventually hired as consultants. "People who become consultants with us have the grey hair and experience to be credible as hands-on advisors," remarked Sweet, "but are typically too independent minded to work in a corporate environment." Once recruited, consultants tended to stay on with IPA. "Retention rate for consultants is 60 percent at the one-year mark, and annual retention rate is 80 percent beyond one year," observed Sage.

Of the 270 IPA consultants, about 75 had come from IPA's largest competitor, George S. May. "Compensation is not the reason these people are with us," Burgess commented.

The pay scales at May and IPA are competitive. We have attracted and then retained so many ex-May consultants because (a) IPA offers a five-day workweek as opposed to a six-day workweek at May and (b) we don't yell and scream at them quite as much as they do at May.

Consultant training comprised an initial 10-day session at headquarters followed by two to five advanced training sessions every year. Only consultants with more than 18 months of experience could be considered for promotion to PMs. Consultants promoted to PMs were required to undergo two weekends of follow-on training in Buffalo Grove.

COMPENSATION STRUCTURE

Business Coordination

Every four weeks, BCs were ranked based on productivity points they had accumulated during the previous four weeks. Attendance was worth 50 points; each unexcused absence led to a 10-point deduction. Number of leads generated did not contribute to points. "Too much focus on writing new leads, in fact, reduces the quality of the leads," remarked Tyler Burgess. Additional points were given only if the leads led to survey sales (see Exhibits 5 and 6).

BCs were ranked on commission basis. "It's not worth the time or the pressure if you are here for the hourly wage," remarked Tyler Burgess. "You might as well work at Taco Bell." Commissions were computed in two-week cycles and were structured differently for the top 25 BCs (in terms of their productivity scores) and the remaining BCs (see Exhibit 6). The average annual compensation for a BC was between $25,000 to $30,000. The highest paid BC, Terrence Perkins, earned $160,000 in 2000. "I get paid very well," noted Perkins, "because I am good at the IPA game." When asked what he meant by the IPA game, Perkins responded: "The IPA game is strictly a numbers game—sheer numbers. In 2000 I had reached my target numbers by Thanksgiving. For 2001 my goal is to earn

EXHIBIT 5 BC Productivity Scores and Compensation Structure

BCs were ranked every four weeks on the basis of their productivity scores. Compensations were computed in two-week cycles.

Productivity Scores

Metric	Points
Attendance	50
Unexcused absence	(10)
Telemarketing sale	50
Executive takeover sale	30
X sale	10

Telemarketing sale   A BC cold-called a potential customer, set the appointment for the FSR, and the FSR sold the survey. A telemarketing sale was worth 50 points to the BC.
Executive takeover sale   On occasions, an FSR was unable to consummate a sale but felt that the contact had potential. The FSR would send the lead to the inside sales department for follow up. If ISRs sold the survey, the BC earned 30 points.
X sale   Every appointment set by the BC department was entered into a database. On occasion, the inside sales department drew its leads from the X database, which contained details of leads generated by BCs that the FSRs had been unsuccessful in selling surveys. When a lead from the X database resulted in a sale, the BC that generated the original lead received 10 points.

Compensation Structure

	Top 25 BCs Compensation = Salary ($9/hr.) + Commission + Bonus			Below Top 25 BCs Compensation = Salary ($9/hr.) or Commission + Bonus, whichever was higher		
Number of Sale	Commission/ Sale ($)	Bonus ($)	Number of Sale	Commission/ Sale ($)	Bonus ($)	
1st–5th	150	—	1st–2nd	200	—	
6th	150	500	3rd–4th	250	—	
7th–9th	200	—	5th	300	—	
10th	200	500	6th	300	500	
> 10th	200	—	7th–9th	300	—	
			10th	300	500	
			> 10th	300	—	

Source: IPA.

$200,000." "Terrence earns more than I do," noted Tyler Burgess, "and I have no problem with that. In fact, I hold Terrence up as a role model for every other BC."

Upon being promoted to zone manager in recognition of his performance, Perkins had become unhappy and dissatisfied. (Zone managers' compensations were entirely comprised of commissions based on total sales in their zones.) "I can make more money just being a really good tele-marketer," he complained. "I didn't want to join management." Burgess eventually acceded to Perkin's request and "demoted" him to a telemarketer on the condition that he work in a special "training room," where new recruits could listen in on his conversations with potential customers and learn his telemarketing technique. Perkins liked this approach, since, "this way, they learn and I don't lose any money because time is money in this business."

EXHIBIT 6   Compensation Structure for FSRs

Compensations were computed in two-week cycles.

Number of Survey Sold	FSR Commission on Normal Sale (% of survey fee)	FSR Commission if One of the Sales Was Hybrid (% of survey fee)
1st	40	50
2nd	55	65
3rd	62	72
4th	75	85
5th	90	100
6th and above	100	100

An average survey was billed at $890; 90 percent of the surveys were billed in the $500–$1,200 range.
Three-way sales were compensated at the normal payout scale. For a hybrid sale, the FSR received the normal payout plus 2 percent of the consulting fees if the project progressed to that stage.
ISRs were paid 33 percent of survey fee collected. (On average, ISR-sold surveys were priced at $350.) Additionally, ISRs earned a bonus of $50 for every survey scheduled for the next day and a $500 bonus for every ISR-sold survey that progressed to consulting.
Source: IPA.

Sales

FSRs' compensation was based entirely on commissions. Burgess commented on this compensation structure: "If we paid our FSRs a base salary plus commission they wouldn't be as hungry to close sales because they would have the comfort of knowing a check was in the mail. Instead, we provide them hot leads and a big upside in commission."

Commissions were based on the number of surveys sold and the amount of survey fees billed and structured progressively, increasing from 40 percent of the survey fee for the first sale to 100 percent of the survey fee for the fifth sale (see Exhibit 7). "In every two-week cycle, our FSRs try to win this 'race for five,'" noted sales development director Tom Ryan. An experienced FSR closed an average of three sales per week and earned between $65,000 and $70,000. The number one ranked FSR earned $220,000 in 2000.

Surveys

Analysts were paid strictly on commission based on consulting services sold. Burgess noted: "If we were to pay a base salary, our analysts would lose some of their zeal for converting a survey into a consulting project. Pure commission gives them more autonomy out in the field—it's just you versus the customer." The commission structure for analysts was divided into four levels, depending upon their accrued experience (see Exhibit 8). The average annual compensation of an analyst was about $80,000. The highest paid analysts earned approximately $300,000 in 2000.

Management Services

Consultants were also paid strictly on commission plus bonus. Commissions were paid on a progressive scale, increasing as the ratio of work done to work contracted increased. In addition, the consultants were paid bonuses for selling and delivering relationship programs to clients (see Exhibit 8). Consultants earned compensation between $40,000 and $65,000 per year, with the highest paid consultant earning approximately $82,000 per year. Burgess defended the relatively conservative compensation offered to consultants:

> We can justify paying this salary range because the kind of people that join us as consultants face a limited job market with few alternative opportunities. Once they join IPA, they are motivated by the possibility of career progression in addition to their compensation. Consultants that are promoted to

EXHIBIT 7   Compensation Structure for Analysts

Compensations were computed in two-week cycles. Top analysts were paid a commission equal to 12 percent of the consulting fee collected; second level analysts were paid a commission equal to 10 percent of the consulting fee collected; third level analysts were paid on the following schedule.

Surveys Converted to Consulting	Hours of Consulting Sold	Commission
1st–5th	>0	5%
6th and above	1st–70th	7%
	71st–130th	8%
	131st–200th	11%
	>200th	12%

Expense Reimbursement

Surveys Converted to Consulting	Circumstance	Expense Reimbursement
1st–5th	Survey site less than 80 miles from analyst home	0
	Survey site more than 80 miles from analyst home	$90 per diem
	Survey requires additional travel day(s)	$50 per travel day
6th and above	Survey site less than 80 miles from analyst home	0
	Survey site more than 80 miles from analyst home	$100 per day
	Survey requires additional travel day(s)	$75 per travel day (departing home) $50 per travel day (returning home)

In addition, analysts receive a mileage allowance of 25 cents per mile.
Source: IPA management.

EXHIBIT 8   Compensation Structure for Consultants

Consulting Commissions	
Consulting Billing (% of the project)	Consultant Commission (% of billing)
0–60	11
61–110	13
>110	16

In addition to commissions, the consultants earned $600 bonus per completed project.

Rewards for Selling and Delivering Relationship Programs to Clients		
Activity	Bonus ($)	Commission
Retainer program	100	16% commission at normal billing rate of $195/hour
Business partner program	500	16% commission at normal billing rate of $195/hour
Term contract program	—	16% commission at reduced billing rate of $145/hour plus transportation home every weekend

Source: IPA management.

PMs triple their compensation. And the number of PMs is growing fast because our company is growing very rapidly.

PMs earned 2.8 percent of the total consulting billings of the projects they managed in addition to the normal payout of consultants when they were fulfilling consultant duties. PMs earned compensation in the $84,000–220,000 per year range.

IPA'S HISTORY[7]

In the summer of 1991, when Burgess and two of his colleagues, Bruce Tulio and Charles Morton, left George S. May, a Park Ridge, Illinois–based consulting firm focused on small businesses, and started a competing business named International Profit Associates, 22 of their former colleagues at May followed them to join the new firm. May retaliated by suing Burgess, his co-founders, and eight other former employees who had joined IPA, for appropriating trade secrets. Although May eventually lost that round of litigation, the 1991 suit was followed by over a dozen suits filed by May, IPA, or individuals with those companies. "They don't like us," noted Burgess, "because they just want to control the marketplace. They want to deny us our right to compete."

IPA faced an uphill challenge in establishing itself as a viable firm, especially given May's legal challenge and the impaired reputations of the founders. All three of the founders had criminal records. In 1989 Tulio had pleaded guilty to having conspired with a drug dealer in the manufacturing of a key ingredient in methamphetamine, commonly known as speed. Morton had been convicted in 1988 in connection with the theft of Hummel figurines from three Pittsburgh stores. And Burgess was a disbarred lawyer who had been convicted of attempted grand larceny.

IPA's early years were a struggle for survival. The company relied for financing partly on the credit cards of its employees. Several creditors had to sue to collect on IPA's allegedly unpaid bills. One of the co-founders, Tulio left IPA in early 1992 after a dispute with Burgess. But after the first few rocky months, business took off. The new company grew rapidly in the small business consulting niche as its four-step approach became increasingly more effective and efficient. As the company expanded, "Charles became ill," Burgess recalled. "I couldn't accept a situation in which everyone except one of the two owners was persevering in their job." In 1998, Morton retired from IPA under board pressure, selling his stake to Burgess for $2.9 million.

In 1998 Burgess initiated a mergers-and-acquisitions company under the IPA umbrella. In 1999 IPA began working on projects with divisions of mid-size firms in the $10–100 million annual revenue range as well as offering telephone coaching for a fee to owners of businesses with annual revenue of less than $500,000. By 2000, IPA, together with its affiliate companies, was recognized as "an advisor to private and public emerging growth companies that provides business valuations, business fund-raising, merger and acquisition assistance, and investor and public relations services worldwide."[8]

JOHN BURGESS

"When John Burgess talks about his life," observed a reporter who had covered Burgess and IPA, "he favors a metaphor about climbing mountains and falling off them. Figuratively speaking, he's done more than his share of both."[9] Born in 1949 in Cranston, Rhode Island, John Burgess was the eldest son in a family of six siblings headed by a father who suffered a nervous breakdown. To supplement the family income, Burgess started selling eggs door-to-door at age 12. At age 16, he dropped out of high school and began his first business—selling fruits and vegetables door-to-door—which he grew to $1,000 per day in revenue within one year.

In 1968, realizing the importance of having an educational degree, Burgess passed his high school equivalency test and began saving money for college. In 1969, Burgess began attending Roger Williams College in Providence, Rhode Island, and simultaneously working as an ingot salesman for Bay State Crucible and Paragon Smelting companies. He earned BS in business administration in 1971 and decided to pursue a graduate degree in law. On his second attempt, in 1972 he was admitted to the New England School of Law in Boston. He had gotten married the same year.

During his first year of law school, Burgess worked during the day selling ingots to support his family and attended law school at night. His workday lasted from six in the morning to past midnight. "The result," he recounted, "was that at the end of the year, for the first time in my life, I was put on academic probation." During his second year of law school, Burgess changed jobs to reduce his working hours. He began working as a soybeans trader for Pillsbury. Upon graduation in 1976, Burgess accepted a full-time position as a commodity trader with Pillsbury in New York and later relocated to its Illinois office. "I was on a salary of $35,000 per year plus bonus," Burgess recalled. "My first year's bonus check came to $75,000." Despite his early success, Burgess left Pillsbury in 1979 under a cloud. Pillsbury sued Burgess for inflating trading profits and charging the firm phantom commissions. The suit was settled out of court "for a nominal sum" according to Burgess.[10]

In 1980 Burgess and his wife moved to a suburb of Buffalo, New York, where he started practicing law. Burgess soon developed a reputation for being a fierce champion of women in divorce cases and his practice flourished. However, a grievance committee investigation, following up on charges that he misappropriated funds from the estate of a deceased client, led to Burgess's disbarment in 1987 and conviction in 1988 on grounds of attempted grand larceny. In 1989, Burgess and his wife filed for personal bankruptcy. They divorced the following year.[11] Reflecting on his checkered background, Burgess reflected later,

"You can't do anything about your past. Your past is your past. But you can make your own future."

His life at its nadir, Burgess joined George S. May in 1990 as an executive survey analyst. "I converted my first two surveys into sales," Burgess recalled. "Then I missed one. I converted 27 of the next 28 surveys into sales. It was a conversion rate unheard of at May." Burgess's progress at May was meteoric. In less than a year, he was earning $12,900 a month and was named chief of the survey department. In 1991, however, he left the company amidst a firestorm of controversy and mutual recriminations and co-founded IPA.

As IPA prospered over the next decade, so did Burgess. He remarried in 1994. In 2000, his annual salary at IPA was about $1 million and his ownership in IPA was worth approximately $100 million, including which, his personal wealth was projected at $120 million.[12] "A personal memory has driven me to make IPA into a success," Burgess reflected during the 2000 Christmas party.

> My first father-in-law was a hardworking Italian immigrant. He mortgaged his house 17 times to build a thriving electrical business. When he died of a heart attack, his son, who had been working with his father for several years, took over the family business. My brother-in-law was a terrific electrician. But the business went bankrupt. I had wondered at that time how that could have happened.
>
> Only when I started working as a small business consultant did the realization strike me that running a business is very different from being a good craftsperson. You have to learn the business of business. Otherwise, big firms that are taking over more and more of the business terrain are likely to overwhelm and consume you, not because they are better at the craft but simply because you don't understand how to run a business. I feel that if I can teach small business owners the business of business, a whole lot of ordinary folks will be in positions to control their own destinies.

References

1. Joseph Rosenbloom, "I'm John Burgess. I'm Here to Help You." *Inc.,* June 2000.

2. Ibid.

3. Ibid.

4. Ibid.

5. Arsenio Oloroso Jr., "This Consultancy's on a Fast Track; but Some People Say They Were Taken for a Ride," *Crain's Chicago Business,* July 29, 1996, p. 1.

6. Ibid.

7. This section draws upon Rosenbloom, "I'm John Burgess. I'm Here to Help You."

8. "FindEx.Com, Inc. Engages IPA Advisory and Intermediary Services to Structure $25–$50 Million Capital Infusion," Business Wire, March 6, 2000.

9. Rosenbloom.

10. Ibid.

11. Ibid.

12. Ibid.

Managing the Organization Through Processes

The discovery in our book thus far that highly effective people and processes are imperative for high-performing professional service firms seems obvious. However, Module Four focuses on how these internal processes connect strategy with implementation (Figure 1). We will see through this module's four cases that few PSFs make this connection in a fluid and dynamic way that leverages organizational capabilities to achieve the desired outcomes. We will also see through these cases how people drive the business at the strategic and tactical level through processes. People determine success or failure. The professionals connect both the external with the internal and the strategic with the tactical to bring organizational success.

In all of the cases we have studied so far in this book we have introduced case protagonists who must connect their PSF's internal systems and structures (Module Three) to the internal processes of the firms. These processes include human capital management (recruitment, training, promotion, performance management [motivation, goal setting, measurement, and evaluation], retention, and succession planning), decision making, and knowledge management.

It has been our intention to highlight why processes are key within PSFs. These organizations traditionally have been transaction oriented with little tolerance for processes that seem administrative in nature and slow down the focus on

This note was prepared by Professor Thomas DeLong, Professor Ashish Nanda, and Dean's Research Fellow Scot Landry.

FIGURE 1

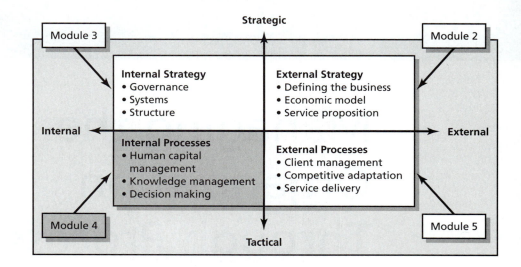

completing the deal or serving the client. However, high-performance PSFs must create processes that leverage both financial and human capital in ways that connect internal with external services that focus on the client.

We emphasize throughout this fourth module that current economic drivers have changed the way many PSFs think and behave relative to human capital management. We also stress that technology has dramatically influenced the way in which organizations think about how to build, share, leverage, transfer, codify, and destroy knowledge. Advancements in technology have also created environments within PSFs that allow professionals to work longer and more intense hours. The professional is now connected to information 24 hours each day through globally networked communication processes. This phenomenon influences the ways in which organizations make decisions. Organizational decision-making processes provide PSFs the opportunity to leverage their intellectual capital in strategic and tactical ways to serve clients. We have seen how those decision-making processes can break down to the detriment of the organization and the professionals who work in them.

HUMAN CAPITAL MANAGEMENT

The human capital management process centers on how to leverage people to achieve high performance. We attempt to answer the following questions: How do we attract, hire, and retain the best people? How do we evaluate them, promote them, pay them, manage them, and outplace them? How do we socialize professionals into the organizational culture? PSFs can sometimes take their human capital for granted. Gradually, PSF leaders are realizing that their professionals are at the very center of the organization's long-term viability and the most important variable for the firm's success.

Only through employee satisfaction and loyalty is excellent client service provided. Excellent service is critical to retaining current clients and also to receiving from them testimonials to win new clients. By emphasizing client relationship management, value creation, and human capital management, PSFs enter into a virtuous cycle in which the three primary constituencies operate in harmony to create shared value (Figure 2). It is through paying attention to this internal cycle of success that the PSF ensures long-term client satisfaction, commitment, and organizational vitality.

KNOWLEDGE MANAGEMENT

We emphasize in Module Four that one of the major tactical issues that PSFs confront is how to build knowledge, collect it, dispense it throughout the organization, store it, control access to it, and destroy it after it is no longer relevant. How can PSFs capture the right information at the right time at the right cost using the best technology in the most advantageous context? What is the relevant role of each professional in the knowledge management process? How can PSFs develop processes to ensure motivation for both the collection of past learning and the

FIGURE 2

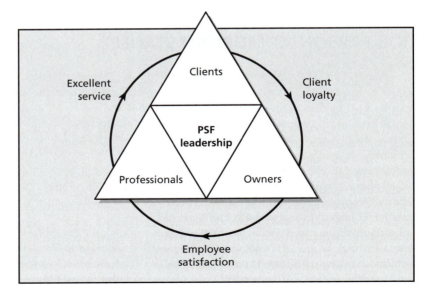

generation of new learning? More important, how do PSFs create a culture where the most helpful knowledge is retained and leveraged?

In our study of PSFs, we understand that few professionals within PSFs enter the most important data into the knowledge management system. Often this is due to either political reasons or because professionals are not rewarded or compensated for these activities. In many cases, PowerPoint slides from final client presentations is all that is shared within firms. When this occurs, the true learning a client team had during an engagement is kept in those team members' collective brains and not disseminated to the firm. This tacit knowledge is the most important knowledge for firms to pass on, since it allows them to learn from their own mistakes and experience and deliver better client service as a result. On the other hand, when copies of presentations are the only "knowledge" available, client service can sometimes suffer, specifically if professionals just repackage a previous analysis for their new client. The most successful PSFs must determine a process that rewards professionals for sharing this tacit knowledge with their colleagues.

DECISION MAKING

The process of decision making within PSFs is critical—it can often either ensure success or failure. Leaders make strategic and tactical errors through dysfunctional processes. The wrong people may be involved in critical decision-making processes. Often internal and external dimensions are not connected through the process.

The way in which the decisions are communicated throughout the firm is essential to long-term success. Professionals want to be involved in the decisions that will affect them. It is up to the leaders of the firms to create processes that enhance commitment to the decisions being made by the professionals.

ROB PARSON AT MORGAN STANLEY

We used the Rob Parson at Morgan Stanley case to discuss performance management issues. Morgan Stanley, under the leadership of John Mack, was in the middle of organizational and cultural transformation. One critical step to achieve that goal was by implementing the 360-degree performance evaluation system. Rob Parson, a star performer, had not behaved in the way required by Morgan Stanley's new culture of teamwork and cooperation. Should this evaluation result affect Rob Parson's compensation and promotion? Should the firm worry if Rob Parson decides to leave without a promotion? Also, a more general question is—How can a PSF use performance management to support organizational change?

The case highlights the complex managerial challenges associated with performance management. How should Rob Parson's manager, Paul Nasr, give the negative feedback? Does Paul Nasr have the political, managerial, and interpersonal skills to be Rob Parson's mentor and coach? This case emphasizes that it requires training at the managerial level in order to implement the 360-degree performance evaluation system successfully.

STRATEGIC SERVICES AT ANDERSEN CONSULTING

The Strategic Services at Andersen Consulting case addresses a pair of issues common to a myriad of PSFs during rapid growth periods: (1) how to expand a thriving business and increase the ranks of a key division in a way that provides organizational symmetry while (2) dealing with internal challenges that growth almost inevitably creates during such periods of expansion.

Specifically in this case, Bill Copacino, newly appointed managing partner of the Strategic Services Division (SSD) of Andersen Consulting for North America, felt pressure to grow his department at the historically rapid growth rate, while protecting a humane and cohesive corporate culture that he considered important to his division's performance as well as its morale. The challenge boiled down to recruit, acculturate, and retain enough competent professionals.

The case addresses issues of internal capabilities and external opportunities and the tension between them. Does the leader focus on external opportunities first or create a sound foundation by focusing on internal challenges? This case forms a natural contrast with the Diamond in the Rough case in that Mel Bergstein, founder of Diamond Technologies, builds the culture from the ground up. Bergstein and Copacino have similar attitudes about human capital. Yet Copacino, as a quasi-outsider at Andersen, has a more daunting and complicated task confronting him. Not that creating a corporate culture is easy, but changing an entrenched one is more complex.

The tensions between centering activities on strategic issues or operational ones set the context and theoretical underpinnings for this module. Bill Copacino must plant a foot in both the external and internal domains simultaneously. Copacino must pay attention to the two external quadrants of external strategy and external process while balancing labor markets and financial markets. This quandry creates the tension of the case and gives readers the opportunity to wrestle with all the challenges that confront managers in PSFs. Through the analysis of this case, readers will also understand how organization theory, socialization, organization economics, hiring, retention, and decision making all affect the nature of a high-performance PSF.

BAIN & COMPANY: MAKING PARTNER

By focusing on the decision choices facing Phyllis Yale and the compensation and promotion committee, the Bain & Company: Making Partner case provides the medium to explore the specific human capital process that centers on professional development and organizational advancement within a PSF. We know from earlier discussions that the promotion, compensation, and succession planning processes are the most important processes to have right for PSFs to function dynamically.

Through the case analysis, readers confront the promotion process and how the firm selects future partners. What makes a good partner in general? Readers could list strong client performance, judgment, teamwork, industry expertise, rainmaking ability, functional skill, potential, management ability, mentoring ability, integrity and trustworthiness, firm-building results, and leadership potential. What characteristics does Bain look for in particular? How much should the promotion process be used to signal the firm's values? Is signaling as a motivation fair to the individuals considered? To what extent has the firm communicated the promotion criteria?

This case also highlights how PSFs are spending more time focusing on human capital processes due to market pressures. Virtually every PSF is concerned with hiring, retention, and development practices and processes. Junior professionals who join these firms now have different expectations regarding incentives, development opportunities, long-term management challenges, and decision-making involvement than new members a decade ago. The more traditional economic paradigm highlighted by the economic pyramid that drove most firms is being questioned, which in turn influences the nature of the processes that are created within these firms (Figure 3).

We hope also that readers have the opportunity to reflect upon their own career experience relative to promotion opportunities. Which of the four junior professionals at Bain would each reader recommend for promotion to partner? Which of the four does each reader relate to the most?

The promotion process takes a significant amount of PSF leaders' time. The reasons for this are that there is a high cost of error and that creating new partners helps determine the future of the firm. From a professional's perspective, partnership promotion is often perceived as the brass ring at the end of a long and arduous journey. A fair and thoughtful process and clear promotion criteria are

FIGURE 3

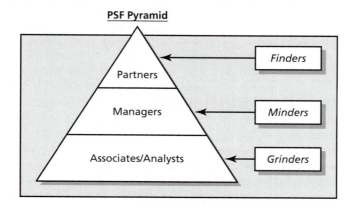

PSF Pyramid

critical for firms to attract junior professionals to join the firm. Having the firm's leadership involved often helps ensure that the process is aligned with other key processes within the organization and that the right signals are being communicated via the promotion decision process.

VENTURE LAW GROUP

Leaders of successful PSF's pay particular attention to the processes of recruitment, selection, socialization, and development of professionals. Craig Johnson's approach to hiring and retention of superb attorneys in the law firm Venture Law Group (VLG) introduces some unique methods of thinking and implementing recruitment and retention strategies of a firm.

Johnson had a vision of how a PSF could be progressive in creating processes that not only meet expectations of professionals but exceed them. Johnson's model of recruiting and incentives is driven by the research on the service profit chain, in which processes are created that enhance employee loyalty. Loyal employees in turn bolster client loyalty. Johnson is clear that he wants zero turnover because he knows that his clients want long-term relationships with his attorneys.

Johnson's obsession with zero turnover (the ideal) or at least low turnover (the goal) drives VLG to create internal processes that push his professionals to think and behave in new ways. He expects professionals to be more creative and connected with leaders of new companies. VLG's new business committee both ensures that only an appropriate amount of new business is taken on and that the type of new work will keep VLG attorneys interested and excited to work at the firm. VLG also developed an outsourcing process to enable them to serve both the needs of its clients and professionals. Lawyers at VLG are able to focus on business that will provide economic returns that exceed profession norms. Thus, internal processes leverage the capability of the lawyers, which in turn increase incentives.

The strength of the VLG case centers on how a PSF leader can link strategic goals (high retention to enable better client service) with specific tactical processes that push the firm forward toward that goal. How many PSFs would turn away as much business as VLG has refused to comply with an internal process? Some professionals may believe that Johnson is overly obsessed with his desire for zero turnover. However, we see that his clarity of purpose pushes the whole system into alignment. The human capital processes support VLG's external strategy of superb client service over the long term.

SUMMARY

A PSF's internal processes must connect its internal and external strategies in order for the firm to maximize its capabilities. These internal processes connect strategy with implementation. Module Four addresses the challenge of creating processes that leverage the most important capital of the PSF firm: its people.

Human capital management is the critical process in PSFs. Knowledge management and decision-making processes help make firms more than the sum of its individual professionals.

We emphasize through these four cases that without excellent processes that are in alignment with client, firm, and professional interests, and capabilities, that PSFs will never be able to ensure *consistent* excellent service. Any PSF can produce excellent results a few times if it has a great team. But as PSFs grow from a small collection of individuals to a larger "firm," how can clients be assured that service will be top-notch regardless of the professionals the firm assigns to the project? A PSF can achieve that goal only through effective training and staffing (human capital management), calling on the firm's broad expertise (knowledge management), and its approach to attacking the client's issues (decision-making). PSF leaders must consider in what ways they will create value for their clients, manage client relationships long term, and manage human capital in ways that encourage and support long-term commitment from both clients and professionals within the system.

QUESTIONS ARISING FROM THE CASES IN THIS MODULE

These are some of the many questions that were raised in our study of the internal organizational processes of PSFs:

- How can performance management processes enhance a PSF's strategic objectives?

- What is the relationship between performance evaluation and compensation at a PSF?

- How can performance evaluation provide a guideline for professionals to manage their career progression proactively?

- How can managers communicate the right message in a performance evaluation session? How can managers coach professionals subsequently?

- How can a PSF maintain its culture and integrate new hires to the firm while experiencing rapid growth?

- How can PSF managers manage expectations of senior executives at the firm, subordinates at the department level, and clients?

- What makes a good partner?

- How much should PSF promotion processes be used to signal firm values? Is signaling as a motivation fair to the individuals considered?

- Do too many PSFs promote only its "stars" and neglect its "solid citizens"? How do professionals organize commitments in order to focus on the whole range of talent within the firm?

- How much does employee turnover cost PSFs? How much can a PSF save by cutting its attrition by 25 percent? 50 percent?

- Why do some firms encourage turnover ("up or out")? What implications does an up-or-out system have on human capital management processes?

- What are the advantages and disadvantages of a new-business committee in PSFs? From a senior professional's perspective? From a junior professional's perspective?

- What criteria should organizations use to determine whether decision-making authority on a subject should be centrally located or decentralized? If decentralized, how does the organization ensure that its decisions will be aligned and of one mind?

- How should PSF leaders handle the issue of seniority versus performance?

- How should PSF leaders weigh performance criteria? How should they communicate these weightings?

- How can partners reach consensus over compensation systems at a partnership?

- How important is a transfer pricing system at a PSF?

- How can a firm retain, build, and leverage its intellectual capital and organizational learning?

Rob Parson at Morgan Stanley (A)

Paul Nasr, a senior managing director in Capital Market Services at Morgan Stanley, pored over the performance evaluation data packet for his star producer, Rob Parson. They were among the most negative he had ever read. Nasr had increasingly sensed that Parson was having difficulty adjusting to the Morgan Stanley culture, but he had not appreciated the extent of his interpersonal problems in working with people inside of the firm. Nasr had also underestimated the degree to which some of Parson's actions had violated Morgan Stanley norms.

Parson was a strong revenue producer and had generated a great deal of new business for the firm. Parson was also sharp-tongued, impatient, and often difficult to work with. From Nasr's perspective, he knew that Morgan Stanley wanted team players, but he felt that he had a responsibility to build a business and that Parson was critical to that effort. Parson was eligible to be promoted to managing director this year. In fact, Nasr had almost implicitly promised the promotion when he recruited Parson to Morgan Stanley. But, with performance evaluations like these, it would be difficult, if not impossible, for the firm to promote Parson.

MORGAN STANLEY

Morgan Stanley, a leading U.S. investment bank since its inception in 1935, was in the midst of an organizational renewal. Under the leadership of John Mack, the firm's new president as of 1993, Morgan Stanley was transforming itself into a "One-Firm Firm." This vision, which Mack and his top executive team developed, was succinctly captured in the firm's mission statement:

> Our goal is to be the world's best investment bank and the Firm of choice for our clients, our people, and our shareholders.
>
> We will succeed by meeting the global needs of our clients—both providers and users of capital—at a level of performance which is exceptional. This commitment to add maximum value will be characterized by extraordinary effort and innovation, and by conducting ourselves with absolute integrity.
>
> Morgan Stanley's people are the source of our competitive advantage. We will distinguish ourselves by creating an environment that fosters teamwork and innovation, by developing and utilizing our employees' abilities to the fullest, and by treating each other with dignity and respect.

The mission statement, and the "one firm" vision were intended to reorient the firm towards an increasingly complex, fast-paced, global industry. The Morgan Stanley leadership recognized that clients interacted with the firm at many different points of intersection. It was important, from a business perspective, to provide a unified face to the customers and also to have mechanisms in place to effectively coordinate work across the firm.

Professor M. Diane Burton prepared this case as the basis for class discussion rather than to illustrate either effective or ineffective handling of an administrative situation. The circumstances and material incorporated in this case have been made available through the cooperation of the individuals and the company involved. Some names and situations have been disguised.

Implementing the new vision was the responsibility of the firm's managing directors. Morgan Stanley, like other professional service firms, had an "up-or-out" promotion system with a steep hierarchy. Managing directors were at the top of the pyramid and as such had to be "standard bearers" for all of the junior staff. (See Appendix A for an overview of the professional positions in investment banking at Morgan Stanley).

CAPITAL MARKETS SERVICES

The Capital Market Services (CMS) division at Morgan Stanley was created as part of an effort to make the firm more responsive to client needs. It was an explicitly interdisciplinary entity designed to serve as a link between the Investment Banking Division (IBD) and the sales and trading arms of the firm, Equity and Fixed Income. The organizational structure was intended to provide clients with more focused attention and service. It also was a mechanism that allowed cross-divisional collaboration and avoided feuds over how to allocate fees across different subunits.

Professionals in Capital Markets Services were organized into market coverage areas, typically industries. They were expected to work with corporate finance professionals, who were viewed as the "stewards" of client relationships. They were also expected to generate business from organizations in their sector who did not necessarily have an existing relationship with Morgan Stanley. Market coverage professionals were described as "entrepreneurs"—like sales people, but responsible and accountable for their own client base. Gary Stuart, a senior market coverage professional, described what it took to excel:

In order to be an excellent producer you have to really understand the business in the industry you cover. That means knowing who the people are, who to talk to, developing relationships. In addition, you need to be extremely good at understanding the markets and have good market judgment. That

takes more than study of the markets. It takes intuitive sense and feel, deal experience, and a certain type of person and way of thinking. You need to truly understand what your client's needs are. You need to have good client relationships so they'll tell you what their real concerns and needs are. But you also need to understand the business they're in and what makes sense for their business so that you can give good advice. You then need to work with product specialists within Morgan Stanley to design the products. It's the synthesis of these things— great relationship skills, great understanding of your client's business, an ability to work with product specialists, as well as great market judgment and understanding of the market. That combination puts you in a position where you can create a business.

Working with clients was only part of the job. Market coverage professionals were also heavily interdependent with other professionals in the firm. As Stuart explained:

You need to work with product specialists to help you design and deliver the products depending on whether it's a preferred stock product or an asset-backed product, etc. But, if you're overly reliant on them, you may miss opportunities. If all you do is drag a product specialist to the client, the deal doesn't always happen. Product specialists don't always understand the client's business— they understand their product. Similarly, if you drag people from the market side out to listen to the client and get a fuller understanding of the market, they don't always get the business because they don't always understand the client, and they don't necessarily understand the product—they understand markets. The market coverage professional is the nexus of all this information—market, product and client. If you understand markets, products, and clients, you have a much better chance of doing business.

PAUL NASR

After becoming president of Morgan Stanley, Mack explicitly sought people who would "shake up the culture." In a major coup, he was able to recruit Nasr, a highly regarded banker in a competing firm, to join Morgan Stanley. Nasar had nearly 20 years of experience and was credited with building a formidable capital markets business. Nasr soon assumed a leadership role in Capital Markets Services for Morgan Stanley. Nasr described the cultural differences he encountered upon joining Morgan Stanley:

> From my perspective, there are a lot of investment banks that have little corporate culture and little infrastructure. These are firms where the "franchise" is not attracting business; individual professionals are. The ability to go out, bring in the business, and write up the ticket depends solely on the entrepreneurial ability of the individual. This means that firms turn a blind eye to certain behaviors, because the pursuit of the business and survival were more important. If you break a few eggs internally to get a ticket written with a major client, nobody is going to raise eyebrows and say, "Hey, slow down. We don't want to break eggs." At Morgan Stanley, this just is not true. Here the franchise matters, the culture is important, and the firm cares a lot about the integrity of the process.

One of the areas where Morgan Stanley had historically been weak was in delivering capital markets services to financial services firms such as banks and insurance companies. This was an area where Nasr had been successful in the past, and he knew that, if he found the right person, he could build a much more profitable business for Morgan Stanley. He described his rationale:

> If you want to be a major player in fixed income capital markets, you cannot take the 30 percent of the market that is generated by banks and financial institutions and say we are not going to be active in it. You have to provide full service to your clients. A firm like Morgan Stanley could not be absent from this segment; it could not be weak in this segment. We had to have a major presence.

To develop a presence in this market Nasr recruited Parson, a young banker who had previously worked for him at a different firm. Parson had been very successful, and had since moved on to become a managing director at a smaller firm where he thought he could have a larger impact. He had a proven track record in financial services and Nasr felt Parson had the type of energetic, entrepreneurial nature that Morgan Stanley needed to penetrate the sector:

> It takes more than a traditional corporate banker to get this job done. It takes somebody who wakes up every morning and wants to turn the world on fire. Rob Parson was the right guy.

ROB PARSON

Throughout his 10 years of experience Parson had built strong relationships with the important players in the banking and insurance industries. He knew that he had acquired a strong reputation, yet when he was approached by Nasr to join Morgan Stanley, he was initially skeptical.

> I am not the typical Morgan Stanley type. I do not fit the profile at all. I didn't go to prestigious schools. I was always a hustler but not academic at all. That doesn't mean I'm stupid; I just never took school seriously.

Parson started college at one of the New York state universities. Somewhat of a rebel, he dropped out after a year and went to California, spending his last teen year running a moped shop on a beach near Los Angeles. Bored, he decided to go back to school and enrolled at California State University, Long Beach. After completing his undergraduate degree he went to the University of Southern California and did a two-year MBA program in a year, "just to get it over with." MBA in hand, and on the advice of an uncle in New York, Parson hustled around Wall Street looking for a job. He reminisced, "I'd never even heard of Goldman Sachs. That's how pathetic I was." He landed his first job at a commercial bank, went through their training program, and ended up working in their savings and loan business, which was booming at the time. With experience in a lucrative field, Parson was highly marketable and moved quickly through three major investment houses. Although he was reluctant to change firms again, Parson was enthusiastic about the opportunity to work with Nasr again:

> There are not a lot of guys in this business that I look at and say, "Wow, that guy's a cut above." Paul is definitely a cut above. He's phenomenal with clients. It's funny, the other day somebody compared me and him, and said, "Gee you're a lot like Paul with clients." I took that as such a compliment. I don't know how he does it—you can go to charm school, you can go to any school you want—but you can never learn to be what he's got.

Parson accepted the job and joined Morgan Stanley as a market coverage professional in the Capital Markets division focusing on financial institutions. He was assigned the title "principal" with the understanding that if he did a good job he would be on the fast track to managing director.

The position that Parson was hired to fill had a reputation for being notoriously difficult to perform and had seen a tremendous amount of turnover at Morgan Stanley. Parson knew the position would be challenging; however, as he reported in his self-evaluation, he initially underestimated the magnitude of the challenge:

> I accepted the opportunity to join Morgan Stanley's Capital Markets effort with the full understanding that the effort was in need of repair. The firm was virtually unranked in

the bank league tables, and in my discussions with many of the important frequent issuers, coverage was scant at best. Many clients, in fact, said they had never been called on by Morgan Stanley, either from Investment Banking or Capital Markets. What I found after my arrival was that the situation was even worse than I had expected.

The firm had done very little capital markets business even with its most important investment banking clients. There had been dramatic turnover in trading coverage. Additionally, and perhaps most importantly, the Bank group was severely understaffed. To compound the challenge, the overall number of transactions was suffering due to high interest rates.

It was widely known in the industry that clients in the financial services segment were extremely competitive and often engaged investment bankers in cut-throat negotiations over how much they were willing to pay in fees. The person filling this role needed to be very much a self-starter. Stuart described the situation:

> You need some aggressive characteristics. You cannot be easily intimidated by clients. You cannot be a person who is easily discouraged, either. You get knocked down a lot more than you do elsewhere. You need to be someone who can stand right back up again. The client base will do things competitively. It will get information or new ideas from you and do the actual deal with someone else. You can't be discouraged when you lose business.

The senior managers in Capital Markets recognized that in order to service this client base effectively, it could not be "business as usual." The financial industry clients moved at a more rapid pace than those in other sectors and were among the most demanding. Nasr, in particular, was sympathetic to Parson's constraints and supported his efforts:

He didn't have time to build consensus around what he wanted to do. He thought that he knew more about his industry and had better market knowledge than the [Morgan Stanley] people around him. And clients in his sector wanted answers in a matter of minutes rather than hours. The Morgan Stanley way was to build consensus. If he waited for consensus, the business would have been transacted away. So basically Rob goes from point A to point B within the time frame that the client has imposed, fulfills the client's demand, but in the meantime has broken every rule within Morgan Stanley to get there. So, people say, "Wow, this guy is not following procedure. We work as a community, not individually. This is not Rob Parson's business. This is Morgan Stanley."

Unfortunately, some people in the firm were not as understanding. The Morgan Stanley way of doing business, as Nasr and others described, was one of consensus building and teamwork. As Nasr explained:

At Morgan Stanley the franchise is very important. You do not impair the internal culture of the firm just to get one extra deal. We would like to maximize our business, but we would not like to maximize it at the expense of our culture, teamwork, and the integrity of the process.

From reading the evaluations and also recalling conversations throughout the past year, it was apparent that there were widespread concerns about Rob Parson's "style." Superiors used words like "volatile" and "abrasive." Colleagues were concerned about his "lack of team player skills." One colleague described how he can appear "cocky, overbearing, flip or insincere." Nasr summarized:

He has created a hostile environment around him. The syndicate guys are not happy with him basically questioning their prices. The traders are not happy with him questioning their knowledge of the markets. And he al-

ways thinks he has the right answer, and the majority of the times he does have the right answer, but every time he comes up with the right answer on his own, a lot of people feel undermined.

As head of the department, Nasr started to hear about the problems Parson was having within the firm. He described how he tried to follow up by explaining to people, "he's a great guy. Give him time. He doesn't know the Morgan Stanley system yet." But the problems continued, and Nasr, who was relatively new himself, was reluctant to wield a heavy hand. He recalled:

Rob would come to my office and say, "What's the problem? What did I do wrong?" And I used to say, "Go and talk to this individual a little bit more." He was so new here, so I tried to go about it in a very diplomatic manner rather than getting him concerned about his position with the firm. He would say, "How'd I screw up this time?" and I would say, "Well, if I were you, I'd do it this way . . . ," but I said it in a very nice, gentle way. Maybe I handled him with kid gloves. But I felt that if I had handled him more aggressively, we would have lost him.

From his own perspective, Parson found some aspects of working within the firm to be very frustrating:

I wondered whether what really mattered was the "form" rather than the "substance." Would the firm rather have the guys that went to the right schools, that say the right things, or a guy like me, who's a little more rough around the edges, doesn't necessarily have the right résumé *per se,* but is generally good at bringing in business?

Despite these problems, Parson was routinely commended for his ability to cross-sell, his willingness to share information and make introductions, and his energetic approach to his job. Stuart described the ways in which Parson was an outstanding contributor:

He makes things happen that wouldn't otherwise happen. He doesn't just go out and pitch business that we already know about. He can actually go out to his client situation where there's no business and create something; talk to the client, figure out a need and create a deal that might not otherwise happen. And, to me, that is an important difference. Not many people can do that. For example, imagine a situation where a client says, "We're going to issue $250 million of preferred stock. Please come out, Merrill Lynch, Morgan Stanley, Goldman Sachs, and talk to me about it, and try to convince me to do it with you." Okay, this is your basic bake-off and a lot of people can do that. That's being good at sales, understanding the product and being an effective marketer. Now imagine that you go out and the client says, "You know what, we don't have any needs. We really don't need to raise funds." Then you have a conversation:

Morgan Stanley: So what are you working on, what are you thinking about?

Client: Well, we're thinking about how to be a little more efficient with our capital.

Morgan Stanley: Well, do you know about these products?

Client: Well, yes, we've heard about those; they don't really apply.

Morgan Stanley: Well, what if we tweaked it a certain way; would that be of interest to you?

Client: No, because we have an accounting issue.

Morgan Stanley: What's your accounting issue?

Client: Well, my accounting issue is we can't account

for those the same way others can.

Morgan Stanley: Hmm. Well, what part of that is the issue?

Client: Well, here's the issue. . .

Morgan Stanley: Let us think about maybe designing something that does work because then, clearly, you might have a need for us.

You come back, you work with product people, you design something, then you go back to the client and make the pitch. You're dealing in a totally different realm. You're going to give me the business because I've created a product that you can use although you didn't think you needed us. You didn't think you had a need. You didn't have a need. We created a need by thinking about what you're doing and how you do it and we make more money doing things that way. And Rob is very good at that.

In the time that Parson had spent working on the financial services sector, he made significant gains in building Morgan Stanley's reputation and revenues. Prior to Parson, the firm had been ranked tenth with a market share of 2 percent. Parson had been instrumental in securing first-time business with more than 10 clients, had secured major deals with existing clients, and was generating substantial revenues for his desk. Now Morgan Stanley held the third rank position with a market share of 12.2 percent. Nasr praised Parson's client relationship skills:

Externally he is the most wonderful guy; his clients love him. Every time they come to New York from anywhere around the world, they want to take him to dinner. And you want to go out to dinner with him because he is probably one of the most amusing, entertaining, and interesting people to be with. People look forward to having meals with him.

Nasr felt that the situation was further exacerbated by the fact that Parson had been the only person that he had hired through a prior personal connection.

> I hired only one individual in Morgan Stanley from my previous life, Rob Parson. The group obviously felt that I was his protector or his godfather. For me, there was the issue of fairness. It was very important not to treat an individual who came from the outside differently from any other Morgan Stanley individual. Also, what signal would I be sending to all of the individuals in the Capital Markets group here? That behavior does not count? Or working together is not important? Or we put money and deals ahead of how we treat each other? Or that it is okay to mistreat our analysts or our secretaries? I think that behavior is unacceptable.

Nasr also reflected on the fact that he himself was relatively new to the organization at the point when he recruited Parson. He described, "If I'd hired him after having been at Morgan Stanley a year or two, I would have talked to him more aggressively about the differences between him and the culture of the firm. But I wasn't yet in a position myself to articulate the differences from that point of view." He summarized the situation:

> Rob Parson is a unique individual. He is unique in his drive. He is unique in his pursuit of business. He is unique in his ambition. His knowledge of markets is excellent and he connects well with clients. And at the same time, he is unique in how many eggs he breaks every day. Everywhere he goes you have to follow him and pick up the broken eggs and put them back together.

Nasr believed that it hadn't mattered that Parson had been "breaking eggs" at his last job because it was such a different place. The question now was how he, Nasr, as a senior managing director at Morgan Stanley, should deal with Parson's performance and the issues it raised.

THE PERFORMANCE EVALUATION PROCESS AT MORGAN STANLEY

One of the important innovations implemented by Mack when he became president of Morgan Stanley was a firmwide, 360-degree performance evaluation process through which all of the professionals in the firm were evaluated by superiors and colleagues as well as subordinates. Top management at Morgan Stanley had introduced the new performance evaluation process amidst great fanfare with the explicit goal of changing the culture of the firm. Mack believed that changing the criteria by which people were evaluated and compensated would encourage employees to conform to a new way of doing business that emphasized teamwork, cooperation, and cross-selling.

The performance evaluation process was also intended to provide comprehensive developmental feedback so that employees could continue to improve their skills in four areas: Market/Professional skills; Management and Leadership effectiveness; Commercial Orientation; and, Teamwork/One Firm Contribution. Evaluators were asked to comment at length on an individual's strengths and weaknesses providing detailed and specific examples. Although the process had been in place for two years, there was little consensus on what it actually meant in practice. One managing director commented:

> There was a cultural feeling, although ill-defined, that someone had to be a "team player." But there wasn't an explicit set of criteria that you could manage people toward or that you, as a professional, could manage your career toward.

In his self-evaluations, Parson recognized that he needed to acquire some "patience" and be less aggressive internally. He also reported feeling that he had done "a poor job at self-promotion." He described wanting to do "a better job communicating internally the extent of my discussions and successes with a broad base of clients across the spectrum of investment banking products." Parson also clearly articulated his long-term career goal: "to be in a senior leadership role in a client capacity, away from the headaches of pure day-to-day administrative duties."

As Nasr read through Parson's performance evaluations (Exhibits 1 and 2), he considered his options. First, he had to decide whether or not the Capital Markets division was going to put Parson up for promotion to managing director. He also needed to complete the evaluation and development summary (Exhibit 3) that would form the basis of Parson's annual performance review. If Parson were a candidate for promotion, the evaluation and development summary would be reviewed by the entire promotions committee, a group of senior managing directors from across the firm who reviewed all candidates and made the final decisions. He would also need to have a conversation with Parson explaining his decision and giving him feedback and developmental advice. Nasr knew that the effectiveness of that session would be very important: first, in terms of Parson's future performance, and second, if the firm decided not to promote him this year, whether or not he would stay.

EXHIBIT 1 Annual Performance Evaluation Data Packet

Robert L. Parson
PRINCIPAL—INVESTMENT BANKING DIVISION
Three Greatest Strengths (provide examples):

Downward Comments
Within IBD

Person A	• Selling skills: Rob has good marketing skills and is always willing to ask for the order no matter how difficult the situation. He has made a big difference with several clients.
	• Aggressiveness/initiative: Rob is a self starter who is unusually aggressive in pursuing the business. Typically, this initiative is constructively channeled toward a trade. Occasionally, he can be too aggressive.
	• Market/product knowledge: Rob knows the fixed income business generally and his segment, in particular, better than anyone else that we have had do this job.

Outside IBD

Person B	• Relationship management: Tireless worker. Rob has done a better job in covering financial institutions than anyone before him.
	• Commitment: Rob is one of the hardest workers in Capital Markets. He seems to take nothing for granted.

Colleague Comments
Within IBD

Person C	• Has strong marketing knowledge readily accepted by client. Willing to do whatever is necessary to move project forward.
	• Works well with regional office to integrate us and use our strengths to manage and develop clients.
Person D	• Rob is responsive to all of my client requests. I asked him to initiate coverage of regions and he was quick to start.
	• Rob also challenges me to be more active. He has introduced me to several clients and he keeps me apprised of all activity.
	• Rob is good with senior client management and knows how to ask the hard questions.
Person E	• Rob has made important progress in the last year, and in particular the last few months. He has been more willing to involve team members with his clients, and this access has clearly led to more business. He covers a tough turf which is not easy given MS's choppy coverage in the past. Good progress on league table data.
	• Improved attitude throughout the year. Demonstrates more initiative, more receptive to pitching business and to allowing team members access to clients. He has seen broader involvement leads to more business and is key to deeper relationships.
	• Aggressive approach to underwritten bid business, important for Firm's overall league table standing.
Person F	• Relationship management: Rob is consistently very thorough about identifying and informing all the internal parties associated with a specific client.
	• Cross-selling: Rob consistently puts key products in front of clients.
Person G	• Keeps me informed: Rob is very good at letting me know what is happening in his area and with my potential clients. Rob has good sources on the Street.
	• Cooperative: Any time I have asked Rob for help he has provided it. We probably need to call on his help more often.
	• Cross-sells: Rob has introduced me to various accounts where he believes investment banking opportunities exist.
Person H	• Rob has made great strides over the year on improving his working relationship inside the Firm. In our work together, Rob has held a positive attitude.
	• Rob's key strengths are as follows: Product knowledge: very good understanding of product or markets. Commercial instincts. Avoids problem deals and has accurate pricing views. Relationship skills. Has numerous strong relationships. Aggressive selling skills. Asks for the sale and makes it difficult for clients to say no.

Colleague Comments
Outside IBD

Person I	• Knows his clients very well. Rob has a very good sense of what his clients' objectives and desires are. For example, he has a good grasp for their funding requirements and what their interest in a potential deal will be.
	• Rob is also very willing to call his clients and get a response or feedback on a particular inquiry. He has no qualms about asking them questions when I want to know something particular about their needs or interests.
	• Rob has been very helpful in cross-selling derivative products by making introductions, giving contact names, and generally pushing our products with his clients.
Person J	• Quality of contacts/relationship with treasury staff at banks throughout the country and willingness to provide introductions for other members of the firm to these people. Also, willingness and ability to cross-sell other groups' products and identify critical issues. This facilitates Rob's participation in other group's presentations/proposals and enhances the clients' perception of the cohesive nature of Morgan Stanley's overall coverage effort.
Person K	• Rob is aggressive in his pursuit of business. I'm impressed as to his attitude in trying to secure a mandate. He often calls upon me in research which none of his predecessors did with any frequency. Great business getter!
	• I find him to be creative in his pitches to customers. If one approach doesn't work he tries another. He is relentless. I've heard back from several of the banks that our "call" has increased significantly since Rob has assumed coverage.
	• He shows good judgment in his client approaches playing always to MS strengths. He has significantly stepped up our profile with financial debt issuers and is helping gain us a role in securitizations which represents a huge opportunity with the banks.

EXHIBIT 1   **Annual Performance Evaluation Data Packet** *(continued)*

Robert L. Parson
PRINCIPAL—INVESTMENT BANKING DIVISION

Three areas in need of further development (indicate suggestions for developing these areas):

Downward Comments
Within IBD

Person A	• Team player skills: Although Rob has made progress here in recent months, he still needs to work at integrating his efforts more effectively with the broader team. Appears to have had problems with McHenry and Pellery on business issues that overlap their areas. Also violated internal policies by extending syndicate invitations which led to $20,000 error. • Personal style: Rob exhibits a volatile personality, at times, that causes problems. Needs to resist the temptation to react too quickly to an emerging problem. Must learn how to treat colleagues with a little more respect. • Management skills: Take a broader strategic view. Where is his business going? How should MS position itself accordingly? We would value Rob's opinions on these issues.

Outside IBD

Person B	• Rob made the most progress in communicating with the MS team. However, it is still the area that he should focus on going forward. Good effort noted but more work to do.

Colleague Comments
Within IBD

Person C	• Understanding of local market. Needs to spend more time in our region and be in regular dialogue with coverage targets. • Presentation tone can be rounded, i.e., as Rob develops, can be less hard-edged.
Person D	• None.
Person E	• Rob still needs to work on a number of areas in order to more fully contribute to the firm. Management and interpersonal skills, very difficult to work for or with. Rob is fun to talk to but is often less than professional. When in a bad mood or temper junior staff analysts and secretaries have been shocked by his language, temper, lack of respect to them and others. This needs to be addressed to ensure his full effectiveness. Most clients want strong team coverage, so he'll have to learn to develop ability for team work. Also to jointly share the work load, responsibility for prep and follow up. • Organization and follow up: Rob needs to work on planning, organization of his coverage effort and consistent follow up. We've seen that not all clients are forgiving on these issues. He is best at short sound-bite conversations. Weakest at strategically plotting turnaround of a client, or long-term pursuit of a prospect or business opportunity. • Judgment and decision making: Rob can be judgmental, rushing to a decision or opinion before having the facts. This includes news on prospective business to pursue, approach, etc. Inconsistent moods can impact his responses and judgments. When Rob controls above issues, he can be an even more successful contributor to our efforts. I like Rob, and enjoy working with him when he's in his calm professional moments. May these times expand.
Person F	• Judgment: Being fully informed is a critical part of the process in reacting to client situations. If Rob would spend more time gathering and evaluating information/feedback, he would probably have fewer overreactions.
Person G	• Rob often is too honest in his assessments, although he is usually correct. He probably needs to take a broader and maybe mature view of our clients and our own people.
Person H	• Work products: spend more time on written products, particularly in bake-off situations. • Presentation skills: Too casual at times.

Colleague Comments
Outside IBD

Person I	• Sometimes, it is difficult to get a response, this is probably because he is busy converting many clients and may not be able to follow up on everything, but it is noticeable on some requests. • Rob is one of the senior CMS covering officers he should take most of a leadership role within the group. This could be demonstrated by more of a presence in the morning meetings, leading by example, etc. Perhaps this is a bit tough to define but he could step up his role in the group.
Person K	• Rob may be pulled in too many directions. He has many projects and pitches underway at the same time which could be detrimental. Does he need more help?

EXHIBIT 2 **Summary of Performance Ratings**

Downward/Colleague Criteria	Direct Manager Score	Downward Average Score	Colleague Average Score
1. Professional Skills			
A. Market and Product Knowledge	—	4.0	4.5
B. Analytical/Quantitative/Problem Solving Skills	—	4.0	3.8
C. Creativity	—	3.0	4.0
D. Initiative and Commitment	—	4.5	4.3
E. Judgment and Decision Making	—	3.0	3.8
F. Versatility	—	3.0	4.3
G. Oral Communication Skills	—	3.5	4.0
H. Written Communication Skills	—	NA	NA
I. Professionalism	—	3.0	4.0
2. Commercial Orientation			
A. Relationship Management	—	3.5	4.3
B. Cross-Selling/Selling	—	3.0	3.7
C. Commercial Instincts/Revenue Contribution	—	3.5	4.0
D. Enhances PBT/Expense Control	—	4.0	3.0
E. Adherence to Firm Policies/Limits	—	2.0	3.5
F. Deal Execution/Project Management	—	4.0	3.8
3. Management Skills			
A. Global Business Management	—	3.0	NA
B. Leadership and Management of People	—	3.0	2.5
C. Evaluation, Development and Coaching	—	NA	2.0
D. Management of Diverse Workforce	—	NA	2.0
E. Management of Firm's Resources	—	4.0	4.0
F. Time Management	—	3.5	3.5
G. Planning	—	3.0	3.7
4. One Firm Contribution			
A. Team Player Skills	—	2.5	4.0
B. Contributes to MS and External related community	—	NA	NA
Arithmetic Average	—	**3.4**	**3.6**
Overall Rating:	—	**3.5**	**2.8**

EXHIBIT 3   Evaluation and Development Summary Form

Evaluation and Development Summary

Evaluatee: Parson, Robert L.	Evaluation Director: Nasr, Paul A.
Title: Principal	Signature:
Div/Dept: IBD/Capital Markets	Date:

Review of Performance

PERFORMANCE SUMMARY, INCLUDING ACCOMPLISHMENTS
Consider objectives in prior year's E&D Summary as well as business objectives set earlier in year. Refer to Self-Evaluation where applicable.

EVALUATION THEMES

Strengths	Comments
1.	
2.	
3.	

Development Areas	Comments
1.	
2.	
3.	

PERFORMANCE OBJECTIVES FOR NEXT YEAR:

Business Goals (list important business and commercial targets).

Professional Development Goals (list important development suggestions to enhance evaluatee's professional effectiveness).

CAREER GOALS (comment on evaluatee's short-term and long-term career goals as described in the self-evaluation):

APPENDIX A   Professional Investment Banking Positions at Morgan Stanley

Title	Career Stage, Including Typical Degree and Professional Experience	Selected Professional Skills/Responsibilities
Analyst	Entry-level position for people coming from an undergraduate college or university.	Acquires relevant financial, accounting, and computer skills. Strives to understand how to analyze data and contribute to the definition of problems and creative solutions. Relates well with clients and establishes good working relationships where appropriate.
Associate	Entry-level position for people coming from an MBA or other graduate program. May or may not have banking experience, but typically has other professional experience. Eligible for promotion to vice president after three to four years.	Understands relevant financial, mathematical, and accounting techniques. Able to analyze data and contribute to the definition of problems and to creative solutions. Relates well with client counterparts and establishes good working relationships. Is an effective representative of the firm.
Vice President	First "officer-level" position at Morgan Stanley. Typically indicates a minimum of three years of professional banking experience and demonstrated technical capability. Eligible for promotion to principal after two to three years.	Displays thorough knowledge of theoretical and applied investment banking techniques. Identifies the key issues and skillfully analyzes problems to reach clear conclusions. Respected for analytical ability. Relates well formally and informally with client personnel at all levels. Commands respect and confidence of clients and has influence. Functions well as team leader.
Principal	Senior officer position. Typically indicates significant level of achievement and responsibility. Eligible for promotion to managing director after three years. Those who are not promoted may in some cases stay with the firm as "permanent principals."	Has mastered theoretical and applied investment banking techniques. Identifies the relevant issues and skillfully analyzes complex problems to reach insightful conclusions. Respected for analytical ability and opinions. Commands respect and confidence of clients. Is sensitive to client's objectives and constraints and is able to identify and create business opportunities. Persuasive with clients. Good negotiation skills. Functions well as team supervisor and leader in the Investment Banking Department.
Managing Director	Most senior level banking position and senior firm leadership position. (Sometimes referred to as "partner.") Indicates the highest level of professional achievement and management responsibility.	Highest level of technical expertise in corporate financing. Significant experience in resolving complicated unprecedented problems. Commands respect for knowledge and insight among vast array of people inside and outside the firm. Highly developed planning and organization skills. Able to persuade and influence others at highest levels (CEOs, presidents). Clients will have complete confidence. Probably well known within the industry and/or sphere of expertise. Displays leadership by clearly, credibly, and consistently articulating departmental visions and strategies. Leads by example.

Strategic Services at Andersen Consulting

In mid-January 1998, Bill Copacino had been Andersen Consulting's managing partner of Strategic Services Americas for two weeks. Working with Strategic Services worldwide director, Peter H. Fuchs, he needed to submit his recommendation for the operating plan for Strategic Services Americas for fiscal year 1999 (beginning September 1, 1998) within the next two weeks. Strategic Services had grown by over 40 percent per year in headcount since 1989, and was now a major player in strategy consulting.[1] Its success was based on its ability to attract top talent and the unique "Business Integration" (BI) value proposition Andersen Consulting offered—combining strategy consulting with process redesign, technology and systems development, and change management—to provide "results not reports" for its clients.

Despite its unprecedented growth rate, Strategic Services remained a relatively small part of Andersen Consulting—about 5 percent of its people and almost 8 percent of its revenues. With the Process, Technology, and Change Management components of the firm growing at nearly 25 percent per year, Copacino and Fuchs were challenged to grow Strategic Services at the level required to increase its relative position in the firm to 10 percent of its people and 15 percent of its revenues.

Fuchs and Copacino needed to decide how Strategic Services could maintain its growth rate. Growing by 40 percent a year had been relatively easy when Strategic Services was much smaller. As the base grew, it took increasingly creative and determined recruiting efforts to keep up with that percentage increase. Finding the MBA hires and experienced hires to meet the goals for 1998 and beyond would be a significant challenge, particularly in a strong economy where there was a huge demand for "the best" people.

Even if Strategic Services could find enough new hires, Copacino was still concerned about Strategic Services' ability to integrate such a large influx of people. He wanted the new hires to feel comfortable so that they could contribute quickly, but he also wanted to ensure that the Strategic Services collegial and humane culture—which he had done so much to foster—would continue to thrive.

As Fuchs and Copacino discussed options, there were no easy answers. Should they continue to try to grow at 30 percent plus per year? Could they maintain the unique culture they had created? Should they consider acquisitions? Was there an effective way to meet their growth targets?

BILL COPACINO

Bill Copacino earned his undergraduate degree in Industrial Engineering from Cornell University and then took an internship at General Electric, rotating through different business areas. He reminisced:

> I was a little unfocused at the time and not enamored with corporate life. A friend of mine was staying with a missionary in Guatemala. I went down there for a vacation. The missionary gave us both room and board while we started a nonprofit company, Agua

Research Associate Catherine Conneely and Abby Hansen, PhD, prepared this case under the supervision of Professor Tom DeLong as the basis for class discussion rather than to illustrate either effective or ineffective handling of an administrative situation.

[1] Average annual headcount since 1989.

del Pueblo ("Water for the People"), to build potable water systems in rural areas. We worked in rural areas where people are downtrodden and have never dreamed they'd have potable water. The community provides in-kind materials and labor. We provide the technology and some funding. I ended up staying in Guatemala for two years. The company just celebrated its twenty-fifth anniversary, and has helped over 400 communities mobilize to obtain pure water and build the foundations and hope for a better life.

Back in the United States, Copacino got an MBA at the Harvard Business School, although he "still didn't know what I wanted to do with my life." A summer consulting job at a company in Chicago helped clarify his direction. He enjoyed consulting, and took a job at Arthur D. Little (ADL) in general management consulting. "I spoke Spanish because of my years in Guatemala, and they gave me leadership of client assignments in South America at a young age. The results were fine, but the process wasn't pretty. It was very anxiety-provoking. You just got trained by whoever you worked with." Copacino subsequently initiated a formal training program at ADL.

In 1989, Copacino joined Andersen Consulting. Although he did not realize it at the time, Copacino was Strategic Services' first "direct entry Partner hire." Andersen Consulting "contacted me through an executive search firm because they wanted to build an Operations Strategy practice. I had assumed responsibility for Operations Strategy at ADL in my early thirties, and built the practice by developing a strong client focus, by creating formal training and a common standard of excellence, and by creating an environment where the best people and best ideas were encouraged, not discouraged."

Copacino rose quickly: he became managing partner of Strategic Services' Northeast Region in 1992, and, in 1994, added the responsibility of heading the division's largest industry practice, Products. Copacino's work ethic, efficiency, and

effectiveness were well known throughout the firm; a fellow Partner called him, "the most productive person I have ever met." The Northeast region grew from 47 to 370 professionals by the end of 1997 under Copacino's leadership, partly because of the collegial culture he promoted. Another executive commented, "Whether you're in London, New York, or Los Angeles, everybody has a Bill Copacino story." A junior consultant in Copacino's division told one:

> Potential hires have one-on-one interviews with consultants here. One afternoon a scheduling problem left a new college graduate sitting outside an office for a long time. A man came out of one of the other offices and asked, "Anything I can do for you—cup of coffee?" The young potential hire said, "I'd love a cup of coffee." The older man brought him one and said, "Let me know if you need anything else." Later the young man learned that Bill Copacino, a managing partner, had brought him the coffee. That doesn't happen at many places.

When he became managing partner for Strategic Services—Northeast, Copacino introduced policies to improve cultural cohesion as well as training—both formal and informal. He hosted recruiting dinners at his home, held frequent Q&A sessions with the business analysts (recruits with bachelors' degrees) and new senior consultants (MBAs). He observed, "we want people to feel good about what they do here." One of his young consultants remarked,

> On my second client engagement, Bill called and said, "I hear there are some problems; what can I do to help?" I told him. He made a few phone calls and fixed the problems. If you ask for help and don't get back to him, he'll call you and ask how things turned out. I've begun to do the same with the business analysts who are junior to me. And it's spreading through the culture. Bill is very influential in this way.

Copacino commented: "There's a revolutionary dimension to what I'm doing here. We're creating a consulting firm that is second to none in terms of the quality of our work and that is distinctive in how we treat our people. We've worked to instill a culture that has a real human dimension and cares for the individual."

THE FIRM

Andersen Consulting had 152 offices in 47 countries in 1998. (See Exhibit 1.) The firm employed over 34,000[2] consulting professionals, generated over $6.6[3] billion in revenues, and was growing at an average annual rate of almost 20 percent per year overall. (See Exhibit 2.) Andersen Consulting was a matrix organization; professionals were organized by competency, by industry, and by region. (See Exhibit 3 for Organizational Matrix.)

The competency groups defined the relevant skill sets that Andersen Consulting professionals brought to client engagements. Worldwide, Andersen Consulting had 17,400 people in the Process Competency, 11,000 in Technology, almost 4,100 in Change Management, and just over 2,000 in Strategic Services. (See Exhibit 4.) Client teams were generally composed of professionals from multiple competencies, under the firm's Business Integration approach. (See Exhibit 5.)

Andersen Consulting's go-to-market strategy was to offer industry experts who would each have particular skill sets that matched the clients' needs. Thus, each major industry practice (Communications, Products, Financial Services, Government, and Resources) had a worldwide organization, marketing operation, and was a profit center. Andersen Consulting developed specialties within those industries as well; Products, for example,

was subdivided into seven segments—Food and Packaged Goods, Retailing, Media and Entertainment, Pharmaceuticals, Travel and Transportation, Electronics and High Tech, and Automotive and Industrial specialties.

In parallel, functionally focused "lines of business" (LOB) allowed the development of very deep functional skills in areas like Supply Chain, Customer Relationship Marketing, Financial Management, Mergers, Acquisitions and Alliances, etc. Engagement teams merged deep skills from the Competencies, Industries and Lines of Business to tailor a consulting team with the mix of skills to address client specific needs and with the ability to understand strategy development through implementation. Andersen Consulting believed these deep skills allowed it to serve its client in a superior fashion.

BUSINESS INTEGRATION MODEL—"RESULTS NOT REPORTS"

The Business Integration (BI) client service model was created in 1989 to tie the competencies together consistently. BI evolved as Andersen Consulting's core strategy and aligned clients' processes, technology, and people with business strategy. Instead of looking at one piece of a client company in isolation, Andersen Consulting used the BI model to consider the entire organization in creating solutions.[4] Most firms, Andersen Consulting leadership believed, offered systems or process consulting without the benefit of determining a strategy first, while well-known strategy boutiques performed strategy consulting, but did not facilitate implementation nor did they have as deep an

---

[2] Includes Strategy, Process, Technology, and Change Management professionals only. Total Andersen Consulting personnel as of December 31, 1997, was over 53,000 personnel (over 34,000 consulting personnel, 10,000 BPM and Enterprises personnel, and over 8,800 administrative/support personnel).

[3] Net revenues for 1997 calendar year.

[4] J.P. Donlon, "Shaheen's Advice Machine," *Chief Executive,* May 1997, pp. 52–57; Adrian Wooldridge, "Doing It Their Way," *Economist,* March 22, 1997, pp. S19–20.

EXHIBIT 1 "We Have a Global Presence"—Andersen Consulting Offices around the World, by Consulting Geography and Office Location

Americas

Andorra
La Vella
Argentina
Buenos Aires*
Brazil
Rio De Janeiro
São Paulo*
Canada
Calgary
Edmonton
Etobicoke
Fredericton
Halifax
Montreal
Ottawa
Toronto*
Vancouver
Victoria
Colombia
Bogotá
Mexico
Mexico City
Monterréy
Puerto Rico
San Juan

United States
Albany, NY
Atlanta*
Austin, TX
Baton Rouge
Boston*
Charlotte, NC
Chicago*
Cincinnati
Cleveland*
Columbus, OH
Dallas*
Denver
Detroit
Florham Park, NJ*
Hartford, CT
Houston*
Indianapolis
Irving, TX
Jackson, Mississippi
Kansas City, Missouri
Las Colinas, TX
MacLean, VA
Memphis, TN
Miami
Milwaukee
Minneapolis
Nashville, TN
New Orleans

New York*
Northbrook, IL
Oklahoma City
Orange County, CA
Palo Alto, CA
Philadelphia*
Phoenix
Pittsburgh
Portland, OR
Raleigh, NC
Rochester, NY
St. Charles
St. Louis
St. Petersburg, FL
San Diego
San Francisco*
Seattle
Springfield, IL
Tallahassee, FL
Tampa, FL
Walnut Creek, CA
Washington, D.C.*

Venezuela
Caracas

EMEAI

Austria
Vienna
Belgium
Brussels*
Czech Republic
Prague*
Denmark
Copenhagen*
Finland
Helsinki
France
Lyon
Paris*
Sophia Antipolis
Germany
Berlin
Dusseldorf
Frankfurt am
Main/Sulzbach*
Hamburg
Munich
Greece
Athens
Hungary
Budapest
India
Bombay

Ireland
Dublin
Italy
Milan*
Rome
Turin
Verona
Luxembourg
Luxembourg
The Netherlands
Eindhoven
Enschede
The Hague*
Nieuwegein
Nigeria
Lagos
Norway
Oslo
Poland
Warsaw
Portugal
Lisbon
Russia
Moscow

Saudi Arabia
Jeddah
Riyadh
Slovakia
Bratislava
South Africa
Cape Town
Durban
Johannesburg*
Pretoria
Spain
Barcelona
Bilbao
Las Palmas
Madrid*
Seville
Sweden
Stockholm*
Switzerland
Geneva
Zurich*
United Kingdom
London*
Manchester
Newcastle
Windsor

Asia/Pacific

Australia
Brisbane
Canberra
Melbourne*
Sydney*
China
Beijing*
Shanghai*
Hong Kong
Hong Kong*
Indonesia
Jakarta*
Japan
Nagoya
Osaka
Toyko*
Malaysia
Kuala Lumpur*
New Zealand
Wellington
The Philippines
Manila*
Singapore
Singapore*
South Korea
Seoul*
Taiwan
Taipei*
Thailand
Bangkok*

*Primary locations of Strategic Services personnel.
Source: Andersen Consulting, December 1997.

EXHIBIT 2 **Andersen Consulting Personnel Growth (1989–1997)**

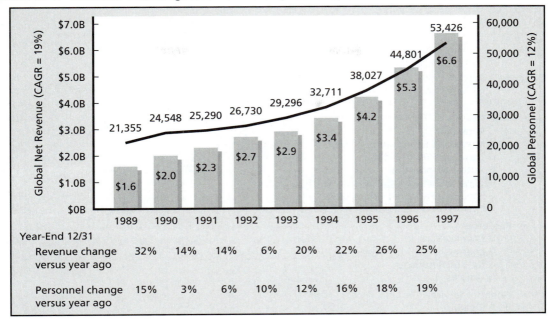

Note: 1997 personnel includes 34,000 consultants, over 10,000 BPM and Enterprise personnel, and 8,800 administrative/support personnel. All competencies and businesses included.
Source: Company documents.

appreciation or understanding of the barriers to and how to achieve successful implementation. According to Fuchs: "If we are to be successful as a Business Integrator, we require 'Point Excellence' or world-class skills in each of the components of the model and the ability to put it together seamlessly." The emphasis on delivering the entire package of consulting services would help deliver "results, not reports," according to the Andersen Consulting slogan. (See Exhibit 6.)

In implementing the BI model, Andersen Consulting's partners concentrated on developing the scale of the strategy practice. Strategic Services was a critical component of BI, because, according to Fuchs:

First, Strategic Services develops top-down strategies which drive the need for the change, process, technology, and human capital di-

mensions. Second, it works to assure that bottom-up initiatives, driven by process, technology, and change competencies are aligned with critical strategic priorities and reflect a strong value proposition for our clients.

Andersen Consulting partners believed that the BI model incorporated a breadth of services which other competitors, such as McKinsey, Booz Allen, and BCG, could not match. Moreover, they believed that the BI model provided a recruiting advantage. Not only would their consultants develop strategic skills and experience, but they would also develop greater general management skills and technology knowledge. Therefore, they felt it provided a richer career option.

Copacino believed Strategic Services offered a unique skill set that became more powerful in the BI framework:

EXHIBIT 3 **Andersen Consulting Organizational Matrix**

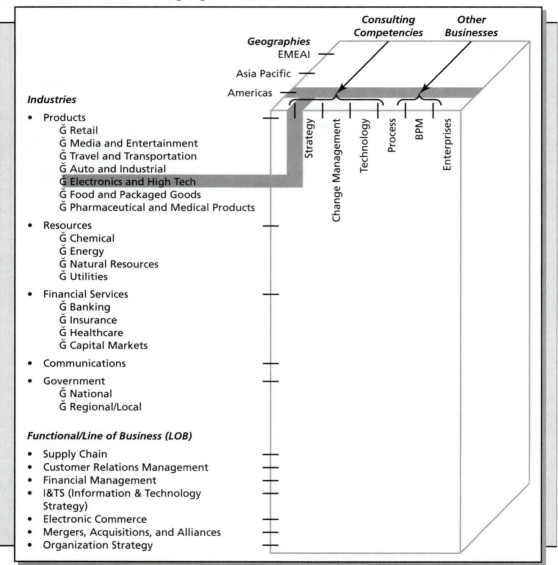

* *A consultant at Andersen Consulting is tied to an Industry or Functional LOB, a Competency, and a Geographic Component.*

Source: Andersen Consulting.

EXHIBIT 4 Andersen Consulting Strategic Services Personnel Growth (1991–1997)

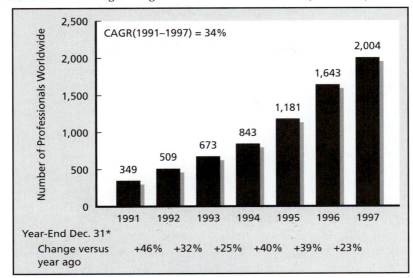

Note: Just over 50 percent of these resources are in the Americas (United States, Canada, and Latin America).
Source: Company documents.

Other practices are methodology-driven. Strategic Services' professionals work with an issue-based, hypothesis-driven problem-solving approach. It's the idea that counts. What makes Strategic Services even more effective is that we can utilize our strategy skills at the same time as drawing on the expertise of our Process, Technology, and Change Management groups to provide integrated, complete solutions for clients. It's a synergistic effect; each of our competencies can and does stand alone, but we're much more effective because we each have distinct skills to bring to the table. As strategists, we feel we can say with confidence that we deliver implementable strategies because we work directly with the other competencies on projects. Moreover, our deep technology skills are a great advantage. In the past, technology was an enabler of strategy. Today, our clients must consider technology as a driver of strategy. We are uniquely positioned to integrate technology as a key part of strategy formulation.

Andersen Consulting's culture in part stemmed from its BI approach. The firm placed a high premium on ensuring that its team members could work together smoothly, both within the Andersen Consulting team and with the clients, who could range from a company's top executive officers to its call center operators. As a result, Andersen Consulting had developed an inclusive, participatory culture.

In addition, the BI approach combined with the industry and regional structures meant that each Andersen Consulting professional belonged to several internal "communities." These multiple points of affiliation helped to draw the collective organization of 34,000 professionals together, by ensuring a substantial amount of interaction between people of different competencies, regions, and industries.

Andersen Consulting's tradition of stewardship played a significant role in its culture. Known for promoting from within, Andersen Consulting

EXHIBIT 5 Andersen Consulting Business Integration Approach

Business Integration (BI) creates unique value for clients by aligning processes, organization, and information technology with key strategic objectives.

<table>
<tr>
<td>

People

- Over 4,000 consultants worldwide
- Leading innovator and practitioner in change management

</td>
<td>

Strategy

- Over 2,000 consultants worldwide
- Second-largest strategy consulting firm in the world
- Leader in IT strategy and supply chain management

</td>
</tr>
</table>

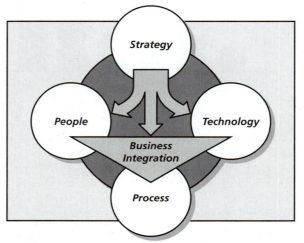

<table>
<tr>
<td>

Process

- Leading systems integrator
- Over 17,000 consultants worldwide
- Deep process design and systems building capabilities
- Leader in SAP installations, resources

</td>
<td>

Technology

- Nearly 11,000 consultants worldwide
- Deep capabilities in all areas of IT
- Palo Alto research center contributing leading-edge advances in IT

</td>
</tr>
</table>

---

spent over $430 million (almost 7 percent of revenues) on training and education programs for its people. Not only did this promote a sense of longevity, Andersen Consulting partners believed that these investments were part of the firm's competitive advantage. No other firm, they believed, had the resources to invest in their main asset—their people—as did Andersen Consulting.

[5] Andersen Consulting estimates.

STRATEGIC SERVICES

In 1997–98, McKinsey & Co., Boston Consulting Group (BCG), and Bain & Co. were Strategic Services' nearest competitors for clients and recruits. McKinsey & Company had almost 3,800 consultants worldwide; BCG had 1,700; Bain & Company had 1,800.[5] (See Exhibits 7 and 8.)

EXHIBIT 6   Andersen Consulting Capabilities versus Competition

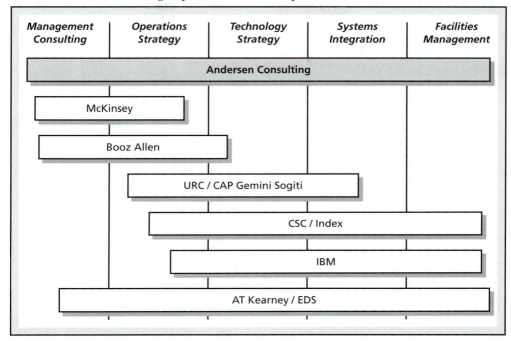

Source: Andersen Consulting, adapted from *Business Week.*

EXHIBIT 7   Competitors Personnel Growth (Historical and Expected)

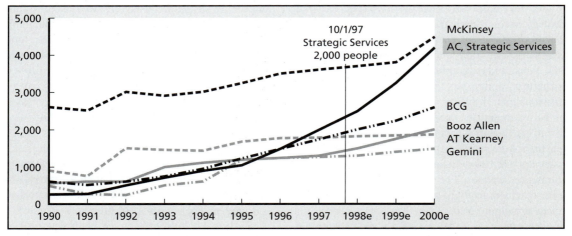

Source: Andersen Consulting estimates.

EXHIBIT 8   Top 15 Global Management Consulting Firms in 1996

Rank	Consulting Firms	Revenues	Low	—	Average	—	High
			Worldwide Growth[a]				
1	Andersen Consulting	$3,115.3					X
2	McKinsey & Co.	2,100.0			X		
2	Ernst & Young	2,100.0					X
4	Coopers & Lybrand Consulting	1,918.0					X
5	KPMG Peat Marwick	1,380.0				X	
6	Arthur Andersen	1,379.6				X	
7	Deloitte & Touche	1,303.0					X
8	Mercer Consulting Group	1,159.0			X		
9	Towers Perrin	903.0		X			
10	A.T. Kearney	870.0					X
11	Price Waterhouse	840.2					X
12	IBM Consulting Group	730.0				X	
13	Booz-Allen & Hamilton	720.0		X			
14	Watson Wyatt Worldwide	656.0		X			
15	The Boston Consulting Group	600.0		X			
15	Gemini Consulting	600.0			X		

Notes: Revenues, less reimbursed expenses, in millions of dollars. Definition of consultant varies. Numbers are for management and IT consulting only. Andersen Consulting revenues exclude Technology and BPM revenues. Total Andersen Consulting revenues as of December 31, 1996 were $5.3 billion, $6.6 billion in 1997 calendar year, and estimated at $8.0 billion in calendar year 1998.

[a] Average growth of 40 largest was 15 percent.

Source: Excerpt from "40 Largest Management Consulting Firms," *Consultant News,* March 1997.

As Strategic Services grew to become the world's second-largest strategy firm, it was evolving from an entrepreneurial unit (large by industry standards, but relatively small compared to Andersen Worldwide) to an even larger, more formally structured entity. By 1997, the practice had professionals in 38 offices worldwide and equaled almost 5 percent of total Andersen Consulting staff. Strategic Services partners made up 130 of 1,100 partners—12 percent of all Andersen Consulting partners. Of 120 new partners in 1997, 30 were in Strategic Services. The ratio of partners and associate partners to total employees in Strategic Services was about 5 to 1.

Professionals in the division were recruited at different entry levels. New college graduates entered as business analysts; MBAs as senior consultants; and experienced hires at levels from manager to senior manager, associate partner, and partner. The working environment in Strategic Services was deliberately humane. One professional commented:

Working 100 hours a week isn't healthy—for you or your firm. Bill Copacino has had a lot of influence on the way we work. We're generally away from our home office from Monday morning to Thursday night, but Fridays are for the office. The whole team gets together. There's a sort of cross-fertilization of ideas, an ability to connect with your colleagues, and an ability to have a better balance by being home more often. The Lunch on Us programs (Andersen Consulting buys) feature presentations from people on client engagements and also from researchers with cutting edge information. If you miss a few Fridays, people say, "hey, where have you been? I haven't seen you."

Copacino provided some practical insight on how he influenced this culture: "If you pay people 10 percent less than they think they're worth, they feel exploited every second on the job. But if you pay them 10 percent more than they think they're worth, they won't feel it's a raw deal if they occasionally work 'til 12 at night. I fight like hell for fair raises and good assignments for people. That's how you build a powerful practice."

He described personal character traits that helped shape his own approach: "I enjoy accomplishing, but I've mellowed to collective accomplishment. I'm 47, and I think, in time, you evolve to a more self-contented point that changes how you think about a lot of things." He referred to "being psychologically-minded" as a useful attribute for a manager, especially in hiring: "Obviously, there's content: benchmarks, references with clients. . . . But in parallel I look for character, a sense of collaboration—how many 'I's' and 'we's' they say in terms of their accomplishments. We try to make logical sense of behavior, and part of it *is* rational. But some of it is emotional. To be a good manager, you need to be able to intuit the emotional dimension. Behavior is driven both by the rational facts at hand, and in part by an individual's make-up and personal history. To be a good manager and to understand people's behavior, you must understand the emotional drivers."

He continued, "A sense of longevity here is one strength of the culture of this firm." The firm encouraged its professionals to set and achieve career development objectives within the organization. Team leaders and professionals developed expectations memos before projects and used a performance appraisal system to measure the professionals' progress toward promotion. New employees received formal training, and oversight from partners or performance counselors as advisors. Advisors oversaw their advisees' midyear and annual performance evaluations and also their overall career development.

CULTIVATING THE CULTURE

Professionals also had several mentors to guide, coach, and help them feel connected to the practice. Copacino emphasized the importance of mentoring by asking junior practice members to list those who had given them formal and informal mentoring during the year, so this information could be fed into the promotion process for associate partner and partner. The firm evolved to a formal 360-degree feedback process.

In the early 1990s, the firm articulated a theme—"People Values Culture (PVC)"—to express the fundamentals of its collaborative work environment. The initials "PVC" caught on so well that consultants referred to the various office buildings as "PVCs" or "PVC sites." To underscore the importance of PVC, Copacino appointed associate partner Paul Wimer (who joined as an MBA in 1989) as "class dean" for the incoming MBA hires of 1997. Like any class dean, Wimer was charged with addressing the group's needs and strengthening its communication with the larger practice. Despite his division's ever-increasing size, Copacino did his best to keep its culture communicative, open, and friendly.

Copacino emphasized Strategic Services' low turnover rate as evidence of two conscious policies: careful recruiting and positive attention to culture. In an industry with 20 percent annual turnover, Strategic Services often saw a large portion of an "entering class" stay with the firm for over four to five years.[6]

---

[6] Of Andersen Consulting's 11 percent turnover, 3 percent was voluntary. Copacino and the other managers believed in informing employees early if the "fit and capabilities" weren't working out.

When Fuchs and George Shaheen (global managing partner/CEO, Andersen Consulting) made the strategic decision to hire experienced professionals in the late 1980s, this broke with some of Andersen Consulting norms. But even with experienced hires moving up from 4 percent to 40 percent of professionals entering in the late 1990s, "homegrown talent" still held the majority of senior leadership positions. Fuchs bore ultimate responsibility for approving experienced hires, but leaders of each industry practice within Strategic Services involved themselves heavily in the selection and hiring—as well as the integration and acculturation—of experienced hires.

THE COMPETITION STIFFENS

In the early 1990s, Shaheen and Fuchs set growth goals for Strategic Services. By the year 2000, Strategic Services should comprise 10 percent of AC's headcount and 15 percent of AC's revenues. The need for the growth was threefold. First, client demand for strategic consulting was increasing substantially, and a large market opportunity existed. Second, clients were increasingly demanding more sophisticated solutions and more specialized expertise with a global perspective, which only a large, global enterprise could provide. Third, to fulfill the Business Integration model, Strategic Services participation was required in an increasing number of client teams.

Fuchs began growing Strategic Services rapidly. He ramped up the Strategic Services presence at blue-chip business schools to bring in a strong base of senior consultants. Recruiting experienced hires was helped by the fact that Strategic Services offered better opportunities and a more attractive culture than many other firms. Andersen Consulting also instituted a long-term strategy of hiring even when business was not booming, which made the firm particularly attractive.

These measures helped grow Strategic Services 36 percent annually from 1991–1995, bringing the total number of professionals to over 1,100. But as Fuchs looked at his growth goals for the second half of the decade, he knew that continuing to grow Strategic Services at a rapid pace would be increasingly difficult, because each year required growing at constant percentages off a larger and larger base. Thus, in 1995, Fuchs commissioned a major internal initiative to examine the challenges and opportunities that existed for professional hiring.

The "Strategic Sourcing" study, commissioned by Fuchs, confirmed several challenges that faced Strategic Services. First and foremost, Andersen Consulting as a whole was growing faster than forecast, roughly the rate of almost 20 percent per year.[7] Thus, the bar was constantly being raised, as Strategic Services sought to become 10 percent of Andersen Consulting's headcount. It was already nearly 5 percent of Andersen Consulting headcount, but Fuchs knew that Strategic Services would have to continue to grow faster than the other competency groups to reach that 10 percent goal.

By the end of 1997, competition for professionals was becoming even more intense. In the experienced hire area, Andersen Consulting was becoming a victim of its own success. With its increased market visibility and stature, it was more difficult to be a "stealth recruiter" at other firms. For one thing, other firms had begun to design clear responses to Andersen Consulting offers (experienced hires' acceptance rate dropped from 86 percent in 1994 to 69 percent in 1996). For another, there seemed to be an industrywide shortage of senior managers, making the competition for recruits much stiffer as well.

On MBA campuses, Andersen Consulting was seeking to attract ever-increasing numbers of senior consultants at the same time that its more well-established competitors (most notably McKinsey,

---

[7] Headcount growth from 1996–1997. Average annual growth for 1995 through 1997 was almost 19 percent.

Bain, BCG, and Booz Allen) were also increasing their hiring. The sustained economic boom also provided students with increased opportunities outside of consulting.

Strategic Services also faced marketing challenges. The growth of Andersen Consulting as a whole brought prestige and market power to the firm, but when students read about Andersen Consulting or met someone from the organization, they typically interacted with the much larger Process competency, not Strategic Services. This meant that potential recruits were often surprised to learn of the size of Strategic Services—by 1997 it was the second-largest strategy consulting firm, behind only McKinsey. Because of Andersen Consulting's reputation, students also often had the misconception that Strategic Services focused primarily on information technology consulting, not the broad array of business strategy and operations engagements that comprised the bulk of Strategic Services' client work.

Finally, Strategic Services began to see its turnover slowly increase, although it was still well under the industry norm. No study had specifically analyzed the increase in turnover, but a number of factors seemed likely. With explosive growth, Strategic Services had lost some of its family atmosphere, despite Copacino and other partners' efforts to reach out to the practice and emphasize inclusion and collaboration. In addition, Strategic Services' increasing prominence made other consulting firms and companies target Andersen Consulting professionals as mid-career recruits.

For Copacino, the single greatest problem as a recruiter was finding enough outstanding senior managers. The organization could only develop them internally at a certain rate, and his assigned growth targets meant recruiting 350 professionals, including as many as 150 experienced hires per year for the Americas for FY99 and growing in years beyond. He commented: "On the campuses, we can still recruit everyone we need. We will probably hire 150 entry-level consultants for the Americas in FY98. But one of the challenges we are trying to think ahead on is, if these numbers go up in subsequent years, how are we going to find enough people, particularly experienced hires? Can we recruit and integrate this many senior people? Will we need to diversify our hiring approach?"

He felt that the experienced hire area was "probably one of the hardest. People who are doing well elsewhere are hesitant to leave their existing firms." Copacino believed that Andersen Consulting had two distinct advantages in experienced hire recruiting—a more friendly and humane work environment and a better package of services for clients because of Andersen Consulting's Business Integration capabilities. Even so, he believed that attracting enough experienced hires would be a problem:

> One of my biggest challenges is to hire 95 senior managers, 43 associate partners, and 14 partners in the Americas this year. We have to ensure that people are going to meet our quality standards and be culturally compatible. We have an internal saying that every experienced hire we bring in should raise our batting average. In other words, be above the mean. Our question becomes, Where do you hire this many people from the outside at this level?

THE IMPENDING REPORT

In many ways, Copacino believed Strategic Services was operating from a position of strength. Its rapid growth over the past eight years was unprecedented in strategy consulting, and was building. Its marketplace visibility had never been higher. And the Strategic Sourcing study Fuchs had commissioned had laid out the options available for Strategic Services to grow. (See Exhibit 9.) Andersen Consulting had anticipated this sourcing challenge, but now was the time to make the tough decisions about which direction to take.

Up until this point, Copacino and Fuchs had been successful in finding enough high-quality people to both "raise the batting average" of the

EXHIBIT 9   Strategic Services Personnel Sourcing Options

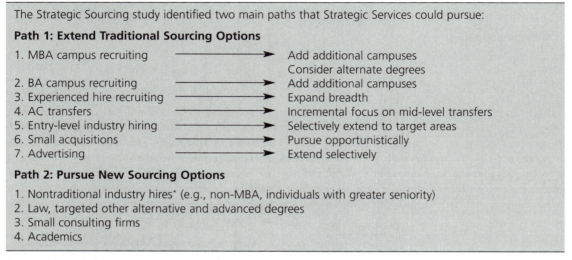

The Strategic Sourcing study identified two main paths that Strategic Services could pursue:

Path 1: Extend Traditional Sourcing Options

1. MBA campus recruiting   ⟶   Add additional campuses
                                                 Consider alternate degrees
2. BA campus recruiting   ⟶   Add additional campuses
3. Experienced hire recruiting   ⟶   Expand breadth
4. AC transfers   ⟶   Incremental focus on mid-level transfers
5. Entry-level industry hiring   ⟶   Selectively extend to target areas
6. Small acquisitions   ⟶   Pursue opportunistically
7. Advertising   ⟶   Extend selectively

Path 2: Pursue New Sourcing Options

1. Nontraditional industry hires[*] (e.g., non-MBA, individuals with greater seniority)
2. Law, targeted other alternative and advanced degrees
3. Small consulting firms
4. Academics

Source: Andersen Consulting Strategic Sourcing study.

practice and grow the practice. But they weren't sure that it would be possible or wise to continue to grow at the 30+ percent rate, given the size of the Strategy practice in 1998. On the other hand, for Strategic Services to take its proper role in the Business Integration model, Andersen Consulting needed Strategic Services' presence on its client teams, and that would mean growing significantly faster than the rest of the firm.

In his report to Fuchs, Copacino believed he had several options. He could recommend focusing on the experienced hire market, to meet the very pressing demand for senior managers. Some at Andersen Consulting believed that Strategic Services should be more aggressive in hiring professionals directly out of industry, without the consulting background that Strategic Services usually sought. This would probably require a new training initiative, to bring them up to speed in strategy consulting. It might also require turning some campus recruiting energies and resources to looking for experienced hires.

Alternatively, Copacino could recommend renewed focus at the entry level, possibly expanding to additional MBA campuses or even to other graduate schools. By emphasizing this group, Andersen Consulting could ensure that its consulting ranks were "home grown" and well schooled in the Andersen Consulting methodology. Strategic Services could redouble its efforts to keep attrition low.

Another possibility would simply be to acquire another consulting firm. Acquisitions, however, had historically been discouraged at Andersen Consulting. Indeed, Strategic Services' initial decision to grow organically rather than by acquisition had been a major factor in sustaining its growth, Fuchs and Copacino believed. Integrating other firms into the Andersen Consulting environment would pose a substantial cultural integration challenge, and Copacino was not inclined to recommend such a course of action. Copacino also could recommend slowing the growth in hiring, no matter what the Business Integration demand or market demand were.

Copacino's decision could not be based solely on how to attract more recruits. He needed to balance his decision with his other priorities. It was imperative, he felt, to maintain the high caliber of the new hires. He wanted to ensure that the practice had cohesion in its approach to problems. He wanted to find ways to make Business Integration work even better for his people and for the clients. He wanted to reinforce "PVC" and assure the solid cultural underpinnings of the practice during its next phase of growth to the year 2000 and beyond. Most of all, his decision needed to reinforce Andersen Consulting's desire to be "the consulting firm of the future."

Copacino knew that his own performance as head of Strategic Services' largest area would be judged based partly on his ability to balance these competing interests and successfully managing the growth of Strategic Services Americas over the next several years. Thus far, Andersen Consulting had seemingly made all of the right moves to establish its position in the marketplace, and had prepared itself well for the sourcing challenges that faced it. His next move, he knew, would be closely watched. With all of these concerns in mind, he sat down to write his report to Fuchs.

Bain & Company, Inc.: Making Partner

We'd like to think promotions are only fact-based, but promotions are inherently both fact-based and judgmental.

Partnership promotion is a make-or-break decision for us.

Tom Tierney, Bain worldwide managing director

In June 1998 Bain's Compensation and Promotion Committee (CPC) met at a beachside resort in Hawaii to review nine candidates for elevation to the rank of vice president, the consulting firm's equivalent of partner.[1] Committee chairman Phyllis Yale, a 16-year Bain veteran and partner in the Boston office, knew that for Bain the stakes were high: partnership was a long-term commitment. Having served on the committee for nearly three years, she realized that its decisions not only had an impact on the strength of the firm's 175-member worldwide partnership, but also sent a powerful signal to Bain's consultants and managers. Maintaining a pool of top quality seasoned consultants was crucial to Bain, which held a leadership position in management consulting, a rapidly evolving industry with revenue growth of nearly 18 percent per annum and annual turnover of about 15 percent.

Candidates were not present for the CPC proceedings. Instead, they were represented by two packages of information, one submitted to the committee by recommending partners from the candidates' local offices, the other by third-party reviewers (themselves members of the CPC) who conducted independent due diligence on each candidate. Local office submissions presented candidates' chronology of case experience and results and numerical scores on critical performance dimensions over their careers and, usually, a cover letter written by the local office head summarizing the local partner group's support. Third-party reviews contained reports of interviews with virtually everyone the candidates had worked with at Bain: partners, managers, and consultants.

Yale and her colleagues determined that, of the nine promotion cases on the agenda, four were particularly challenging. Over the next several hours, CPC members would debate whether these four Bain managers, each of whom had several years of service and a long list of accomplishments, were ready to become Bain partners.

THE CONSULTING INDUSTRY IN 1998

During the 1990s corporate initiatives on reengineering, downsizing, early retirement, consolidation, and outsourcing had fueled both the supply and demand for consultants worldwide. In 1997 total industry revenues worldwide grew to $73 billion, up from $62 billion in 1996 and $51 billion in 1995. A prominent industry research group pre-

Senior Research Associate Perry L. Fagan and Professor Ashish Nanda prepared this case with the advice and guidance of Professor Michael Y. Yoshino as the basis for class discussion rather than to illustrate either effective or ineffective handling of an administrative situation.

[1] Bain & Company was a corporation. Bain executives used the term "partner" to convey the mutual commitment and sense of partnership that each vice president was supposed to bring to the firm.

dicted a $114 billion global consulting market by the year 2000.[2]

The ease of entry for newcomers (not much investment was needed to declare oneself to be an "independent consultant") and competitive advantages of larger firms (brand equity, diversified client base, broad geographic coverage) accounted for the hourglass structure of the consulting industry, its firms divided into the very large and the very small. Consulting firms with fewer than 10 professionals accounted for three-quarters of the industry's 360,000 employees, and about half of industry revenues.[3] A handful of firms, on the other hand, had, through acquisitions, mergers, and global expansion, grown into consulting behemoths, "one-stop" shops that offered a wide array of consulting and other professional services. The one-stop shops notwithstanding, most consulting firms generated the bulk of their revenues from one type of work. Information technology (roughly 64 percent of the market), compensation and benefits, and management/strategy consulting were the three largest specialties. Bain was recognized within the industry as a leading strategy consulting firm.

Within specialties, competition for clients and recruits was intense. In fact, consulting firms claimed that competition for recruits—with investment banking and venture capital firms and high-tech start-ups as well as other consulting firms—was more intense than competition for clients.[4]

Traditionally, consulting firms hired directly from the top graduate business schools, absorbing up to 25 percent of top MBA program graduates annually. But with high rates of growth and a shortage of elite business school graduates, some firms had begun to look beyond their usual sources of recruits to nonbusiness professional schools, PhD programs, and industry.

Retention, a perennial challenge, was made even more difficult during the 1990s by the tight market for skilled labor. Few consultants professed long-term commitment either to their respective companies or to consulting as a career. Remarked one: "I'm interested enough to do it for a few years because of the experience I'll gain and the industry contacts." Added another: "I don't know if I've found my niche or whether there's another niche to come."[5]

BAIN & CO.

Founded in 1973 by Bill Bain, Tennessee-born son of a food wholesaler, and seven colleagues, Bain & Co. grew rapidly in the 1970s and 1980s. Revenue climbed from $34 million in 1982 to almost $200 million in 1989. Recalled one former employee: "We were oozing success."[6]

In the late 1980s, just as the founding partners were transitioning management of the company to the next generation, Bain experienced financial difficulties. Buffeted by a downturn in the U.S. economy, the firm suffered a slowdown in growth and painful layoffs.

Under a new partnership structure led by Tom Tierney, the company rebounded in the 1990s. Tierney had joined Bain in 1980 after graduating from Harvard Business School, was promoted to partner and named vice president in 1983, appointed managing director of Bain's San Francisco office in 1987, and was elected worldwide managing director in 1993. In 1998, he was serving his second three-year term.

Bain had always emphasized achieving tangible results for clients (see Exhibit 1). It maintained an

[2] Kennedy Information Research Group (www.kennedyinfo.com).

[3] Peter Haynes and Dolly Setton, "McKinsey 101," *Forbes,* May 4, 1998, pp. 130–35.

[4] Tim Bourgeois, director of research, Kennedy Research Group as quoted in Jay Berry, "Good-bye to the Lush Management Consulting Life?" *Journal of Management Consulting,* November 1998, pp. 22–26.

[5] Brian Palmer, "Is It Time to Join the Consultants?" *Fortune,* August 3, 1998, pp. 251–52.

[6] Keith H. Hammonds, "Can Bain Consultants Get Bain & Co. Out of This Jam?" *Business Week,* February 11, 1991, p. 52.

EXHIBIT 1   **Bain Mission Statement**

Bain & Company's mission is to help our clients create such high levels of economic value that together we set new standards of excellence in our respective industries.

This mission demands:

- The Bain vision of the most productive client relationship and single-minded dedication to achieving it with each client.

- The Bain community of extraordinary teams.

- The Bain approach to creating value, based on a shared competitive and customer focus, the most effective analytic techniques, and our process of collaboration with the client.

We believe that accomplishing our mission will redefine the management consulting business, and will provide new levels of rewards for our clients and for our organization.

Bain Values

- Bain exists to provide results through strategy to our clients, and extraordinary opportunities for our people.

- Our client results—and our ability to attract and retain the best people—drive our long-term business success.

- Delivering results requires partnership with client general managers who are committed to change.

- We are generalists; however, expertise is an increasingly important ingredient of our competitive success.

- We are entrepreneurial and meritocratic, but we work as teammates in a variety of extraordinary teams.

Bain & Company is a business which should yield among the highest returns in our industry over time.

Source: Bain & Company.

audited "scoreboard" tracking clients' share prices over the years (see Exhibit 2). The compensation process reinforced this results focus by tying partners' compensation in part directly to the long-term results achieved by their clients. The consequence, in the words of Asia managing director Mark Daniell, was

> quite a unique focus on very practical bottom-line results for clients. We differentiate ourselves from the usual strategy consultants that write reports in that our whole corporate culture is structured around very

practical measurable results for clients. That means that we work in situations where there is a possibility of creating effective results for our clients.[7]

Pursuing its focused strategy of results-oriented advice to large, established multinational companies on corporate strategy, Bain grew rapidly from 1992 to 1998, experiencing compound annual revenue growth in excess of 20 percent, increasing consulting staff from 640 to more than 2,000, and expanding its partner group from 55 to 175. In 1998, Bain's practice spanned 25 offices in 18

---

[7] Jennifer Jacobs, "Bain & Co. Aims to Boost Asian Operations," *New Straits Times (Malaysia),* May 12, 1998, p. 6.

EXHIBIT 2   The Bain "Scoreboard"

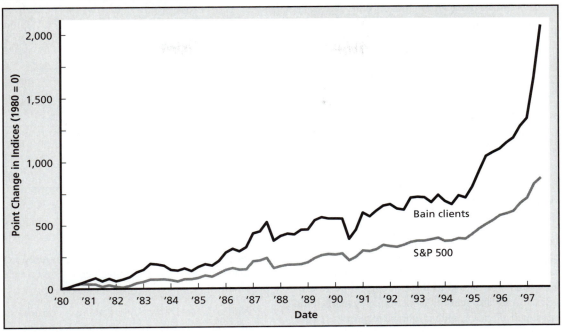

Note: Methodology and data attested to by Price Waterhouse LLP through September 1997.
Source: Bain & Company.

countries across six continents. Bain's worldwide revenues were thought to exceed $500 million.[8] Since its founding Bain had worked with more than 1,500 clients, "from every economic sector, in every region of the world."[9]

THE PARTNER PROMOTION PROCESS

The CPC made partner promotion decisions twice a year, in June and December[10] (see Exhibit 3).

The process for June promotions began roughly in mid-March. By mid-April the CPC received all the documentation for the candidates up for promotions. Decisions made in June were announced roughly July 1. A similar timeline was followed for December promotion decisions.

Career Progression of Bain Professionals

Bain had a relatively flat hierarchy with five levels: Associate consultant, consultant, manager, vice

[8] The top-tier in strategy practice was widely considered to comprise Bain, McKinsey ($1.1 billion), and The Boston Consulting Group ($655 million). Source of revenue estimates: *Consultants News,* June 1998, p. 9.
[9] Bain & Co. fact sheet.
[10] The CPC was one of Bain's three main governing bodies. The other two were the Policy Committee and the Nominating Committee. The Policy Committee set policies on strategy, firm finance, personnel, and compensation. The Nominating Committee proposed candidates for chairman of the board, managing director, the Policy Committee, and the CPC and acted as a watchdog on governance issues.

EXHIBIT 3 Bain's VP Promotion Process

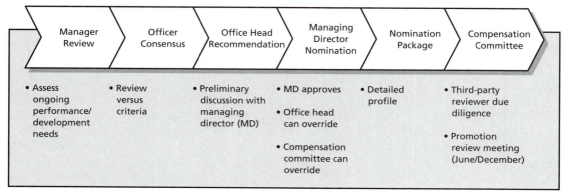

Source: Bain & Company.

president, and director. Associate consultants typically joined Bain right out of college, and stayed with the firm for two to three years before returning to graduate school. Consultants usually held advanced degrees, and might have previous consulting experience at another firm, or as associates at Bain. Consultants were promoted to managers, roughly after three years, and managers to vice presidents, after a few more years. For consultants joining Bain post-MBA promotion to vice president was usually five to eight years out. "If you are the best in the company, you'll take five years to partner, otherwise, more like seven," a VP had remarked. Vice presidents were akin to partners in other consulting firms. Five or more years after being named vice presidents, some of the VPs were named directors. Tierney reflected on career progression of Bain consultants.

> Our people are incredibly important to us. Each and every consultant hired into Bain is welcomed with the expectation of being promoted to partner one day. So right from day one we offer our consultants rigorous and frequent performance feedback that helps them calibrate their efforts and address issues before they become problematic.

"Soon after you arrive at Bain you quickly get feedback on how you are doing," concurred a vice president.

> Within 12 to 18 months of being a consultant, you have a strong indication of your trajectory. Likewise for managers; within 18 months you have explicit feedback regarding your partnership promotion prospects. A lot of self-selecting out of the firm takes place. Some people feel they will not be able to make it or conclude that partnership is not for them. In addition great job opportunities lure many of our people away from consulting. About half our turnover occurs because people move on to these opportunities. The net result of this self-selection is that over the course of time many consultants leave Bain. In my class 19 people started with me seven years ago as consultants, and today three are left.

Getting Nominated

Candidates were nominated by their local partner groups in consultation with Tierney. Local offices sought to strengthen their own organizations through promotion recommendations and the local partners typically invested a lot personally and professionally in their respective candidates. As worldwide managing director, Tierney held veto power over all local office nominations; a candidate could not come before the CPC without his blessing. Moreover, he could (but seldom did) nominate candidates over the objection of local offices. Tierney explained his role in the process.

> I pick up the promotion candidates usually a year ahead of time and have an ongoing dialogue with the local office. I have to really dig down to explore whether all the local partners agree, whether there is a minority that is not fully comfortable, what their views and concerns are. I have to identify people who probably won't make it and push the local office to invest more aggressively in developing them before their names come up formally before the committee. Once I give a tentative green light, a package is developed and the candidate is usually passed right on to the committee.

CPC's Decision-Making Process on Partner Promotions

The CPC comprised Tierney plus seven members, all Bain partners (see Exhibit 4). Committee members, elected by Bain's worldwide partner group by slate, served three-year terms, staggered to ensure continuity. CFO Len Banos served the CPC as an ex-officio member. According to Yale, the committee was responsible for:

- making a set of compensation recommendations independent of office heads;

- serving as the final decision making authority on promotions; and

- acting as third-party advisor to office heads on partner management issues.

Twice a year the committee was presented with a set of promotion nominations together with local office recommendations. In making its promotion decisions (which were subject to neither formal review nor appeal), the CPC had to take a firmwide

view and weigh the strengthening of local offices against the maintenance of Bain's "one-firm" strategy.

Calibrating across offices while sorting reality from advocacy was difficult. Remarked a London-based senior partner who was also a CPC member: "It's hard to read between the lines; the local office recommendation tends to be a little sales-oriented. You know: 'This guy walks on water; that woman has done this or that great thing.' Personally I view this document as the starter package, a requirement because we need to have a baseline of information."

To achieve cross-comparisons and get an independent fix on them, candidates were also evaluated by CPC members identified as their third-party advisors. "It is really a two-step process," explained a committee member. "The local partner interviews people first and then somebody from the committee will come in and interview the same people." "Each of the seven committee members," Yale elaborated, "is assigned to a set of offices as a third-party advisor. The third-party advisor does due diligence on promotion candidates from his or her set of offices (chosen geographically removed from the third-party reviewer's home office to avoid conflicts of interest) by interviewing all of the related people to understand the subfacts, what really happened, what really went on, what the issues are with someone."

Local office nominations were calibrated and verified through interviews lasting 30 minutes each of 15 to 20 people per candidate. Noted a Bain veteran: "They interview anybody that a candidate has ever worked with, a consultant, a manager. . . . It is a lot of data. The job here is really to see how these people would stack up against others, not just in the local partner group. Committee members don't interview the candidates themselves. Not that it's off limits and not that it's forbidden, it just tends not to be done. Although the candidate need not be informed, usually they know that the process is going on." Sometimes the candidates supplied raw materials (e.g., basic facts of their client assignments and so forth) for the

EXHIBIT 4   Compensation and Promotion Committee Member Profiles

A director in the Paris office, **Jean-Pierre Felenbok** joined Bain in 1981 and was elected to the partnership in 1987. A leader in the practice areas of retail/consumer goods, high technology, and financial services, he had previously worked as a civil engineer. Felenbok held an MBA from Harvard Business School and Master of Science degree from MIT. Mr. Felenbok was also a graduate of Ecole Nationale des Ponts et Chaussees. He had been published in such publications as *Harvard Business Review, Financial Times, EFMA,* and *Revue Banque.*

A director in the Boston office, **Dave Johnson** joined Bain in 1985 and was elected to the partnership in 1990. A leader in the practice areas of manufacturing, financial services, and utilities, he had previously worked as a regulatory economist for New England Telephone. Johnson held an MBA with distinction from Harvard Business School and a Bachelor of Arts in economics with highest honors from the University of Rhode Island.

A director in the London office, **Paul Rogers** joined Bain in 1986, having previously worked as a European brand manager for Procter & Gamble. He advised clients across a wide range of industries and issues, and had particular experience helping companies within branded and consumer goods. Rogers had received an Open Exhibition from Cambridge University and studied corporate finance at the London Business School.

A director in the London office, **John Smith** had been with Bain since 1983. Based in Boston until 1993 Smith's client assignments emphasized multinational companies, restructuring, strategic acquisitions, and buyouts. From 1993 until 1995 Smith was responsible for Eastern Europe and served as director of Bain Link, a Soviet joint venture with Bain. Until recently he had been working out of the Munich office supporting Swiss and other multinational companies. Prior to joining Bain, Smith was a project manager at British Leyland, U.K. and project engineer at CERN, Geneva. He held an MBA with honors from Columbia Business School and an Honors degree in mechanical engineering from Hertfordshire University in England.

A director in Bain's Boston office, **Paul Smith** was one of the leaders of the company's Telecommunications and Technology practice. Smith held a Bachelor of Science degree in computer science and mathematics with highest honors from the University of California at Los Angeles and was a graduate, with highest distinction, of the Harvard Business School.

A director in the San Francisco office, **Elisabeth Walsh** joined Bain in 1983 and was elected to the partnership in 1990. Co-head of the West Coast health care practice, she had more than 12 years experience working with clients in such areas as growth strategies, corporate reengineering, and portfolio/business unit strategies. Prior to joining Bain, Walsh had worked as an associate in Merrill Lynch's Health Care Finance Group and as an economist with the U.S. Department of Energy. She held an MBA with distinction from Harvard Business School and a Bachelor of Science in economics and international relations with highest honors from the University of California.

A director in the Boston office, **Phyllis Yale** joined Bain in 1982 and was elected to the partnership in 1987. Yale focused on the health care and financial services industries. Prior to joining Bain, she had been a commercial lending officer at Citibank. Yale held an MBA with distinction from Harvard Business School and a Bachelor of Arts degree in economics with honors from Harvard and Radcliffe Colleges. She served on the boards of directors of Planned Parenthood and Lexington Montessori School.

Source: Bain & Company.

local office nomination package. "We generally don't go back to the client," observed Yale, "although their views are often included in the local office nomination packages in the form of supporting letters."

Once all the data had been collected, the CPC met to review the candidates. A typical CPC meeting lasted several hours, but could take longer if consensus was slow to emerge or more data were needed for particular candidates.[11] Nominated candidates were discussed in turn, their cases presented by the third-party reviewers. "Usually the committee quickly figures out which of the candidates have no chance of making it this time around or which clearly cross the bar," remarked Yale. "We end up spending most of our time discussing candidates who are on the margin." A preliminary vote was usually taken for the easier candidates; if a unanimous decision was quickly achieved the candidates' names were written on a blackboard. Voting was postponed for the more difficult cases. After each candidate had been discussed at length, members returned to the more difficult cases for further vetting.

The committee sought, but did not require, unanimous agreement on all candidates. A two-thirds majority was required to ratify a promotion; usually unanimous agreement was obtained. Once decisions had been rendered on all candidates, the committee "stared down the list" of the new partners to gain an overall sense of the group. If members were comfortable with the list and no further discussion was required, the meeting adjourned.

It fell to CPC committee members to inform each candidate's office head of the committee's decision. The office head then notified the candidate, usually in person, and informed the rest of the partner group, usually by group voicemail. Accepted candidates were asked to sign a new partner contract that included a noncompete provision and a pledge to stay at Bain for at least one year. After all contracts were signed (usually two weeks

after the committee's decision), an official announcement from Tierney was posted in all Bain offices. Names of rejected candidates were not made public.

A committee member recalled:

> This time last year, seven nominations made it past the committee out of the ten that had made it to the committee. There were another five that were raised but didn't make the committee, which is a typical ratio. Some of those five might never make the committee, but most are just postponed. There may be another half dozen to a dozen that didn't pass the local committee and make it into the fifteen that came to Tom.

Promotion Criteria

"Partner skills are broader than manager skills," Tierney observed.

> Before you become a partner you can often get away with simply being smart and analytical and a good team player. Being a partner is all about trust and judgment. You continue to apply the skills you had earlier, but analysis is no longer your output; it becomes the input into your decisions. The big step is that, all of a sudden, other executives are saying to you, "I'm going to entrust the success of my company and my career in part to you."

Within Bain there seemed to be broad agreement that partners were "entrepreneurial and energetic," "committed to building an enterprise," "client-oriented," "smart," and "possessing a one-firm mind-set." "A Bain partner's defining characteristics are a focus on results and value creation, client relationships and communication, and team-building skills," remarked one partner.

In 1992 Bain had developed a detailed set of formal criteria for promotion to vice president (see Exhibit 5). "We are the guardians of the promotion

---

[11] In the latter case the committee might adjourn the promotion discussion for a few hours and conduct other business while the third-party reviewer collected further data.

EXHIBIT 5 **Bain VP Promotion Criteria**

Criteria	Performance Guidelines

• Client
  —Value addition
  ➤ Brilliant insights
  ➤ Package insights to move client to act
  ➤ Process to achieve results (minimize yield loss)
  ➤ Build organization capability
	• Demonstrated ability to solve clients' toughest strategic problems (strategy and implementation)
	• Real value and results created for clients
	• Consistent success over period as manager (review past two years)
	• Demonstrated value addition in different client and analytic situations
	• Positive referrals for Bain received from client
	• Work in another office or on a multiple office assignment
	• Ability to effectively manage multiple case teams and workstreams

—Relationship
  ➤ Viewed as an expert in case-specific area
  ➤ Consulted by client beyond immediate project scope
	• Demonstrated leadership in helping to create, manage, and expand a CEO/high-quality, flagship relationship
	• Driven strategic agenda and thought processes
	• Highly valued by senior client
	• Multiple situations
	• Significant role with a senior management-level decision maker

—New business development
  ➤ Proposal structuring
  ➤ Process management
  ➤ Selling support
	• Significant role either within existing relationship or with new client development (strategic clients)

• Asset building
  —People assets
  ➤ Treat people with respect/caring
  ➤ Manage resources appropriately
  ➤ Investment in specific programs
	• Average or above on surveys
	• Basic minimum citizenship on recruiting/training
	• Viewed as a team player by peers

—Practice ➤ Support on codifying insights/ specific practice area support	• Significant contribution on at least one dimension: —Defined as Highly Leveraged Achievements; or —Agreed to by line VP/office head

—Brand
  ➤ Support on conference/article development
  ➤ Pro bono/community networking
—Office/firm leadership
  ➤ Responsibility for/contribution to office or one firm development	

• Promotes Bain values/adheres to operating principles	• Respected/admired by peers/subordinates

EXHIBIT 5   Bain VP Promotion Criteria *(continued)*

Criteria	Performance Guidelines

• Future potential for growth and contribution
  ➤ To build new client relationships
  ➤ To contribute to intellectual capital and other asset building
  ➤ Potential as flagship client head
	• Subjective assessment

Source: Bain & Company.

criteria," remarked a CPC member. These criteria notwithstanding, Yale cautioned, "we don't get or look for cookie-cutter candidates. Promotion is based on merit and contribution, which are difficult to evaluate—and not tenure, which is easy to measure. This makes the promotion decision so complex." Added Tierney: "There is no hard and fast timetable for promotion. We pride ourselves on being a true meritocracy. Tenure is not that important at all. People are promoted when they're ready, based on merit, results, and teamwork."

In evaluating candidates against the promotion criteria the committee focused in particular on "repeatability" of high quality results across multiple client engagements. "A big issue for us is ensuring consistent performance at a partner-like level," remarked a CPC member.

> It's always a fine line to bet on the future potential or to bet on what's proven in the past. Future potential is very important. But I think we as a group tend to focus more on "have you done it; have you walked the walk" versus "do we believe you have potential."

Concern over repeatability had led the CPC to reject several candidates from the same office in the previous promotion cycle. "We felt the office had proposed a number of very high trajectory people for whom we just felt there was a little too much betting on the come," a member of the committee explained. "We wanted to send a signal that

we want to see consistent, repeatable performances of vice president caliber as a condition for partnership."

Another CPC member reflected on past promotion decisions.

> I've been on this committee for five years, been the chairman for two years. In my view, if we have made mistakes they've been in the direction of promoting too soon rather than promoting too late. The problem with moving people too fast is that once you become a partner there's a lot of new and complex pressures. It is better to get firmly across the line when you really have the tools in place to face the added pressure, as opposed to just squeak across the line. We make promotion decisions every six months. In the grand scheme of things, is six months a big deal?

The Rejection Decision

Unlike at some other professional service firms, promotion rejection at Bain did not imply an automatic termination of the employment relationship. "We don't have an up-or-out system at Bain," observed Tierney. "If you don't make it once you can be nominated again for promotion and the CPC will take a fresh look at you. Even if you fail again and don't make partner, we still expect you to maintain life-long relationships with Bain and try our best through counseling and advice to ensure that you remain a productive and happy member of the Bain team."

Rejection could, however, unleash negative emotions. "When I didn't get promoted the first time before the committee," recalled one junior partner,

> although I maintained a brave front outward, inward I was angry and disturbed. The day I was rejected by the committee I scheduled three job interviews. But then, everyone on the promotion committee, including Tom Tierney as well as my mentor, talked with me. They told me to keep on doing what I was doing for another six months and everything would be all right. I kept on working and, indeed, I was promoted in the next go-around.

In contrast, another junior partner who had also been rejected on his first attempt remarked that "for me, the process reinforced two-way trust, especially around meritocracy. The way they run the process reinforces the idea that you are not merely picking up a brass ring. For me, it was reenergizing."

THE CANDIDATES FOR PROMOTION

The four candidates on whom the CPC members were focusing—Annie Gonzalez, Dave Chew, Peter Smythe, and Evelyn Planck[12]—were veteran Bain managers with distinguished track records and staunch local office support.

Annie Gonzalez

Annie Gonzalez had joined Bain as an associate consultant in 1989 after earning a BS (electrical engineering) from Stanford University. She was promoted to consultant-in-training in 1991 and to consultant in mid-1992, left the following year to

attend Harvard Business School, and returned as a consultant after earning her MBA. She was promoted to manager in early 1996. This was her first nomination to the CPC.

The local partner group was very enthusiastic about Gonzalez's candidacy. (See Exhibit 6 for extracts from local partners' comments in the nomination package of all four candidates.) They summarized their evaluation of her candidacy as follows:

> Her intellectual leadership and ability to get strategy into clear action with client buy-in are strengths multiple standard deviations from the norm. She is the one we put confidently into our most difficult client situations where she performs exceptionally. [We endorse] her promotion with high expectations based on demonstrated successes despite her otherwise more limited time at Bain. This is a true case for meritocracy.

Third-party interviews largely concurred. Gonzalez's case team scores, which comprised feedback on her performance from all members of her case teams, were routinely greater than 4.0 (out of 5.0).[13] Her upward feedback scores, which reflected the views of more junior case team members, were above average for managers. She was sometimes seen as a perfectionist and "at the sole center of synthesis, though this is reflective of the complexity of strategic issues posed to her." Gonzalez was also seen as occasionally tending toward micromanagement, despite which, the local partner group believed that she had helped codify and build two of Bain's most important industry practices in her office. Her colleagues also praised her for being a strong contributor to recruiting and for working to advance Bain's recruiting methods and processes.

"Clearly, she has been a star," Yale reflected with respect to Gonzalez's profile. "Her candidacy

---

[12] The candidates' names and some biographical details have been disguised to protect anonymity.
[13] The average case team score for partner promotion candidates was 4.0 out of 5.0.

EXHIBIT 6 **Extracts from Local Partner Comments in the Nomination Packages**

Annie Gonzalez

Annie is an extraordinary Bain talent. We start this way only to acknowledge that her otherwise shorter tenure as a manager may initially raise questions, but, collectively, we view her as one of the unique few for whom meritocracy on results, value addition and client relationships shines through so clearly. Both her results to date plus expected trajectory and contribution place her among the top few we've experienced and, therefore, among the limited set we felt should break any norms.

She has excelled within two of Bain's largest client successes and opportunities the last two to three years. She is clearly seen and identified as the intellectual horsepower behind many of the significant client successes by her Bain teams, VPs, and clients.

On one client she managed the capital budget work that has delivered $5 billion in NPV. She was instrumental in the early years of the relationship in establishing the value of Bain. Her relationships and work extend throughout the senior management team and the insights of her work and depth of relationships have led directly to further requests for Bain work over the last couple of years.

On another case she led the work resulting in a major acquisition—a $1 billion plus deal and fundamental step shift in the client's strategy. She has continued to be integral to the client relationship and has been identified with generating additional client demand for Bain. Bain's current efforts in arguably one of the most core strategic issues for the client is in part a result of her work, insights and value creation to date.

She is able to go very deep on the most complex issues for our biggest clients and "hit" insights and results. Her confidence and respect earned with the most senior clients is further testament to her capabilities and contributions.

Dave Chew

Dave has been at the center of the total reorganization of a well-known global private bank and asset management company, resulting in a doubling of the client's stock price. He also evaluated two deals for a private equity company with little supervision. The client held him in high regard and on numerous occasions commented favorably on him, unsolicited. In addition, he won over a very proud, defensive, talented, creative entrepreneur who saw no value from an outside consulting firm and reached total consensus on the way forward. Client sales doubled as a result.

He moved core processes evaluation and implementation ahead at a manufacturing company by getting up to speed on a complex process quickly, earning the respect of the sponsor, and getting the sponsor on board with the whole program. He focused on how we would have the most impact in the shortest amount of time. The engagement achieved significant re-engineering and implementation of structural changes recommended, which led to a significant profit improvement.

Dave has rapidly integrated into the Bain culture through his zeal for value added and results, his contribution to the office and firm through recruiting and training, and his interaction with other offices as manager of global cases. His actions not only exemplify Bain values but also act as an inspiration to others to follow suit.

Peter Smythe

Peter's client and internal assignments over the last two and a half years have allowed him to demonstrate clearly outstanding capability and consistent contribution on each VP promotion criteria well above performance thresholds.

At one client he is currently playing a critical leadership role and is helping lay the groundwork for growth in the relationship. He has been positioned with the client as the day-to-day leader of the work

(continues)

EXHIBIT 6 Extracts from Local Partner Comments in the Nomination Packages *(continued)*

(equivalent to a junior VP) and is performing extremely effectively in this role. The output of the teams to date has been very well received, supported, and promoted by a broad array of managers, and it is clear that we are gaining significant momentum relative to our most direct competition within the client.

Peter's work directly saved [an important client] $67 million over the course of one year, and identified another $30 million of potential opportunities. On [another case] Peter improved a client's defection recovery rate by 12 percent, resulting in value to them of nearly $400 million. At [another client] he managed approximately $2 million per month in revenue for Bain.

A key to our success at [one of the clients] has been Peter's extraordinarily strong client management skills. Our day-to-day client contact is an extremely volatile and even abusive individual. Peter has taken on this client as a project and is building a strong relationship with him, allowing the team to be successful in the value creation process.

Evelyn Planck

Evelyn has demonstrated the ability to arrive at the right answer on complex strategic issues that convince management to make bold strategic moves. She has the ability to win the respect and confidence of senior client management, including the CEO and strategy director of a major European telecommunications company, who relied upon her during the firm's recent merger. She has demonstrated the ability to roll over work on her assignments, which last year resulted in $3 million in additional revenues.

Evelyn has the potential capability to land major new clients based on her participation in new client development opportunities. In these situations Evelyn has come across with credibility and professionalism. She possesses strong team management skills supported by clear direction and high levels of team productivity. She is firmly committed to Bain values and is consistently supportive of the Bain partner and manager group. In addition, she has the ability to listen for feedback and to act upon it in her own development.

is testing our minimum time standard. We would like to make examples of promoting bright people early to demonstrate the meritocracy in our system, but we all worry that such candidates sometimes hit a massive wall later on in their careers and simply 'flame out.'"

Dave Chew

Dave Chew joined Bain in January 1995 as a manager. He held an advanced degree in chemical engineering from Carnegie-Mellon University (graduating in the top 5 percent of his class) and an MBA from Wharton. He spoke English and Mandarin Chinese. Prior to Bain he had worked two years with a high tech company and three years as a consultant at another consulting firm. This was his first nomination to the CPC.

At Bain Chew had worked with a variety of clients in retail, private equity, tobacco, and banking on assignments in corporate strategy, loyalty, rationalization and process implementation. He had managed the recruiting function for his office and served on multiple occasions as a trainer. Chew had demonstrated consistent improvement over time in his case team scores (despite a heavy workload). His most recent scores were significantly above average.

Local partners had supported his nomination (see Exhibit 6). They summarized the rationale for promoting him to partnership:

We unanimously support Dave for promotion to partner. He is effective both externally and internally, he has charisma and has demonstrated the ability to lead and generate insights and business for clients and Bain. He is a role model for achieving results and will be a significant future contributor to the partner group.

Although generally concurring with the gist of the local office nomination, Chew's third-party reviewer added:

His strengths are also his weaknesses. His zeal to go for value and to serve the client has, in the past, taken a toll on his workload and his ability to step back and focus on only the most critical issues. It has also led to communication problems with his fellow team members and has alienated him somewhat from more junior people in the office. In a couple of cases his direct reports refused to work with him again and in one instance a team member left the firm. Dave was made aware of these issues and has improved over time.

A CPC member remarked:

Dave is a great client person, adds tremendous value, works very hard, inspires clients, and is great at consulting. He is friendly, the type of person you would like to go to dinner with. But he is so passionate in his drive to do what's right for the clients that he ends up working his teams too hard. So he chews people up internally. His team members are unhappy—one even quit—and although he has been improving over time it's been rough around the edges. I am worried about the kind of message we might be sending to the rest of the organization if we promote him.

Peter Smythe

Peter Smythe joined Bain as a summer associate in 1990 while enrolled at Harvard Business School. After graduating in 1991, he returned to Bain full time as a consultant. In February 1994 he was promoted to manager. Smythe held a Bachelor of Commerce degree from a leading Canadian university, with majors in accounting and finance, and prior to business school had worked for four years as an M&A consultant at another consulting firm. This was his first nomination to the CPC.

Smythe's major assignments as manager had included clients in automotive, not-for-profit, transportation, financial services, diversified manufacturing, and defense industries. His assignments included formulating order-to-delivery strategies, operations and organizational restructuring, restructuring of airport services, customer loyalty, and reengineering. Smythe's local partner group rated him exceptional on all performance dimensions: positive effect on firm spirit; intellectual capability; value creation; case team management; client relationships; selling potential; intellectual contribution to the firm; and people development.

Smythe's dossier included glowing recommendations from his local partners (see Exhibit 6) as well as several letters from current and past clients praising him for his outstanding performance, including one from a "volatile" client. The client wrote:

Peter has been extremely valuable to us because of his ability to quickly grasp a key financial understanding of our business and then focus and pursue value-added opportunities to substantially improve our business results. Personally, I am very grateful to Peter for setting us on a course that will reap benefits for many years to come that are far greater than anyone could imagine at the beginning of the assignment.

Smythe had headed up consultant recruiting in his local office since mid-1994, had been extensively involved in a number of client development initiatives, and had played a major role in selling casework to five new clients. He was a significant contributor to worldwide experience sharing, particularly as part of Bain's Financial Services Practice, and several Bain offices had emphasized results from one of his engagements in speeches and client development initiatives. Smythe had also been invited to speak at the Direct Marketing Association Loyalty Conference.

Smythe's office head summarized his candidacy:

> Peter is an extraordinarily talented and mature individual and has continued to do an outstanding job for us on every dimension. He has continued to be an outstanding contributor to the success of our office and has the full support of the partner group. We believe he will be an exceptional VP and continue to be a major contributor to Bain's success over the long term as a member of our partnership. We strongly recommend he be promoted during the current promotion cycle.

Third-party interviews generally agreed with the local office assessment of Smythe's candidacy. The third-party reviewer felt that Smythe was well rounded and had demonstrated success on multiple dimensions. The reviewer also knew that business needs in Smythe's local market were not sufficiently strong to justify expanding the local partner base. Owing to recent induction of several industry hires at the partner level, the local partner group's pyramid was already too top heavy for its current client base.

Smythe's ex-wife had settled in the city where his Bain office was located. She had custody over their two children, five and two years of age, with Smythe having visitation rights. The third-party reviewer knew that Smythe would be unwilling to relocate at this stage of his life. The other partners in the office were in their late thirties and early forties and had strong local ties.

Evelyn Planck

Evelyn Planck joined Bain in March 1990 and was promoted to manager in April 1992. She was a graduate of Oxford University, had earned an MBA from INSEAD, and, prior to joining Bain, had worked for the European Union in trade policy with a focus on telecommunications.

During the prior three years Evelyn had worked almost exclusively in Bain's worldwide Telecommunications and Technology practice group. She was considered one of the firm's leading telecom experts.

This was Planck's second nomination to the CPC. Six months earlier the committee had rejected her nomination with the conclusion that she "needed to demonstrate consistency in client impact and relationship building for a longer period before being promoted to partner."

Her partner group was very supportive of Planck (see Exhibit 6). The nominating partners reiterated their support and described her fit with Bain values.

> The significant success which Evelyn has brought Bain through her client work over the last six months is ample evidence of her continued progress. As in December, the partner group believe that Evelyn is ready to be promoted to partner at Bain & Company.

> Evelyn embodies most of the classic beliefs that founded our company. She demonstrates a passion for having a significant impact with clients and sets some of the highest standards for the quality of her work. She works exceptionally hard, but tries to set an example for others to have a fairly balanced life. She has been very proactive in praising the work of her team in public settings and is a role model for others in terms of her people management skills and her professional standards.

Planck had contributed to a 1996 worldwide consultant training program, offering some of the modules and organizing European participation. She was also responsible for revamping Bain's M&A training program. In addition, she had been "enthusiastically involved" in consultant recruiting at INSEAD from 1990–1996.

Observed Yale: "Evelyn is clearly bright and very capable within her specialty, but minimum thresholds on all the criteria are still necessary for promotion. The question we have to address here is whether to promote a niche player or to look only for a generalist."

THE JUNE DECISION

As the promotion committee began to focus on and debate these four candidates, a senior partner remarked: "Partner promotion decisions are very, very hard. These decisions really get to the crux of what Bain & Company is all about. It's a question as basic as who are you going to marry. You have to work with these people for the rest of your life."

Venture Law Group

> Perhaps VLG should acknowledge that the people we attract are so talented and the opportunities in Silicon Valley so diverse and appealing that we have to accept losing a steady stream of our people to other opportunities. But I'm not prepared to accept that yet.
>
> *Craig Johnson, VLG chairman*

Dressed in silk pajamas and smoking jacket and holding a martini glass, Craig Johnson, chairman of Venture Law Group (VLG), entered VLG's 1998 Halloween celebration escorted by his "angels,"[a] two VLG attorneys and a paralegal who had recruited him for the role. It was a tradition at the nearly six-year-old firm that Johnson, or "Charlie" as he referred to himself that afternoon, would dress up in costume and make a big entrance for the Halloween celebration, to which nearly all of VLG's 80 lawyers and 130 administrative professionals brought their families, the children traveling from office to office "trick-or-treating." Johnson's cheerful mood was to be short-lived, however. "As we were making our rounds," he recalled,

> Jim Brock and Bob Zipp, both VLG directors, approached me and said they would be leaving VLG to form their own consulting firm, BZ Partners, to advise early-stage Internet start-ups in exchange for equity. Jim had helped to start Yahoo! but had turned down the general counsel position in 1996 to stay at VLG and become a director. He saw

the Yahoo! general counsel make more than $100 million in less than two years while he was still at VLG, doing well by traditional standards, but nowhere near as well had he joined Yahoo!

> Jim and Bob had been exploring with the VLG board of directors, the ways they could have a bigger piece of the start-up equity that was going to VLG, but I still was surprised and disappointed by their decision. I was stressed and uncertain what I could do to retain them and other VLG attorneys.

Retention had been an obsession for Johnson, who understood the costs of attorney and staff turnover on start-up clients that needed close, intense legal support to get to market, as well as the internal morale problems it generated (seeing friends leave and requiring others to work harder to serve clients) and the hiring and training costs it incurred.

Although he had seen 21 professionals leave the firm, Johnson was particularly distressed by Brock's and Zipp's resignations. The first two partners to decide to leave VLG, they had been supporters of the

Dean's Research Fellow Scot Landry prepared this case under the supervision of Professors Thomas DeLong and Ashish Nanda as the basis for class discussion rather than to illustrate either effective or ineffective handling of an administrative situation. This case is based on a class project by Anthony Wang (HLS '99) entitled "Venture Law Group."

[a] "Charlie's Angels," a popular ABC-TV private detective show from 1976–1982, featured the owner of a private detective agency who never appeared on camera and interacted with his three female detectives and their male business manager exclusively through a speakerphone.

firm's "zero-voluntary turnover" goal (see Exhibit 1). In the face of their departures, Johnson wondered whether this goal was attainable.

We've done what we can to make this a great place to work and to be responsive to em-ployee suggestions. We have an economic model that will make those who stay wealthy. But given the "economic hurri-cane" sweeping through Silicon Valley and the stories of general counsels making hun-dreds of millions overnight, is there any-

EXHIBIT 1   About VLG

Venture Law Group specializes in representing deal-intensive technology companies, both public and private, and investment firms that support these companies. Our goal is to treat our clients as business partners, to combine excellent legal skills with good business judgment and to play an active role in helping our clients succeed. As our clients succeed in building their businesses, we will succeed too.

If We Accept a Client, We Will Do a Great Job. We have limited capacity and can only accept a small portion of the startups or other companies who approach us for representation. But we promise that if you are accepted as a client of VLG, we will use all our efforts, contacts and judgment to make your business a success.

We Are Experts in Representing Deal-Intensive Companies. Our lawyers are all top graduates from top law schools and are recognized throughout Silicon Valley as being among the best at what we do. We are experts in helping young technology companies grow, prosper and avoid legal problems and have worked with dozens of companies from startup through the initial public offering and beyond. We specialize in securities law (venture capital financing, public offerings and underwritings), mergers and acquisitions and complex corporate partnership transactions. We will provide you with a list of client references. Feel free to contact them.

We Are Responsive. We promise to return your phone calls and messages quickly. We will keep you posted on projects and deadlines and will welcome your input on priorities. We will ask you to respond to periodic client satisfaction questionnaires to see how we're doing.

We Write Agreements in English. You'll find our agreements are short, complete, and understandable. Shorter, clearer agreements are tougher rather than easier to do. If something isn't clear, ask us to explain it.

We Have Technical and Business Backgrounds. Although being an engineer or having a business background isn't a requirement for a good business lawyer, it helps. Most of us worked prior to law school and have background in computer science, civil engineering, mathematics, market research, accounting, finance, the life sciences and other fields. The academic background of the lawyers serving you and their work experiences will be provided to you.

We Choose Our Clients as Carefully as They Choose Us. Our firm isn't for everyone. We represent clients, particularly technology companies and investors, where our brand of total commitment, partnership and expertise will add the greatest value. We typically have an ownership stake in the companies we represent. We request that we be allowed to attend board meetings. We educate all our employees on who our clients are and what they do. We believe this familiarity with our clients motivates our employees to provide better service. We are making an investment in a relationship that we hope will pay off for client and law firm alike. We get excited about what our clients are trying to do and want to be active participants in helping build your business!

(continues)

EXHIBIT 1 About VLG *(continued)*

We Are Highly Automated. Visit our firm and you'll see what we mean. Our goal is to be the most highly automated firm in the United States, and we're well on our way. Labor is very expensive in law firms (salaries for attorneys and staff account for most of the operating expenses), so we think it's only logical to leverage the talent of our best people through extensive automation training and systems. You'll notice the effect of our automation in our high quality work, our rapid turnaround, and our cost effectiveness.

We Strive for Zero Voluntary Attorney Turnover. We try to provide meaningful career paths for all our attorneys in order to minimize the client disruption and problems created by high attorney turnover often found at larger law firms. We promote beginning attorneys who meet our tough grading standards to senior attorneys in four or five years and to directors two to three years after that, giving them early and real feedback on how they're doing. We want to attract the best attorneys and keep them, for the benefit of our clients.

We Are Flexible and Fair in How We Bill. We provide full itemized billing information on all bills, including people working on the account, their hours and rates and detailed descriptions of what they did. We expect our clients to advance any significant out-of-pocket expenses such as filing fees and to sign our standard legal services agreement. We do not bill for routine phone and fax charges, routine photocopying, word processing and the like (they're included in our rates). Large copying or other jobs will be sent to an outside service or will be billed by us at cost. On certain transactions where we are able to estimate accurately the approximate amount of legal work involved, we are willing to quote fixed fees in writing. We expect prompt payment of our bills, but are flexible in timing of payment if a company has not yet received funding. In short, we want to treat our clients fairly and to be treated fairly ourselves.

Source: VLG webpage, www.vlg.com, accessed on February 10, 2000.

thing we can do to help our firm better retain our employees? Is zero voluntary turnover possible?

CRAIG JOHNSON

Craig Johnson grew up in Arcadia, California, and attended Yale University, where he majored in Russian history and took several courses in computer science. Upon graduation in 1968, he entered the Peace Corps, traveling to Ethiopia to teach high school English for two years. "After returning from the Peace Corps in 1970," he recalled,

I took a job as a systems programmer with Burroughs in Pasadena in early 1970. I applied to both law schools and computer science PhD programs. After being admitted to

several schools, I reflected on the fact that all the good management jobs at Burroughs seemed to go to people with JDs or MBAs, and not to the engineers. So I ultimately chose Stanford Law School because I believed I would have greater career choices as a lawyer and wanted to return to the West Coast.

During his first two years at Stanford, Johnson "was mostly interested in environmental law," and was president of the Stanford Law School Environmental Law Society, and externed for a semester at the Natural Resources Defense Council's new office in Palo Alto. He was very close to accepting a job with the Bureau of Land Management of the U.S. Department of Justice, but ultimately grew disillusioned with environmental law, "since much of it seemed so negative to me, suing to block projects based on the pretext of an inadequate environmental impact statement."

"To be near my parents," Johnson recalled,

I took a job at a small, 25-lawyer, Los Angeles corporate law firm, Parker Milliken Kohlmeier Clark & O'Hara, in the summer after my second year. There I had the chance to work with some small San Diego software companies for one of the partners. I loved the work and client contact. When I returned to Stanford I realized there were a number of similar companies nearby in what was just starting to be called Silicon Valley. The largest law firm in Palo Alto at the time was 10 attorneys. I interviewed with all of them and ultimately decided to join Wilson Mosher & Sonsini as attorney number 11. When I started in September 1974 the stockmarket was headed straight down, to 500. It wasn't obvious I had made the right choice.

Johnson's career progressed rapidly at the firm, renamed Wilson, Sonsini, Goodrich, and Rosati (WSG&R) in 1978, apace with the firm's earning a reputation as a legal powerhouse. Under the tutelage of John Wilson and Larry Sonsini, Johnson earned the respect of his colleagues and early-stage entrepreneurs, eventually garnering a seat on the executive committee, his own 15-lawyer fiefdom, and an annual draw of $1.1 million.[1] He was widely regarded by entrepreneurs as someone who could be counted on to help with financing and management recruitment as well as deal structuring, his "platinum rolodex" reflecting a number of deep relationships with the venture capital community. By the early 1990s, it was clear, according to venture capitalist Richard Kramlich of Menlo Park's New Enterprise Associates (NEA), that Johnson "was really the number two person at WSG&R."[2] In 1992 *California Lawyer* named Johnson a member of its all-California legal "dream team." (See Exhibit 2 for Johnson's biography).

His stellar reputation and seven-figure income notwithstanding, Johnson gradually became discouraged with the direction WSG&R's business was going. Twice he tried and failed to convince his colleagues to open a satellite office on Sand Hill Road, near 75 of the leading venture capital firms. Many of his colleagues were averse to the idea of a branch office a mere five miles from

EXHIBIT 2 **Craig Johnson Biography**

Venture Law Group chairman Craig Johnson graduated magna cum laude from Yale in 1968, spent two years teaching with the Peace Corps in Ethiopia, and subsequently worked as a systems programmer for Burroughs Corporation in Pasadena. After graduating from Stanford Law School in 1974, he joined the Palo Alto law firm of Wilson, Mosher & Sonsini (later Wilson, Sonsini, Goodrich & Rosati). Johnson left WSG&R in 1993 with 13 other attorneys to start VLG, which subsequently grew to 95 attorneys and included among its clients companies such as Yahoo!, eToys, Chemdex, Netcentives, and Phone.com.

Besides co-founding VLG, Johnson was the co-founder of several other companies, including Garage.com, Financial Engines, and Grassroots.com (where he was the acting CEO).

Johnson was recognized in 1986 by the *San Jose Mercury News* as one of Silicon Valley's "rising stars," named as a member of *California Lawyer's* all-California legal "dream team" in 1992, and identified by *Business Week* in 1997 as one of Silicon Valley's top 25 "movers and shakers" and by *Red Herring* in 1999 as one of Silicon Valley's top nine "power brokers." He lived with his three sons in Portola Valley, California, and was active in a number of community activities, including DayTop Village, Inc. and The Exploratorium.

Source: VLG.

headquarters.[3] Johnson had also been concerned by turnover and growth at WSG&R. Growth from 10 to roughly 250 lawyers during his 18 years there, together with the expansion and maturation of companies on the client roster, had diluted the firm's focus on the early-stage companies that were Johnson's practice and passion.[4] Moreover, the size of the partnership had prevented Johnson from guaranteeing promotion to his star subordinates and some consequently left. Johnson began to perceive a philosophical difference between himself and Sonsini: "Larry," he recalled, "wanted to follow clients up the food chain. He wanted to create a firm that could do everything, high or low end, in all practice areas. Wilson, Sonsini has a chance to be the best traditional firm ever. They have a great future. But I wanted to do something different and avoid becoming a traditional pyramidal structure."

DREAMING OF A NEW TYPE OF FIRM

Johnson recalled feeling "very depressed" after failing in his second attempt, in August 1992, to launch the Sand Hill Road office and seeing yet another key associate decide to leave WSG&R. "I went to bed on a Friday evening," he recalled,

> and had a dream. I got up around five A.M. the next morning and, still in my pajamas, sat at the dining room table and wrote it all down, amassing 15 single-spaced pages by dawn. The process was like taking dictation; I wasn't passionate about it because it didn't seem quite real. In fact, I was deeply skeptical about the dream's central theme of launching a new firm; I was not about to throw away a million dollar-plus annual income from a firm I loved and had helped to build for 18 years without a lot of investigation. But obviously my mind had been processing a lot of the issues subconsciously. My former partners at Wilson, Sonsini later pointed out that many of the ideas for VLG

had been ones I had suggested to the executive committee at Wilson, Sonsini almost a decade earlier.

Johnson's vision of the new firm was a pure-play on technology start-ups, a firm that would leverage technology instead of associates to allow partners to get deeply involved in their clients' business issues. Johnson began to discuss his idea with close friends and partners. "The few partners in my group with whom I discussed the idea," he recalled, "were immediately enthusiastic. So gradually I started to take the idea more seriously. However, we didn't finally decide to leave Wilson, Sonsini until mid-January 1993."

On February 2, 1993, two days after WSG&R paid bonuses to his group, Johnson announced his resignation to the executive committee. Reading a statement, "resignation isn't something I've been thinking about for a long time," Johnson remarked. "I went to bed on a Friday evening with no idea about leaving the firm and woke with the reasons for leaving fully formed in my mind. . . . The conclusion now seems inevitable."[5] The reaction of the WSG&R partners, according to Johnson, was "utter and complete shock. No one," he observed, "had seen this coming. I had been very well compensated and regarded. People knew me as one of the primary 'boosters' of the firm. They thought a law firm not engaged in litigation and a broader portfolio of law would surely die. They figured I must have been mentally imbalanced to throw away 18 years and a seven-figure income from Wilson, Sonsini."

The *National Law Journal* wrote that Johnson's resignation "sent shock waves through Silicon Valley." But Johnson was sure he wanted to pursue wholeheartedly his own vision. "I loved Wilson, Sonsini," he emphasized, "but I had a dream of a different business model and I couldn't turn to Wilson, Sonsini to execute it. It was a massive risk for me. If VLG hadn't worked out, I'd probably be in a sleeping bag on a San Francisco street."

Thirteen of the 14 lawyers in Johnson's group, including all of the partners, as well as 20 other employees close to the group, resigned with Johnson. They took many elements of the WSG&R cultural heritage with them. "We wanted," explained Johnson, "the same culture of excellence, valuing excellent legal work, which John Wilson and Larry Sonsini had instilled in me. We wanted to continue investing in clients; Wilson, Sonsini had been investing since the late 1960s. And, most important, we wanted to maintain the tradition of treating people well."

The key uncertainty was whether clients would also migrate to VLG. "With the exception of two senior clients who were close personal friends, I had not discussed the plans for VLG with any clients prior to my resignation," recalled Johnson.

"Somewhere between a Traditional Law Firm and a Venture-Capital Firm"

Johnson based the new firm's business model on the framework of a venture-backed start-up. "We are," he emphasized, "part investment bank, law firm, VC fund, and consultant." The name said as much. Rather than proclaim the names of its founding partners, the moniker Venture Law Group evoked the nature of the practice. As a pure-play on technology start-ups, the business model was radically different from that which characterized traditional law practices.

"Many traditional firms do not consider start-ups good clients since they are a higher risk not to pay fees," Johnson explained. "We, however, consider entrepreneurs to be the most interesting, most challenging, and most profitable clients. We want our model to appeal to entrepreneurs."

A significant percentage of compensation, for VLG as for WSG&R and other Silicon Valley firms that advised start-up ventures, took the form of equity investments in clients.[b] "Because we're so involved early on in the business as well as the legal strategy," a VLG partner explained, "we like

to participate on a financial basis."[6] "Clients," according to VLG senior attorney Laurel Finch, "appreciate the fact that, by investing, we're on the team; plus, they're used to it now and have come to expect it."

Trumpeting its goal to be the "most highly automated firm in the United States," VLG exploited technological automation fully to enhance efficiency and reduce client costs (see Exhibit 1). VLG enlisted all of its attorneys to create a comprehensive set of on-line forms and annotations that covered all aspects of VLG's practice and hired full-time "research and development" attorneys whose sole responsibility was to research legal topics and maintain the automated forms system, thereby significantly reducing the time taken to perform legal tasks. VLG also developed a system that afforded the firm's lawyers desktop access to all firm financial data, including current billings and collections. Lawyers recorded on-line their time, as well as detailed information on all firm clients. VLG also provided its lawyers with home computers and high-speed DSL lines through which they could access the firm's network.[7]

Philosophy and Core Values

Johnson credited the book *Built to Last,* which he described as the "best business book I ever read," with "confirming our early vision for the firm. It exactly describes," he explained, "what we're trying to do. Our core values are our DNA."[c] "We hadn't identified our core values," he recalled. "*Built to Last* said all visionary companies had core values, so, at a VLG retreat at Pebble Beach, we tried to identify what ours were. Six people raised their hands and we listed their suggestions in order of the hands raised. We looked at the list and said, 'That's who we are.' It took us a total of 10 minutes!" (Exhibit 3 lists VLG's core values.)

"Most firms choose a superstar model where a junior attorney needs to latch on to a 'superstar'

[b] Equity interests, however, were not in lieu of hourly fees.
[c] James C. Collins and Jerry I. Porras, *Built to Last: Successful Habits of Visionary Companies,* Harper Collins: New York, 1994.

EXHIBIT 3   VLG Core Values

We want to provide an ever-increasing level of service and value to our clients.

We value partnership and teamwork in working toward common goals and are not overly hierarchical or formal.

We want to be the best at what we do and attract the best clients. We want to hire and retain the best attorneys and the best staff.

We are innovative and value innovation as an end in itself

Family and fun are important to us.

We want to provide opportunities for all VLG employees to meet their personal objectives.

Source: VLG.

partner in order to rise in the firm," observed a recently promoted director.

> At VLG, we have an entrepreneurial approach in which we're rewarded for building up our practices. We don't have to be a pyramidal structure, which often promotes the wrong behaviors. Also, we reward responsibility credits instead of origination credits when determining annual compensation. Origination credits create a zero-sum game. I hate to compete against my teammates. Responsibility credits encourage us to help each other out and share client responsibility.

Early Struggles

Initially, VLG struggled financially, going without compensation for the first six months as expenses, start-up costs, and investments soaked up much of the firm's early revenues. Johnson recalled of this time that he and the other partners "were very concerned with our survival. We were anxious," he added, "about our junior partners with young kids and mortgages. I felt a heavy responsibility to them."[8] But once VLG began to build its client roster, according to Johnson "we started to pay ourselves and then make up the back pay. We also added Jim Brock and two others from Wilson, Sonsini to our team, giving us a total of 17 attor-

neys. Later that year, 15 attorneys joined us from Morrison & Foerster."

In early 1995, VLG's business suddenly took off. Recalled Johnson: "We had expected that maybe 50 percent of our former clients at Wilson, Sonsini would dribble over to us. In fact, only 2 out of 100 did not come. It was no disrespect to Wilson, Sonsini; it was a testament to the bond we developed based on our service. Clients told us, 'You're our team. We've been with you for eight years.'"

VLG also began to get cold calls from the general counsels (GCs) of major companies, among them, Intel, which had heard about VLG's staffing structure and sought to retain the company to handle one to two deals per month. "VLG's model is, I think, a model for the future in the emerging technology niche," remarked Intel's GC.[9]

VLG soon faced much more work than it could handle. By mid-1995, recalled Johnson, "we were in the middle of a full-fledged crisis." Added director Don Keller: "We were so swamped: the only way we could survive was by turning down deals. Otherwise, we were going to kill ourselves and kill our associates."[10] VLG was aided in August 1995 by the immigration of Joshua Green and 10 other attorneys from Brobeck, Phleger & Harrison to VLG. Remarked Johnson, who was buoyed by this third wave of attorneys joining the firm, "Josh had been a longtime friend and respected competitor. He was the only non–Wilson, Sonsini attorney I considered for VLG when we started. I actually had dinner with him the night before my resignation announcement. After two years of dinners, mostly just exchanging ideas, Josh decided to join VLG. I was thrilled." But the addition of another major rainmaker exacerbated, not alleviated, the problem of too much work.

Establishing Focus

A financially successful 1995 notwithstanding, Johnson worried that VLG might have strayed from its alternative model of focusing on start-ups. Flattered by the opportunities, it had accepted assignments from big-name companies such as Intel

Corporation and Goldman Sachs, diluting emphasis on start-up ventures. At the same time, some partners were taking on several high-risk projects. The number of unfunded start-ups it was already handling was affecting how many more VLG could accept.[11]

To keep VLG focused on its mission, Johnson and the other partners decided to centralize the client selection process. In lieu of individual partners unilaterally accepting business, a New Business Committee (NBC), a group of five rotating attorneys, was to review all proposals and accept only those it determined (a) would bring in high-quality work, (b) had a good chance of paying off, and (c) were consistent with the firm's mission. (Exhibit 4 depicts the NBC's selection matrix.)

EXHIBIT 4   VLG's New Business Committee: Selection Matrix

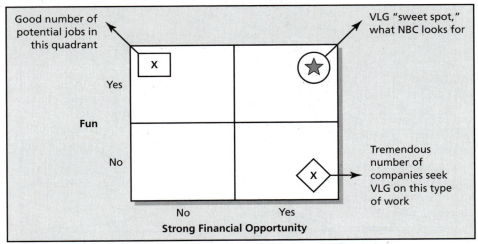

VLG's Goals

We want to . . .

- work with fewer companies per attorney;
- have more fun;
- add more value;
- spend less time;
- earn more money;

. . . than other law firms.

"The NBC set a higher threshold for client acceptance," recalled Johnson.

It was scary initially to say no to prestigious firms. Many other law firms thought we were crazy to turn away work. But we needed to say no to survive. Our people were overworked. After saying no a few times, clients began to compete to get us. It benefited us that we were more selective. Some clients started issuing press releases to say we accepted them. It was a badge of honor for them.

Although it took some decision-making authority away from them, the NBC was generally welcomed by VLG directors. Remarked one: "I think we have much less marginal work now . . . the type of work that tends to drive an attorney crazy." (See Exhibit 5.) Junior attorneys were grateful because the NBC eliminated much of the drudgery that accompanied low-end work. Even large firms appreciated VLG's rationale for restricting client acceptance. Stated Oracle Corporation's GC: "Unlike other firms that will take anything that comes in the door as long as it's paying, they really want to make sure that they serve their clients well."

EXHIBIT 5 **VLG Target Market**

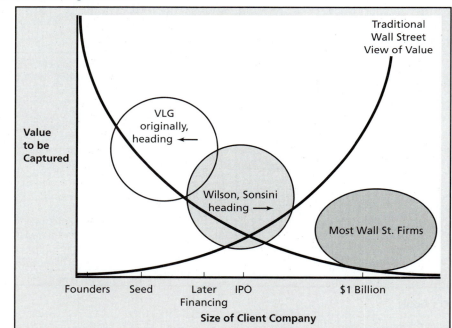

Lawyers' Experience

Seed
- High emphasis on judgment
- Risky
- Equity

Huge Client
- Uncreative
- Low margin
- Low fun
- Dehumanizing
- Attorneys as commodities

"We currently accept less than 5 percent of the companies that approach us for representation," emphasized Johnson. "We want the best, but not the most, companies as clients. 'Best' means the ones with the greatest financial and innovation potential. Companies brought to us as completed packages—financing, management, strategy, etc.—aren't as interesting to us as companies with missing pieces, which we can help to supply." (Exhibit 6 plots VLG market share; Exhibit 7 describes VLG "Game Plan.")

One of the clients that did make it past the NBC selection process was Yahoo! Johnson explained how VLG developed a relationship with Yahoo! founder Jerry Yang.

> Jerry was bored with his PhD and his main hobby was with the World Wide Web. He told us that he and one of his friends collected website links and posted them. He wanted to brainstorm about how to make it a business. Jim Brock had several meetings with the company founders, meetings for which VLG never charged a fee. We asked if he was trying to be the yellow pages of the web. We asked if there was anything proprietary in the business and we agreed that

there wasn't. But we all thought it was a really interesting idea. So we introduced them to Sequoia Capital, which put in $1 million for 25 percent of the company. VLG invested $30 thousand. If we had continued to hold it, today it would be worth $100 million.[d]

As word of VLG's business model spread, entrepreneurs began to show up at VLG headquarters sans appointments to try to be "discovered" by Johnson.[12] Many of the firm's attorneys compared these entrepreneurs to aspiring actors arriving in Hollywood.[13] Between 1996 and 1999, VLG continued to experience rapid growth in profits, professionals, and clients. It helped launch Yahoo!, eToys, Chemdex, and Netcentives, among many other firms. (Exhibit 8 presents VLG's growth figures.)

VLG's Value-Creation Cycle

"The key focus of VLG is client service, not market share," explained Johnson.

> We're trying to be the best at providing coaching and legal advice to high-potential, early-stage companies.[14] We have far fewer

EXHIBIT 6 **Top Law Firms Competing for Venture-Backed, High-Tech Clients (1996–1Q 1997)**

Firm	Office	Market Share (%)
Wilson, Sonsini, Goodrich & Rosati	Palo Alto	11.2
Cooley Godward Castro Huddleson & Tatum	Palo Alto	6.4
Brobeck, Phleger & Harrison	San Francisco	4.6
Venture Law Group	Menlo Park	4.3
Fenwick & West	San Francisco, Palo Alto	2.6
Hale & Dorr	Boston	2.5
Gray, Cary, Ware & Freidenrich	San Diego, Palo Alto	2.3
Gunderson, Dettmer, Stough, Villeneuve, Franklin & Hachigian	Menlo Park	2.2

Sources: VentureOne; Alex Gove, "Nine of High Tech's Top Power Brokers. And They're Not VCs," *Red Herring*, October 1999, p. 114.

[d] The firm owned 1 percent of Yahoo, but sold its stake for approximately $2 per share shortly before the company's initial public offering. (Alex Gove, "Nine of High Tech's Top Power Brokers. And They're Not VCs," *Red Herring*, October 1999, p. 114.)

EXHIBIT 7   **Venture Law Group "The Game Plan"**

Mission

- To be the premier service provider for select technology start-ups providing legal, business, and strategic advice and assistance

Core Values

- Remain focused and concentrate our efforts on areas of legal service where we can provide exceptional value
- Insist on excellence and seek constantly to improve the quality, usefulness, and value of our services to our clients
- Provide an environment where our employees can have productive lives and careers and reasonable risks and make significant investments to accomplish our goals
- Provide opportunity for individual growth, creativity, and career satisfaction in the achievement of our established goals
- Create a set of values and culture which will assure VLG's continued success and enable it to founders and future generations
- Meet our obligations of good citizenship in our community

Value Proposition

What are we selling?	Access (seed capital, VC, bankers, strategic partners) Creativity (strategy; solve problems) Execution (deals) Experience (legal, deal, business)

Comparison with Traditional ("Bricks and Mortar") Law Firms

	VLG	Traditional Law Firm
Vision	Premier service provider for select technology start-ups from inception through major transactions	Premier law firm for technology companies
Ideal client	High-profile start-up, large equity position requiring small number of billable hours (e.g., Hotmail, BabyCenter, Lightera, Garage.com)	High profile, public company paying large legal fees (e.g., Cisco, Intel, Microsoft, Sun Microsystems)
Economics	Equity with acceptable cash	Cash with minimal equity (if shared by all partners)
Service offering	Strategic services only; partner with other law firms (e.g., Orrick) to increase equity with minimal dilution	Full service; giving up legal revenue is heresy
Internal politics	Consensus; most partners generate substantial equity	Tension; few partners (less than 1/9th) generate substantial equity
Organization	Small and focused	Large and leveraged
Marketing	Established VLG brand name consistent with the vision	Mixed message
Associate opportunity	Intensive training and opportunity to implement the value migration strategy; equity opportunity	Great legal training; may provide some start-up work (but it will be a small percentage of total workload)

Source: VLG.

EXHIBIT 8 VLG's Growth (1993–1999)

Year	Revenues ($MM)	Attorneys
1993	3.0	14
1994	6.0	27
1995	13.0	45
1996	20.0	60
1997	26.0	70
1998	41.0	80
1999	53.0	95

Source: VLG.

companies per attorney than our competitors. We try to have a cycle in which we meet many possible clients, select start-ups that we feel have high potential, add value by helping to "package" them, get equity right, help them build the company and become successful, and then get compensated well. To do this, the fee model doesn't work. We need equity.

We focus on advising deal-intensive, high-tech companies in the early phases of development and seek to handle only corporate matters, with an emphasis on complex securities transactions. To do this, we need to be highly automated and to stay relatively small, never expanding beyond 75 lawyers in one office.

VLG developed its revenue model to appeal to clients that lacked free cash to cover legal fees. VLG could be counted on to devote substantial time, from a few weeks to a few months, to developing a business plan and financing strategy for a struggling venture, at no cost to the client until it received financing.[15] "Since many come to us before they receive funding," Johnson explained, "we only turn the meter on when we actually get down to doing substantive legal work, as opposed to business counseling." VLG sometimes entered into delayed-payment or modified-fee-agreement deals with startup clients attempting to secure financing.

Given its emphasis on start-ups, VLG's lawyers often became heavily involved in the planning phase of client ventures, sometimes even before a client company had a name. During the start-up phase, VLG often helped clients to structure stock and options packages to attract specific investors, and introduced clients to prospective investors and board members.[16] According to Johnson, much of VLG's coaching occurred in this stage.

We believe in the ideas of our clients and often will become core members of their teams, helping them execute critical projects. The decisions that start-ups make in their first few months are critical. Getting started is a lot like launching a rocket. If the rocket is a tenth of a degree off at launch, it can end up 1,000 miles off downrange. For example, although start-ups often have a difficult time allocating equity to their employees, they have even more problems deciding how and when to raise financing. Only a small percentage of the companies that approach us have already received venture funding, and we often play an active role in helping them secure initial financing. Almost 100 percent of our start-up clients eventually receive venture funding. Many of our biggest client successes, some of which are multi-billion dollar companies today, give VLG a lot of credit for their success.[17]

Once client companies were funded and up and running, VLG handled only what Johnson termed "the fun stuff": securities, mergers and acquisitions, and other transactional legal work. VLG preferred to delegate more routine legal help to an in-house GC or another firm. "Our active outsourcing of business to our competitors," remarked Johnson, "sends most traditional lawyers into fantasyland. They think we've got it all wrong. But you have to understand our strategy. We don't want to staff up to represent the IBMs. I had plenty of opportunity to do that kind of work at Wilson, Sonsini, and I didn't like it. "[18]

Internal Organization

VLG had three tiers of attorneys. Of 80 attorneys at the end of 1998, 21 were directors, 13 senior attorneys, and 46 associates. Johnson explained career progression at VLG.

Initially, attorneys take four to five years before being promoted to senior attorney through an up-or-out process. Senior attorney is a badge of honor, a permanent tenure spot. It involves a major bump in compensation and they can participate in the stock investment program. Senior attorney was a novel concept at the time in law firms. We modeled it on investment banks. After a few years, senior attorneys are promoted to directors.

Annually, 40 percent of junior attorneys' 1,900 to 2,100 billable hours was allocated to one director's team, 40 percent to another, and 20 percent to entrepreneurial time, for which attorneys chose the director with which to work.[19] Directors averaged fifteen clients and each client engagement usually involved a director, senior attorney, junior attorney, and paralegal.

"In our first few years here," explained one junior attorney,

we must engage in the "necessary evil" of learning transaction and legal techniques. While I'd rather be providing more value-added counseling, like the firm is known for, I understand the desire to make us well-schooled attorneys. Without this legal knowledge we'd likely fall into the trap of becoming "BSers" like many other lawyers. It is frustrating sometimes, however, when friends from school or others in my personal network call me and want to talk about their start-up. I'd love to spend more of my time helping them out.

Attorneys, senior attorneys, and directors were expected to become deeply involved with each client's business. VLG's focus on seed-stage companies had organizational benefits, according to Johnson. "We've flattened the traditional pyramidal law firm staffing model, which can work if your client is IBM, but when you're working with an early stage company they want more partner and senior-attorney time." Owing to VLG's low ratio of partners to associates, new attorneys assumed more responsibility earlier. VLG's attorneys were also able to avoid some of the problems associated with serving mammoth clients. "Big companies have a tendency to treat their lawyers like socket wrenches," remarked Johnson. "That is the antithesis of what we want to do at VLG."[20] VLG's senior lawyers were limited to advising 15 to 20 companies at one time compared to the 30 to 50 companies a partner at a more traditional firm might service.[21]

Compensation

Employee compensation included a base salary and a profit sharing bonus. Points were reallocated to every attorney yearly by a rotating compensation committee, which by policy could never include the chairman. For receptionists and other employees, most compensation came from their base salary. For senior directors, over 80 percent of compensation came from profit-sharing points.

Remarked Johnson:

We seek to pay our people at or above the highest level of comparable compensation among our major Silicon Valley competitors. We expect that in the near future VLG attorneys will earn more than lawyers at almost any other law firm in the United States, including partners in the major Wall Street firms. We won't earn as much as partners in successful VC funds, and there may be a few GCs that do better. But VLG attorneys will do better than almost every other attorney, especially given the benefits of having an investment portfolio of such opportunities rather than betting on a single company.

VLG set senior attorney base compensation close to that of new partners to discourage attrition.

Junior attorneys' salaries were competitive. "Cash flow is not an issue in this job," remarked one. "However, my wife is VP of Human Resources at a start-up. Many of my friends also work in start-ups. It would be great if we had options here, like my wife and everyone else has at start-ups."

Everyone, from junior secretaries to senior partners, received a slice of VLG's profits via the profit-sharing bonus plan. Four times annually, at the end of each quarter, the firm subtracted its expenses and overhead from its revenues and divided what was left. "It's very exciting," enthused fifth-year associate Sharon Hendricks. "We get together and everyone talks about how the firm has done in the last quarter. Then they distribute the checks."[22] "I have no idea how many points others have," remarked one attorney, "but I had 3,000 when I joined three years ago; I have 21,000 now. The firm does a projection each year of what it thinks a point will be worth. If it's worth $1 next quarter, I'll get a check for over $20,000!" (Exhibit 9 tracks VLG's point bonus history.)

VLG's investment fund (VLGI) constituted the third part of attorney compensation. Partners and senior attorneys contributed pro-rata shares of their net distributions in the form of loans to the investment fund, which purchased small equity positions (usually investments of between $10,000 and $25,000 per company) in VLG client companies before they went public.[23] A director who personally brought in a particular client personally invested 10 to 20 percent, VLGI the remaining 80 percent to 90 percent, of the total invested. As inside advisors, VLG lawyers were bound by a standard lockup period that prevented them from trading pre-offering shares within 180 days of a public offering. Because most of VLG's stock holdings were classified as "restricted securities," SEC rules required VLG to hold its pre-offering shares for at least one year.[24] Whereas a typical venture capital firm backed 10 to 20 new companies per year, VLGI invested in more than 200 companies in its first five years. In 1998, its total distribution was $3 million. "In 1999," Johnson estimated, "it should be in the neighborhood of $30 million. In 2000, we think it may approach $100 million."

THE CHALLENGE OF ATTORNEY RETENTION

Johnson's views on turnover bordered on obsessive. He cited turnover as "one of the major reasons I left Wilson, Sonsini. Clients benefit from long-term relationships with their attorney team," he emphasized.

EXHIBIT 9 VLG Point Bonuses

VLG shared its profits with all employees by paying out earnings each quarter based on the number of "points" employees held. VLG annually forecasted the point value for planning purposes. At the end of each quarter, the Executive Committee determined the amount of profit that was distributable as point payouts, thus determining value per point. Point value fluctuated from year to year based on the market for legal services and expenses. The number of points attorneys held increased annually with their salaries. Over time, points became a more significant portion of total compensation.

Year	Annual Budgeted Amount	Actual Payout	Actual Value Based on 1,000 Points
1996	$1.55	$2.05	$2,050
1997	$1.85	$2.13	$2,130
1998	$2.13	$3.25	$3,250
1999	$2.60	$4.53	$4,530

Source: VLG.

Many of our clients didn't realize how attached they became working with the same attorneys year after year. Since law is an information business, it is inefficient for clients to lose information that is stored in peoples' heads. When someone left the firm, a dozen gaping holes of information opened up in the practice. Service could fall off a cliff. It takes a different type of firm to focus on retention. I view turnover as a piece of metal in acid, destroying what we've spent a hard time building. I take pride in recruiting people and holding them.

VLG's focus on emerging companies made turnover more of an issue. Attrition for any reason was especially disruptive to emerging companies, which, owing to their tight launch timelines, could ill-afford redundancies or readjustments. "Clients are not happy when we need to restaff," observed Johnson. "It's really destructive to client service because all the legal knowledge and history of the company disappear with the attorney and the new attorney and the company start at ground zero again. There's no way to make it positive from the client's point of view."

Frequent staffing changes arising from attorney turnover might be interpreted as a lack of concern for client relationships or a sign of organizational instability. In addition to its negative effects on client service, turnover hurt VLG internally as well, incurring costs associated with hiring and training new attorneys and lost productivity as a consequence of vacant positions. Observed attorney Laurel Finch, "Turnover affects morale, because when friends leave it makes everyone unhappy. Also, because we staff leanly, turnover kills those forced to pick up the slack." Johnson echoed Finch's comments.

I believe turnover is extremely expensive for the firm and many of its most significant costs are hidden ones. It's not just the headhunter fees we pay to recruit replacements and the loss of productivity, it's the loss of information about clients and their history

and businesses. Turnover degrades the level of service a law firm can provide its clients. Clients hate it, too, but have come to accept it as inevitable. We haven't.

Reasons for Attorney Turnover at VLG

VLG had experienced moderate levels of turnover (see Exhibit 10). "The most frequent reason a person leaves VLG is to work for a company as in-house counsel or in business development," reported senior attorney Keith Miller. "Very seldom do attorneys choose to leave VLG for other law firms." Added Finch: "The main reason people take a GC job at a start-up is the money. For example, one third-year associate left here to go to Babycenter. About 20 seconds after joining he was worth $4 million."

As for management-initiated attorney turnover, Johnson remarked that "a quarter to a third have left for performance reasons. We take our reviews very seriously," he emphasized. "The reviews are fair and constructive. We've had a number of attorneys who have bounced back from poor reviews to become stars. But those who accumulate a number of bad reviews are asked to leave. VLG is like a cult," Johnson continued. "A new attorney either starts to 'get it' and becomes more excited or doesn't. We can tell when someone has figured us out. It's like joining an academic fraternity or sorority or a guild."

About 10–20 percent of VLG turnover was motivated by external personal considerations, according to Johnson. "I do my best to encourage them to stay," he reflected. "For example, Mary Beth Younger, a fabulous associate, moved to Sioux Falls where her husband got a position managing a $100 million hedge fund. She wanted to follow him, considering the opportunity that her husband faced. But we installed a high-speed connection to allow her to continue working with us by telecommuting."

Johnson emphasized that he was the most troubled when attorneys left "because they thought they were getting a better deal elsewhere." Com-

EXHIBIT 10   Venture Law Group Turnover (January 1997–December 1999)

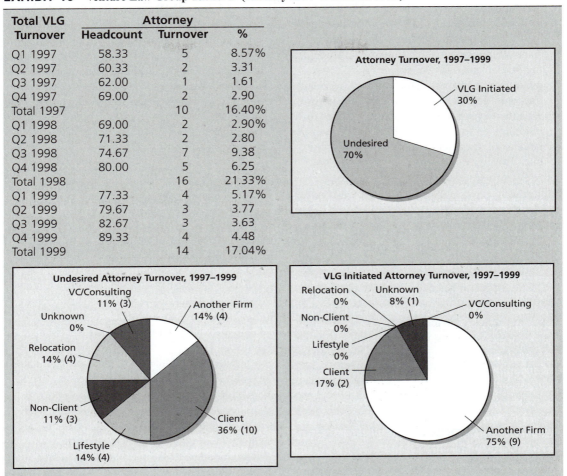

Total VLG Turnover	Headcount	Attorney Turnover	%
Q1 1997	58.33	5	8.57%
Q2 1997	60.33	2	3.31
Q3 1997	62.00	1	1.61
Q4 1997	69.00	2	2.90
Total 1997		10	16.40%
Q1 1998	69.00	2	2.90%
Q2 1998	71.33	2	2.80
Q3 1998	74.67	7	9.38
Q4 1998	80.00	5	6.25
Total 1998		16	21.33%
Q1 1999	77.33	4	5.17%
Q2 1999	79.67	3	3.77
Q3 1999	82.67	3	3.63
Q4 1999	89.33	4	4.48
Total 1999		14	17.04%

Source: VLG.

petition for talented employees from non–law-focused businesses was particularly acute in Silicon Valley because of the concentration of emerging businesses and business-related services offering lucrative opportunities to experienced individuals. Headhunters for venture capital firms, top consulting firms, and investment banks approached VLG attorneys, some of whom chose to give up law in favor of a business interest.

"Money is not an issue in Silicon Valley," remarked Johnson.

Plenty of money can be found here. We exist in an unbelievable cauldron of opportunity where people can literally make fortunes overnight. Take the case of Mike Jacobson who left [VLG competitor] Cooley Godward to join eBay as general counsel. Nine months later he already had equity worth $100 million!

The downside to VLG being the leading law firm representing high-growth, early-stage companies is that other firms keep tugging at our talented people. As a result, our attorneys are constantly exposed to great opportunities. Especially young attorneys with many years ahead of them can afford to put chips on the roulette wheel. If the companies fail, they figure they can always come back to VLG.

Some turnover was triggered by diverging views of what VLG's business model should be in the future. Some directors sought to ensure that the firm's client base remained sufficiently diversified to guarantee continuing cash flow and low equity risk. Other directors wanted VLG to place even greater emphasis on working with seed-stage firms. The pace of growth, too, was often an issue. Attorneys tended to perceive VLG to be growing either too quickly or too slowly. Observed Johnson, "Young attorneys want support as they become more senior, which necessitates growth. But as our equity investments become more important, some people are beginning to perceive growth as dilution."[25]

Johnson's Approach to Minimizing Voluntary Turnover

Johnson's approach to those considering leaving for a start-up was to emphasize VLG's diversified portfolio and variety of challenges versus the riskiness and monotony of entrepreneurial ventures. The argument offered sufficient reason for many attorneys to stay. "Each attorney over a five-year period gets the opportunity in aggregate to invest in a number of companies that would surpass your investment if you joined one company," noted attorney Keith Miller. "We don't have to build a better mousetrap or create a better product to be the entrepreneur. And yet we are rewarded like entrepreneurs."

VLG also sought ways to reduce attorney workloads. "While we work as hard as other firms, we are doing everything we can to reduce work," explained Johnson. "We recognize that we can improve retention by doing this. For example, we recently limited the number of companies any attorney can work on and are strongly encouraging directors to outplace less interesting work to other law firms. We hope in the future to make much more money doing much less work than at other law firms."

Recruiting

Selection and recruitment of new associates was particularly critical. "Our zero voluntary turnover goal can be helped by diligence in the recruiting stage," Johnson emphasized.

Despite all our other activities, we want to be a law firm. We'll always recruit from the top 10 percent of students at Harvard, Stanford, Yale, and a few others. We want our associates to master legal skills. In our view, one can't be an excellent business advisor without being an excellent business lawyer first.

Having said that, the candidates that consider VLG often decide between VLG and Goldman Sachs or VLG and McKinsey. They seek to get heavily involved in business. They end up choosing VLG because they realize that there is no exposure to early-stage companies at places like McKinsey or Goldman. We want people with excellent records of achievement in law school who want to be business strategists and who want to learn the law fundamentals in their first few years and who want to practice law long term to master their craft.

Two recent recruits reflected on their experience with VLG. "Before being introduced to VLG, I wasn't sure that law was right for me," recalled Scott Ring, who joined the firm in 1998 after graduating from Kellogg's JD/MBA program.

I did not enjoy law school as much as business school. I found that the people who really enjoyed law school were theoretical in nature. I'm more practical. I came to Silicon Valley on a recruiting trip thinking that I'd work in a high-tech company or a VC firm. I had heard many things about VLG so I wanted to meet them. After five hours here I went to the airport and called my wife and told her this place was the one I wanted to join.

Disenchanted with law while working at Kirkland Ellis in New York City, attorney Gene Yoon moved to VLG in 1998. "While at Kirkland I never thought about staying to be a partner," he reflected.

I considered jobs in investment banking and consulting before coming to VLG. But I really wanted to work with high-technology start-ups and be out here in Silicon Valley. I figured if I would be here it would be better to go with a focused Silicon Valley firm than be part of a full-service national firm's office. VLG provided a great opportunity to do that. The business model was attractive, the place was tough, and people worked really hard. By choosing VLG I didn't leave the law, but I joined a company, too.

JOHNSON PONDERS HIS NEXT STEPS

Still reeling from the resignations of Brock and Zipp, Johnson was told by partner Mark Silverman in December 1998 that he was leaving to go to VLG client Drugstore.com as its vice president and general counsel. "The economic hurricane in Silicon Valley is creating tsunamis of wealth overnight," reflected Johnson:

Naturally, people wanted to take advantage of that. Immediately after Mark's announcement, Michael Hall, another founding director of VLG, told me he was jumping to Latham and Watkins because he wanted to practice law more than be a business advisor.

We are compensating our attorneys well, but some partners making $500,000 to $600,000 think they are working for "chump change." We are addressing the workload issues, I believe people have faith in our promises that we'll do everything in our power to have fewer companies per attorney, have more fun, add more value, do our work in less time, and earn more money that other firms.

Part of my legacy is the quality and spirit of VLG as an organization. This can only be achieved if we keep our human capital here on Sand Hill Road. Would any changes to our business model stem the tide? Or is it simply a money issue? Should we allow greater participation in the VLGI at lower levels? Or would we have many attorneys who have achieved their financial goals leaving the firm for less demanding roles elsewhere? What if people become so rich that they no longer have to work? Have I done enough to build the kind of organization I dreamed about years ago?

References

1. D. M. Osborne, "Start-Up Fever," *The American Lawyer,* July/August 1996.

2. D. M. Osborne, "When Is a Law Firm not a Law Firm?" Inc., May 1998, p. 82.

3. Osborne, "Start-Up Fever."

4. Osborne, "When Is a Law Firm not a Law Firm?"

5. Osborne, "Start-Up Fever."

6. Osborne, "When Is a Law Firm not a Law Firm?"

7. Osborne, "Start-Up Fever."

8. Ibid.

9. Ibid.

10. Ibid.

11. Ritchenya Shepherd, "Radical Plan: Turn Down Work," *The National Law Journal,* October 26, 1998.

12. Alex Gove, "Nine of High Tech's Top Power Brokers. And They're Not VCs," *Red Herring,* October 1999, p. 114.

13. Ibid.

14. Osborne, "When Is a Law Firm not a Law Firm?"

15. Ibid.

16. Osborne, "Start-Up Fever."

17. Gove, "Nine of High Tech's Top Power Brokers."

18. Osborne, "Start-Up Fever."

19. Shepherd, "Radical Plan: Turn Down Work."

20. Osborne, "Start-Up Fever."

21. Osborne, "When Is a Law Firm not a Law Firm?"

22. Osborne, "Start-Up Fever."

23. Ibid.

24. Ibid.

25. Ibid.

Serving Clients Effectively

In previous modules we have stressed that high-performing PSFs must align their systems and structures with their internal processes. Module Five emphasizes that its imperative for these internal systems and processes to be connected to the external processes of client management, competitive adaptation, and service delivery. These three external processes are at the very core of PSF success in the marketplace.

The goal of serving clients effectively is to exceed their expectations in order to create a long-term, mutually beneficial relationship. We demonstrate through these three cases that the external processes must be concerned with ensuring the promises made to clients are kept. If the competitive marketplace is changing quickly, the external client relationship process must deliver information to firm leaders to allow firms to adjust their internal processes and systems in order to serve the current market most effectively.

We also emphasize through this module that PSF leaders must balance the needs of their firm with the needs of the professional who is delivering the service and the client who is receiving the service. If the firm provides the appropriate incentives to the professional, satisfaction increases. This employee satisfaction, in turn, enhances the client service that is delivered, which creates client

This note was prepared by Professor Thomas DeLong, Professor Ashish Nanda, Dean's Research Fellow Scot Landry, and Ying Liu (MBA 2001).

loyalty. This cycle of success creates the economic value that supports the ongoing relationships within the cycle.

Most important, this cycle only works if the PSF makes and then delivers on promises made to the client. Clients' perceptions of service are then influenced by the nature of the service offered, the nature of the relationship developed, and the delivery versus the promise. Effectively managing client relationships and expectations is the key to building a sustained professional service business.

COMPETING THROUGH PROCESSES

PSFs must know how to achieve competitive advantage through service excellence and the delivery of quality products. We emphasized in Module Four that the human capital, decision-making, and knowledge management processes must be in alignment in order to create processes that compel professionals to exceed client expectations. It is also clear that in many firms there are a number of touch points between client and provider. Through effective client relationship management we know that both the provider and client win by leveraging those interactional touch points.

PSFs must increase their knowledge about client businesses and their competitive markets and simultaneously develop services and products that align with the capabilities of the professionals who provide the services. Ensuring a proper communication process to get market information into the heart of the firm will help firms adjust to better serve client needs.

SERVING CLIENTS EFFECTIVELY

This module focuses on the client service process and emphasizes just how demanding this process is when clients often are not clear about what they want as an end result or what they want from the provider. We emphasize throughout the module that it is critical to build and leverage relationships to achieve the results that are valuable for both the clients and providers. This endeavor is no easy task. Many PSFs fall by the wayside when they do not meet client expectations or there is little value added to the economic model of the clients. They begin to overpromise and underdeliver in order to retain clients, but end up losing clients in the end.

The externally oriented process of investing in clients and building mutual trust is critical for long-term success (Figure 1). Readers will form their own opinions about whether face-to-face interactions remain a key variable in building the trust necessary for long-term viability after witnessing the e-consulting practices in the professional services arena. The cases in this module will help readers understand marketing in both relationship and transactional businesses and the relationships between service promise and delivery, and client satisfaction and loyalty.

FIGURE 1

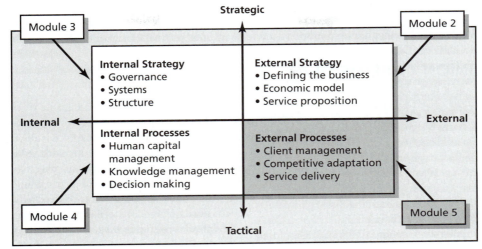

&SAMHOUD

We start with the &Samhoud case, which bridges Module Four and Module Five. Obsessed with employee satisfaction, Salem Samhoud, founder of &Samhoud, developed recruitment and professional development processes, a satisfying work environment, and a shared culture. This is his unique approach to client service relationship management: defining internal professionals as customers.

This case introduces the links between employee productivity, satisfaction, and loyalty; customer satisfaction and loyalty; and firm profitability and growth. Salem Samhoud tried to build his consulting firm based on the service profit chain theory. He believed that in order to add value to clients, the firm would have to invest in professionals first. The firm might suffer from short-term expenses, but in the long run, benefits from employee satisfaction and loyalty would outweigh upfront investments. Salem Samhoud wanted to build an organization that lasts.

This case is unique because it allows readers to consider the issue of under what circumstances to terminate a client and what the criteria should be for keeping a client. Salem Samhoud's dilemma of whether to terminate one of the firm's major clients is universal to most PSF leaders and managers. Should &Samhoud terminate the client because consultants do not learn from this client assignment and are dissatisfied with little progress? Or should &Samhoud keep the client because the firm's short-term revenus and profit will be hurt without this client?

We also highlight methods to motivate professionals through this case. Unlike the International Profit Associates case in Module Three, Salem Samhoud relies on intrinsic rewards and internal motivation to build employee satisfaction and loyalty, instead of using cash as an extrinsic reward. The &Samhoud case shows that committed professionals will exceed client expectations and create clients that are committed to the firm.

THE UNION CARBIDE DEAL

The Union Carbide Deal case examines the important dimensions of client relationship management in the context of closing a deal. Through the eyes of Bruce Jamerson we learn the classic lesson that a number of small activities have a cumulative effect and can add up to a long-term relationship that adds value for both client and provider. Conversely, arrogance and assumptions play havoc when clients need assistance and PSFs take long-term relationships for granted.

The Union Carbide Deal also illustrates the connection of external processes with internal processes. As client needs change, external processes are affected before the internal processes. Client relationship managers must help ensure that the information they gather during the selling process is communicated to the organization; in a way that the organization can continually improve its structure and processes to serve clients better.

The PSF must reevaluate how it defines itself to clients. Is Diamond Technology Partners a technology consulting firm or a strategy consulting firm? Is Morgan Stanley a client-first organization or an arrogant, elitist organization that only treats clients well as long as they are producing revenues for the bank? In this case we see that Morgan Stanley thought it had little need to worry because it assumed the relationship with Union Carbide was secure. Morgan Stanley was blindsided by its arrogance.

As we study the processes at First Boston, we can see that the firm struggled with a common PSF dilemma—the appropriate balance of rewards for shorter-term and longer-term activities. Jamerson gambled that investing in the Union Carbide relationship would pay off someday. Readers might speculate whether or not Jamerson would get paid well if the Union Carbide deal did not go through. Unless he produces a specific transaction that brings revenue to the firm quickly, will Jamerson be seen as a "hanger-on" and be asked to leave the firm? Do firms often classify stars only as the most effective short-term producers? Perhaps Jamerson is not seen as a star in the system because he is doing what he is supposed to do and focusing on the long term. The PSF conundrum is that the more you follow what you think is right and focus on the long term, it calls into question whether you can focus on the short term simultaneously.

The Union Carbide case is a useful case in order to study the way firms define problems with and for clients. First Boston defined Union Carbide's problems more broadly, while Morgan Stanley took a more narrow approach. As is common in client service, the case illustrates how a PSF defines a client problem in a way that is not connected with reality. So Jamerson, to win the business, must endure disparate goals from clients and senior managers and create a solution that is in the best interest for the client. How do you manage the process of getting a deal done when client and organization have different interests?

This case underscores the importance of context in the decision-making process of the client and the proposals made to the clients. Carbide had been kicked around since the Bhopal disaster. The organization wanted to be treated with dignity and like a Fortune 50 company. The First Boston proposal, at the margin, satisfied this desire more than the Morgan Stanley proposal, just as the Salomon proposal was rejected for being too gradualistic. Carbide's urgency to act fell on resonant ears at First Boston, which had its own reasons to flex its muscles. First Boston's proposal solved the problem with the patient's heart. Jamerson had put in his time to earn the firm the opportunity to compete, the firm was desperate to get the business and was willing to risk its balance sheet. One sees the focus on connections that won First Boston the business from Morgan Stanley.

JILL GREENTHAL AT DLJ

In the Jill Greenthal at DLJ case, we focus deeply on how investments in client relationships can be leveraged into business opportunities. We emphasize through this module there are certain challenges facing professional services firms in traditional transactional businesses. Jill Greenthal is an example of a producer manager who swims against the currents by emphasizing that long-term relationships are good for both clients and providers. The case illustrates how to build trust over time, particularly if clients are initially skeptical that the service provider is only interested in generating revenues for the short-term bottom line.

This case is yet another example of the internal and external challenges PSFs often have in motivating professionals to think past the next deal. Jill Greenthal wins over a very tough client in a very competitive market by focusing both on the short and long term simultaneously. We see how she, as a managing director, manages internal politics to leverage internal capital and human resources to achieve a desired outcome that serves both client and provider.

Another important issue that emerges through the Jill Greenthal case is whether clients are more committed to firms or to individual professionals they deal with at the firm. Greenthal began her relationship with Leo Hindery when she worked for Lehman Brothers. When Greenthal switched to DLJ, Hindery and John Malone moved to DLJ as well. Their relationship was portable.

We also highlight the importance for firms and individuals to assess how to create loyalty with clients. It takes us back to the discussion in Module Three where we saw how the Morgan Stanley Dean Witter merger pushed the leadership to reassess the client, firm, and professional triangle. Jill Greenthal has to weigh her loyalties to client and firm and balance the tensions between both systems.

The Greenthal case is a prime example of a firm and a professional that take into consideration not only client management, but competitive adaptation and service delivery. Greenthal is obsessed with listening to her client and adapting her recommendations based on what will enhance the long-term relationship between DLJ, Greenthal, TCI, and Leo Hindery. While Greenthal is balancing these demands, her internal team is watching every move to evaluate how she leverages the external processes to enhance client value. Greenthal has added pressure because senior management is watching her every move as well, knowing that completing this deal will put the firm at another level of play in the eyes of other clients, future clients, and competitors.

SUMMARY

External processes ensure delivery of promises through client and project management, and nimble adaptation to competitive dynamics. The external processes of client management, competitive adaptation, and service delivery are only as effective as the internal processes they rely upon. There is low probability that PSF providers will exceed client expectations if their human capital and decision-making processes are not aligned with the process of managing client expectations. Excellent service delivery cannot occur if service providers are not focused on adapting to current environmental contexts that drive client strategies.

It is imperative to note that Samhoud's success with applying the service profit chain theory, Greenthal's success over a nine-year period with TCI, and Bruce Jamerson's success with Union Carbide were a result of professionals who not only had eyes focused on the transactional, short-term clock but also managed long-term relationships. These three examples underscore how excellent service delivery transpires within firms that have a modicum of alignment. These firms derive success because of an obsession with understanding their own internal and external processes and leveraging those processes to deliver excellent results that stand over time.

QUESTIONS ARISING FROM THE CASES IN THIS MODULE

These are some of the many questions that were raised in our study of the client service processes of PSFs:

- Should a PSF focus on people who the firm pays, that is, employees, or people who pay the firm, that is, clients?

- What are the criteria PSF leaders should use in deciding whether to accept a client, serve a client, or terminate a client?

- What are the signs when the PSF professionals are working harder than the client?

- In serving a number of clients, what is an appropriate balance between short- and long-term activities?

- Are clients more tied to their relationship manager/partner at the firm or the firm itself? How do firms try to ensure that it is to the firm? How do partners try to ensure that the relationship is portable if they leave the firm?

&Samhoud Service Management

On June 20, 2000, as Salem Samhoud, founder of Dutch consulting firm &Samhoud, stepped down from his train at the Utrecht stop, he hardly noticed the hundreds of bicycles parked next to the station. Samhoud's mind was churning out possible outcomes of a difficult decision: whether or not to continue the nine-year old consulting relationship with &Samhoud's largest client ConneXXion, Netherland's major public bus transportation company.

One year earlier, Samhoud had promised himself that, unless circumstances changed drastically, on his fortieth birthday, his firm would terminate its relationship with ConneXXion, a client that generated 25 percent of &Samhoud's revenue in 1999. He had reasoned that (a) &Samhoud needed to diversify its client base away from public transportation; (b) several of &Samhoud's top consultants, including rising star Frank Bierkens, were getting burned out by the lack of progress with ConneXXion's management team; and (c) ConneXXion had failed to show marked organizational improvement despite &Samhoud's persistent efforts.

With only six days left to his fortieth birthday, Samhoud was having second thoughts about acting on his promise. Samhoud had slated the next four years at &Samhoud primarily to realigning internal organizational practices and developing a tier of senior consultants who would lead &Samhoud in establishing a global presence.[1] Internal focus, however, meant that less time would be devoted to generating new business, making it difficult to "fire" a large client. Besides, the financial ramifications for &Samhoud of terminating ConneXXion would be serious, especially since &Samhoud's profits were expected to decline in 2000. "In the wake of tremendous growth over the past few years," Samhoud averred,

> in 2000 we have focused on aligning compensation, the evaluation system, and the nature of our partnership. When you get internally focused and realign systems, you can't be out generating profit. We expect our profit to be significantly lower in 2000 than in 1999.

Samhoud walked into his office, greeted the receptionist, and proceeded to the dining area. After pouring himself a cup of coffee, he stared out onto the firm's Japanese garden. Even though keeping his promise would have severe financial repercussions, Samhoud reflected that not keeping it might be even more deleterious to the firm. The client's inability to make substantive progress was creating frustration and dissatisfaction among &Samhoud consultants, which in turn jeopardized the retention of key consultants—&Samhoud's future leaders.

SALEM SAMHOUD

The only child of a single mother, Salem Samhoud grew up in Apeldoorn, a small town in the eastern

Research Associate Monica Mullick prepared this case under the supervision of Professors Thomas DeLong and Ashish Nanda as the basis for class discussion rather than to illustrate either effective or ineffective handling of an administrative situation.

[1] Inspired by the Olympics, Samhoud viewed long-term planning in four-year increments.

part of the Netherlands. His fondest memory was of playing soccer with the neighborhood children. Samhoud was never a serious student, failing his high school examination not once, but twice. His mother was so upset that she refused to speak to him for three months. "Her silence was what whipped me into shape," joked Samhoud. As he gradually began to take his studies more seriously, Samhoud developed a bent for academics.

Samhoud attended Nijenrode University, known as the Harvard of the Netherlands. To help pay for school, he washed dishes in the university cafeteria where he learned "the true meaning of work." Samhoud hated the elitist attitude of many of the professors and students and refused to join the popular social club on campus because he felt it was too exclusive.

After university, Samhoud attended graduate school in Lyon, France, where he earned his MBA. After graduation, Samhoud entered the business world as a sales and marketing analyst with the multinational consumer products company Unilever. Eager to experience a new country and culture, Samhoud moved to Africa's Ivory Coast in 1986 where he sold printed textiles for Unilever in Togo and Niger. Over the next three years, Samhoud felt increasingly bored and unchallenged by the "mindless process of selling consumer products."

Soon after returning to Netherlands, Samhoud caught up with college friend Cees Arends who had also been disillusioned by his first business experience. Samhoud and Arends realized that they both shared a passion for the service industry. "I was raised in the service industry," Samhoud explained his personal intrigue. "My grandparents owned a hotel and my mother was a secretary and a house caretaker for a lawyer."

ARENDS & SAMHOUD

Having felt the dissatisfaction of working at product-focused organizations, Samhoud and Arends became obsessed with the idea of converting product-focused organizations into customer-focused systems. This customer-focus formed the foundation in 1989 of their start-up consulting firm Arends & Samhoud.

Samhoud and Arends set up their first makeshift office in Arends' apartment where they brainstormed on how to find a client. They wanted to target a sector where many customers could be impacted but competition for consulting services was low. In a country of 14 million people and 17 million bicycles where 10 percent of the population spent at least 20 minutes riding public transport daily, public transportation appeared a logical choice.

Samhoud and Arends filmed impromptu interviews with passengers and employees of Centraal Nederland, one of the Netherland's major public transportation companies, and captured their dissatisfaction and resentment. In November 1989 they played the homemade video before Centraal Nederland's board. Samhoud recalled the meeting:

> Central Nederland's board agreed to meet with us, two unknowns, because we were determined. We told them: "We know your customers and we want to share what we know." They were stunned by our video and shocked into the undeniable realization: Centraal Nederland's management did not understand either their customers or their employees. It had never even occurred to them to listen to their customers and employees for insight into the company's problems.

Soon after the November 1989 meeting, Centraal Nederland hired Arends & Samhoud on a six-week $19,000 dollar contract to determine why customers were dissatisfied with public transport and propose a solution to remedy the problems. "The very best feeling is scoring a soccer goal," observed Samhoud. "The next best feeling is winning a contract." During the first three weeks of the project, Samhoud and Arends spent all their time trying to learn the industry by visiting more than 20 satellite offices of Centraal Nederland's state-owned parent company, the United Regional Public Transport Company (VSN). "We had to learn the transportation business in three weeks," recalled Samhoud. "All we did was listen and ask questions."

Over the next two years, Arends & Samhoud sold several projects to VSN. At the end of 1991, Arends and Samhoud decided that instead of taking home their share of profits at Christmas, they would enroll in a Harvard Business School executive education course focused on service profit chain. Service profit chain is a management theory that suggests that a firm's profitability and growth hinge upon customer satisfaction, which, in turn, is a result of having satisfied employees.[2] "I loved the course," Samhoud reflected upon his time at HBS.

> When Cees returned home, the first thing he did was get his diploma framed. I lost mine. But I did buy and read over a hundred books that addressed the subjects of customer and employee satisfaction. I became obsessed with learning everything I could about employee and customer satisfaction. I learned that in order to add value you have to invest in your employees first and then your customers. In the short term, you may lose money, but in the long term you win—this idea is both philosophical and practical. I came to believe that, based on my beliefs and understanding about employee and customer satisfaction, I could build a company that could one day be the McKinsey of service firms.

During 1992, Arends & Samhoud focused on teaching the service profit chain concept within VSN. However, progress was slow because VSN had a monopoly over the entire public transport system in Holland giving it little impetus to change. In 1993, Arends & Samhoud revenue had

grown to $1.39 million from $1.17 million in 1992, a 27 percent year-over-year increase.

As Samhoud and Arends gained visibility as experts in the transportation sector, their views in support of privatization quickly became known publicly. Samhoud and Arends believed that introducing competition would create an impetus for VSN to focus on its customers and employees. To that end, Samhoud and Arends contacted Vancom, a transportation company based in Chicago, IL, whose CEO had "Dutch roots," to discuss the prospect of entering the Dutch transportation market. In early 1994, the Dutch government opened the public transport industry to foreign companies. With the help of Samhoud and Arends, Vancom entered the industry, posing an immediate threat to VSN.

Samhoud and Arends' role in introducing competition in the public transport industry led VSN to discontinue entirely its relationship with Arends & Samhoud. To diversify their client portfolio, Arends & Samhoud began focusing its efforts in the financial services arena.

Even as the competitive landscape of the transportation sector was shifting dramatically and new business opportunities were emerging for their consulting firm, Samhoud felt Arends' interest in building the firm was waning. Recalled Samhoud:

> When public transportation was opened up to competition, Arends and I became well known and began appearing in the press and on television as nongovernment "transportation experts." It was very gratifying and easy to get caught up in all the attention. I believe that is what happened to Arends. His focus became too external. We began having divergent views on our commitment to, and the end goal of, the firm.

Arends and Samhoud could not concur on how to grow the firm, mentor their junior professionals,

---

[2] James L. Heskett, W. Earl Sasser, Jr., and Leonard A. Schlesinger, *The Service Profit Chain* (New York: The Free Press: 1997).

or diversify into other industries. Samhoud wanted to build a world-class consulting firm, and to achieve this he wanted to invest in his employees, whereas Arends wanted to focus more on marketing. To manage this tension, Samhoud and Arends agreed to split their responsibilities within Arends & Samhoud. Samhoud would focus internally, and Arends would center his activities on marketing the firm's services. Over time, however, their philosophical differences had become so pronounced that Samhoud sensed the partnership was breaking apart. Listening to a speech by the Netherland's Olympic volleyball coach confirmed his inclination to sever the partnership. Samhoud recalled the speech:

> Describing his strategy for going for the gold in 1996, the head coach said: "It is time to put into place new systems, new people, and new combinations if we want to become gold medal winners." Suddenly, it became crystal clear to me. Arends and I would have to break apart and refocus our efforts separately.

Samhoud and Arends officially disbanded in 1996. Samhoud took a personal loan of $1.3 million, representing 26 percent of the firm's 1995 revenue (see Exhibit 1), and bought out Arends' share

in the firm. Arends joined Vancom, which had captured 20 percent of Holland's transportation market, as director. Having lost his partner and his biggest client VSN, Samhoud was faced with rebuilding his firm.

&SAMHOUD

Between 1996 and 1998 Salem continued calling the firm Arends & Samhoud, but in 1998, Samhoud and his team renamed the firm &Samhoud, keeping the ampersand sign to signify the partnership the firm entered with its clients and employees (see Exhibit 2), and formulated &Samhoud's vision: Together, with our clients, we will build a brighter service future; we will create the most pleasant firm to work for and work with; we are dedicated to bringing out the best in people and achieving the best results.

By June of 2000, with headquarters in Utrecht, Holland, and satellite offices in Cologne, Germany, and Stockholm, Sweden, &Samhoud had grown to 100 employees and $8.5 million annual revenue. Its client base had expanded beyond transportation to telecommunications, energy, and financial services.

Business Practice

&Samhoud was committed to improving client performance using the service profit chain approach. &Samhoud Germany director Edwin Winter described the challenges of using the approach: "It takes at least two years for the service profit chain to pay off. Therefore, it's a challenge to attract clients because they want to see short-term results."

Although there was no "typical" client engagement, &Samhoud implemented a consistent methodology and philosophy through most projects. Projects were staffed with 2 to 10 professionals, and revenue per project ranged from $21,000 to $635,000. Projects lasted from three to nine months and were divided usually into three phases. During the first phase, &Samhoud introduced the

EXHIBIT 1 &Samhoud Key Growth Metrics

	Revenue ($US)	Consultants
1990	559,889	3
1991	533,369	5
1992	1,172,275	7
1993	1,388,655	21
1994	2,646,209	36
1995	4,947,641	39
1996	6,633,889	50
1997	5,996,487	72
1998	6,666,498	77
1999	9,257,022	94
2000	8,281,703	91

Source: &Samhoud management.

EXHIBIT 2
&Samhoud
Sample Business
Card

Source: &Samhoud.

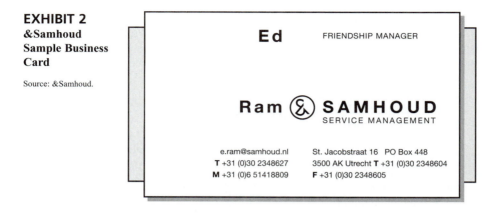

client to service management theories, starting with a discussion of the linkages that constituted the service profit chain.

After the client had agreed with the conceptual basis of the service profit chain, in the second phase, the &Samhoud team would walk the client through a self-evaluation process to understand the firm's mission, core values, and long-term goals. The process also provided &Samhoud consultants the opportunity to identify the client management team's personal goals. &Samhoud would then present a number of exercises to help define the scope and direction of the project by identifying the strategic processes on which the engagement would focus.

One exercise, called "C3 marketing" (C3 stood for Check, Choose, and Cherish), involved showing clients how to estimate economic value of satisfied customers, target those customers, and deliver services to them. From C3 marketing, the client learned how to segment customers into different categories, and the financial impact of gaining or losing a particular customer segment. C3 marketing also helped create an operational strategy to attract and retain target customers. "Value strategies" encompassed another set of exercises that &Samhoud conducted for its clients. Value strategies emphasized the achievement of product leadership and operational excellence through regularly measuring, using the balanced scorecard ap-proach, and improving employee and customer satisfaction.

The third phase of &Samhoud's engagement involved specific interventions to achieve the desired short- and long-term goals. The interventions typically comprised projects to remedy former dysfunctional practices and create new focus and excitement among customers and employees. This phase also involved creating metrics to measure the effectiveness of the change efforts.

Employee and Customer Relationships

Founded on the principles of "intensity, authenticity, and life-long friendship," &Samhoud sought to integrate these qualities in both their customer relationships and their employee relationships.

Recruiting and Professional Development

Samhoud was convinced that "customers can always see what is happening in the heads of consultants. Therefore, you have to have consultants who love what they do and where they work." Since "in consulting, the major risk is hiring the wrong people," &Samhoud had created a recruiting process to attract professionals with values similar to that of the firm. "Unlike other consulting firms," noted senior consultant Frank Bierkens, "we screen first for attitude and then for smarts." From printed job advertisements (see Exhibit 3) to final round interviews which consisted of group discussions, presentations, and debates on ethical dilemmas, &Samhoud's recruiting process honed in on candidates' personalities, values, and ability and desire to deliver excellent service.

Samhoud wanted to instill in his organization the idea of life-long personal and professional progression. His mantra was, "I believe in risk taking and supporting others in realizing their dreams. As our professionals work to keep their dreams alive, energy is infused into the firm." When, for instance, junior consultant Nur Hamurcu wrote a proposal outlining a four-week service project in Kenya, Samhoud not only approved the project, but also contributed funds to it and allocated two consultants to work on the project with him. Hamurcu reflected on the project:

> &Samhoud's philanthropic arm called Foundation funded the project. While I love my traditional consulting projects, I also want to contribute my services to make a difference outside the business community. Foundation provides people like me the opportunity to use our talents to the utmost.

However, Samhoud and his colleagues were also well aware of the risks in running a "feel-good dream-making" firm—lack of standardization, analyses that lacked quantitative rigor, and casual relationships with clients. Senior consultant Joost Preyde expressed his concern about potential tensions between personal and business relationships: "The idea of friendship can go too far with clients. We can lose the business atmosphere because we have allowed our friendship to take over. The relationship risks becoming too personal, casual, and unprofessional."

Samhoud wanted his firm to stand as an example to its clients in creating a work environment where employees were highly satisfied. To measure employee satisfaction &Samhoud used the balanced score card to monitor on a quarterly basis three key areas of the consultants' life: personal

work, knowledge sharing, and loyalty (see Exhibit 4). Results from this assessment provided an indicator of how consultants viewed &Samhoud's environment and helped &Samhoud's management directionally predict employee retention, performance, and client satisfaction.

"Friendship" Management

Integrating "intensity, authenticity, and life-long friendship" in client relationships meant placing demands not only on themselves, but also on their clients, requiring the creation of a two-way relationship in which both the consultant and the client were responsible for reaching shared goals. Consultant Anne Geurtsen described &Samhoud's philosophy:

> Our competitive advantage is creating a process where expectations play a major role. We are not as prescriptive as McKinsey. We interact more with the client and through this interaction the project gets defined. We expect the client to be involved in the action planning and implementation. We are good at keeping the mirror in front of the client.

Firm Culture

&Samhoud professionals referred to their firm as having an "open culture" where direct and honest communication was encouraged. "The work we do can be replicated," opined consultant Edwin Winter. "Our philosophy and our culture make us unique and competitive." Samhoud was particularly proud of "an intangible yet valuable benefit" the firm offered its professionals, a benefit he loosely described as the company's "spirituality." Some consultants described "spirituality" as the motivation and passion that drove consultants to meet and exceed client expectations. Others interpreted it as the energy in the company that simultaneously allowed autonomy to lead change and cohesiveness to produce synergies. Samhoud noted, "When you can't or won't put spirituality,

EXHIBIT 3 &Samhoud Job Advertisement

YOU &SAMHOUD

You
As a starting junior consultant you will work on a range of various projects. You feel that professional and personal development in a results-focused environment is important. You recognize yourself in the following profile:
- ¥ You have the drive to work hard and aim for perfection;
- ¥ You are not afraid to be vulnerable and are a good listener;
- ¥ You stimulate others to develop themselves;
- ¥ You take responsibility and act after your own instincts;
- ¥ You feel that having fun at work is very important;
- ¥ You have clear ideas on customer-focused service management

&Samhoud Service Management
&Samhoud Service Management is a young, dynamic consultancy in the area of service management, where there is an informal environment and thinking and acting are equally important.

All employees recognize themselves in our core values: intensity (giving everything you have), authenticity (staying yourself and experiencing freedom) and lifelong friendship (touching people, having openness and loyalty).

Choosing people and having fun at work is very important to us. Because &Samhoud chooses people we have specially created an extra space in the name of our company; every employee is able to put his/her name before the character: &.

Markets
&Samhoud actively operates in the following markets:
Labor market, energy, mobility, telecommunications, e-business, financial services and government.

Competencies
The markets above are served from our competencies:
- — Change Management
- — Communication & Experience
- — Customer Relationship Management
- — E-service
- — People Leadership
- — Process Redesign
- — Vision, Strategy, Team, Leadership
- — Applied Research

Career possibilities
Your career with &Samhoud is what you make of it yourself. Employees are able to develop in several directions, depending on their goal. &Samhoud forces you to think about your goal and on how to reach it. Of course you will be well coached in doing so.

As a graduate from university you will be hired as a junior consultant. You will simultaneously work on different projects and learn different aspects of the consulting and implementation business. You will learn about the different markets we operate in. You will work within a team and will be given the opportunity to develop your qualities and strengths.

Apply
Visit our website for more information: ww.samhoud.com. Or phone/mail Bibi van Hoeflaken on
e-mail address: b.vanhoeflaken@samhoud.nl or telephone number: +31 30 234 8683.

Source: &Samhoud.

EXHIBIT 4 &Samhoud Balance Scorecard Assessment

KNOWLEDGE AND EMPLOYEES

PERIOD: APRIL TO JUNE 2000

1. In the following table please tick to what extent you are satisfied with the sharing of knowledge by other business units.
(Please check one box per row and leave the row of your own business unit blank.)

Sharing Knowledge	Don't Know	Very Dissatisfied	Dissatisfied	Neither Satisfied or Dissatisfied	Satisfied	Very Satisfied
Change in service						
Communication and events						
Efficiency support						
NetVenture						
Strategy and concepts						
Traffic and transport						
K3						
Recruiting to retain						
Corporate support						

2. The following table addresses matters concerning the organization of your work.
(Please tick only one box per row)

Responsibility	Very Dissatisfied	Dissatisfied	Neither Satisfied or Dissatisfied	Satisfied	Very Satisfied
The amount of responsibility I am allowed to carry					
The freedom I feel in my work the way I want					

Possibilities for Growth	Very Dissatisfied	Dissatisfied	Neither Satisfied or Dissatisfied	Satisfied	Very Satisfied
The possibility to learn a lot					
The possibility to realize my ambitions					
The extent to which I have to push myself to the limit					

Balanced Score Card	Percentage
What percentage of your BSC action plan have you realized	

Feedback/Openness	Very Dissatisfied	Dissatisfied	Neither Satisfied or Dissatisfied	Satisfied	Very Satisfied
The feedback I receive on my achievements are (generally)					
The appreciation I get when I give feedback					
The ability to be myself					

(continued)

EXHIBIT 4 &Samhoud Balance Scorecard Assessment *(continued)*

Team Spirit within Business Units	Very Dissatisfied	Dissatisfied	Neither Satisfied or Dissatisfied	Satisfied	Very Satisfied
The team spirit within my business unit					
The amount of time my business unit (BU) leader has for me (BU leaders: leave row blank)					
The quality of coaching by my BU leader (BU leaders: leave row blank)					
The quality of coaching by others					

Team Spirit and Cooperation between Business Units	Don't Know	Very Dissatisfied	Dissatisfied	Neither Satisfied or Dissatisfied	Satisfied	Very Satisfied
Change in service						
Communication and events						
Efficiency support						
NetVenture						
Strategy and concepts						
Traffic and transport						
K3						
Recruiting to retain						
Corporate support						

Pressure of Work	Very Dissatisfied	Dissatisfied	Neither Satisfied or Dissatisfied	Satisfied	Very Satisfied
My work-life balance					

General Satisfaction	Very Dissatisfied	Dissatisfied	Neither Satisfied or Dissatisfied	Satisfied	Very Satisfied
In general I am a _____ employee					

Discipline	Grade between 1 (lowest) and 10 (highest)
How does &Samsoud score on discipline?	

Pride	Yes	No	Sometimes
Do you tell others of your business unit with pride?			
Do you tell others of &Samhoud with pride?			

Loyalty	Yes	No	Sometimes
Do you tell others of your business unit with pride?			

Your name (not obligatory):

. . . .

Would you like to discuss your answers with your business unit leader?

Yes   No

Thank you for completing this questionnaire.

Source: &Samhoud.

attention, and energy into employees, only then will employees want to be compensated with more money."

Samhoud professed a lack of interest in the idea of making exorbitant amounts of money. "I don't believe that capital in itself has any rights," he observed. "I don't have much respect for people who make money from money. Money will never get to me." It appeared that Samhoud's perspective was shared by many of his colleagues. Noted consultant Ed Ram: "At &Samhoud, we don't drive BMWs. We take public transport."

Respecting balance in one another's lives was another important part of &Samhoud's culture. Samhoud explained his philosophy on vacation time: "My goal is to take at least two months a year off where I cannot be reached by the firm. When I am on holiday, I do not call the office, and I do not accept any calls from the office. I assume that they can make decisions without me. They have the authority to do so."

CONNEXXION

VSN and &Samhoud in 1999

In 1995 the Dutch government ordered the breakup of VSN into two stand-alone companies: VSN1 to service the central region of the Netherlands and VSN2 to serve the northern and southern regions (see Exhibit 5). Controlling approximately 60 percent market share in regional and local road and rail transportation, VSN1 serviced more than one million customers daily across the central region of Holland. In 1998, VSN1 workforce totaled almost 13,000 employees, 8,000 of which were bus drivers.

In January 1999, Cees Anker was named director of VSN1. Anker, who had been an Arends & Samhoud client in the early 1990s, had remained Samhoud's personal friend even after the business relationship between VSN and &Samhoud had ended. He phoned Samhoud to share his frustration about lack of internal alignment at VSN1 and to seek Samhoud's input.

Anker followed the phone conversation with a request to &Samhoud to assist VSN1 in a change management project titled "Connecting 2000." Samhoud, although reluctant because of VSN's past inability to change, established a formal client relationship with VSN1.

The First 100 Days

VSN1 and &Samhoud concurred that the principal objective of the first 100 days of Connecting 2000 would be to establish direction for VSN1. &Samhoud consultants began the project by presenting service management theory to VSN1's management team, including concepts of vision, service profit chain, customer value equation, C3 marketing, value strategies, and balanced score card. With &Samhoud's guidance, VSN1's management team created the following goals:

Mission	Bringing people together
Core values	Reliability Enthusiasm Entrepreneurship Fun
Goal	To become the best public transport company from a customer's point of view within the next three years
Value strategy	Operational excellence

"We are no longer a public transport service company," ConneXXion director of strategy and development Geert Eikelboom proclaimed ConneXXion's new way of thinking. "We are now a service provider in the passenger mobility service. We are going to manage this company from the demand side, not the supply side."

The Second 100 Days

The second phase of Connecting 2000 included initiatives to (a) gain insights into employees, customers, competition, and costs; (b) standardize

EXHIBIT 5 Historical Organization of VSN and the Evolution of ConneXXion

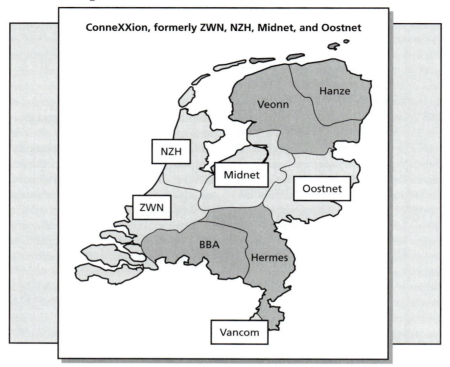

Prior to 1995, Holland's public bus transportation system, divided into urban and regional (i.e., nonurban) markets, was entirely government owned and operated. State-owned transit company VSN (United Regional Public Transit Company) controlled the regional bus market by forming an umbrella over eight smaller providers which were geographically distinct: Veonn and Hanze made up the northern region; BBA and Hermes made up the southern region; and ZWN, NZH, Midnet, and Oostnet made up the central region (formerly known as Centraal Nederland). Collectively, VSN had power over 19,000 drivers and generated annual revenue of 2 billion guilders.

In 1995, government pressure along with the introduction of foreign competition, American Vancom, succeeded in unlocking monopolistic VSN by forcing it to divide into two stand-alone companies: VSN1 and VSN2. VSN1 controlled the central regional providers while VSN2 controlled the northern and southern regional providers. During the last half of 1998, two transactions caused VSN2 to dissolve: one, UK-based public transport company, Arriva, bought northern regional providers Veonn and Hanze for 155 million guilders; two, Hermes and BBA divested to operate as stand-alone companies. VSN1, still in control of the central regional bus market, was renamed ConneXXion in May 1999.

Source: &Samhoud management.

service offerings and processes (including travel demand estimation, travel scheduling, customer service, quality control, and bus maintenance) throughout the VSN1 system; and (c) launch VSN1's new name, ConneXXion, and new image.

To understand the employees' perspective, &Samhoud conducted focus group sessions with VSN1 management and bus drivers. Asked how they perceived the new name, ConneXXion, one bus driver reflected the disinterest of his colleagues when he said: "We don't care about a new name. To me, a new name only means receiving a new uniform with a new logo. All that I am looking forward to is some new clothes." Eikelboom added:

> The drivers don't give a damn about their management. That is particularly worrisome since the quality of our service is driven by the quality of our personnel. We have good buses, good systems, but our drivers are the key variable; 60–70 percent of our costs goes to driver salaries.

"Top 26,000" Event

&Samhoud senior consultants Frank Bierkens and Ed Ram worked with VSN1 management team for several months to create their new image and new name. Their goal was that the name ConneXXion should inspire employees and instill confidence among customers that the old bureaucratic, government-run VSN1 no longer existed.

In May 1999, the name ConneXXion was welcomed with a gala event for the top 500 employees of the company. In response to Eikelboom's and others' opinion that "the key issue at hand was how to get the bus drivers to embrace change," the next major event, slated for January 2000, would include all 13,000 ConneXXion employees and their significant others, an event appropriately named the "Top 26,000." &Samhoud viewed the Top 26,000 event, estimated to cost $3.4 million, as a potential landmark in the history of VSN1, one that would proclaim, "We value our employees."

When gas prices rose from $2.59 per gallon in January 1999 to $3.21 per gallon in October 1999 implying an $8.5 million dollar increase in ConneXXion's annual operating expenses, ConneXXion's senior management canceled the Top 26,000 event without discussing their concerns or intentions with &Samhoud. Eikelboom summarized ConneXXion's dilemma:

> We are in a very low profit margin business, between 5–6 percent, which makes management risk averse. But some of us don't realize that we must take risks to raise profits. When our employee satisfaction is low, our sick leave is high. Even a 1 percent decline in sick leave translates into an increase of $3.4 million in profit—enough to cover the cost of the Top 26,000 event. The sudden cancellation of the Top 26,000 event led &Samhoud to question ConneXXion's commitment to creating an organization focused on employee satisfaction.

The Third 100 Days

The third phase of Connecting 2000, the implementation phase, included initiatives empowering employees to excel as service providers, offering standardized services to customers that met quality requirements, and measuring employee satisfaction.

&Samhoud consultants worked rigorously with ConneXXion executives to create an employee satisfaction tool using the balanced score card to monitor the morale of ConneXXion employees. The previous survey had been circulated annually and had a response rate of only 27 percent. The new survey, consisting of only 10 questions, would be implemented every three months starting in April 2000. Even though &Samhoud consultants believed the new survey was much better at measuring employee satisfaction, ConneXXion's human resources director never followed up on the initiative and continued to administer the former questionnaire with dismal results.

ConneXXion's 1999 revenue was $910 million, relatively unchanged from 1998. Eikelboom reflected on the Connecting 2000 initiative:

> We've conducted rigorous customer investigations and we have implemented Connecting 2000. The information generated by this process will drive our strategy and operations. Our new name has come from this process. Our employees have come away from the process with a feeling of inclusion. Connecting 2000 has brought together our frontliners, the bus drivers, and our management team so that they can learn from one another. However, not all bus drivers believe in Connecting 2000.

CONNEXXION GROUP

In March 1999, ConneXXion's parent company, formerly VSN and now renamed ConneXXion Group, was jolted by unexpected criticism from Holland's minister of public transport, the governmental body that supplied ConneXXion Group with funds to run its subsidiaries. ConneXXion Group chairman Frans Sevenstern, Anker's boss, reflected:

> The government used to just give us money to run a timetable to transport people of Holland from one place to another. We viewed customers as a bother. After competition was introduced into the transport business we had to rethink our whole business. The transportation minister felt we had not reduced costs enough and we had not increased our customers' use of public transportation. That is why I turned to &Samhoud.

Together &Samhoud, Sevenstern, and Anker organized a strategic operating committee that would create a "vision program" for ConneXXion Group. The strategic operating committee, comprised of ConneXXion Group chairman Sevenstern and the directors of each subsidiary, met with Samhoud and Bierkens in three sessions. During

these sessions the following goals of the ConneXXion Group were agreed upon:

Mission	To make and keep people mobile
Core values	Honest, open, and reliable Entrepreneurial Surprising and innovative
Mission	To make and keep people mobile Enthusiastic and having fun
Goal	To become Europe's best solver of mobility problems within three years
Value strategy	To broaden and to enlarge the customer market

In December 1999, the ConneXXion Group's board of directors and &Samhoud consultants participated in what Bierkens characterized as "a breakthrough discussion" on implementing the ConneXXion group's new vision. "We had a very emotional, cathartic meeting," recalled Bierkens. "After being involved with the company for so many years, it felt as if we had finally reached a turning point." It was the first time that all the directors of the ConneXXion Group had agreed on a common vision. The commitment from all the participants was unanimous.

Soon after Christmas, however, ConneXXion Group's management team decided not to move forward with the new vision. A few senior managers were convinced that the new direction would not be accepted by the employees. Bierkens vividly remembered his disappointment:

> I was sick of it. The vision statement clearly laid out concrete initiatives of implementing the new direction. When ConneXXion Group went back on their commitments, I realized that there was no unity among the ConneXXion Group management team. They did not respect the core values that

they themselves had formulated only a short time before. Nothing had changed. We were still dealing with the old bureaucratic and political VSN. We at &Samhoud decided we did not want to work for the board of directors. From that day on, we have only worked for Cees Anker, the director of the subsidiary ConneXXion. And I told Salem I wanted out of the client relationship altogether.

SAMHOUD'S VOW

On June 10, 1999, while playing golf with ConneXXion Group chairman Sevenstern and &Samhoud project leader Frank Bierkens, Samhoud made his vow.

ConneXXion must show signs of improvement. Otherwise, I am not doing my job as your advisor. Frans, you are retiring as ConneXXion chairman at the end of 2000. My goal is to quit working for ConneXXion in June of 2000 when I turn 40 unless things change.

Now, one year later, in June of 2000, the time had come for Samhoud to follow through on his commitment to terminate &Samhoud's relationship with ConneXXion despite the potentially severe financial implications of the decision. Samhoud wondered what to do with an organization that acted as if it did not want to be helped. Reflecting over the nine-year relationship, he contemplated what he could have done differently along the way to commit ConneXXion more fully to the change process. "Should I keep working with ConneXXion because we need the short-term financial support? I'm just not sure there is any hope with this client."

The Union Carbide Deal (Abridged)

On November 3, 1986, after a three-hour board of directors meeting, Union Carbide decided to accept First Boston's proposal to embark on a $2.5 billion recapitalization program. Jamerson and his associates' efforts had paid off. Jamerson had reason to be excited: He had changed a weak relationship between First Boston and Union Carbide into one that would generate tens of millions of dollars in revenue for his firm. In the highly competitive world of investment banking, it was a particularly sweet victory, since First Boston had won the business from Union Carbide's traditional banker, Morgan Stanley.

UNION CARBIDE AND ITS INVESTMENT BANKS

In 1983, Carbide had revenues of $9.1 billion and was ranked thirty-seventh among the Fortune 500. Petrochemicals, industrial gases, and metal and carbon products were historically Carbide's bedrock product lines. The future growth of the company, however, lay elsewhere. As Warren Anderson, chairman of the board and chief executive officer, reported in his "Letter to Stockholders" in the 1983 Annual Report, "Our specialty, consumer, and service businesses—the entrepreneurial segments of our portfolio—will play an increasingly important role in the economy of the decade ahead, and in Carbide's future performance." Those business segments included such

products as Eveready batteries, Glad bags, and Prestone antifreeze, and together contributed 45 percent of the company's revenue.

Despite its size, Carbide was not a major player in the capital markets. Carbide had not issued equity since its initial public offering in 1917, and most of its debt offerings were privately placed with institutional investors such as insurance companies, rather than underwritten by an investment bank and sold to the public markets. During the 1970s, some funding and merger and acquisition activity occasionally brought Carbide in touch with the market and with various investment banks. Although Morgan Stanley did most of this work, other firms participated in cases where they possessed needed expertise. Goldman Sachs, for example, was the dealer for Carbide's commercial paper program. J. Clayton Stephenson, who in 1954 began working at a West Virginia plant and in 1982 was named chief financial officer, summarized Carbide's financial activity through the early 1980s: "We used investment bankers only intermittently."

As Carbide's "relationship bank," Morgan Stanley managed some debt offerings, assisted with some divestitures, and conducted several advisory studies on various aspects of Carbide's financial strategy. Stephenson recollected, "Morgan Stanley had long held a privileged position. It was based largely on close personal relationships between senior managers in the two companies. In 1983, other investment banks felt they were breaking their pick calling on us."

Senior Lecturer Thomas DeLong prepared this case as the basis for class discussion rather than to illustrate either effective or ineffective handling of an administrative situation. It is an abridged version of an earlier case prepared by Jeffrey Bradach under the supervision of Professor Robert Eccles and Professor Dwight Crane, The Union Carbide Deal, HBS No. 288-065.

Union Carbide's relationship with Morgan Stanley made Carbide an unlikely business prospect for First Boston in 1983. Nonetheless, account officers were assigned to all major companies regardless of perceived potential, and George Weiksner, a First Boston managing director, was to watch for opportunities at Carbide. (Managing director is the highest position at First Boston, followed by vice president, associate, and analyst.) He was not optimistic about his prospects for generating much business.

In mid-1983, Carbide let several investment banks know that it was accepting proposals on how it might finance the purchase of a ship. Bruce Jamerson and Bob deVeer, vice presidents in First Boston's Project Finance Group, put together a presentation and won the business. The $140 million deal was extremely complex and required working closely with many Carbide administrators. A deal of this size, though, did not necessitate the involvement of senior management at Carbide. Jamerson recalled that "although I didn't get to know any senior people, I worked with the junior treasury people, their lawyers, accountants, and others. In the process I got to know many of the people and, importantly, I got to know the company from the inside."

During the subsequent two years, Jamerson, an eager 33-year-old vice president, willingly invested his time and energy on the account even though no managing director had much hope for it. Because the ship package involved several refinancings, it provided an opportunity for him to keep in frequent contact with Carbide people. Still, First Boston was unable to establish a relationship with the key financial decision maker at Carbide, Clayton Stephenson. His tanned face and silver hair made him look like he stepped out of central casting to play the role of a chief executive officer. And indeed, he was mentioned as a possible successor to Warren Anderson.

Stephenson was involved in virtually all key decisions facing the company. When poisonous gas leaked from a Carbide plant in Bhopal, India, in late 1984, killing some 2,000 people, Stephenson was one of a few executives charged with managing the crisis. The accident rocked the company and dramatically affected its financial condition. Three days after the disastrous gas leak, an article in *The Wall Street Journal* suggested that the company might declare bankruptcy. Carbide's stock price slid precipitously, and the credit rating on its bonds was downgraded by Moody's from A2 to A3. The litigation generated by the accident haunted every move the company made.

THE GAF TAKEOVER ATTEMPT

Eight months after the gas leak, in August 1985, GAF, a company one-tenth the size of Carbide, began purchasing Carbide stock and for the second time in less than a year Carbide's future seemed in doubt. GAF's chairman, Sam Heyman, had a reputation as an aggressive corporate raider, winning control of GAF in a takeover battle two years earlier. Heyman's stake in Carbide grew from 5.6 percent in early August to 9.9 percent by the end of the month. Carbide management was wary and they turned to Morgan Stanley for assistance.

Stephenson recalled that "when we knew there was a raider out there, we put together a team of three: the president, the general counsel, and myself. We involved the board at an early stage, too." The team needed advice quickly "and Morgan Stanley was an easy and practical road to go down; they knew more about us than anyone else. This was not a time for comparison shopping. You go with who you know."

Carbide moved aggressively to defend itself. In the last week of August, an announcement was made that 4,000 jobs, 15 percent of Carbide's workforce, would be eliminated within a year. Furthermore, plants would be closed, businesses sold, and some of the surplus in the company's overfunded pension fund would be tapped. The cash generated by these actions would be used to buy back 15 percent of Carbide's stock, which would increase earnings per share and support the price of the stock. While Ed Van Den Ameele, a Carbide spokesman, told the New York Times (August 1, 1985, p. D7) that "this is a plan we have been working on for quite some time," the GAF threat certainly accelerated its implementation.

During the fall of 1985 Heyman was kept at bay, but his interest in Carbide had not subsided. On December 8, GAF made a tender offer of $68 a share for approximately 70 percent of Carbide's shares. (On August 1, the stock closed at $50 per share. With the persistent rumors of a takeover, the stock traded up to $63 by December 1.)

The next week the board of directors met to consider the GAF bid. Morgan Stanley outlined the options available to Carbide. After spending a week studying alternatives, the board decided that the GAF offer was inadequate and that the best way to stymie GAF's advances was to offer Carbide shareholders a package of debt securities and cash in return for their shares. Carbide shareholders would thus be able to choose between GAF's cash offer and their own company's exchange offer. Depending on the size of GAF's stake in the company, Carbide was committed to buy back anywhere from 23.5 to 47.1 million shares (approximately 70 percent of the outstanding stock).

On January 8, after a month of ratcheting up its tender offer price to $78 a share, GAF withdrew its offer. Shareholders who accepted Carbide's exchange offer, including GAF, obtained a substantial profit. Thus, despite failing to obtain control of the company, GAF walked away with an $81 million after-tax profit for its efforts when it took advantage of Carbide's exchange offer.

Carbide, however, had been forced to sell a major portion of its business and had placed itself in a precarious financial position. In the end, Carbide bought back 55 percent of its shares, which resulted in the issuance of $2.5 billion in new medium and long-term fixed-rate debt. Its debt to equity ratio soared from 39 percent to 72 percent. And Carbide paid dearly for the debt. The three debt issues had a weighted average interest rate of 14.2 percent. Carbide's bond rating fell again, this time from A3 to Ba3. The new debt moved Carbide from an "investment-grade" company to a "noninvestment grade" company.

Soon after the dust settled, Carbide started to chafe under the large debt burden. Stephenson recalled that "while some were celebrating our victory, we knew we were in trouble. We had only completed phase one of a long series of battles. We wanted to be able to run the company as a business, not as an investment banking exercise."

Not only was Carbide hampered by the onerous debt burden, but also the convenants on the newly acquired debt severely restricted its activities. John Clerico, who had been promoted to Carbide's treasurer just the day before Heyman's tender offer, remarked that "we had to pretty much call the bank if we wanted to buy or sell anything." Clerico pointed out that "the financial constraints affected the culture of the company. Managers in different divisions were unable to pursue good ideas, which was counter to the independent, entrepreneurial culture of the company. Financial considerations constrained strategy."

Carbide's first task was to reduce the interest expense. In February 1986, Carbide invited several investment and commerical banks to bid on interest rate swap advisory. Jim Sawyer, Clerico's assistant, called Jamerson and invited First Boston to make a presentation. (Sawyer and Jamerson were both graduates of MIT's Sloan School of Management and had met there at a First Boston recruiting presentation.) Carbide was betting that interest rates would fall and wanted advice on how, and at what price, to swap its fixed interest rate obligations into floating interest rates that would decrease if its bet was correct.

Four investment banks (Morgan Stanley, First Boston, Goldman Sachs, and Salomon Brothers) and two commercial banks (Morgan Guaranty and Bankers Trust) made presentations to Clerico and his staff. First Boston won. Sawyer recalled that "First Boston was the only investment bank that truly understood our needs. We wanted advice on how to price swaps—First Boston understood that. The other banks wanted to *do* swaps with us, which certainly conflicted with our desire to have advice on how to price them." Clerico believed that the loss of the swap deal did not disturb Morgan Stanley too much because it was not an area of strong emphasis for the investment bank.

"I was elated," said Jamerson. He now had something to talk to Clerico about on a regular basis. In Clerico's new position it was crucial that he know what was happening in the capital markets. Jamerson knew that. "I started sending him economic reports, chemical industry surveys, and First Boston Flash Reports on opportunities that he might find useful. If I can help him do his job better—and he looks good to his boss—we both win." The reports, coupled with the ongoing swap program, served Jamerson well in his efforts to develop a working relationship with Clerico. Beginning in February 1986, Jamerson and Clerico talked on the phone once or twice a week. By September, Carbide had swapped over $700 million of their debt.

Jamerson's pursuit of Carbide business complemented his pursuit of promotion at First Boston. In March 1986, Jamerson moved from Project Finance, where he served as product specialist, to the Natural Resources Group, where he was given account coverage responsibility. Along with switching departments, Jamerson received his first customer call list. He asked that Carbide be placed on it, since he had effectively managed that account for some time. George Weiksner had moved to the Technology Group the previous year and Tony Freeman, a managing director, had assumed account management responsibility for Carbide. Freeman agreed to relinquish day-to-day management of the account to Jamerson, although nominally he remained the senior member of the firm assigned to Carbide.

During the spring and early summer, Carbide sought ways to generate cash to reduce its debt burden. At Carbide's request, Morgan Stanley made several presentations to Stephenson and Clerico regarding an equity issue. At the same time Morgan Stanley assisted with the GAF takeover defense. On April 22, the business was sold to a group of investors in a leveraged buyout

(LBO). The purchase was funded by First Boston's LBO group. Jamerson had nothing to do with the deal; he purposely stayed away from it because in this instance First Boston was working for the buyers of the business and not for Carbide.

Jamerson talked to Clerico several times in the spring about issuing equity or swapping the debt for equity. "I knew there was no way Carbide would stay in its existing financial condition," said Jamerson. The nagging problem of a large amount of high interest rate debt with restrictive convenants remained. A few meetings with Clerico entailed full presentations by First Boston on the impact of an equity offering on Carbide's situation. Although Stephenson and Clerico were interested in doing an equity offering, they were unconvinced that the ideas on the table would solve their problems.

The Carbide/First Boston relationship took another step forward when in July First Boston agreed to finance the buyback of some of Carbide's high-yield bonds on the open market. The bond-buyback idea emerged out of a conversation between Jamerson and John Kolmer, a managing director and head of First Boston's High Yield Sales and Trading Department. Although in different departments, Kolmer and Jamerson spoke frequently about the bond market and Jamerson's accounts. Kolmer knew that the first call date on Carbide's bonds was three years away, and he believed "there was no way Carbide would be able to wait that long." They both agreed it made sense to purchase some bonds now, since the three issues were currently less expensive compared to other, similar issues. Kolmer also thought interest rates were going down, which would make the bonds more expensive to buy back later.

Clerico was interested in Jamerson's idea. It had added appeal to Clerico because Morgan Stanley had earlier expressed reluctance to provide the same service to Carbide. Kolmer and Jamerson visited Danbury, Connecticut (Carbide's headquarters), the next week and made their pitch. Kolmer said he was certain that he could bring in the bonds at low prices: "I told Clerico I was so confident that I'd sell him the bonds at today's prices." After some discussion, Clerico and Kolmer agreed that First Boston would purchase approximately $200 million of the bonds, hold them in inventory, and Carbide would have the option to buy back the bonds at cost plus accrued interest and a trading commission. Even though the profits on the deal were modest, Kolmer was happy to buy back the bonds. "I knew that this was an entree deal. I was willing to do it for nothing with the hope that we might get future business."

A few days later, First Boston quietly commenced buying the bonds. No consolidated list of bondholders existed, since most of the bonds had been recycled from the original bondholders (former Carbide stockholders who obtained the bonds in the earlier exchange offer) to institutional investors. At the start nobody knew where the bonds were, but during the six-week buying period Kolmer acquired a substantial amount of market information. By the end of August, First Boston had purchased $207 million of Carbide's bonds, or about 8 percent of the issue.

On September 2, Clerico called Jamerson and said Stephenson wanted to meet with the people at First Boston. After spending many months considering gradualist solutions to their situation, and coming to the conclusion that it would take five to seven years to relieve the debt burden, Robert Kennedy (who was appointed chairman and CEO in April 1986), Stephenson, and Clerico decided to explore "more sweeping and comprehensive ideas," recalled Clerico. Part of the reasoning noted by Stephenson was that "we weren't really getting what we wanted from Morgan Stanley, so we decided to broaden our conversations and to talk with others." In addition, officers at Carbide had been taking a broader look at their use of both commercial banks and investment banks. They concluded that it would be helpful to have more investment banking firms involved in their business, just as they had multiple commercial banks. As Clerico said, "We thought that to get Carbide back on track would require the expertise of many people, not just one investment bank."

A lunch meeting of the Carbide and First Boston people was set for September 10. It was held in a private dining room on the 44th floor of First Bostons' midtown Manhattan office. Peter Buchanan, chief executive officer of First Boston, Jamerson, Freeman, and Brian Finn, an associate from the Mergers and Acquisitions Department with expertise on corporate restructurings, attended from First Boston. Stephenson and Clerico represented Carbide. Sitting next to each other in the elegant, wood-paneled dining room, Buchanan and Stephenson discussed Carbide's situation. Stephenson told Buchanan, "There is lots of money to be made here if you come up with a creative solution to our situation." Buchanan's presence at the meeting reflected the magnitude of the opportunity.

Stephenson also let them know that he had asked Salomon Brothers, Morgan Stanley, and Goldman Sachs for their ideas. Stephenson said they were looking for sketches of proposals, and that they would give all four banking firms access to internal documents and personnel so that they would fully understand Carbide's situation. Once the company decided on a course of action they would pay the chosen investment bank to develop further its ideas. Speed was important. The Tax Reform Act of 1986 had increased the capital gains tax, making financial actions before the end of the year more attractive.

Carbide had three objectives. First, it sought to reduce its interest expense by substituting lower-cost capital for the high-cost debt currently on the books. Second, it wanted the covenants on the debt relaxed in order to have more operating flexibility. The second objective was a problem because covenants were extremely difficult to amend. A change required the consent of 80 percent of the bondholders. Making matters even more difficult was that even though Carbide sought to relax the covenants, they also wanted to ensure that they would not be vulnerable to a corporate raider again.

Carbide's third objective was to give Robert Kennedy a "clean slate." Stephenson noted that

Kennedy was "discontented with the capital structure. He was a builder and was working toward building the 'new Union Carbide,' but he was hampered by the financial situation of the company. He provided this entire effort with support and a sense of urgency."

THE PROPOSAL

A flurry of activity at First Boston followed the meeting. Suddenly the firm had a good shot at a giant piece of Carbide business. Jamerson met with Dick Bott, a managing director who was co-head of the Investment Banking Group, and requested the necessary manpower. Bott suggested that Jamerson meet with Bob Calhoun, a managing director who had recently formed the Restructuring Group and who was widely respected throughout the firm.

"I had just formed the Restructuring Group a month earlier," said Calhoun. "We were a part-time advisory group made up of a few people from different parts of the firm. Our goal was to serve as a resource to account managers who had clients interested in restructurings." (Calhoun's new group focused on healthy companies that needed to restructure to defend against raiders. There was also an existing reorganization group in the Corporate Finance Department that worked on restructuring of companies in Chapter 11 bankruptcy proceedings.)

By this time, Jamerson also realized that the proposed task extended beyond the scope of a vice president. "This was a big ticket item, and we needed the big bats. I was not too proud to realize that," said Jamerson. One of Jamerson's colleagues remarked, "Not only was it an issue of whether Jamerson was senior enough to deal with the client, it also wasn't clear that he had the muscle to master all the product groups." Given the substance and the magnitude of the task, Calhoun was the perfect person to serve as the senior account manager. Freeman, who had since been assigned responsibility for calling on industrial clients in the United Kingdom, stepped back into the picture, since he had some experience working with Carbide.

Although Jamerson knew that a managing director should be involved in the deal, he expressed some concern. "You want to be *the* guy, both to the client and internally. You must be perceived to be of that stature to succeed." In the end, while Calhoun and Freeman offered a guiding hand, Jamerson was responsible for managing the work. It had been largely his efforts that made a nonexistent relationship into one that might yield enormous revenues.

The clock was running and First Boston needed to come up with a proposal. Richard Kauffman, an associate who had recently joined Calhoun's Restructuring Group, was asked to help with the proposal. Kauffman remembered that "it wasn't really clear who was responsible for coming up with a solution. In fact, we didn't have a good handle on the problem." A task of this magnitude cut across organizational boundaries in the bank, and simply getting people together for a meeting was difficult. For several days Jamerson, Freeman, Calhoun, Kolmer, Kauffman, and Mark Lightcap, a managing director from High Yield Sales and Trading who reported to Kolmer, discussed the issue endlessly.

Pressure mounted when Carbide visited First Boston's New York office on September 23 for a follow-up meeting. Carbide officials were disappointed because a formal presentation of ideas was not made. Although the meeting was still productive, it was clear that First Boston would have to have concrete suggestions for the next meeting to be held a week later on October 1.

The key problem was figuring out how to obtain the consent of 80 percent of the bondholders—the number required to amend the debt covenants. As Carbide's problem came into sharper focus, so did its options: a tender offer to buy the bonds for cash or an exchange offer in which new securities would be offered for the old bonds. John Kolmer was convinced that the only way to get 80 percent of the bondholders to tender their bonds was to offer cash. "I was adamant about this approach. A cash offer had the best, and maybe only, chance of getting 80 percent of the bonds in." Along with the higher probability of success, the cash tender offer had other advantages. First, Leon Kalveria, a vice president from High Yield Finance, worked with outside legal counsel and determined that a cash tender offer would be the quickest approach. Second, the financial impact of the recently ratified tax bill favored the cash tender offer over the exchange offer. Third, the strategy avoided the uncontrolled distribution of equity shares to the bondholders. After its experience with corporate raiders, "Carbide didn't want to have its equity washing around the market," noted Jamerson.

Calhoun concurred, "The cash tender offer was the obviously superior thing to do. To solve the client's problem we had to figure out a way to do it." The difficulty with the approach was coming up with the $3 billion in cash needed to buy back the bonds. This amount was higher than the face value of $2.5 billion, but the market value had risen and some premium would be needed to gain acceptance of the offer. (Part of this $3 billion would be used to buy the $207 million of bonds that First Boston had previously purchased for Carbide, but as agreed, the company would obtain these at First Boston's cost plus commission, not at the tender offer price.)

"We immediately looked at what Carbide's commercial bank financing capabilities were and what it might be able to do in the capital markets," said Jamerson. Jamerson immediately met with Bill Clark, a vice president in the Bank Finance Department. Clark had also worked for several years at Morgan Guaranty, one of the major commercial banks working with Carbide.

Clark told Jamerson he was convinced that the commerical banks would lend Carbide $2 billion. During the most recent negotiations with commercial banks (before the idea of a tender offer was on the table) $1 billion in new bank credit facilities had been offered to Carbide. "I was con-

fident that the banks would lend another $1 billion, as long as specific assets were earmarked to repay the bank debt." Clerico also told Jamerson that, as a part of an overall recapitalization program, Carbide could divest businesses worth approximately $1 billion within a few months. With these assets available, a total loan of $2 billion from the commercial banks appeared to be reasonable.

This left $1 billion to be obtained in the capital markets from a new equity issue and a private placement of securities. Jim Freeman, a managing director and the co-head of Equity Sales and Trading, was involved in early discussions with Jamerson about the feasibility of an equity issue. "Freeman told me that the market could absorb $500 to $600 million in new Carbide equity," said Jamerson. At the same time, Jamerson met with the First Boston Private Finance Department and asked it to determine the amount and type of securities that could be privately placed with institutions. Tom Keaveney and Sean Twomey, a managing director and a vice president, believed they would be able to place between $200 and $500 million of short-term debt securities. Kauffman was assigned the responsibility of analyzing Carbide's financial position and assessing the financial impact of a cash tender offer. Carbide's recent financial maneuvering had wreaked havoc on their financial statements, leading one banker to comment, "No one had seen clean financials for two years." Kauffman, who was given substantial access to the available data, plowed through Carbide's financial statements line by line, trying to understand what the new, slimmed-down Carbide would look like after a cash tender offer. This torturous process led him to remember the project as "one of the worst I've ever worked on."

As the informal discussions prior to the October 1 meeting continued, Jamerson and Calhoun raised the idea of First Boston making a bridge loan to Carbide to cover this gap. They and Freeman met with William Mayer, a managing director and one of four senior members of the firm who made up the Executive Committee, to explore the feasibility of making a bridge loan. Mayer's approval was needed for such transactions. As he said, "We don't want salesmen having the ability to commit the capital of the firm." Jamerson explained the Carbide situation to Mayer, emphasizing that in the event of a tie, Carbide would probably give Morgan Stanley the order. The ability to offer financing for the deal would differentiate First Boston.

The other issue facing Mayer was whether First Boston had the capacity to lend $1 billion to Carbide. He knew that another bridge loan of over $1 billion was being considered. First Boston was representing Campeau, a Canadian retailer, in its attempt to buy Allied Stores. Mayer had to be sure that First Boston could handle the unlikely, but possible, occurrence of both bridge loans happening simultaneously. After examining First Boston's own borrowing capacity and the internal capital of the firm, he determined that the firm could commit up to $1 billion to Carbide.

Calhoun and Jamerson managed the blizzard of activities that First Boston undertook to prepare for the October 1 meeting. Calhoun recalled, "I was working on five or six other projects at the time, but this was certainly the biggest. I probably met with people two or three times a day." Jamerson worked full-time on the proposal, spending every other day at Carbide headquarters gathering information. "I worked seven days a week from 8:00 A.M. until 11:00 P.M."

In just a few weeks the contours of First Boston's proposal came into focus. A plan to obtain 80 percent of the bonds was created, the tender offer price was determined, and financing mechanisms adequate for the purchase of the bonds were proposed. Help was solicited from several departments or groups within the banking firm, but marshaling resources was not a problem. "Big deals attract a lot of attention," observed Calhoun. "Once key people are involved—and the deal looks big—you don't have much trouble getting people to help even if they are in different departments."

WINNING THE SUPPORT OF MANAGEMENT AND THE BOARD

Jamerson, Calhoun, and Kolmer visited Carbide's Danbury headquarters on October 1 and gave their presentation. Dave Batten, a First Boston managing director with substantial new equity issue experience, also took part. Stephenson agreed with their assessment that a cash tender offer was the optimal solution. Most important, First Boston, through its bridge loan facility, offered the means to finance the deal. Stephenson still had concerns about the financial implications of the plan. He wanted to be certain that Carbide would be able to wipe the bank debt and bridge loans off the books promptly and that earnings per share would not be reduced.

At a second meeting on October 13, Jamerson, Calhoun, Jim Freeman, Tony Freeman, and Clark outlined the plan in greater detail. Stephenson was concerned about the size of the premium being paid for the bonds; it would fall directly out of the owner's equity line on the balance sheet. For him "it was vital to hear Jim Freeman say we could take the equity deal to market." Scenario after scenario was examined. The financial analysis was a subject of great consternation because the results depended heavily on an uncertain number, the percentage of the bonds that would be tendered.

The three other investment banks made presentations to Carbide, and each offered entirely different ideas. Goldman Sachs analyzed several approaches but did not offer a specific recommendation. Salomon Brothers did an extensive analysis of the bond market and told Carbide that the premium necessary to buy back the bonds would be excessive. They recommended that Carbide continue to pursue a gradualist approach and slowly buy back the bonds. Carbide appreciated Salomon Brothers' candor, but disagreed with their view. Morgan Stanley did not believe that Carbide had the resources to make a cash tender offer, so they suggested that Carbide make an exchange offer: swap the existing debt for equity and new, cheaper debt. After First Boston and Morgan Stanley each made two formal presentations, Carbide management decided it wanted First Boston as the financial advisor on the deal. Calhoun observed that "Carbide wasn't really choosing so much among investment banks as it was choosing among different proposals."

"What clinched the deal was that First Boston could and would put up the necessary money," said Stephenson. "Morgan Stanley clearly had no stomach for this." Though economic reality swayed Stephenson, he was also very impressed with the First Boston team. "They put a very good looking group in front of us with some very good ideas." Stephenson and Clerico were particularly impressed with Bob Calhoun, head of the Restructuring Group. Stephenson remarked that Calhoun "is one of the steadiest and most thoughtful investment bankers I know."

"Morgan Stanley was stunned when we told them that we gave the business to First Boston. They were obviously very distressed," Stephenson went on. The most senior managing directors at Morgan Stanley contacted Stephenson to discuss the matter. Stephenson recalled that, after some reflection, "Morgan Stanley agreed that they had not followed up the account appropriately; they had not worked aggressively to solve Carbide's predicament."

Even though Stephenson was impressed with the organizational capabilities of First Boston, there was actually some confusion below the surface. The three leaders—Calhoun, Jamerson, and Tony Freeman—formed an amorphously structured management team. "It wasn't entirely clear who was in charge," said one banker associated with the deal. Once First Boston received the order from Carbide management, Calhoun reduced his involvement: "I spent about an hour a day on it." Freeman and Jamerson, however, worked full-time on the deal. Freeman was responsible for "implementation" and Jamerson was accountable for the "day-to-day orchestration" of the deal. More than one team member mentioned the fact that the distinction between Jamerson's and Freeman's jobs was vague.

Kauffman and Randy Hazelton, an analyst, continued to work with Carbide's financial staff between October 15 and November 3, the date of the board meeting. Kauffman was responsible for the financial analysis and the management of the equity offering, which involved doing due diligence and preparing the "red herring," the preliminary prospectus for the equity offering.

In three months, Carbide's entire capital structure was altered: a nascent idea in early October had developed into a set of deals that gave the company an entirely different balance sheet by the end of the year. With the help of First Boston, Carbide achieved its goals of lower debt, reduced interest expense, and less restrictive covenants. It could approach the future with new flexibility and vigor.

First Boston also met its objectives. With the completion of the equity and private placement offerings, First Boston's bridge loan was paid down from nearly $1 billion to $100 million in just a few weeks. The package of transactions garnered revenues to First Boston exceeding $70 million, and it was in a strong position to do future business with Carbide: "We finally established a strong relationship with Union Carbide," said Jamerson.

Virtually all the First Boston bankers agreed that the Carbide deal was a great experience. With characteristic flourish, Tony Freeman remarked that "this was the Olympic Games of investment banking." In discussing the deal with Jamerson six months after it occurred, we could not help being swept up in this enthusiasm. He would leap from his chair and reenact the meetings associated with the deal.

Even though the financial rewards for individuals at First Boston were significant, the sense of having participated in something "big" was the most salient memory people had of the deal. Although Kauffman possessed a rather jaundiced view of the experience because of the long hours and grueling detail, even he conceded that "there was a certain sense of excitement involved in doing the equity deal." Six months after the deal he moved from Investment Banking to the Equity Capital Markets Group: "My experiences on the Carbide deal enabled me to meet these people and I was impressed with them." Twomey confessed that the one-month period during which the deal was happening "generated a lot of stomach acid. But that is what this business is all about. I wouldn't want a steady diet of these but one or two a year are great."

Gookin was even more ebullient about his experience. "This was a great deal—the biggest tender offer ever done, the biggest bridge ever done, and a Christmas tree of refinancing transactions. I also became an expert on debt tender offers." On a more personal level he said, "This was a great credibility builder for me. I got to work with a multitude of organizations within the firm." He also developed relationships with the Carbide people. "I now regularly call on several people who work for Clerico."

Stephenson believed that the recapitalization was a success. "The president of the company was able to go to the shareholders with a clean slate in 1987." In a June 1987 *Corporate Finance* article (p. 54), Stephenson described the plan as "a surgical, quick, neat, trim, clean silver bullet sort of solution." That same article concluded that "for Union Carbide shareholders, it is without a doubt a most successful restructuring."

As for whether First Boston earned its fees, Stephenson responded, "I think they did given the fee structure that obtains in the industry." His satisfaction with First Boston's work, however, did not lead to the conclusion that it was now Carbide's exclusive "relationship" bank. "Carbide's aggressive financial strategy attracted the attention of many investment banks," said Clerico. "Now a number of them are quick to call on us with new ideas." Still, Carbide's investment banking relationships, old and new, endured. "Morgan Stanley has a very strong person assigned to the account, and things are back on course," said Stephenson. Clerico's assessment was similar: "Morgan Stanley and First Boston are equal runners on anything that comes down the road."

Jill Greenthal at Donaldson, Lufkin & Jenrette (A):
The TCI/AT&T Deal

> A deal like this would be a once-in-a-lifetime transaction for me.
>
> *Jill Greenthal, managing director, Donaldson, Lufkin & Jenrette*

Jill Greenthal joined her team on the terrace adjoining the conference room in which 40 corporate decision makers, bankers, and advisors had convened for the day. AT&T CEO Michael Armstrong had assembled what seemed like a small army to work out possible deal structures for a joint venture between telecommunications and cable industry giants AT&T and TCI. The transaction (with a combined valuation of close to $80 billion) had the potential to dramatically alter the landscape of the telecommunications and cable industries. (For proposed structure, see Exhibit 1.) Those present, moreover, stood to gain considerable reward and recognition. Greenthal, managing director at Donaldson, Lufkin & Jenrette (DLJ), one of the three investment banks at the conference, explained the purpose of the meeting:

> AT&T was preparing to face the eventual entry of the Regional Bell Operating Companies into its consumer long-distance business. AT&T proposed to combine its consumer long-distance operations with TCI's cable assets, thus giving it the potential to enter the local telephone market with a bundled offering. Before considering any kind of combination, we all needed to agree on

the value of AT&T's and TCI's businesses. Valuing AT&T's consumer long-distance operations was particularly challenging. The business had never been separately valued before—there were confusing technical, legal, and tax issues—and had a difficult-to-value brand name.

Greenthal had worked long and hard cultivating relationships with John Malone and Leo Hindery of TCI over the course of a decade. She had forged her way up the "food chain" of transactions, taking on increasingly larger, more prominent, and more prestigious transactions. For this current negotiation, which could lead to a breakthrough deal in the industry (and in her career), she had assembled an eight-member "A" team at DLJ.

The "all-hands" meeting on May 30, 1998, was the culmination of a series of meetings that had taken place between the disparate groups that spring. The negotiating parties had reached what seemed like an impasse. Greenthal described the sentiment in the room:

> After several hours of complicated structuring and valuation presentations by different bankers, it was clear that there were major

Research Associate Sarah Thorp prepared this case under the supervision of Professors Ashish Nanda and Thomas DeLong as the basis for class discussion rather than to illustrate either effective or ineffective handling of an administrative situation.

EXHIBIT 1   AT&T and TCI—Proposed Deal Structure, May 1998

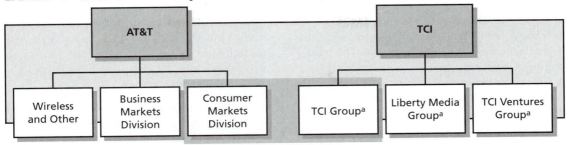

Proposed Deal Structure

ᵃ TCI Group: domestic cable assets.
Liberty Media Group: programming assets.
TCI Ventures Group: international assets and businesses and noncable and nonprogramming assets.

Source: AT&T's proxy statement and prospectus.

differences of opinion. We were all growing increasingly skeptical that getting agreement between the two companies on the value of AT&T's business would be possible.

AT&T, counseled by its financial advisors CS First Boston and Goldman Sachs, had claimed that its brand and long-distance business were worth well in excess of the valuation which TCI and Greenthal's team had determined.

Malone had begun to wonder aloud why he would want to combine TCI with AT&T's troubled consumer long-distance business. Mindful that Malone was a no-nonsense straight-shooter who wouldn't think anything of walking out on a proposal that didn't seem right, Greenthal wondered what, if anything, her team could do to help find a better alternative.

JILL GREENTHAL

Education and Early Career

Jill Greenthal had grown up in Wisconsin—a Green Bay Packers[1] fan with three brothers. Moving to Boston after high school, she attended Simmons College, a small liberal arts school for women. After earning a BA in economics, she moved to New York to sell industrial chemicals for Union Carbide and, in the fall of 1981, matriculated at Harvard Business School (HBS).

During business school, Greenthal decided to explore job opportunities on Wall Street. She spent a summer interning at Goldman Sachs. Upon graduation, she accepted a position as an associate at Smith Barney. Nine months into her work at the firm, Smith Barney was approached for help with selling a small television station. At the time, the firm had no formal media group. Greenthal volunteered to work on the deal. "I was curious about the industry," she explained,

> because my HBS friends were interested in media, as was my husband, Tom, who had also been a sectionmate at business school. Upon being signed up, I tried to learn everything I could about the business. By the time the deal had closed I had gotten the media bug and realized that I needed to go and work for someone who understood the media investment banking business.

Greenthal discovered that Lehman Brothers was one of the few investment houses with a

---

[1] Wisconsin's professional football team.

media group. Four people strong, the group was headed by Fred Segal, who Greenthal characterized as "a brilliant and demanding banker." Hired by Segal in 1986 as a second-year associate, Greenthal soon became his lieutenant. The following year, business exploded. Segal and his small team of bankers closed 35 transactions, establishing themselves firmly in the media and entertainment arenas.

Career Moves

In the winter of 1990, having decided that living and working overseas would be an important learning experience, Greenthal and her husband moved to their respective firms' London offices. Greenthal continued her media work for Lehman; her husband Tom Eisenmann moved to McKinsey's London office. Five months after they arrived, Segal announced he was leaving to join Salomon, whereupon Lehman asked Greenthal, eight months pregnant at the time, to return to New York City to run its media group. The couple returned to New York in August 1990. Greenthal was promoted to managing director in 1991.

The media industry went through a fallow period from 1989 to 1992, with a downturn in highly leveraged transactions. "[It] was a crossroads for media investment banking," observed an industry reporter. "While some saw it as the dark days of investment banking, Jill Greenthal viewed it as a blessing in disguise." "Difficulties during the 1989–1992 period," reflected Greenthal, "caused everyone to retrench, figure out how to run their businesses better. It sorted out the people who understood the industry from the people who did not. . . . People who didn't have a commitment to the business moved on."[2]

In 1994, when her husband resigned from McKinsey to pursue a doctorate at HBS, Greenthal gave up running the media group and began

working primarily as a producer for Lehman in Boston.

By 1995, Greenthal had earned a reputation as a savvy, exacting banker. DLJ's head of high-yield research Mark Grotevant, who had previously held the same position at Lehman, recalled her work in media and communications:

> The companies in Jill's portfolio included the most dynamic, entrepreneurial firms in the marketplace, such as Comcast, TCI, and Time Warner. Her approach was not the typical "what-can-we-do-for-you" followed with profit-maximizing execution. For her, client relationships were more of a process than a simple binary proposal. She made sure she understood client's business as well as, if not better than, her client. She wanted to know their strategy and was constantly in conversations with them about the right thing to do. Jill was opinionated. She challenged them and I'm sure at times was in disagreement with them. The client viewed her as a partner.

Said Carl Vogel, former Jones Intercable CFO and ex-EchoStar and ex-PrimeStar president, of Greenthal: "She's bright, aggressive, and understands the business very, very well."[3] Just as these attributes served her in negotiating deals, Greenthal had also earned a reputation among some of her peers at other investment banks of being somewhat formidable. "Those who sit on the opposite side of the negotiating table from Jill learn quickly to beware," explained a colleague. "She has a sharp tongue. She has an edge to her. You can't get anything past her."

Attracted by her reputation as a bright and tenacious banker, investment banks were eager to hire Greenthal. Greenthal, meanwhile, began to wonder "if Lehman Brothers was the right place for me to continue to work," she recalled. "Unfortunately,

---

[2] Price Colman, "The Deal Makers," *Broadcasting & Cable* 127, no. 49 (December 1, 1997), p. 61.
[3] Ibid., p. 60.

at the time, the firm was struggling with many internal issues."

The DLJ Offer

Among those that were recruiting Greenthal aggressively was DLJ. She recalled the initial contact by her former HBS sectionmate Jim Alexandre in the fall of 1995:

> Jim mentioned that DLJ would be a great platform for media and telecommunications. He told me DLJ wanted to strengthen its specialty group for the industry and was willing to open a Boston office for me. I spoke with Tony James [investment banking head], Joe Roby [DLJ president], Garrett Moran [vice chairman of investment banking], and John Chalsty [the CEO].

DONALDSON, LUFKIN & JENRETTE

Company Background

Dick Jenrette and partners Bill Donaldson and Dan Lufkin founded Donaldson, Lufkin & Jenrette in 1959, shortly after graduating from Harvard Business School. The firm's first product, new to Wall Street at the time, was in-depth research designed to serve professional institutional investors seeking additional information to improve investment performance.

By 1996 DLJ had emerged from a research boutique to a fully integrated investment and merchant bank and was ranked in the top 15 investment services firms. But research remained DLJ's core competency. "Wall Street firms tended to have personalities based on how they started," explained Dennis Leibowitz, DLJ's equity research analyst in broadcasting and cable, who had been ranked for 20 years on the *Institutional Investor* all-star list and was widely regarded as the "dean of the cable television industry."

> DLJ was started as a research firm. In fact, everyone who has run the firm—all except

for Joe Roby—came from research. For this reason we have a different mentality. Goldman Sachs and Morgan Stanley are known for banking, Salomon for trading. With us, research was always the cornerstone.

Relative to its competitors, DLJ distinguished itself as a haven for entrepreneurial bankers by keeping management ranks thin and affording young bankers opportunities to assume greater responsibility earlier than was typical in the industry. Comparatively unburdened by bureaucracy and internal politics, DLJ's senior management focused on driving organizational efficiency and left external relationship building, pitching business, and executing deals to the professionals. "Our business is personal," observed James, describing the firm's culture. "Here, you don't have the business card that allows a mediocre person to be successful. Our people need to have individual strengths. It helps tremendously if you are a brand in the context of DLJ."

Lines of Business and Organization Structure

Over the years, DLJ had expanded its lines of business, initially into equity, then merchant banking, and later high-yield debt. It had consistently ranked number one in high yield since the early 1990s and was known for advising mid-market companies. In 1996 the firm had sales of nearly $3 billion and employed 5,900 people in 17 offices in the United States and 11 offices in Europe, Latin America, and Asia. Its businesses included securities underwriting; sales and trading; investment and merchant banking; financial advisory services; investment research; venture capital; and asset management.

DLJ comprised four principal operating departments: banking, equities, fixed income, and financial services. The banking department was organized into two main units: banking products groups and industry specialty groups. (Exhibit 2 provides an organization chart.) Banking products groups included professionals with in-depth product knowledge (in mergers and acquisitions, high

EXHIBIT 2A Donaldson, Lufkin & Jenrette, Inc. and Subsidiaries
Principal Operating Groups

Group Headcount

	1996	1997	1998
Banking	856	1,170	1,608
Equities	675	770	1,025
Fixed Income	789	826	891
Financial Services	2,970	3,589	4,139
Other	595	698	802
Total	5,885	7,053	8,465

Group Net Revenues ($ millions)

	1996	1997	1998
Banking	$853	$1,220	$1,487
Equities	564	598	656
Fixed Income	505	664	617
Financial Services	828	1,009	1,248

Group Pretax Profits ($ millions)

	1996	1997	1998
Banking	$266	$382	$416
Equities	149	119	25
Fixed Income	122	200	166
Financial Services	142	158	186

Source: DLJ Factbook, October 8, 1999.

yield, private placements, and equities), and industry specialty groups comprised individuals with industry-specific expertise. Usually the bankers in the specialty industry groups were the ones who forged relationships with clients. Together, the industry and the products groups provided an "integrated," industry-intensive approach to executing investment banking deals. (Exhibit 3 compares DLJ's mergers and acquisitions activities.)

The Media and Communications Group

Media and Communications, the most profitable of DLJ's 18 industry groups, was the group ag-

gressively courting Greenthal. Created in the mid-1980s, the group, led by Bob Johnson, had performed mostly small to medium-sized transactions during the early 1990s. In 1996, the group employed approximately 30 people working on 100 deals and bringing in close to $400 million in total revenues. The largest media and telecommunications deal—a public offering transaction in 1993—had been valued at $930 million. Its largest merger had been valued at $2.3 billion. "Historically, the media group at DLJ had done some important mid-size financing deals in the U.K. and U.S. cable, cellular, and satellite industries," ob-

EXHIBIT 2B   **DLJ Investment Banking Business Groups**

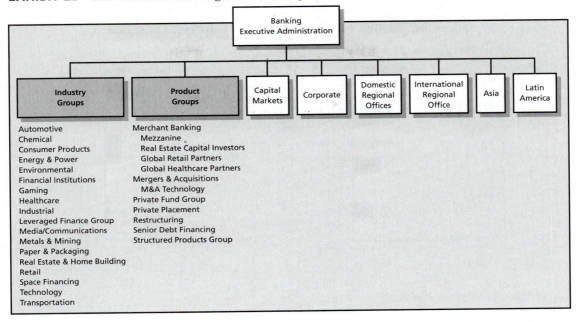

Source: Donaldson, Lufkin & Jenrette.

served a media and communications associate, "but we hadn't done much M&A work."

The Mergers and Acquisitions Group

Herald Ritch and co-head Joel Cohen had built DLJ's M&A group starting in the early 1990s. "The M&A group," recalled Ritch, "had really been small potatoes until 1991 when we began to grow. In 1993, we had approximately $50 million in revenues and every year thereafter we set a record, growing to approximately $200 million in revenues in 1996." Observed Jimmy Neissa, a managing director of the group, "We have done well with entrepreneurial companies that have strong CEOs who make it their business to be involved in everything. We have done less well with large bureaucratic institutions that have too many people making decisions."

JILL GREENTHAL AT DLJ

Greenthal's Recruitment

Desirous of expanding the media business further and feeling that the group was getting short on talent, James approached Leibowitz for advice on recruiting someone with market impact. "Leveraging research is critical to our business," explained James. "So we are always trying to find bankers the research analysts respect. Dennis respected Jill. We had no doubt that she respected Dennis, and so we asked him to initiate contact with her."

Greenthal was contacted first by her former HBS sectionmate at DLJ, followed by Roby. After meeting several DLJ executives, Greenthal accepted their offer and joined DLJ in February 1996. "The decision turned out to be a no-brainer," Greenthal recalled.

EXHIBIT 3A   Mergers and Acquisition Transaction Volume and DLJ's Ranking

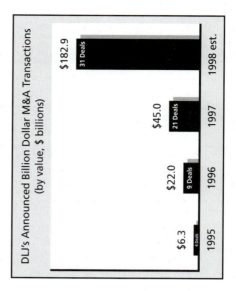

Domestic Completed M&A Transactions[a]
($ billions)

| 1994 | 1995 | 1996 | 1997 | 1998 est. |
| $295 | $436 | $642 | $764 | $1,338 |

[a] This represents all M&A transactions in the world (not just for DLJ).

DLJ's Announced Billion Dollar M&A Transactions
(by value, $ billions)

$6.3 (4 Deals) 1995
$22.0 (9 Deals) 1996
$45.0 (21 Deals) 1997
$182.9 (31 Deals) 1998 est.

[a] This represents all M&A transactions in the world (not just for DLJ).

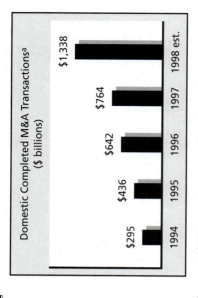

Global Completed M&A Transactions[a]
($ billions)

| 1994 | 1995 | 1996 | 1997 | 1998 est. |
| $493 | $767 | $1,103 | $1,338 | $2,115 |

[a] This represents all M&A transactions in the world (not just for DLJ).

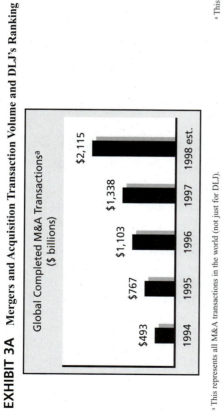

DLJ's Global and Domestic M&A Rankings

| | Global | | Domestic | |
	$ Value	# Deals	$ Value	# Deals
1998 (est.)	11	8	12	1
1997	11	9	9	5
1996	12	13	11	7
1995	14	13	11	8

Rank order compared to other investment banks.

Source: Securities Data Company.

EXHIBIT 3B 1996–1998 Completed Merger and Acquisition Deals for Small, Medium, and Large Markets

1996 Small Markets—Deals $200M or Less

Rank	Advisor	Number of Transactions	Amount ($ millions)
1	Salomon Smith Barney	93	$7,4760
2	Merrill Lynch & Co. Inc.	64	5,909
3	Deutsche Bank AG	76	5,906
4	Goldman Sachs & Co.	55	5,528
5	Donaldson, Lufkin & Jenrette	47	4,157
6	Lehman Brothers	38	3,442
7	Morgan Stanley Dean Witter	34	3,267
8	Credit Suisse First Boston	33	3,167
9	Warburg Dillon Read	31	2,866
10	Bear Stearns	30	2,320

1997 Small Markets—Deals $200M or Less

Rank	Advisor	Number of Transactions	Amount ($ millions)
1	Goldman Sachs & Co.	69	$7,633
2	Deutsche Bank AG	82	7,434
3	Salomon Smith Barney	74	6,687
4	Morgan Stanley Dean Witter	47	5,140
5	Donaldson, Lufkin & Jenrette	68	5,131
6	Merrill Lynch & Co.	57	5,076
7	Bear Stearns	35	3,924
8	Banc of America Securities LLC	51	3,864
9	Credit Suisse First Boston	36	3,820
10	Lehman Brothers	45	3,563

1998 Small Markets—Deals $200M or Less

Rank	Advisor	Number of Transactions	Amount ($ millions)
1	Donaldson, Lufkin & Jenrette	85	$8,335
2	Salomon Smith Barney	81	6,524
3	Morgan Stanley Dean Witter	56	6,446
4	Deutsche Bank AG	52	4,948
5	Goldman Sachs & Co.	44	4,842
6	Banc of America Securities LLC	55	4,353
7	Merrill Lynch & Co. Inc.	42	4,212
8	Lehman Brothers	44	4,056
9	Credit Suisse First Boston	37	3,038
10	JP Morgan & Co. Inc.	30	2,983

1996 Medium Markets—Deals between $200M and $500M

Rank	Advisor	Number of Transactions	Amount ($ millions)
1	Goldman Sachs & Co.	45	$13,725
2	Morgan Stanley Dean Witter	36	11,637
3	Merrill Lynch & Co. Inc.	33	10,027
4	Salomon Smith Barney	31	8,867
5	Deutsche Bank AG	22	7,390
6	Donaldson, Lufkin & Jenrette	20	6,632
7	Lazard Houses	17	5,667
8	Lehman Brothers	16	5,515
9	Credit Suisse First Boston	18	5,292
10	Bear Stearns	18	5,202

1997 Medium Markets—Deals between $200M and $500M

Rank	Advisor	Number of Transactions	Amount ($ millions)
1	Morgan Stanley Dean Witter	45	$16,078
2	Goldman Sachs & Co.	46	15,972
3	Merrill Lynch & Co. Inc.	39	14,430
4	Salomon Smith Barney	40	12,892
5	Donaldson, Lufkin & Jenrette	31	9,607
6	Deutsche Bank AG	27	8,851
7	Credit Suisse First Boston	21	6,292
8	JP Morgan & Co. Inc.	16	5,155
9	Lehman Brothers	16	5,077
10	Lazard Houses	13	4,246

1998 Medium Markets—Deals between $200M and $500M

Rank	Advisor	Number of Transactions	Amount ($ millions)
1	Donaldson, Lufkin & Jenrette	53	$17,055
2	Goldman Sachs & Co.	47	16,224
3	Merrill Lynch & Co. Inc.	48	15,338
4	Morgan Stanley Dean Witter	48	14,424
5	Salomon Smith Barney	37	11,519
6	Credit Suisse First Boston	32	9,333
7	Deutsche Bank AG	28	8,792
8	Chase Manhattan Corp.	25	8,258
9	JP Morgan & Co. Inc.	24	7,636
10	Lazard Houses	17	6,328

1996 Large Markets—Deals over $500M

Rank	Advisor	Number of Transactions	Amount ($ millions)
1	Morgan Stanley Dean Witter	61	$170,469
2	Goldman Sachs & Co.	58	128,528
3	Merrill Lynch & Co. Inc.	49	127,147
4	Lehman Brothers	25	77,517
5	Salomon Smith Barney	38	70,351
6	Credit Suisse First Boston	25	61,802
7	Lazard Houses	19	47,851
8	JP Morgan & Co. Inc.	22	46,320
9	Deutsche Bank AG	14	41,935
10	Bear Stearns	9	40,012

1997 Large Markets—Deals over $500M

Rank	Advisor	Number of Transactions	Amount ($ millions)
1	Merrill Lynch & Co. Inc.	73	$171,785
2	Goldman Sachs & Co.	78	156,092
3	Morgan Stanley Dean Witter	73	156,087
4	Salomon Smith Barney	42	86,509
5	Credit Suisse First Boston	38	80,256
6	Bear Stearns	18	61,867
7	Lazard Houses	20	53,465
8	JP Morgan & Co. Inc.	19	52,185
9	Donaldson, Lufkin & Jenrette	30	41,905
10	Lehman Brothers	23	36,507

1998 Large Markets—Deals over $500M

Rank	Advisor	Number of Transactions	Amount ($ millions)
1	Goldman Sachs & Co.	100	$414,309
2	Merrill Lynch & Co. Inc.	84	387,512
3	Morgan Stanley Dean Witter	87	283,474
4	Salomon Smith Barney	57	255,152
5	Credit Suisse First Boston	52	210,456
6	Lehman Brothers	44	191,836
7	JP Morgan & Co. Inc.	29	153,383
8	Lazard Houses	28	152,014
9	Banc of American Securities LLC	10	94,584
10	Chase Manhattan Corp.	19	89,025

Source: Thomson Financial Securities Data.

DLJ appeared to be a great place to work. It was not political; it was not bureaucratic. The management under Joe Roby and Tony James was brilliant. It had a great equity and high-yield practice and its M&A group was growing. I liked the firm's entrepreneurial focus. Its advisory and underwriting products matched up well with my clients' interests. I decided to come on board as a managing director in February 1996.

Greenthal discerned DLJ's approach to business as quite different from Lehman's. "At Lehman," she observed, "we concentrated on very large companies, which took a long time to cultivate. We were encouraged to do transactions with Fortune 100 companies and to be patient with them. DLJ's business is more focused on the bottom line."

Contributing to DLJ's Media Business

One of Greenthal's first priorities upon joining DLJ was to persuade Christine Mott, who had worked as an analyst with her at Lehman, to also move to DLJ. Only weeks after Greenthal had moved, Mott joined DLJ, bringing with her, Greenthal believed, an "encyclopedic understanding" of many of Greenthal's clients. "It takes a certain kind of person to work with Jill," explained Mott. "It took several months of working with her and toughing it out before I completely understood her drive and tenacity. She's tough. Not everyone wants to work with her, but those who eventually do appreciate her intellect and integrity."

Mott admired Greenthal's thorough approach to business. "Jill is exacting and patient in dealing with her clients, which typically are large firms. She communicates frequently with many different decision makers on the client side." Mott was frustrated at times, however, by Greenthal's approach to pitching business. "We often disappointed potential clients," she explained,

not telling them what they wanted to hear about their company's value. Jill would say to them: "This is the realistic level we can get you on an IPO or a bond offering." On occasion, we would lose their business because other banks would come in and highball the value. I'd be so discouraged that we hadn't gotten the deal. We'd later see that as time passed and the deal was completed it would end up getting done at the level that our team had predicted. Jill knew I was frustrated and she would always say: "Remember Christine, it's a long race; these companies will remember that we gave them the right advice."

Mott observed that Greenthal worked with clients for months, often without an engagement, simply keeping in touch off-hours and offering free advice. "It had to be tough on her," observed a client, "in an industry that compensates investment bankers on transactions and fees that come in by year end." Greenthal was unperturbed. "Over time, as DLJ's base of business grew," she explained, "our management gave us more leeway to make reasonable decisions about short-term and long-term relationship building."

Nor was compensation a problem for Greenthal. "I think the firm really does compensate you for the effort that you put into generating both near-term and longer-term business," she explained.

I don't know what the magical formula is. Compensation is very flexible, open-ended, and ambiguous. At the end of the year Tony James looks at the absolute revenues I contribute to the firm. But he also looks at the other objectives of the firm—the quality of the client's business, for example. I know he is asking, "Are they good names, or marginal? Are they high-caliber companies? Will they create new business for us?" We have such a flat organizational structure that management seems to know what's going on with everyone all of the time. So when it comes to bonus time, you know they've done a good job talking to the people you work with and understanding how much time and energy you put into the business. In the end, it seems to all work itself out mysteriously in year-end bonuses. The message management conveys is: "We think you're smart and we will pay you for today's business as well as for the potential business you are developing."

Working with the M&A Group

When Greenthal needed to work on an M&A deal, she would partner with an M&A managing director to jointly staff the deal team. The team typically included a vice president and an associate or analyst (depending on deal complexity) from either group.[4] Selecting appropriate team members was challenging, "when there are so many egos involved," observed one junior associate, "as is typical in this industry, especially in any M&A group." Neissa explained: "Finding the brightest analyst isn't always the best thing to do; oftentimes it has to be someone with the personality or a sense of humor or style that complements the leader of the specialty industry group."

After a couple of early transactions, Greenthal earned a reputation in the M&A group as a brilliant banker. "Jill really doesn't even need an M&A person," remarked Neissa. "She can do it all herself." Working with Greenthal was recognized, as one associate put it, as "a learning opportunity. When it came to the cable industry she knows where everybody is buried. She includes us in important meetings and decisions. And her deals tend to be high profile." But Greenthal, direct, unrelenting, and tough, had also become known in the

M&A group as a banker who "does not suffer fools gladly." Some of the strong egos in that department had clashed with, and been bruised by, hers.

TELE-COMMUNICATIONS, INC.

The Media and Telecommunications Industry

Government deregulation and technological innovation in the mid-1990s opened a window of opportunity for reshaping the telecommunications industry. The Telecommunications Reform Act of 1996 made it possible for cable and local and long-distance telephone companies, earlier prohibited from cross-investing, to enter one another's markets. For the first time, telephone companies could offer television services and vice versa.

Concurrently, the Internet had grown in popularity and new technologies had increased both the amount and type of information that could be transmitted. Coaxial cable, on which the cable industry had relied until the late 1990s to transmit signals to subscribers, was beginning to be replaced, in part, by higher bandwidth fiber-optic cable that could carry more video, data, and voice channels. By 1996, a cable modem-equipped digital "set-top box" that provided high-speed Internet access and interactive programming had been introduced to the market. "Digital compression" was allowing broadcasters to squeeze more channels of video programming through the existing conduits. An era of faster and more economical communication services was being ushered in.[5]

Convergence, the increasing possibility of transmission of video, interactive data, and tele-

---

[4] Generally, professionals in investment banks comprised analysts (typically recent college graduates in entry-level positions), associates (promoted analysts or MBA recruits), vice presidents, directors/senior vice presidents, and managing directors (capable associates were promoted to vice presidents and, after a few years, to managing directors). Managing directors could, over time, become the equivalent of partners.

[5] This paragraph draws information from W.H. Donald, "Industry Profile," *Broadcasting & Cable, S&P's* Industry Survey, July 8, 1999, pp. 1-8; "Cable and Other Pay Television Services," *U.S. Industry Profiles,* 1999, pp. 1–10; and "Digital Interactive Television," *Encyclopedia of Emerging Industries,* 1999, pp. 3–18.

phone service over the same broadband pipes, caused an extraordinary explosion of business transactions in telecommunications, cable, and entertainment industries. TCI's Malone and Leo Hindery, at the forefront of this revolution, were, according to an industry observer, "two cowboys at the head of the pack."[6]

TCI HERITAGE AND LEADERSHIP

Texas rancher Robert Magness founded Tele-Communications, Inc. (TCI), a cable company, in 1956, moved it to Denver in 1965, and hired former Bell Labs engineer John Malone in 1973 to take control of what had become a $5 million-per-year company.

John Malone

A Yale-educated engineer with a PhD in operations research, Malone was also a financial genius. Brought to TCI in 1973, he rescued the then almost bankrupt firm and persuaded Wall Street to embrace cable.

In the late 1980s Malone oversaw the company's purchase of more than 150 cable companies and the largest U.S. movie theater operator, United Artists Entertainment. TCI also invested in major television channels such as Discovery, Black Entertainment, and American Movie Classics.[7] An article in *Fortune* magazine called him "the Darth Vader of cable" who had "over 25 years negotiated hundreds of deals with bankers, cable companies, regulators, and TV networks. Complex financial arrangements," it observed, "were second nature to him. In the 1990s," the article continued, "Malone set out to be the Vanderbilt of the information

highway, bringing convergence into the homes of America. In 1992 he promised 500 channels; in 1993 he tried to jumpstart the revolution by merging with Bell Atlantic."[8]

"You tend to remember meetings with John C. Malone," mused Ronald Grover in a book review in *Business Week:*

> Big, square-jawed, with a ready wit and an intense dislike for those who disagree with him . . . he tends to speak his mind and take no prisoners. . . . "Phone companies are never going to be the winners in this race," I recall his telling me as we sat in his Denver office in early 1995, a year after his celebrated $35 billion merger with Bell Atlantic Corp. had cratered. "They have too many layers of detritus weighing down their cost structure. You know, whale shit."[9]

DLJ's Herald Ritch described Malone as "a decisive entrepreneur. He likes people who could go toe-to-toe with him."

Mott described the TCI organization, circa 1997, as "a three-headed conglomerate" (see Exhibit 1). One affiliate was Liberty Media, which held programming assets such as the Discovery Channel and Fox Sports; the other was TCI Ventures, which had investments in such companies as @Home and Sprint PCS; the largest was TCI, a cable company with 14 million subscribers. The total market capitalization of the three affiliates was nearly $33 billion.

Its large size and leadership position in the cable industry notwithstanding, TCI had, according to an analyst report, "reached a tricky balance sheet position by early 1997 and was experiencing poor operating performance."[10] Another observer reported that as early as October 1996 "the cable

---

[6] Jeanie Stokes, "TCI President Hopes to Energize Stock," *Bloomberg News,* May 18, 1997, p. 4.

[7] Edward W. Desmond, "Malone Again," *Fortune* 137, no. 3 (February 16, 1998), p. 67.

[8] Ibid., pp. 66–69.

[9] Ronald Grover, "John Malone and the Cable Tangle," *Business Week,* September 28, 1998.

[10] Dennis H. Leibowitz and Karim Zia, "Telecommunications, Inc.: The Empire Strikes Back," *Equity Research: Broadcasting & Cable,* Donaldson, Lufkin & Jenrette, March 18, 1998, p. 3.

television giant (estimated 1997 revenues $8.1 billion) had stunned investors by reporting an unexpectedly large $31 million loss for the third quarter. Even worse, 70,000 subscribers had defected. Shareholders responded by dumping the stock, causing its price to plunge to $10.75," almost 65 percent below its 1997 high of approximately $30.[11]

Compounding the disappointing financial results, Bob Magness, the founder, passed away at the end of the year. Malone appeared to have gotten away from the day-to-day management of the business and there were rumors that his health was poor. In February 1997, needing to resurrect TCI from operating troubles and financial woes, Malone hired Leo Hindery to help him.

Leo Hindery

A Stanford MBA graduate, Hindery had served as CFO and acting COO of *Chronicle Publishing Company* and, before that, as managing director and CFO of Becker Paribas, a New York investment banking firm. In January 1988, he formed InterMedia Partners, a cable TV company in which TCI became an investor.

In 1995 InterMedia led a $2.2 billion buyout of Viacom cable TV systems, making InterMedia Partners, which had no cable subscribers five years before, the seventh-largest cable operator in the country. In 1996 he helped InterMedia materially improve its customer base as well as cash flow.

In February 1997 Hindery was hired by TCI, which had a roughly 50 percent equity stake in InterMedia. According to *Bloomberg News*: "Malone was banking on Hindery to repeat that performance at TCI—reverse last year's $813 million loss and attract new customers."[12]

Hindery, known for arriving at work at 5 A.M. and "never tolerating double talk," was determined to fix the company. "I had a busted company that I

was confident was going to fix itself on operations," he recalled, "and, by way of a series of transactions, we were also committed to changing the perception of the company and the industry." Upon joining, Hindery found TCI in upheaval. In a last-ditch effort to combat out-of-control spending that had swelled the workforce 18 percent in 1996 to 38,500 and left warehouses bulging with equipment, in November 1996 Malone had ordered 2,500 jobs cut and temporarily halted shipments from some suppliers.

GREENTHAL AND TCI

Building the Relationship

One of the leading firms in her industry, TCI, according to Greenthal,

> was an active company with many different business affiliates. It was entrepreneurial and financially very aggressive, always doing cutting-edge transactions with multiple companies. Understanding TCI meant understanding John Malone, because he loved to move pieces around. You never knew what was going to happen next. You would focus on one transaction in one corner of the company and meanwhile something entirely different would be taking place in a different area. You had to be like an air traffic controller—focusing on one but keeping track of others about to take off. Frankly, at times I found it frustrating! At the same time I knew TCI was worth sticking with because the firm was so active that new opportunities for innovative deal making were always coming through.

Greenthal had first become acquainted with TCI while at Lehman Brothers. "My early work," she recalled,

[11] Duff J. McDonald, "Stocks with 9 Lives," *Money 26,* no. 3 (March 1997), p. 115; Datastream International. TCI Stock Price, December 15, 1997.
[12] Jeanie Stokes, "TCI President Hopes to Energize Stock . . . ," *Bloomberg News,* May 18, 1997.

included issuing commercial paper.[13] Later, we did some medium-term note business and then some debt business. I sold some cable properties to TCI. The breakthrough deal was a tracking stock project.[14] In 1994, while at Lehman, we took Liberty Media, one of TCI's three core businesses, out in the form of a tracking stock.

The work on Liberty Media in collaboration with First Boston strengthened Greenthal's relationship with TCI and helped her develop expertise in tracking stocks. "At the time, Jill, or for that matter, any investment banker, didn't know much about tracking stocks," recalled Mott, who had worked with Greenthal on TCI transactions.

TCI was the first company to create a tracking stock for a business that didn't have earnings; the entire concept was really pushing the envelope. To create the stock we didn't just look at their income statement and cash flow; we actually had to comb through their assets and find out where each one belonged. We broke the company into four different units: its core cable business, Liberty Media and programming, and Technology Ventures and International Business. We had to figure out what was in each business and how we could value them. At least 100 investments within TCI had to be allocated among the groups. It was an interesting puzzle.

Maintaining the TCI Relationship at DLJ

Before Greenthal's arrival, DLJ's relations with TCI had been spotty at best. "The firm's book of business had generally not been with large-cap companies," Greenthal explained, "so TCI's size made dealing with them unusual for DLJ." "Until Jill came," added James, "we had done only a few assignments with TCI where we had secondary roles."

Although projects with TCI remained smaller relative to some of the other deals in her portfolio, Greenthal continued to invest time in the relationship. "Jill had much more client maintenance with TCI than normal," observed James. Even as TCI experienced the upheavals of 1996, "we stayed with them through the turbulence," Mott recalled, and "a lot of people at TCI were coming and going."

In 1996 Greenthal was rewarded for her persistence by participation, jointly with Merrill Lynch, in the TCI Ventures creation and the TCI Satellite spin-off and related high-yield financing.[15]

Strengthening the Relationship

When in February 1997 Hindery joined TCI as COO, perhaps no one was more pleased than Greenthal, who had over the years worked intensively with him at InterMedia. Prior to Hindery's arrival, TCI had worked with other investment bankers, primarily Merrill Lynch. "When Leo came in, he was given authority over finance," recalled Leibowitz, "and he was prepared to use it, since he had his own ideas about finance issues."

In October 1997, soon after Armstrong had joined AT&T as its new CEO, he, Malone, and Hindery began discussing potential combinations of some of AT&T's assets with a TCI affiliate. Hindery chose to take Greenthal's advice on this project, even though the TCI affiliate had usually used

---

[13] Commercial paper is short-term unsecured promissory notes issued by a corporation. The maturity of commercial paper is typically less than 270 days; the most common maturity range is 30 to 50 days or less. (source: Yahoo Financial Glossary, biz.yahoo.com)

[14] A tracking stock is designed to track the earnings performance of a particular business unit or group of businesses within a firm.

[15] One of TCI's affiliated companies, TCI Satellite, owned an interest in PrimeStar, a joint venture between cable and satellite that offered direct-to-home business.

two other banks. "Though Jill did not have deep expertise in the affiliate's business," Mott, who worked on the project with Jill, recalled, "she was quick to find a specialist from our technology group at DLJ to help us. With his help we were able to impress TCI that in our desire to work with them and do a great job we had gotten to know their affiliate's business cold."

THE DEAL

In the winter of 1997 Malone and Hindery began a series of private conversations with AT&T's Armstrong about a possible joint venture between AT&T's consumer long-distance business and TCI's cable business. Armstrong, desirous of forming a "consumer company" that would offer cable, long-distance, and local telephone service, wanted Malone and Hindery to consider a "carve out" of TCI's cable business that could be merged with AT&T's consumer long-distance business.

Choosing the Banker

When it came time to think about hiring a banker to help negotiate the consumer company venture, Hindery was faced with a dilemma. "I knew this upcoming transaction was going to be an enormous deal," he recalled.

I had to decide. Should I go with Jill alone? Or should I go with her and add a partner? Or should I go elsewhere? It would have been rude to dismiss Jill because she was involved at the time in some other deals we had going. So, it was appropriate to determine whether Jill should migrate over to what we knew would be the biggest deal in the industry. On the other hand, because I had many relationships with many banks, it seemed only fair to consider others in addition to Jill to do the deal. The industry doesn't appreciate exclusive relationships between companies and bankers; you often end up leaving too many fund-raising opportunities elsewhere, and large companies are not inclined to handle those consequences.

Ultimately, Hindery chose to engage Greenthal, with DLJ as the sole bank. "Jill was one of only a half dozen superstars in media investment banking," he explained.

She stood out because of her attitude. Here was a banker who took an interest in her clients in an industry where many people are simply interested in printing the ticket. She had a sense of continuity and progression. She shared well. She was easy to like and even easier to respect. Moreover, she was stunningly bright, someone Malone himself would call on the phone. She was willing to surround herself with people as talented as she was and not resent it. It's tough in a place where everyone wants to be the star.

Assembling the Deal Team

When Greenthal caught wind that the smaller deals at TCI were perhaps leading to "something bigger," she knew it was time to find a partner in the M&A team. She had her eyes on Neissa—one of Ritch's "golden boys," known for his excellent work, easy temperament, and friendly disposition. One day in September, she knocked on his office door. "Jill came into my office and closed the door," Neissa recalled. "She told me that something was up between TCI and AT&T. 'I need a partner,' she explained. She said that she needed someone from our group to be her opposite, to challenge her, and to help her through the conceptual work and the implementation of the deal."

By spring 1998, Greenthal and Neissa felt that it was time to bring more DLJ staff on board the project. Mott was already deeply involved in the relationship with TCI. Neissa joked that together, Greenthal and Mott "knew more about TCI's assets than did many TCI employees." Tony Belinkoff, a telecommunications specialist, also came from the Media and Telecommunications Group. Neissa recruited Lee LeBrun, an experienced vice president who Neissa chose carefully. "It had to be someone who could handle working such an opportunity with Greenthal and Mott. They were known for being perfectionists." LeBrun was to oversee Ehren Stenzler, a promising young analyst who had recently graduated from Wharton. Max Jellinek, a young analyst who had worked on other deals with Neissa and Stenzler, was also brought on board. (Exhibit 4 provides pictures of the team.)

EXHIBIT 4 **DLJ's Deal Team**

Jill Greenthal
Managing Director

Tony Belinkoff
Managing Director

James Neissa
Managing Director

Herald Ritch
Managing Director

Christine Mott
Associate

Lee LeBrun
Vice President

Ehren Stenzler
Analyst

Max Jellinek
Analyst

Media and Communications Group | **Mergers and Acquisitions Group**

It was a potentially huge deal for DLG. The transaction, if successful, would dwarf any other the firm had facilitated thus far. Financial rewards (typically 0.5 percent commission on the deal) would be very generous. In addition, the deal would add cachet to the DLJ name and firmly establish the firm as an industry leader in the very active media and telecommunications industry.

With each recruit held to secrecy, the work began. The team was charged first with building a financial model to value AT&T's businesses and identifying parts of TCI that might enter into a joint venture with AT&T. "There were so many individual businesses within both TCI and AT&T," explained Stenzler.

> Each needed to be valued differently. Our job was to value all of the different pieces of TCI's businesses and at the same time stay on top of the valuation of AT&T's businesses so we could understand where AT&T's bankers—Credit Suisse First Boston and Goldman Sachs—would be coming from in our upcoming meeting.

Through careful and intense work over four weeks, the DLJ team determined that a TCI-AT&T joint venture could combine together businesses worth $80 billion.

DIFFERENCES OF OPINION

TCI's senior managers and lawyers and the DLJ team met AT&T's senior managers, lawyers, and bankers in the grand conference room at AT&T's corporate headquarters on Saturday, May 30. Early in the meeting it became obvious that the valuations diverged considerably. The AT&T team presented "aggressive numbers," according to a DLJ team member, regarding the valuation of their consumer business.

"We ran through the numbers and just couldn't figure out how to make the deal work," Greenthal elaborated. "We were not even on the same page as AT&T's bankers from a valuation standpoint. They had rationalized that they should be compensated for the AT&T brand. We felt that their business faced significant competitive pressure and hence couldn't command anywhere near the value that they were suggesting."

"Two hours into the conversation," Neissa recalled, "we walked onto the terrace, concerned. Some of us felt there was not even a prayer that the joint venture could materialize."

Leadership and Change Management in PSFs

ACHIEVING BALANCE AMONG THE FOUR QUADRANTS

The first five modules of the casebook focus on providing readers with a macro and micro view of how professional service firm leaders must direct their attention on both the internal and external dimensions of the firm, how they function strategically and tactically, and, importantly, how they connect these dimensions to allow their organizations to thrive. PSF leaders must manage both for their future and for their current clients within the context of the internal structures, systems, processes, and professionals that comprise the organization.

We emphasize through the first five modules that a theoretical framework is at the core of how we think about PSFs. The framework hangs on two dimensions: level (strategic versus tactical) and focus (external versus internal). Juxtaposing

This note was prepared by Professor Thomas DeLong, Professor Ashish Nanda, Dean's Research Fellow Scot Landry, and Ying Liu (MBA 2001).

these two dimensions orthogonally yield four quadrants. We assert that to be successful, a PSF needs to achieve balance across these four quadrants. We underscore throughout these modules that the four-quadrant model can be used as a lens rather than a rigid framework in which to "fit" the examples, cases, and discussions.

We have developed the theme of the book on the premise that PSFs were originally created to help other organizations leverage capabilities and reduce risk. PSFs make promises to clients and then rally their organizations to deliver on those promises. Exceeding client expectations is the goal of high-performing PSFs, as it ensures repeat business and client referrals to help with new business.

We also emphasize that as the complexity of business challenges has increased, the world of PSFs has become more challenging. This has manifested itself in many forms, leading PSFs to question many of the assumptions on which they have been created. One example is the change in retention of young professionals within PSFs. No one could have predicted that turnover rates of professionals at all levels of the organization would be such a challenge for these firms.

These new outcomes have caused PSFs to question how to organize, how to create processes, how to think strategically about their capabilities and their competition. They are looking for organizing principles that will assist them in leveraging their capabilities to serve clients. At the end of the day, all PSFs are looking for ways to attain high levels of performance. What becomes more challenging is that there are competing values that create inherent tension within organizations. These tensions must be managed strategically in order to guide the organization in the direction it wants to go. These competing values have different assumptions around motivation, information processing, decision making, power and influence, leadership roles, managerial roles and behaviors. The four-quadrant model provides a lens that helps the leaders of PSFs think about how to position the firm strategically, how to compete in the market place, and how to organize the firm internally around systems and structures. It also provides an explanation as to why certain processes are critical to sustain the long-term viability of the enterprise.

LEADERSHIP AND CHANGE MANAGEMENT

Module Six moves from analysis of each quadrant to an analysis of how the quadrants are interrelated both with each other and with a singular unit of analysis. This six-session module emphasizes the skills and values that we believe successful PSF leaders possess: balance between producing and managing, change management and leadership skills, and the ability to cope with ever increasing demands on one's time.

We will see in this module's cases that a leader sets a direction along with strategies for the PSF, aligns the right people and communicates with them about the vision of the PSF, and motivates and inspires people to head toward the vision.[1] We will introduce different approaches to setting up visions and strategies, communicating those visions within the organization, and motivating professionals to achieve those visions. The four-quadrant framework we have introduced in this book applies to all the cases in this module. The alignment of strategies and tactics externally and internally is key to achieving visions and managing changes.

CAMBRIDGE CONSULTING GROUP: BOB ANDERSON

We begin Module Six with the Cambridge Consulting case because the firm faces a myriad of process and people challenges that require leadership at the senior management level and within departments. It represents a situation in which the protagonist must balance a number of processes that need to be intertwined and managed simultaneously. The case also highlights that in PSFs owners, producers, and managers are often the same person. This phenomenon becomes more pronounced the higher one moves up the organizational hierarchy.

Bob Anderson must learn how to balance the inherent tensions of producing and managing simultaneously. Everyone in the firm has high expectations of him, including himself. His subordinates have high expectations about their own careers and the role Anderson should play relative to their careers. Further, Anderson wants to prove to his colleagues and senior management that he is a star because of his ability to contribute revenues to the bottom line.

The case creates the scenario where readers must prioritize and evaluate which processes must be focused on first. The case also highlights the economic leverage model that guides most PSFs. Anderson realizes through his own behavior that the firm's philosophy around scale, scope, and growth rate, all influence how he views the world and how senior management expects their managers to behave.

The most important learning in the case surrounds the tension between the roles of manager and producer. Anderson, like most professionals, made a name for himself early in his career with his production and technical expertise. Many individuals attracted to PSFs are primarily transaction-oriented and care less about the processes that focus on identifying strategic direction and creating commitment to that direction because these activities take time away from transaction-oriented tasks. Anderson's success as a producer can be quantified and more easily measured than his contribution to human capital management. Further, the firm has not figured out its reward systems to reinforce effective management practices. Thus, professionals at all organizational levels experience career development challenges.

All PSFs wrestle with the balance of internal human capital demands and external client demands. Externally, producers tend to earn more respect from other professionals within the system. PSFs must create processes that take into

---

[1] J. P. Kotter. "What Leaders Really Do," *Harvard Business Review,* case no. 90309, 1994.

consideration the tension PSF leaders face between these two roles and that manage the inherent conflict between them. PSF producer-managers must be clear about their personal goals and agendas in order to get feedback regarding whether they have a reasonable balance between the two roles.

CHARLOTTE BEERS AT OGILVY & MATHER WORLDWIDE

The Charlotte Beers at Ogilvy & Mather Worldwide case focuses on how Beers, Ogilvy & Mather's first outsider CEO, tried to lead a senior team to form a vision for the world's sixth-largest advertising agency. Beers understood that a good vision could provide both a strategic and a motivational focus for the firm, and that a long-term, consistent change strategy could be powerful. The case illustrates traits of successful leaders, such as the ability to inspire and motivate through passion and candor, a high-commitment style, and the ability to command and seek accountability.

The case emphasizes not only the importance of having a vision of the firm, but also the process of forming the strategy. Beers had to form communication channels to keep different constituencies of the firm headed toward the new vision. Should Beers encourage debates among her diverse team members? How can a leader make different stakeholders agree on a firm vision? Beers also had to align internal structures and systems in order to implement the new vision. At the old Ogilvy & Mather, organizational structure, staffing, incentives, and compensation systems were misaligned. How can Beers deal with this management challenge? Can Beers act both as a leader and as a manager?

LEHMAN BROTHERS: RISE OF THE EQUITY RESEARCH DEPARTMENT

The Lehman Brothers case begins with the rise of Lehman Brothers' equity research department under the leadership of Jack Rivkin. Rivkin transformed the equity research department from an insignificant organizational entity to the highest-ranking research department on Wall Street. He set the vision for the department and implemented drastic changes by overhauling the old system. Specifically, Rivkin built the department from scratch by ensuring internal alignment of the department's values, processes, and systems.

Jack Rivkin aligned the research department's strategy and tactics externally as well as internally. The department's external strategy was to become the number one research team on Wall Street. With that goal in mind, internal strategy and processes were implemented, such as the performance evaluation system and the recruiting and training system, and so forth. One of the unique approaches was that Rivkin chose to play the role of "Mr. Outside." By hiring Fred Fraenkel as "Mr. Inside," Rivkin allowed the department to be governed under both leadership and effective management.

Rivkin's leadership was also reflected in client management. He created a work environment that professionals enjoyed, and he treated professionals as internal clients. Like what we have seen in the &Samhoud case, professionals in turn worked in teams and increased the department's creativity and focus to serve clients.

This case also sets the context for the research department's rise within the parent company's domain. Leaders at a department level will need to consider the parent company's strategy and sometimes will be constrained if their objectives are not aligned. How should Rivkin manage the relationship of the research department with the rest of Lehman Brothers? Can the research department have a totally distinct culture from the rest of the firm?

ALEXANDER BANDELLI

We include in Module Six another example of a leader who parachuted in from outside a system to confront the challenges of transforming a dysfunctional professional service firm. Bandelli went about trying to articulate a strategy, gain commitment to the strategy, and execute on that strategy. In trying to accomplish this, Bandelli relied on change management and project management skills he developed as a consultant.

Bandelli knew he needed to build a team to focus on the change needed. Bandelli must decide through a process of organizational triage where to begin his efforts.

As he begins his assessment of the situation with his organization, he must prioritize activities that center on team-building processes. He must hire a downtown, central office team. He must find new office space, evaluate and possibly terminate people on the old team, review individual business plans, create suburban territories and offices, and hire a rainmaker or two.

In terms of change leadership, Bandelli knows that he must create a vision/mission statement, formalize sales meetings, train new hires, create cost controls, hold monthly budget reviews and forecasts, and create administrative processes that will enhance the way in which the office operates. Some of the tasks include determining best practices, establishing account management systems, creating official legal forms and processes, and redesigning the marketing and research departments. Bandelli asks himself where he should begin to ensure organizational success.

The processes of project and change management are built upon the assumption that relationships will be enhanced through the interaction between professionals. This assumption is grounded on the premise that trust can be built. Trust has as its cornerstone confidentiality, accountability, and responsibility. Once trust is established the project leader has the opportunity and challenge to teach and consult. These important dynamics are supported by the ability to listen, do what is best for the team members, and teach the members how to get where they want to go.

There are five focusing steps that can help project teams become more attuned to achieving the desired outcome. These steps provide a framework for focusing on the key leverage points in the process: (1) select the leverage points; (2) exploit the leverage points; (3) subordinate everything else to the above decisions; (4) elevate the leverage points; and (5) before making any significant changes, evaluate whether the leverage points will and should remain the same.

This framework allows the team to remain centered and grounded on the task at hand. Once the leverage points are identified, the team or team leader can plan the project using six steps: (1) clearly state the objectives of the project and the project plan; (2) determine the desired outcome and the tasks required to meet them; (3) determine the logical relationships between tasks and needs; (4) estimate the resource requirements, task duration and costs; (5) evaluate the plan according to budget and timing restrictions; and (6) always reevaluate.

Bandelli knows that he will not have a second chance to make the office successful. He knows that he has an old guard of professionals waiting for him to fail or succeed and who have little patience for the "educated" new kid on the block. Bandelli has to weigh what the cost will be in terms of having people change to a new way of doing business. He will have to assess whether or not there is a collective desired outcome. He has to determine quickly how he will manage the future, the specific deliverables, the organization/administration of the team, and the overall team attitude. These are not activities that evolve over time but must be confronted soon so that barriers do not arise in the process of achieving the project goals.

We emphasize change and project management in this module because as we study PSFs it has become apparent that even though Bandelli parachutes into this challenging project from outside the organization, professionals within PSFs must become competent in these skills if they hope to succeed long term in these organizations. The ability to multitask globally and to simultaneously leverage the internal and external processes (alluded to in earlier modules) underscores the importance of achieving competency in this arena.

TOM TIERNEY AT BAIN & COMPANY

The Tom Tierney case illustrates how interpersonal leadership leverages both individual, group, and organizational competencies. Tierney has the ability to manage financial and human resource capital. He has a belief about how to use resources through management skills emphasizing the use of time, people, and his own competencies. Furthermore, as the worldwide managing director, Tierney has the opportunity to put governance systems and structures in place to balance internal resources. The case also introduces the challenges of developing senior professionals of a PSF.

The case highlights how leaders must understand timing as it relates to making human resource decisions. For all practical purposes there is no problem in the Miami office. Why is Tierney meddling? Is this the outcome of a PSF that has become too internally focused? What signals is Tierney trying to send?

Apparently Bain's leadership team believes in a checks and balance system that takes more administrative time than some professionals might want. Can Bain and Tierney afford the time and energy to push for change in an area that shows no sign that change is needed? The skill of interpersonal leadership in the context of not only running a firm but also smaller entities within the firm is central to the success of the firm and the leader who is leading the change process.

INFOSYS

The Infosys case highlights the elements of leadership that lead to success as PSFs follow a global strategy. Narayan Murthy, Infosys's founder, chairman, and CEO, led the firm to serve global clients from its headquarters in India. During the firm's history, Infosys experienced market slowdowns and unfavorable business environments. But Murthy focused on ensuring service quality and strengthening client confidence in order to build long-term client relationships. Internally, Murthy tried to provide employees with a diversity of work experience and an entrepreneurial work environment. Employees were empowered at Infosys, and they also shared ownership of the firm.

We include this case to show an international perspective of leadership. As a leader in a multinational PSF, Murthy had to manage growth across countries and manage across diverse cultures simultaneously. How can a PSF operating in a third-world country satisfy clients from a first-world country? Should Infosys accelerate its pace to go global? The case also touches upon Murthy's leadership traits. His modest yet ambitious demeanor, his business ethics and integrity, and his global perspective motivated employees at Infosys.

As Infosys grew, Murthy had to decide how to position the firm to take advantage of the technology wave and stay ahead of competitors for the future. How can Infosys move up the value chain? How can Infosys continue its growth without losing its entrepreneurial work environment? How can Infosys sustain its success?

SUMMARY

This module covers significant ground. In our discussions on change leadership and project management in PSFs, we emphasize leadership in setting the organizational and market strategies and tactics of PSFs.

The first case in the module deals with the dilemma of being a producer-manager. Bob Anderson at Cambridge Consulting Group faced challenges and had to learn quickly how to convert himself from a producer to a producer-manager. In addition, the first case highlights the importance of leadership in setting strategic direction for the group and managing internal resources and talent within the organization to sustain success.

This module also includes cases concerning change management and leadership in periods of transition. The Charlotte Beers case illustrates that strong leadership is the most critical dimension in changing a PSF. Leadership is required to set the vision for the firm's future, while managers have to figure out ways to align internal systems and processes within the vision. In Alexander Bandelli, the protagonist accepts a position where he must confront a myriad of challenges to achieve promised results. In Tom Tierney at Bain and Co., the worldwide managing director of the firm must make key decisions surrounding the transition of power within a key office. It also brings to our attention the subtle issues around career management. In these cases we emphasize the importance of mastering the service delivery process (making promises, parallel processing to ensure that all elements of the team pull together, and delivering on commitments) to ensure that clients are delighted. These cases also stress the three key imperatives required for teams to work effectively: honesty, trust, and mutual respect.

The module also includes cases that focus on leading a PSF to success. The Lehman Brothers case emphasizes the power of leadership in turning around a research department. The question is how to sustain that leadership and how to manage relationships with senior executives and with other divisions of the investment banking firm once the research department becomes successful. The Infosys case gives us an example of a modest, yet strong leader that has led an Indian IT firm to success on a global scale.

QUESTIONS ARISING FROM THE CASES IN THIS MODULE

These are some of the many questions that were raised in this module:

- What are the best ways to prepare for and deal with the tensions of being a producer-manager in PSFs?

- What processes can PSFs establish to help transaction-oriented producers make effective transitions to producer-managers?

- With incredible demands for production and for management tasks, what are the best ways to balance work-related demands with personal matters?

- As a producer-manager, who should you approach for help if you are struggling with balancing the two roles?

- How do you encourage older partners to leave the firm when they do not want to leave? What is the career progression path for the younger generation? Has this path been communicated clearly to the firm's professionals?

- Should PSF leaders be worried about lateral hires? Will they be acculturated or will they dilute the firm's old culture and values?

- What additional challenges does a leader face if he or she comes to the PSF as an outsider and has to redirect the firm to a new vision?

- Do leaders and managers have different qualities? Can a leader be an effective manager simultaneously?

- Should leaders hire professional managers to separate their roles? Is the combination of "Mr. Outside" and "Mr. Inside" the only solution?

- Can subunits of a PSF maintain their own unique culture?

- How can leaders in public sectors motivate employees with nonmonetary rewards?

- How do leaders create a sense of urgency in the organization? How do they create the need to change?

Cambridge Consulting Group: Bob Anderson

As the 747 circled and climbed eastward out of Los Angeles International Airport, Bob Anderson began to unwind from the grueling 48 hours in Los Angeles. As managing partner of the High-Technology Group of the Cambridge Consulting Group (CCG), he had spent two long days defining a consulting project for a rapidly growing biotech company. Now, while some of the junior members of his team were doing preliminary data gathering, he was flying back to Boston to meet with another client.

Since the computer had not placed anyone in the other seat of his row, he was left to his own thoughts as he sipped a glass of white wine. Not surprisingly they turned to CCG and the Technology Group. What did surprise him was that in the relative quiet of the first-class cabin, with no immediate pressures, his thoughts drifted to how he was doing at the end of his second year as group head, something he never had enough time to reflect on. The reflections which filled his head were mildly disturbing, because he began to wonder if, in spite of the great year his group had had, he was really doing such a great job of managing. Was he positioning the group well for the longer term with clients, vis-à-vis the intensifying competition, and was he developing younger staff and the organization to handle the rapidly growing number of clients?

THE FIRM

CCG, with revenues of $85 million, had been highly successful during the past decade. The firm had 52 partners and operated offices in Boston, Chicago, San Francisco, and Toronto, as well as in London and Singapore. The firm's success was reflected in its record profits in each of the prior three years. These profits were generated by a particularly strong showing in working with rapidly growing firms, including high-tech ones, as well as a strong practice in implementing mergers and acquisitions.

Much of the firm's success was attributed, by both industry observers and its partners, to the firm's rich traditions and strong reputation among its clients. Where many in the industry argued that it was difficult to hold long-term relationships with the same clients, CCG partners believed that the trust and confidence of its clients were a key to the firm's past and future success. The best way to meet these clients' needs was to tackle any client problems or opportunities with team effort and provide long-term service. In fact, CCG partners prided themselves on being able to put together a team of outstanding talent drawn from anywhere in the firm to meet a client's needs.

With the firm's rapid growth and a desire to hold the number of partners relative to the professional staff constant, each recent year saw an increasing number of the firm's activities being conducted by nonpartners, vice presidents, and more junior professionals (associates). To fill the need for its growing cadre of vice presidents and associates, the firm actively recruited at major graduate business schools in the United States, especially Columbia, Harvard, Stanford, and Wharton. In fact, over 70 percent of its professional hires in the past five years had MBA degrees from such schools.

THE HIGH-TECHNOLOGY GROUP

At 42, Bob Anderson headed a group that included one other partner, five vice presidents, and 15 associates. Bob had graduated from Williams College with a major in economics and had subsequently worked for a large consumer products firm. After two years with the company, he went on to the Harvard Business School from which he graduated with high distinction. He joined CCG immediately after business school and was made a partner 10 years later at age 38 and after two years was put in charge of the High-Technology Group.

This group was one of four within the firm which focused on a particular type of industry. The others were banking, transportation, and retailing. Other clients were serviced by a pool of consultants, who usually maintained relationships with companies in specific geographic areas such as the Midwest, Southeast, or West Coast.

The focus of the High-Technology Group was on companies whose basic strategy was in new technology, whether it be electronics, computers, pharmaceuticals, or biogenetics. While the group had been successful before Bob assumed its leadership, its performance in the past three years had been nothing short of spectacular. Gross billings had grown at a compounded annual rate of 26 percent, and its success rate in attracting new clients (closure rate) had grown from 20 percent to 50 percent in the last three years.

As Bob ruminated about the group, he recognized all of these as signs of his successful management. And he added to them the strong relations he and the other consultants in the group had developed with their clients. They understood these rapidly growing companies well and had earned the respect of their top managers.

ANDERSON'S CONCERNS

In spite of all these positive signs, Bob was uneasy as he sipped on a second glass of wine. One source of concern was the other partner in his group. John Burgess was in his late forties and had been involved with their high-tech clients for almost a decade. John knew the consulting issues related to these companies and did a good job in serving them. Yet he was not forthcoming with new ideas and was not productive in developing new client relationships; nor did he go out of his way to provide guidance to the vice presidents or associates, except when they were working directly with him on a project.

Bob had always suspected that John was surprised and resentful when Bob was asked to take the leadership of the group instead of him. Bob had always been respectful of John's opinions, but realized that he had not asked for his help in leading the group. What had evolved was a polite but distant relationship between them.

As the group had grown and the pressures on him had built up, he had occasionally wished John would come forward and offer to share the burden, but he didn't. He now realized he resented this. In fact, he found himself feeling quite angry. He felt that John was getting rich as a result of his efforts, while only doing what was needed to handle their established clients.

Having sunk into this reverie, he hardly noticed what he was selecting from the tray of appetizers the flight attendant held in front of him. In fact his thoughts leapt on to his five vice presidents. All had excellent B-school credentials, were in their early thirties, and all had been very effective as associates. He had inherited three of them from his predecessor and had pushed for the promotion of the other two, including Jane Reynolds, one of a small number of female vice presidents in the firm. The five of them were the workhorses of the group, he knew. They worked long hours and got the job done. He wasn't so far away from being a vice president himself that he couldn't remember the frustrations they must have and the stress of the long hours and the constant travel. The hoped-for reward in addition to money: partnership! That's what made it all worthwhile. But given the ceiling on new partners and the growth in the firm, there was no way they were all going to make it. Maybe one or two of the five, but no more.

That reminded him of a conversation he had had with Jane on another transcontinental flight last summer. It started innocently enough. He'd thought he'd ask her how things were going, to show interest. That was something that Jerry Davis, vice president of professional development, had suggested might be useful to help understand his staff's attitudes. Anyway, it had sure backfired. Initially Jane expressed concern about business problems—did they understand the long-term competitive situation? Why were there so many misunderstandings and arguments with the staff in other offices? What could he do to help with the chronic understaffing she and other vice presidents faced? How could they teach the associates, when they were so busy? All of this he had heard from the other vice presidents—so it seemed like normal griping. But then she got more personal. She was not getting any feedback from him about how she was doing, or about her chances to make partner. All she heard were rumors. She worked "like the devil" to the detriment of her marriage. She seemed to think a divorce was a distinct possibility. It had been a disturbing conversation—it reminded him of that line from *My Fair Lady:* Why can't a woman be more like a man? At the time he thought, maybe she had too much scotch. After all his efforts on her behalf, her complaints had left him feeling angry. Now, six months later, he was wondering—was she saying things that his other vice presidents felt but were too afraid to say? If so, he had more problems than he thought.

Then he connected another set of events and concluded he might really have serious problems with his vice presidents. Nine months earlier, Bill Prince, another vice president, had come to him with the news that he had just been offered a key job in the Midwest with a newly formed consulting division of a large public accounting firm. Because his wife wanted to stay in Boston, Bill said he wasn't inclined to consider it seriously. Besides, the immediate compensation was much lower than he was receiving at CCG. Yet the offer and the opportunity to make partner there led to several conversations about his future at CCG. In one of them Bill made a comment which now seemed more ominous than it did originally. Bob could remember it verbatim:

> You know December is the worst time of the year for me. I get a huge bonus. I earned $300,000 last year, which made me one of the highest paid guys at my tenth HBS reunion. But what's sad is I don't feel good about it. When I get the bonus news in December, I don't get any other feedback— How am I doing, what are my future prospects—to be a partner? What do I need to prove to make it?

Bob now wondered whether that offer had really been unsolicited or whether it was Bill's way of getting attention.

As the supper tray was cleared away, Bob reached into his attaché case to do some reading and analysis in preparation for tomorrow's meeting. But he found it difficult to concentrate. Not only was he wondering about his vice presidents, he also began to recall several recent encounters with his associates.

THE ASSOCIATES

The 15 associates were all under 30. They all had MBAs from prestigious business schools and had ranked high in their classes. Having been with the firm for three years at the most, they were still learning about consulting in general and CCG in particular.

What immediately came to mind was Jerry Davis's comments at the partners' meeting last year. He said that the associates felt disconnected from the firm and needed more direct contact with the partners. Bob had been among the majority who greeted this news with a hoot and a moan. He remembered one of the other partners saying, "It's a tough world out there; these associates need to learn to swing on their own. We can't coddle them." And Bob had silently agreed. Even when the chairman had jumped in to support Davis, Bob remembered thinking, "My associates are hard working. They are turned on, really doing the job!" He still believed this was fundamentally true, but now he realized he didn't have any hard evidence one way or the other. In fact, he rarely had time to speak to associates unless they were working on matters of immediate concern to him.

Bob tried to square Davis's information with his own impressions of his hard-working associates. Were his associates that dissatisfied? After all, they were the cream of the crop from their business schools, and they were getting paid very high compensation and were doing challenging work. Nobody was quitting! Yet on the other hand, he knew he spent virtually no time with them, and the vice presidents and other partners in the group probably didn't have much time or interest in them either. There were no rewards passed out for developing associates. Rewards came for developing business. He had to admit it was very different now from his own early experience after joining the firm. Ten years ago there were fewer associates and the good ones seemed to find a partner to whom they could attach themselves and learn.

He tried to turn his attention back to the preparations for tomorrow's client meeting. After all, even if there were real problems with both the vice presidents and the associates, he couldn't deal with them at 39,000 feet. Tomorrow afternoon he'd think about all of this some more.

THE CHANGING MARKETPLACE

Putting these concerns aside was no solution, he realized. He'd been procrastinating in the same way about doing any long-range thinking about his business. David Lipscomb, the partner in charge of the Boston office, had been pressing him for ideas about the longer-term issues in the high-technology industry, but Bob never had time to think about them. He rummaged through his at-taché case for the sheet of paper on which he had jotted down several strategic questions he wanted to answer for himself and David:

> What impact would a decline in defense spending have on the business? Are we vulnerable to foreign competitors? Are major international firms like McKinsey and Booz Allen going to focus on emerging firms that are so important to CCG? What do the mega-mergers in the telecommunications and pharmaceutical industries mean for our high-tech clients? Is it a threat or an opportunity for them and for us?

What bothered him most was that he remembered making those notes on a prior transcontinental trip last spring—over six months ago.

THE TIME BIND

Time—that was really the heart of the matter. Whatever else he should be doing—dealing with his partners, sorting out the vice presidents' and associates' concerns, doing strategic thinking—there weren't enough hours in the day to do it. He was already working too many 12-to-14-hour days, to say nothing of weekends. He was driving the business development effort through his personal contacts with present and future clients. He had to get into the details of his projects because the clients were paying for his talent. Besides, he enjoyed it and was good at it. In fact, he recalled how much he resented having to take time out to interview new candidates at Wharton and Stanford last fall. And he really disliked being placed on firm committees. It was a nice honor and indicated that the Management Committee recognized his abilities and contribution, but he needed more work like a hole in the head.

As the seat-belt sign went on indicating the beginning of their descent into Logan Airport, he reached one conclusion. Jane Reynolds wasn't the only one who had problems at home. If he spent any more time on CCG business, he might have to kiss his own marriage goodbye. Barb had said over dinner the other night that she'd gladly trade some of his income for more of his time for herself and the two kids. Her repetition of this theme was becoming increasingly vehement. He knew what she was saying because the kids were already 12 and 14 and sometimes he felt like he hardly knew them.

He found himself in an increasingly discouraged mood as the plane landed. Maybe there was nothing to be done but to keep plugging along. Maybe he should try to sell the office partners on the idea of assigning him a vice president as a group administrator. One of the other partners had done this. Oh, hell, he thought—I've spent six hours fretting over all this nonsense, and I still have to get ready for tomorrow's meeting.

Charlotte Beers at Ogilvy & Mather Worldwide (A)

It was December 1993, and during the past year and a half, Charlotte Beers had found little time for reflection. Since taking over as CEO and chairman of Ogilvy & Mather Worldwide in 1992, Beers had focused all her efforts on charting a new course for the world's sixth-largest advertising agency. The process of crafting a vision with her senior management team had been—by all accounts—painful, messy, and chaotic. Beers, however, was pleased with the results. Ogilvy & Mather was now committed to becoming "the agency most valued by those who most value brands."

During the past year, the agency had regained, expanded, or won several major accounts. Confidence and energy appeared to be returning to a company the press had labeled "beleaguered" only two years earlier. Yet, Beers sensed that the change effort was still fragile. "Brand Stewardship," the agency's philosophy for building brands, was not well understood below the top tier of executives who had worked with Beers to develop the concept. Internal communication efforts to 272 worldwide offices were under way, as were plans to adjust O&M's structures and systems to a new set of priorities. Not the least of the challenges before her was ensuring collaboration between offices on multinational brand campaigns. The words of Kelly O'Dea, her Worldwide Client Service president, still rang in her ears. "We can't lose momentum. Most change efforts fail after the initial success. This could be the prologue, Charlotte . . . or it could be the whole book."

OGILVY & MATHER

In 1948, David Ogilvy, a 38-year-old Englishman, sold his small tobacco farm in Pennsylvania and invested his entire savings to start his own advertising agency. The agency, based in New York, had financial backing from two London agencies, Mather & Crowther and S.H. Benson. "I had no clients, no credentials, and only $6,000 in the bank," Ogilvy would later write in his autobiography, "[but] I managed to create a series of campaigns which, almost overnight, made Ogilvy & Mather famous."[1]

Ogilvy's initial ads—for Rolls-Royce, Schweppes, and Hathaway Shirts—were based on a marketing philosophy that Ogilvy had begun developing as a door-to-door salesman in the 1930s, and later, as a pollster for George Gallup. Ogilvy believed that effective advertising created an indelible image of the product in consumers' minds and, furthermore, that campaigns should always be intelligent, stylish, and "first class." Most of all, however, David Ogilvy believed that advertising must sell. "We sell—or else" became his credo for the agency. In 1950, Ogilvy's campaign for Hathaway featured a distinguished man with a black eye patch, an idea that increased sales by 160 percent and ran for 25 years. Other famous campaigns included Maxwell House's "Good to the Last Drop" launched in 1958 and American Express's "Don't Leave Home Without It," which debuted in 1962.

[1] David Ogilvy, *Blood, Beer, and Advertising* (London: Hamish Hamilton, 1977).

Gentlemen with Brains

David Ogilvy imbued his agency's culture with the same "first class" focus that he demanded of creative work. Employees were "gentlemen with brains," treating clients, consumers, and one another with respect. "The consumer is not a moron," admonished Ogilvy. In a distinctly British way, collegiality and politeness were highly valued: "We abhor ruthlessness. We like people with gentle manners and see no conflict between adherence to high professional standards in our work and human kindness in our dealings with others."[2]

At Ogilvy's agency, gentility did not mean blandness. Ogilvy took pride in his agency's "streak of unorthodoxy." He smoked a pipe, refused to fly, and peppered his speeches with literary references and acerbic wit. He once advised a young account executive, "Develop your eccentricities early, and no one will think you're going senile later in life." In a constant stream of letters, he made his dislikes clear: "I despise toadies who suck up to their bosses. . . . I am revolted by pseudo-academic jargon like *attitudinal, paradigms,* and *sub-optimal.*" He also exhorted his staff to achieve brilliance through "obsessive curiosity, guts under pressure, inspiring enthusiasm, and resilience in adversity." No one at Ogilvy & Mather ever forgot the full-page announcement he placed in the *New York Times:* "Wanted: Trumpeter Swans who combine personal genius with inspiring leadership. If you are one of these rare birds, write to me in inviolable secrecy."

In 1965, Ogilvy & Mather merged with its partner agencies in Britain to form Ogilvy & Mather International.[3] "Our aim," wrote David Ogilvy, "is to be One Agency Indivisible; the same advertising disciplines, the same principles of management, the same striving for excellence." Each office was carpeted in the same regal Ogilvy red. Individual offices, however, were run independently by local presidents who exercised a great deal of autonomy.

David Ogilvy retired in 1975. Succeeding the legendary founder proved daunting. "The next four chairmen," commented one longtime executive, "did not have his presence. David is quirky; they were straightforward, middle-of-the-road, New York." Ogilvy's successors focused on extending the network offices internationally and building direct response, marketing research, and sales promotion capabilities. Revenues soared in the 1970s, culminating in record double-digit gains in the mid-1980s (see Exhibit 1). The advertising industry boomed, and Ogilvy & Mather led the pack. Nowhere was the agency's reputation greater than at its New York office, heralded in 1986 by the press as "the class act of Madison Avenue."

Advertising Industry Changes

The booming economy of the 1980s shielded the advertising industry from the intensifying pressures of global competition. Companies fought for consumer attention through marketing, and advertising billings grew—on average, between 10 and 15 percent per annum. Brand manufacturers—challenged by the growth of quality generic products and the diverse tastes of a fragmented mass market—created multiple line extensions and relied on agencies' creative powers to differentiate them. As business globalized, so did agencies. Responding to clients' demands for global communications and a range of integrated services, agencies expanded rapidly, many merging to achieve economies of scale as "mega-agencies" with millions in revenues worldwide.

After the stock market crash of 1987, companies reconsidered the value added by large advertising budgets. Increasingly, many chose to shift resources from expensive mass media and print

[2] David Ogilvy, *Confessions of an Advertising Man* (New York: Atheneum, 1963).
[3] *Dictionary of Company Histories,* 1986.

EXHIBIT 1   Selected Financial and Organization Data

1984–1988

	1984	1985	1986	1987	1988
Revenues (in thousands)	$428,604	$490,486	$560,132	$738,508	$838,090
Net income (in thousands)	25,838	30,247	26,995	29,757	32,950
Operating profit (in thousands)	49,191	45,355	47,764	57,933	65,922

Source: The Ogilvy Group Annual Report, 1988.

1989–1993[a]

	1989	1990	1991	1992	1993
Total annual billings (in thousands)[b]	$4,089,000	$4,563,700	$5,271,000	$5,205,700	$5,814,100
Revenues (in thousands)	592,600	653,700	757,600	754,800	740,000
Percent change in net income[c]	NA	4.7	-2.8	1.9	5.3
Operating margin	NA	6.4	4.1	4.9	7.6

[a] Financial information for 1989–1993 is not comparable to 1984–1988 due to the restructuring of the company following sale to WPP Group, plc. It is the policy of WPP Group, plc not to release revenue and net income information about its subsidiaries.
[b] Represents an estimate by Advertising Age of the total value of all advertising and direct marketing campaigns run in a given year.
[c] The percent increase or decrease is given from an undisclosed sum at base year 1989.
Source: *Advertising Age.*

campaigns toward direct mail, cable, telemarketing, and sales promotion. Fixed fees began to replace the agencies' historical 15 percent commission on billings. Long-standing client-agency relations were severed as companies sought the best bargains. Viewed by some as ad factories selling a commodity product, the mega-agencies were challenged by new, "boutique" creative shops. The globalization of media and pressures for cost efficiencies encouraged companies to consolidate product lines and to sell them in more markets worldwide. They, in turn, directed agencies to transport their brands around the world. The advertising agency of the 1990s—often a loose federation of hundreds of independent firms—was asked to launch simultaneous brand campaigns in North America, Europe, and the emerging markets of Asia, Latin America, and Africa.

Organizational Structure

By 1991, Ogilvy's 270 offices comprised four regions. The North American offices were the most autonomous, with office presidents reporting directly to the Worldwide CEO. Outside North America, presidents of local offices—sometimes majority stakeholders (see Exhibit 2)—reported to country presidents, who in turn reported to regional chairmen. Europe was coordinated centrally, but—with significant European multinational clients and a tradition of high creativity—the region maintained its autonomy from New York. To establish a presence in Latin America, Ogilvy obtained minority ownership in locally

EXHIBIT 2 Percent of Regional Offices Owned by O&M Worldwide

	Number of Offices	100%	> 50%	< 50%	0%
North America	40	80	20	0	0
Europe	97	63	24	8	5
Asia/Pacific	66	57	36	7	0
Latin America	48	25	6	21	48

owned agencies and formed partnerships with local firms. The last region to be fully formed was Asia/Pacific, with the addition of Australia, India, and Southeast Asia in 1991 (see Exhibit 3 for organization chart).

Between and across regions, "worldwide management supervisors" coordinated the requirements of multinational clients such as American Express and Unilever. WMSs served as the point of contact among multiple parties: client headquarters, clients' local subsidiaries, and the appropriate Ogilvy local offices. They were also respon-

sible for forming and managing the core multidisciplinary account team. More important, they facilitated the exchange of information throughout the network, attempting to ensure strategic unity and avoid operating at cross-purposes.

Over time, Ogilvy & Mather came to pride itself as "the most local of the internationals, the most international of the locals." Local delivery channels and the need for consumer acceptance of multinational products required specialized local knowledge and relationships. Local and global clients also served as magnets for each other:

EXHIBIT 3 Ogilvy & Mather Worldwide Organization Chart, 1991

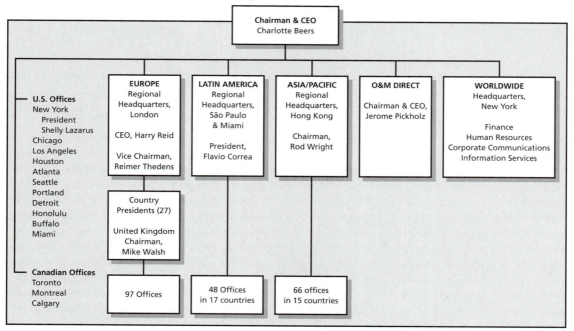

without local accounts, country offices were unable to build sufficient critical mass to service multinational clients well; without multinational accounts to draw top talent, the agency was less attractive to local clients.

With a "light center and strong regions," most creative and operating decisions were made locally. The role of Worldwide Headquarters in New York, staffed by 100 employees, was limited largely to ensuring consistency in financial reporting and corporate communications. Key capital allocation and executive staffing decisions were made by the O&M Worldwide board of directors, which included regional chairmen and presidents of the most powerful countries and offices such as France, Germany, the United Kingdom, New York, and Los Angeles.

The Ogilvy offices represented four core disciplines: sales promotion, public relations, advertising, and direct marketing.[4] Sales promotion developed point-of-purchase materials such as in-store displays and flyers. Public relations offices worked to promote clients' corporate reputation and product visibility. Advertising focused on mass marketing, establishing the core of a client's brand image through the development and production of television commercials, print campaigns, and billboards. Direct marketing created and delivered targeted advertising—from mail order catalogues to coupons and television infomercials—designed to solicit a direct response from consumers. While the latter three resided within the regional structure, O&M Direct was an independent subsidiary. In the late 1980s, the Ogilvy board of directors decided to focus on advertising and direct marketing, the firm's chief competitive strengths. Unlike advertising, Direct's business in the 1980s remained chiefly local, but expanded explosively. By 1991, O&M

Direct had received numerous industry accolades and was ranked the largest direct marketing company in the world.

"Beleaguered" Ogilvy & Mather

As clients demanded lower costs and greater service, Ogilvy & Mather—like many large agencies at the time—was slow to make adjustments. In 1988, Ogilvy was ranked the sixth-largest advertising firm in the world. As one executive remembered:

> Everything was going well. All we had to do was wake up in the morning and we were plus 15 percent. So why did we need to change? Our vision was "just keep doing the same thing, better." We failed either to recognize or acknowledge what were the first real indications that life around here was about to change fundamentally.

In May 1989, WPP Group Plc, a leading marketing services company, acquired Ogilvy & Mather for $864 million.[5] WPP, led by Harvard Business School–trained Martin Sorrell, had already purchased the J. Walter Thompson agency for $550 million two years earlier.[6] The takeover was hostile, with agency executives—including CEO Kenneth Roman—opposed. "It was a shock," explained one longtime executive. "We were a proud company with a constant stock market growth, the masters of our destiny. Suddenly, we were raided." Within months of the takeover, CEO Roman resigned. "Ken had absolutely nothing in common with WPP. There was a lack of trust, an air of conflict, adversaries, and invasion," remembered another. A number of top creative and account executives followed Roman, leaving Ogilvy & Mather for other agencies.[7]

---

[4] The number of Ogilvy offices by discipline in 1994 were as follows: 83 Advertising, 60 Direct Response, 12 Promotional, 23 Public Relations, and 92 in other areas, including highly specialized market research firms.
[5] Christie Dugas, "The Death of Ogilvy and an Era," *Newsday,* May 17, 1989.
[6] Ibid.
[7] "Change Comes to Fabled Ogilvy," *New York Times,* April 12, 1992.

Graham Phillips, a 24-year Ogilvy veteran, was appointed Roman's successor. One executive who worked with Phillips described him as "a brilliant account guy and a very good manager who identified our need to become a total communications company. But few would describe him as an inspirational leader."

In 1989, the agency lost major advertising assignments from Unilever and Shell. In 1990, Seagram's Coolers and Nutrasweet withdrew their multinational accounts.[8] Account losses in 1991 proved particularly damaging to the New York office, the agency's center and standard bearer. "If New York thrives, the world thrives. If New York fails, the world fails" went a familiar company adage. New York's client defections were explained by one executive as a failure in leadership: "The office was run by czars with big accounts. People got used to a highly political way of working and work deteriorated." In 1991, Campbell Soup withdrew $25 million in business, Roy Rogers $15 million, and American Express—the account for which Ogilvy had won "Print Campaign of the Decade"—pulled out $60 million.[9] "Losing American Express had symbolism far beyond what the actual business losses were," recalled one Ogilvy executive. "People who were loyal Ogilvy employees, believers for years, disengaged. They threw up their hands and said, 'This place is falling apart.'"

Despite declines in revenue, the agency found itself unable to adapt to clients' changing demands. Budgets were not reduced at local offices, even as large clients pushed Ogilvy to streamline and centralize their accounts. "We were a high-cost operation in a low-cost world. There was a lack of financial discipline, a lack of focus on cost, and a lack of structured decision making on business issues," noted one executive. Another faulted the firm's tradition of local autonomy and failure to institute systems for managing collaboration:

"We were spending a lot of money at the creative center without cutting back locally—building costs at both ends."

Recalling the atmosphere at the time, another executive concluded, "A shaken confidence permeated the whole company. We talked about change and what we needed to do ad nauseam, but nothing was happening. We tried to work within the old framework when the old ways of working were irrelevant."

At the end of 1991, Phillips stepped down as CEO, telling the press: "I have taken Ogilvy through a very difficult period in the industry. I had to let go people whom I had worked with for 27 years, and that wears you down." In April, Charlotte Beers was appointed CEO and chairman of Ogilvy & Mather Worldwide, the first outsider ever to lead the company.

CHARLOTTE BEERS

The daughter of a cowboy, Beers grew up in Texas, where she began her career as a research analyst for the Mars Company. In 1969, she moved to Chicago as an account executive with J. Walter Thompson. Once there, she cultivated success with clients Sears, Kraft, and Gillette, combining a southern Texan charm with sharp business acumen. Beers rose quickly to senior vice president for Client Services.

At Thompson, Beers was known for her passionate interest—unusual in account executives—in the philosophy of marketing. Commented Beers, "I try never to discuss with clients only the stuff of business. I focus on advertising as well—on the ideas." Once described on a performance evaluation as "completely fearless," Beers earned a reputation for her ability to win over clients. Colleagues retold the story of how Beers impressed a

---

[8] "Beers Succeeds Phillips at O&M Worldwide," *Adweek,* April 13, 1992.
[9] "Operation Winback," *Advertising Age,* February 1993.

roomful of Sears executives in the early 1970s by taking apart, then reassembling, a Sears power drill without skipping a beat in her pitch for a new advertising campaign.

In 1979, Beers became COO of the Chicago agency Tatham-Laird & Kudner. Her success in winning the mid-sized agency several new brands with Procter & Gamble helped turn the firm around. Accounts with Ralston-Purina and Stouffer Foods followed. Beers was elected CEO in 1982 and chairman of the board in 1986. In 1987, she became the first woman ever named chairman of the American Association of Advertising Agencies. One year later, she led TLK through a merger with the international agency Eurocome-RSCG. Tatham's billings had tripled during Beers's tenure, to $325 million.

Beers Takes Over

Beers's appointment, recalled O&M veterans, created initial apprehension. Commented one executive, "She was from a smaller agency in Chicago and had not managed multiple offices. O&M is a worldwide company, and she had never worked outside the United States. And, she was not from Ogilvy." Added another, "This is an organization that rejects outsiders."

Her approach quickly made an impression with Ogilvy insiders. "It was clear from day one that Charlotte would be a different kind of leader. Full of life. Eyes open and clearly proud of the brand she was now to lead. Here was somebody who could look around and see the risks, but wasn't afraid to turn the corner even though it was dark out," said one executive. "We had leaders before, who said all the right things, were terribly nice, did a good job, but they didn't inspire. Charlotte has an ability to inspire—Charlotte has presence." Commented another executive, "She is delightfully informal, but you always know that she means business." Within two months of her appointment, Beers dismissed a top-level executive who had failed to instigate necessary changes.

Activate the Assets

"When I took over," recalled Beers, "all the press reports talked about 'beleaguered' Ogilvy. My job was to remove, 'beleaguered' from our name." In her first six weeks, Beers sent a "Hello" video to all 7,000 of Ogilvy's employees. It began:

> Everybody wants to know my nine-point plan for success and I can't tell you that I know yet what it is. I'm building my own expectations and dreams for the agency—but I need a core of people who have lived in this company and who have similar dreams to help me. That's going to happen fast, because we are rudderless without it. David [Ogilvy] gave us a great deal to build on, but I don't think it's there for us to go backwards. It's there to go forward.

Beers concluded that people had lost sight of Ogilvy's still impressive assets—its vast network of offices worldwide, its creative talent, and its distinguished list of multinational clients. "We must," she told senior executives, "activate the assets we already have." In her second month at Ogilvy, Beers observed a major client presentation by the heads of five O&M offices:

> It was a fabulous piece of thinking. We had committed enormous resources. But in the end, they didn't tell the clients why it would work. When the client said, "We'll get back to you," they didn't demand an immediate response, so I intervened. "You saw a remarkable presentation, and I think you need to comment." Ogilvy had gotten so far from its base, that talented people lacked the confidence to speak up.

For Beers, her early interactions with a key client symbolized the state of the company. "He kept retelling the tale of New York's downfall: how we blew a major account in Europe and how our groups fought among one another. The fourth time I heard this story," remembered Beers, "I interrupted. 'That's never going to happen again, so let's not talk about it anymore. Let's talk about what we can accomplish together.'"

Beers spent much of her first months at Ogilvy talking to investors and clients. For Wall Street, she focused on the quality of Ogilvy's advertising. "I refused to do a typical analyst report," she said. "When the Wall Street analysts asked me why I showed them our ads, I told them it was to give them reason to believe the numbers would happen again and again." Clients voiced other concerns. "I met with 50 clients in six months," recalled Beers, "and found there was a lot of affection for Ogilvy. Yet, they were also very candid. Clients stunned me by rating us below other agencies in our insight into the consumer." Beers shared these perceptions with senior managers: "Clients view our people as uninvolved, distant, and reserved. We have organized ourselves into fiefdoms, and that has taken its toll. Each department—Creative, Account, Media, and Research—are often working as separate entities. It's been a long time since we've had some famous advertising."

To restore confidence both internally and externally, Beers maintained that the agency needed a clear direction. "I think it's fair to say Ogilvy had no clear sense of what it stood for. I wanted to give people something that would release their passion, that would knit them together. I wanted the extraneous discarded. I wanted a rallying point on what really matters."

For Beers, what mattered was brands. "She is intensely client- and brand-focused," explained one executive. "You can't go into her office with financial minutia. You get about two seconds of attention." Beers believed that clients wanted an agency that understood the complexity of managing the emotional as well as the logical relationship between a consumer and a product. "I became confident that I knew what clients wanted and what Ogilvy's strengths were. It was my job to be the bridge." Beers, however, was as yet unsure what form that bridge would take or how it would get built. One of her early challenges was to decide whom to ask for help in charting this new course:

> I knew I needed their involvement, and that I would be asking people to do much more than they had been, without the benefits of titles and status. I avoided calling on people on the basis of their titles. I watched the way they conducted business. I looked to see what they found valuable. I wanted people who felt the way I did about brands. I was looking for kindred spirits.

The "Thirsty for Change" Group

Over the next few months, Beers solicited ideas for change from her senior managers, asking them to give candid evaluations of disciplines and regions, as well as of one another. In a style that managers would describe as "quintessential Charlotte," Beers chose to meet with executives one-on-one and assigned them tasks without regard to their disciplinary backgrounds. She commented, "I was slow to pull an executive committee together. I didn't know who could do it. It was a clumsy period, and I was account executive on everything—everything came to me." At first, some found the lack of structure unnerving. Noted one executive, "People weren't quite sure what their roles were. It caused discomfort. We began to wonder, 'Where do I fit? Who is whose boss?'" Another added, "She was purposely vague in hopes that people would stretch themselves to new configurations." Several executives, though cautious, found Beers's talk of change inspiring and responded with their ideas.

By May 1992, Beers had identified a group whom she described as "thirsty for change." Some were top executives heading regions or key offices; others were creative and account directors who caught her eye as potential allies. Her selection criterion was "people who got it"—those who agreed on the importance of change. All had been vocal about their desire to move Ogilvy forward. She sent a memo inviting them to a meeting in Vienna, Austria, that month:

Date:	May 19, 1992	HIGHLY CONFIDENTIAL
From:	Charlotte Beers	
To:	LUIS BASSAT, President, Bassat, Ogilvy & Mather—Spain	
	BILL HAMILTON, Creative Director—O&M New York	
	SHELLY LAZARUS, President—O&M New York	
	KELLY O'DEA, Worldwide Client Service Director, Ford and AT&T—London	
	ROBYN PUTTER, President and Creative Director—O&M South Africa	
	HARRY REID, CEO—O&M Europe, London	
	REIMER THEDENS, Vice Chairman—O&M Europe, Frankfurt	
	MIKE WALSH, President—O&M, United Kingdom, London	
	ROD WRIGHT, Chairman—O&M Asia/Pacific, Hong Kong	

Will you please join me . . . in re-inventing our beloved agency? I choose you because you seem to be truth-tellers, impatient with the state we're in and capable of leading this revised, refreshed agency. We want to end up with a vision for the agency we can state . . . and excite throughout the company. Bring some basics to Vienna, like where we are today and where we'd like to be in terms of our clients and competition. But beyond the basics, bring your dreams for this great brand.

BRAND STEWARDSHIP

The Vienna meeting, recalled Beers, "put a diversity of talents in a climate of disruption." Having never met before for such a purpose, members were both tentative with each other and elated to share their perspectives. Two common values provided an initial glue: "We agreed to take no more baby steps. And it seemed clear that brands were what we were going to be about."

Beers asked Rod Wright, who had led the Asia/Pacific region through a vision formulation process, to organize and facilitate the meeting. Wright proposed a conceptual framework, based on the McKinsey "7-S" model,[10] to guide discussion of the firm's strengths and weaknesses. He also hoped to generate debate. "We don't have passionate arguments in this company. We avoid conflict, and debates go off line. When you use a framework, it's easier to depersonalize the discussion."

Reactions to the discussion ranged from confusion to disinterest. "It was theoretical mumbo-jumbo," commented one participant, "I tend to be far more pragmatic and tactical." Added another, "I don't have much patience for the theoretical bent. I wanted to get on with it." Wright admitted, "They rolled their eyes and said, 'You mean we've got to do all that?'" Beers agreed: "The B-school approach had to be translated." As the discussion unfolded, the group discovered that their personalities, priorities, and views on specific action implications diverged widely.

One debate concerned priorities for change. Shelly Lazarus diagnosed a firmwide morale problem. She argued for restoring confidence with a pragmatic focus on bottom-line client results and counseled against spending much energy on structural changes. Mike Walsh agreed but insisted that the group take time to articulate clearly its vision and values. But Kelly O'Dea had become frustrated with Ogilvy's geographical fragmentation and argued that anything short of major structural changes would be insufficient.

Participants were also divided on whether the emerging brand focus was an end or a starting

[10] Wright's model included 10 issue categories: shared values, structures, stakeholders, staff, skills, strategy, suggestions, solutions, service systems, and a shared vision.

point. The "creatives" in the group[11]—Luis Bassat, Bill Hamilton, and Robyn Putter—flanked by Beers, Lazarus, and Walsh were interested primarily in finding an effective vehicle for communicating O&M's distinctive competency. An eloquent statement, they felt, would sell clients and inspire employees. The others—O'Dea, Wright, Harry Reid, and Reimer Thedens—wanted a vision that provided guidelines for an internal transformation. Summarized Wright, "One school of thought was looking for a line which encapsulates what we do: our creative credo. The other was looking for a strategy, a business mission to guide how we run the company."

Yet another discussion concerned the route to competitive advantage. Bassat, Putter, and Hamilton, commented one participant, felt that Ogilvy had lost sight of the creative product in its rush to worry about finances—"we'd become too commercial." A recommitment to better, more imaginative advertising, they believed, would differentiate the firm from its competitors. Reid and Thedens, architects of a massive reengineering effort in Europe, insisted on financial discipline and tighter operations throughout the company as the only means of survival in the lean operating environment of the 1990s. Wright and Thedens added the O&M Direct perspective. Convinced that media advertising by itself was becoming a commodity product, each pressed for a commitment to brand building through a broader, more integrated range of communication services.

At the close of the meeting, remembered one attender, "There was a great deal of cynicism. 'Was this just another chat session?' we asked ourselves. But, we also had a sense that Charlotte felt right. She fit."

In August 1992, the group reassembled at the English resort Chewton Glen. Members presented Beers with their respective lists of priorities requiring immediate attention. Taken together, there were 22 "to do" items ranging from "examine the process by which we develop and present creative ideas" to "improve our delivery of services across geographical divisions." Beers recalled, "No one can focus on 22 things! I was so depressed, I stayed up all night and wrote a new list." She delivered her thoughts the next day:

> I think we have hit bottom and are poised for recovery. Poised but not assured. Our job is to give direction for change. So here is where I start. For 1993, we have three—and only three—strategies. They are:
>
> 1. *Client Security.* Let's focus our energy, resources, and passion on our present clients. It takes three years to replace the revenue from a lost client. Under strategy one, there's a very important corollary: We must focus particularly on multinational clients. This is where we have our greatest opportunity for growth and where our attitudes, structure, and lack of focus have been obstacles.
>
> 2. *Better Work, More Often.* Without it, you can forget the rest. Our work is not good enough. Maybe it will never be, but that's OK—better to be so relentless about our work that we are never satisfied. You tell me there's nothing wrong with our credo, "We Sell, or Else," but you also say we need some fresh thinking on how to get there. We must have creative strategies that make the brand the central focus.
>
> 3. *Financial Discipline.* This has been a subject of high concentration but not very productively so. We simply have not managed our own resources very well, and that must change.

These 1993 strategies were linked to the emerging vision by a declaration: "The purpose of our

---

[11] Within advertising and direct marketing, "creatives" develop the art and copy for each media outlet of a brand campaign.

business is to build our clients' brands." One participant recalled, "The idea of brand stewardship was still embryonic. Charlotte clearly understood it in her own mind but was just learning how to communicate it. She used us as guinea pigs to refine her thinking." But some expressed concern: "There was no disagreement that the 1993 strategy was correct. It was fine for the short term but we needed a long-term strategy."

Through the fall of 1992, group members worked to communicate the strategy—dubbed the "Chewton Glen Declaration"—to the next level of managers. Beers directed her energy toward clients, working vigorously to win new and lost accounts. She spoke about the emotional power of brands, warning them of the abuse inflicted by agencies and brand managers who failed to understand the consumers' relationship with their products. Ogilvy & Mather, Beers told clients, was uniquely positioned to steward their brands' growth and development. Clients were intrigued. By October, O&M boasted two major successes: Jaguar Motor Cars' entire U.S. account and the return of American Express's $60 million worldwide account.[12] The press hailed, "Ogilvy & Mather is back on track."

Worldwide Client Service

The Chewton Glen mandate to focus on multinationals heightened the need for better global coordination. Although Ogilvy had pioneered multinational account service in the 1970s, the firm in the 1990s remained "segregated into geographic and discipline fiefdoms" that hampered the development and delivery of brand campaigns worldwide. Noted O'Dea, "What most clients began to seek was the best combination of global efficiencies and local sensitivity, but we were not set up to facilitate that. We had the local strength, but international people were commandos with passports and begging bowls, totally dependant on the goodwill of local agencies and their own personal charisma."

In the fall of 1992, Beers asked O'Dea to head a new organization, Worldwide Client Service, that would "tap the best brains from anywhere in the world for each account." O'Dea envisioned dozens of virtual organizations, each focused on a multinational client, with multiple "centers" located wherever their respective clients maintained international headquarters. Under WCS, members of multinational account teams became "dual citizens," reporting both to their local office presidents and WCS supervisors. One WCS director noted, "International people coordinating multinational accounts used to be regarded by the local offices as staff. We thought we were line; the clients treated us like line; but internally, we had no real authority. What WCS did was give us teeth by giving us line responsibility for our accounts—tenure, profits, growth, and evaluation of local offices."

WCS brand teams were structured to mirror their clients' organizations. Some WCS directors served largely as consultants, while others ran highly centralized operations, with a core team responsible for the entire creative and client development process. "We had to reinvent ourselves in the client's footprint," remarked the WCS account director for Kimberly-Clark. His counterpart at Unilever agreed but noted that current trends favored centralization. "Speed, cost-efficiency, and centralization are our clients' priorities. What matters is not just having good ideas, but getting those ideas to as many markets as possible, as fast as possible."

By 1993, O'Dea began to travel the world presenting the possibilities of transnational teams without borders. "Good sell-ins had to be done. Office heads had to understand that there were no choices—global accounts had to be managed horizontally. We'd be dead if we didn't do it," said Reid.

Tools for Brand Stewardship

"The first six months were high excitement, high energy, and a steep learning curve," said Beers. "That was followed by 12 months of disappoint-

12 "Operation Winback," *Advertising Age,* February 1993.

ment and frustration. It didn't look as if we were getting anywhere." In December 1992, Beers asked Robyn Putter and Luis Bassat, two of the firm's top creative talents, for help in developing the emerging notion of "Brand Stewardship." They answered: "If we are to be successful, we must 'audit' our brands. We must ask the kinds of questions that will systematically uncover the emotional subtleties and nuances by which brands live." Beers took their insight directly to existing and prospective clients. One manager remembered:

> Clients immediately bought into Brand Stewardship. That created pressure to go public with it before we had every "i" dotted and "t" crossed. We didn't have a codified process, but Charlotte would talk to clients and we'd have to do it. Clients came to O&M offices saying, "I want a brand audit." And, our offices responded with, "What's a brand audit?" One client asked us for permission to use the term. We had to move quickly, or risk losing ownership of the idea.

Beers responded by asking a group of executives to elaborate the notion of a brand audit. Led by Walsh, they produced a series of questions designed to unveil the emotional as well as the logical significance of a product in the users' lives: What memories or associations does the brand bring to mind? What specific feelings and emotions do you experience in connection with using this brand? What does this brand do for you in your life that other brands cannot? The insights gathered from these questions—which became the brand audit—would, in Beers's words, "guide each brand team to the rock-bottom truth of the brand." Focusing on two of Ogilvy's global brands—Jaguar and Dove—Beers's working group struggled to articulate in a few words and images each brand's unique "genetic fingerprint." The result was O&M's first BrandPrint™:

- A Jaguar is a copy of absolutely nothing—just like its owners.
- Dove stands for attainable miracles.

Crafting a Vision

As the "technology" of Brand Stewardship developed, the senior team continued to wrestle with the formulation of a vision statement. Some argued, "We have the vision—it's Brand Stewardship." Others maintained that Brand Stewardship was but a tool to be used in attaining a yet undefined, future state. Further, as O'Dea explained, "Nearly everyone had had some contact with Brand Stewardship and WCS but they viewed them as separate and isolated actions without a strategic context."

The solution to the impasse, for some, was to include a larger group in the vision formulation. "We needed to decide collectively what we were going to be. If you have 30 people deciding and 30 people who have bought into the vision, then they have no reason not to go out and do it," reasoned Wright. Walsh agreed: "You get the 30 most influential people in the company to open their veins together—which hasn't happened in a very long time." Others, including Beers, worried about losing control of the end result. Advocates for a larger group prevailed, and the entire O&M Worldwide board of directors along with eight other local presidents attended the next meeting in July 1993 at the Doral Arrowwood, a conference center in Westchester, New York.

The purpose of the meeting, explained one of the organizers, was to get final agreement on the vision and where brand stewardship fit in. Feedback from clients on Brand Stewardship and WCS was used to guide the initial discussion. Participants' recollections of the three-day event ranged from "ghastly" to "painful" and "dreadful." Noted Lazarus, "It seemed an endless stream of theoretical models. Everyone was frustrated and grumpy."

The turning point, Beers recalled, took place at the end of a grueling first day, when one person voiced what many were thinking: "He said, 'There's nothing new here. I don't see how Brand Stewardship can be unique to Ogilvy.' This was very helpful. One of the negatives at Ogilvy is all the real debates unfold outside the meeting room." The next morning, Beers addressed the group: "Certainly, the individual pieces of this thinking are not new. But to practice it would be remarkable. I have heard that in any change effort, one-third are supporters, one-third are resisters, and one-third are apathetic. I'm in the first group. Where are you?"

With Beers's challenge precipitating consensus, attenders split into groups to tackle four categories of action implications. One group, which included Beers, was charged with crafting the specific wording of the vision. A second began to develop a statement of shared values that would integrate traditional Ogilvy principles with the emerging values of the new philosophy. "That was hard to agree on," recalled Wright. "At issue was how much of the past do we want to take forward." The third group worked on a strategy for communicating the vision to all levels and offices throughout the company. Plans for a Brand Stewardship handbook, regional conferences, and a training program were launched. A fourth group was asked to begin thinking about how to realign titles, structures, systems, and incentives to support the new vision.

After heated brainstorming and drawing freely from the other three groups to test and refine their thinking, Walsh remembered that, finally, "there it was: 'To be the agency most valued by those who most value brands.'" Summing up the meeting, one attender said, "There had been an amazing amount of distraction, irrelevance, and digression. I didn't think we could pull it together, but we did." (See Exhibit 4 for the final version of the Vision and Values statement.)

EXHIBIT 4   Statement of Vision and Values, 1993

To our people, our clients, and our friends—

The winds of change are blowing through Ogilvy & Mather. We are raising the sights of everybody in the company to a sweeping new vision:

TO BE THE AGENCY MOST VALUED
BY THOSE WHO MOST VALUE BRANDS

Not that we have ever been unmindful of the importance of brands. Quite the contrary. Our new thrust gets a big boost from ingrained Ogilvy & Mather strengths. Its roots lie in the teachings of David Ogilvy that reverberate through our halls. We have always aimed to create great campaigns with the spark to ignite sales and the staying power to build enduring brands.

What's new is a restructuring of resources, an arsenal of modern techniques, and an intensity of focus that add up to a major advance in the way we do business. We call it BRAND STEWARDSHIP — the art of creating, building, and energizing profitable brands.

The new techniques and procedures of Brand Stewardship have already proved their value for many important brands. As I write they are being put to work for others. In March we will launch them formally — in print, on tape, and throughout the Ogilvy & Mather network.

This will affect the working habits of every professional in the agency, to the benefit, I am convinced, of every brand we work for. I predict that it will bring out the best in all of you — creatively and in every other aspect of your work — and add a lot to the pleasure and satisfaction you get out of your jobs.

As a first formal step the Board of Directors is putting forward the new statement of Shared Values on the facing page. You may notice that several of the points are taken from principles that have guided the company since its start — principles that were most recently set on paper in 1990 when David Ogilvy brought our Corporate Culture up to date.

Thus the Shared Values perform two functions: they *expand* our culture to reflect inexorable change, and in the same breath they *reinforce* its timeless standards.

All vital cultures — national, artistic, corporate — tend to evolve as conditions change, preserving valuable old characteristics as new ones come into the spotlight. In just that way these Shared Values now take their place at the forefront of the dynamic culture of Ogilvy & Mather.

Charlotte Beers
Chairman, Ogilvy & Mather Worldwide

The market in which we compete is not a static one. To progress toward our new Vision will demand restless challenge and frequent change. The values we share, however, the way we do things day-to-day, will remain constant.

We work not for ourselves, not for the company, not even for a client. We work for Brands.

———

We work with the client, as Brand Teams. These Teams represent the collective skills of our clients and ourselves. On their performance, our client will judge the whole agency.

———

We encourage individuals, entrepreneurs, inventive mavericks: with such members, teams thrive. We have no time for prima donnas and politicians.

———

We value candor, curiosity, originality, intellectual rigor, perseverance, brains — and civility. We see no conflict between a commitment to the highest professional standards in our work and to human kindness in our dealings with each other.

———

We prefer the discipline of knowledge to the anarchy of ignorance. We pursue knowledge the way a pig pursues truffles.

———

We prize both analytical and creative skills. Without the first, you can't know where to go; without the second, you won't be able to get there.

———

The line between confidence and arrogance is a fine one. We watch it obsessively.

———

We respect the intelligence of our audiences: *"The consumer is not a moron."*

———

We expect our clients to hold us accountable for our Stewardship of their Brands. Only if we have built, nourished, and developed prosperous Brands, only if we have made them more valuable both to their users and to their owners, may we judge ourselves successful.

MOVING FORWARD

Through the fall of 1993, Beers and her senior team worked relentlessly to spread the message of Brand Stewardship throughout the agency. It was a slow, sometimes arduous, process. By the end of the year, they had identified several issues that they felt required immediate attention.

Spreading the Gospel

Compared to clients' enthusiasm, reactions to Brand Stewardship within the agency were initially tepid. Across disciplines, employees below the most senior level lacked experience with, and knowledge of how to use, the principles of Brand Stewardship. O'Dea remarked, "Brand Stewardship has not seeped into everyday practice. Only a minority of the O&M population truly understands and embraces it. Others are aware of Brand Stewardship, but not deeply proficient. Many are still not true believers."

Account executives who misunderstood the concept were at a loss when their clients demanded it. Planners expressed confusion about how to use Brand Stewardship to develop a creative strategy.[13] Recalled one executive, "People didn't understand such basic things as the difference between a BrandPrint and an advertising strategy."

Greater familiarity with the process did not always mitigate opposition. Admitted Beers, "We didn't always have much internal support. It did not sound like anything new." Another problem was that a brand audit might suggest a change of advertising strategy. "Doing an audit on existing business can be seen as an indictment of what we have been doing," noted one executive. Lazarus concluded:

It will only be internalized throughout the organization with experience. I did a Brand Stewardship presentation recently with some of our account people. The client was mesmerized. They wanted the chairman of the company to see the presentation. Now, that had an effect on the people who were with me. I can bet you that when they make the next presentation, Brand Stewardship will be their focal point.

Perhaps the greatest resistance came from the creative side. "We've got to get greater buy-in from the creative people," noted Walsh. Their initial reactions ranged from viewing the BrandPrint as an infringement on their artistic license—"I didn't believe in recipe approaches. They can lead to formulaic solutions," said one early convert—to the tolerant skepticism reported by another: "The creatives tell me, 'If it helps you get new business, that's great, but why are you in my office talking about this? I have a deadline and don't see what this has to do with creating advertising.' But you can't develop a good BrandPrint without cross-functional involvement."

Others questioned the relevance of Brand Stewardship for O&M Direct. While clear to Beers that Brand Stewardship clarified the rewards to clients from integrating advertising and direct marketing, some were slow to see this potential. Dispelling the popular notion that direct encourages short-term sales while advertising builds brands over the long term, Thedens argued, "You can't send a message by mail that contradicts what you show on television. Both disciplines sell and both build the brand."

One executive concluded that the biggest problem was insufficient communication: "Anyone who heard it firsthand from Charlotte bought in. From the moment she opens her mouth to talk about brands, you know she has a depth of understanding that few people have. The problem is that, until recently, she has been the only missionary."

---

[13] Account executives managed the agency's contact with clients, bringing in new accounts and coordinating information flow between other functions and the client. Planners worked with account executives to establish creative marketing strategies.

Although the senior team had started "taking the show on the road," Walsh felt they were too few for the magnitude of the task: "The same six or seven people keep getting reshuffled. The result is that follow-through is not good." O'Dea, however, pointed out that the new missionaries had different tribes to convert. He emphasized the importance of translating the vision into a new role for each employee:

> We need to move beyond a vision that is useful to the top five percent of account and creative people, to one that has meaning for everyone at Ogilvy. The Information Systems staff should see themselves as brand stewards, because without information technology, we can't respond with appropriate speed. I want the Media people to say, "I will not buy airtime on these TV shows because they don't fit the BrandPrint." Creatives at O&M Direct developing coupon designs must be as true to the BrandPrint as creatives in advertising. Everyone must see themselves as co-stewards of the vision.

Local/Global Tensions

Success in 1993 winning several, large multinational accounts created further challenges for the embryonic WCS. Their goal of helping clients to develop a consistent brand image globally created tension in the firm's traditional balance of power. WCS pressed local agencies to give priority to brands with high global development potential over local accounts. For local agencies, however, local accounts often provided the most stable revenue stream and greatest profit. Further, in their zeal to exercise their newfound "line" responsibility, WCS supervisors were viewed at times as overstepping the bounds of their authority.

While tension had always existed between the centers and local markets, the increasingly centralized brand campaigns exacerbated conflicts. "Local agencies were used to always giving the client what they wanted," explained one WCS supervisor, "I had to start telling them to stop over-servicing the client." Some balked. Local expertise had always been one of Ogilvy's greatest competitive strengths. As one senior executive explained, "Certain local offices have not responded well to some of the advertising created centrally. One downside of global work is that it can end up being middle-of-the-road. When this happens, it's bad for an office's creative image locally."

But with costs escalating both centrally and locally, many felt that "the local barons" had to be reigned in. "How do we help our clients globalize," asked Walsh, "when our local management will conspire to keep them geographically oriented?"

For smaller agencies, issues of creative pride and autonomy were especially salient. Under the new system, the central WCS team developed the BrandPrint and advertising campaign with input from local offices. Local offices then tailored execution to regional markets. But while large offices usually served as the center for at least one global account, smaller offices, explained one WCS director, "are more often on the receiving end now. They begin to feel like post boxes. How do you attract good people to smaller offices if they never get to run big accounts?"

Beers felt that maintaining flexibility was key. "Some of our competitors—McCann Erickson is a good example—are excellent at running highly centralized campaigns. For us to view WCS that way would be a mistake. WCS should build upon, not diminish, our local strength." Creative and execution roles, she explained further, should shift according to the locus of the best ideas or relevant resources:

> I want to continue to cultivate the tension between local and center. The easiest thing would be to have far more dominance centrally. It is more efficient, and the clients like it, because they invariably wish they had more control at the center. The reality is that nothing substitutes for full-blown, local agencies where the people are talented enough to articulate the heart of the brand, to

interpret it in a sophisticated way, and—if necessary—to change it. If you have messengers or outlets, you will never execute well. The best ideas have unique, local modifications. One brand campaign we tested, for example, was an absolute win around the world, except in Asia, where the humor did not translate well. Our creative director in Asia worked with the idea, and it became the print campaign we use globally.

Also on her mind was the brewing controversy about how to split fees and allocate costs between WCS and local offices. Agency compensation on large accounts consisted frequently of fixed fees that were negotiated up front. With new clients, it could be difficult to estimate the range of Ogilvy services needed and the extent of local adaptation that would be required. Agencies in more distant markets were asked to contribute—sometimes without compensation—when the need for additional local work was discovered. Local presidents complained that, although WCS accounts pulled their people away from local accounts with clear-cut billable time, their portion of multinational fees was small. WCS, on the other hand, maintained that they were being forced to absorb more than their fair share of local costs.

Beers recounted one specific incident that unfolded in December. "Kelly told me that one of our offices had refused to do any more work for a client, because they did not have any fees. I said to him, 'I think you ought to talk to them about our new way of working and how much promise there is in it. Give them more information. If they still can't see their way, have them come to me.' You ask for collaboration," she concluded, "but occasionally you act autocratically."

As conflicts continued to erupt, senior management was divided on the solution. "We have highly individual personalities running our offices. With 272 worldwide," one account director observed, "it's been like herding cats." Debate swirled around the degree of management structure required. Lazarus advocated commonsense resolu-

tions between the global account director and local agency presidents: "In our business, the quality of the work that gets done all comes down to the people who are doing it, not to bureaucratic structures. If you create the right environment and you have the right people, you don't need a whole structure." Others, O'Dea and his WCS corps included, insisted that organizational changes were necessary to make Brand Stewardship a reality agency-wide. Walsh agreed: "What we don't have is a structure, working practices, remuneration, praise of people—all based on Brand Stewardship." Referring to the trademark Ogilvy color, Beers offered her perspective:

> We have to make Ogilvy "redder." The finances should follow our goal of killing geography as a barrier to serving the brand. . . . Let's get the emotional content high and the structure will follow. We have people in the company who would prefer it the other way, but I want to get it done in my lifetime. So much of what happens at Ogilvy is cerebral, thoughtful, and slow. We can't afford to move at a "grey" pace.

At the end of 1993, yet another issue had come to the fore. With large multinational accounts, some WCS heads controlled billings that easily surpassed those of many countries in the network. The agency, however, had always accorded the greatest prestige and biggest bonuses to presidents of local offices, countries, and regional chairmen. Brand Stewardship now required top-notch brand stewards and organizations centered around products and processes rather than Ogilvy office locations. "I ask people to collaborate, but I don't pay them for it. This company has never asked its feudal chiefs to consider the sum," observed Beers. She pondered how to attract the best and the brightest to WCS posts, knowing she would be asking them to leave the safety of turf to head brand-focused, virtual organizations.

The "thirsty for change" veterans believed another hurdle would be learning to work better as a team. Said Lazarus, "I don't think we make a lot of group decisions. We talk about it, but decisions tend to get made by Charlotte and by the specific individuals who are affected." But implementation revived many of the debates of the first Vienna meeting. "I think we are all still very guarded," explained Walsh. "As each meeting goes by, it's a bit like a lump of ice slowly melting—our edges getting smoother all the time." Lazarus hoped that team members would grow "comfortable enough to disagree openly with one another." Battling a culture she had once described as "grotesquely polite" was still on Beers's list of priorities as she considered the group she had assembled to help carry the change forward.

By December 1993, Charlotte Beers assessed the year's progress: "Clients love Brand Stewardship. Competitors are trying to copy it. And internally, we lack consensus." She wondered what course of action in 1994 would provide the best stewardship of the Ogilvy brand.

Lehman Brothers (A):
Rise of the Equity Research Department

In August 1992 Lehman management distributed an all-hands memo announcing that Jack Rivkin would leave the firm "as a result of differences over the future direction of the equities business" to be replaced by Lehman fixed-income executive Paul Williams.[1] "We were white-faced and slack-jawed and couldn't believe it," recalled a Rivkin associate. "This was an absolute bolt from the blue. If there were long-standing disagreements, they were well hidden."[2]

Rivkin, a charismatic and beloved leader, had taken Shearson Lehman Brothers' research department from relative obscurity to the highest ranking research department on Wall Street within three years.[a] A flagship of the firm since the late 1980s, the research department had enjoyed low analyst turnover and had produced one star analyst after another. Fred Fraenkel—Rivkin's trusted lieutenant from April 1987, first as associate director of equity research and, when Rivkin became worldwide head of equity division in spring 1990, as global head of equity research—was left pondering over whether he ought to change some of the department's practices or leave things unchanged and continue building on Rivkin's legacy.

THE SHEARSON LEHMAN MERGER

In May 1984 Lehman Brothers Kuhn Loeb was acquired by Shearson American Express. (Exhibit 1 presents a history of Lehman Brothers.) "The acquisition was opportunistic," recalled Shearson chief operating officer Jeffrey Lane. "Lehman was a currently troubled, but storied franchise. Getting into trouble forced it into our arms. It was a golden opportunity for us." Peter Cohen, CEO of Shearson American Express, was named chairman of Shearson Lehman Brothers; Sandy Weill, architect of Shearson's expansion and erstwhile president of American Express, left the firm in early 1985 (see Exhibit 2 for a short biography).

The merger gave Shearson access to Lehman's underwriting business and impressive list of clients. Lehman received $2 billion of much-needed capital and gained access to Shearson's powerful distribution capability. A disciplined retail powerhouse, Shearson was reputed on Wall Street for its management systems and cost controls. Remarked one former Lehman partner: "The guts of Lehman were screaming out for the orga-

[a] Research department rankings were compiled in *Institutional Investor* magazine's annual October All-America Research Team (colloquially called "all-star") rankings of analysts and research departments.

nization and management Shearson possessed."[3] Observed Lane: "If we could get retail and wholesale respecting each other and working well together, we could own the world."

Despite the merger, however, Lehman employees wanted nothing to do with the "inferior people" of Shearson, who they nicknamed "Corned Beef With Lettuce," for Cogan, Berlind, Weill, and Levitt, individuals who had led Shearson during its formative years in the 1960s.[4] Recalled Judy Sanders, who in September 1986 became head of human resources for capital markets for the merged unit: "We acquired Lehman Brothers, where everyone thought that they were smarter and better and

EXHIBIT 1   **Lehman Brothers History, 1850–1990**

Lehman Brothers Heritage

In 1849 Henry Lehman and his brothers Emanuel and Mayer founded a dry-goods store in Montgomery, Alabama. Lehman Brothers became extremely successful during the pre–Civil War cotton boom by accepting raw cotton in place of cash payments for various products. The firm was instrumental in establishing the New York Cotton Exchange in 1870. In 1887 Lehman Brothers bought a seat on the New York Stock Exchange.[a]

Lehman Brothers underwrote its first IPO in 1899 for the International Steam Pump Company and later, with Goldman Sachs, participated in underwriting one of the most promising companies at that time, Sears Roebuck. Herbert Lehman, son of Emanuel Lehman, after serving as a Lehman Brothers partner from 1908 to 1929, became governor of New York from 1933 to 1942 and a U.S. senator from 1950 to 1956. Robert Lehman, grandson of Emanuel Lehman, led the firm from 1925 until his death in 1969.

The firm had always been viewed as an entrepreneurial organization. Its partners were independent, paid individual bonuses based on seniority and individual profits, rather than as a fixed percentage of firm total profits (as was the custom at many investment banks). The individual partners exerted tremendous power in business dealings, quoting investment banking fees on the basis of their personal judgment and enjoying generous expense accounts.

Failure to control costs led to losses in the early 1970s. Brought in as CEO to return the firm to its past prominence, Lehman's top investment banker Peter Peterson cut partners' expenses, implemented strict departmental budgets, and focused on specific market segments (primarily debt issues and large equity financing). The firm regained its fame for both innovation in financial products and the caliber of its people and in 1977 merged with another prestigious securities firm, Kuhn Loeb & Co., to create the investment bank Lehman Brothers Kuhn Loeb.[b]

In 1983 just two months after Peterson had named him co-chief executive officer, top trader Lewis Glucksman replaced Peterson as chairman in what was viewed by many as an inside coup. "There was a war taking place between investment banking and capital markets," recalled Shearson chief operating officer Jeffrey Lane. "I guess on a temporary basis capital markets won. Peterson left the company. Lou Glucksman became the chairman. Then the company really got into trouble."

Traditionally a "free spirit" organization with almost no management system, Lehman became riven by dissension and weakened in an environment increasingly requiring intensified interdivisional communication and coordination. Entering 1984 with insufficient capital to survive as a consequence of in-house fighting and business downturn, the firm began to seek a white knight that could bail it out of its troubles.

In May 1984 Lehman Brothers Kuhn Loeb was acquired by Shearson American Express.

[a] "Lehman Brothers," Vault Reports, Inc., www.vaultreports.com, 1999, accessed August 1, 1999.
[b] Ibid.

EXHIBIT 1 Lehman Brothers History, 1850–1990 *(continued)*
Timeline of Key Events

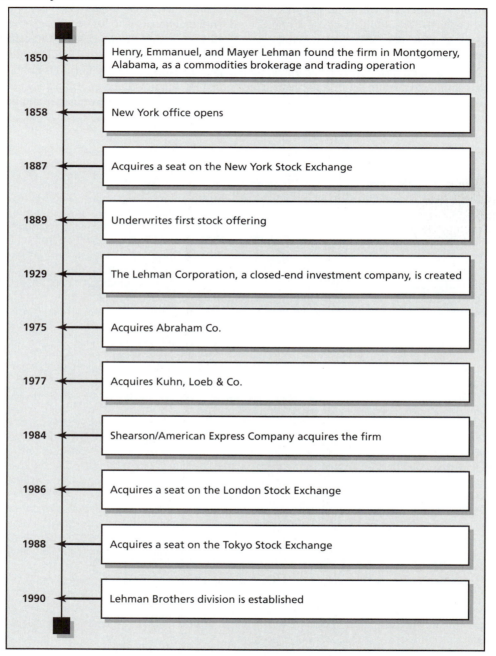

1850	Henry, Emmanuel, and Mayer Lehman found the firm in Montgomery, Alabama, as a commodities brokerage and trading operation
1858	New York office opens
1887	Acquires a seat on the New York Stock Exchange
1889	Underwrites first stock offering
1929	The Lehman Corporation, a closed-end investment company, is created
1975	Acquires Abraham Co.
1977	Acquires Kuhn, Loeb & Co.
1984	Shearson/American Express Company acquires the firm
1986	Acquires a seat on the London Stock Exchange
1988	Acquires a seat on the Tokyo Stock Exchange
1990	Lehman Brothers division is established

Source: "Lehman Brothers—Who We Are, www.lehman.com/About/Who/Docs/about, accessed on August 1, 1999.

EXHIBIT 2 Profiles of Key Case Protagonists

Stephen Balog After earning an MBA from the Wharton School (and a BS in mechanical engineering from Bucknell University), Balog worked for several years for such companies as Merck and Interactive Data Corporation before joining Prudential in 1983 as an analyst covering electronics—connectors, semiconductor production, testing, and measurement equipment. He left Prudential in 1987 after becoming a ranked analyst and was hired by Rivkin and Fraenkel as a member, and later became head, of Lehman Brothers' technology group. Balog came from a family with deep roots in investment banking; his father had built one of the most powerful research departments on Wall Street at Drexel Burnham Lambert.

Fred Fraenkel Fraenkel had joined Goldman Sachs in 1974 after obtaining an MBA from the Wharton School. Within a year, the banking team with which he was associated was ranked number one by Greenwich Associates. Fraenkel left Goldman in 1976 to run a cellular business in which his family had invested. After taking the firm public within three years, he returned to Wall Street, joining E.F. Hutton as an investment strategy analyst. He moved to Prudential in 1982 but, dissatisfied with the firm's research strategy, left in 1986 with a handful of colleagues to launch a family of index mutual funds.

Richard Fuld Fuld had joined Lehman in 1969 as a commercial paper trader. An MBA from New York University, Fuld had been named partner in 1978 and been a key lieutenant of Glucksman when the latter rose to power in 1983 at the old Lehman Brothers.

Jack Rivkin Rivkin had graduated from the Colorado School of Mines in 1962. Upon receiving an MBA from Harvard Business School in 1968, he joined Laird Inc. as a security analyst. He subsequently worked as a security analyst in the airline and aerospace industries for Mitchell Hutchins, which named him associate director of research in 1973. When Paine Webber acquired Mitchell Hutchins in 1977, Rivkin became director of research for the combined operations. That same year, Paine Webber/Mitchell Hutchins research department, for the first time in the existence of both Paine Webber and Mitchell Hutchins, received *Institutional Investor* magazine's highest All-America Research Team ranking. Rivkin exited research operations in 1980 to accept an appointment as Paine Webber's CFO. Rivkin also ran Paine Webber's institutional brokerage and asset management operations, serving as a president of Paine Webber Capital from 1985 to 1987.

Sandy Weill Devastated when Wall Street rejected him at age 21, Weill had joined Bear Stearns as a stockbroker after a year as a Wall Street messenger. In 1960 he co-founded Shearson predecessor Carter, Berlind, Potoma & Weill. Weill then built the Shearson franchise by acquiring several smaller investment firms. Weill was chairman of Shearson Hayden Stone before its merger with American Express in 1981.

cleverer than we. They were damned if they were going to let Shearson, this upstart organization, tell them what to do."

Untroubled by stories of conflict between Lehman and Shearson employees that began circulating soon after the merger, American Express chairman and CEO James D. Robinson III remarked: "Any Harvard versus Yale kind of competitive vibrations are all to the good. The cultures are clashing just as I hoped they would."[5] The conflict, however, seemed to sap the combatants' energies. One senior Lehman Brothers' employee recalled that "too many partners' offices . . . were dark at 6:00 [P.M.]."[6] Few attempts were made to generate new business. Exceptions to Shearson's famed cost control systems began to emerge, making the revenue/cost ratio of the merged firm more like Lehman's than Shearson's.

The "Friday Massacre"

Senior management made Bruce Lisman, a former all-star banking analyst who had become Lehman's research manager in July 1981, responsible for the merged firm's research department. Shearson's popular director of research, John Connolly, a former all-star auto analyst, was fired. On an infamous Friday in May 1984, Lisman walked around the research department firing a number of ex-Shearson analysts. He quit Shearson Lehman the following Monday to run research at Bear Stearns. Shortly after the "Friday massacre," most of the remaining former Shearson analysts and some former Lehman analysts quit the newly merged firm. Recalled Fred Fraenkel, who was running research operations at Prudential at the time: "First, they lost a lot of talent that they fired for no reason other than that they were from Shearson. Second, Shearson Lehman became a place that no research director or research analyst would seriously consider joining."

Desperate to replace Lisman quickly, management asked Eliot Fried, a former all-star aerospace analyst and former research director at Shearson who had been promoted in 1982 to chief investment officer, to again take on the responsibility of research director.

JACK RIVKIN TAKES CHARGE

In November 1986 Herb Frieman, head of capital markets at Shearson Lehman, offered Jack Rivkin the job of head for its global equity research department. Before moving on to become CFO, Rivkin had built Paine Webber's research department during 1977–1980 into a powerhouse that drove the rest of the firm's businesses (Exhibit 2 lists the profiles of the key protagonists).

Rivkin agreed to join Shearson Lehman in February 1987. "Herb Frieman and [Shearson COO] Jeff Lane made me an offer that was financially very difficult to refuse," he recalled, "I got them to

tie to the package some incentives, minor incentives for getting the firm into the top 10 amongst research departments, fairly major incentives for getting the firm into the top five."[b]

Jack Rivkin

"I enjoy working with bright, energetic people, and I'm not very tolerant of other types," remarked Rivkin.

> There's an intensity to managing a service organization with these kinds of people. It is always a work in progress and requires hands-on management. You spend an enormous amount of time individually with the analysts. You need to do a lot of apparently little things that may not look like they relate directly to the business but are critical to reinforcing a culture and an attitude.

"Politics is not his strength," observed Jane Rivkin, who had been married to Jack Rivkin since 1964.

> He likes autonomy and has never liked interference from above in his group's workings. And he speaks his mind. He has no problem contradicting his boss. So, sometimes he comes across as being not respectful of authority. But whatever Jack does, from golf to fly-fishing to work, he does with intensity, passion, and determination.

"Jack infects people around him with his work ethic and enthusiasm," recalled Rivkin's secretary Regina Taylor. Taylor, who had worked with Rivkin since 1980, when he was Paine Webber's CFO, and later moved with him to Shearson Lehman Brothers, added: "I have heard stories about Jack, when he was a teenager in Oklahoma, waking up at 4 A.M. to pick peas in the fields, then going to his second job in a school cafeteria, then attending school, and still ranking first in his class."

---

[b] In 1986 Lehman's research department was ranked number 15 on the *Institutional Investor*'s All-America Research Team.

Taking Stock

"When I got to Lehman, the research department was a mess," recalled Rivkin. "It got no respect. The offices were scattered around hodgepodge. There was no physical structure that said, 'This is an important part of the firm.' There were no systems in place, no use of electronics, no use of computers, no use of networks to capture and efficiently deliver information." Elaine Garzarelli, one of the most recognized research analysts at Shearson Lehman in 1986, commented on the situation: "The department wasn't disciplined. The few meetings we had were held on a freewheeling, as-needed basis. People did whatever they wanted to do. They didn't have to talk at regular meetings; they didn't have to submit reports at certain times. Absolutely no mention was ever made of the *Institutional Investor* All-America team."

As at other investment banks, Shearson Lehman's research department was treated as a cost center; revenue-producing departments—investment banking, retail, and institutional business—covered its cost. Pointing out that Merrill Lynch's and Goldman Sachs' research budgets were more than twice Shearson Lehman's and arguing that the firm needed only modest increases in investment banking, retail, and institutional businesses to cover an increase in research expenses, Rivkin was able to negotiate with senior management agreement on a near doubling of the department's size, from roughly 35 analysts and 35 support staff to approximately 60 analysts and 60 support staff.

Building from Scratch

In January 1987, a month before formally joining Shearson Lehman, Rivkin arranged a luncheon meeting with the firm's analysts at which he took them through the seven S's.[c] "Our objective is to be the best in the business," he told them,

and the objective for each of you is to become recognized as an expert in your industry by all of the constituencies that you touch. When someone calls a corporation or an institution and asks the names of the best analysts, I want our analysts to be on top of those lists. In order to achieve these objectives, we are going to run this department like a business, all seven S's aligned with one another.

Immediately after joining the firm, Rivkin met individually with all the analysts. He discussed their products, what they thought was right and wrong with the organization, and what they thought ought to be changed. He impressed upon them his vision of building one of the best research departments on Wall Street and was little moved by complaints that the sales force was not selling research products aggressively. Often in the past, research and sales departments had engaged in mutual recriminations, the retail executives criticizing the poor quality and persistent delays of analysts' reports and the analysts using the sales force as scapegoats for poor sales of research reports. Remarked an associate: "Jack's view was that the product should sell for itself and should not need a stellar sales force."

Morning Meetings

Rivkin ruled that Monday, with rare exceptions, would be a day in the office and instituted a fortnightly, mandatory attendance Monday lunch to introduce some discipline to the organization and facilitate sharing of ideas and issues by analysts. Next, Rivkin restructured the morning meetings. These meetings were critical, since it was through them that analysts reported to institutional sales people new developments that they, in turn, conveyed to clients.

Lehman's morning meetings were conducted on the research floor at 8:45 A.M., about the same

---

[c] McKinsey's 7-S model was popular among business executives as an approach to ensure effective operations through alignment among strategy, structure, systems, staffing, skills, style, and shared values.

time Lehman's clients would be meeting in anticipation of the 9:30 A.M. opening of trading. Because their recommendations were made too late to impact on clients' immediate trading behavior, Lehman traders paid little attention to the information the analysts shared with them in the morning meetings. At these loosely structured meetings, "analysts sometimes spoke without written notes and salespeople often read newspapers," recalled Rivkin. The First Call system that electronically distributed analysts' updates and recommendations did not get Lehman's First Call notes until 2 P.M. on the afternoon of the day of the call, too late for them to have any impact on clients' decisions.

Rivkin changed the morning meeting time to 7:45 A.M. and, subsequently, to 7:30 A.M., and required analysts to submit their reports in writing before appearing at the morning meetings. Rivkin also changed the venue for the morning meetings, convening them on the trading floor. Explained Rivkin:

> I wanted our sales trader to immediately call up his counterpart and say: "Just wanted you to know that our analyst just raised her estimates on company X." It would generate a chain reaction, since the institutional trader would go into his morning meeting and say: "Lehman's analyst just raised her estimates on company X." The institutional trader would be happy with Lehman because he would have gotten valuable information that he would have used to contribute meaningfully in his morning meeting. And chances would be that Lehman would be mentioned in our customer's morning meeting. In order for this chain reaction to be set off, it was critical that our sales traders listening to the morning meeting be able to use the information immediately to advise their institutional counterparts. So I moved the meetings to the trading floor. In the beginning the traders weren't too keen on the move. They soon became a lot more interested, though, as they

began noticing that their clients were taking more of their calls because now they were offering information instead of just reading them the trades.

One of Rivkin's first hires was Michael Skutinsky Jr., who had worked for him at Paine Webber since 1982 building one of the first institutional sales systems on Wall Street. Rivkin knew Skutinsky to be an "unusual person" who possessed both a technology background and a comprehension of the research business. "He could explain technological advances to research analysts without dropping acronyms," observed Rivkin. Skutinsky developed a system for getting analysts' notes into First Call. When analysts spoke at morning meetings their notes would already be available to the salesmen as well as entered in First Call.

A "Public Shooting"

Two months into his job, Rivkin shared with the analysts his perception that "although it was a bleak scenario, there also was a tremendous opportunity for improvement." Privately, he thought, he had to "quickly get the analysts to understand that I was serious about turning it around."

Rivkin asked Fried, the previous director of research ("He was a great analyst and investor but an uninterested manager. Other analysts loved talking to him about stocks, but they didn't ask him about the business. That was not what Eliot wanted to discuss," recalled Rivkin) to look for other opportunities within the firm. Fried left the department in March 1987. Next, Rivkin fired a ranked analyst who was following a minor industry. "The retail people wanted this guy shot," recalled Rivkin,

> and, frankly, I wanted to shoot somebody; he just happened to be in the sights. He had a pathetic track record; his analytical work was incomplete and shoddy; and he had lost money in a pretty good market. The reaction within the department to his firing was surprise and fear that I was serious. And the reaction from the institutional sales personnel

was mixed. In spite of how bad he was, at least he was ranked, even though in a minor industry. Was I making things better or worse?

Jack and Fred: "Mr. Outside" and "Mr. Inside"

"I got lucky with Fred," recalled Rivkin, referring to his April 1987 hire of Fraenkel. "His joining us basically doubled the energy at the top of the research department. I got him to join as my number two and I got the company to accept him on the same sort of incentive schedule that I was so that our incentives would be aligned."

Fraenkel and some of his colleagues had left Prudential in 1986 to launch a family of index mutual funds. "It was a great idea, but horrific timing," recalled Fraenkel. "When the 1987 crash came our company ended up being sold to a mutual fund complex in Boston and everybody went their own separate way." About that time, Rivkin contacted Fraenkel. Observed Fraenkel:

Jack knew a whole lot about how to structure a research department; he knew a lot about how to change a research department. But he had been out of research for so long that he didn't know the players and he didn't know all the operating ins and outs any longer. His challenge was to take the research department from fifteenth rank to fifth. That was a lot of ground to cover if you really didn't know exactly who to hire and exactly what to do with the department. He figured out quickly that he needed a partner. So I was his second hire, which is very unusual. You go into a research department and management expects you to hire some big name analysts. The first thing you do is say: "I need somebody to help me." That's not really cool when you've been hired as a big-ticket guy. But he did it.

Fraenkel, like Rivkin, viewed the Shearson Lehman research department's circumstances as at once desperate and holding considerable potential. "Shearson Lehman," he reasoned,

was perhaps the only one of the several Merrill Lynch wannabes on Wall Street that, given its big retail and investment banking operations, had a real potential to become a financial monolith. And Jack and I had tremendous freedom to do whatever we wanted in the research department. We could have put a neutron bomb in there and make everybody disappear; we could have rolled up the carpets and brought in Ouija boards—nobody would have known. People outside the department didn't understand it and didn't want to know about it.

The chemistry between Rivkin and Fraenkel was obvious from the start. "Fred and Jack were like Yin and Yang," observed a Shearson Lehman analyst.

They were great complements to each other. What one lacked, the other one had. Jack was the strategic thinker. He was always looking ahead. Where can we be a year from now? How can we get better? Are we pushing for out-of-the-box thinking? He was the one who could illuminate his vision. And Fred was the one who knew how to get there. He understood and believed in Jack's vision. He just got it done. And Jack and Fred were synchronized right off the bat. One of them could just say the other one's next word. You never felt that there was an ego barrier between them. You just felt comfortable coming to either of them.

"Jack," observed Skutinsky, "was the outside person, the visionary thinker, Fred the inside person, the operational head. Jack was like a CEO, shaking hands, meeting division heads, interacting with and appeasing banking, retail, and institutional sales contingents, and offering the macro view. Fred was the COO who would talk with the analysts about valuations. When you needed a pat on your back he was there to pat you; when you needed to get whacked in the head he was there also, to whack you."

ESTABLISHING SYSTEMS AND PROCESSES

Systematizing Analyst Activities

Rivkin expected analysts to initiate at least 125 client calls per month. He asked analysts to record their client contacts—outgoing calls, incoming calls, and visits—and anything significant discussed during their conversations. An analyst might conclude from a meeting with an XYZ mutual fund buy-side analyst, for example, that "it looks like XYZ might be a buyer of ABC airline stocks." Copies of the analyst's notes were distributed to salesmen and traders on the accounts.

Copies of client contact records were also inputted to the control system, which generated a report that detailed analyst contacts. Everyone who accessed the system—analysts and salespeople alike—knew who was making calls to whom and how often. Salespeople began to use the report to pressure analysts who were contacting few clients to make more calls. "Once the report card on analyst contacts was electronically pinned up on a board," Skutinsky recalled,

> all the analysts began trying to get to the front section of the rankings, no one wanted to be near the end. From the correlations between calls made and analyst ranking it was obvious that analysts who were dialing the accounts were in fact dialing for success. People realized that in trying to become a top analyst you sell some steak and you sell some sizzle. You had to have good research to get client support, but talking to clients also helped. The analysts started asking one another: "How do you make so many calls? Where do you find the time?"

To introduce some uniformity and discipline to the process by which analysts made recommendations, Rivkin established an investment committee that met weekly, but could also meet at a day's notice upon an analyst's urgent request. Rivkin, Fraenkel, and strategist Mike Sherman were permanent members, research analysts were named as rotating members, and it also included representatives from retail and asset management. Analysts who wanted to change their recommendations would have to submit to a critique by the committee. Incomplete or unsatisfactory reports were sent back to the drawing board. A ranked analyst elaborated on the role of the investment committee: "If I decided to change a recommendation, I had to present my thesis before an investment committee. I would have to answer a barrage of questions to explain why I was changing my recommendation. The questions exposed me to multiple perspectives from different areas of the firm."

Performance Evaluations

Performance evaluation had not been Shearson Lehman's strong suit. Recalled Sanders: "The employees themselves rarely had an opportunity to say: 'Here's how I think I did.' It was usually a one-way review. Jack was very different," Sanders continued, recalling Rivkin's overhaul of the performance review process.

> He knew that people were not going to have fun or succeed if they were continually asking themselves, "How am I doing?" Jack asked people to come to the performance review sessions with their own sets of expectations. And then, he engaged them in discussions, setting high, yet achievable goals. He maintained a careful, written record, and followed up on a quarterly basis. People knew where they stood. They understood what they needed to accomplish and what support was available to help them.

Performance reviews, conducted twice a year, took three weeks of management time in January and two weeks in May. "We collected enormous amounts of objective measurements," recalled Fraenkel.

We counted everything: how many calls they made; how many pages they published; how their recommendations panned out. Then we made subjective judgments on analyst performance against the backdrop of the enormous objective data. By and large the analysts felt that the process was very fair, as opposed to our just saying to them, "You get this much bonus. Why? Because that's what I think you're worth." If anybody wanted to argue about compensation they had to argue against the backdrop of the data that had been compiled.

In July 1987 a rating system named BONUS was implemented to help Rivkin measure analysts' performance. "The acronym for our rating system is BONUS," remarked Rivkin, "and that's how the analysts are going to be paid, bonuses based on their performance." Graphs charted stocks' price performance against analysts' recommendations on the stocks, enabling management to match analysts' hold, buy, and accumulate recommendations against stock performance and identify missed upticks and downticks. Management could compare analysts against peer groups, sectors, and other benchmarks. A commission tracking system, "the analysts' bottom line," according to Skutinsky, was developed to determine how much agency commission business analysts were bringing into their stocks relative to the norm. Unlike the client contact report, the commission system was shared only between management and the analysts being rated.

Teena Lerner, who joined Wall Street in 1982 to follow biotech stocks, elaborated on Rivkin's focus on measurement:

> Anything that he could, Jack wanted to measure: number of calls, trading commissions, written reports, client visits. But there were no secrets. The numbers were out there for everyone in the department to see. He developed a business plan with metrics on which he held analysts accountable. I had never heard about a business plan on Wall Street.

One of Lerner's colleagues, a ranked analyst, recalled:

> Noticing that the research department had a history of taking a lackadaisical attitude and the absence of a cultural bond, Jack and Fred pulled sharply on the leash. Suddenly, there was pressure and stress that shell-shocked some of us. We began saying that Jack and Fred's approach was "II [get ranked by *Institutional Investor* magazine] or die." There was a sense that if you didn't make II, you would be out of the place. A lot of us worked 12–15 hours a day, 7 days a week, 365 days a year. But the great thing was that in my class, 95 percent of us made II within the first year and a half. It was so special. I remember talking to competitors at Merrill who were amazed at how fast we were developing analysts into stars.

Inducting "Rate Busters"

Rivkin initially hired only a few people, not necessarily ranked analysts. "We didn't have to necessarily hire a number one ranked analyst," explained Fraenkel, recalling Rivkin's guidelines on the type of analysts to bring into the department, "but the person we hired had to bring something that did not exist in the department. We would hire somebody who really knew how to make phone calls or was truly an industry expert. Their practices, we hoped, would rub off on the others."

The first major hire into the department, a ranked airline analyst from Drexel, Helane Becker, occurred three months after Rivkin joined the firm. Rivkin characterized her as "a marketing demon. She made more calls to clients and put out more First Call notes than seemed humanly possible," he recalled. "I had worked for Fred Fraenkel at Prudential Securities," observed Becker, "and, as much as you can trust anybody on Wall Street, I trusted Fred. In 1987 Fred invited me to a dinner with him and Jack. Over dinner they shared their ambition of building a top-of-the-line research department and invited me to become one of the cornerstones of that department. It sounded an exciting opportunity to work for people that I knew and trusted."

Stephen Balog, the second ranked analyst to join the firm, had covered the semiconductor sector for Prudential. Balog, in turn, built his team by hiring a few "rate busters," carefully recruited analysts who would be far above the norm on at least one of the dimensions of importance to analysts. Not every star hire worked out; rather than absorb their expenses for long, Rivkin quickly negotiated their exits.

Hiring Process

Rivkin developed for recruitment an interview process that required several senior people in the equity research department to meet candidates, typically MBA graduates from top business schools. Becker explained her approach to the recruitment interviews: "A lot of people are smart. But the key question is who is intuitive. In the end, you need to make fast decisions with imperfect information. And the analyst should be able to change his or her mind. We used to ask some bizarre questions just to find out how fast somebody was able to think on their feet."

Following the interviews, the interviewers met as a group to review each candidate individually and fill out forms, designed by Rivkin, that contained questions such as: What did you like most? What did you like least? What concerns do you have? Who does this person remind you of? What would be your worry if the analyst were to be hired? "The post-interview review meeting was like a Quaker gathering," recalled Sanders. "Rivkin made sure everyone understood that we would have to live with this person every day. The 10 or 12 of us who had met the candidate decided by consensus. There was neither pulling of rank nor counting of votes. If anybody was really concerned about a candidate the group would pass." Fraenkel recalled his "four-qualities" test:

I tried to figure out whether the interviewee had the intellectual capacity and the work ethic to become an industry expert. If those two qualities didn't exist, then nothing else mattered. The third question was whether the interviewee was capable of representing those two qualities to clients, orally or in writing, so that they could be recognized. All you can do in this business is call, visit, or write—that's it; there's no other way to gain recognition for expertise. The fourth part was our magic bullet. I asked myself whether the interviewee was someone people were going to like. And if he or she wasn't, I would take a pass and let them go.

Strategist Mary Farrell commented on Rivkin's approach to evaluating candidates: "One of Jack's biggest strengths is his ability to identify the best people. He didn't make many hiring mistakes. It all had to do with his unusual interview technique. He didn't spend any time on meaningless questions and went directly after the in-depth topics. He was trying to understand what a person was really thinking and what made that person intellectually different from others. In a single interview, he would try to assess if a person could perform under pressure as well as that person's quantitative and communication skills. Furthermore, he looked for nice people. Jack believed in maintaining a fun environment in which analysts would work together in teams without hostility."

Rivkin was emphatic about who he would *not* hire. "I have a 'no jerk' policy," he declared. "No matter how good an analyst may be, given the structure we are trying to create here I am not going to bring a jerk into the department. To me, a jerk is someone difficult to manage, marching to his own drummer, not interested in what was going on within the department and within the firm. We are just not going to have people like that here." Recalled Balog: "Jack was very clear in telling us that life's too short to have prima donnas in the department even if they might be number one ranked people. Even if we could get them we didn't want to deal with jerks. We wanted people that were well rounded and could have fun with others so that it became a fun place."

Cherry Picking from E.F. Hutton

In November 1987 American Express acquired E.F. Hutton, necessitating rationalizations in areas in which the firms had duplicate capabilities. Between 5,000 to 6,000 people were laid off, mostly from E.F. Hutton.[7] Some of the Shearson Lehman departments, Fraenkel recalled, "literally had E.F. Hutton employees come to auditoriums and once the auditoriums were filled, announced, 'You are all dismissed.' Jack and I," he added, "were among the few people trying to hire Hutton people."

Rivkin and Fraenkel visited E.F. Hutton's office every day for 10 days and interviewed everyone in the research department. Having worked for E.F. Hutton, Fraenkel knew many of its analysts. Following the interviews, Rivkin and Fraenkel would meet and decide for each industry covered whether Shearson Lehman analysts or their E.F. Hutton counterparts were better. "On several occasions," recalled Fraenkel,

> we concluded that the Hutton analyst was better than the Shearson Lehman analyst. Letting go of the Shearson Lehman analysts was sad, but it was business. By being smart about the rationalization process we dramatically upgraded our department. We also bought undying loyalty from people that we saw promise in, people whom anybody else might've blown away, but we kept. For the next few years no one else on Wall Street even tried to hire those people because they knew they would be loyal to us for having been given a fair chance.

"There was very little cherry picking going on in other departments of Shearson Lehman," recalled Balog. "The general approach was: 'Our guys win; your guys are dead.' People were just using E.F. Hutton as a spare parts bin to pick up a few good people. Jack and Fred were much more heads-up in following a systematic approach."

Among those Rivkin and Fraenkel succeeded in getting to join them from E.F. Hutton were seven ranked analysts.

Two weeks after Josephine Esquivel, an HBS graduate, started on Wall Street in June 1987 Shearson Lehman had bought her employer, E.F. Hutton. Esquivel, who was interviewed by Rivkin and Fraenkel and hired into the Shearson Lehman research department, was struck by the contrast between their expectations of the research department and the investment bankers' expectations:

> Lehman's bankers used to joke that putting together Lehman, fifteenth in rankings, and Hutton, sixteenth, would create a research department that would be thirty-first. That is how bad the reputation of the two research departments was! Bankers were the ones that had the relationships. Analysts were just peripheral people that you brought along to the final dance. Jack wanted to make the analysts into superstars. He believed that they could be much more important than before to investment bankers in closing transactions. The good ones would have even better relationships than the bankers.

Training

Developing people through education and training was a passion for Rivkin. "Jack is always looking for opportunities to teach people around him," noted Taylor.

> Take me for example. As his secretary, I make work life smooth for Jack. I will get his lunch if he is in a rush. But Jack is always giving me business plans to read, educational videos to view. He lets me talk to lawyers and presidents of companies. He has encouraged me to continue my education and just lets me run with as much as I want to do. Thanks to his encouragement, today I am also a registered broker.

"Jack would sit down with all the analysts," recalled Lerner, "and try to help us figure out how to get recognized and ranked. He would preach to us to do something original and then broadcast it as loud as we could. When he reviewed our research reports, we would receive them back with his green comments scrawled all over."

Fraenkel and Rivkin shared a common vision for building Shearson Lehman's research department. Recalled Fraenkel: "Jack and I both strongly believed that the value of an analyst to an investment bank should come from their industry expertise, not just stock-picking ability. We told our analysts to become the best industry experts and we would show them how to become successful. That was an attractive proposition to our analysts. Analysts who live or die on stock picking are very scared."

Rivkin and Fraenkel developed a 13-week training program aimed, according to Fraenkel, specifically at converting the analysts' industry expertise into high-quality analysis. "We were not going to teach the semiconductor analyst how to differentiate between Pentium and the 386," he remarked.

> We were going to help him with a training program to monetize that knowledge. So we stole everything we thought valuable from everybody else on Wall Street and pinched it into our training program. We stole First Boston's idea of calling institutions on the phone to get their votes to improve our analysts' ranking. We stole the written product delivery processes of Goldman Sachs and Merrill Lynch. We were totally shameless. As a result, an industry expert entering our training program could be accelerated fairly dramatically into a recognized analyst.

"We were very systematic at the time when Wall Street was not systematic," reflected Lerner. "Fred gave lots of nuts and bolts lessons on how to conduct one-on-one meetings, how to conduct group meetings, how to deal effectively with different kinds of clients within a group meeting context, how not to say stupid things to the press."

The best people in the department were asked to teach whatever they were best at and to share their worst mistakes. "The training sessions served two purposes," Rivkin explained. "One was bringing people up to speed so they understood how to do their jobs effectively. But the second part was recognition of our experts. We asked some of our rate busters and top analysts to offer training sessions on subjects like making a marketing call, balance sheet analysis, creating something special in your research, dealing with investment banking, and so forth." Becker remembered: "Fred and Jack recruited me to Shearson with the mandate to mentor the young, enthusiastic people and show them how to become good analysts. Jack specifically wanted me to teach analysts how to use trading, write good research reports, and make 150 phone calls a month." Participants in the training sessions, held once every week, for three hours, averaged a dozen to 15 people throughout the year and ranged from recent MBA graduates to 50-year-olds who had been analysts for 25 years.

Esquivel, who became a ranked analyst in less than a year, one of the shortest times in Wall Street history, attributed her success partly to Lehman's training program. "There was always something to take away from the training sessions," she recalled. "We went through all the different aspects of what our job entailed: from stock picking to how to talk to the press, how to talk to the client, how to talk to the salespeople. We learned how to do all this to our best ability and build our franchise molded to our strengths. And the camaraderie that the training sessions built was unbelievable." Balog agreed that the training had a positive impact on the work atmosphere of the research department. He observed:

> People came to understand the importance of marketing, learned various techniques to become successful, and at the end of the course had a great party. But it was also an experience like hazing, like being initiated into a fraternity or a sorority, that strengthened people's bonds. Fred would act like an idiot and people would just love it. The entire class would go out some evenings, come

in the next morning absolutely hung over, and the people that had been through the class would see the new participants come in all hung over and remember their times together. It strengthened the feeling that this was a fun place to be in.

The Miracle of 1988 and 1989

Shearson Lehman Hutton's research department jumped from fifteenth in *Institutional Investor*'s rankings in 1987 to seventh in 1988, the first year of Rivkin's stewardship. Recalled Fraenkel:

> Our earlier decision to hire only nice people really helped us. Nice people got much better reception from the outside world in a voting sense and were better team members. By the second year our training program had been unbelievably successful. People who had been in last year's training program were getting onto the *Institutional Investor* All-America Research Team. Everybody in the firm said, "A miracle is occurring. We have no idea what they're doing, but they're doing good."

When the department's ranking climbed to fourth in 1989, American Express chairman James Robinson III sent personalized notes of congratulations to everyone who made the rankings that year. Shearson Lehman Hutton president Lane remarked of Rivkin and Fraenkel: "They are both extraordinary professionals. They are bright; they are interesting; they know their business; they did what they were supposed to do. They have ended up at the top of the heap. They did it in a very professional, nice way. I think they did an extraordinary job."

MANAGING THE RESEARCH DEPARTMENT

Rivkin believed the most important attribute of a research director to be a "genuine respect for the people who are working for you. These," he maintained, "are professional, very capable people who are viewed as a cost center and pulled at by every constituency. You have to respect and protect your people. You have to buffer them against all of the demands on their time." Remarked Frankael: "Jack and I made it clear to everybody in the research department that they didn't work for us, we worked for them. If they had problems we were going to fix them. People would come in and talk about their work, their personal lives; we would listen. Our job was to listen to our people and solve their problems." Recalled Taylor: "People would line up in front of Jack's office, like at the church confession, waiting to talk to him about their personal dilemmas."

Nurturing "The Conscience of the Company"

When analyst Marvin Roffman was fired from Janney Montgomery Scott in 1990 for questioning the financial stability of client Donald Trump's casino empire, Rivkin immediately wrote a letter to *The Wall Street Journal* criticizing Janney Montgomery Scott. The message to the Shearson Lehman Hutton research department was clear: analysts can and must be independent thinkers.[8] "Not only did Jack understand what we did," remarked Esquivel, "but also he loved, believed in, and stood up for what we did."

Rivkin characterized the research department as "the conscience of a company." Recognizing that sell-side analysts were under constant pressure to produce favorable reports on client companies, he went out of his way to create an atmosphere in which they felt secure and protected.[9] He preached constantly that the research department's mission was to produce the most timely, creative, and comprehensive research in the industry built on integrity, objectivity, and outstanding service. Shearson Lehman investment banker Richard Thaler offered an investment banker's perspective:

> Jack and Fred brought focus to the research department and integrated it with trading, retail, and investment banking. Organiza-

tionally, we looked real sharp. Research, retail, sales, and trading people worked together closely to get business. The investment bankers knew up front the positions of our analysts. We had remarkable success in pitching banking deals because we had great research and we also knew what institutions were thinking. Jack made sure that research people were also involved in determining if the firm should participate in a potential deal, if so, then at what price, and how to position and sell the deal to investors. The analysts were paid a commission based on banking revenues—15 percent of banking fees in the first year, with a tail of five years—which also motivated them to help investment banking. But if push came to shove and there was a conflict between research and investment banking, Jack always protected the analysts' independence.

Lerner, however, differed in her perspective on the research analysts' independence from the other departments. "We became rather arrogant," she recalled.

We respected the traders. But we looked down on the sales force as incompetent. And we saw the bankers as total mercenaries. All the bankers wanted us to do is to help sell their deals, and we were going to resist their pressure and uphold truth and justice. I had no clue how Jack was able to pull off this situation where we had complete autonomy and very little to do with the rest of the firm. We didn't particularly cooperate with the investment bankers or care about them.

Observed research investment banking officer Brian Nolan: "Jack protected the analysts from the politics of the organization. People knew that if ever there was a conflict there was no doubt that Jack was always going to support the analysts versus anybody else, and so they trusted him implicitly." Analyst Greg Nejmeh, who joined Shearson in October 1981 and began covering building and

construction industry group in summer 1987, recalled a particular episode as representative of Rivkin's support to analysts.

Shearson Lehman was the lead manager of a large equity offering for a company I covered. I had certain reservations about consensus earnings estimates following the offering and so issued a neutral rating on the stock. It is unusual for a lead manager to not issue a buy rating, particularly immediately after a deal. Jack backed me completely even though he took a lot of heat on my behalf. In the end, I was vindicated. Without question, the extent to which Jack supported and protected me contributed to my allegiance and loyalty to him, and sent a powerful message of independence and autonomy to the rest of the department.

Building a "Basketball Team"

"The problem with most big research departments," reflected Becker, "is that the research director is not seen. The position is very impersonal. Jack, in contrast, was very accessible." Rivkin envisioned research department operations in sports metaphors. "Merrill Lynch," he explained,

is like a baseball team; individual players fill positions and bat. Occasionally they throw a ball to one another, but that's about all the interaction they have with others on the team. If a position falls vacant the team buys a good player from the free agent market. The other part of the analogy is that the manager of such a team is usually underground half the time. Goldman Sachs is like a football team with very good coaching, but the coaches call the plays all the time. What I was trying to do was create a basketball team, where the players would be interacting and the coaches would be on the sidelines. So we began setting up industry-focused teams within the departments. And we came down hard on people who could not or would not fit with this team approach.

To help ingrain team-mentality in the research department, Rivkin ruled that analysts' client presentations had to reference at least two compatriots. "I don't want to hear 'I–I–I' in the presentation," he insisted. "I want to hear 'We' and I want to hear other people's names. Believe me, that's going to come back to you in spades. Number one, other analysts will do that for you. Overall, your visibility will increase. Second, it's going to increase the sense among clients that we're a team."

Fraenkel named leaders for each team and, as teams jelled around their new heads and solidified, delegated greater responsibilities to the team leaders, who were paid 20 percent additional compensation for their added responsibilities. "Jack and Fred were trying to build teams around individual superstars," recalled Esquivel. "They were always trying, through onsite work and offsite meetings, to get people to work together across sectors and functions." Nejmeh elaborated: "We would get together in industry sectors to have breakfast and discuss forces affecting our industries, and try to draw inferences about larger trends where some commonality seemed to exist. The sharing of information and exchange of ideas not only made us collectively better as a department but also made us more astute as individual analysts." Over time, Shearson Lehman Hutton's research teams became well known on Wall Street for their cohesiveness and internal rapport.

The Amgen Call

In 1988 biotechnology analyst Lerner got the notion that the small biotech company Amgen and its marketing partner Johnson & Johnson were sitting quietly, for strategic reasons, on the drug erythrofruidin, which was going through the approval process. "My colleague Mimi Willard, a hospital supply analyst," remembered Lerner,

came to me with a question related to a product which was being jointly produced and promoted by Johnson and Johnson, a company Mimi was following, and Amgen, a company I was following as a biotech analyst. We approached the question like a PhD research project. We just sat down and figured out what research had to be done to identify the potential size of the market for the product. Whereas other analysts had identified only one potential market, Mimi and I thought more broadly and identified several potential secondary markets. To estimate the size of these markets, we had two senior analysts (ourselves) and three junior analysts dividing up the field work. Some called oncologists, others called surgeons, yet others called Switzerland because the product was already on the market there. The combined answer pointed us in one direction: this was going to be a blockbuster product with multiple secondary markets.

"Once Teena [Lerner] described the potential of the drug," Fraenkel recalled,

everyone in the health care group set aside their careers for two weeks and began working on this project with her. Every analyst and every assistant made calls. They called about 100 hospitals and pharmacies around the world, estimating the market potential for the drug. Once they had the data together, they knew Amgen had a multibillion dollar drug on its hands. No research department could have possibly made this estimation with just one analyst and an assistant. That's basketball, people getting joy out of making the assist not just the basket, giving up the spotlight for a teammate.

"Our call was so contrary to the position taken by other analysts on Wall Street," Lerner added, "that at that time some people thought that we were crazy. But we had done the research. And we had this incredible support from our management. Lehman pulled all stops in releasing our report, even putting ads in *New York Times* and *Wall Street Journal*. I attribute that call on Amgen for being primarily responsible for my jumping from number three position on the *II* list to number one.

Everybody likes controversy, especially if it leads to positive results."

Casual Fridays and Offbeat Off-Sites

"Jack recognized that a lot of people on Wall Street want psychic income as much as they want dollar income," reflected Thaler. "They like a place where it is fun, where they are respected, and have an impact. At places where it is just about money, there is no loyalty. But if your leader and team provide you the psychic income, you are very loyal to the leader and the team."

"Jack would have parties and retreats," recalled Garzarelli. "He was always gathering everybody together for meetings, creating a family-like atmosphere. He and Fred would get together and bring a cake on people's birthdays, even for secretaries. They would both take me out to lunch once a year and just talk about how things were progressing."

Shearson Lehman Hutton analysts often compared their research department to a graduate school. Rivkin introduced casual Fridays and encouraged analysts to establish home offices so they could spend more time with their families and also have a place away from the investment bank pressures in which to write their reports in peace.

Unique to the department were two-day, off-site analyst meetings that Rivkin organized every year. Wanting to nurture an out-of-the-box culture, Rivkin recruited outside speakers to talk about unconventional subjects at the analyst meetings. One year a consultant conducted sessions on the left brain/right brain dichotomy. Teams of "left-brain dominant" and "right-brain dominant" analysts were assigned similar tasks. "The difference between how the two groups approached their tasks was so stark," recalled Rivkin, "that the analysts immediately realized that you have to recognize who you are, but even more important, you have to understand the person you are going to communicate with and tailor your communication accordingly."

At another off-site meeting attended by everyone—Rivkin, Fraenkel, analysts, economists, administrative staff—the participants went through team-building exercises. Upon return from the off-site, recalled Skutinsky, "No longer were people saying: 'There goes the chief economist Mr. Barbara.' Instead, they were saying: 'Gee, that's Bob, who was leaning backward and hugging the consumer analyst, trying to stay on the platform [in one of the exercises] at the off-site.'"

The off-sites were not all fun and games. Skutinsky, for example, once offered a presentation on the technology of minicomputers explaining the potential points of failure. A psychologist talked about the "age wave," how the baby boomer population's moving through life would affect stock market preferences of the investing public. The department discussed special reports—such as *View from the Year 2000,* a 1992 prognostication of the future; *Beyond Borders,* on international developments, and *Core of the Universe,* in which analysts picked the companies "you should buy as an investor as the core of your holdings regardless of how the market was doing at that time"—that were subsequently presented to a broader audience.

Gender-Blind Management

The research department was embedded in an organization and industry with its own culture that was, in some ways, at odds with the culture Rivkin had nurtured. "Lehman and, in fact, most of Wall Street had a powerful culture that allowed only a particular type of person to succeed," recalled Sanders. "Everything from the clothes you wore to the jokes you told telegraphed whether you would be in the in-group or not."

Rivkin, Sanders believed, emphasized equal opportunity at the research department. "Jack would bring in anyone who could succeed in the job," she recalled; "it didn't matter what they looked like, because he didn't care. Imagine how people like me felt to work with somebody like him in a business that many consider highly sexist.

He was like this wonderful little island in the middle of a massive ocean." One analyst recalled a meeting attended by some senior sales executives at which Rivkin, she, and another female analyst were present. "Midway through the discussion," she said, "a salesman turned to us and asked: 'So what do the girls think of ____?' Jack turned to us and said that we didn't have to answer that question."[10] "Jack has an outstanding reputation going back to the dark ages of early 1970s," recalled Farrell,

> when children were seen as cumbersome burdens on woman analysts and some investment bankers would meet clients at places where women were not allowed. It was during those times that Jack promoted Margo Alexander—one of the first women on Wall Street to be so named—to research director at Paine Webber. I joined Paine Webber partly because of his reputation for building a woman-friendly environment. I had one child, I wanted to have a second child, and Paine Webber was the only firm where I felt I could successfully balance my professional career and family.

"Fred and Jack were willing to give women a shot at a time when most firms were not," observed Esquivel. "During the late 1980s," recalled Lerner, "a top bulge bracket firm developed an unsavory reputation of being a particularly difficult place for women to work. Some people from that firm would brag that every woman that worked there had quit. In my view, the joke was on them. They were passing up on potentially 50 percent of good people. At Lehman, we felt we were building a meritocracy. People were hired not because they were the 'right gender' but because they were good at what they did and they got along well with others."

"We figured very early on that a woman can be just as good an analyst as a man," explained Fraenkel.

> So we had totally sex-blind recruitment and evaluation processes. In recruiting, if we saw a woman we thought was a better candidate than a man, we hired her, period, end of story. As our department evolved, if I were asked who were better analysts, the women or the men, on average, I would say it was the women. I have no idea why, but that's my observation. The head of our health care group was a woman; the head of our consumer group was a woman; the head of our financial group was a woman; and they were among the best in our department. We just had several really good female analysts.

By the end of 1989 Shearson Lehman Hutton's research department was nearly 30 percent women, one of the highest percentage in the industry; its percentage of equity ranked analysts who were women (39 percent) was the highest of all the major investment banks (see Exhibit 3).[11]

Best of the Best

In 1990 Shearson Lehman Hutton was ranked number one for the first time on the *Institutional Investor*'s All-America Research Team. Rivkin had made good his promise to build the best research department on Wall Street two years early. (Exhibit 4 charts the evolving profile of the research department.) Robinson visited the research department to present Rivkin and Fraenkel with leather jackets.

Nejmeh described analysts' surprise on achieving top ranking: "If Lehman could have achieved top five status (from fifteenth when Jack took the reigns), senior management would have considered that a highly commendable achievement. Perhaps Jack in his private moments had visions, but I don't think any member of the department had expected that to happen when Jack joined. So, being ranked number one generated a remarkable feeling of accomplishment."

"The research directors of other Wall Street firms were flabbergasted," recalled Fraenkel. "They couldn't believe that we had just come out of nowhere and taken the number one spot away from

EXHIBIT 3 **Gender Comparisons in Research Department at Shearson Lehman Brothers versus Security Industry**

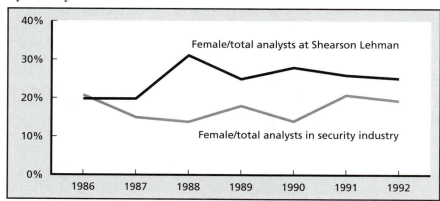

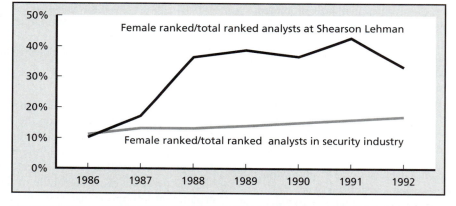

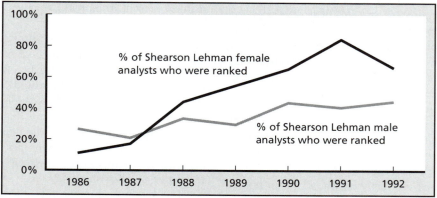

Source: Created by casewriters.

EXHIBIT 4   Shearson Lehman Brothers Research Department Profile, 1986–1992

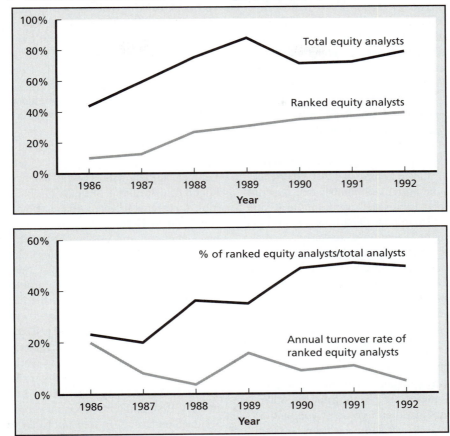

Source: Created by casewriters.

them." Fraenkel attributed the department's rise to team spirit. "Our people," he said,

> liked working at Lehman. They liked the people they were working with. They were better analysts than they would be somewhere else because of the people in their team helping them and giving them insights into their industry. Our competitors were offering them jobs with hundreds of thousands of dollars more salary, yet they didn't find it worthwhile to dislodge from what they had here.

Analysts, generating among the highest numbers of reports in the industry and covering large numbers of companies, credited the research department's environment with fostering creativity and boosting productivity. Shearson Lehman Hutton reports did more than crunch the numbers; they came to be distinguished by their liveliness. In 1990, for example, Katherine Hensel, a second teamer in the regional bank industry, posed as an executive trying to lease space in suburban office towers in the region she was covering. Finding many empty spaces, she correctly warned investors about industry prospects in her heralded "Beam Me Up, Scotty" report.[12]

"It was so much fun working with people who really enjoyed working together," reflected Lerner. "We really felt that we were climbing together toward a shared goal. It was an exciting and nice place to work." Recalled Becker: "I loved going to work everyday. I loved what we were doing and what we were building. It was fun." Added Nejmeh: "It was magical. I would wake up in the morning and just could not get there fast enough. I really felt that I was a part of something special and consider myself very fortunate to have had that experience."

Thanks to being ranked number one, "recruiting was no longer an issue," according to Rivkin. "People wanted to join the department. Everything was just going great and we were starting to make a lot of money. We began to take the research operations global." But being number one also created some tensions with other operations in the investment bank. Balog recalled that jokes about the ages of some of the analysts became both more strident and more frequent. "One banker," he recalled,

> told me, "I can't bring your 'Doogie Howser' analyst to my company."[d] And the kid was an all-star. Some of the people from the other departments just didn't get it. If you paid a lot of money to get someone from another investment bank, everybody would be ready to fall at their feet. But if you developed a young all-star, he or she would find it difficult to earn people's respect.

REALIGNMENT AT SHEARSON LEHMAN HUTTON

Corporate Travails

Even as its research department was rising in rankings, Shearson Lehman Hutton was experiencing difficulties in investment banking. In a consolidating and increasingly competitive industry, the firm's market position in various categories of investment banking had been slipping during the 1980s (see Exhibit 5). Subsequent to a March 1987 public offering of Shearson Lehman Hutton shares at $34 per share that left American Express owning 60 percent, Nippon Life 13 percent, and Shearson insiders 6 percent, the firm's position deteriorated rapidly. The collapse of the stock market in 1987, the real estate and junk bond markets decline at the end of 1980s, and its money management unit, Boston Co., reporting false profits of $30 million in 1988, together left Shearson Lehman Hutton with a weak balance sheet and hundreds of millions of dollars in bad loans. (Exhibit 6 presents selected financial data for Shearson Lehman Hutton, 1986 to 1989.) "We would have managed the difficulties if we had strong management," reflected Shearson Lehman Hutton president Lane. "But people just weren't getting along. I was clearly part of the problem in that I was not agreeing with a lot of the decisions that were being made. When senior management doesn't get along well, the road just caves in. From 1987 through 1990, American Express became a progressively less happy place to work."

An attempt to sell $250 million of new equity having failed, the firm experienced a capital crisis in early 1990 and CEO Cohen and president Lane resigned under fire. To forestall bankruptcy, American Express increased its stake in Shearson Lehman Hutton to 87 percent in return for a $1.3 billion bailout investment and installed its own chief financial officer, Howard Clark, as the company's new chairman and chief executive.[13]

Reorganization at Lehman Brothers

The Shearson Lehman Hutton colossus was reorganized into two operating divisions, generating rumors that American Express was planning to sell one of these units. Retail brokerage and asset management were grouped into the new Shearson Lehman Brothers Division, led by Jonathan Linen, to serve individual investors. Investment banking

---

[d] "Doogie Howser" was a 1980s television program about a young genius who was a physician.

EXHIBIT 5   Security Industry Trends and Shearson Lehman Hutton Rankings, 1980–1989

Percent Share of Total Capital of U.S. Securities Firms

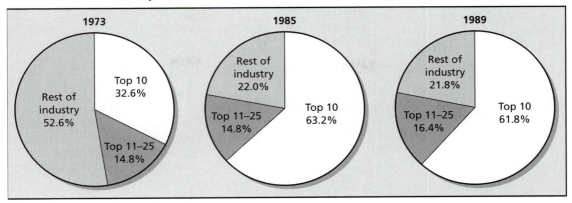

Source: "Downsizing or Rightsizing?" *Investment Dealers' Digest,* October 29, 1990.

Security Industry Pretax Return on Equity

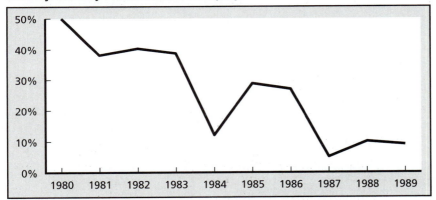

Shearson Lehman Hutton Industry Ranking, 1980 versus 1989		
Market	**Rank 1980**	**Rank 1989**
Worldwide issues	4	7
U.S. issuer worldwide	3	6
Domestic market issues	4	6
Investment-grade debt	5	6
Convertible debt	1	15
Junk debt	2	2
Mortgage-backed securities	2	7
Asset-backed securities	NA	8
Preferred stock	1	2
Common stock	3	5
IPOs	1	4
Municipal debt	3	3

Source: Miriam Bensman, "The 1980s: The Decade That Transformed Corporate Finance," *Investment Dealers' Digest,* January 8, 1990.

EXHIBIT 6   Shearson Lehman Hutton Selected Financial Data, 1986–1989

(all figures are in $ millions)	1989	1988	1987	1986
Income Statement Data[a]				
Revenues:				
Commissions	$ 1,938	$ 1,515	$ 1,151	$ 938
Investment banking	963	1,321	760	882
Market making and principal transactions	1,269	1,129	818	983
Interest and dividends	7,341	5,635	3,349	3,344
Investment advisory fees	684	648	450	316
Other	306	281	221	285
Total	12,501	10,529	6,749	6,748
Expenses:				
Compensation and benefits	3,163	2,972	2,045	1,919
Interest	7,128	5,376	3,159	3,187
Other	2,054	2,062	1,392	1,162
Total	12,345	10,410	6,596	6,268
Income before taxes and special adjustment	156	119	153	480
Net income	$ 110	$ 96	$ 101	$ 341
Balance Sheet Data[a]				
Total assets	$63,548	$84,840	$66,599	$53,911
Total liabilities (excluding long-term indebtedness)	54,582	76,683	61,115	49,301
Long-term indebtedness	6,766	6,411	3,741	3,336
Total stockholders' equity	2,200	1,746	1,743	1,274
Total capital (including equity and subordinated debt)	5,310	4,899	3,640	2,571

[a] The income statement and balance sheet data include Hutton, acquired January 13, 1988, Premier Unit Trust Administration, acquired June 15, 1988, and State Street Bank (Switzerland), acquired November 7, 1988, from their respective acquisition dates.
Source: Shearson Lehman Holding Inc. Annual Report, 1989.

and capital markets were grouped into the new Lehman Brothers Division, headed by Sherman Lewis and Richard Fuld, to serve large corporations and institutional investors.

Fuld was a family man who decorated his office with family pictures, an "unbeatable squash player" and legendary Wall Street trader, acknowledged by many to be "the ultimate honest man" and "a very smart guy, tough as nails."[14] Reputed for having led the fixed-income division to great success in the dark days of the late 1980s, Fuld girded up to rebuild investment banking and capital markets at Lehman Brothers.[15]

Until 1990 Lehman Brothers' equity operations had been fragmented among several groups as-sembled together through acquisitions and suffering from infighting. The two groups in equity operations that had distinguished themselves were over-the-counter (OTC) trading department led by Peter DaPuzzo and the research group led by Jack Rivkin.

In spring 1990 Fuld combined all of Lehman Brothers' equity functions—research, trading, and sales—into one worldwide equity division that would report jointly to DaPuzzo and Rivkin, who, in turn, would report to Fuld. Fraenkel was named to succeed Rivkin as global head of research and Balog was named to Fraenkel's erstwhile position as associate director of research (see Exhibit 7 for the Shearson Lehman Brothers organization chart).

EXHIBIT 7   Shearson Lehman Brothers Partial Organization Chart, 1990

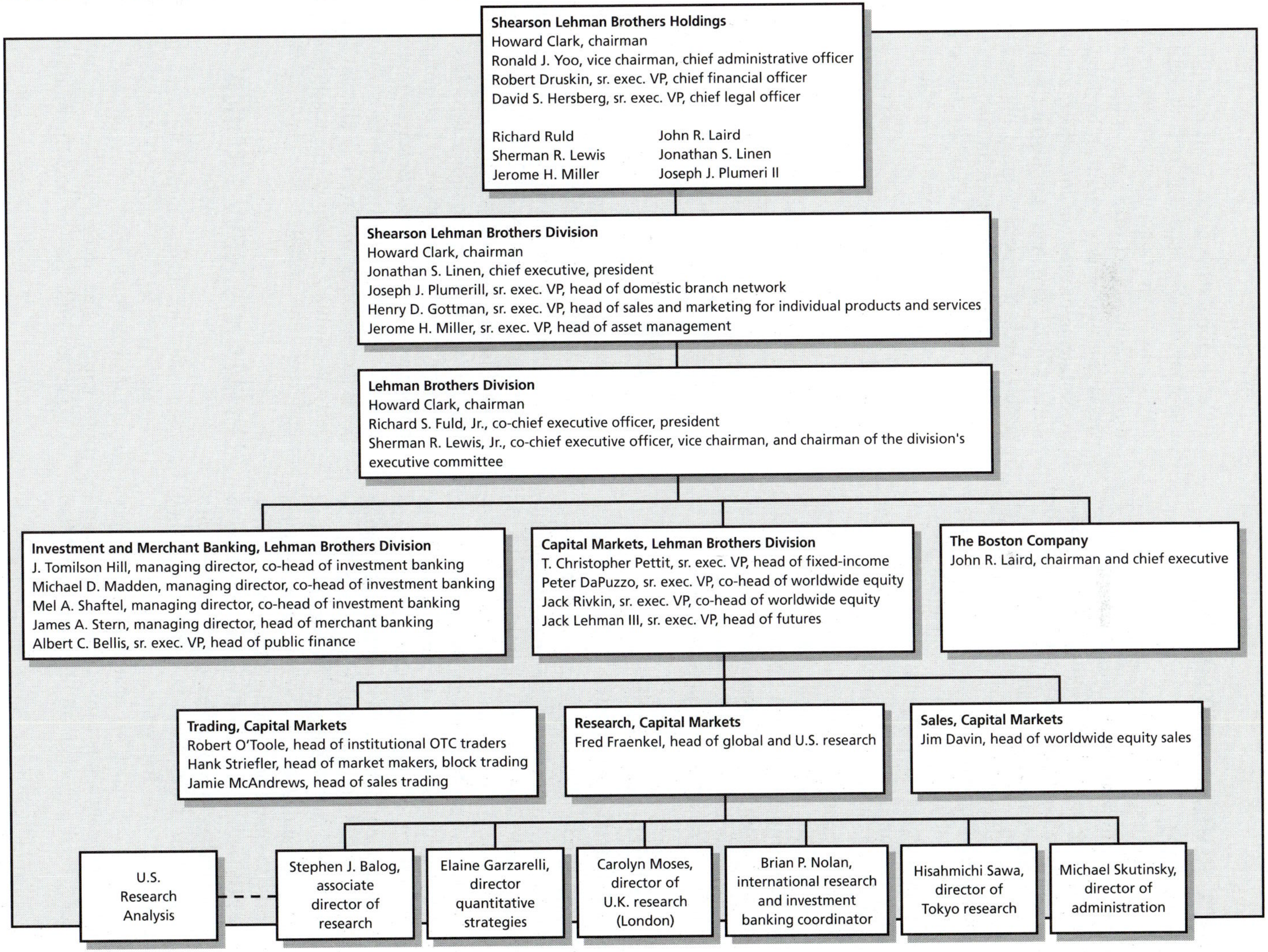

Shearson Lehman Brothers Holdings
Howard Clark, chairman
Ronald J. Yoo, vice chairman, chief administrative officer
Robert Druskin, sr. exec. VP, chief financial officer
David S. Hersberg, sr. exec. VP, chief legal officer

Richard Ruld   John R. Laird
Sherman R. Lewis   Jonathan S. Linen
Jerome H. Miller   Joseph J. Plumeri II

Shearson Lehman Brothers Division
Howard Clark, chairman
Jonathan S. Linen, chief executive, president
Joseph J. Plumerill, sr. exec. VP, head of domestic branch network
Henry D. Gottman, sr. exec. VP, head of sales and marketing for individual products and services
Jerome H. Miller, sr. exec. VP, head of asset management

Lehman Brothers Division
Howard Clark, chairman
Richard S. Fuld, Jr., co-chief executive officer, president
Sherman R. Lewis, Jr., co-chief executive officer, vice chairman, and chairman of the division's executive committee

The Boston Company
John R. Laird, chairman and chief executive

Investment and Merchant Banking, Lehman Brothers Division
J. Tomilson Hill, managing director, co-head of investment banking
Michael D. Madden, managing director, co-head of investment banking
Mel A. Shaftel, managing director, co-head of investment banking
James A. Stern, managing director, head of merchant banking
Albert C. Bellis, sr. exec. VP, head of public finance

Capital Markets, Lehman Brothers Division
T. Christopher Pettit, sr. exec. VP, head of fixed-income
Peter DaPuzzo, sr. exec. VP, co-head of worldwide equity
Jack Rivkin, sr. exec. VP, co-head of worldwide equity
Jack Lehman III, sr. exec. VP, head of futures

Sales, Capital Markets
Jim Davin, head of worldwide equity sales

Research, Capital Markets
Fred Fraenkel, head of global and U.S. research

Trading, Capital Markets
Robert O'Toole, head of institutional OTC traders
Hank Striefler, head of market makers, block trading
Jamie McAndrews, head of sales trading

Stephen J. Balog, associate director of research

Elaine Garzarelli, director quantitative strategies

Carolyn Moses, director of U.K. research (London)

Brian P. Nolan, international research and investment banking coordinator

Hisahmichi Sawa, director of Tokyo research

Michael Skutinsky, director of administration

U.S. Research Analysis

JACK RIVKIN AT THE EQUITY DIVISION

DaPuzzo, who had successfully managed retail equity trading as well as institutional OTC sales and trading before 1990, was a street-smarts trader and hyperactive motivator and Rivkin a long-term planner. The two split their responsibilities: Da-Puzzo ran trading, Rivkin research and sales. They decided to build the equity operations slowly. "We're not going in with big guns, writing big tickets," DaPuzzo remarked. "We'd get burned that way. We are doing it gradually."[16]

The new equity division's first year was successful. Its first birthday party was attended by some 200 people in colorful party hats and tee shirts; morale was high; Lehman was gaining market share; and the division's revenues were up by double digits relative to the previous year.

Rivkin Initiates Changes at the Equity Division

When DaPuzzo departed at the end of 1991, Rivkin began to put his own stamp on the equities division, introducing, among other things, his famous off-sites. All functions of the equity division participated in an off-site held in New York City at which the participants were divided into 40 teams and given the "3x" challenge, which was to come up with an idea that had the potential of tripling business. A $65,000 reward was offered for the winning idea. To encourage the out-of-the-box thinking demanded by the contest, team members were asked to paint one another's faces the evening before. The next assignment was for each team to create a painting in two halves, one-half representing Lehman as it was then, the other half as they expected it to be in five years.

Rivkin also inducted his associates into key positions. Tom Bianco was named head of risk management, Fred Fraenkel of research, and Mike

Rulle of global derivatives. Head of equity syndicate Tony Brooks also reported to Rivkin, and Nolan, a longtime associate, was promoted to head of research in Tokyo after serving as a liaison between research and investment banking.[e] These appointments created rancor among some of the professionals who had not worked with Rivkin earlier. "Jack is trying to build his own empire with people who owe him," remarked one Lehman official. "The only problem with Jack's plan is there are way too many traders on that floor who loved working for Peter [DaPuzzo]."[17]

Fraenkel and Balog continued Rivkin and Fraenkel's tradition of two-person leadership of the equity research department. "Now I was Mr. Inside and Fred Mr. Outside," Balog remarked. "I got heavily involved in the internal workings of the department, and Fred dealt more with the external constituencies that interacted with the research department." According to Skutinsky, however, the "Mr. Outside/Mr. Inside" dynamics changed after Rivkin's promotion. "We lost some of the outside traits," he averred. "Instead, we got two very good people who were both inside-oriented."

Although Lehman Brothers' overall financial performance declined in 1992 (Exhibit 8 presents selected financial data for Lehman Brothers, 1991 and 1992), the equity division's revenues continued to be strong. 1991 and 1992 continued to be good years for the Lehman Brothers' research department; in both years it was rated as the best research group on Wall Street (Exhibits 3 and 4 chart the evolving profile of the research department from 1986 to 1992).

LEHMAN'S NEW TROIKA

When Sherman Lewis retired in June 1990 J. Tomilson Hill III was named Lehman Brother's co-CEO with Fuld. Hill, a mergers and acquisitions expert, had joined Lehman in 1982 after working for First Boston and Smith Barney. He

---

[e] Bianco and Nolan had worked for Rivkin at Paine Webber.

EXHIBIT 8 **Lehman Brothers Holdings, Inc., Selected Consolidated Financial Data**
($ millions, except per share data)

	12 Months to 12/31/91	12 Months to 12/31/92
Revenues		
Interest and dividends	$4,909	$5,404
Less: Interest expense	4,569	4,928
Net interest and dividends	340	476
Principal transactions	1,211	1,192
Investment banking	468	674
Commissions	495	446
Other	50	65
Total revenues	7,133	7,781
Net revenues	2,564	2,853
Noninterest Expenses		
Employee-related	1,370	1,551
Other	965	1,411
Reserves and other charges	144	245
Total noninterest expenses	2,479	3,207
Pretax Income	85	(354)
Net income	169	(245)

Source: Raphael Soifer, "Lehman Brothers," Brown Brothers Harriman & Co., November 13, 1996.

had run the M&A department before becoming co-chief executive officer and head of investment banking for the Lehman Brothers division.

In 1991 Lehman Brothers co-CEOs Fuld and Hill were joined by Fuld's protégé, Chris Pettit, as Lehman Brothers' chief operating officer.[18] Fuld and Hill were to focus on strategic planning, Pettit on executing the plans. A former West Point All-American lacrosse player, Pettit had joined Lehman's fixed-income division in 1977. One longtime Lehman partner described Pettit: "Military is a good definition of Chris. He is a very good manager, both of people and of businesses. But whether he is very original in terms of his style, or he brings much in the way of new ideas or strategic thinking to the firm, is doubtful."[19] Judy Sanders recalled Pettit as

a person of great personality and enormous charm. He was dynamic, inspiring, and interesting. He was so charismatic that if he said, "Jump out that window," we would say,

"When?" One of his favorite techniques in leading people was to have them rally around him against a common enemy. Sometimes that common enemy was Shearson's management. Sometimes it was American Express. Most often it involved money and how much bonus Chris's people would receive. His ability to create an us-versus-them culture was amazing.

Their extreme loyalty to Pettit led to the less charitable observers calling his associates "Moonies" or "Khmer Rouge." "There is a lot of nervousness in the firm about these guys," remarked a senior Lehman Brothers officer. "Especially on the investment banking side there is a lot of apprehension about just how intense these guys are."[20] Fuld argued on behalf of Pettit's disciplined management style: "If you associate fixed income with disciplined management, then you're right. Why shouldn't this philosophy guide all our businesses? If you're not going to be accountable and be disciplined in how you handle your people, and if you aren't going to run your business the way we ran [fixed income], then you're not going to make the trip with us."[21]

RIVKIN'S DEPARTURE

In August 1992 Rivkin abruptly left Lehman Brothers. One version of what had transpired leading to his departure was that Fuld and Hill had expressed dissatisfaction with Rivkin's performance as sole head of the equity division in the summer of 1991.[22] Another version held that Rivkin was building a sense of momentum in the equity group, but had an irreconcilable conflict with Pettit. Remarked one source: "It's been building over the last three or four months and this was a real blowup. This was a screaming match about control between Pettit and Rivkin."[23]

Rivkin's Viewpoint

"I was fired," Rivkin later recounted.

> and I could see it coming. Lehman was being run by the fixed-income people. Here we were, this equity business, which is very different from the fixed-income area, painting people's faces and doing all that stuff, yet bringing in results. We created an easygoing team spirit in the equity division, complete with dress-down days. That created a real flap because people weren't doing that in fixed income. Chris was all upset about this. "How can you do this?" he questioned. "This really destroys discipline." I replied: "What's the big deal if they're working together and producing the numbers?"

Rivkin first saw some unwelcome signs in the summer of 1992 when his suggestion that equity and fixed-income derivative groups be integrated was perceived by some as an attempt to expand the scope of his authority. This was followed by an incident that grew out of Lehman Brothers' involvement in what was to be the largest block trade on the stock exchange to that time. Goldman Sachs, Morgan Stanley, and Lehman Brothers were planning to place a bid as a group to buy a large block of U.S. Steel stock and resell it. Rivkin communicated the terms of the deal to Fuld and Hill but, even as the deal was almost ready, Fuld and Hill had not yet decided whether Lehman Brothers should agree to its terms. "They kept coming back with suggestions like, 'Maybe it ought to be a quarter of a point lower,'" recalled Rivkin.

> As good a trader as Dick is, he was thinking in a fixed-income mentality characterized by Tom Wolfe in *The Bonfire of the Vanities*— "Just imagine that a bond is a slice of cake . . . every time you hand somebody a slice . . . a tiny little bit comes off, like a little crumb, and you can keep that." Goldman Sachs and Morgan Stanley were getting antsy. I tried to call Dick to get his final decision. He wasn't there. So I called [Shearson Lehman chairman and CEO] Clark and said to him, "Howard, either we're going to be a part of what will be an historic trade, or we're not. This is the price. What do I do? I want to do this trade." "Do it," he replied. And so I did the trade. Even though Lehman made a lot of money on the trade subsequently, Dick was very upset because he had not been involved in the final decision.

Shortly after his phone conversation with Clark, Rivkin was called to a meeting with Fuld, Hill, and Pettit that ended with a negotiated settlement whereby Rivkin would leave the firm.

"The day he left Lehman," confided Regina Taylor,

> Jack came to say goodbye to all the equity people. Standing in the middle of the trading floor, surrounded by the equity professionals, he said: "Look to your right. Look to your left. They are the reasons why you should keep the momentum going even though I will not be here with you." It was an emotionally charged moment. Some people were crying.

Jane Rivkin remembered the events surrounding Jack Rivkin's departure from Lehman Brothers:

> Jack called me in the morning and said, "Don't worry. Everything is OK, but I have had to resign from Lehman." I started crying. I asked him: "Do we still have health insurance?" Jack told me not to worry. We decided to take some time off and almost immediately left for France. We received so many phone calls, letters, and visits. I was touched by how supportive people were. In retrospect, the resignation was a relief for Jack and a relief for me. A lot of Jack's tensions were gone. My biggest concern quickly became how to keep him occupied during the 24 hours a day that he would be home.

Rivkin's Associates' Perspective

"I was in Ireland with my future husband meeting my in-laws when I got a call that Jack was leaving," recalled Josephine Esquivel. "I turned pale. I didn't know what to do. I remember feeling, 'Oh God, now the golden run of our department is really over.'" Added another research analyst:

> Jack's termination came as a huge surprise to us, primarily because Jack had always done a phenomenal job of protecting the analysts from firm politics and making them feel safe within their own world. Jack's departure was probably the first indication to the analysts that the world around us wasn't as rosy and friendly as we had thought it was.

Another analyst, however, perceived "an air of inevitability about his departure because Jack just didn't fit the mold and didn't try to either. He told me about one or two run-ins he had with Dick Fuld, and I figured, 'You don't have too many of those before your chances are used up.'" The analyst explained Rivkin's departure in terms of a mismatch between his personality and Lehman's culture.

Lehman has a very closed culture. You either grow up in the culture, which is primarily fixed-income business culture, or not. You're never accepted into it. Fuld and Pettit both came from this business. They had worked together for more than two decades. Jack was never going to fit into that fraternity because there's nothing you can do to fit into something like that; you either were with them for 20 years or you weren't. So that was one strike against Jack right there. The other thing about Jack is that he speaks his mind, and I think that that was unacceptable within the Lehman Brothers culture. Yes, he created a great research department and led it for several years, but he antagonized several people by saying what he really felt about things. That harmed him much more than the success of the research department helped him.

Sanders had noticed growing tension between Pettit and Rivkin and attributed it to their different management styles. "Chris had a real need to control people and Jack was a person he couldn't easily control," she recalled.

> Jack believed in running his business the way he thought it was important to run the business. He did his own thing and didn't often ask for permission. Chris did not like that and came to believe that Jack wasn't much of a team player. You could only be a team player with Chris by doing things exactly the way Chris wanted you to do them.

"Jack crashed and burned," observed Teena Lerner, commenting on Rivkin's firing, "because he is so smart and he knows it. And he comes across as someone who doesn't care what others think about his actions. He annoyed a lot of people because he didn't respect those he thought of as less intelligent or less capable. Finally, one day, he bumped into someone politically stronger who blew him away."

"Jack was terrible politically," noted Mary Farrell. "He didn't suffer fools and he didn't suffer bureaucracy. He was happy to turn over the reins to his people and trust them. He could not understand why people above him could not do that." Helane Becker agreed. "Jack is the kind of person," she observed, "who just wants to be told what needs to be done and be left alone. And people who were running Lehman at that time didn't like that. You could see the handwriting on the wall. It seemed only a matter of time before Jack would be pushed out. And yet, when I found that Jack was fired, I was devastated."

"I saw him do some things that I knew were going to make management angry," Fraenkel said, recalling the events leading to Rivkin's exit:

> Jack is a very bright guy who doesn't want people who don't understand his business telling him what to do. He hired some people he liked and moved some he liked to po-

sitions of responsibility in the equity division without consulting anybody above him. One of his appointees was a person he named to head equity trading. In Lehman, you didn't just name somebody to head trading without consulting Dick Fuld and Chris Pettit, who were considered world-class traders. And Jack did that. We just held our breaths and said: "Oh God! He's really going to get them mad." Nothing happened for a couple of months. Then, one day, Fuld, Hill, and Pettit had an hour-long meeting with Jack, after which they called me to a meeting and told me: "Jack Rivkin has been terminated." I asked them: "What do you want me to do?" They replied that they wanted me to still run the research department. Somewhat flabbergasted, I agreed.

References

1. Ron Cooper, "Lehman's Equity Division Stunned by Loss of Chief," *Investment Dealer's Digest,* August 31, 1992, pp. 6–8.

2. Ibid.

3. Beth Selby, "Can Shearson Save Its Lehman Legacy?" *Institutional Investor,* December 1985, pp. 57–60.

4. Jill Andresky Fraser, "The Annotated Lehman Prospectus," *Institutional Investor,* November 1993, pp. 62–68.

5. Anthony Bianco, "American Express: A Financial Supermarket That Works," *Business Week,* June 2, 1986, p. 78.

6. Selby, "Can Shearson Save Its Lehman Legacy?"

7. Cary Reich, "Today Hutton, Tomorrow. . . ," *Institutional Investor,* March 1988, pp. 81–91.

8. Anita Raghavan, "Jack Rivkin, High-Profile Research Head at Smith Barney, Is Removed in Shake-Up," *The Wall Street Journal Europe,* October 23, 1995, p. 31.

9. Ellen E. Schultz, "Wall Street Grows Treacherous for Analysts Who Speak Out," *The Wall Street Journal,* April 5, 1990.

10. Janet Lewis, "The Rise of Woman Power," *Institutional Investor,* December 1989, p. 176.

11. "How the Firms Stack Up," *Institutional Investor,* December 1989, p. 178.

12. Ibid.

13. "AmEx's Shearson Move Draws Fire," *USA Today,* March 6, 1990, p. 3B. Nippon Life held the remaining 13 percent.

14. Ron Cooper, "Can a Troika Take Lehman Up a Level?" *Institutional Dealer's Digest,* August 24, 1992, pp. 16–22.

15. Robert Clow, "Fuld's Gold," *Institutional Investor,* July 1998, pp. 47–51.

16. Ibid.

17. Philip Maher and Ron Cooper, "Rivkin Starts Realigning Lehman Equities Divisions," *Investment Dealer's Digest,* August 17, 1992, p. 5.

18. Cooper, "Can a Troika Take Lehman Up a Level?"

19. Ibid.

20. Ibid.

21. Ibid.

22. Ibid.

23. Ibid.

Alexander Bandelli (A)

Alexander brings a whole new vision to our business.

John Orrico, president, Transaction Services: Eastern Region

Alexander Bandelli, who had only been the district manager of Ronsini & Fitch (R&F) in Boston for a scant two months, leaned back on his chair in a private room at the Harvard Club, looked at the casewriters, and said "That's what I have been doing for the past 60 days." Since February 11, 1998, when R&F announced to the world that Bandelli was in charge of the Boston office (including two smaller offices in Newton, Massachusetts, and Portland, Maine), Bandelli had been talking to staff and collecting as much information as possible. He had a two-year contract to change the nature of business from a sales-based individualized process to a collaborative team service-based management environment. This would involve changing the mind-set of the real estate brokers from product orientation to a customer focus.

Senior management at R&F in Chicago saw the introduction of new blood to the Boston office as an experiment. Bandelli had been drafted to turn the culture on its head and bring not only the Boston office but help bring R&F into the twenty-first century. A distinct culture had grown up around the older, established real estate brokers. Boston had a reputation of being a club with a set of brokers who had been doing business one way for many years.

Bandelli continued: "I attended R&F's national meeting a couple of weeks ago. This gave me time to examine the list of priorities I made based on issues I've seen at the office and compare these issues with challenges facing the company nationally. I know I have to build a team." With the clock ticking, Bandelli had less than two years to turn the office around. The remaining question for Bandelli was how and where to start.

ALEXANDER BANDELLI

Prior to joining R&F, Bandelli served as principal of the consulting firm, the Parthenon Group, providing strategy development and senior advisory services to Fortune 1,000 companies. He previously spent four years with CB Commercial Real Estate Services, Inc., negotiating more than $80 million in lease and sales transactions for commercial retail properties. A native Bostonian, Bandelli graduated from Harvard University with a bachelor's degree in economics and an MBA from the Harvard Business School. Bandelli epitomized the Boston mentality with his thick accent, excitable personality, and absolute passion for his mandate.

THE REAL ESTATE INDUSTRY[1]

The real estate industry underwent a difficult period in the early 1990s due to challenging market

---

Research Associate Catherine Conneely prepared this case under the supervision of Thomas DeLong as the basis for class discussion rather than to illustrate either effective or ineffective handling of an administrative situation.

[1] Information in this section is taken from Society of Industrial and Office Realtors, *Comparartive Statistics of Industrial and Office Real Estate Markets* (Washington, DC: Society of Industrial and Office Realtors, 1997), pp. 1–16; and Urban Land Institute, *Market Profiles 1997: North America* (Washington, DC: Urban Land Institute, 1997), pp. 25–32.

conditions. All markets suffered, but the industrial and office property markets, which were the focus of R&F, were hit particularly hard. The Boston market was comparatively small, even "parochial," and the office relied on the industrial and office practices. Going into the mid- and late 1990s, its profitability seemed to lag behind the rest of the group, although the Boston market had recovered to become the strongest real estate market in history. The Boston Ronsini & Fitch office benefited from this and showed substantial revenues, but was barely profitable and lagged behind the top four to five companies in the market as it was not perceived as a quality service provider.

The Boston office serviced the metropolitan Boston area of over 1,500 square miles (see Exhibit 1). By the late 1990s, the economy was growing steadily, with unemployment dropping to 3.7 percent in early 1998 in Massachusetts. Population had also increased slightly to 3.84 million residents in the metropolitan area. The retail market (e.g., shopping malls) showed signs of recovery as retail sales increased by 8 percent in 1996 due to a rise in tourism and continued economic recovery. The key industries in the area included high technology, financial services, health care, education, and biotechnology.

Of the 10 major markets, which contain 1.6 billion square feet of the U.S. office industry, Boston accounts for 6.8 percent, with 108 million square feet and is sixth in size. Boston real estate firms had access to an even smaller inventory, and the massive migration of firms to other states and the vast downsizing of a Massachusetts mainstay, the defense industry, was difficult to overcome. There was a slow improvement, however, as the vacancy rate in the Boston market decreased from 17.1 percent in 1996 to 13 percent in 1997. Typical lease rates for good-quality industrial and warehouse space ranged from $3.85 to $5.75 per square foot.

The office property market (3.5 billion square feet nationwide) had also been through some tough times. The market had been saturated in the 1980s as speculators overbuilt office complexes which could not hold their inflated prices in the recession of the early 1990s, selling for as little as one-third of their value. Despite dire predictions that the bottom would fall out of the office property market as clerical workers were being replaced by office automation, it was discovered that information technology staff had more than replaced those displaced by innovation. The office market in Boston totaled 108 million–plus square feet with an overall market vacancy of 9.6 percent in 1996. Average rents were between $26.50 per square foot downtown, $22 in Cambridge, and $24 on Route 128, and had been increasing steadily to reach $40–50 per square foot downtown, $35 in Cambridge, and $30–35 on Route 128 by 1998 with vacancy down to 4.9 percent.

RONSINI & FITCH[2]

Most Ronsini & Fitch offices had recovered from the depressed market of the early 1990s. By 1998, R&F was one of the nation's largest publicly traded commercial real estate services firms with offices (including affiliate offices) in 85 markets and approximately 4,000 professionals and staff, providing transaction, management, financial, and strategic services to clients. R&F serviced clients internationally through the European headquarters in London.

R&F was founded as a residential brokerage company in Northern California in 1958. Commercial and insurance brokerages soon followed, as well as property and asset management and real estate development services. R&F went public (traded on both the New York Stock Exchange [symbol: GBE] and the Pacific Stock Exchange) upon the completion of a 1981 merger with GMR Properties of Jacksonville, Florida, and began a pattern of growth with the acquisition of well-

[2] Information in this section is taken from the Ronsini & Fitch website.

EXHIBIT 1 Boston Metropolitan Area

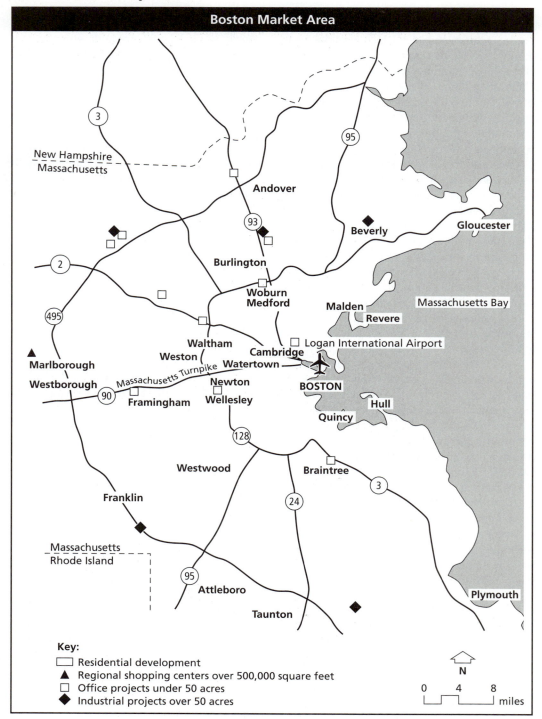

Source: ULI Market Profiles: 1997, Boston.

established real estate firms throughout the country. R&F had been in bad shape after the real estate crash of the late 1980s, going through five CEOs in six years. The company was near bankruptcy and was forced to restructure in the early 1990s by closing unprofitable offices, divesting nonstrategic businesses, and refocusing efforts on core businesses. There was a clear turnaround with the elevation of Neil Young to CEO in 1996, who started by cleaning up the R&F balance sheet. Young had a vision of R&F as a service company rather than merely a transactional company. R&F sold the residential operation in 1994.

A wholly owned property and facilities management subsidiary (Axiom Real Estate Management, Inc., acquired by R&F in January 1996) was renamed Ronsini & Fitch Management Services, Inc., in September 1997. The company also instituted a national affiliate program to help it expand in markets where it did not have a formal presence.

During 1997, the company relocated from San Francisco to Northbrook, Illinois, a suburb of Chicago. In fiscal year 1997, R&F and affiliates were involved in more than 16,000 transactions worldwide, valued at approximately $16.1 billion. Through its Management Services subsidiary and affiliates, R&F managed a total portfolio in 1998 of over 110 million square feet valued at over $12 billion (see Exhibit 2 for financial information).

THE FUTURE OF REAL ESTATE

The real estate industry was undergoing a major transformation towards the end of the 1990s. The industry was consolidating, and continued securitization of the real estate business was pushing real estate companies to offer one-stop shopping for all service, extend coverage nationwide, and implement a more sophisticated value-added ser-

EXHIBIT 2 **Financial Highlights, Year Ended June 30, 1996–1997 (US$ thousands, except share and staff data)**

	1997	1996
Operating Results		
Total revenue	$228,630	$193,728
Net income before nonrecurring items[a]	12,840	1,640
Net income	19,101	2,102
Per Share Data (fully diluted)		
Net income (loss) before nonrecurring items[a]	.63	(.13)
Net income (loss)	.93	(.10)
Average shares outstanding	20,427,140	8,870,720
Balance Sheet Data		
Cash and cash equivalents	16,790	13,547
Working capital	16,985	8,064
Total assets	36,696	29,658
Long-term liabilities	12,700	42,462
Stockholders' equity (deficit)	12,923	(12,475)
Additional Data		
EBITDA[b]	17,629	7,418
Staff at year end[c]	3,800	2,900

[a] Nonrecurring items consist of the company's deferred tax benefit, other nonrecurring expense/income, and extraordinary items.
[b] Earnings before interest expense, income taxes, depreciation and amortization, adjusted to exclude nonrecurring items.
[c] Includes employees and independent contractors.
Source: Company documents.

vice requirement. R&F management foresaw that the current trends would continue to evolve the industry as clients expected, and demanded, better service from their brokers.

As well as focusing on improving the service side of the industry, there was also a movement toward national accounts, "to better manage client requirements for more services in more markets through a single point of accountability." According to Bandelli, the industry was "moving toward managed brokerage systems; meaning that management must allocate the resources of an integrated systems of services and geographic locations in contrast to the traditional model where the broker found business and executed it." Bandelli recognized that real estate was sales and service and the same people had to do both. Bandelli was confident that the salesperson could focus more on service.

R&F IN BOSTON

When Bandelli joined the Boston office in early 1998, it was made up of 28 sales professionals, spread out between three offices. The company came to Boston in 1986 with the purchase of the prestigious local real estate firm of Leggatt, McCall, and Warner. R&F had hoped to buy into Leggatt's great reputation and top position locally, but when the original partners left in 1989 upon the expiration of their contracts (followed by a second wave of people leaving), R&F found that those who had made Leggatt's reputation were no longer with the firm.

Despite the difficulties in measuring market share of real estate companies, management knew that R&F was not one of the top five firms in Boston. R&F was clearly seen as a second-tier firm by peers and customers. While the Boston office had revenues of $9 million in 1997 (from fees and commissions on sales and leasing), the top firms' revenues were between $12–15 million.

The financial performance of the office with regard to revenues was good, but profits were poor.

Earnings before interest, tax, and depreciation represented only 5 percent of revenues—some $400,000 on $9 million—in sharp contrast to an industry average of 15 to 20 percent. In addition, Bandelli found that only three or four of the brokers at the firm were responsible for 50 percent of revenues representing $1 million in revenues per person per year—the standard for "stars" in the industry. The top three brokers in the Boston office made $1.9 million, $1.5 million, and $1.2 million respectively in 1997 (for a total of $4.6 million), earning between them over 50 percent of the office's total revenues ($8.7 million).

THE FIRST 60 DAYS

Looking back on his first 60 days, Bandelli acknowledged that the circumstances in the Boston office "more or less met my expectations. The people who hired me were honest about the situation and I was not surprised with what I encountered there." Bandelli continued: "For the first 30 days, I talked to people and listened. For the second month, I talked to people more and got involved with issues." The three major problems Bandelli saw with the office concerned finance, culture, and brand equity.

The financials were dismal, and the office ran on a very thin gross margin. Expenses at the office were over budget. For example, the office "seat" cost per broker was over $90,000 in contrast to the R&F average of $60–70,000 (the Boston market average was approximately $75,000). Revenue was divided between brokers (taking 50 percent for fees with sliding scale up to 68 percent on highest dollar earnings) and the office for overhead and profit. In fiscal 1997, participation, which is the payout to the brokers in the form of advances against earnings, at the firm was at 65 percent, but should have been only 55 percent. The reasons for such high levels of participation were because half the brokers (14 out of 28) did not earn enough to cover their advances and some earners were in very high brackets.

Brokers were paid on a "draw" system, which gave brokers advances against their earnings over the year (the amount of the advance was established by a "bogey number" of three components—salary, benefits, and reimbursed expenses.) Fourteen brokers of the Boston staff were not making budget, in fact, they were not even hitting their compensation numbers. In any real estate office, it was to be expected that some of the newer, less well established staff would not bring in the same revenue stream as experienced brokers. The office could tolerate some investment in young brokers, but Bandelli also found that the office was supporting a start-up retail group of four highly paid brokers who were not from the area and had difficulty bringing in revenue to support their division. In addition, there were several older brokers who were having bad years, and several inadequate new hires.

The office did not have a great reputation in the local market. Bandelli spoke to numerous clients and people in industry who gave him a similar response: the R&F Boston office was not providing the level of service necessary to compete in the market. The perception from their peers was that the office did not have a lot of talent and was seen as having a weak team.

Bandelli felt the poor reputation stemmed from the office culture or lack thereof. Most brokers were reluctant to share information with each other. The traditional decision point in a real estate transaction for the broker was Should I split my commission with another broker to help me win and service this client? But now the emphasis was on service, and Bandelli was challenged to replace the traditional decision point with one which examined: How can we best create a relationship with the client? The compensation structure, rewarding brokers for quantity, also made it difficult for people to think of service. Leggatt has successfully had a salary and bonus structure, which facilitated team work and client service. Although Bandelli felt the compensation structure must eventually be adjusted, he did not see it as the best or only way to guide the organization and manage the business. He felt management could become

the decision maker and it would be possible to create a team service environment within the current compensation structure.

THE THREE Cs

Bandelli saw the problems in terms of the "Three Cs": lack of communication; lack of cooperation; lack of collaboration. According to Bandelli, "team members drop the ball on opportunities. We have weak people making decisions." Brokers in the Boston office knew the weaker members of the team. The stars were, therefore, reluctant to share opportunities with the less capable members of the team. Bandelli found he had a few "problem children" in the office as well. "About 30 percent of the people think what I'm doing is great and get on board right away, about 40 percent are on the fence, and the final 30 percent will never get on board. The issue was how to make that happen."

Bandelli said: "For me, this is a unique opportunity to do something that will really stretch me as a manager. I can see that the office is not performing, and I want to make this the best firm in Boston. I have the security of a two-year contract so I can make the difficult decisions."

READY, AIM. . .

"General management jobs, in general, are much different than consulting," Bandelli continued. "There isn't enough time to do everything. It's easy [in consulting] to figure out priorities and figure out what you have to do. The difficulty is to know when to act on the right issues. You have to trust yourself and trust the decisions you are making and . . . pull the trigger. The way to succeed is by doing things and taking action." He continued: "I have already drawn up a rough list of priorities and I had time to go over the list at the national R&F conference." Bandelli's list of priorities covered team building, team retention, office administration, financial analysis, service delivery, creating processes, and attracting new clients.

First on Bandelli's list of priorities was team building. Bandelli was concerned at the lack of specialization in some areas of real estate practice at the Boston office. He discovered it would be necessary to hire a downtown team as "downtown leasing is the heart and soul of the Boston real estate business," and R&F had practically no presence in downtown Boston. The property management side was also lacking—property owners did not typically think of R&F when looking for a company to manage their property. Both the investment division and retail division also needed leaders. In particular, getting the newly developed retail group on its feet was not only time consuming but also a revenue drain. Bandelli also planned to hire a suburban team and consolidate the suburban office in Newton with the downtown Boston office. (Expanding the downtown office in itself would be another headache: the current space was too small for the consolidated staff to work out of.) Bandelli would have to tread very carefully.

In conjunction with creating a suburban team, Bandelli planned to create suburban territories defining markets and responsibilities, as there was an obvious lack in R&F's coverage of the areas the office purported to cover. "Brokers would be assigned to a territory, becoming specialists in that area rather than overall generalists. This would show up the gaps in the Boston office coverage and increase broker accountability."

According to Bandelli, "Recruiting is a full-time sales job, people in real estate careers hit peaks and valleys." Based on the real estate broker's career cycle, Bandelli saw himself putting in place a recruiting database. In order to make room for new people, Bandelli knew he would have to fire many of the nonperforming brokers, as well as some of the stars who were contributing to the deal-oriented culture of the office. Making this task more difficult was the lack of termination process. Bandelli realized he would have to create standards for monitoring performance and establish a paper trail before he could start an office sweep.

Another priority was team retention. Bandelli was adamant about keeping the younger people who were not yet established brokers. Once R&F had invested in their training, Bandelli foresaw a problem with retention. Bandelli also planned to introduce performance reviews for brokers. The difficulty with measuring performance in the deal-based real estate industry was that brokers gauged performance by how much money they made. Bandelli saw that in his pursuit of a service-based business, he would have to define new methods of measuring success, for example, how much repeat business a broker or office got, how many potential client presentations did brokers give, how many presentations was R&F invited to attend, and perhaps most important, how much of the business the office and brokers went for were they actually awarded.

Bandelli continued: "The first thing is to define the group vision and values and get buy-in for the objectives. I plan to hold an off-site meeting with brokers to set values. I want a shared set of values to be the guiding force of the organization versus dollars." Bandelli also planned to formalize sales meetings, hosting in-house training topics, outside speakers, and market review—"basically, I want to put in place a platform and a system for doing business."

Another headache for Bandelli was the information collection and sharing processes, which would have to be revamped. R&F had no system in the Boston office for tracking exclusive clients, new and existing client contracts, or new business opportunities. Bandelli visited other offices to gain insight into R&F's best practices. He had been to the New York office and was impressed with the prospect tracking system database there. He was determined to put in place a similar knowledge management system to share intellectual capital through the Boston team.

R&F had a companywide product for real estate processes, which allowed the company to offer a consistent approach around the country while giving individual offices the ability to create templates for local business situations. Bandelli planned to introduce the product as soon as possible. "Consistency is lacking in the office," he said, "and this product provides a detailed process and deliverables and will help us improve our presentation skills." Bandelli also wanted to establish an account management system—he had found that many of the brokers had a lackadaisical attitude to maintaining and recording their client contacts and relationships.

Another aspect of creating a team vision could be achieved through "rookie" training. New brokers would be trained in-house and sent to various R&F training seminars. Bandelli was concerned about "how to teach sales skills."

Adding to the cultural issues was the office infrastructure. Bandelli came to an office with high turnover of administrative staff, old computer systems, and lack of defined processes. "Everything here is a fire drill," he exclaimed, "we are constantly reinventing the wheel. The business operations manager only started last year and she is completely swamped. I have to spend time with her and create a work plan to lay out the goals and objectives of the office for the coming year." With administration, Bandelli saw he would have to develop an entire management plan from job descriptions to performance standards and measurement to training. Even such basics as official legal forms were unavailable in the office. "There are no set forms or contracts in Boston office, the brokers have been using their own forms up to now," Bandelli said. Bandelli wanted to redesign the marketing and research departments as well. "We have to give the brokers the best available tools to do their jobs. The research and marketing functions must be world class."

Financial problems also abounded in the Boston office. Bandelli knew he needed to create a cost control plan and fix accounting irregularities, with the goal of hitting budget in 1998. He wanted to establish monthly budget reviews (which meant staff would have to have 30-day plans) and

monthly revenue forecasts, so he could follow up with individuals as part of performance tracking.

. . . FIRE

Bandelli's list of priorities required "a lot of personal discipline and time management skills to pick priorities. I have two primary goals: one is team building and the second is processes and culture and how to deliver a different level of service. I need to spend 40 percent of my time on recruiting issues, another 40 percent fixing processes, and the remaining 20 percent on financial and other administrative and personnel issues."

"Time management is a big issue for me," Bandelli continued. "I don't have a big staff. I could just show up every day and react to things. With human assets, everything is so time consuming, since the best thing is to spend time with people. I have to assess at end of each day if I am closer to my priorities. I need to make progress on team building and recruiting everyday, the rest is not important if the players are not in place."

"The first thing I have to do is change the culture, so that people can be part of something that is fun. Even though I think things are beginning to change already (I'm selling to people in the halls, around the water cooler, etc.) I won't be able to create a vision with some of the brokers who are set in their ways. Firing some of the top performers may be the catalyst to change the culture. Once word gets out that there is a new vision at R&F in Boston, I will be able to hire better brokers. Money alone isn't enough to attract the caliber of broker this office needs without also creating a different way of doing things."

Bandelli's three-page list of priorities needed a timeline. For the most part he knew how he would implement the many changes needed at the Boston office; but he sought a timeline to fit the tasks within the less-than-two-year time frame his superiors had given him.

Tom Tierney at Bain & Company (A)

As managing director I worry whether there is momentum inside the partnership. Do we have the right people in the right places? Is the glue of the partnership working? Are we making the right decisions the right way? Are people developing themselves as fast as possible?

Tom Tierney, worldwide managing director, Bain & Company

"My job is to help our partners succeed," declared Tom Tierney, worldwide managing director (MD) of Bain & Company.[a] In his role as chief executive officer, Tierney was responsible for managing Bain's internal operations and overseeing the appointment, compensation, and career progress of Bain partners, including the firm's 15 office heads. At any given time Tierney's agenda could include as many as two dozen partner-related career issues. "Often," he explained, "I have to help partners realize it's time for a change in their assignment before they do. Office heads can be particularly challenging. Frequently, I face the difficult task of convincing an office head to step down before they feel ready. It's against human nature to give up your power base voluntarily."

In December 1998 Tierney faced a difficult situation with Granville Harris, the 41-year-old head of Bain's Miami, Florida office.[b] "Granville does not want to step down," Tierney explained. "He founded the office nine years ago and a large part of his ego and self-image are tied up in running it. But he is no longer fully effective in that role.

Also, we cannot afford to have one of our most valuable revenue-producing partners continually bogged down by the many management duties that come with being an office head. He just doesn't have enough time to spend with critical clients."

By all accounts, Harris had built the office into a highly profitable business staffed by 100 persons. The office had been financially successful and since its founding had grown 50 percent annually. "But like anyone who has been in the same job for so long," observed Tierney,

> he needs a change. And the office needs a change. I need to convince Granville to rotate out, find his replacement, and do so in a way that keeps him at Bain and ensures a smooth transition in Miami.

THE CONSULTING INDUSTRY IN 1998

During the 1990s advances in technology and telecommunications fueled corporate policies of

Senior Research Associate Perry L. Fagan and Professor Ashish Nanda prepared this case with the advice and assistance of Professor Michael Y. Yoshino as the basis for class discussion rather than to illustrate either effective or ineffective handling of an administrative situation.

[a] Bain & Company was a corporation owned by its roughly 175 vice presidents. In practice, Bain executives used the term "partner" to convey "the mutual commitment and sense of partnership that each vice president was supposed to bring to the firm."
[b] The location of the Bain offices and identity of its partners have been disguised.

reengineering, downsizing, early retirement, consolidation, and outsourcing, which contributed, in turn, to a dramatic rise in the supply of and demand for consultants worldwide. Total industry revenues worldwide were estimated at $85 billion in 1998, up from $73 billion in 1997 and $62 billion in 1996. Revenues for the top 50 consulting firms were expected to grow 27 percent to $54.8 billion in fiscal 1998, compared with a 22 percent increase to $43.3 billion in fiscal year 1997.[1] A prominent industry research group predicted a $113 billion global consulting market by the year 2000.[2]

Ease of entry for newcomers (little investment was needed to declare oneself an "independent consultant") and the competitive advantages of larger firms (brand equity, diversified client base, broad geographic coverage) accounted for the hourglass structure of the consulting industry, firms being divided into the very large and very small. Consulting firms with fewer than 10 professionals accounted for three-quarters of the industry's 360,000 employees and about half of industry revenues.[3] In contrast, a handful of firms had, through acquisitions, mergers, and global expansion, grown into consulting behemoths. Although some one-stop shops offered a wide array of consulting and other professional services, most consulting firms generated the bulk of their revenues from a single type of work. Information technology (roughly 64 percent of the market), compensation and benefits, and management/strategy consulting were the three largest specialties.

Within specialties, competition for clients and recruits was intense. Some consulting firms claimed that competing for recruits—against not only other consulting firms, but also investment banking and venture capital firms and Internet start-up companies—was more intense than competition for clients.[4]

Traditionally, firms hired directly from the top graduate business schools, absorbing up to 25 percent of MBA graduates annually. But rapid growth and a shortage of elite business school graduates had led firms to begin to look beyond their usual sources to second-tier business schools, nonbusiness professional schools, PhD programs, and industry.

Retention, a perennial challenge, was made more difficult during the 1990s by a tight market for skilled labor in the United States. Firms lost, on average, about one out of five employees annually, turnover being highest among younger consultants.[5] Few consultants, entry level and partner alike, professed long-term commitment either to their respective companies or to consulting as a career. Remarked one: "I'm interested enough to do it for a few years because of the experience I'll gain and the industry contacts." Added another: "I don't know if I've found my niche or whether there's another niche to come."[6]

BAIN & COMPANY IN THE 1990S

Founded in 1973 by Bill Bain, Tennessee-born son of a food wholesaler, and seven colleagues from the Boston Consulting Group, Bain & Co. grew rapidly in the 1970s and 1980s. Revenue climbed from $34 million in 1982 to almost $200 million in 1989. Recalled one former employee: "We were oozing success."[7]

However, in the late 1980s, just after the founding partners sold their majority interest in the firm, Bain experienced financial difficulties. Approximately 90 employees were laid off in April 1988, another 220 professional and support employees worldwide (including 167 in the company's Boston headquarters) in October 1990 as part of a broad restructuring program. Altogether, Bain had reduced its workforce by 17 percent to about 1,000. Revenues reportedly fell by 10 percent in 1990, the first decline in Bain's history.[8]

In June 1991 Bain completed a management buyout, transferring ownership from the eight founding partners to approximately 60 partners who became the new firm owners. The firm rebounded, growing quickly in scale and scope. Revenue grew by roughly 25 percent per year from 1992 through 1999 (see Exhibit 1). Worldwide revenues were believed to exceed $500 million in 1998.[c] Consulting staff increased from 640 to more than 2,000, the partner group from 55 to 175.[d] Bain also expanded internationally, from 12 to 26 locations worldwide with 16 offices outside the United States.

Bain pursued a focused strategy of selling results-oriented advice on corporate and business unit strategy to large multinational companies. Since its founding Bain had worked with more than 1,500 clients "from every economic sector, in every region of the world." The firm maintained an audited "scoreboard" that tracked clients' share prices over the years. Partners' compensation was partially linked to the long-term results achieved by their clients.

Bain also expanded aggressively into new sectors, including private equity consulting, technology and telecommunications, and e-commerce. Under the banner "Consulting Plus," the company began to co-invest in private equity and venture capital funds (the latter primarily in e-commerce start-ups) and to take equity positions in clients in lieu of fees. Bain also made substantial investments in its internal capabilities, notably in professional development, training (through Bain Virtual University), and knowledge management (through its Global Experience Center).

EXHIBIT 1

Bain's Revenue Trend, 1992–1999

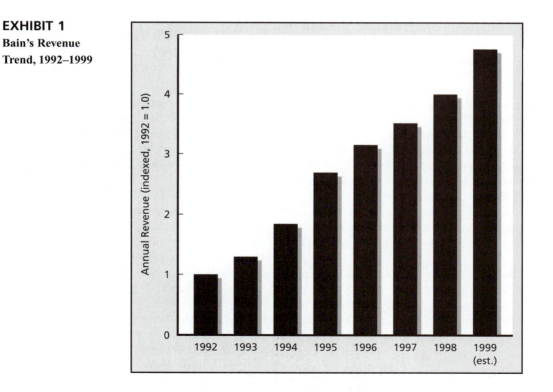

c The top tier in strategy practice was widely considered to comprise Bain, McKinsey ($1.1 billion), and The Boston Consulting Group ($655 million). Source of revenue estimates: *Consultants News,* June 1998, p. 9.
d In 1999 roughly a third of Bain partners were outside hires (including returning alumni).

GOVERNING BAIN

Bain's financial crisis had prompted a radical change in the way the firm was managed. "When Bill Bain left we lost the governance system overnight," explained a senior partner. "We had to start all over again." Added another veteran:

> We changed our philosophy in 1990. We transitioned from being controlled by a single individual to a management model involving a lot more people. We started to run the firm like a partnership where individual partners had a say and a role in running the firm.

Three governance committees were set up: a Policy Committee (PC) that set firm strategy, a Nominating Committee (NC) that put forth nominations for senior leadership positions, and a Compensation and Promotion Committee (CPC) that set partner pay and voted on candidates for partner. The company also added a nonexecutive chairman of the board who served primarily as an external ambassador and high-profile client "rainmaker" and a worldwide managing director (MD) who, as chief executive, managed the firm. Bain's office heads reported directly to the MD, along with practice leaders and corporate staff (see Exhibit 2).

Nominating Committee

The five-member NC proposed candidates for chairman of the board, MD, the PC, and the CPC.[e] The NC also acted as a "watchdog" on governance issues. "The partnership elects them to be objective decision makers," explained Tierney. "They sit above the fray. They also do a lot of homework. They don't propose a candidate without conducting one-to-two-hour personal interviews with 60 percent or 70 percent of the partnership. It's very, very rigorous. And they do it every year because there are always slots to fill on the governance committees." Added NC chairman Crawford Gilles:

> The NC also acts as the general partner of the firm, which gives it quite extraordinary powers, powers that we hope will never be used. If there were to be a major rift within the firm, a fundamental disagreement between the different governing bodies, the general partner could step in and, for example, replace the MD, replace the chairman of the board, or override the PC.

Any Bain partner except the chairman of the board and MD was eligible for NC membership. Current members of the PC and the CPC could serve, but could not comprise more than 40 per-

EXHIBIT 2 **Bain Governance System, November 1999**

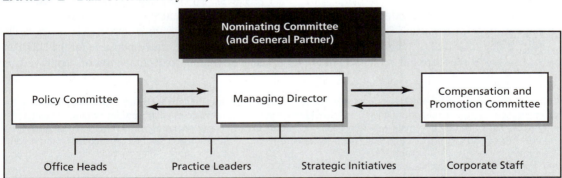

[e] The NC could have as few as three members.

cent of the NC. Candidates for the NC were required to "represent the long-term interests of the firm," had to be "discreet enough to handle sensitive personnel information," and were required to possess "global knowledge" of Bain's partner group. Emphasized Gilles: "We look for absolute trust, and someone who would put the long-term interests of the firm above all else."

The partnership at large voted directly for individual candidates to fill open slots on the NC. The candidates who received the greatest share of votes (weighted by partner equity share) were appointed and served a single three-year term up to a maximum of three consecutive terms.[f] Other Bain governing bodies filled openings through a single slate put forward annually by the NC and voted on by the partnership. NC members (as well as members of all other Bain committees) held staggered appointments, which, according to Tierney, "keeps the committees evergreen. When I first took over as MD," he recalled, "there were no term limits. I, for one, insisted that there be term limits because I've seen people wear out their welcome. Very rarely does someone leave when they should leave."

Gilles explained Bain's approach to electing partners to governance positions:

We designed our process to avoid the problem of having losers. We researched this in the early 1990s and could not find another professional services firm employing open elections where losers continued to play an ongoing role in the firm. The people who lost tended to leave. At the time we felt we had so few leaders around we could not afford no lose those people. We were also concerned that the election process would become divisive, leading to more factionalism and less of a one-firm culture.

NC members earned a standard allocation of 5 percent of their time for participating on the committee. "It's quite an honor, but it's also a lot of work," observed Gilles. "At least one year out of the three it takes up 20 percent of your time, and some months it's more like 50 percent." NC members were evaluated by the MD, with input from the NC chairman.

Elected by the full committee and rotated annually, the chairman of the NC was responsible for calling and conducting meetings, establishing agendas, making assignments, and preparing for the Bain partnership an annual report on the NC's work. The chair, although prohibited from disclosing sensitive personal information, was required to disclose to the partnership, and provide a brief rationale for, the proposed slate to be ratified.

Policy Committee

"The PC," explained Tierney, "functions essentially as the executive committee of a board."[g] The PC was responsible for the firm's long-term success and for determining overall strategy. "Unlike most other firms," observed a former committee member, "at Bain we don't have a single leader responsible for strategy. We do it by committee."

The PC set compensation policies based on the CPC's recommendations. It approved annual budgets and investment programs, safeguarded long-term assets, was responsible for the MD's annual evaluation and compensation, approved the

---

[f] All votes for committee positions were equity-weighted. Equity interest was determined by each partner's cumulative compensation, which, being performance driven, could rise and fall in successive years, irrespective of tenure. Equity interest did not constitute a formal ownership claim. Retiring partners did not "cash out" of the firm. According to Tierney: "The going concern value of Bain is entirely based on reputation. Reputation can be damaged easily and quickly if we make mistakes with our clients. For that reason we do not cash out our partners. They are paid annually based on the multiyear results they achieve for the firm."

[g] Being a corporation, Bain was required by law to name an official board of directors. Separate from the PC, it comprised roughly 60 senior partners, including the MD and chairman of the board. The board was a component of Bain's legal, rather than management, structure.

termination of partners, and, in consultation with the NC, could propose governance changes to the full partnership.

Excepting current members of the NC and CPC, any Bain partner was eligible for membership on the PC. The committee typically comprised 7–10 members, including the MD, who was generally an active member, and the chairman of the board. Gilles described the personal qualities Bain sought in members of the PC:

> We look for people who have demonstrated excellence in the craft of consulting, who have run our largest client relationships, and who as a result are very respected inside the firm. These are people of high integrity who put the firm's interest ahead of their own. The ability to lead a group of partners is paramount.

Although it sought broad geographic representation on the PC (and its other committees), Bain claimed not to use quotas in the selection process. Members were elected annually to three-year terms and limited to two consecutive terms. Member performance was assessed by the MD, with input from the PC chairman. The PC chairman, whose role, like that of the NC chairman, was to call and conduct meetings, establish agendas, make assignments, and produce an annual report of the committee's activities, was elected by the full committee and rotated annually.[h]

The PC's job had become more difficult as Bain had expanded. "It has served the firm well over the years, but we may be outgrowing this model," observed Tierney. "With tiny time allocations, committee members are increasingly disconnected from many details of our complex and rapidly expanding firm. Furthermore, our decision cycle time is slowing during a period when I believe it needs to accelerate."

Compensation and Promotion Committee

The eight-member CPC helped to set annual compensation for all Bain partners except the MD (whose compensation was set by the PC) and ratified all promotions to partner and director.[i] Committee members spent considerable time and effort collecting performance feedback from operational units.[j] The committee was charged with calibrating performance feedback from different sources to ensure consistent application of compensation policy across offices. The committee was also authorized to propose changes to compensation policy.

Excepting the MD, who was automatically a member, members of the PC were not eligible for membership on the CPC. Candidates were expected to be reliable and discreet. A past member of the CPC said: "We look for individuals who are particularly good listeners, people who exhibit a lot of empathy, and people who are trusted."

CPC members, like PC members, were elected as part of the single annual slate for openings across Bain's governing bodies, served three-year terms, and were limited to two consecutive terms. Individual terms were staggered. Members' work on the committee was evaluated by the MD, with input from the CPC chairman.

Chairman of the Board

As a high-profile "role model and spokesperson for the values, ethics, reputation, and client focus of Bain, both internally and externally," the chairman of the board was expected to give frequent

---

[h] The MD could not serve as chairman. In consultation with the MD, the chairman also appointed a nonvoting secretary to the committee.

[i] Partners with a minimum five years experience were eligible for director. The director title carried no additional compensation.

[j] For details on the CPC process for promotion to partner, see "Bain and Company, Inc.: Making Partner," HBS no. 899-066.

press interviews and conference speeches, and conduct top-level networking on behalf of the firm. The chairman also served as a senior counselor to the MD in a nonexecutive role, but was not directly accountable for firm management.[k] Only a modest time allocation was given for the chairman's role, however, since the bulk of the chairman's time was expected to be devoted to client work.

Only directors were eligible for Bain's chairmanship. Candidates were expected to be "among the most respected directors and role models with a deep understanding of client value-addition, respected leadership of their peer group, and skilled in promoting Bain's reputation and values." Candidates were proposed by the NC and elected by the partnership. An automatic member of the PC, not permitted to serve on the CPC or NC, the chairman served a three-year term and was limited to three consecutive terms. The chair's performance was evaluated by the PC and MD. A sitting chair could be removed only by a two-thirds vote of the directors.

The chair since 1993 had been Orit Gadiesh, a graduate of Harvard Business School and veteran of the Israeli army who had joined Bain in 1977.

Managing Director

Shortly after its restructuring in 1993, Bain & Co. combined the president and chief executive officer positions formerly held by Bill Bain into a single MD position responsible for global management of the firm. The MD was responsible for all operational aspects of the firm, including preparation of an annual budget and three-year growth plans for all Bain offices, but, unlike other Bain partners, was not expected to undertake client work. The MD also appointed all office heads, practice heads, and corporate department heads and, according to Tierney, was

> responsible for the P&L of the company, the welfare of the partnership, and for imple-

menting the strategy of the company. How the MD allocates resources, motivates people, and manages the evolution of the partnership is pretty much up to the MD. It is a complex and challenging leadership position within our partnership.

People know that what the MD thinks of them is incredibly important to their careers. The MD can determine their pay. The MD can sideline people. It's very unusual for someone to make the PC without the MD's support, because the NC doesn't want to put people onto the PC who aren't going to work well with the MD.

Candidates for promotion to partner had to be approved by the MD before they could be considered by the CPC. The MD could put partners on probation and, with approval of the PC, fire partners for poor performance. Annually, the MD, with input from and ratification by the CPC, made compensation decisions for every partner in the company. "If the committee disagrees significantly with the MD," observed Tierney, "it has final decision-making authority. In reality, we almost always reach consensus."

Finally, the MD was expected to integrate the various elements of Bain's governance system. "The MD is very much at the hub of the wheel of our governance system," maintained Gilles. "It's a very difficult role to play. The MD is really the only person who can pull different committees together to make sure that they're in sync with each other and with what people at the office level are trying to do on a day-to-day basis."

Candidates for the MD position had to be directors of the firm and among Bain's most respected client officers, as well as demonstrate skills and interest in management, administration, and leadership. MD candidates were proposed by the NC and approved by majority vote of the full partner group. MDs served a three-year term with a three-term limit. The MD automatically served

---

[k] The chairman also called and conducted board meetings.

on the PC and CPC, but was not permitted to serve on the NC.

The MD's compensation was set by the PC according to a predetermined formula based on the MD's contribution to overall firm performance. A sitting MD could be removed only by a 67 percent vote of the partnership.[1] According to Tierney, the subcommittee's role in evaluating the MD was

to set the MD's "highly leveraged activities" (HLAs), and to compensate based on the MD's performance against them. At the beginning of the year the MD proposes to the PC what Bain's priorities should be. That translates into a couple of pages of HLAs, which are usually weighted. Last year, 50 percent was on what we call "running the plant," all the day-to-day tasks such as budgeting, partner assignments, and so forth. The other 50 percent concerned longer-term strategic initiatives, for example, entering a new market.

At the end of the year the PC evaluates the MD against the HLAs. It collects data, including interviewing 30–40 partners, and then provides feedback, both verbally and in writing. Usually the written version takes anywhere between 5 and 15 pages. Each HLA is assigned a grade of "does not meet," "meets minus," "meets," "meets plus," or "exceeds."

The overall evaluation might influence the MD's cumulative compensation, plus or minus 10 percent. The issue is not so much the compensation as it is the feedback. As MD I don't want to get a "meets minus" on anything. The system creates alignment between the MD's agenda and the firm's agenda; it provides a feedback loop for the MD and, at the margin, it offers financial motivation.

The MD's annual evaluation was never made public. "Some of the topics the partnership isn't even aware of," explained Tierney. "These are highly confidential, and could involve sensitive personnel decisions." Some activities, according to Tierney, were too sensitive even to disclose to the members of the PC who evaluated the MD.

Regional Operating Committees

The MD oversaw three regional operating committees composed exclusively of office heads. The North American Operating Committee (NAOC), which comprised Bain's six primary office heads in North America, met monthly by telephone and quarterly in person. NAOC decisions ranged from resource allocation to client development priorities to compensation levels for new consultants. In Asia, Tierney convened during the first quarter of every year a meeting of partners from offices across the continent to discuss the firm's three-year plan and strategy for the region. The European office heads also met periodically to discuss cross-country strategic and operating issues.

TIERNEY AS MD

Tom has to run a democracy and a fascist state at the same time.

Senior Bain partner

Tom is an extraordinary project manager and multitasker. He is very productive. Nothing sits on his desk for more than 24 hours, and one of his gifts is an ability to simultaneously manage a few dozen different initiatives and ideas, some of which have two-year cycle times and some of which have two-hour cycle times. He is very organized. He doesn't spend a lot of time pondering the inevitable. He

---

[1] Removal of a sitting MD required board approval. The rules were the same for removing sitting members of Bain's governance committees.

tends to be very practical. He's very disciplined all the way around. Disciplined in terms of time, disciplined in terms of priorities. If the spinach has to be eaten, he eats it first.

Senior Bain partner

"Looking back," mused Tierney, "I never expected I would be CEO of Bain & Company. In fact, I never expected I would stay at Bain for more than two years. But I love what I do." At 45, Tierney had spent almost 20 years at Bain, 13 in management, including six years as office head in San Francisco. He had joined Bain in 1980 upon graduating from Harvard Business School (see Exhibit 3 for Tierney's bio). Elected Bain's first (and only) MD in 1993, Tierney was nearing the end of the second of his three possible terms.

As office head in San Francisco, Tierney's responsibilities had included managing the office and leading important client engagements. He had also helped to lead Bain into private equity consulting. During his tenure the San Francisco office had grown into the second largest in the company.

EXHIBIT 3   **Management Bios**

Tom Tierney   Tierney joined Bain & Co. in 1980 upon graduating from Harvard Business School, from which he received an MBA with distinction. A California native, Tierney earned a BA in economics, with highest distinction, from the University of California at Davis, which honored him as the year's most outstanding graduate. He was named a vice president of Bain in 1983 and managing director of the company's San Francisco office in 1987. Tierney specialized in leadership, strategy development, and the management of professional service firms. Prior to his study at Harvard, he had served as manager of Field Cost and Planning for Bechtel, International in Arzew, Algeria.

Tierney served on the boards of directors of the Institute for Higher Education, United Way of Massachusetts Bay, Committee for Economic Development, and Catholic Charities. He was a Trustee of the Woods Hole Oceanographic Institution and Overseer of the Hoover Institution and WGBH, a member of the Advisory Council of Harvard Business School, Stanford Business School, and the Boston Symphony Orchestra, and a former director of the Bay Area Council, Bay Area United Way, and University of California, Davis, Alumni Association.

Tierney lived with his wife and two children in Wellesley, Massachusetts.

Granville Harris   During his 15 years with Bain, Harris had advised top-level managers in a wide range of industries and had been a leader in Bain's business strategy and automotive, manufacturing, retailing, financial services, and consumer products practices. More recently, Harris had become a firmwide leader in the areas of free trade and privatization of government-owned industries. He was frequently called upon to speak and write on these topics.

Harris had obtained an MBA with high distinction from Harvard Business School and a BA in Japanese, magna cum laude, from Brigham Young University. Prior to joining Bain, he had worked in the financial services and real estate industries. Harris served on the board of the Miami Council of Civic Affairs and was involved in numerous other civic and religious organizations.

Oliver Bradshaw   Bradshaw joined Bain in 1985 and was elected to the partnership in 1991. A leader in the practice areas of aerospace and defense, telecommunications, and transportation, he led efforts in strategy development and implementation, M&A valuations and integration, organizational reengineering, and market and competitive assessment. Bradshaw had also developed considerable experience with clients in real estate, waste services, and consumer goods. Prior to joining Bain, Bradshaw had worked for five years at Bankers Trust in New York and Shawmut Bank in Boston. He held an MBA from Harvard Business School and a BA in economics, with honors, from Amherst College.

Tierney's success in San Francisco had led to his appointment as MD. "This was by no means an obvious outcome for me," Tierney explained. "Taking on the MD role meant having to move to Boston. As a fifth-generation Californian, this was almost unthinkable. It also meant having to give up a significant amount of client work. Finally, I was taking on the leadership of the firm in a tough turnaround situation."

Seven years later, Tierney estimated that he received roughly 300 voice mails and dozens of e-mails per week. By the first of every year more than 100 days of his calendar were already booked. Tierney described a typical day.

If I'm in town, which is probably 50 percent of the time, I usually get up around 5:00 A.M. and work out for 45 minutes. I can listen to voice mail while exercising. I cannot answer, but I can get through those that don't require a response. It also makes exercising a lot less painful. I will be in the car by 6:15 or so.[m] I will then get back on voice mail while I drive and by the time I get into the office I will have my voice mail close to complete. I am almost always one of the first people in the office, which I have been my whole career.

At 6:45 I grab a cup of coffee and finish the voice mail on speakerphone while going through the *Wall Street Journal* and other business periodicals. By 7:30 I have gone through faxes, e-mails, and voice mails. Usually, I don't schedule anything until 8:30, so I can prepare for meetings or make a few random phone calls.

I tend to schedule my days tightly, in 30 or 60 minute increments with no break in between. Meetings and scheduled phone calls cover everything from a strategic issue that we are wrestling with to a specific client or personnel issue. They may be with partners anywhere in the world or with one of my staff people. In between meetings the phone rings. I inevitably get backed up.

I eat a light lunch while I'm conducting a meeting or listening to voice mail at the middle of the day. If I'm in town I try to get out of the office by 6:00 P.M. Most people stay later than that. On the way home I go through voice mail. Voice mail tends to creep up later in the day. Seven to nine P.M. is absolute family time. I adore my wife and our two sons, age 12 and 5. Despite my demanding schedule I try to spend every free moment with them. I don't watch television. I don't play golf. I read at least one business book each month.

Tierney's direct reports, which had grown significantly during his tenure, in 1998 included 15 office heads, 10 practice heads, five department heads, the VPs of marketing and human resources, the chief of staff, the CFO, and a few others. This growing span of control was causing him increased stress as the company expanded. "My main complaint as MD," confided Tierney,

is that I spend so much of my time managing that I don't have a chance to go deep on long-term issues when I want to and when I should. I just run out of time. A second complaint is that a lot of what I do I've done over and over again. For example, next week we have a NOAC meeting. Because it's my thirtieth meeting, it's not quite as stimulating as it used to be. It also bothers me that by the very nature of my job I'm unable to take direct accountability for a lot of heavy client work. Sometimes I feel almost ceremonial. It can be frustrating.

Managing Partners

"I want to be known for making a difference, for helping talented people make the most of their lives," remarked Tierney.

---

[m] Tierney owned a 1998 BMW 528i and a 1965 Corvair, his first automobile. He had rebuilt the Corvair engine three times.

Once I asked a founder of the firm: "Does the firm exist for its people, or do the people exist for the firm?" His answer disturbed me. He said that people exist for the firm. What is the firm? Something registered somewhere. The firm exists for people to collect together with others who share their values and ambitions to achieve something that is personal and meaningful to them. It's a facility; it's a liberator; it's a focus mechanism for energies. People do not exist for it; it exists for them.

Tierney considered partner allocation and motivation his most important priority as MD. "How you allocate partner time," Tierney insisted, "not only affects the motivation of the individual in trying to get people to perform their best, but it has enormous influence on the overall economics of the business. The difference between 5 percent growth and 25 percent growth is whether you can harness the horsepower of the partnership. It's like an engine. If the engine's finely tuned you can get another 25 or 50 horsepower out of it."

As a result, Tierney devoted much of his time to placing the right partners in the right jobs (see Exhibit 4). "I continually have to give people a 're-potting,' a new challenge," he explained. "People get stale. I've observed that you have to repot people every three to four years. They have to have something new and exciting. I've also reached a conclusion that most of the time they won't come to you and ask for that. They want to be, as one of my partners said, recruited."

Tierney related an example of one ongoing "recruitment" effort.

For the past eight months I've been trying to get a partner in our Hamburg, Germany, office to move to Manila, the Philippines. You could not find two cities that are more different. I can't order him to go to Manila. I can't say to him, "if you don't take your kids, take your wife, and move to Manila, I will fire you." I can't do that. That is bad management. If word got out that I was

threatening him just because he wouldn't move, I wouldn't have my job. Much of my job is based on trust and mutual respect. You have to have the ability to influence people without using the nuclear weapons of removing them from their job or demolishing their compensation (although the possibility that those weapons could be used gives me enormous power).

I can try to persuade him or convince the office head to persuade him. I can enlist other partners to help sell the move. I can offer him a significant cash bonus or an office head position. I can give him a round-trip ticket to return to Hamburg in 36 months so that he and his wife know there's a definite end date to the assignment.

Bain's office heads were frequent targets of Tierney's recruitment efforts. He recounted an earlier effort to influence office heads to grow their offices in support of Bain's corporate strategy.

Many of them didn't want to grow aggressively enough. Now we're at the point where most offices have inculcated our minimum 10–15 percent growth target. I've got that wired into the mind-set. But early on I had to really push. We would usually get to a point where an office had about 50 people. Then they would often declare, "We don't want to grow. We're just the right size. We know everybody; we can all be in the room together." But in our business you've got to grow, just like you must constantly improve quality. You can't stand still.

Partner Feedback

Opinions about Tierney were generally favorable. "Tom is very good at the *quid pro quo* game," observed a senior partner. "He remembers when he owes you, and over time it balances out. He is also a good listener. He has few weaknesses." Added another: "Tom has emerged as someone who has world-class interpersonal skills. He doesn't get

EXHIBIT 4   Abridged Text of "Constellation Leadership for Competitive Advantage" Speech Delivered by Tom Tierney to UC Davis Business Partners, April 14, 1999

The organizational chart has become merely an artifact. The boxes don't count anymore, except as a navigational map that a new person to the company may need to pull out once in a while. What counts is what is inside those boxes. Talent. And what really counts is how that talent relates to and develops other talent in the company outside any individual box, how talent pulls together around a company's mission and pushes outward following entrepreneurial mandates that profitably grow the firm. You can think of it as a constellation, defined by stars in key positions that are subject to the forces of gravity that pull in and rotation that push out. Getting those forces right is critical. But getting stars in the right places is the hardest part of all. There is tremendous competition for top talent. Star wars are today's reality and competitive advantage goes to the firm that can win and motivate the brightest stars. It goes to the company that manages its organization around these stars and creates the forces that bind and propel them. It goes to the managers that master what I call "constellation leadership."

Let's go over the principles of constellation leadership. Constellation leadership requires first that organizations establish the highest possible standards for performance, then that they upgrade key jobs to meet those standards.

The practice of constellation leadership also requires that HR become a line function and that the organization invest executive time and cash in identifying and hiring that top talent into key positions. You need to invest whatever it takes. *At Bain we invest about 150K per hire.* And as general managers, you need to assume personal accountability for the results.

Constellation leadership requires that an organization clearly articulate a unique and compelling mission, which, in fact, becomes an integral part of its value proposition. This is your strategic gravity. It serves to bind together talent in purpose and commitment. The CEO becomes, in effect, the keeper of the mission, the steward of who imprints it on employee hearts and minds through constant communication and pushes it out to the periphery of a company's activity. This is about the power of passion. If people are passionate about a cause they will work harder and more aggressively execute the organization's strategy.

Constellation leadership requires a business to manage itself around stars and give its teams specific entrepreneurial mandates, aligned with the mission and reinforced by appropriate practices of compensation, review, and promotion. Here, general managers invest time primarily in deciding which key stars go where, and in developing policies that create impetus for their strategic behavior and parameters or standards for entrepreneurship, information sharing, and accountability.

Finally, constellation leaders inspire strategic behavior within their organization; they raise performance standards, and they measure performance against those standards to keep everyone on course.

We all know that constellations don't appear overnight. The stars we see in the heavens have taken millions of years to form. Companies will need to move a lot faster than that, but the analogy still holds: if you get started, you will get there. Indeed, the winners of today's corporate star wars will be the companies that get their forces right and create and motivate their organization around constellation leadership. And when your company does this, it will find its stars shining on a vast sea of opportunity as the next century brings increasing turmoil, both stronger undertow and bigger breakers. With star talent and an organization that acts strategically, you can catch the waves.

emotional and can really motivate people. I am puzzled to this day as to how he evolved because at the time he was appointed MD there was nothing in our culture valuing or rewarding those skills."

"One of the criticisms of Tom is that he's not close enough to the clients anymore," observed a former member of the PC.

> Tom has very strong internal strengths. We needed strong controls on the business back in the early 1990s. But as the firm has matured I believe that a person in Tom's position would carry more credibility with the partnership if he spent a little bit more time on the external side. There is a tendency for global client heads to feel superior to Tom because they have led client engagements whereas he has simply managed and led the firm. I suspect that his successor will probably have more of a track record with important clients.

A senior partner agreed.

> Tom's job is complicated by the fact that he is working in a culture where client heads drive everything. There's an attitude of, "My client is better than your client, so please give me my choice of people in the office." There is a star system inside Bain. You are king of the hill if you have a very significant relationship with a company whose stock price is doubling every year.

Another former member of the PC observed:

> Tom's ability to actually spend time with the people who report to him has diminished now that we have 175 partners and not 60. Sometimes he will come on with his "let's get things done" attitude and drop something on an office head or a practice head that seems unreasonable and out of the blue because he hasn't spent enough time culti-

vating the idea. Other firms at this scale have moved to a structure with regional heads. But we haven't changed yet. We still use a small partnership model, and that has put a strain on Tom.

A Bain director explained the challenge Tierney faced:

> Tom is caught between a rock and a hard place. On the one hand, Bain is a partnership and so he has to be deferential in how he treats people. On the other hand, people want leadership. Tom gets pulled in two different directions and some people criticize him for not being decisive enough. At other times people say he's acting too much like a boss. It all depends on who's on the receiving end. People who have not been on the receiving end of Tom say "Oh, he's still not being directive enough." And people who have been on the receiving end say, "Oh, he's sticking his nose where it doesn't belong." It's almost schizophrenic.

Tierney realized that Bain's rapid expansion had made it increasingly difficult for him to maintain close contact with the partnership. Its current operating plan called for the firm to double in size within five years. Looking ahead Tierney knew that the challenges facing the MD would only grow more complex.

THE MIAMI OFFICE

In 1989 two Bain consultants, Granville Harris, then a junior partner, and Oliver Bradshaw, a Bain manager who worked under Harris, put forward a bold proposal to Bill Bain and the firm's founding partners (see Exhibit 3 for bios of Harris and Bradshaw).[n] "We wanted to recreate the magic of the Bain brand in Miami," observed Harris. "At the time the firm was in financial trouble and we

---

[n] Bain professionals began as associates and progressed through consultant, manager, partner, and director.

felt the culture back in Boston was changing, and not for the better." Recalled Bradshaw:

> We set out to do something quite entrepreneurial. We had a large client in Colombia. It took us 13 hours to get there from Boston via Miami. We loved Bain, but were frustrated with the travel. We were also looking for a new challenge and more recognition inside the firm. We believed that area of the country was set to grow. So we sat down and created a business plan, which we took to Bill Bain and the founding partners. Incredibly, they said yes.

> Bill Bain's philosophy was to have large offices. He believed large offices gave the firm scale benefits, for example, a large experience center and a large research library. Back then, if Bain started a new office it was usually done in a big and extremely thoughtful way and involved a large number of senior partners. And here Granville and I were going off practically alone! Many people inside Bain thought we would not be successful. Some wanted us to be merely a satellite office of Boston, but we wanted more operating control. We were mavericks.

Harris, Bradshaw, and five others from Boston opened the Miami office in July 1990 with a single client. "Then the wheels came off," recalled Bradshaw. "We lost our one and only client the first month we were there. We almost didn't make it." Soon thereafter they found another client and the office took off.

"Since we opened we have exceeded plan every year," emphasized Harris.

> When we started in Miami Bain was perceived to be unstable, and so we developed a bit of an independent streak. We felt like we could do things ourselves. At the time compensation was driven by local office per-

formance.[o] Because of that, we were perceived by some as too financially oriented, even greedy. Once we became successful and the firm started to become more successful, they started managing us more tightly and we resisted a little bit. We felt like we were very capable of managing ourselves. I think there's still a little bit of that in Miami.

As office head Harris was responsible for the Miami office's overall financial performance. He managed partner and consultant utilization, the annual budgeting process, the three-year planning process, and office administrative staff (including their professional development and overtime hours). He also set annual recruiting targets for the office and the recruiting budget.

Of Tierney, with whom he had frequent interactions, particularly on the NAOC, Harris observed: "Tom in his formal role is a controller. Informally, he has been a friend and mentor, someone who has given me fatherly advice. I have a strong, healthy sense of respect for him. Occasionally, he has also sought my advice."

PLANNING A "REPOTTING"

> I've made it plain from day one that I expect office heads to work at a job five to seven years and then to rotate out. I don't want to create master sergeants who get "long in the tooth" and stop learning. Their capabilities stall out and younger partners may not work for them because younger partners don't want to work for the guys running a kingdom; they want to work for partners helping them succeed.

> *Tom Tierney, worldwide managing director,*
> *Bain & Company*

---

[o] In a move initiated by Tierney in 1997, Bain changed its North American compensation policy to reflect a single bonus pool

Although the Miami office had been financially successful and since its founding had grown 50 percent annually, Tierney felt the time had come to replace Harris as the office head. "In spite of his many years as office head," Tierney reflected, "he is still the Lone Ranger business-getter, an individualistic, make-it-happen guy. I've been hearing complaints from some of the consultants that the office is not team oriented. We now need less of an entrepreneur and more of a manager in the office head role."

Unbeknownst to Bradshaw, he had become Tierney's choice to replace Harris. In addition to client work, the 40-year-old Bradshaw managed all professional human resource functions in Miami, including training, staffing, and career development. "Oliver has been Granville's number two from the beginning," explained Tierney. "He's been patiently waiting in the wings for Granville to step down, but Granville is finding it hard to let go." Unlike other positions at Bain, office heads were not subject to formal term limits. "I think Oliver is the best choice to succeed Granville," Tierney continued.

> He may not have as much client experience as Granville, but he is more experienced in the arena of professional development. But as would be expected, no one has the full support of the partners in Miami. I will have to build consensus around Oliver and give him enough air cover to make his transition. But Granville has to want to support it. The transfer won't work unless you move somebody in that everybody will endorse.

"Rotating an office head takes a lot of work on Tom's part because he's got to get the incumbent to agree that the timing is right," concurred a former member of the PC. "He's also got to find another candidate in the office who is acceptable to him, and to the partners in the office, and at least tolerable to the former office head. A poorly executed office head transition is morale destroying and economically disruptive. It is very costly."

"You need to treat the outgoing office head with respect and to make sure that that person feels they are moving on to a big job," added a senior partner. "Everyone has to feel they're growing, especially the kind of competitive and talented people we have in the partnership. I think it would be very difficult to take someone who's been running an office for many years and then just make them a generic partner again."

The Breakfast Meeting

In December 1998 Tierney knew he would have to soon decide how to convince Harris to rotate out and devise a plan to insert Bradshaw. "I have to be careful," he concluded.

> I wouldn't like Granville to leave the firm. Even with my planting the seed and getting others to plant the seed, he is not very receptive to stepping down. But for the sake of the office and his own development, he's got to step down. In the past it has often taken me a long time to convince entrenched office heads to step down. Given how difficult it can be, it is tempting to leave him in there. After all, the office is doing great financially. But that is not good for Granville, or for Bain.

Tierney scheduled a breakfast meeting with Harris in Miami.

References

1. Elizabeth MacDonald, "Consulting Firms Post Record Growth in Revenue, but May Face Slowdown," *The Wall Street Journal,* June 10, 1999.

2. Kennedy Information Research Group website, accessed November 17, 1999.

3. Peter Haynes and Dolly Setton, "McKinsey 101," *Forbes,* May 4, 1998, pp. 130–35.

4. Tim Bourgeois, Kennedy Research Group, quoted in Jay Berry, "Good-bye to the Lush Management Consulting Life?" *Journal of Management Consulting,* November 1998, pp. 22–26.

5. MacDonald, "Consulting Firms Post Record Growth."

6. Brian Palmer, "Is It Time to Join the Consultants?" *Fortune,* August 3, 1998, p. 252.

7. Keith Hammonds, "Can Bain Consultants Get Bain & Co. Out of This Jam?" *Business Week,* February 11, 1991, p. 52.

8. Ibid.

Infosys Technologies, Limited

Our goal is for Infosys to be on the short-list of every Fortune 500 CEO and CIO whenever they have a business problem that requires information technology to resolve.

N.R. Narayan Murthy, chairman, Infosys Technologies

INTRODUCTION

N.R. Narayana Murthy, chairman and CEO of Infosys Technologies, Limited, one of India's leading software companies, had ample reason to be happy on January 3, 2000. The firm was growing rapidly and moving from strength to strength. (Exhibit 1 provides Infosys's summary financials.) Since March 1999, when Infosys had made its debut on the NASDAQ stock exchange, the company's stock price in the United States had risen more than sevenfold (see Exhibit 2). The firm had just been named India's most admired corporation by India's leading financial newspaper (see Exhibit 3). Yet, Murthy felt that the firm had a long way to go before reaching its goal of becoming a globally respected corporation providing high-quality technology solutions to business problems.

ORIGINS AND EARLY GROWTH OF THE INDIAN COMPUTER INDUSTRY[1]

The early days of computing in India were dominated by public research organizations. ESSO Standard Eastern Inc., Exxon Corporation's Indian subsidiary, installed the first commercial computer in 1961. Thereafter, computers, incorporating both hardware and system software were imported by Indian organizations from international computer suppliers, such as IBM, Digital Equipment Corporation, Burroughs, Sperry, and Honeywell. Indian software development focused on writing for these systems software applications for use within India.

However, one Indian firm, Tata Consultancy Services (TCS), was focused on the international market. India had a low per capita income and yet possessed the second-largest English-speaking scientific manpower reservoir in the world as well as a well-functioning technical education system. Its national institutes, engineering colleges, and universities graduated more than 60,000 technically trained knowledge workers each year. TCS, recognizing that Indian firms were advantageously placed in offering skilled programmers for software development at low cost, began offering software services through contract programming, that is, Indian programmers writing software for foreign companies at their respective sites.

During the 1970s, Indian government restrictions on the import of computers, except for use in software exports, led to few advanced systems being imported. Software development suffered from lack of a computer base. Government rules on foreign ownership of Indian firms were tightened in 1977. Rather than dilute ownership and risk losing control, IBM and other computer com-

EXHIBIT 1 Infosys Financial Data, 1994–2000

Year Ending March 31 (Rs. million, except ratios and per share and shareholder data)								
	81–82	93–94	94–95	95–96	96–97	97–98	98–99	99–00e
For the Year								
Revenue	1.2	300.8	577.0	934.1	1,438.1	2,603.7	5,127.4	9,214.6
Operating profit (EBITD)	—	97.1	198.6	339.5	500.6	886.1	1,917.5	3,788.8
PAT	0.4	80.9	133.2	210.1	336.8	603.6	1,329.2	2,859.5
At Year End								
Share Capital	—	33.5	72.6	72.6	72.6	160.2	330.7	330.8
Reserves	0.4	253.5	552.0	725.8	1,055.8	1,569.4	5,413.6	8,002.3
Loan fund	—	—	63.4	42.6	—	—	—	—
Gross block	—	82.7	253.2	468.6	712.9	1,051.4	1,689.2	2,840.3
Capital investment	—	71.3	252.3	155.5	273.1	344.1	716.8	1,598.7
Net current assets	0.6	139.4	324.7	411.7	542.0	972.3	4,729.6	6,121.3
Financial Ratios								
ROCE (%)	97	43	32	33	40	46	64	46
Debt/Equity ratio	—	—	0.10	0.05	—	—	—	—
EPS (Rs.)	—	1.22	2.01	3.18	5.09	9.13	20.10	43.23
Market capitalization	NA	1,910.2	3,484.2	3,556.7	7,310.4	29,634.2	96,728.0	593,381.7
No. of shareholders	7	6,033	6,526	6,909	6,414	6,622	9,527	46,314

EBITD: Earning before interest, depreciation, and tax; PAT: profit after tax (from ordinary activities);
ROCE: return on capital employed; EPS: earnings per share from ordinary activities; e: expected; NA: not applicable.
Source: Infosys.

EXHIBIT 2 Infosys Technologies Stock Price Performance

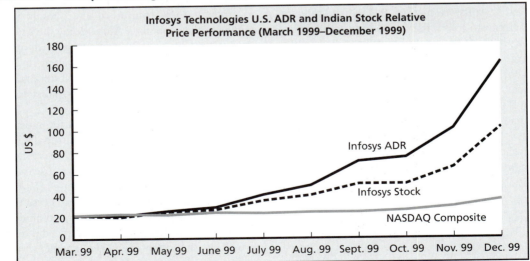

Source: Datastream.

EXHIBIT 3   India's Most Admired Companies

Rank	1987	1990	1992	1994	1996	1998	1999
1	Hind. Lever	Tisco	Tisco	ACC	Hind. Lever	Glaxo	**Infosys**
2	Tisco	Telco	L&T	ITC	Tisco	Hind. Lever	Hind. Lever
3	Telco	Hind. Lever	Telco	L&T	Indian Hotels	Ranbaxy	Wipro Infotech
4	Colgate	Glaxo	Siemens	Guj. Ambuja	Asian Paints	MRF	Asian Paints
5	ITC	L&T	Glaxo	Telco	Tata Electric	Indian Oil	Reliance Ind.
6	L&T	ONGC	Hoechst	Raymond	ITC	**Infosys**	L&T
7	Indian Hotels	Bajaj Auto	Titan Watch	Glaxo	Telco	Coca Cola	Satyam Comp.
8	Philips	Colgate	Pfizer	Maruti	Glaxo	Cipla	Ranbaxy
9	Bajaj Auto	Siemens	Hind. Lever	P&G	L&T	L&T	NIIT
10	Reliance & Glaxo (tied)	Bombay Dyeing	Raymond	Hind. Lever	Nestle	East India Hotels	Johnson & Johnson

Sources: "Survey of India's Most Admired Companies," *The Economic Times,* January 3, 2000 (for 1999 rankings); "India's Most Respected Companies," *Business World,* July 12, 1999, pp. 20–25 (for 1987–1998 rankings).

panies chose to divest their stakes in their Indian subsidiaries and leave the country.

Several Indian firms sprang up to fill the void left behind by the departing foreign firms. These firms offered Indian businesses assistance in importing computers, software development and maintenance, and low-level data-processing functions. As their capabilities grew from servicing the tiny Indian software market, the Indian software firms began to look offshore, hoping to arbitrage on the relatively lower labor costs of skilled Indian software programmers. U.S. software programmers cost their firms a minimum of $100,000/year, whereas U.S.-based personnel from India cost about $75,000/year.[2] Once the Indian cost advantage had become apparent, several firms sprouted in the late 1970s, offering to foreign firms "bodyshopping" services, so called because they essentially provided "bodies" at lower cost to write specific software.

NARAYAN MURTHY

I'm a capitalist in my mind, a socialist in my heart.[3]

Narayan Murthy

Born on August 20, 1946, Murthy had grown up, one of eight siblings, in a middle-class family in the South Indian state of Karnataka. He had earned bachelor's and master's degrees in electrical engineering and computer sciences from Mysore University and the Indian Institute of Technology, Kanpur, respectively. The 1950s and 1960s were the heyday of socialism in India, as the government took control of the "commanding heights of the economy." Attracted by the socialist ideal of equality, in 1974, while writing an operating system for an airline cargo system in Paris, Murthy campaigned for Francois Mitterand, who was making his second bid as a socialist for the presidency of France.

Murthy was surprised that even the most die-hard among the French socialists nursed the belief that wealth-creation was a more effective leveler of class distinctions than pure redistribution. While traveling home by train through the Communist heartland of Eastern Europe, he saw neither the efficient state nor the happy comrades he had dreamed of. Instead, he experienced a repressive state and often-frightened people (he was briefly imprisoned in Bulgaria over espionage charges[4]). He came to believe that "every human being needs incentives to move forward, be it in the form of according money, recognition, or fame. The government is not the instrument to create wealth. It is the job of the government to create an environment and provide for the infrastructure and mindset to create wealth."[5]

In 1974, Murthy returned to India and joined Systems Research Institute (SRI) in Pune. SRI tried to solve, through systems theory and operations research, complex computing challenges faced by government-owned enterprises. He produced reports that "gathered dust" by his account. In 1977, he joined Mumbai-based Patni Computer Systems (PCS). One of the several Indian firms that had sprung up in 1977 when the foreign firms exited India, PCS imported, installed, and supported Data General computers in India.

In 1981, Murthy and six of his associates at PCS left the firm against the advice and counsel of family and friends to found Infosys Technologies with an initial capital of rupees 10,000 (approximately $1,100 at that time). Years later, Murthy recalled that the people who seemed most enthusiastic about his forming Infosys were his ill-wishers —they were certain that he would fail and be stigmatized for life.[6]

INFOSYS'S FIRST DECADE: 1981–1991

All of Infosys's founders were professionals who came from conservative middle-class backgrounds. "We all prize fairness, dignity, and respect," observed Infosys co-founder K. Dinesh. "And we brought complementary strengths to the table, without treading on each others' toes." In 1983, attracted by its pleasant climate and access to a pool of talent from its numerous engineering colleges, Infosys relocated in Bangalore, capital of the south Indian state of Karnataka.

Murthy and his co-founders wanted to create a "different" kind of company. Nandan Nilekani, a programmer in his mid-twenties in 1981, the youngest of Infosys's co-founders, explained:

In contrast to the kinds of firms that have dominated Indian business—the too personal family-owned and run companies and the too impersonal multinational corporations—we wanted to build a different kind of firm. We wanted to build a firm that was professionally owned and professionally managed, with good corporate governance, good employee management, and good ethics. We wanted a firm that promised a "fair deal" to all its stakeholders—shareholders, employees, and customers alike.

However, getting started as a new venture was quite a challenge, given the bureaucratic constraints imposed by the government. "It took us nine to twelve months and as many as 15 visits to Delhi to get permission to import a computer," Murthy recalled. "It took us one year to get a telephone line in 1983. We had to rely on debt since the IPO route was constrained. The Indian central bank's permission had to be sought for travel abroad. Data communication was very difficult." Dinesh reflected that despite these constraints, being a software services company gave Infosys a flexibility that start-ups in other industries might not have. "All that was required to succeed initially," he remarked,

was that our people needed to go on-site. The customer typically took care of everything else. We could start the business without much capital and still have big dreams. Right from the start, we wanted not just to be successful but to be a trailblazer.

Until 1986, Infosys had only one major customer, Databasics Corporation, whose software package Infosys helped customize for Databasic's customers. In 1986 Infosys entered into a short-lived joint-venture with Kurt Salmon Associates with Kurt Salmon marketing, and Infosys delivering, software services.

"The Near Death Experience"

In 1989 Infosys's efforts to intensify sales efforts in the United States were constrained by Indian government regulations on setting up foreign offices. In addition, the U.S. government severely restricted the number of B-1 visas it issued each year. Infosys could no longer send its programmers freely to customer locations in the United States.

Believing that Infosys, a "small, unknown company, with no brand equity," was as good as dead, one of its original founders left to pursue opportunities on his own in the United States, and the remaining founders seriously considered quitting the firm. "I can vividly recall that in 1989 the founders had a marathon meeting," reminisced an Infosys founding partner,

in which, for hours, we went round the table describing how difficult doing business was and listing all the constraints within which we were operating. After about six hours of complaints and laments, a view began to emerge that we should be prepared to sell the business for any offer of $1.5 million or more. Murthy had been quiet throughout the meeting, listening to everything that was said, and absorbing the other co-founders' views and concerns. But when sale of the company began to appear a very real possibility, he spoke up. "I am confident that the company will succeed eventually," Murthy said. "If any of you want to leave, I will be happy to buy you out." There was a total silence for a few minutes. Then Nandan spoke up. "If you are staying on," he said, "then I am in it with you." One by one, every one of the other four co-founders changed their viewpoints and expressed a desire to stay on. "Let this be the last time we talk about selling the company under duress," Murthy admonished.

"I was so sure the firm was going to succeed in the long run," recalled Murthy, "that I had no hesitation in offering to buy out the skeptics. But I had no money to back up my offer. Had even one of the co-founders taken me up on the offer, I wonder where I would have raised the money to buy him out."

Infosys struggled to grow through the 1980s, finishing its first decade with 1991 revenues of rupees (Rs.) 50 million (then less than $2 million).

THE DECADE OF HEADY GROWTH: 1991–2000

To be a highly respected name in the global market for [software] services and products, and to continue to realize a significant portion of revenues from exports.

> *Infosys's long-term goal, reiterated in its annual reports*

"The Seminal Point"

Although in 1986, the Indian government, realizing that India had the potential to be a software export powerhouse, had formulated a computer software policy that loosened several restrictions and established new incentives, the Indian software industry had remained mired in the "license-and-permit raj" of extensive regulations and controls. In 1991, trying to overcome a balance-of-payments crisis, the government launched a program of economic liberalization that included relaxation of several trade and exchange controls and dismantling the "license-and-permit raj."

Murthy referred to India's 1991 economic reforms as a "seminal point. Had it not been for the reforms," he added, "Infosys would have ceased to exist." The 1991 reforms allowed firms to open offices abroad, travel easily, and hire foreign consultants. The reforms also eased access to capital markets for private companies, making equity financing a viable option. Encouraged, in February 1993 Infosys tapped the Indian capital market for its initial public offering (IPO).

The General Electric Lesson

In 1989 General Electric (GE) became an Infosys customer and, within three years, came to account for approximately 40 percent of Infosys's revenues. Attempting to take advantage of its bargaining power as Infosys's largest client, GE began exerting intense pressure on Infosys to reduce its rates. Infosys responded by terminating its relationship with GE. After a one-year transition period, during which all of Infosys's work at GE was handed over to other companies and in-house IT personnel, Infosys exited the relationship.

"The important lesson for us," recalled an Infosys executive, "was to never be dependent on one customer for more than 10 percent of our business, a tenet we have faithfully adhered to ever since." Thus, in financial year 2000, its largest customer accounted for 10 percent, and the five largest customers for 33 percent, of its total sales. Infosys followed a similar approach to maintaining a diverse mix of clients, turning down work if that led to concentration in any one industry.

Maintaining Excellence

The Indian government reforms of 1991 had opened new opportunities for Infosys but ironically had also intensified competition. Multinational (MNC) behemoths such as IBM began planning to reenter India to set up development centers and take advantage of its pool of low-cost skilled talent. Dire predictions began circulating among industry experts that Indian firms such as Infosys were "finished," since they would be unable to compete in the war for skilled talent. "The entry of MNCs into India was a do-or-die moment for Infosys," recalled Murthy.

> We had two options at that stage. The first was to lobby the government aggressively to keep the MNCs out. But all of Infosys's founders were firmly opposed to doing any such thing. It was not the honorable thing to do. We could not have maintained our sense of self-respect had we done so. The other option for Infosys was to introspect and understand why potential employees might consider working for Infosys instead of firms such as IBM or Oracle.

Infosys managers realized that two critical reasons why employees might be attracted to foreign firms were compensation and work environment. Management addressed the compensation challenge by ensuring that Infosys employees' salaries were in the top 10–15 percent of the salaries offered by companies in its peer group. In addition, in a major departure from the practices of other Indian firms, Infosys began issuing to its employees stock-option warrants, vested after five years.

To counteract the second pull of MNCs on potential employees, Murthy invested a substantial part of the proceeds from Infosys's IPO in relocating Infosys to a better facility. Feeling that potential employees perceived Indian companies at a disadvantage relative to multinational firms because they had "glitzy and luxurious offices," and wanting to provide "a world-class facility for a world-class company," Murthy opened a new office complex for Infosys in the outskirts of Bangalore. Featuring a gymnasium, basketball courts, and tennis courts, the new complex seemed more like a college campus than a corporation.

"I'm glad we took the route of becoming more competitive with foreign firms in the war for talent rather than lobby with government to keep foreign firms out," reflected Murthy. "We came out with a lot of innovations. As a result, we grew many-folds in sales and market capitalization. The only way to survive and grow is by putting our own house in order."

Overseas Development Centers and the Push for Quality

Even as the Indian government was easing restrictions, Indian software firms were moving up the chain of value-added services from bodyshopping contracts to off-shore development contracts (ODCs)—Indian programmers writing software in India for foreign companies. (Exhibit 4 offers international cost comparisons for software development; Exhibit 5 provides productivity comparisons between Indian and U.S. firms.) ODCs offered greater arbitrage opportunities than bodyshopping

EXHIBIT 4 International Cost Comparisons in Software Development, 1994

Country	Indexed cost	
	Programmer	Systems Analyst
USA	1,164	1,124
Japan	1,293	1,185
Germany	1,351	1,196
France	1,135	1,307
Britain	781	1,287
Mexico	652	658
India	100	100
Russia	80	84
China	75	80

Source: *The Economist* (1994), quoted in Ghemawat et al., "The Indian Software Industry at the Millenium," HBS 700-036, Ex. 6.

(the average fully loaded salary for software professionals in India was about $13,000/year compared to $75,000/year for an Indian programmer in the United States[7]) but also greater risk for the client. In bodyshopping, the client could strictly control the parameters of the project and closely monitor the software development process. An ODC required the software supplier to control and monitor software development on behalf of the client. During the 1980s, foreign clients did not have much confidence in the Indian software firms' ability to deliver on offshore projects. In 1988 ODCs comprised only 10 percent of the Indian software exports.

Infosys was one of the leaders among Indian firms in pursuing ODC opportunities. Constrained by U.S. government visa restrictions from sending its professionals freely to the United States, Infosys management decided, in Dinesh's words, to "convert a threat into an opportunity" by investing in processes that would enable them, and build client trust in their ability, to do more work "here" (in Bangalore) and less work "there" (on-site).

Infosys managers recognized that, thus far, quality had been a function of "personality-dependent excellence" and, to become a hallmark of Infosys, it needed to be institutionalized. To build

client confidence and internal processes, Infosys established a formal quality group. All programmers and new recruits were required to undergo a three-day quality orientation. Project managers underwent training in how to manage for quality, and all employees were trained in quality estimation and measurement. Management also began paying greater attention to customer-satisfaction surveys and incorporated these in the performance evaluation process. Since several European organizations demanded International Standards Organization (ISO) certification from their service providers, Infosys, seeking to expand into Europe, sought and received ISO 9000 certification, further raising quality awareness within the firm. In 1998, Infosys became the first Indian company to receive for its processes level 4 certification of the Software Engineering Institute's (SEI) capability maturity model and was on track to receiving level 5 certification in 2000. Only 2 percent of the companies assessed by the SEI worldwide had achieved level 4 or higher certification; less than 40 firms had level 5 certification.

Infosys's Global Development Model: GDCs and PDCs

Within Infosys, ODCs were called GDCs, global development centers, to emphasize the concept that development centers would be located in globally optimal destinations, whether in India or abroad, whether overseas from the client or within the country depending on cost considerations.

Most GDC work focused on writing customized software for installation at client sites. A typical project required a small team of project leaders to first travel to their client's location to ascertain the client's priorities and specifications. Following this, the project leaders would return to India and supervise a team, typically of 20 to 50 professionals, sometimes in more than one GDC (to facilitate teams with different types and levels of expertise to work in parallel without being co-located) as the project proceeded to completion. A small group of people typically stayed on-site with

EXHIBIT 5 Indian versus U.S. Software Firms' Productivity Comparisons, 1998

Parameters (US$ 000)	Indian Firms					U.S. Firms				
	Infosys	NIIT	Tata Infotech	Satyam	Wipro	CTP	Keane	Mastech	Sapient	TSC
Sales/employee	32.0	30.0	33.1	27.8	30.3	166.2	93.3	80.3	134.2	209.0
Operating cost/employee	21.3	20.1	28.4	17.4	20.9	139.8	79.2	69.2	103.8	177.2
Operating profit/employee	10.7	9.9	4.7	10.4	9.4	26.3	14.1	11.1	30.3	31.8
EBIT/employee	8.2	9.2	4.6	6.9	8.1	23.8	11.5	10.9	29.8	28.0
Net profit/employee	7.5	6.3	3.5	6.1	5.6	13.5	6.6	6.4	18.3	16.2

CTP: Cambridge Technology Partners; TSC: Technology Solutions Company; EBIT: earnings before interest and tax.
Source: P. Ghemawat et al., "The Indian Software Industry at the Millenium," HBS 700-036, Ex. 7

the client, interacting with the home base via satellite-enabled communications on issues such as changing specifications, obtaining clarity on issues, getting permission for changes, and so forth. Once the project was completed, a team would travel to the client's site to install the software, test it, and train the client's staff.

Over time, Infosys had begun serving mission-critical software systems to high-profile clients such as Nortel, Reebok, and Nordstrom. For example, beginning in 1992 with simple tool development for Bell Northern Research, an R&D division of Northern Telecom (as Nortel was then called) generating $200,000 of revenues, Infosys's relationship with Nortel blossomed by 1998 into intense collaboration with core R&D engineering groups and even working with Nortel clients generating $8 million in revenues. The Seattle-based retailer, Nordstrom, hired Infosys to create customized software to handle inventories centrally while allowing tailoring to vary with local tastes. The software was subsequently installed on their systems all over the United States.

As management confidence in its delivery capability strengthened, Infosys began to take on an increasing share of the risk involved with software development. To build long-term relationships, Infosys began offering some of its clients "managed software solutions"—fixed-time, fixed-price projects with quality guarantees that took away several of the risks that clients commonly faced in outsourcing software projects. These clients were so satisfied with Infosys's delivery against its promises that, by 1998, more than 75 percent of Infosys's revenues came from repeat customers. Clients benefited from GDCs in two ways—the lower overall cost of software development; and a 24-hour work cycle (the Indian programmers worked while their U.S. counterparts slept, and vice versa) enabled by broadband communication that allowed rapid implementation of software projects.

As an increasing number of projects began to flow in, Infosys began locating its GDCs in cities—Bangalore, Chennai, Coimbatore, Pune, and Man-

galore—that were rich in engineering and technical colleges. "Proximity to engineering colleges afforded us relatively easy access to a base of young graduates with strong analytical skills," remarked an Infosys executive in 2000. "It also allowed engineers from all over India to work for Infosys and yet live as close to their homes as possible. Today, we are not just a Bangalore company, but an Indian company with a Bangalore base. Tomorrow, we will be not just an Indian company with global reach, but a global company headquarted in India."

Murthy emphasized that the firm's GDC model included work at both ODCs and proximity development centers (PDCs), teams of Infosys employees located close to the customers. Infosys had set up PDCs in Fremont and Boston. Comprising both marketing and development personnel, PDCs focused on aspects of implementation that required physical proximity to customers. Management expected the PDCs to both improve customer satisfaction and manage expectations better. "The GDC model," opined an Infosys executive, "will help change the image of Infosys from purely an offshore development company to an all-purpose global IT-based problem solver. If implemented correctly, it will convince customers that Infosys can deliver on any software project, wherever it is located, and whatever its scope, with maximum customer comfort."

Software Services and Products

"I work with four business principles," reasoned Murthy.

> First, predictability of revenues. Every year you must be able to say, "Next year my revenues will be so much." Second is the sustainability of those predictions. Once you have predicted, you must make sure that the business actually comes. Third is the profitability of those revenues. Fourth, it's not sufficient to have just predictability, sustainability, and profitability—you need to have a "de-risking" model. Our de-risking model

says that we must have a balanced portfolio of markets, technologies, and practices.[8]

To achieve these four business objectives, Infosys complemented its offshore software development service with other software services and products.

Software Maintenance

Infosys provided software maintenance services, especially maintaining legacy systems inherited from previous generations of computers. The almost 11-hours difference in time zones between India and the United States was leveraged to provide maintenance services to U.S.-based systems while usage was low. Rejecting the popular image of software maintenance, Murthy observed: "Maintenance is only 5 percent bug-fixing. Most of the work lies in organically evolving the software to keep pace with changes in the marketplace."

Software Reengineering

Software reengineering helped clients migrate to new technologies without jettisoning existing systems that were rich in functionality. Companies that had a significant proportion of their existing systems in mainframe-based technologies but wanted to migrate to client/server-based models or companies that used nonrelational databases and wanted to move to using relational databases were examples of these kind of customers.

Y2K Compliance

During the late 1990s, several IT firms, Infosys included, worked with clients to ensure that the software they were using was "Y2K compliant," that is, free of a particular bug that could generate errors based on the logic of the programs and cause tremendous losses. This involved painstaking line-by-line parsing of software to identify and remedy the bug. The cost of fixing the problem in computer systems was estimated at approximately $300 billion worldwide.

Several Indian software companies took on contracts from U.S.-based companies to make their systems Y2K compliant. Infosys managers were aware that Y2K was a "cash cow" but could also be "a dangerous addiction with painful withdrawal symptoms." Between 1996 and 1999, even as global Y2K-related business expanded, Infosys's Y2K-related revenues declined from 31 percent to less than 20 percent of revenues, reflecting management's focus on reducing Y2K exposure. Management aggressively increased the budget for retraining software engineers on Y2K-related projects in new areas of expertise, including enterprise resource planning (ERP) and e-commerce.

ERP and E-Commerce Consulting

Infosys executives expected its new ERP and Internet units to generate significant revenues in the future. ERP systems included consulting services, customization of ERP packages to suit customer needs, and training customer personnel to run and maintain the software. Infosys had also developed an Internet consulting practice, offering services to companies ranging from getting started on the Internet to full-scale e-commerce solutions. In 1999 e-commerce consulting contributed 19 percent of Infosys's total revenues.[9] Besides generating new revenues to replace Y2K-related revenues, implementing e-commerce solutions would also engage Infosys's software programmers in an exciting and challenging field, and help Infosys build deep domain knowledge in e-commerce.

Product Development

As early as 1988, Infosys attempted to diversify from software services into software products. Sensing that the technology solutions that banks in developing countries needed would be different from the ones in vogue in developed countries, the firm conceived and developed Bancs2000, a software package for retail and corporate banking. Although Bancs2000 received "good" product reviews, its sales over the next decade were middling at best, never approaching the promise that initial market analysis had projected. "We had thought we could be both a services and a product company," reflected Dinesh.

> But we realized that product development requires a different, venture-capitalist mindset. It requires a willingness to stomach a J-curve cash flow—negative cash flows for several years before seeing positive returns—whereas services are cash positive from the get-go. Competition is also more intense in product business. Because of the much larger economies of scale in product development, a product company cannot afford to be number three or four in its market segment; it has to be number one or two. Employee lifestyles are also different in product and services companies.

When in 1993 Infosys designed and sold to GE's appliances unit a warehouse management software solution, it again faced the opportunity of converting this solution into a product. Rather than run the business within Infosys, the firm, in 1996, co-invested with venture capitalists such as Draper International in a new firm, Yantra Corp., based in Acton, MA, to market and sell the software product, named Eagle, to U.S. companies.

Murthy did not rule out Infosys ever doing product development again. If innovative product ideas came out of work done in the new e-commerce solutions area, for example, Murthy speculated that some variant of the Yantra model would be used, with Infosys playing the role of venture capitalist. Infosys itself, would remain a focused services company. For product development to be attractive in its own right, Murthy observed, "the product we develop must be large, lending itself to big ticket sales, and offer significant scope for services, such as training and installation—more like SAP and less like Microsoft." Added Nilekani, who had been named chief operating officer in 1998: "Software products become commoditized. Services are where the action is. And whereever there are services to be offered, we'll be there."

INTERNAL STRUCTURE AND PROCESSES

Organization Structure

Exhibit 6 lists Infosys's founders, board members, and governance council members. Till 1999 Infosys was organized around nine strategic business units (SBUs). Each SBU was run as a self-contained organization, with functions like sales, marketing, and delivery services coordinated within. In addition to allowing each area to focus deeply on what it did best and develop domain expertise in its own area, this structure helped the firm develop the next generation of Infosys leaders by giving SBU managers a free hand as CEOs of their SBUs. Over the years, Infosys had built a core of expertise in a variety of areas, ranging from banking and finance to retailing and telecommunications. The telecommunications practice had built such deep relationships with some of its clients that entire SBUs were set up to deal with specific clients such as Nortel Networks, helping Infosys deepen and broaden the relationships.

To take advantage of potential economies of scale across the different business units, in October 1999, the firm was reorganized into practice units (PUs) organized by geography, with dedicated sales and software delivery organizations. Although each PU had coordinators for support functions, human resources, finance, education, research, quality, IS, and administration were among the 10 functional groups that offered centralized support to all the PUs. A centralized domain competency group was established to nurture skill development and deployment for the entire company. Exhibit 7 provides an organization chart of the firm.

Management Style and Values

When Infosys was founded in 1981, the founding team established as an article of faith their belief that their company would live or die by the quality of their people. Infosys's head of strategic planning S. Sukumar observed: "For a professional

EXHIBIT 6 Infosys Founders, Board of Directors, and Management Council

Infosys Founders
N.R. Narayana Murthy
Nandan M. Nilekani
N.S. Raghavan
S. Gopalakrishnan
K. Dinesh
S.D. Shibulal
Ashok Arora[a]

[a]Mr. Arora quit in 1989 to pursue other opportunities in the U.S.

Board of Directors, 2000

Name	Designation
N.R. Narayana Murthy	Chairman and CEO
Nandan M. Nilekani	MD, president, and COO
Susim M. Datta	Director
Deepak M. Satwalekar	Director
Ramesh Vangal	Director
Marti Subrahmanyam	Director
Philip Yeo	Director
S. Gopalakrishnan	Deputy MD
K. Dinesh	Director
S.D. Shibulal	Director

MD: managing director

Management Council, 2000

Name	Designation
Nandan M. Nilekani	MD, president, and COO
T.V. Mohandas Pai	SVP—CFO, Facilities
Ajay Dube	VP—delivery (Europe)
P. Balasubramanian	SVP—Domain competency
V. Balakrishnan	AVP—Finance
Basab Pradhan	VP—Sales (WENA)
Depak Sinha	Sr. manager—Computers and Communication
K. Dinesh	Director—HRD, IS, Quality and Productivity and Communications Design
Girish Vaidya	SVP—Banking Business Unit
S. Gopalakrishnan	Dy. MD—Customer Service and Technology
Hema Ravichandar	SVP—HRD
Jan DeSmet	VP—Business Consulting
Phaneesh Murthy	SVP—Sales and Marketing and Communications and Product Services
M.S.S. Prabhu	SVP—Engineering Services and Consultancy
A. Raghavan	AVP—Quality and Productivity
Raghupathi Bhandi	SVP—Delivery (Enterprise Solutions)
Rajiv Kuchhal	AVP—Communications and Product Services, Nortel and PCC, Development Center (Mohali)
S.D. Shibulal	Director—Customer delivery
P.R. Sobha Meera	VP—Sales (CENA)
Srinath Batni	SVP—Delivery (WENA)
Vasudeva Rao	SVP—Delivery (CENA)
S. Yegneshwar	VP—Education and research

VP: vice president; SVP: senior vice president; AVP: assistant vice president; CENA: Canada and North America; WENA: West North America.
Source: Infosys.

EXHIBIT 7 Infosys Organization Chart, January 2000

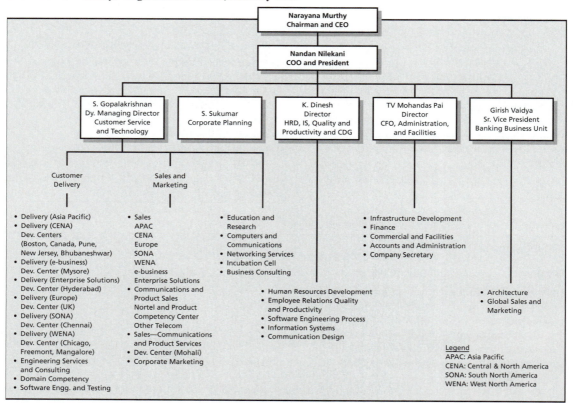

Source: Infosys.

services firm, it is not a cliché, it is a survival imperative!" From its early days, Infosys's founders paid attention to what they called "the important things"—employee empowerment, wealth-creation, wealth-sharing, an open culture that gave respect to ideas regardless of where they originated from, an emphasis on training, and building leaders.

Murthy believed in leadership by example. He would breeze into the office at 7:30 A.M. every day, work ceaselessly for 12 hours (or more), and then return home. "I don't go for parties," he remarked, "and I don't watch TV."[10] In 1996 Murthy was named IT businessman of the year by *BusinessWeek;* in 1999 he was conferred with the Sir Visweswaraiah and the Rajyothsava awards by Karnataka government and industry associations and named businessman of the year by *Business India.* Marveled an observer: "He's got time for everyone. Sometimes, you wonder if the man ever says no to anyone. The humility, the tranquility, and the straightforwardness, so far alien attributes to the world of Indian business, have been all honed to a nicety—and converted into a trademark management style."[11] Responded Murthy: "On a scale of one to ten," he remarked, "I will give myself six as a leader."[12] Pointing to Murthy's legendary modesty, an executive commented: "Infosys's values are steeped in a middle-class mentality."

"One of our biggest challenges at Infosys is running a first world firm in a third world country," reflected Murthy.

Every morning, our professionals leave the warm embrace of their homes, where there is so much love and affection for them but there are few physical amenities. Then they travel through miles of dirty, rutted roads on the sides of which they see so much misery, sorrow, and pain. The travel brings them to a campus that is as beautiful and well kept as the best in the world. Immediately upon arrival, they start working to the standards and expectations of their first world clients. And every evening, they traverse this journey through cultures in reverse. This culture shock is very tough on our smart and sensitive professionals. But just as the annealing process of rapidly heating and then rapidly cooling a metal makes the metal stronger, I believe that these frequent and rapid transitions between cultures makes our professionals stronger and tougher, so they can become robust bridges between cultures.

One of the tenets that Murthy practiced and preached was that Infosys employees act with integrity in all situations, even at the risk of losing business. "Our value system can be summed up in one sentence: 'It is better to lose $100 million than a good night's sleep,'" he said. "And the softest pillow is a clear conscience. Never, ever do anything that is illegal or unethical, vis-à-vis society, competitors, or customers."[13]

An Infosys employee who had joined the firm in 1996 said that she had learned that the most distinguishing characteristic of Infosys was its "people, people, people." She added: "Compared to other companies my college mates joined, the only things that really matter at Infosys are 'ideas' and 'execution.' Ideas flow nonhierarchically and senior employees interact with junior colleagues with informality. Whenever I have had apprehensions about some issues, I have gone straight to my superiors, something I could not have dared to do at any other Indian company."

Hiring, Training, and Retention

"If there is one challenge that the Indian software industry faces," observed Murthy,

it is: how do you recruit, enable, empower, and retain the best and brightest professionals? We don't have a demand limit. We have a supply limit. That's where the challenge is. Those of us who will be able to do this can grow much faster.[14]

Infosys scouted for talent at the top Indian universities and engineering colleges, recruiting from 55 colleges nationwide. The firm was one of the sought-after employers at India's leading engineering colleges, such as the six Indian Institutes of Technology. In 1998 the firm received 75,000 job applications for 1,500 positions; in 1999 it received 184,000 applications and made 3,300 offers.[15] "In India, software is the industry of choice for bright young people," noted Nilekani, "and Infosys is the company of choice for software professionals."[16] Recent recruits emphasized that they were attracted to Infosys by the diversity of work experience it promised and an informal work culture.

Prospective employees were tested not for computer programming, a skill Infosys executives believed could be taught easily, but for (a) analytical and problem-solving skills to help dynamic learning, the key to success in an industry where the state of the art changed rapidly; and (b) communication skills—not just language skills but the ability to get ideas across in both interactive and noninteractive situations—essential to developing deep and long-term relationships with clients. New employees underwent a 14-week orientation and training program that included courses on programming, working with specific tools, and software applications. In consideration for this training, Infosys recruits signed a bond to stay with the company for at least one year.

Unlike other Indian software companies, Infosys abjured asking its professionals going abroad on assignments to sign bonds pledging ongoing loyalty. In 2000, professional turnover rate at Infosys was approximately 10 percent, about half the industry average. A "large fraction" of this turnover, in the estimation of senior vice president of human resources Hema Ravichandar, comprised those who left Infosys for higher education, typically with Infosys's blessings. On occasions, the professionals sent to overseas clients "hunted" for and won local jobs overseas. A few left the firm to set up their own entrepreneurial ventures. Rarely did professionals leave Infosys for Indian rivals. "The chance to get some high-flying stock has done much to keep programmers from leaving," noted an observer.[17] "It's not the golden handcuffs [that keeps you in the firm]," countered a 34-year-old multimillionaire Infosys executive, "You feel you need to contribute here."[18] "I would contemplate moving from Infosys," reflected a manager who had joined Infosys in 1994,

> if (a) the people and environment changed for the worse, and (b) the work became dull and repetitive. On the latter score, I have no concerns. We are doing very interesting and challenging work. On the first, however, I am concerned by the furious pace at which Infosys is adding people. Our employee base has grown from about 3,000 in early 1999 to over 4,500 by early 2000. The place is becoming impersonal. I barely know half the people I see in the corridors anymore. What makes Infosys different is its open, nonhierarchical culture. I worry if we have the ability to adequately assimilate and train so many new employees in our habits.

"We've done certain things to keep the organization nimble while handling growth," Murthy reasoned. "We have created small units of 300 each within the organization—each of these are self-contained units and the bonding among the people is very, very close."[19] The rapid growth had helped the firm offer career growth opportunities to its professionals. "We are growing so fast," noted Ravichandar, "that many people with two to three years experience are getting into managerial roles."[20] However, an employee with three years experience at the company complained of the sudden increase in responsibility. "You land up at the client site," he remarked, "and all of a sudden, you've got far more responsibility than you can handle. Leadership is basically thrust on you and you learn to cope with it. Help is available, but you have to seek it. But you need to know that, and nobody tells you that it is available." Countered another Infosys employee: "You can create a role for yourself. I don't have to become a project manager if I don't want to. I can focus on the technology and become a technical consultant."[21]

Outstanding Performance

Following its initial public offering (IPO) in 1993, Infosys floated several bonus issues. By 1999, it was estimated that an Infosys employee who had joined the company at the time of its IPO and had held on to options would be in possession of Infosys stock worth more than rupees 10 million (approximately $250,000). As of May 2000, the firm's stock option plan had made 400 Infosys professionals U.S. dollar millionaires.[22] In 1999 Infosys was named India's most admired company, ahead of multinational and family-owned companies (see Exhibit 3). Started in 1981 with a $250 investment, the company was expected to earn $61 million on sales in excess of $200 million in the year ending March 2000.[23] "We have conveyed a message," Murthy averred,

> that it is possible to live in India and add value to the nation. The Infosys experiment has demonstrated that it is possible to create wealth legally and ethically, create quality jobs and a challenging work environment, and leverage sweat equity in this country.[24]

Infosys was not the only Indian software firm to record outstanding performance in the decade of the 1990s. The removal of government controls had proved to be a major catalyst for the Indian software industry's growth, from $10 million in 1986 to $2.2 billion in 1997 (see Exhibit 8). Between 1993 and 1997, software industry grew at an annual rate of 52.6 percent. Software exports grew from $200 million in 1993 to $1.08 billion in 1997, an annual growth rate of 48 percent. Hoping to win a greater share of the lucrative ODC business, Indian software companies increased their quality focus, seeking ISO 9000 and Software Engineering Institute certifications. In 1997, contract programming and offshore development made up 58.7 percent and 30.2 percent respectively of all software exports. (Exhibit 9 lists Indian software export destinations; Exhibit 10 names the top 10 Indian software exporters.)

The ADR Offering

In March 1999, Infosys tapped the public markets again, this time in the United States, with a $75 million issue of 1.8 million American Depository Receipts (ADRs) priced at $34 each on the NASDAQ stock exchange, becoming the first Indian company to be listed on an American stock exchange. The offering tapped into American investors' appetite for emerging-markets-based information technology firms to raise capital for Infosys's continued expansion. To this reasoning, Murthy added three more:

First, a successful IPO, and subsequent chart-busting performance will draw attention to Infosys, and by extension, its service offerings. This will increase Infosys's name recognition in U.S. markets and boost the comfort level of Infosys's premier customers. Being listed on the NASDAQ can be a crucial first step to our goal of getting into the rolodexes of the CEOs and CIOs of Fortune 500 companies.

Second, as Infosys expands the scope and scale of its services, Infosys has to become considerably more global in its presence. The global delivery model, with its emphasis on both local and remote elements in the implementation of IT projects, requires Infosys to boost its local presence, closer to client sites. The ADR will allow us to offer our international employees U.S.-denominated stock options, thereby linking their compensation to the firm's overall success and making it comparable to their peers in other technology companies.

Third, the ADR can serve as a valuable currency if we wish to acquire companies with deep domain knowledge, tools, and skills in chosen niche areas rather than build in-house expertise.

Concurred an observer: "Beyond these concrete advantages [of raising capital and attracting international talent by offering stock options] lay something a bit more ephemeral, touching on matters of status. Despite a roster of big-name North American clients, Infosys was battling the crass Western perception that a smart, honest, reputable company could never come out of a country where cows still run in the street. A NASDAQ listing would give a stamp of approval."[25]

Over the next nine months, the ADR prices rose more than sevenfold, 150 percent faster than the price of the underlying Infosys shares, and the firm's market valuation was close to the $25 billion mark (see Exhibit 2).

CHALLENGE FOR THE FUTURE: BUILDING A FIRST WORLD COMPANY

To be a truly global company, we should raise capital where it is cheapest, produce software where it is most cost effective, and sell our services where it is most profitable.

Narayana Murthy

EXHIBIT 8 The Indian IT Industry, 1995–2000

	1994–95		1995–96		1996–97		1997–98		1998–99		1999–2000	
	Rs. b	$ m	Rs. b	$ m	Rs. b	$ m	Rs. b	$ m	Rs. b	$ m	Rs. b	$ m
Software												
Domestic	10.7	350	16.7	490	24.1	670	35.1	950	49.5	1,250	72	1,700
Exports	15.4	485	25.2	734	39.0	1,083	65.3	1,750	109.4	2,650	171.5	4,000
Total	26.1	835	41.9	1,224	63.1	1,753	100.4	2,700	158.9	3,900	243.5	5,700
Hardware												
Domestic	18.3	590	35.6	1,037	37.8	1,050	45.0	1,205	42.4	1,026	62.0	1,450
Exports	5.5	177	1.2	35	10.3	286	7.4	201	0.2	4	3.7	86
Total	23.8	767	36.8	1,072	48.1	1,336	52.4	1,406	42.5	1,030	65.7	1,536
Peripherals												
Domestic	4.6	148	6.7	196	6.5	181	8.3	229	13.6	329	18.7	435
Exports	0.2	6	0.2	6	0.5	14	0.7	19	0.7	18	1.2	27
Total	4.8	154	6.9	202	7.1	195	9.0	248	14.3	347	19.9	462
Training	3.3	107	5.0	145	6.6	183	9.4	263	12.5	302	17.2	400
Maintenance	4.4	142	5.9	172	6.6	182	8.2	221	9.8	236	11.3	263
Networking and others	1.1	36	2.4	710	5.6	156	7.2	193	9.8	237	13.3	310
Grand total	63.5	2,041	98.9	2,886	137.0	3,805	186.6	5,031	247.8	6,052	370.8	8,671

Source: Nasscom, www.nasscom.org, accessed April 16, 2001.

EXHIBIT 9

Indian Software Export Destination, 1999–2000

e: estimated.
Source: Nasscom, www.nasscom.org accessed April 16, 2001.

Region	% Share
North America (U.S. and Canada)	62.0
Europe	23.5
Japan	3.5
Rest of Asia, Australia, and New Zealand	6.5
Rest of the world	4.5

"My role as chairman and CEO," remarked Murthy,

is to make sure the organization is successful not just in the present but also in the future. We have just completed our infancy. We are toddlers now. We will become adults if we can show longevity for 40 years. And to do so, we need to establish global brand equity. If you ask people in the United States, Europe, or Japan: "Which is the company you want to outsource software to?" we want them to say "Infosys." We aren't there yet. To get there, we need locals to build relationships. They understand the local culture. We also believe that Infosys

has a responsibility to create jobs in the markets from which we derive revenues. So, we are hoping to become not just an Indian company but a global firm. But if we want to become a truly global firm, we need to refine not only the art of selling internationally but also the art of recruitment, compensation, and training on a global basis, and the art of teamwork across borders.

In the early 1980s, Infosys's main competitors were companies such as Tata Consultancy Services, whose stock-in-trade was remote software services. "To some extent," commented Murthy, "we still compete with them. But Infosys's future

EXHIBIT 10 Top Ten Indian Software Exporters, 1998–2000

	1998–1999		1999–2000e	
Rank	Name	Exports (Rs. b)	Name	Exports (Rs. m)
1	Tata Consultancy Services	15.2	Tata Consultancy Services	18.2
2	Wipro Infotech	6.3	Wipro Technologies	10.4
3	Pentafour Software	5.1	Infosys Technologies	8.7
4	Infosys Technologies	5.0	Satyam Computer Services	6.6
5	NIIT	4.0	HCL Technologies	6.3
6	Satyam Computer Services	3.8	NIIT	5.5
7	Cognizant Technology Solutions	2.9	Silverline Technologies	4.3
8	IBM Global Services India	2.3	Cognizant Technology Solutions	4.1
9	DSQ Software	2.2	Pentamedia Graphics	3.9
10	Tata Infotech	2.2	Pentasoft Technologies	3.5

e: estimated.
Source: Nasscom, www.nasscom.org accessed April 16, 2001.

lies in moving further up the value chain, in executing more complex projects for our customers, with higher value-addition. We want our clients to give us problem statements, rather than simply ask us to implement solutions that have already been devised." Observed a research analyst: "Infosys's prospects are bright. It has cost-effective, highly skilled talent, but will have to convince customers that they should hire it for more than just low-cost work."[26]

In the higher-value space, Infosys's competitors would be the likes of Cambridge Technology Partners (1999 revenues $612 million, EBIT $81 million), Electronic Data Systems (1999 revenues $17 billion, EBIT $1 billion) and the Big Five accounting firms. But even as Infosys was moving up the value chain, it was losing the advantage of lower employee costs. Infosys's India-based employee costs (16 percent of total costs) were rising 25 percent per year and non-India–based employee costs (21 percent of costs), were rising at 10 percent per year.

It was imperative, Murthy and his team believed, that by the time the cost advantage disappeared, Infosys should execute several "marquee" projects, build significant brand equity in its client space, sharply boost its domain knowledge, and become a truly global company, in terms of its client mix and employees. Just as important, observed Nilekani, would be keeping the level of excitement and focus amongst its employees high and maintaining the small company environment and entrepreneurial spirit as the firm grew larger. Nilekani believed that for veteran professionals to stay motivated and new employees to choose Infosys as a career option, Infosys management needed to share with the employees the excitement and challenge of being a part of Infosys—often characterized by Murthy as "a first world company in a third world country"—embarking on the "great journey" of taking on first world companies several times its size, with several times its financial heft and name recognition.

References

1. *"Tata Consultancy Services: Globalization of Software Services,"* July 1997, Stanford University Graduate School of Business case study no. SM-18; and C.R. Subramanian, *India and the Computer,* Oxford University Press, 1992.

2. Adapted from "HCL America," HBS case no. 393-030

3. "The Asiaweek Power 50," *Asiaweek,* May 26, 2000, p. 66.

4. "From India to the World," *Asiaweek,* May 26, 2000, p. 87.

5. Srikant Srinivas, "Human Touch to Wealth," *Economy and Business,* September 20, 1999, pp. I–II.

6. Talk at TiE-Atlantic meeting, Burlington, MA, April 1998.

7. Avnish Bajaj, Michael Kadyan, Devtosh Khare and Suvir Sujan, *"The Indian Software Industry,"* HBS Industry Note.

8. Yogesh Sharma, "The Lightning Spark," *Silicon India,* August 1998, pp. 50–52.

9. "From India to the World."

10. Rahul Joshi, "Infosys Has Completed the Infancy Stage," *The Economic Times,* January 3, 2000.

11. Ibid.

12. Ibid.

13. Partly derived from Sharma, "The Lightning Spark."

14. Sharma, "The Lightning Spark."

15. R. Sukumar, "Infosys: Wealth and Values," *Business Today,* January 7, 2001, p. 131.

16. Claire MacDonald and Jagdish Rattanani, "Programming for Profits," *Asiaweek,* June 1999, p. 59.

17. Ibid.

18. Ibid.

19. Joshi, "Infosys Has Completed the Infancy Stage."

20. R. Sukumar, "Infosys: Wealth and Values."

21. Ibid.

22. "From India to the World."

23. Ibid.

24. Sharma, "The Lightning Spark."

25. Eric Pfeiffer, "From India to America," *Forbes ASAP,* August 23, 1999, pp. 19–24.

26. Sadanand Dhume, "Life after Y2K," *Far Eastern Economic Review,* September 16, 1999, p. 59.

Becoming a Professional

PERSONAL LEARNING

The final module focuses on helping readers become better prepared to grow and develop as their careers progress within PSFs. The management of one's career is a dynamic process that involves professionals and their networks inside and outside the firm. Essential elements of a successful professional at a PSF include a proactive career management approach, effective processes of giving and receiving feedback, a clear ethical perspective, and balance between private and professional lives, among others.

PROFESSIONAL ETHICS

The first and second cases of this module center on the issue of professional ethics. In Tim Hertach at GL Consulting, the protagonist must decide whether he should confront his boss over billing practices that he considers questionable or whether he should avoid a confrontation to protect his career and protect his ability to fight more politically prudent battles later. In Professionals' Quandaries, we consider five caselets in which professionals confront ethical dilemmas. Four of these caselets were developed from real situations. The goal of these sessions is to allow readers to further their own thinking on how to determine when they face

This note was prepared by Professor Thomas DeLong, Professor Ashish Nanda, Dean's Research Fellow Scot Landry, and Ying Liu (MBA 2001).

an ethical situation and, when faced with an ethical situation, to know how to deal with it appropriately.

STRATEGIES FOR SUCCESSFUL STARTS AND PERSONAL BALANCE

We conclude the module with two cases that resonate with most readers. In The First Six Months: Launching a PSF Career, one caselet considers two different strategies for getting off to a good start in a PSF career. Another caselet focuses on practical tactics for recovering from a slow start. The goal of these caselets is to provide readers the opportunities to reflect on practical real-life game plans for ensuring a successful launch to their careers. In our final case of the module, we move into choppy waters by discussing how to balance work with personal lives. This discussion is very relevant for those working or planning to work in PSFs because professionals in these organizations are convinced they work harder than others in other professions. We offer some strategies to help maintain some sense of balance between professional and private life, and we discuss coping mechanisms that may assist the professional succeed in an ever-turbulent business sector.

TIM HERTACH AT GL CONSULTING

Professionals must confront ethical issues daily. It is part of the world in which they live. Consultancies set their own ethical standards. Individuals within those practices have the opportunity to assess ethical situations in the context of self-interest. Tim Hertach meets the enemy and perceives the enemy is not only within the firm but running the firm. He has invested time and energy into his internal relationships and is doing well. Through the GL Consulting case we see a few activities that seem questionable to the protagonist. We question whether Hertach was showing courage or being foolhardy. We question which of his behaviors were those that illustrated less than professional judgment. We have to wrestle with whether or not the train has come off the track for GL Consulting or for Hertach or for both.

Our discussion centers on how one frames an ethical context. When do we take risks and stand up to be counted? Or do any of the options outlined in the case merit a second analysis as we study the behavior of Hertach? We conclude the case by identifying how to balance ethical and personal concerns and how to determine when to raise an issue to the point of questioning ethical behavior of colleagues. We ask what price we will be willing to pay to take a stand for our ethics (like Hertach did).

One potential framework[1] centers on 12 questions: (1) Have you defined the ethical problem correctly? (2) How would you define the problem if you stood on

---

[1] Laura L. Nash, "Ethics without the Sermon," *Harvard Business Review* reprint no. 81609, November 1981.

the other side of the fence? (3) How did this situation occur in the first place? (4) To whom and to what do you give your loyalty as a person and as a member of the corporation? (5) What is your intention in making this decision? (6) How does this intention compare with the probable results? (7) Whom could your decision or action injure? (8) Can you discuss the problem with the affected parties before you make your decision? (9) Are you confident that your position will be as valid over a long period of time as it seems now? (10) Could you disclose without qualms your decision or action to your boss, your CEO, the board of directors, your family, or society as a whole? (11) What is the symbolic potential of your action if understood? If misunderstood? (12) Under what conditions would you allow exceptions to your stand?

PROFESSIONALS' QUANDARIES

The five caselets within the Professionals' Quandaries case study are real situations that professionals have faced in their careers. "Spaulding v. Zimmerman" addresses the issue of the professional responsibility that the doctor, lawyer, and insurance executive have to Spaulding. Must they tell him of his potentially life-threatening condition? Is there a difference between their professional responsibilities and their human responsibilities?

The "Stacey Duquette" caselet focuses on the obligation of junior professionals when they become aware that leaders of the firm have misrepresented the firm's capabilities in order to win new business. Should Duquette take action and, if so, what steps she should take? We focus on the difference between "espoused ethics," of a professional and the "ethics-in-use." If all consulting firms misrepresent themselves and overpromise, does it lessen any obligation Duquette or her firm has to their clients?

The "Lisa Jordan" caselet centers on the conflicts of interest faced by professionals in PSFs that have multidisciplinary practices. Jordan, a leading technology research analyst, is approached at her firm's Christmas party by a colleague from the corporate finance department. She believes that her colleague deliberately "mentions" that the firm is up to win a high-profile equity underwriting engagement in the next week in order to get Jordan to delay publishing a report that will opine that firms in the potential client's industry have overpriced stocks. Jordan feels that the Chinese wall in her firm has been breached, but she wonders what she should do based on the information she now has. We consider the question of how professionals should balance collegiality against professional responsibility.

The "Carlos Garcia" caselet concerns the professional issues regarding the paying of bribes in certain third-world countries. If bribes are the way business gets done in a country how should professionals reconcile that with their espoused ethics or even the ethics-in-use that the firm professes in other countries? The "Dexter Simmons" caselet focuses on the practice of professionals misrepresenting themselves in order to obtain data for their clients. Readers again consider the question: If every other firm (or every other professional in my firm) is doing this, is it ethical for me to do it?

As we wrap up the case, we consider five important questions: (1) Why are ethics particularly critical for professionals? (2) In what circumstances do ethical quandaries seem to arise more often? (3) Must all professionals "grow up" and lose their "innocent" ethics in favor of adopting a professional ethics-in-use or relative ethics? (4) How should professionals ensure that they do not slide down an ethical slippery slope? (5) What do professionals gain by being ethical?

TRADE-OFFS: JUGGLING CAREERS IN PSFs WITH PRIVATE LIFE

The discussion of the protagonists who are trying to balance private and professional life gives us an opportunity to reflect about our own careers and the dynamics in play as we make career-related decisions. We end the book with this subject to highlight its importance and to allow readers to integrate previous learning from the book with personal beliefs they have regarding the appropriate balance between private and professional life. We also discuss the warning signs that manifest themselves in the context of dyadic relationships. One of the central goals of this case is to have readers realize the importance of having a strategic plan for their private lives.

The key teaching objectives of the case are (1) to underscore the fact that professionals tend to focus more on work because success is most often better defined, specified, and quicker to achieve at work than at home; (2) to discuss how the intangibility of the PSF work products often causes these organizations to set up artificial barriers and hurdles so that professionals might demonstrate commitment to the organization; (3) to promote understanding of the powerful role that organizational culture plays in the balancing act between the demands of work and family; (4) to highlight warning signs that indicate that the personal support system in a relationship is out of balance; and (5) to introduce the theory that identifies patterns and implications for healthy, dynamic family system functioning. These patterns extend into the family system to influence how its members interact, as well as how the family makes decisions as a system.

All those who want success in PSFs and desire a fulfilling private life know the difficulty of balancing the two. Part of the ethos and economics of PSFs is to leverage their human capital by working professionals long hours. Professionals with strong potential within the organization are routinely expected to show their willingness to sacrifice—often at a distance from their home bases and support systems. The challenge of managing a relationship with an ambitious spouse, and the added responsibility of children, provides the structure and ingredients of the three caselets.

The case provides readers with the opportunity to explore the conflicting tensions of professional and private life within the context of committed, two-career relationships with children, as well as a single parent with children. It directs our attention to two bedrock issues: What does success mean when one is simultaneously attempting to function as a spouse, parent, and professional? Further, how do all these challenges interrelate?

It is important to note that while the protagonists in the case are confronting the challenges of child-rearing and career, all of the challenges have a generic component. The learning outcomes apply to all professionals who have support systems and careers. It is much less significant whether those relationships be with partners, friends, relatives, children, parents, or others than that they exist and must be balanced with the demands of work and one's own personal goals. More important, the case gives readers the opportuntiy to think strategically about the ways in which they plan moving forward to balance private and professional life.

THE FIRST SIX MONTHS: LAUNCHING A PSF CAREER

The case is divided into two caselets that cover very different issues. The first caselet sets a context in which two best friends are making a bet regarding whose strategy will be most effective in achieving success in the first six months of their careers. With very similar backgrounds and education, they will be joining the same consulting firm but will approach the first six months very differently. Both contestants are well aware of each other's strategies. While they both share the same goal to quickly achieve star status, their strategies and the trade-offs they are planning to make are very different. Both friends are confident that their respective approaches are right. The case outlines the differences in approach between the two friends and allows readers to determine for themselves which elements of both strategies they will take as their own as they launch their careers.

Liam Quinlan's approach to beginning his job is based on breadth of focus. Do not go deep too quickly. Focus on learning the overall client needs for the business and worry less about learning the technical dimensions of a particular function. Having not to focus on depth, Quinlan is freed up to self-promote and let others know in discrete ways how competent he is. Quinlan believes that no one will realize how competent he is unless he discretely sells himself.

Quinlan believes that networking should be done with peers and managers who are responsible for his day-to-day performance. He will focus on learning the ropes and ethos of the organization before striking out in one particular area of expertise. Once he has impressed his peers and managers through his interest in them and in learning the system, he can focus on the technical expertise later. The underlying theme for Quinlan is networking with as many people as possible. This theme holds true in activities centered on recruiting as well. Quinlan hopes that others will make the leap and believe that he will be excellent with clients as well. Quinlan wants to throw the net wide and develop relationships through the system as fast as he can in hopes that others will sell him. He also wants to dispel any fears that his universe only revolves around the Harvard Business School.

Quinlan plans on accepting the assignments he receives and gaining a reputation for being a team player and being easy to work with. Quinlan will keep some perspective with the management of time and create a work ethic that illustrates that he has a life outside of Barker Consulting. He also plans on taking a generalist approach by connecting with a number of mentors and sponsors at different levels throughout the institution. This will allow Quinlan to meet those professionals with whom he will want a long-term relationship well past the six-month time frame.

In contrast to Quinlan, John Sheehan thrives on the technical and analytical aspects of his work. He is anxious to prove himself to managers and colleagues alike that he is very good at the work itself. He wants to focus on one or two client problem areas where others will know and recognize him due to his work. His self-concept is wrapped up in the work he does in totality. Sheehan has no need to go out and "glad hand" because he knows that his work will stand for itself. He believes in the organizational review and performance evaluation system that Barker Consulting has created to monitor and evlauate its professionals. Sheehan does acknowledge that he will reach out to others senior to him as long as they have interest in those practice areas that leverage his analytical talents. Sheehan firmly believes that once others see his work they will sell him to others. If the time arises when Sheehan has extra time on his hands he wants to focus on expanding his knowledge and drive home the point that he will be the best technician in the firm. Clients will seek him out because they will know that he delivers work that exceeds expectations.

Sheehan wants to leverage his HBS experience through networking with the workforce that has a common experience. It will be too much to reach out to others in ways that do not bring more immediate results to the bottom line. Over time, Sheehan plans on branching out and creating the network that will serve him when he is more senior in the organization.

Sheehan plans on "pushing back" if necessary to get the right assignment with the right partner. He is intent on getting an assignment with a high-profile partner that will allow him to focus on his work and worry less about the politics of the system. The only part of managing image that Sheehan believes in strongly is centered on his work ethic. He wants to make it clear that he is the first to arrive at work and the last to leave. He also is clear about wanting to find a star performer who will run interference for him and teach him the ropes. Sheehan believes that it is important to hook on to a star who will take him on the journey as the star moves up the system.

We end the caselet with two questions intended to help readers define the type of professional they want to be perceived as early in their careers: (1) Which of the two would readers hire if they were running the new start-up group? (2) If you were a colleague at Barker Consulting, who would you rather work with as a team member?

The second caselet focuses on one young professional who has just received the shocking news from his mentor that he has been evaluated a "Category III." As far as Steve DiGiovanni is concerned, he has failed at his new profession and he has only been there for six months. This was his first review since graduating from the Harvard Business School. The protagonist must listen to the comments made by others about him and respond somehow to this information. As DiGiovanni sits silently, hoping that he would never have to respond, he must do something with the thoughts racing through his head. Is the feedback accurate? How should he respond? Should he leave the firm immediately? We then consider the very practical and tactical elements of responding to negative feedback. It is 10:30 A.M. and you have just finished your performance evaluation discussion with Ed Egan. What do you do now as Steve?

What can be done to turn around a bad performance evaluation? What do you do with a subordinate or individual when you have lost or are losing confidence in that person? Some of the specific behaviors we suggest are (1) keep breathing; (2) make a list of what attributes, abilities, and talents got you there in the first place; (3) make a list of success stories where the person influenced an organization or where the person felt successful; (4) do not dwell on the situation, but get back to your activities with the awareness that some of the activities will need to be done using different processes; (5) get busy learning something new about your expertise, a client, a product, or a process. Dwelling on the status quo will create a cycle of failure that will only amplify the negativity of the situation.[2]

The following points summarize general learning about successful careers in PSFs: (1) Professionals who want to thrive in PSFs must be strategic in the first six months of the career to achieve maximum leverage from their efforts, (2) There are professional skills that can be learned that will influence the outcome of one's career, (3) To be successful there are concrete, actionable steps that can be taken to increase the probability of exceeding the expectations of the firm and the expectations of the professional, (4) It is critical to understand the best way to approach networking and building relationships within the organization, (5) Most professionals will experience disappointment by not meeting expectations of a superior in an organization. It is critical to understand what actions to take when one's performance does not meet the expectations of someone in the organization.[3]

THE SPILLOVER EFFECT

The consequences of trying to balance private and professional life is that many professionals feel that there is never enough time for either role: professional or contributor in private life. Many professionals report that they feel guilty no matter how they split their time. They perceive that there is so much to accomplish that regardless of effort, they have not done enough. They feel a constant scarcity of time.

As the professional shifts from one role to the other there is a feeling that one is abandoning the other role. This recurring feeling causes tension and stress that spills over in relationships at home and at work. Evans and Bartolome emphasize

---

[2] J. H. Heskett, W. E. Sasser, and L. A. Schlesinger, *The Service Profit Chain*. New York: Free Press, 1997.
[3] For more specific tactics in PSFs, we refer readers to "Career Strategies and Tactics in PSFs," *Harvard Business School* no. 800-375.

in their research that it is typically easier to block personal tensions from home and focus on work as opposed to blocking work challenges and concentrating on personal life. They suggest that the environment at work is more conducive to task focus because the goals and objectives are so explicit.

There are generic principles that will assist the professional in the process of balancing private and professional life. These strategies become more important the higher one moves up the firm hierarchy because responsibility, learning, and compensation all increase.

Acknowledge the Pull toward Work

PSFs make it a practice to have clear and explicit measures for success. Clarity around tasks, roles, and functions are critical in achieving high performance. Thus, we move to the arenas of our lives where the criteria for success are clear and explicit. At work, professionals get feedback in a myriad of ways. Professionals are involved in tasks that can be intellectually challenging, interacting with interesting colleagues. At home, the criteria for success are less clear. How does a professional determine if he or she is successful in private life? Success is measured long term. For the professional, feedback and satisfaction may be more immediate as one works on projects, whereas work in private life may not give the professional immediate feedback for long periods of time.

It is imperative that the family support system makes the goals of the family explicit. What are the desired outcomes for the family? Is there ever a sacred time for the professional and the support system? Few couples make strategic decisions, so the more explicit organizational goals traditionally carry the day.

Know the Meaning Events Have for Other People

If a person's central focus is his or her own agenda it is difficult to relate with what is important to others. If a person's goal is to accomplish his or her things-to-do list it becomes problematic to be attentive to the wants of others. Additionally, there is a litany of activities that are important to someone. Some of those activities are as mundane as planning quiet "think" time early in the morning. It may be exercising, or it may be a family ritual or holiday—the Thanksgiving parade, the family vacation, or the visit to a particular relative. These activities may not be important to others, but a professional can make the assumption they are important because he or she values them.

The central point to this strategy is to understand that what is important to one person may not be important to others. The opposite also holds true. Employees, family members, and people within their support systems all have particular patterns, habits, celebrations, and so forth that bring meaning to their lives. What may be important to a five-year-old may hold little interest to a father. A short dramatic presentation at school with actors selected from the second garde may be only a bother for an executive.

At work, PSF professionals have commitments, family priorities, and so forth. Resentment builds over time when professionals perceive that the boss's agenda always comes first. Does the boss know what is meaningful to the key people at work? How much should the boss know? How can a boss go about figuring out what is important to those people close to him or her?

Take Time Early in Relationships

In 1986, during an HBS class session on "balancing work and family" Dr. Barry Brazelton was invited as a guest. While speaking to the students, he told a story of a time when he brought a four-month-old child into a classroom to illustrate how attentive the child was. But he also highlighted how parents often underestimate their influence on children.

While Brazelton held this child in front of the class, he asked the mother to talk quietly to the baby while standing behind Brazelton, out of sight of the child. As the mother whispered, the baby began to squirm with his mouth puckered when hearing the mother's voice, realizing that nourishment was nearby. The mother quietly stepped away and was replaced by the father. As the father spoke quietly, the baby began to arch his back and react very differently than when the mother spoke to the baby. There was clearly a different movement pattern, a different reaction to dad than mom.

Finally the father left and Brazelton asked a stranger to stand behind him and talk quietly to the child. The baby responded differently again. Three voices, three distinct reactions to the baby. A student observing this raised his hand to ask a question. He stated, "you mean that I can make a difference by the way I interact with the baby? I consider myself reasonably well educated yet I believed that my interactions with my children would really make a significant difference when they were older. I figured when the child was old enough to play tennis, go skiing, that is when I could leave my fingerprints on my children." Often we rationalize our behavior with children to justify our actions, so that we can accomplish those tasks that we believe are important. Research indicates that fathers play an important role in the development of children at a very early age (Lamb, 1990).

This private–professional tension arises in a particular way because the early years of the professional's career are key in launching a successful career. Taking time early in the relationship of children means taking the professional away from a crucial time for technical development and socialization in the profession.

Competing agendas emerge countless times as the professional makes choices that impact the degree to which success is defined at work. Awareness of these competing demands is the beginning in recognizing the myriad resource and allocation choices that emerge over time.

Take Time with Key People

There are a few activities more important than hiring excellent talent. Equally important is what we do with the talent once we have hired them. The socialization process is absolutely critical to the future success of the professional and the organization. In the 1980s, for example, few investment banking firms would hire lateral partners because the firm culture would reject the lateral hire. Regardless of how hard the individual joining the firm worked, the other partners believed the new hire was an outsider. Senior bankers needed to spend more time supporting the lateral hires.

The key people professionals identify at work and home need the professionals' time. When one makes assumptions about these relationships danger looms around the corner. A senior vice president could not fathom that one of her key direct reports would walk out on her. A head of sales at an investment bank could not understand when his best salesman left for a better offer. A manager of a mid-size consumer goods company thought his wife was kidding when she informed him she wanted a divorce. A professor at a leading business school stood up and walked out of a school counselor's office when informed that as a father he needed to spend more time with his children. Quality time has become a trite rationale for not focusing on key people and investing time in them.

Protect Private Time

Organizations make a practice of defining for us what the metrics are for success. The measurements are clear. Thus, we move to arenas of our lives where it is easiest to measure success. Work demands are clear, explicit, and well articulated. At home they are not. Few partnerships block out time to plan and think strategically about what their intentions are.

More and more family dynamics are taking on the look of a stock car race. Family members each have their own tasks and demands. The kitchen of the home becomes the "pit" where family members drop off materials and race to the next meeting or demand. Sometimes the family members may spend a few minutes at mealtime when they nod and acknowledge one another before racing to the next activity. But fewer and fewer families connect in an organized way on a daily basis.

The home becomes more a place to race through rather than receive nurturing from others. Home becomes a way station, a very brief oasis rather than a place to receive psychological and emotional nurturing. Little surprise that relationships experience stress when sacred time is not more organized and focused.

How do you measure success? How do you protect your time and the relationship? If you have a family, how do you protect that system from external demands? Few families protect or block time other than for holidays or vacations. Is there weekly time blocked out for family? What signs indicate to you whether your family life is successful or unsuccessful? Have you discussed your criteria with your family?

Be Aware of Agendas

Two MBA students involved in a class project to meet requirements for graduation committed to a project that involved collecting data, diagnosing the data, creating a summary of the data, and making a presentation to senior management. Throughout the interaction with their client company, the HBS students often showed up late for appointments. When they arrived they shared with their clients how busy they were, how hard they were working, and how many demands they had on their schedules. The clients later explained to the professor supervising the project,

> Your students seemed to be so full of their own agendas and schedules that it never felt like they asked about our work. They communicated implicitly that their work was more important than their relationship with us. We were simply a means to an end for them. They were friendly, competent folks but full of themselves and their world. After a while, we quit looking forward to our interactions with them and set our sights on when the project would be over. We would be reluctant signing up for another project with you.

Implicitly, the students communicated a far more profound message to their clients. Unknowingly, the students made it clear that the client was fortunate to have the privilege of working with HBS students. When the professor discussed the situation with the students in a debriefing session they initially became defensive but quickly realized what they had done. Their reaction turned from defensiveness to embarrassment. They realized that in unconscious ways people communicate clearly the magnitude of their agendas and, in so doing, how important they are in accomplishing those tasks set forth on those agendas.

Understand Stress

Stress manifests itself physically, psychologically, and behaviorally. Stress can be viewed as a chronic illness when it is long term. While it can create positive short-term results, long-term stress is a pollutant to the human system. Further, the more we learn about stress, the more concerned we should be.

There are many causes of professional stress. Stress results when individual expectations about a particular context, situation, or experiences do not match one's internal expectation of the experiences. Professionals find themselves in organizational situations where either the expectation of their role does not match what their manager expects or what they expect of themselves. When their capabilities are being underutilized, they experience stress. When they are being expected to accomplish more than is possible, they experience anxiety.

Stress occurs during times of change, from new geographical locations, to new employment venues, to new relationships, to promotions, to new family members, to deaths. The uncertainty of preparing for new challenges with unfamiliar structures, systems, and processes raises the level of concern both physically and psychologically. Throwing oneself into a new situation means there may be a cost to the change. The cost may be in a loss of productivity or efficiency.

PSFs rely on meeting the demands of clients. The management of the client demands and managing many clients simultaneously may cause unrealistic demands on the professional. How does the professional meet client expectations and the internal demands inherent in PSFs? Junior professionals want time and attention. There are budgets, performance evaluations, team management meetings to hold, and new clients to see. There is travel. There is time away from support systems. There are clients who need constant attention. Over time, the cumulative pressure adds up. The pollutants that are created over time are due to a number of factors. When unresolved conflict continues over time, pollutants build up. When the professional never manages ongoing demands caused by time pressures, stress builds.

As professionals assume new responsibilities or join new organizations, perceptions and expectations are often violated. Professionals may have a bimodal reaction to assuming new responsibilities in new organizations. Either the professional feels overloaded with new information, new people to meet, and new challenges to learn how the organization works, or the professional experiences "underloading," where talents and capabilities are not being used as the professional expected.

The simple process of dealing with change can cause unrealistic pressures and stresses on the professional. The simple process of change pushes some to experience anxiety, which in turn influences various chemical responses in the human system. Did I take the right job? Should I have moved the family internationally? What about school? What about day care? What happens if my boss moves and I have to report to someone else? What happens if functional responsibilities shift and I am left without a mentor?

The process of self-improvement often produces stress. Professionals need to identify their managerial weaknesses. In what situations do they micro manage? When do they exhibit perfectionist tendencies that gradually wear down colleagues and subordinates? Unclear roles and responsibilities can provide tension both in the system and in the individual. Clarity drives short-term pain from the system and hones in on longer-term outcomes. As long as organizations have few mechanisms in which professionals receive feedback and create a developmental plan for improvement, dysfunctional organizational behaviors may continue to influence long-term output of the professional.

Another central cause of stress is unresolved conflict. When tensions never get resolved in our professional and private lives, the system cannot cope with the constant pressure on the body. Conflict resolution is critical to healthy systemic functioning. This does not mean that conflict is bad. It can be useful in creating dialogues that push teams to better answers to tough questions. The problem arises when the conflict persists over time. This tension becomes a pollutant for the individuals and for the organization as well.

Recent research suggests that while short-term stress may be vital for enhancing productivity, chronic stress breaks down the body's functions and prepares the body for disease. Prolonged chronic stress begins to break down our immune systems and central organs and will continue to play havoc on the system. Stress manifests itself in the way we feel, the way we think, and the way we act or behave. Feelings are typically overstimulated when stress occurs, feelings of impatience, irritability, anger, loneliness, and a sense of insecurity, anxiety and depression.

The thinking processes during stress typically become less focused. Creativity can be impaired. Simple decisions are heightened and become dilemmas. Subjectivity is impaired. We can become unfocused more often or irrational, or we can experience feelings of being rushed or disorganized and perceive to be overwhelmed most of the time. These responses or symptoms to stress become cumulative, slowly breaking down the processes that manage and maintain healthy psychological functioning.

The third way we experience stress manifests itself physically. The symptoms show up as ongoing exhaustion, nervousness, insomnia, high blood pressure, nervous twitches, headaches, and stomachaches. These are but a few of the ways in which stress makes us less alert, less focused, and less able to meet new challenges.

In addition, stress can be produced from external experiences that threaten to affect how we see ourselves and others see us. Through our reactions to the experiences, we may strike out with anger, sarcasm, complaining, or attacking others through words and deeds. For others the reaction is one of withdrawal, confusion, justification, rationalization, and blaming others for our situation.

Learn How to Cope with Stress

Coping with the myriad challenges and requisite spillover takes strategic planning for the professional. By prioritizing demands, building in "dead time," and having courage to delegate, the professionals can significantly help themselves cope with stress and keep perspective.

Professionals must learn how to recognize stress in themselves and in others. They must be aware of the clues that are subtly given by others that they may miss either intentionally or unintentionally. The warning signs are there.

Once professionals recognize that they need to change the way they internalize experiences to get better long-term results, they can get support from many areas. Personal sources range from spouse/partner to other family members to a confidant or a friend. Work sources range from colleagues, co-workers, managers, and mentors to more generic work-sponsored activities like retreats, conferences, and so forth. Finally, community groups and professional counselors can play a temporary role in creating the support of a professional who may need to recalibrate old behaviors and create new behaviors that are more helpful to long-term, high-quality performance and overall satisfaction.

There are five specific tactics that every professional should practice:

- *Create gaps*—Build specific breaks in the day that are sacred. No interruptions. No calls. No emergencies. It may be as much as two 15-minute breaks during the day where there are no demands. The gap may be filled with exercise, meditation, relaxation, drawing, or playing an instrument. The key is to switch focus from work.

- *Prioritize*—Decide what is urgent and important. Decide what must be done at work and in one's private life. What cannot be delayed? Decide who the key people are in your life and allocate time on your calendar for them. Notice when you begin to slip back into your habits of ignoring the priority list and get back on track.

- *Delegate*—Individuals drawn to PSFs tend to be perfectionists who genuinely believe they do what they do best. They are typically technically competent in their field. Thus, it is problematic to delegate work to others. At the end of the day, the professional is quite convinced that the person receiving the assignment cannot do it as well as him- or herself. We resist delegating knowing eventually the work will circle back in our hands. Stress can be managed as we give up our illusions that if we do not complete the assignment personally that the client will suffer. The irony is that the perfectionist ends up suffering due to excessive micromanaging.

- *Recognize the warning signs*—What are the warning signs for you when your life is out of balance? What do you want others to do about it? How does your partner show signs of stress? What does your partner want you to do? Do you know what the warning signs are for the key people at work? What do they want from you? How will your reaction influence work and how the task is accomplished? How have you become a barrier for others because of your reaction to physical and psychological pollutants?

- *Manage stress proactively*—The keys to coping with stress rest with stepping back and gaining a perspective. The foundation of change is withdrawing temporarily and keeping the macro view that the long-term effects of the current behavior are too great. Talk to someone and build and maintain a support system and be very clear about what the values are that drive the intended behavior. Professionals are task driven and goal driven. To reflect and be aware of physical symptoms and reactions is difficult. Keeping a light touch becomes imperative to the regeneration process.

SUMMARY

This module covers significant ground. The cases on learning, feedback, ethics, and success and balance in PSFs emphasize that work in PSFs is complex, demanding, personally challenging at times, and incredibly fulfilling when one can strike the proper balance. Striking this balance never occurs reactively; rather, professionals must proactively manage their lives in a way that they make reasonable trade-offs in their professional and personal lives. Rest assured there are many successful and satisfied consultants, investment bankers, lawyers, money managers, accountants, venture capitalists, and so forth.

We have attempted in this module to be as practical and specific as possible. We sought to enliven the discussions with real-life examples of concerns that readers of this book have expressed a need to discuss. By placing Module Seven at the end of our book, we intend that readers could integrate what you have learned about the organizational and market strategies and tactics of PSFs with how they as professionals will apply them in their careers.

We hope the journey through Module Seven is a unique and personal one for each of you. We hope the cases raise questions in your mind that allow you to further define and improve your approach to managing your career and life within PSFs. This learning will be a dynamic process throughout your career. We wish you good luck and all the best!

QUESTIONS ARISING FROM THE CASES IN THIS MODULE

These are some of the many questions that were raised in our study of this module.

- To what extent do we frame our management decisions with an ethical perspective in mind?

- How do individuals within a given professional practice assess ethical situations versus self-interest?

- At what point in the learning and career development of a professional can ethics be taught as a discipline? How will the focus on ethics as a subject bring about behavioral change?

- Is it possible to create a potential framework that guides the ethical decisions we make in professional service firms?

- To what extent is there a difference between our professional and human responsibilities in the context of business?

- In what circumstances do ethical quandaries seem to arise more often?

- What are the strategies that guide a new recruit when joining a new professional service firm?

- To what extent do new hires in professional service firms have degrees of freedom to try new skills and approaches in the performance management process?

- How do professionals manage their lives so that they are able to balance the trade-offs between career pressures and family demands?

- How do professionals deal with the artificial barriers and hurdles that often arise to demonstrate commitment to the organization?

- What are the warning signs that indicate that the personal support system in a relationship is out of balance with work?

Tim Hertach at GL Consulting (A)

Walking to his car outside the Chicago headquarters of GL Consulting, Tim Hertach was looking forward, after a hectic couple of weeks at work, to spending the three-day Memorial Day holiday with his wife. Hertach's career and stature at GL Consulting LLP (GLC) had progressed rapidly; he was viewed as a leader among the cohort of recently promoted partners and was routinely praised by clients. But something was troubling him. "I was pondering over a dilemma while leaving the office that Friday night," recalled Hertach.

> I had just helped win a large project at Parks Food. It meant a lot for the firm and obviously for my career. But I couldn't get out of my mind a comment my colleague had made. He had described a billing practice at another client that, on the surface, appeared to be questionable. I had squelched any possibility of following such questionable practices in the Parks Food project. But I was left wondering whether it was my responsibility to probe deeper into our firm's billing practices with other clients.

TIM HERTACH

Early Childhood and Schooling

Hertach had grown up just outside Reston, Virginia. An introverted child, he struggled in school and at forming friendships. He had almost failed first grade and was required to attend remedial education programs until the fourth grade. "I was

overweight as a kid and was mocked by my classmates," Hertach recollected.

> Often they would call me "professor" or "egghead." I guess they thought I was smart even if my teachers did not. I remember once, in the fourth grade, giving away money I had saved from my modest weekly allowance and earned doing extra chores to some of the kids that were nice to me at school. My parents, owners of a small, local, and highly successful accounting firm, provided little emotional support as they were consumed by the demanding needs of their clients. At times they made the problems I faced at school worse by expressing their frustration with my mediocre academic performance.

In seventh and eighth grades, Hertach's academic performance improved dramatically once he was placed in some advanced classes that he enjoyed, though he still had difficulties socially. In 1974, at age 13, Hertach left home to attend Deerfield Academy, a private boarding school in Massachusetts. Although his social and academic experiences continued to be uneven, his participation, in the summer of 1977, in the Colorado Outward Bound School, a wilderness-based personal development program, did boost his self-confidence.

Upon graduation from school, Hertach, rejected by a number of universities because of his spotty academic record at Deerfield, was finally

Dean's Research Fellow Scot Landry prepared this case under the supervision of Professors Ashish Nanda and Thomas DeLong as the basis for class discussion rather than to illustrate either effective or ineffective handling of an administrative situation. Certain names, titles, and key terms have been disguised to maintain confidentiality.

accepted at Oklahoma State University in Stillwater, Oklahoma. Finding the transition from a small, private, elite, East Coast boarding school to a large midwestern public university difficult, Hertach followed his 1978–1979 freshman year with a year in Volunteers in Service to America (VISTA), a government-run program that employed volunteers to assist the economically disadvantaged. "It was one of the most rewarding and important experiences of my life," he recalled. "I worked with a neighborhood association in Baltimore, Maryland, formed many close relationships, and felt, for the first time in my life, accepted by a community." Upon returning to Oklahoma State in 1980 Hertach flourished, achieving high grades, becoming president of his fraternity, and leading several other major campus organizations.

Hertach's First Job: Weston Consulting

Upon graduating from Oklahoma State in 1983 with a BS in chemistry and a minor in business, Hertach joined Weston Consulting. Among the world's largest consulting firms, Weston set aggressive sales targets and asked its managers and partners who failed to meet their targets to leave. The firm's competitive, high-pressure environment took its toll on professionals; morale was low and turnover among consultants averaged 25 percent. In the course of working on a wide range of projects, Hertach encountered situations that made him feel increasingly uneasy. "On my first project," he recalled,

> I was on a team that designed and implemented a large computer system that we knew, in the later stages of the project, wouldn't work, but we never told the client. On another team we violated the client's bidding guidelines. In the second instance, I confronted the partner in charge and we were able to reach a compromise that I felt resolved the issue. After these two experiences I came to the conclusion that Weston's

high-pressure environment to generate revenue caused some "good people to do bad things."

Working for a Nonprofit

Hertach entered Harvard Business School's MBA program in the fall of 1986. Upon graduating in 1988, unlike most of his classmates who sought jobs in corporations, investment banks, or consulting firms, he joined Habitat for Humanity, a nonprofit organization that built housing for economically disadvantaged families. Hertach's decision was driven by a dramatic event that occurred during the summer of 1986, just before he started business school. "I was almost killed in a car wreck that summer," recalled Hertach.

> Two people traveling with me died and I was thrown free, suffering only minor injuries. That experience showed me that life was short and that if I wanted to do something I ought to do it sooner rather than later. I had always admired Habitat and decided to work for them immediately after HBS.

Hertach enjoyed the experience. "The people in the organization were dedicated and compassionate individuals," he observed. "I made many great friendships, learned a tremendous amount about managing projects and teams and had a lot of fun. It seemed that we were making a real, meaningful impact in the lives of others." (Exhibit 1 summarizes Hertach's career values.) In April 1991 Hertach married Linda Howard; his wife was an artist and shared many of his interests.

After working with Habitat for three years Hertach decided to seek a change. "I felt as though I was no longer as challenged as when I had started," he reasoned.

> My next promotion would take me into administration rather than running the projects I so enjoyed doing. The compensation I was receiving was low, as to be expected at a nonprofit, and would remain so for as long as I stayed with the organization.

EXHIBIT 1   **Tim Hertach's Career Values**

Desired job characteristics feedback for Timothy Steven Hertach.

This chart summarizes what you seek in terms of an ideal job, with the most important characteristics higher in the chart. Additionally, the chart tells you what relative weight you attach to each characteristic. For example, a bar that is twice as long as another bar tells you that you consider the former factor to be twice as important as the latter.

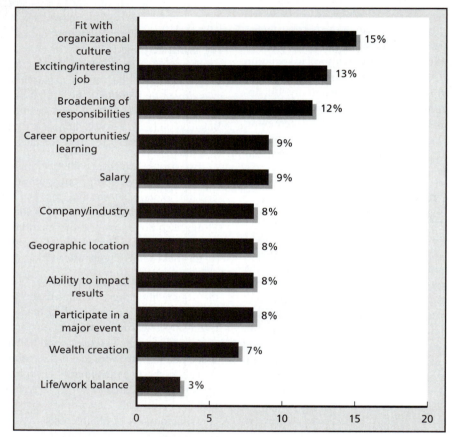

The chart was developed by Hertach's taking a self-assessment test in August 1999 with Korn/Ferry Futurestep.

Since my only source of wealth was what I earned working, I was concerned that I would not be able to support my family if I stayed at Habitat. And I missed some of the challenges and faster pace of the for-profit world.

Hertach Rejoins the For-Profit Sector

Hertach left Habitat in August 1991 to join the Bec Company, a medium-size consumer products company, as director of strategic planning. He was soon promoted to vice president of production planning and customer service and made responsible for managing an 18-person department that controlled the production of 5,700 products at seven manufacturing facilities, managed inventories, and resolved problems with retail customers such as Wal-Mart, Kmart, Sears, and JC Penney. "It was a tough job," recalled Hertach. "I was always challenged and learned a tremendous amount. Fortunately I had a department filled with dedicated and experienced people."

But the firm, having experienced a leveraged buyout in the mid-1980s, was suffocating under a mountain of debt. "I thought that Bec's future might be limited," Hertach recollected, "and I did not have a high regard for most of the senior management team." In August 1993 Hertach moved from Bec to Consultants Limited (CL), a small consulting firm that had been conducting a business process reengineering project at Bec.

At CL Hertach sold and delivered business process reengineering projects to governmental agencies and consumer products companies. But the firm was having financial problems and decided to exit a number of businesses, including Hertach's area, reengineering, and focus exclusively on packaged software implementation. Although he could have stayed on at CL by relocating, Hertach chose to leave the firm since he did not want to focus only on implementing software. "At the time CL was going through merger negotiations with a much larger firm, GL Consulting," Hertach recalled. "CL partners introduced me to some of the senior partners there. Although CL did not eventually merge with GL Consulting, I received an offer from them and decided to join the firm in January 1996."

TIM HERTACH AT GL CONSULTING

GL Consulting

An established, respected, fast-growing consulting partnership, GL Consulting had more than 40 years' experience executing strategy, process improvement, information technology, operations, and logistics projects for some of the largest and best-known companies in the world. Client firms responding to quality surveys conducted during and at the conclusion of projects almost universally reported that they were very satisfied with GLC's services and would recommend the firm to others. Reflecting its emphasis on delivering high-quality, results-oriented consulting services, GLC's work came mostly from repeat clients. Unlike many large firms that frequently staffed projects with people with little or no relevant experience, GLC was reputed in the industry for maintaining a high ratio of experienced to inexperienced staff on projects. Remarked a senior GLC partner: "One of the few ways to get fired from GLC is to screw up a client engagement."

In addition to client focus, tight control of compensation, administrative and other overhead expenses helped make the firm highly profitable. Competitors and industry analysts alike generally viewed GLC positively. Many considered it a "sleeping giant," believing that it could greatly increase its market share if it were to become more aggressive. A frequent acquisition target of other consulting firms, GLC routinely rejected such overtures, since the senior partners at GLC wanted to remain independent.

A Friendly Culture

GLC was perceived by outsiders to have solid, experienced people who delivered tangible results to clients. One industry analyst characterized it as the kind of place anyone would be proud to work at. Hertach felt that GLC had a friendly, congenial atmosphere. Cooperation was emphasized and individuals enjoyed considerable latitude and freedom in determining their career focus. "I was surprised at how little direction I was given when I joined the firm," he recalled. "Basically it was up to me to decide what I wanted to do." When he talked with other professionals who had joined GLC from other consulting firms, they particularly emphasized how little conflict and internal politics they had encountered relative to their previous experience.

Sales targets for managers and partners that were lower than at most other major consulting firms fostered a less-intense work environment. Compensation, including bonuses, was tied more closely to seniority than to individual performance. Working on weekends was the exception; most consultants worked only 40 to 60 hours per week.

Consultant turnover at GLC averaged 10 to 12 percent per year, about half to one-third what other large consulting firms experienced. Hertach felt that one reason for the low turnover was that very capable people remained at GLC (even though they knew that they could make more money elsewhere) for cultural and lifestyle reasons. He heard several stories of GLC partners and consultants rebuffing executive recruiters offering job opportunities with compensation increases of 30 to 50 percent.

Traditionally, GLC had promoted from within, but as the firm grew rapidly in the mid-1990s, it became necessary to hire outside professionals (from other consulting firms and from industry). Bringing in outsiders occasioned no discernible internal dissension, most long-time employees seeming to realize that outside hiring was necessary to continue growing the business. GLC, like most consulting firms, struggled to find qualified people who fit its culture; some of its outside hires were successful, others not.

Hertach's Debut at GLC

Hertach was one of the experienced hires. In January 1996 Hertach joined GLC as a senior manager in a newly formed practice area that was responsible for selling and delivering multifunctional consulting projects that required a mix of strategy, systems, and process improvement services. "I had joined GLC even though I had other, more lucrative offers," Hertach stated,

> because I had found a firm that shared my values of placing the clients' interests first, delivering high-quality results, and treating one another with respect. However, my fit

with the firm's culture was somewhat uneasy. I considered myself to be idealistic, creative, and a broad business thinker who was quick to draw conclusions. I learned that these traits were often at odds with GLC's conservative culture dominated by individuals who were specialists and engineers by training.

In late 1996 Hertach was appointed manager for a fairly large project reporting to two partners, GLC chairman Mark Williamson and senior partner Bob Morton, who was relatively new to the firm. Hertach and Morton quickly became friends, in part because they shared similar opinions about GLC's strengths and weaknesses.

Morton, 10 years Hertach's senior, soon became his mentor. Hertach admired Morton's positive attitude. Realizing that he could learn a lot from him, he became Morton's confidant and sought to work with him as often as possible. Morton reciprocated by bringing Hertach into major sales efforts and creating opportunities for Hertach to lead large projects and firmwide management initiatives. "By late 1997," Hertach recalled,

> my career at GLC was going very well, thanks largely to Bob Morton. I had helped him sell several large engagements, was starting to be quoted in the press, delivered a presentation at a major trade show, and served on several internal GLC committees. Additionally, I was asked to lead a consulting project I had helped to sell: to create and launch a new business unit for a large company. It was definitely the most interesting, successful, and enjoyable stage of my career and I was very enthusiastic about my work. The firm recognized my accomplishments in these areas and promoted me to the partnership in January 1998.

In 1998 Hertach spent most of his efforts developing a new practice area. Although his investment in the new business line adversely affected Hertach's sales, management continued to reward him with more responsibility. "I enjoyed working at GLC and continued to build experience, contacts, and knowledge," recalled Hertach.

> Early in the year I was appointed, through Bob Morton's support, to head a committee of senior GLC partners responsible for coordinating marketing efforts throughout the firm. I was quoted in about 20 articles in the general, business, and trade press on a wide range of business and consulting issues. And I was selected to travel to Europe to deliver a presentation at an industry conference. Overall it was a successful year.

Taking Stock

As 1998 drew to a close and he prepared for his annual review with his direct superior, head of the strategy practice Phil Mabree, Hertach reflected on his impressions of GLC and his plans for the future. Although he believed that the day would eventually come when he would no longer be challenged and would seek to do something else, Hertach nevertheless saw himself working for GLC for the foreseeable future. "On the positive side," he explained,

> GLC was a profitable and growing firm. It placed high, but not unreasonable demands on its employees. It tried to treat everyone fairly, taking into account individual circumstances when making staffing assignments and treating people with respect. The firm always tried to do what was right for the client rather than simply maximize firm revenue—the opposite of what I had seen at Weston. I felt that the firm was very well managed and wrote personal notes to both chairman Mark Williamson and president Lester Simpson of GLC thanking them for their efforts.

> But GLC, like any organization, was far from perfect. I didn't think Mark and Lester provided a clear or inspiring vision for how to grow the firm. They would periodically send memos to all the partners extolling them to sell more and raise hourly rates. Many of the partners ridiculed these memos. I felt these memos were basically pointless, equivalent to telling a basketball team to score more points than its opponents, an obvious goal everyone understands, when the real problem was figuring out how to do so. I discussed this with Mark and Lester, but they, even when pressed, could not explain how to grow the business other than to say, "we need to work harder selling larger projects."

> GLC had not built Internet or enterprise resource planning software practices early enough, thereby ceding leadership in these important growth areas to other firms. The firm was also not investing enough in infrastructure. Our accounting system was hopelessly outdated and inflexible; and we lacked methodologies. I felt that we were way behind our competition in these and other infrastructure areas and simply not spending enough to catch up.

Hertach was generally viewed positively. On several occasions senior partners had told him that they "needed more people like you at GLC in order to grow the firm." In 1998 he was presented an award for outstanding firmwide performance. Mabree stated in Hertach's 1998 year-end annual performance review:

> Tim performs well in highly creative situations and in managing and coordinating others. His verbal skills are very strong. He builds very strong relationships both with clients and other GLC personnel. He enjoys business development and will be strong in this area as he builds his experience, network of contacts, and skills.

> Tim is very much a team player, willing to suboptimize his position or performance if it benefits the client or the firm.

> He is also a natural entrepreneur, taking great satisfaction out of creating something new such as the firmwide marketing cam-

paign for food, drug, and consumer packaged goods.

In terms of areas for improvement, Mabree offered the following feedback:

Tim needs to continue to learn more about GLC culture, policies, and procedures. Sometimes in his effort to get something done, Tim violates the norms, culture, and procedures of the firm. He does, however, learn from these instances and rarely makes the same mistake twice.

Tim is, at times, more blunt in expressing his opinions than is the norm at GLC. He needs to continue to be sensitive in his communication with others.

Hertach fully agreed with Mabree's feedback. Yet, he believed that his communication style, characterized as blunt in the review, was an asset when dealing with clients. "I rarely had conflicts with my clients over my communication style," he reflected.

I frequently received commendations and thank-you notes from them and they usually gave my projects very high ratings on the evaluation forms that they periodically filled out. They appreciated my honesty and it helped me form many close friendships. In fact, often times my only regret was that I was not being honest enough with them. On occasions I foresaw problems developing, but did not, out of respect and friendship, address them with sufficient force. As a result, in some cases, I was not effective in helping them confront and solve some significant problems that, in turn, harmed their organizations or careers.

THE REVALUATION PROPOSAL

"Proposal to Enhance Value"

Preparing to attend GLC's annual worldwide partners meeting in February 1999, Hertach was intrigued by a two-hour block of time earmarked for a session cryptically titled "Proposal to Enhance Value." The first 90 minutes of the session were devoted to a presentation of the proposal by two senior GLC partners. "The longer I listened, the more annoyed I became," recalled Hertach.

They kept presenting slides and talking about the benefits of their proposal without describing the proposal itself. I started to have a very bad feeling regarding what we were about to hear. Finally, an hour into the presentation, the partners described their proposal. They recommended quadrupling the valuation of a partnership unit. The units that each partner held would vest at their new valuation after five years.

The partners making the presentation stated that the new valuation would be a more accurate estimate of the true value of the partners' equity in GLC and would help the firm minimize dilution when acquiring other firms. They said that the firm's financial advisors had put together numerous cash flows using various assumptions that showed the revaluation would be advantageous for the firm. They also said that the firm's bankers, lawyers, and accountants had all provided favorable opinions and recommended implementing it, and GLC's board of directors supported the plan.

The last half-hour was devoted to questions and answers. The first was a request to get a copy of the presentation they just delivered. The presenters answered that they would not distribute it because "the proposal might change." As the question period proceeded, Hertach, too, raised his hand. Once recognized he said:

Maybe I don't understand something about this proposal but it appears to me that the 20 percent of the senior partners that own 80 percent of the firm will get a huge windfall from this whereas the remaining 80 percent of the partners will be left trying to pay for it.

The silence that suddenly enveloped the room was broken by one of the presenting partners responding with a long, somewhat rambling explanation. After the meeting was adjourned, several partners came up to Hertach and told him that they shared his concerns. One senior partner slapped him on the back and said with a smile, "I see that they taught you a few things at the Harvard Business School." Hertach smiled back weakly, sick with anger over a proposal that he felt mortgaged the future of the firm.

Later that evening Hertach met his mentor Morton. They got into an intense argument over the relative merits of the revaluation. It soon became apparent to Hertach that Morton strongly supported the proposal.

After the partnership meeting, GLC's board of directors named a committee of senior partners to take input, answer questions, and make a final recommendation to the board. Although several mid-level and new partners privately expressed their concerns to Hertach, he remained one of a handful of people who publicly objected to the committee regarding the proposal. His requests for copies of the cash flows, comments other partners had submitted, and the opinions provided by the firm's financial advisors were denied, making Hertach "angrier, frustrated, and more concerned."

Adoption of the Revaluation Proposal

A slightly revised proposal was put to partnership vote in May 1999 and passed with about 80 percent of the units voting in favor. When asked, the senior partners would not reveal how many of the actual partners, rather than units, voted in favor of the proposal. Hertach remembered his reaction:

> It was over. On paper I was instantly $250,000 richer, or would be if I stayed with the firm for five more years. And this amount could increase, perhaps substantially, over that time. But, even though Bob Morton relentlessly championed the new valuation approach, extolling its virtues whenever he had the chance, I remained unconvinced. I believed instead that the senior

partners had set up a system that would allow them to cash out with a huge windfall, draining capital from the firm, leaving the younger partners in the lurch. I especially disliked the way the proposal was presented and the way in which the senior partners withheld information. On top of everything else, Bob Morton and I were no longer on speaking terms.

All the partners at GLC knew of Hertach's opposition to the proposal. Several partners that he barely knew voiced their concerns privately to him. Many expressed frustration that henceforth they would have to invest significantly more money, about 80 percent of their annual bonus, to buy the new more expensive units whereas, in the past, they typically had to invest roughly 30 percent of their bonus to make their annual unit purchases. One mid-level partner told Hertach that he did not support the proposal but felt he had to stay at GLC because his units could be worth several million dollars in five years. Once his new units vested, he planned to cash out and leave the firm. Several younger partners acknowledged to Hertach that they had begun listening interestedly to the pitches from executive recruiters (whose intensity of calls had increased dramatically because they "smelled blood in the water") because they wanted to have an exit strategy "in case things do not work out."

In mid-1999 the senior partners publicly announced that the change had been successful. They had expected about seven partners to leave because of the change, but so far, none had. However, revenue at the firm had been sliding over the past six months and so the managing partners began, once again, to push partners to raise hourly rates and sell larger projects.

THE BILLING CONTROVERSY

As the revaluation process unfolded over the first half of 1999, Hertach, despite his disappointment, continued to sell work and deliver consulting services. He was even given additional responsibilities when Mabree put him in charge of the firm's food, drug, and consumer packaged goods strategy practice. Hertach soon found himself in the middle of a new controversy. He was part of a team proposing a multimillion-dollar consulting project for Parks Food, a leading but troubled company. The firm's chief financial officer inquired whether GLC would be willing to defer a portion of its fees until its recommendations were implemented and tangible results achieved, a type of billing arrangement GLC usually sought to avoid.

GLC's Billing Practices

GLC customarily billed clients for three categories of expenses: consulting fees referred to as fees for professional services, travel expenses, and administrative expenses. Fees for professional services were calculated by multiplying the number of hours consultants worked by their respective hourly billing rates. Airfare, lodging, and meals expenses were passed through to clients at cost; GLC did not share with clients the substantial rebates it received from airlines, hotels, credit card companies, and its corporate travel agent.[1] The last category of expenses was administrative.

Fees for professional services typically accounted for 75 to 80 percent of a project's cost. Although GLC preferred to bill clients fees as incurred with no maximum amount, which placed the risk of a project requiring more effort or running longer than expected squarely with the client, few consulting projects were sold in this manner. Many companies, desiring consultants to share some of the risk for completing work on time and on budget and needing to know approximate project costs in advance for budgeting purposes, preferred a billing approach of fees as incurred up to a maximum amount.[2]

Performance-linked payment schemes, such as the one being requested by Parks Food, also referred to as "contingent fees" in the consulting industry, were not used widely. Under an arrangement termed "gain sharing," one of the two major variations of this approach, GLC billed clients an amount based on a percentage of the financial improvement attributed to the project (e.g., a percentage of savings resulting from an inventory reduction project). The other approach typically added a bonus to a fixed fee if specified performance or quality criteria were met or exceeded. Although it did not actively pursue performance-linked payments, GLC did, albeit infrequently, agree to such arrangements. Its experience with such arrangements had been generally bad. In a number of cases, even with long-term clients, disagreements arose over whether results were realized and amounts to be paid. Almost invariably, clients ended up paying more for the work than they would have otherwise because GLC charged more to compensate for the additional risk it incurred and the time consumed in closely monitoring results.

Administrative expenses charges were supposed to cover GLC's support and administrative expenses. These expenses being a mix of different items, billing was quite complicated. This category included client-related administrative expenses such as courier services and outside commercial printing. By far the largest component was an overhead charge equaling roughly 7 percent of total fees.

Although calculated almost entirely on a percentage basis, administrative expenses were shown

---

[1] Some clients requested that travel expenses incurred by GLC on their projects follow their own more restrictive corporate guidelines or that GLC establish a maximum cap, either a set dollar amount or a percentage of fees. In most instances, GLC agreed to do so.

[2] These were two of the five types of billing approaches used by GLC and most other large consulting firms: (1) fees as incurred (no maximum); (2) fees as incurred (up to a maximum amount); (3) fixed fee; (4) performance-linked fees (contingent upon some quantifiable milestone or result achieved); and (5) value billing (charging clients for a portion of the expected value created through provision of the consulting service).

on the invoice in dollars. As fees went up and down, so did administrative expenses. The few clients that eventually figured out that they were paying a percentage-based overhead charge rather than a direct expense objected verbally and often refused to pay it. GLC did not require clients that challenged the overhead charge to pay it. (Exhibit 2 provides a sample invoice.)

GLC Responds to Parks Food

GLC's response to Parks Food's request for a performance-linked scheme was complicated by two factors. One, the GLC team, aware that a competitor also bidding on the work had agreed to the request, feared that if it did not offer to make some comparable concession it would lose the bid. But aware also of Parks Food's reputation for being contentious and litigious with its vendors, the GLC team worried that if it agreed to the deferral and won the bid it might never get fully paid for its work.

One partner on the team suggested that GLC "instead offer them a discount like we did Bolton Machine [a longtime, multimillion-dollar GLC client], then increase our rates to make up the difference." Hertach remarked to the group that this did not sound ethical and the option was discussed no further.

EXHIBIT 2   **GLC Sample Invoice**

GL Consulting LLP[a]

Invoice

Through December 13, 1997

Attention of:

Jeff Higgins
Chief Financial Officer
Bolton Machine
54 Western Avenue
North Saddlebrook NJ 04712

Client: 12555
Project: 26453
Invoice: 97-62345
Project description: Implementation of redesigned product development processes and systems

Fees for professional services:	$265,780.00
Travel expenses:	43,345.11
Administrative expenses:	70.38
Interest charges:	0.00
Total due:	$309,195.49

Questions regarding this invoice or payments should be directed to Accounts Receivable department at 212-555-8332. Terms: Net in 90 days, thereafter 1.5% monthly interest is charged. All forms of payment should be made payable to: GL Consulting LLP.

[a] GLC also offered alternative invoice formats that were more detailed, although most clients received the version shown above. In the more detailed versions "fees for professional services" were broken down by individual consultant, and/or "travel expenses" were shown by category (e.g., airfare). More detail regarding "administrative expenses" was not available on any invoice format. Bolton Machine, on December 13, 1997, was not paying the 7 percent overhead charges normally included under "administrative expenses."

Ultimately GLC offered no fee concessions to Parks Food. Fees and expenses were to be billed as incurred with a fee maximum of $2.2 million. Expenses were estimated to be about 25 percent of the fees. The client was to be invoiced monthly, payment due within 90 days. Even though a competing consulting firm had agreed to a fee deferral, GLC was selected, in large part owing to the strong relationship the GLC team had established with the Parks Food executive team. The Parks Food team was particularly impressed with the experience, empathy, and understanding the GLC team had demonstrated for the pressures and issues Parks Food faced and with the GLC team's action bias in proposing to launch pilot tests after only six weeks of analysis.

HERTACH PONDERS FURTHER INVESTIGATION

"I was thrilled that we were able to win the Parks Food account *and* do it above board," recalled Hertach,

> but the comment made by my colleague about how billing had been handled on the

Bolton account began to gnaw on me. That partner implied that GLC had done something questionable. Did I have a responsibility to bring the issue up to senior management? If the client or any other outsiders found out that the firm had behaved poorly with Bolton, then GLC's reputation would suffer. On the other hand, was it appropriate to investigate GLC's past practices with clients that were not my own?

Professionals' Quandaries

SPAULDING V. ZIMMERMAN[1]

In 1956, David Spaulding was badly injured in an accident while he was a passenger in a car driven by John Zimmerman. Spaulding sued Zimmerman for medical expenses and other damages.

During the legal proceedings, a medical specialist appointed by Zimmerman's insurer examined Spaulding. The doctor found a previously undetected aortic aneurysm, which might have been caused by the accident. The doctor did not inform Spaulding of this diagnosis. The insurance company and Zimmerman's attorney also chose not to inform Spaulding of this dangerous condition. Soon after, Spaulding accepted a $6,500 settlement.

Spaulding's own doctor eventually discovered the aneurysm during a routine examination, and Spaulding underwent immediate surgery. Spaulding sued, arguing that vital information had been improperly withheld from him.

STACEY DUQUETTE

Stacey Duquette's first 18 months at the strategy unit of Barker Consulting (BC), a technology integration consulting firm, had gone extremely well. She really liked the firm and the people and felt that she had made the correct decision upon graduating from Harvard Business School (HBS) to choose BC over offers from other leading strategy firms. The partners on her first four engagements in the Energy & Resources practice had given her stellar feedback and the firm graded her "at the top of the top tier" in her first annual review.

After returning from a three-month maternity leave in January 2000, Duquette requested and gained permission to work on internal projects out of the firm's Houston office so that she could be with her young daughter and husband each night. BC asked Duquette to conduct a review of all the 118 enterprise resource planning (ERP) projects that the firm's strategy practice had recommended to, and business integration practice had implemented for, clients. When in late February she presented her findings, based on project reports and client surveys, to 60 strategy partners at their annual meetings, Duquette was praised for her "tremendous insights and recommendations."

A week after her presentation, Duquette was approached by Phil Hollis, a partner from her home office. Hollis told her that the following Monday he would be recommending to his client Nelson Industries, a large multibusiness conglomerate, an ERP project that could generate $10 million consulting revenue for the firm.

Hollis asked Duquette to accompany him on the presentation "just in case Nelson has a few questions too data-specific for [Hollis] to answer." At the presentation, Hollis never called on Duquette to answer Nelson executive's queries, responding instead to their questions, she recalled, with statements such as, "As Stacey has studied,

[1] Adapted from L.R. Patterson, *Legal Ethics,* 1982; based on Spaulding v. Zimmerman, 116 N.W. 2d 704 (Minn. 1962).

the average Barker ERP project has improved operating income by 18 percent, with the best seeing over 35 percent improvement and no client seeing less than 10 percent." Duquette sat silently during the presentation, stunned that "not only was Phil not referring to me when addressing questions about actual performance results of ERP projects, which were much lower than his figures, but also he was exaggerating past results." As they traveled back to the airport, Hollis turned to Duquette and said that he thought "the presentation went extremely well" and that he was confident that "Nelson's gonna choose us." He thanked her for her presence and support.

Immediately upon returning to the Houston office that afternoon, Duquette went to see her peer-mentor, Vicki Wish. Also an HBS graduate, Wish had joined BC a year prior to Duquette and had recently been promoted to engagement manager, a year earlier than the norm. Duquette later recalled their conversation.

> I told Vicki that I was very concerned about something Phil had done and needed her immediate advice. (Vicki had worked with Phil on two projects.) I told her that I believed that Phil, in an attempt to win the business, had intentionally misled a client on how much benefit it could expect from an ERP project. Vicki literally laughed in my face. She asked me to "grow up." She told me, "*Everyone* oversells in this business. It is a fact of life in the profession. If BC doesn't oversell, we will lose business to all the other firms that continually oversell their performance. Clients know we're giving them the ideal case. They're smart enough to apply a discount factor to our, and everyone else's, claims."
>
> Phil's actions earlier in the day had unnerved me. Vicki's advice was even more unsettling. As I got up, disappointed and

disheartened, she gave me a hug and said, "Don't be naïve, Stacey. It's a tough world. If you want to succeed in this firm and in this business, you have to become comfortable overselling yourself and your firm."

LISA JORDAN

In 1995 Lisa Jordan graduated from Harvard Business School and joined the well-known investment bank TLG as a sell-side analyst following the software sector. Sell-side analysts were considered Wall Street's "financial detectives," its "wizards of odds."[2] Institutional and retail investors based their investment decisions partly on the recommendations contained in the reports prepared by the analysts.

In October 1999 *Institutional Investor* magazine named Jordan as a third teamer on the All-America Research Team in software and data services sector. The magazine annually named in its All-America Research Team the top four or five security analysts covering various sectors.

Referred to as the analysts' Oscars, rankings were very valuable to the investment banks. Client companies liked their stocks to be followed by ranked analysts, since that gave visibility to their stocks. Investment banks with in-house ranked analysts often had an advantage in landing deals. Although a "Chinese wall" separated research analysts from investment bankers, there often was an unspoken understanding that the banks' analysts would follow investment banking client firms. Some observers also argued that "the analyst today is an investment banker in sheep's clothing," because they rarely gave negative evaluations to firms that were investment banking clients.[3] Typically, analysts' year-end bonuses were determined partly by the investment banking activities in their sectors. Ranked analysts were rewarded handsomely by their firms. Whereas

[2] N.R. Kleinfield, "The Many Faces of the Wall Street Analyst," *New York Times,* October 27, 1985, S. 3, p. 1.
[3] Jeffrey M. Laderman, "Who Can You Trust?" *Business Week,* October 5, 1998, p. 148.

senior unranked analysts earned $250,000 to $400,000 annually, first-team analysts earned $2 million to $5 million.

At age 31, Jordan had become one of the youngest recipients of star honors at her firm. Her research reports had come to be highly respected for carefully addressing industry fundamentals and backing assertions with detailed financial and valuation analyses. Many retail investors closely followed her recommendations. Her 1999 accomplishment was especially significant since she had taken time off from her job to try and earn a spot on the U.S. Olympics speed-skating squad in February of that year. She had come tantalizingly close to representing her country.

At the firm's Christmas party that year, Jordan met one of her colleagues from the corporate finance department, Brian Tovar. Tovar and Jordan had been section-mates at HBS, had joined TLG in the same cohort, and had stayed in touch over the years. Six months previously, Tovar had taken charge of the group within the corporate finance department servicing software firms.

Conversation at the Christmas party turned to how Tovar was adjusting to his new responsibilities. Tovar was particularly excited about the prospects of TLG underwriting a highly anticipated equity issue of a software firm. The software firm would be choosing its underwriter from among TLG and three other banks within the next four days.

Jordan almost bit her lips. Although Tovar had not mentioned the name of the software firm, Jordan knew from her research that Tetrasoft was actively considering issuing equity. And she was in the midst of putting finishing touches to a report, in which she had opined that several software companies, including Tetrasoft, were overpriced. She knew that a negative research report would infuriate Tetrasoft's executives and put TLG's investment banking team at a disadvantage.

Jordan left the party pondering what, if anything, she should do. Should she postpone releasing her report by a week? A number of her reports had come out late the previous year because she had been traveling or had needed additional information.

CARLOS GARCIA

After graduating from Harvard Business School in 1990, Carlos Garcia returned to his home country and took a job at Gonzalez & Moreno (G&M), a business and government consulting practice. Given his business background, Garcia was surprised when in his very first project he was given exclusive responsibility for implementing a government engagement. The partner to whom Garcia was reporting on the project briefed him that he had been given a fairly straightforward and routine project to "get his feet wet." The client was a large foreign consumer goods company that wanted to establish a domestic subsidiary in time to realize benefits from the expected passage of a liberalization package later that year. Garcia was instructed that G&M had assured the client that G&M would "do what it takes" to incorporate and secure the permits necessary to build three factories in the northern province.

While visiting the northern province, a government official told Garcia that "his car had broken down. He told me that the only way that he would be able to put in the 'extra time' necessary to get the permits completed was if a 'miracle' happened and he found a new car with keys in the ignition parked in his driveway the following Saturday." Garcia brought this situation to his boss who responded forcefully, "Remember, we never had this conversation. Realize that this project is really important to our client and to our firm, there's considerable leftover funding in the northern province's budget, and you are overall in charge of the project."

DEXTER SIMMONS

Dexter Simmons was thrilled that he was finally staffed—three weeks into his ten-week internship at Beantown Consulting, a top-tier strategy firm—

on an engagement at Barresi Manufacturing, a large player in the automotive parts industry. Simmons had joined Beantown for his summer internship at the end of his first year of MBA at Harvard Business School.

After being introduced to Barresi executives and having lunch with his Beantown team, Simmons sat down with his engagement manager Markus Hensler for a briefing on the client's situation, Beantown's project scope and purpose, and the contribution expected from Simmons.

Hensler told Simmons that he would be surveying firms in the industry that both supplied and sourced parts from Barresi's 10 largest competitors. Hensler added that this survey would need to be conducted in "stealth mode." He explained that the firms Simmons contacted should not know that he worked for Beantown or was on an engagement for Barresi. He told Simmons to "have fun with it. Tell them you are a student at Harvard Business School—which is true—doing a research project—which is kind of true, since this is like a research project. Be creative; try different names; just make it believable to the respondents."

Simmons must have shown some discomfort, because Hensler got up from his chair, shut his office door, solicitously put his arm around Simmons, and said, "Trust me, Dexter. I've been in this business for five years. It's standard operating procedure in projects such as this. Our staple is information. Your target group will never give us the information we need for this project if they know who we are."

After the briefing, Simmons returned to his office in a former storage room at Barresi headquarters, thinking, "I've always wanted to be a consultant. I can't believe that the job requires me to lie—on the first day of my first project no less! What should I do?"

Trade-Offs:
Juggling Careers in Professional Service Firms with Private Life

All professionals face conflicting responsibilities as they attempt to balance work and private life. Long hours are simply part of the ethos of professional firms—a fact that recent graduates of professional schools must deal with as they simultaneously build careers, networks, and personal relationships. This case portrays three situations connected to professional service firms, focusing on the tensions and trade-offs they experience as they confront the challenges of work and relationships in their own unique ways. Although the fundamental theme of this case—the inescapable tension between personal and professional responsibilities—is so broadly applicable that one might call it universal, the characters in this case represent only three situations of interpersonal dynamics.

DARCY AND MAX: FROM SOUTH YARRA, AUSTRALIA TO HARLEM, NEW YORK

We always kept an illusion that everything was perfect.

Darcy McCormack

Max Edwards was 18 years old when he met Darcy McCormack at the University of Melbourne, Australia in 1984. Both from strong Catholic family backgrounds, they married seven years later in 1991. After graduating from the University of Melbourne Law School, Max accepted a job in a prestigious law firm, while Darcy, who had graduated from the School of Arts, was a fashion editor for a chic fashion magazine. The Edwards were the poster couple for the "yuppie" lifestyle, living in a charming one-bedroom condominium on Darling Street, South Yarra—Melbourne's answer to New York City's Fifth Avenue/Upper East Side.

Bars and Stars to Stars and Stripes

Max explained his decision to attend business school in the United States. "I wanted to be a player in Australian business. I looked around and saw that the most successful businesspeople all had MBAs from prestigious American business schools." Darcy added, "He considered Harvard Business School, but he wanted to be closer to Wall Street." Max applied and was accepted to Columbia Business School. Darcy became pregnant six months before they were to leave for the States. Darcy commented, "Everything seemed to happen quickly, and decisions seemed easy to make. For a moment we considered postponing Max's admission and our trip to the United States, but I said go for it. We both have that supportive attitude with each other."

In August 1993, the couple left Australia for New York City. Max said, "We showed up in New York with two suitcases and $20,000 in cash and were allocated a small one-bedroom student housing apartment in Harlem. Actually it was Morn-

Research Associate Monica Mullick prepared this case under the supervision of Professors Thomas Delong and Ashish Nanda. HBS cases are developed solely as the basis for class discussion. Cases are not intended to serve as endorsements, sources of primary data, or illustrations of effective or ineffective management.

ingside Heights, but Darcy liked to say that we lived in Harlem. We had no idea what we were getting ourselves into." Darcy remembered, "Our apartment was terrible. It had nothing, no furniture or anything. That first night we slept on the floor. There I was six months pregnant, in Harlem, sleeping on a towel. As bad as it was, we never even thought of going back." Max and Darcy slowly furnished their apartment, pushing an old armchair 47 blocks to their apartment from 86th street to 125th street.

Jack Is Born

Max was extremely ambitious and worked vigorously to make ends meet. During the semester, he was a teaching assistant for several classes, tutored a number of students each day, and still managed to rank at or close to the top of his class. "In the beginning, I respected him for how hard he worked," said Darcy.

Darcy's mother, a doctor, came from Australia to help with the last weeks of the pregnancy. Darcy recalled:

> Mom was obviously upset with the way we were living. When I went into labor, my mother gave me a $100 bill and hailed a cab. I told the driver that I was in labor and I only had a $100 bill. He said he didn't have change and to find another way to the hospital. I walked all the way to Park Avenue, before I could find a cab.

Their baby, Jack, was born toward the end of Max's first semester, which was about the time the Edwards ran out of money. Max called home and told his dad that they needed about $40,000. But all his family could offer were good wishes and prayers. They had supported Max through college, and there were still another six children to educate. Fortunately, over Christmas break, Max made some additional money doing some work for his former law firm's New York office. He continued tutoring students and took four teaching assistant positions.

The Dream Job

Darcy said:

> We were young when we got married and Jack joined us very quickly. We had never talked about kids until they were here. We hadn't planned or talked about how we would handle our careers. Max expected not to have kids until he was 35. But I wanted two kids before I turned 30. I always wanted to have kids and a career. I believe that you can follow your dreams. It is hard, but you can make it work.

Six weeks after Jack was born, Darcy was offered her dream job working for a major international fashion photographer. They were out of funds and it was the opportunity of a lifetime. Max added, "My wife is a very ambitious person. She is intelligent, independent, very strong willed, and tough to the world." The Edwards hired a nanny, and Darcy went back to work.

An Offer from a Major Investment Banking Firm

Max was still doing well at school and between his first and second year at Columbia, he accepted a summer associate position at Rothman Brothers in Mergers and Acquisitions (M&A). It was a prestigious position, because the firm historically only extended one or two summer offers in M&A at Columbia. Max considered this opportunity a dream come true: the perfect entry position to make him a player in the corporate major leagues. He thought he had found his calling. He loved it, but he knew there would have to be sacrifices along the way. Max wanted Darcy's approval. He explained:

> I kept telling Darcy that investment banking was a tough life. There is a ton of traveling and ungodly hours. I tried to get her to socialize with some of the other bankers' wives at Rothman Brothers to have her get a better feel for what life was like married to a banker. But she kept insisting that she didn't

want to have veto power over my career choices. She felt it was unfair to put her in that position.

Max received an offer in the M&A group at Rothman Brothers during his second year in school. Max accepted the job. He worked one day a week through his fourth semester at Columbia. It helped pay the bills and he was enthralled with the work.

Max was not scheduled to start work full-time until August, so after graduation, he took a job as an office boy for $10/hour for an Australian linen importer. The nanny's hours coincided perfectly with Max's 8:00 A.M. to 6:00 P.M. schedule and Max looked forward to spending more time with his family. Rothman Brothers called, however, and asked if Max wanted to start his new job early. He readily accepted and started in July 1995, several weeks ahead of the 12-week training program.

Max worked six- and seven-day weeks and 12- to 20-hour days for the next 18 months. One of his first deals was with Wafer in Chicago, during which he did not see his family for several weeks at a time. "He never came home; he loved the work and was starting to feel the internal pull of the company. He kept bringing home those stupid Wafer dinosaur cookies. We didn't want Wafer cookies, we just wanted to see him," Darcy exclaimed. During the deal Jack turned two years old and Max almost missed his son's birthday. Max commented, "I didn't think it was appropriate to ask for Saturday off. I really lost my perspective!"

Max was on the fast track at Rothman Brothers. He received great feedback from his bosses and loved what he did. The work was both challenging and rewarding for Max. He had tremendous responsibility and was getting huge exposure. Max believed he needed two years to establish himself at work. "I didn't think I had a choice but to focus my energy there." He added, "In M&A at Rothman Brothers, they give you a series of deals, and once you are on board you just can't jump off the train. You are the guy, and the deals keep coming in the door."

Another Child?

Darcy's job was also going well. She worked 9:00 A.M. to 6:00 P.M. and had weekends off. Three times a year she traveled to Paris for fashion shows. Darcy truly loved her job. Although she found it hard to be on her own while Max was working so much, she also wanted another child. Communication between them was not great. Max was ambivalent about adding to the family. Although they were a dual-income couple, Max's base salary was relatively low, and with New York City rent, a nanny, and so forth, the Edwards could not seem to get ahead financially. Max felt another child would be a bad economic decision and increased strain on the marriage. But it was what Darcy really wanted, and Max eventually supported the decision. "The more we tried to get ahead the greater the pressure we felt at home," he said. Was it all worth it? There was no end in sight.

JENNIFER AND STEVE: OIL AND WATER

If I had come out of business school at age 30 with a child, I would have never taken a job in investment banking. This is a fast-paced and very demanding industry. I chose it for that very reason. I thrive on the pace and challenge, but I strive for the ultimate in my personal life also, and sometimes the two don't go together—at least not at the same time. I started out without planning ahead except to know that I wanted success in my job and success at home. I've learned that at any given time you evaluate trade-offs as they present themselves. You never know what the future holds, so I don't make decisions about what might happen three years from now. I believe you need to decide what you want to do, and then go for it.

Jennifer

Jennifer and Steve met the first night of freshman year at college, and began dating. After graduation, they continued to date. Jennifer worked as an analyst at an investment bank in New York City. Steve worked for a consulting firm in Hartford, Connecticut. They first talked about marriage right before they left to get their MBAs (at the same business school). They planned to get married after graduation.

Just out of business school and before the wedding, Steve accepted a job with a company in the health care industry. He commented:

> I liked the location: New York City. I liked the functional area: finance. It was an area that I wanted, but in which I had no previous professional experience. And I liked the idea that the corporation actually makes things, as opposed to financial services. We make things that help people feel or look better—things like prescription and over-the-counter medicines, infant formula, and medical devices.

Jennifer accepted a job with an investment banking firm. They recognized that they were joining two completely different cultures. Jennifer started work in a fast-paced, intense environment, with long hours. Steve's position ramped up more slowly. As he moved up in the company, pressures increased. The difference between their two work cultures meant that Steve's trade-offs would come at a later time than Jennifer's.

As Steve put it:

> I would say that in the 14 years I've been with this company, I've been continually challenged. After two years, I was selected by the CFO for a position that put me into contact with him on nearly a daily basis, making significant decisions for the company. In terms of subsequent jobs, I've progressed reasonably quickly and have stayed pretty challenged. The pace has certainly quickened as I've moved up the ladder.

Jennifer spoke candidly about the challenges she faced as a woman in the investment-banking world. "By the time I started in September, I was married. I was afraid to tell anyone at work about the change in my 'condition.' I did not want anyone to treat me differently. Three months into the job I still felt I had to apologize about getting married. I worried they were thinking, 'Oh God, a woman in investment banking. She'll want to be home within two years with kids.'" Jennifer was disappointed to find very few female role models upon whom to pattern her career.

Heading to Wall Street

Investment banking was not conducive to the newlywed lifestyle, but Jennifer and Steve worked conscientiously to free their schedules for time together. Jennifer worked the infamously long I-banking hours as an associate. She loved her work and drove herself hard to succeed. But the feeling of having to apologize for taking time off never seemed to dissipate. Jennifer added:

> Steve never complained in those associate years. I would do anything I could to finagle some time with him. I would kill myself on a project for three straight weeks, knowing I could steal a weekend at the end. I worked smarter and aimed to build a reputation for delivering.

Jennifer discussed the trials, tribulations, and challenges of attracting the next generation of high-quality people to a field that does not place much value on lifestyle: "A lot of women and men today are choosing careers outside of investment banking. They aren't giving it a shot because of the implications it has on lifestyle. When I entered the business, it was less acceptable to admit to lifestyle concerns and priorities."

Jennifer set general objectives and plans for her life that would not be compromised. She wanted to "do it all. I wanted significant success in my business, marriage, and I wanted to start a family by the time I turned 30." Jennifer felt effective time management was the key to everything. She believed that if she built a strong reputation at work she would be able to deal from a position of strength. Jennifer felt she had to achieve the title of vice president before having children. She felt a promotion would give her more leverage with her company and the firm would be more willing to work with her on her terms. She suggested, "The VP title was so critical and important because I did not want others to think I was on a different track. I was a banker."

Steve considered the decision to have a family from his own point of view:

> I've always felt strongly about family, but it's easy to balance a mid-level position in a company and a wife. It's a different ball game to balance a senior-level position, two children, a commute, etc. I still feel strongly that if I move too far in the direction of either career or family, then I won't be happy or satisfied, and I will try to move back to the middle, the position of balance. At the end of the day, though, my family is the most important thing to me.

Despite the differences in their professional lives, the couple knew they complemented each other. Jennifer remarked, "Steve reins me in on occasion, and I don't even know it. I am very high strung and he is very capable of calming me down, setting priorities, and thinking longer term. It's a nice balance." Steve agreed: "I share Jennifer's perspective on this. She has made me more high-strung than I normally am, but for the most part I am an easygoing individual. We strike a good balance. At times I will have to tell her to chill out and at other times she will attempt to light a fire under me. I think we both have taken the positive aspects from each other's tendencies."

Aye Carumba

About three years into their careers, Steve and Jennifer were dining on the Upper East Side of New York City at a Mexican restaurant called Carumba's and the subject of raising children came up seriously for the first time. Steve's early thinking was that when the couple had children, Jennifer would quit her job and be a full-time mom, but this discussion revealed that Jennifer was completely sure she did not want to quit work. It would not be an option for her to stay at home.

Julie was born in 1989, just after Jennifer turned 30, and right on Jennifer's schedule. Jennifer commented, "The first three months of Julie's life I didn't leave her side. I wanted to be with her every waking moment." Jennifer returned to work, but found the hours and the separation from her child unacceptable. Jennifer decided that she was either going to quit or work part-time. She negotiated with the firm to switch to a four-day workweek. She did that successfully until she got pregnant with Sam, the couple's second child. Jennifer again reduced her workweek, this time to three days. Her strong will continued to show through.

> I thought that many in the firm believed I would quit, but I came back three days a week. That is the only way I could still work and be the kind of mom I wanted to be. But the whole time I worked part-time, I felt different. I was worried that people were mentally relegating me to the "mommy track." It really bothered me, but there was not much I could do about it. It was a great consolation to me that I was completely confident in my decision to work part-time.

Returning Full-Time

In 1992, a senior officer at her company contacted Jennifer with an offer of a full-time job working for the CEO. Jennifer first discussed the new opportunity with Steve, and then, "took about two more minutes to accept the offer. I am an ambitious person. I wanted to become a managing director and take on a leadership role. I wanted to test myself. When this full-time opportunity came up with the CEO, I had to accept."

The Kids, the Commute, the Challenges

Jennifer and Steve talked about their children non-stop. Jennifer said,

I am obsessed with their well-being. When I'm with my kids I try not to let them see me down, tired, or upset. I see myself as a role model, especially for my daughter. I already feel additional demands from the kids as they are getting older, but I think you can do it all—work, family, marriage—and be successful at all of them. I seem to have to be around more and more. I am trying to build the type of relationship with my children that I had with my parents.

Jennifer became a managing director at her firm by the end of 1996 and was assigned additional responsibilities through 1997. Steve was a star at his company, yet his success brought increasing challenges to find more time at home. As he became more senior in his corporation he spent more time on the road, leaving for full weeks at a time. With the increasing demands of work, the pressure of the commute from Greenwich, Connecticut, to Princeton, New Jersey, where he now worked, had intensified for Steve. He rented an apartment in Princeton, so he could stay there a couple of nights each week.

Survey Says?

Steve set the tone: "As we get older everything gets turned up a notch. It's like a kick-off return man in a football game. Everything seems to be converging on us at once. The commute increases, jobs get more serious, and the kids need more time." Jennifer said, "Over time, as the children get older and we get more senior in our jobs, the pressures only increase, and it just keeps getting tougher." Steve reflected on his life, and looked toward the future. "I have the perfect wife, perfect career, perfect health, and perfect kids. No couple has worked as hard to get where we are. But I just keep thinking of that song, 'Cat's in the Cradle,' and I know things will have to change." Jennifer added, "There are definitely days when I lose it, and I think to myself, what am I doing? I think I should be at home, but I realize I also need the fulfillment and challenge of my work."

Steve and Jennifer agreed there were a number of decisions that would have to be made in the next few years. They would need to make further trade-offs. Should one or both of them redirect their careers? If so, which one, and how? What would happen if Steve were named CFO and his time commitments at work continued to grow? Would moving closer to Princeton be a reasonable compromise? When would they feel financially secure, and what would be the implications of that security? Steve concluded: "It's a tough call. It's about time to go back and have another strategic discussion."

JULIA MCLAUGHLIN

I want my two daughters to know they can do whatever they want to do and be whatever they want to be. I want to prove to them that they can do it without being dependent on someone else for their livelihood. In that, I hope to be their role model.

Julia

Julia Adams met Mark McLaughlin in September of 1989 at Rensselaer Polytechnic Institute in graduate school. They became close friends and dated sporadically throughout the year at RPI. Upon completion of an MS in industrial engineering, Julia returned to Frisco Products in Rochester, NY, to take a position as a general supervisor of manufacturing. Mark returned to Solutions, the Baltimore, Maryland–based software company that had sponsored his graduate studies. In November of that year Mark invited Julia to Maryland to attend a Hunt Club Ball and at Christmas he proposed. Over the course of their 18-month engagement, they ultimately ended up living together in Michigan where Julia was promoted to an account manager at General Motors and Mark took a software engineering position at Ford. They were married in May 1992. Julia explained:

Weddings take on a life of their own once set in motion. Upon reflection, I had misgivings about marrying Mark. We were very different people and I wasn't head over heels in love. However, we were good friends, and I believed I was supposed to get married, so I did. Determined to make it work, we started planning a family immediately. I always wanted to be a young mom so I could run and play tennis with my kids and build the kind of close relationship that my Mom and I shared.

In February 1994, Julia gave birth to a daughter, Erica. Convinced she could "do it all!" Julia resumed work after the six-week maternity leave that General Motors allowed:

I was on the fast track at Frisco Chassis and I did not want to do anything to jeopardize my position so I returned to work full-time as expected. I also had this precious little girl and I wanted to be the best mom possible so I made the extra effort to keep breastfeeding her. I felt like supermom: up all night with Erica, working and traveling all day for the company, doing laundry and trying to keep house, etc. Still, despite all my efforts I was overwhelmed with guilt that Erica was the first kid to get dropped off at day care in the morning and the last to get picked up in the evening.

Massachusetts

When Erica was 10 months old, Julia's mom offered to retire from teaching to watch Erica full-time if Mark and Julia would move back to the Boston area. Julia's dad was equally excited at the prospect of having his grandchildren around. Exhausted and sensing that this alternative was the best for Erica and Mark, Julia jumped at the offer, although it meant giving up her career at Frisco. As a software engineer with considerable expertise, Mark was inundated with career options. Julia received an offer from a small automotive sup-

plier, Tires Plus, where she joined in on a reengineering effort that involved reorganizing the company. They moved in with Julia's parents in January 1995. By March they had bought a home in Lynnfield, three miles from Julia's parents:

Mark had never felt compelled to focus on Erica or on housework so being near my mom made a huge difference in my life. My mother helped me with the grocery shopping and laundry and Erica thrived with so much attention and love. I was promoted to manage a business unit and my job was transferred to a town 20 miles south of Boston. I was now commuting 45 miles through horrendous traffic each way. I arranged my schedule to get up at 4 A.M., drive to the gym and run six miles, get to work by 6:15 A.M. and stay until 6:00 P.M. This way I was giving the company a solid day's work, but was available for as many of Erica's "awake" hours as possible.

After seven months at Tires Plus, Julia and Mark received great news, Julia was pregnant again. In June 1996, Julia gave birth to a second daughter, Eliza. At 10 lbs, 22" Eliza was a big, beautiful baby but was born with a hole in the soft part of her palate. At nine months, Eliza spent three days in the hospital getting her mouth repaired, after which she needed to be taught how to drink from a cup, no small feat for an infant or mother.

Taking care of a toddler and an infant who needed special care created a strain on Julia's mom who suffered from rheumatoid arthritis. To help her mom and aid in Erica's development, Julia found a suitable day care program for Erica three mornings a week.

With so much to balance, Julia found herself more and more distant from Mark:

I was trying so hard to make everyone happy and to keep everything working smoothly but over time I realized how very unhappy I was in my marriage. I resented that Mark did not pull his weight with the girls or with housework. I also felt he took my parents for granted. I got to the point that I could not stand it anymore. Mark kept insisting that everything was perfect. While we had been married four years, I struggled with trying to find a way to make things better but there was just not enough of a foundation for us to build on.

Harvard Business School

Later that year, one of Julia's subordinates applied and got accepted to HBS and encouraged Julia to get her MBA as well. "I applied somewhat on a whim, only to HBS. In a way, I thought it would give me much more time with the girls. The acceptance letter was shocking to me as I never expected to get in. I felt like it was the kick I needed to ask Mark for a divorce. Mark agreed and suddenly I had a new lease on life. My mom told me she would help care for the girls. She was incredibly supportive of me and the HBS experience." Julia's mother explained:

My reaction to Julia's acceptance at HBS was multifaceted. On one hand I was thrilled and delighted that she would have the opportunity to do something most people can only dream of, and it had come at a time when her life was filled with turmoil and unhappiness in her marital situation and she needed a positive experience. This was the basis for my reservations about the adventure. Her work at Tires Plus was very demanding but rewarding, and she had worked out a lifestyle that tried to balance her work life and give her valuable time with her two girls. Like most working mothers she has guilt about the amount of time she can spend with them. I love spending my days with her girls, but I'm not their mom, and Julia and I both know how much they need her. However, the opportunity to attend HBS was too important to abandon; so with the hope that she would be up to the challenge physically

as well as intellectually, we decided to work together to make it happen.

Julia was accepted into the January Cohort of the Class of 2000. Julia sold her home to pay for HBS, and she and the girls moved in with her parents. "I was so excited about the fresh start. When I got my new computer and was prompted for a password, I chose 'freedom.'"

Julia and her parents worked out an implicit agreement for caring for Erica and Eliza. "When I'm at school, my folks are in charge. When I'm home, I have responsibility for the girls. For the most part, it works for the girls too—but it has sometimes been difficult for me to see the girls run to my mom with problems instead of running to me." Still, everything worked out well as Mark and Julia maintained an amicable relationship and the girls had a consistent support system.

The time at HBS was a difficult but rewarding experience for Julia. Like many students, Julia spent the first term convinced that she would hit the screen. Living 20 miles from campus imposed additional time constraints. Eventually she got the hang of the routine, arriving at school by 7 A.M. and reading cases between classes to get a jump start on the next day. "I missed the girls so I would finish my cases at home at night to be near them. My parents have pictures that show me sitting at the dining room table reading a case with Erica drawing at the table next to me, and Eliza standing in my chair behind me braiding my hair." Second year allowed for a little free time. Since Julia's job search was confined to the Boston area, she was able to work in more time with the girls and participated in some of their school events.

Job Search

While a number of manufacturing firms contacted Julia because of her background she was most drawn to consulting. An elite consulting firm in Boston soon contacted Julia, and she liked the professionals she met at the firm and was excited to receive an offer.

But Julia started to have second thoughts as she reflected on the amount of travel that might take her away from home. "The kids will miss you—are you sure you're doing what's right for the kids?" Julia recalled her mother asking her. Julia wondered whether she would even get to see her daughters every weekend, given Mark's visitation schedule with the girls. After considerable internal turmoil, Julia declined Phoenix Group's offer.

Six weeks later, Julia began to reconsider her decision. "I started to realize that my heart was with Phoenix Group, particularly after a number of my close HBS friends had accepted positions there." Julia spoke with Greg Pappas, head of HBS recruiting at Phoenix Group about her concerns. "Greg replied that Phoenix Group would find a way to make it work," Julia remembered, "and I vowed to work incredibly hard, both in the morning when the girls were asleep and also on the weekends when Mark took the kids." Greg Pappas, head of recruiting at HBS for Phoenix Group averred:

Obviously, we were very impressed with Julia, her credentials and her abilities. I had felt all along that despite her relatively unique personal situation that she was a remarkable fit with the culture of Phoenix Group. We were very disappointed (and a little shocked) with her decision in late January to decline our offer. So, you can imagine that when she called me and indicated that she wanted to reopen discussions regarding the possibility of a change of heart, I was surprised but anxious to understand her situation. It was then that I really came to understand her decision-making process. In this day and age, and with individuals like Julia, firms do not have the luxury of not being creative when confronting individual personal situations. When she asked me could we make it work, I looked at her with every confidence in the world and said, "Sure. That's an easy one."

Looking toward the Future

As Julia completed her vacation with the girls in June 2000, her thoughts turned to the impending challenges and adjustments the first year on the

EXHIBIT 1   **Julia McLaughlin's Espoused Demand System**

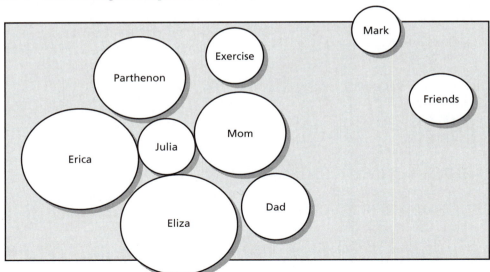

job would present her, her daughters, her parents, and Mark. One change Julia and her parents made in preparation was to buy a home together in Winchester. "Neither of us would have been able to buy it individually, but together we are able to make it work." Julia stated.

Asked when she would begin dating, Julia responded "I just can't fit that in right now. My priority is to be with the girls as much as possible (see Exhibit 1)."

The First Six Months: Launching a PSF Career

LIAM QUINLAN
AND JOHN SHEEHAN

Sitting on the patio at Shay's Pub on a warm and sunny Tuesday afternoon in early May 1999, Liam Quinlan clinked his wineglass to John Sheehan's beer mug in celebration of the completion of their final Harvard Business School exam. "It's hard to believe," Sheehan toasted, "that in less than a month we'll both be carrying our daughters across the stage to shake Dean Clark's hand and we'll be done here at HBS. These 18 months have gone so fast!"

Quinlan and Sheehan had spent considerable time together at HBS as next-door neighbors in Soldiers Field Park, members of the same first-year study group, fathers of three-year-old best friends, and husbands of co-presidents of the HBS Partners Club. "But John and I couldn't be more different," Quinlan averred. "Yeah, we hate each other," chuckled Sheehan, "because Liam refuses to recognize that he went to the wrong school, supports the wrong ball club, thinks the East Coast is the place to be, and prefers wine! At least HBS is making him a little smarter because he's decided to follow me to Barker [Consulting]."

The two classmates enjoyed pointing out, even exaggerating, their differences. Quinlan had attended the U.S. Naval Academy graduating in 1992; Sheehan graduated from the U.S. Military Academy at West Point in 1993. Sheehan, a die-hard Yankees fan, "took tremendous pleasure" from forcing Quinlan, a Red Sox fanatic, into

watching the Yankees win the 1998 World Series. Yet both were excited to begin careers in the newly created start-up practice at Barker Consulting, a top strategy firm—Quinlan remaining in Boston and Sheehan traveling to Barker's San Francisco office.

"I can't wait until our six month reviews" Quinlan remarked, "as those free plane tickets to the Bay Area will be nice in the depth of winter." Sheehan and Quinlan had made a bet, unbeknownst to their wives, that the one with the lower performance rating after six months would send plane tickets to the other to come and visit. "Although I certainly want Liam to succeed," Sheehan interjected, "he's *definitely* got the wrong strategy. In six months, I'll be much more interested in his admitting that I was right than actually getting the plane tickets, although Judy and Jennifer [Sheehan's wife and daughter] will enjoy coming back East to see Kate and Tiffany [Quinlan's wife and daughter]."

The two soon-to-be consultants had first realized their different strategies while reading the other's final paper for the *Self-Assessment and Career Development* (SACD) course. SACD students were required to include in their papers their strategies for ensuring a quick start in their new jobs. "While we shared the same goal—to quickly earn 'star' status at Barker—our strategies and the trade-offs we were planning to make were *vastly* different," recalled Quinlan. "We couldn't both be right and yet we were both confident of our respective approaches. I suggested that we boil down our ap-

Dean's Research Fellow Scot Landry prepared this case under the supervision of Professors Ashish Nanda and Thomas DeLong as the basis for class discussion rather than to illustrate either effective or ineffective handling of an administrative situation.

proach into the key differences, put the differences on paper, each hold ourselves accountable for committing to our strategy for the entire six months, and make the wager to add some extra fun and significance to the debate. Time will tell which one of us is right." (See Exhibit 1 for a chart of Quinlan's and Sheehan's differences.)

STEVE DIGIOVANNI

Feeling his insides "begin to boil" and trying to deal with the "shocking news," Steve DiGiovanni sat in Barker Consulting's New York office, across a desk from his partner-mentor Ed Egan. Egan had

EXHIBIT 1 Differences in Quinlan's and Sheehan's Strategies for Early Success at Barker Consulting

Category	Liam Quinlan	John Sheehan
Breadth versus depth of knowledge	I want to be viewed as having a "solid handle" on a wide array of start-up client issues.	I seek to knock my analysis "out of the park" and become a recognized knowledge expert in one or two client problem areas.
Self-promotion	Respecting cultural norms, I'm going to self-promote as much as possible. Most people will only know how well I'm doing if I tell them.	I plan to let my work and contribution pretty much speak for itself. I will trust Barker's review system to ensure that people know about my good work.
Networking	Going directly to partners at the outset will make me seem like a bottom-kisser. Instead, I will network extensively with peers and well-regarded managers, get a sense from them for how the organization really works, and let my peers and managers talk me up to the partners.	I will network intensively with partners in my areas of interest. If I can demonstrate how quickly I've picked up depth of knowledge, they'll get a really good feel for me and support me in front of others.
Extra work	I'll become heavily involved in HBS recruiting and office-based parties. I want to meet many people and let people know I'm someone who cares about the firm and is great with people. If they think I'm a people-person, by extension, they'll think I'll be great with clients.	If I have "extra" time, I'll do something extra to build knowledge and go-beyond-the-call in my current engagement(s). I want the partners I work with to see that I'm focused and that I deliver the best work. I first want to become known for intellectual rigor and for results that help clients. I'll do the firm-based "soft stuff" later in my career, when I am measured for it.
HBS ties	I'm going to try to build relationships with people from other schools. I don't want people to classify me as "a HBS guy." People from other schools have negative connotations of HBS grads.	I'm planning to network and spend time with people who share the HBS background. HBS alumni make up 20 percent of the firm, and it will be easier to get to know them and share experiences than with non-HBS types. Most people from other schools flock around their own—it's only natural for people to bunch with others from their alma maters.

EXHIBIT 1   Differences in Quinlan's and Sheehan's Strategies for Early Success at Barker
Consulting *(continued)*

Category	Liam Quinlan	John Sheehan
First assignment	Although I'll do my best to identify a project I like and get on it, I don't want to get a reputation for being "hard to please" and "tough to deal with," particularly as a HBS grad.	I'm going to make sure my first assignment is with a great partner and on a high-exposure project. If I need to push back a lot, I will. I want to get on the right playing field initially and work with the stars. This may require patience and a few diplomatic "no's." People will forget about the push-back if the project is ultimately successful.
Face time	If the Barker people know I'm committed to doing great work and having strong values in my personal life, they'll respect my choice of how I structure my time.	I want people to know I'm totally committed to doing well at Barker. For the first six months anyway, I'll normally plan to be the first at work and the last to leave.
Mentors	In about six months, I hope to have four or five mentors at Barker: one or two peer mentors, two or three manager mentors, and one or two partner sponsors. Over time, I will ask more partners to join my "personal board of directors."	I want to get one *great* partner mentor. I want to work with *the* star in the organization, connect with that person, and develop close personal and professional bonds with that person. If I have more than one mentor, great, but one great mentor-sponsor is all one really needs.

just handed DiGiovanni his official written performance evaluation, which indicated that DiGiovanni had been classified a *Category III* performer (out of five classes; a Category III was equivalent to being rated in the middle of his class). DiGiovanni had fully expected that he would be rated a *Category I* "star." This was his first review since he graduated from Harvard Business School six months previously.

DiGiovanni listened superficially as Egan rattled through some positive comments contained in the review. His emotions welled up when Egan got to the "Points for Discussion" section, which contained the following bullets:

- Steve's work has been good and has met expectations but not exceeded it.

- Steve has contributed solidly but not stood out in his client or firm-building projects.

- Steve once misstated facts in a key client presentation at Walsh Manufacturing. At the end of the project, Walsh chose not to hire Barker Consulting for a follow-on project. Steve's mistake was only one of the many factors leading to Walsh's decision, but it did contribute to Walsh's perception that the Barker team was not fully prepared.

- Steve needs to work on being more polished in front of clients.

- Steve's peer-mentor reported that she spent much less time with Steve than her other three mentees.

Picking his eyes up from the paper, Egan focused on DiGiovanni, remarking:

> I really like you Steve and want you to succeed. I've seen it happen sometimes that our forced curve can be really harsh to some people. In your class, you have some people who the firm considers not just stars but *superstars*. They have many advocates and sponsors already in the firm.
>
> Please realize that there are many partners in this firm who were not rated Category I or II in their first review. I really believe you have the potential to become partner here if you work hard at it. I'm sorry you're so obviously disappointed.

DiGiovanni sat silently, hoping Egan would continue talking, since he wasn't ready to respond yet. Thoughts were quickly racing inside his head: What's really going on here? Am I getting screwed? Have I failed? Should I ask for time to sort this out? Should I respond emotionally and say this is B.S.? Is Egan the person I want to talk this out with? Should I start calling headhunters this afternoon?

Index